Person and Act and
Related Essays

THE ENGLISH CRITICAL EDITION OF THE WORKS
OF KAROL WOJTYŁA / JOHN PAUL II

VOLUME 1 ❧ *Person and Act* and Related Essays

EDITORS

Rev. Antonio López, FSCB, General Editor

Carl A. Anderson

David S. Crawford

Nicholas J. Healy

Grzegorz Ignatik

David L. Schindler

KAROL WOJTYŁA

VOLUME 1

Person and Act and Related Essays

TRANSLATED BY GRZEGORZ IGNATIK

FOREWORD BY CARL A. ANDERSON

The Catholic University of America Press
Washington, D.C.

Copyright © 2021

The Catholic University of America Press

All rights reserved

The paper used in this publication meets the minimum requirements of American National Standards for Information Science—Permanence of Paper for Printed Library Materials, ANSI Z39.48—1984.

∞

Design and composition by Kachergis Book Design

Library of Congress Cataloging-in-Publication Data

Names: John Paul II, Pope, 1920–2005, author. | Ignatik, Grzegorz, translator. | Anderson, Carl A. (Carl Albert), 1951– writer of foreword. | John Paul II, Pope, 1920–2005. Osoba i czyn. English.

Title: "Person and act" and related essays / Karol Wojtyła ; translated by Grzegorz Ignatik ; foreword by Carl A. Anderson.

Description: Washington, D.C. : The Catholic University of America Press, [2021] | Series: The English critical edition of the works of Karol Wojtyła/John Paul II ; volume 1 | Includes bibliographical references and index.

Identifiers: LCCN 2020056953 | ISBN 9780813233666 (cloth ; permanent paper) | ISBN 9780813233673 (ebook)

Subjects: LCSH: Act (Philosophy) | Personality. | Philosophical anthropology. | Phenomenological anthropology.

Classification: LCC B105.A35 J64513 2021 | DDC 128/.4—dc23

LC record available at https://lccn.loc.gov/2020056953

CONTENTS

Foreword to the English Critical Edition by Carl A. Anderson   vii

Introduction to the English Critical Edition
by Rev. Antonio López, FSCB   xi

Preface to Volume 1 of the English Critical Edition
by Grzegorz Ignatik   xxv

Acknowledgments   xxxix

I. PRE-1969 SYNOPSIS AND FRAGMENTS

1. *Person and Act*: A Synopsis   3
2. *Person and Act*: The Introductory and Fundamental Reflections   36
3. Person and Act in the Aspect of Consciousness: A Fragment of the Study *Person and Act*   59
4. *Person and Act*: The Reflexive Functioning of Consciousness and Its Emotionalization   74
5. *Person and Act*: Subjectivity and Subjectivism   87
6. Person and Act in Light of Man's Dynamism   90

II. PERSON AND ACT

Introduction   95

Part 1. Consciousness and Efficacy

1. Person and Act in the Aspect of Consciousness   121
2. The Analysis of Efficacy in Relation to the Dynamism of Man   161

Part 2. The Transcendence of the Person in the Act

3. The Personal Structure of Self-Determination   207
4. Self-Determination and Fulfillment   251

Contents

Part 3. The Integration of the Person in the Act

5. Integration and Somaticity — 295
6. Integration and the Psyche — 330

Part 4. Participation

7. (*Supplementum*): An Outline of the Theory of Participation — 377
   Afterword — 415

III. POST-1969 RELATED ESSAYS

1. Introductory Statement during the Discussion on *Person and Act* at the Catholic University of Lublin on December 16, 1970 — 419
2. Symposium on *Person and Act* (Lublin—Catholic University of Lublin, 1971) — 423
3. The Afterword to the Discussion on *Person and Act* — 433
4. The Personal Structure of Self-Determination (A Lecture for the Conference on St. Thomas) — 457
5. The Person: Subject and Community — 467
6. Participation or Alienation — 514
7. A Letter to Anna-Teresa Tymieniecka — 532
8. Subjectivity and "the Irreducible" in Man — 536
9. The Degrees of Being in Phenomenology and in Classical Metaphysics: Introduction (to the Discussion from the Point of View of the Phenomenology of Action) — 546
10. The Transcendence of the Person in the Act and the Auto-teleology of Man — 554
11. *Theoria* and *Praxis* in the Philosophy of the Human Person — 567
12. *Theoria* and *Praxis*: A Universally Human and Christian Topic — 575
13. The Author's Preface to the First English Edition of *Person and Act* — 586

Texts Marked by the Critical Apparatus — 589

Footnotes Marked by the Critical Apparatus — 623

Editorial Notes — 627

Bibliography — 641

Index — 653

FOREWORD TO THE ENGLISH CRITICAL EDITION

Carl A. Anderson, Supreme Knight, Knights of Columbus

The body of work left to us by St. John Paul II is both enormous and profound. I am reminded of an anecdote related in the preface to the book *Augustine*. In it, the author recalls the words on a plaque hanging over the case of St. Augustine's writings in a Sevillian monastery: "Anyone who says he has read all this is a liar."[1]

One might pause to consider whether a similar, if less severe, maxim applies to the writings of St. John Paul II—albeit for a different reason. Though the quantity of work left to us by this saint will challenge even the most voracious readers, *access* to it has been an even more significant challenge. There has been no publisher's equivalent of a monastic collection of all his writings in English. Except for official papal addresses and documents preserved and disseminated by the Vatican, his works have been scattered around the published world in single folios and limited collections. As this particular volume attests, the published works could sometimes benefit from a new translation and attentive discernment regarding non-authorial edits. Moreover, since different manuscripts have piqued the interest of readers and publishers in varying countries, English-language audiences have faced the challenge, even in the case of published texts, of working across multiple languages and translations and of dealing with textual idiosyncrasies. This further complicates the task of building a coherent understanding of this saint's theological and philosophical thought, which is expressed in writings that often reveal his mystic passion for God, his psychological appreciation of the intricacies

---

1. Christopher Kirwan, *Augustine*, The Arguments of the Philosophers (New York: Routledge, 2009).

of human persons, his poetic keenness for language's communicative precision and expressive imprecision, and his pastoral urgency for serving the people of God with the richness of God's love and truth.

Needless to say, when the Knights of Columbus encountered the chance to acquire the rights to collect and translate into English the entirety of St. John Paul II's works, the decision seemed one of duty rather than of luxury. There is a clear need to present his thought in a unified fashion so as to further enrich those who knew him and introduce his work to the ever-growing body of humanity who did not know him.

This project marks the second time the Knights of Columbus have collaborated with a distinguished academic institution to make available a scholarly edition of the collected works by a great saint of the Catholic Church. Previously, the Knights of Columbus's financial assistance enabled the completion of the Yale Edition of the Complete Works of St. Thomas More. Over nearly four decades, Yale University Press published twenty books by St. Thomas More in fifteen volumes.

The importance of a complete and coherent collection of the works of St. John Paul II is even more pronounced when one considers the works' author: a pope and saint who was monumental in terms of both his personal holiness and his contributions to theological and historical realms—factors that shaped a generation of Catholics bearing his name. Even before entering the 1978 conclave that would elect him the vicar of Christ for the universal Church, Karol Wojtyła's writings had a relevance for the world. Diverse in genre and topic, they reveal the depth with which this man grappled with various issues of importance—whether spiritual, theological, anthropological, philosophical, metaphysical, poetic, historical, familial, political, sexual, or patriotic. And yet, both individually and as a whole, his writings tend to transcend the specific genres he impacted, to highlight the central topic illuminating all the others: God, the "fully Self-sufficient Being" who is the "necessary ground of ... all created beings, including man."[2]

Primary among these topics is the multifaceted puzzle of the human person, a subject also treated, with detrimental consequences, by the competing twentieth-century ideologies. At the parish of Wiśniowa,

---

2. John Paul II, *Memory and Identity: Conversations at the Dawn of a Millennium* (New York: Rizzoli, 2005), 8.

Karol Wojtyła exhorted young people: "Defend your humanity. This is the great heritage of Christianity, the great heritage of our faith: that we think highly of mankind and we set high standards for mankind. This is the only way to attain high regard for mankind."[3] John Paul II saw that each person has within him the seed of greatness, a greatness that needs to be called forth and given room to flourish.

As a new generation grapples with age-old challenges in constantly changing environments, this saint's words remain a relevant and important contribution to the questions of the human heart, including those about what it means to be human, the dignity of human life, and the meaning of and desire for love. This collection of his works, which begins with the present volume, sets forth the writings not just of a pope and intellectual but of a "holy father"—writings that express ideas that took shape within him as well as ideas that shaped him, shaped the Church, shaped a generation, and ultimately shaped the world.

---

3. Adam Boniecki, *The Making of the Pope of the Millennium: Kalendarium of the Life of Karol Wojtyła* (Stockbridge, Mass.: Marian Press, 2000), 407.

INTRODUCTION TO THE ENGLISH
CRITICAL EDITION

Rev. Antonio López, FSCB

We are honored to introduce the English Critical Edition of the Works of Karol Wojtyła/John Paul II (ECE). In doing so, it is fitting first to clarify the significance of St. John Paul II's philosophical and theological reflections for both the Church and the growth of the human spirit. In what follows, we also explain the aims of this project and the criteria that have guided our most important decisions.

I

Just as the alternating sun and rain, heat and cold of the seasons reveal the fruitfulness hidden within a seed, so, too, the historical unfolding of the Church's life discloses, without ever exhausting, the full form and richness of the mission of a saint. Only time will bring to light the true depth and fruitfulness of St. John Paul II's mission; hence, the publication of his works a little more than a decade after his passing hardly allows for a full account of their importance. This introduction therefore will not elucidate where St. John Paul II (1978–2005) stands vis-à-vis the "greats," that is, St. Leo I (440–461), St. Gregory I (590–604), and St. Nicholas I (858–867). Nor will it attempt to characterize the influence his earlier philosophical work may have had on the development of phenomenology or moral philosophy in general. While the ECE may help readers answer these and many other questions, the more fundamental concern here is to clarify the nature of Christian tradition so as to better perceive the depth and meaning of his works.

The time of the Church is different from the simple succession of years and, more importantly, from world history. In the latter, entirely worldly societies take their bearings from specific places, times, or myths, and thus consider themselves to be moving further and further away from their origins. Our preoccupation with the rise and fall of civilizations, peoples, and cities, as well as single human existences, is a lucid and transparent witness to this. Each encounters others, ripens in its own identity, and, when coexistence is no longer feasible, tends either to be absorbed by another or to merge with it. However complex and rich such processes may be, they nevertheless have only a limited time frame in which to grow out and away from their origin before ceasing to be. Besides this relation between societies and the origin from which they derive their identities, there is also a common presupposition guiding this perception of the succession of historical eras that is important to mention here. In our technological culture, the significance of societies or persons tends to be measured scientifically and sociologically by the success with which they radically opposed what came before. This culture also believes that individual accomplishments and the unparalleled possession of power determine life's worth. Nowadays, quantity replaces quality, and hegemonic aloneness substitutes for fruitful identity. In this regard, what comes afterwards not only stands as heir to its predecessor but also supersedes and, to a certain extent, eliminates it.

By contrast, the time of the Church—within which one can perceive the significance of a saint—is paradoxical in at least two senses. First, her origin lies at the beginning yet remains present: "I am with you always, to the close of the age" (Mt 28:20). Of course, since the Church is formed by men and women who have been made one with Christ in baptism and who are called to transfigure the world in Christ's light, the time of the Church remains inseparable from world history. Her time also knows the flourishing and dying of eras, and no stage of her existence is absolute. Yet, the origin of the Church is a unique event: the "handing over" (*traditio*—tradition) of the Father's only begotten Son (Jn 3:16, 1:14) who, having taken on flesh through the Virgin Mary, gave himself to the end in the Spirit (Heb 9:14) so that all may receive eternal life. The Church's origin, then, is this *traditio*, that is, Christ's giving over of his very self, an event in which Christ has made known all that he heard from the Father (Jn 15:15; Rom 8:32). Christ died to redeem man and to give his Spirit, the Spirit of the Father, who guides those who receive him into all truth (Jn 16:13). He allows man to enter into the Word of the Father, to become a son in the Son (Jn 1:12; Gal 4:4–5), and to pray to the Father (Rom 8:15). Through the Spirit, the person of Christ remains sacramentally present in history. In the Eucharist, it is his very self that abides, and Christ remains in all those who by participating in it are incorporated into him. They constitute his body, which is the sacramental Church (Acts 9:4). The Eucharist gives birth to the Church who makes this same Eucharist possible. The memory of the Church's origin, celebrated every day in the Eucharistic sacrifice, is ever alive and life-giving (Lk 22:19–20; 1 Cor 11:24–25). It is also constantly renewed through liturgical prayer, contemplation of the Word of God, and participation in Christ's suffering. The Church's origin is also her permanent source. Thus, there is nothing farther from the nature of Christianity than reducing "tradition" to the handing on of memories, customs, ideas, or artifacts of foregone events to future generations; nothing more distant from it than evaluating the quality of the present times or the work of a given person in terms of a mechanical repetition of what was inherited. It would thus be misleading to approach St. John Paul II's thought in order to evaluate "how far" he brought the Church's tradition, what of it he undid, and what quantitative impact his tireless efforts had on the world. In fact, rather than a simply finite human endeavor—that is, an endless, horizontal progression through the free enactment of possibilities—time for the Christian mind is both a deepening of the ever-present, ever-new event of God's love in history and a further unfolding of his glory so that God "may be everything to every one" (1 Cor 15:28).

While the abiding presence of the Church's origin thus characterizes, in a first sense, the paradoxical nature of the time of the Church, the Church's origin is marked in a second sense by its capacity to hold together past and future in the present. The present is an ever-new presence of what has already taken place: the Father has revealed his face (Jn 14:9; 6:46) in his perfect image (Col 1:15; Heb 1:3) and has, in a manner that surpasses all understanding (Eph 3:18–19), offered his love for man once and for all (Jn 16:27; Heb 10:10). In this regard, the time and existence of the Church never grow beyond or away from Christ. Rather, they grow within him whose being, love, and existence are coextensive. To see how this "present" is not a fixation with past events, it is important to recall that Christian memory, which deepened the understanding of the Hebrew people, is not the remembrance of a past event but the recognition and celebration of its presence. The history of the Church, from this point of view, is her becoming ever more present to the abiding and bottomless mystery of the Christ-event. Time, in this sense, is for man the possibility of increasingly being conformed to and living the act of God. God became flesh, died, rose again, and sent the Holy Spirit so that the human person may dwell in him (1 Cor 3:16). However, because the Church, including her history, is Christ's "body, the fullness of him who fills all in all" (Eph 1:23), the time of the Church is also characterized by a "not yet." The Holy Spirit leads the Church's *traditio* toward her eschatological fulfillment by incorporating her response to God's love into Christ's very offering of himself to her and to the Father. God wishes to reveal his glory through the transfiguration of those whom he makes his own and whose lives and works, through the Spirit, are conformed to Christ, the beloved Son of the Father.

Rather than the "novelty" or quantifiable "impact" it may have, the significance of the saint's mission is thus determined by the mysterious fact that, through it, the very content of God's being and loving design for man is present anew in a specific time in history. In the saint's life and work, human existence, with all its drama and questions, meets God's eternal and ever-new Word spoken to man in his historical time. The saint is thus a "synthesis," a coming together of the horizontal axis of human questioning and endeavors and the vertical axis of God's response to history. In this sense, the life of a saint is an exegesis of the event of Christ; its beauty, truth, fruitfulness, and attractiveness depend on its assisting others to see the figure of Christ and his mission. In keeping with the understanding of *traditio* outlined above, such exegesis of Christ's figure and mission cannot be understood as the offering of some translation of his words and deeds, as if the saint were merely a "mediator" who, placed between his contemporaries and Christ, would be able to interpret rightly (i.e., to actualize or efficaciously implement) Christ's unique newness. As St. Paul says, it is sheer foolishness to regard *gnosis* as capable of reaching further than faith (1 Cor 1:25), or, in other words, to hold that one could know the divine mysteries better than the Spirit of God and explain them to the people of a certain historical era. Rather, the saint's exegesis of Christ's redeeming, nuptial love is the radiating proof of the presence and ever-new fullness of Christ. It is only by such witness that the saint is fruitful for the Church and the world.

The mystery of the event of Christ's incarnation—which includes his suffering and death on the cross, his ascent to the Father, and their sending of the Spirit of truth—the very mystery of the triune God that Christ reveals, and God's loving plan for man are so endlessly profound that they always call for ever-new contemplation, participation, and more precise exposition. It is, then, both the superabundant richness of the event of Christ and the nuptial dimension of God's love for man that call for man's response and ground his reflection. Thus, the philosophical and theological responsibility to ponder, contemplate, and communicate these mysteries does not entail bringing to light aspects of Trinitarian and Christological dogma left untouched by Christ, as odd as this may sound. Nor does it mean that the history of the Church is the limited time given to enlightened human acumen to discover the remaining hidden pieces of the divine and human puzzle. Rather, while the task of teaching is a human work, it is more fundamentally Christ who, through his Spirit, brings every human being into a deeper realization of the Father's ever-ancient and ever-new beauty, truth, goodness, and justice, which are, in a word, the love that he embodied. Only in this sense can we say that the reflection offered by a saint contributes to the development of doctrine. Genuine development, rather than a growing *out of* is a growing *into* the bottomless and luminous mystery of Jesus Christ—the one who, as Son of the Father, is always the Father's perfect Word; who, with the Father, is eternally fruitful in the Spirit; and who, as son of Mary, is also man's redeemer and destiny. The saint's theological and philosophical contribution, in this regard, is measured according to its obedient and grateful collaboration with the unfolding of a divinely revealed truth.

The re-presentation of the mystery of Christ, as already mentioned, does not happen abstractly, as if man's endeavors, accomplishments, and troubles were irrelevant to God's self-revelation, or as if the human being were simply a channel indifferent to what flows through him. Rather, in the saint, the theological exposition of the divine mystery captures both the most pressing questions of the saint's time and the exact answer God wishes to give to a specific age. The saint, therefore, not only embodies the question and drama of his historical era but is also given a thought or insight into the divine mystery revealed in Christ, which then becomes his task to obediently, gratuitously, and laboriously unfold so that all persons may become reacquainted with the "whole," that is, with the truth of God and of man. This "synthesis," therefore, is not the putting together of human ideas but the re-presentation of the central event of Christianity as pertinent to the history and questions of the living generation. As such, the saint's mission also has a prophetic dimension: it clears the way for a new path that leads to a deeper, fuller participation in man's true good. The saint's exposition of divine truth—which, like that of the Fathers or Doctors of the Church, can at times take the form of veritable treatises—always follows the form of the original "tradition" at the Church's source. In other words, the saint's elucidation is genuine so long as it is a personal expression of this *traditio*, if it is a response to the redemptive love of Christ that precedes it. The saint's theological and philosophical exposition is the expression of his participation in Christ's self-gift through the very gift of his human existence. Love is both the form and content of the divine Logos, and all human imitation is called to participate in and express the same form and content. In this sense, the thought of a saint, and in our case of St. John Paul II, can be understood only "from within," that is, as an outflow of his inner dialogue with God and of the mission entrusted to him.

The mission of the saint is such a precise, concrete, and truthful response of God to the question of an age that it is common for it to be at first misunderstood, persecuted, and rejected altogether. The greater the role a saint is called to play in history, the more intense the opposition he meets. The wealth and light that come from him are so vast, deep, and revealing that people stand corrected—that is, purified, sustained, and guided toward a more genuine perception of the mystery of God and man as well as a freer, more responsible abandonment to this mystery. Of course, that which a saint is given to live and express also includes more culturally and historically determined elements. Yet, the missions of the saints are also endowed with essential elements that remain a permanent treasure of the Church. The fact, for example, that the Albigensian heresy no longer stands does not mean that the Dominican order has lost its raison d'être; nor does the fact that Italian immigrants in the United States no longer need the support of the Missionary Sisters of the Sacred Heart of Jesus imply that Mother Cabrini's order has become insignificant. The task to communicate the truth and beauty of God that is contemplated (*contemplata aliis tradere*), as well as to witness and educate to the truth of Christ's love, remains. We, however, are not just to abstract what is essential and come up with a précis of "free-floating" concepts that, while dazzling, have lost their capacity to radiate Christ's life—like specimens stored in glass boxes that still draw the admiration of collectors and onlookers. The essential must be perceived within the whole form of the saint's life. Besides what is simply transitory, human reflections always contain elements that will be proven inadequate. This, however, is never a reason to dismiss someone's thought altogether. The Church continues to benefit, for example, from St. Augustine's profound account of faith regardless of his inadequate exposition of predestination, just as she still receives so much light from Aquinas's theological reflections, even though he was not the best of scriptural exegetes.

The question of our times, as St. John Paul II himself acutely identified and deeply felt, concerns the mystery of the human person. The modern world simultaneously exalts and banalizes the human person. Today there is, for example, a naïve and exhilarating trust in man's capacity to master the cosmos and, more importantly, to master his very person through biotechnological means. Such means render him increasingly capable of enhancing whatever he wishes to improve or amending whatever causes him to suffer. Society, work, and man's relation to other persons—as well as to his own sexually differentiated body—are all subjected to a freedom that no longer knows any intrinsic relation to what is truly good. Man thinks his freedom is sufficient unto itself. Ironically, however, this exaltation of man's subjectivity in every realm (anthropological, sociological, political, economic, etc.) has turned him into an object governed by an ever present, albeit invisible, bureaucratic system. Recalling the annihilation of millions at the hands of the different totalitarianisms that held sway through much of the twentieth century, as well as the systematic elimination of the most vulnerable, especially the unborn and the elderly, in contemporary liberal regimes, allows us to see the reduction of the human person to an object at the service of ideologies whose bold promises unfailingly effect man's demise.

The Christian faith is always sensitive to man's constitutive need to know who he is. The faith also confronts the world with an extremely high and demanding image of man. Nevertheless, in light of our cultural context, one can say with Hans Urs von Balthasar that "the real target of today's intense assault on the Church's creed" is precisely the contention that the human being, man and woman, is created in the image of God and called to participate in God's triune communion of love.[1] The question of the mystery of the person—created male and female and called to a communion of persons—preoccupied Karol Wojtyła from the very beginning of his philosophical work and priestly ministry. From early on, he busied himself with the meaning of human action as revelatory of the mystery of the human person as well as with man's pursuit of his true good in the nuptial relation between man and woman. He expressed this in great detail in a well-known letter to Henri de Lubac when still archbishop of Kraków:

> I devote my very rare free moments to a work that is close to my heart and devoted to the metaphysical sense and mystery of the PERSON. It seems to me that the debate today is being played on that level. The evil of our times consists in the first place in a kind of degradation, indeed in a pulverization, of the fundamental uniqueness of each human person. This evil is even much more of the metaphysical order than of the moral order. To this disintegration, planned at times by atheistic ideologies, we must oppose, rather than sterile polemics, a kind of "recapitulation" of the inviolable mystery of the person.[2]

This concern to think through and to propose the full dignity of the person continued throughout his years as supreme pontiff. *Redemptor hominis* (1979), the *Catechesis on Human Love* (1979–84), *Mulieris dignitatem* (1988), *Veritatis splendor* (1993), the *Letter to Families* (1994), and *Fides et ratio* (1998) are some of the many fundamental texts that witness to this ongoing reflection on the nature and existence of the human person.

Created in the image of God and called to communion with him, the

---

1. Hans Urs von Balthasar, *Man Is Created*, vol. 5 of *Explorations in Theology*, trans. Adrian Walker (San Francisco: Ignatius Press, 2014), 371.

2. Henri de Lubac, *At the Service of the Church: Henri de Lubac Reflects on the Circumstances That Occasioned His Writings*, trans. Anne Englund (San Francisco: Ignatius Press, 1993), 171–72.

human person remains incomprehensible outside of the Christian revelation of the triune God. For this reason, a deepened understanding of the mystery of the human person demands a more profound consideration of the mystery of God. As St. John Paul II indefatigably showed, the indispensable elucidation of the human being as gift instead of as self-creative freedom would remain at the moral level were it not grounded in the mystery of the triune God. Equally so, the relation between sexually differentiated persons would fail to overcome romantic reductions of love were it not centered on the God who, in Christ, revealed himself as a triune communion of persons. The years of his pontificate not only allowed St. John Paul II to deepen his previous anthropological reflection, as the encyclicals on the triune God show (*Redemptor hominis*, *Dives in misericordia*, and *Dominum et vivificantem*), but also gave him the opportunity to unfold further the mystery of God as love and, by this light, to develop the theological meaning of the person. The mystery of the triune God and the mystery of man illuminate each other. The *Catechism of the Catholic Church*, written during his papacy and approved by St. John Paul II, explains well what it means that God is love (1 Jn 4:8): "God himself is an eternal exchange of love, Father, Son and Holy Spirit, and he has destined us to share in that exchange" (no. 221). In light of the tri-personal love revealed in Christ, the human being also realizes that created being is gift and that he in particular is the creature that God willed for his own sake. Man, in this way, discovers who he is only through a reciprocating gift of himself.[3] The significance of the work and mission of St. John Paul II, as they unfolded both before and during his papacy, is thus rightly

---

3. St. John Paul II frequently cited *Gaudium et spes*, no. 22: "The truth is that only in the mystery of the incarnate Word does the mystery of man take on light. For Adam, the first man, was a figure of Him Who was to come, namely Christ the Lord. Christ, the final Adam, by the revelation of the mystery of the Father and His love, fully reveals man to man himself and makes his supreme calling clear." It was in light of this passage that he also read no. 24: "Indeed, the Lord Jesus, when He prayed to the Father, 'that all may be one ... as we are one' (Jn 17:21–22) opened up vistas closed to human reason, for He implied a certain likeness between the union of the divine Persons, and the unity of God's sons in truth and charity. This likeness reveals that man, who is the only creature on earth which God willed for itself, cannot fully find himself except through a sincere gift of himself." Indeed, it is Christ's revelation of God's love that reveals how God's being, on the one hand, and created, non-subsistent being, on the other, are to be analogically understood as gift, and how human action and nuptial love find their truth and meaning when they reveal and participate in the gift-character of man's being. Second Vatican Council, Pastoral Constitution on the Church in the Modern World *Gaudium et spes* (December 7, 1965).

approached when seen within the *traditio* of the Church as an answer God gave through him to the questions that most preoccupy our era. The ECE offers his profound theological and philosophical thought to English readers with the hope that, through it, what God wanted to give the Church and the world in St. John Paul II may continue to be a source of enrichment.

II

The English Critical Edition of the Works of Karol Wojtyła/John Paul II consists of two parts, the first containing the works of Karol Wojtyła and the second those of John Paul II. The decision to publish both parts, and not simply the first one, derived from the editors' conviction that his work must be seen as a unity. Undoubtedly, everything published before his election to the See of Peter lacks the magisterial value that belongs to his papal writings. Yet, the author is one and the same, and his thought progressed and matured throughout the years of his pontificate. Indeed, one would have difficulty fully understanding documents such as *Redemptor hominis* or the *Catechesis on Human Love* if one were unfamiliar with texts such as *Person and Act* or *The Lublin Lectures* (with all their surrounding documents), or with his works on the family and his pastoral writings and speeches to youth, families, priests, and religious. The reverse is also the case. Wojtyła's elucidation of the meaning of human love (as we see, for example, in *Love and Responsibility*), work, religious freedom (addressed in several articles and in his contributions to *Dignitatis humanae* during the Second Vatican Council), and human action deepened and became more precise during his pontificate. While keeping the appropriate distinctions, it is thus superficial to separate the two phases of his production and to categorize Wojtyła's works simply as "philosophical" and John Paul II's reflection as "theological." This is not only because, on the one hand, there are theological texts in the pre-papal years and, on the other hand, the pontificate's theological reflection is supported by a robust, albeit mostly tacit, metaphysics (see, for example, *Veritatis splendor*, *Fides et ratio*, and *Catechesis on Human Love*). It is also because Christian existence, as we have seen, entails conformity with Christ the Logos and as such is philosophical by nature. The banal view that tends to draw a wedge between the reflection of Wojtyła and that of John Paul II also tends to consider his philosophy an incipient moral phenomenology that resists letting go of some Thomistic insights. Such a view is also prone to label his theological reflection as "magisterial" and hence to disregard it either because of its pastoral overtones or because it is somehow deficient with respect to contemporary academic standards. It may be the case that his philosophical essays require further development and that the magisterial framework—which demands that everything said be in service of the faith and not a platform enshrining private theological opinions—at times precludes a more systematic account of a given topic. Yet, both reductions seem to be guided by a common goal: to justify disregarding what was given through him. This, of course, cannot be understood to mean that his philosophical work is comparable to that of Plato or Aristotle, or that his theological reflections tower among those of Gregory of Nyssa and Leo I. St. John Paul II never sought to better his predecessors but only to humbly continue their work by expounding the novelty that Christ brought with himself. As we mentioned already, the full form of his work and its fruitfulness for the Church and the world will be disclosed only by the history of the Church. Our clarification, then, simply seeks to explain how an undue separation of the works of Karol Wojtyła/John Paul II weakens them as a whole.

A word is now needed to explain what is meant by "critical." In its first part, the ECE offers the English translation of the works of Karol Wojtyła, most of which were originally composed in Polish. This part is comprehensive and wishes to render available to a wider readership what Wojtyła wrote and said as a philosopher, teacher, priest, and bishop before being elected pope. Different versions and editions of texts are compared, and the differences are marked by a critical apparatus. For reasons of length and the proportionally few readers who master the Polish language, the Polish original will not be printed. Meticulous work done by Prof. Grzegorz Ignatik, translator and editor of these manuscripts, at the different archives where Wojtyła's texts are gathered (Kraków, Rome, and Lublin) has proven to be very fruitful. In fact, his efforts have helped resolve open questions regarding some seminal texts such as *Person and Act* and have led to the discovery of many unpublished texts now being made available for the first time. Whereas until now Wojtyła's published texts have been made available as individual books, such as *Love and Responsibility* and *Sources of Renewal*, each volume of the ECE gathers texts, lectures, and other documents that belong together thematically. The volumes of the first part are thus ordered around a given subject and then chronologically within each subject. Let us offer two examples from the first part's sixteen projected volumes. The first volume presents *Person and Act* along with all other texts related to its content and written both before and after its publication. The second volume offers *The Lublin Lectures* as well as essays that deal with the ethical nature of human acts and lived experience.

Following these two volumes, the general schedule for publication of the first part is organized thematically into volumes as follows: (3) anthropology, including manuscripts on the person and man's experience of action, as well as works on Scheler, such as Wojtyła's habilitation thesis; (4) ethics, including manuscripts on moral theology and Catholic social teaching; (5) love, marriage, and the family, including *Love and Responsibility* and his manuscripts concerning Paul VI's *Humanae vitae*; (6) theological essays, including his studies on St. John of the Cross; (7) the nature and mission of the Church; (8 and 9) his interventions at the Second Vatican Council, as well as his reflections on the work of the council, its interpretation, and those texts dealing with its pastoral implementation, such as *Sources of Renewal*; (10–13) retreats, sermons, and pastoral documents; (14) literary works, consisting of poems, dramas, and meditations.

The second part of the ECE is organized according to criteria that distinguish it from previous collections of the papal works. Given that the twenty-seven volumes of the *Acta Apostolicae Sedis* and the fifty-seven of the *Insegnamenti di Giovanni Paolo II* already contain the papal texts in chronological order, the second part will offer an English translation— either one previously published and now republished or one original to the ECE—of the texts deemed most important from a theological or philosophical perspective. Thus, unlike the first part, the second is not comprehensive. Another main criterion pertains to the ordering of the volumes. The texts are not gathered chronologically as they are in the *Acta* and *Insegnamenti*. These two series are invaluable for those wishing to retrieve a specific document or to find out, for example, what St. John

Paul II said during his apostolic trip to Mexico or during the first year of his pontificate. However, since most readers are interested in knowing what St. John Paul II said on a given issue, the fifteen projected volumes of the second part of the ECE are ordered thematically. Thus, each volume will gather all relevant texts regarding a topic such as Christology, marriage and family, the priesthood, the nature of the Church, or theological anthropology. As with his pre-papal works, many of these texts have already been published as single books or encyclicals. However, there is no published volume that offers English readers every relevant document on a given topic.

Both parts of the ECE keep the critical apparatus to an indispensable minimum. It is better to let the texts speak for themselves than to offer an interpretative key that could explain everything about a certain theme—for example, the significance of the sexual difference for understanding the *imago Dei*—or guide the reading of the text in a certain direction. Where necessary, editorial decisions are explained and, with regard to the second part, indexes provide references to texts not published in the ECE yet pertinent to the subject matter at hand. The last projected volume in the series will contain a set of comprehensive indexes.

We cannot conclude this introduction without expressing our deep gratitude to Supreme Knight Carl Anderson and the Knights of Columbus, who acquired the English copyright to the works of Karol Wojtyła and John Paul II and entrusted the John Paul II Institute at the Catholic University of America in Washington, D.C., with the editing and publication of the ECE. Without their financial magnanimity and constant support, the John Paul II Institute would not be able to serve the mission of the Church by offering the English Critical Edition of the Works of Karol Wojtyła/John Paul II. We would also like to thank the Catholic University of America Press and its director, Trevor Lipscombe, for their commitment to publish these works and for their invaluable guidance.

PREFACE TO VOLUME 1 OF THE ENGLISH CRITICAL EDITION

Grzegorz Ignatik

The first volume of the English Critical Edition of the Works of Karol Wojtyła/John Paul II (ECE) has as its central theme Wojtyła's work *Person and Act*. The purpose of this preface is to introduce that work without offering an interpretation of Wojtyła's philosophical thought. The preface thus presents, first, a brief outline of the contents of volume 1 according to the order of their creation and publication. Second, against the backdrop of the problems with the first English edition of *Person and Act*, it provides the textual basis for and main principles of the work of translation. Finally, it explains the critical apparatus used in this volume.

The Chronological Genesis of *Person and Act*

It is difficult to determine the exact timeframe in which *Person and Act* was written because Karol Wojtyła's manuscripts rarely contain dates. The earliest noted date for this work is 1964. This date accords with Wojtyła's statement in the introduction to *Person and Act* that the initial phase of its composition coincided with his participation in the Second Vatican Council, and, more specifically, with the drafting of the pastoral constitution *Gaudium et spes*. Wojtyła's work on *Person and Act* continued beyond its first publication in 1969.

Pre-1969 fragments

On January 29, 1965, Wojtyła submitted two initial chapters of the early version of *Person and Act* (which correspond to the introduction and chapter 1 in the book editions) to be published by the Catholic University of Lublin in a collection entitled *Pastori et magistro*.[1] However, only the beginning of chapter 1 was published in that collection.[2] In 1968, the journal *Studia theologica Varsaviensia* published another part of chapter 1.[3] The beginning of chapter 2 was also published in 1968 in the collection *O Bogu i o człowieku*.[4] Being at times quite different from the 1969 Polish edition, these early texts provide a unique insight into *Person and Act* and are therefore included in this volume of the ECE.

Book editions

The first full Polish edition of *Person and Act* was edited by then Fr. Marian Jaworski and published in Kraków in 1969. It had limited subheadings and no footnotes.

Around 1975, Wojtyła began to review *Person and Act* to prepare it for translation into English. At some point before 1979, Wojtyła revised the first edition of the Polish text (1969), which involved reworking both the introduction and chapter 1 as well as making corrections to chapter 2. He also developed and incorporated an extensive system of headings and subheadings, complementing and sometimes replacing the old headings. Lastly, Wojtyła wrote footnotes in collaboration with others such as Sr. Emilia Ehrlich, OSU, and Andrzej Półtawski, who helped him with his research. Wojtyła sent updated parts of *Person and Act* to the translator, Andrzej Potocki, while collaborating with the editor of the English edi-

---

1. Pastori et magistro: *Praca zbiorowa, wydana dla uczczenia jubileuszu 50-lecia kapłaństwa Jego Ekscelencji Księdza Biskupa Doktora Piotra Kałwy, Profesora i Wielkiego Kanclerza KUL* [*Pastori et magistro*: A collection published to celebrate the fiftieth anniversary of the priesthood of His Excellency Bishop Piotr Kałwa, professor and chancellor of the Catholic University of Lublin], ed. Andrzej Ludwik Krupa (Lublin: Towarzystwo Naukowe Katolickiego Uniwersytetu Lubelskiego, 1966). The complete text sent to the Catholic University of Lublin is stored in the Kraków archives, catalogued under AKKW CII 13/128 as "Osoba i czyn: artykuł do księgi pamiątkowej na 50-lecie kapłaństwa Bpa Piotra Kałwy."

2. "Osoba i czyn w aspekcie świadomości (Fragment studium 'Osoba i czyn')" [Person and act in the aspect of consciousness: A fragment of the study *Person and Act*], in Pastori et magistro, 293–305.

3. "Osoba i czyn: Refleksywne funkcjonowanie świadomości i jej emocjonalizacja" [*Person and Act*: The reflexive functioning and emotionalization of consciousness], *Studia theologica Varsaviensia* 6, no. 1 (1968): 101–19.

4. "Osoba i czyn na tle dynamizmu człowieka" [Person and act in the perspective of the dynamism of man], in *Problemy filozoficzne*, vol. 1 of *O Bogu i o człowieku*, edited by Bohdan Bejze (Warsaw: Wydawnictwo SS. Loretanek-Benedyktynek, 1968), 201–26.

tion of *Person and Act* (or *The Acting Person*, as it was then translated), Anna-Teresa Tymieniecka. The first English edition of *Person and Act* was published in 1979 as a part of the book series entitled Analecta Husserliana. Other non-Polish editions followed. The German edition was published in 1981, the Italian and Spanish editions in 1982, and the French edition in 1983.[5]

The second Polish edition of *Person and Act* was edited by Prof. Andrzej Półtawski and published in Kraków in 1985. This edition included not only the revisions that Wojtyła himself introduced into the text in preparation for the 1979 English translation but also a plethora of other editorial interventions made by Półtawski. Because almost all editorial changes appearing in the 1985 Polish edition were made before or in 1979, we can also call the second Polish edition the 1979 edition.

The third Polish edition was published in Lublin in 1994 and reprinted in 2000. This edition was based on the second Polish edition (1985), though its editorial board introduced its own changes into the text.[6] These changes, however, are mostly stylistic in nature.

Post-1969 writings related to *Person and Act*

As is evident, Wojtyła continued to discuss and develop the themes studied in *Person and Act*. This work found its expression in various articles and lectures, which are presented anew in this volume of the ECE. In December 1970, Cardinal Wojtyła and other philosophers participated in a Lublin symposium in which several professors and lecturers of the Catholic University of Lublin discussed his book *Person and Act* published in 1969. Wojtyła's introductory and concluding remarks to this discussion were published in *Analecta Cracoviensia* in 1973–74. In 1976, Wojtyła published an article entitled "Osoba: Podmiot i wspólnota" [The

---

5. Hence, the earliest non-Polish editions are *The Acting Person*, trans. Andrzej Potocki (Dordrecht: D. Reidel, 1979); *Person und Tat*, trans. Herbert Springer (Freiburg im Breisgau: Herder, 1981); *Persona e atto*, trans. Stanisław Morawski, Renzo Panzone, and Rosa Liotta (Vatican City: Libreria editrice Vaticana, 1982); *Persona y acción*, trans. Jesús Fernández Zulaica (Madrid: BAC, 1982); *Personne et acte*, trans. Gwendoline Jarczyk (Paris: Le Centurion, 1983).

6. The three main Polish editions of *Person and Act* are thus *Osoba i czyn*, ed. Marian Jaworski (Kraków: Polskie Towarzystwo Teologiczne, 1969); *Osoba i czyn*, ed. Andrzej Półtawski (Kraków: Polskie Towarzystwo Teologiczne, 1985); and *Osoba i czyn oraz inne studia antropologiczne*, ed. Tadeusz Styczeń, Wojciech Chudy, Jerzy W. Gałkowski, Adam Rodziński, and Andrzej Szostek (Lublin: Towarzystwo Naukowe Katolickiego Uniwersytetu Lubelskiego, 1994; repr. 2000).

Person: Subject and Community], in which he analyzed in more detail the relation between personal subjectivity and the human community, a problem outlined in chapter 7 of *Person and Act*. In addition, Wojtyła wrote several articles on the topic of the person and his action, which he presented at events such as conferences in Poland and abroad in the years 1974–77.

In light of all these developments, the first volume of the ECE consists of three parts. The first part contains the pre-1969 synopsis and fragments of *Person and Act*. The second part is the central work, *Person and Act*. The third and last part includes post-1969 texts that are closely related to *Person and Act*. Chronological and publication details concerning all these texts are provided in editorial notes. It is worth pointing out that many of these texts have never been translated into English. All texts from part 1 and articles such as "Introductory Statement during the Discussion on *Person and Act*" and "The Afterword to the Discussion on *Person and Act*" are published in English here for the first time. Furthermore, several texts published in this volume have never been published even in Polish (except "The Author's Preface to *Person and Act*"). These texts include "*Person and Act*: A Synopsis," "Symposium on *Person and Act*," and "A Letter to Anna-Teresa Tymieniecka." All texts published in this volume of the ECE are new English translations from the Polish.

The Present Critical Edition of *Person and Act*
Controversies surrounding the first English edition

The international community of thinkers interested in Wojtyła's philosophical work has long been aware of two main problems with the 1979 English edition of *Person and Act* (entitled *The Acting Person*), translated by Andrzej Potocki and edited by Anna-Teresa Tymieniecka. The first of these problems is unauthorized editorial interventions in the text of *Person and Act* by Tymieniecka, a devoted phenomenologist and long-standing friend of St. John Paul II. The second problem, closely related to the first one, is an unfaithful and inconsistent English translation of the Polish text.

On the one hand, the documents dated 1975–77 and stored in the Kraków archives indicate that Wojtyła discussed topics pertaining to *Per-*

son and Act with Tymieniecka and that these conversations in some way influenced the changes he made to the first Polish edition of the book. As mentioned, Wojtyła made a number of revisions to that edition and sent the updated sections of the text to Potocki to be translated into English. On the other hand, Tymieniecka herself undertook the revision of the text by making her own changes to it and allegedly obtaining approval for them from Wojtyła.[7] Through her revisions, Tymieniecka changed the text to align it more closely with her own phenomenological sympathies, as if she were a coauthor of the definitive version of *Person and Act*.[8] Her changes included, for example, removing almost all references to St. Thomas and Aristotle, replacing Latin terms and phrases with English substitutes, and adding phenomenological language and even names (e.g., those of Husserl and Heidegger). Unfortunately, it is impossible to identify which changes may have been approved by or come from Wojtyła, given that original corrections sent to Potocki are unavailable and that there are no indications of them in the English text itself.

Naturally, the question arises whether and to what extent the revised English text influenced the text of the second and third Polish editions of *Person and Act*. In a private conversation in June 2018, Andrzej Półtawski, the editor of the second Polish edition, vehemently denied that Tymieniecka had anything to do with the Polish text published in 1985. Nonetheless, in agreement with Tymieniecka, Półtawski claimed that the 1969 edition of *Person and Act* was underdeveloped and, hence, that it needed further improvements to more fully express the author's thought. It is certain that both he and the editors of the third Polish edition of *Person and Act* (1994) introduced editorial interventions into their respective versions of the text. In the present critical edition, the scholarly apparatus marks all known revisions made to the successive Polish editions of *Person and Act*, whether made by Wojtyła himself or by others, thus en-

---

7. Anna-Teresa Tymieniecka, editorial introduction to *The Acting Person*, by Karol Wojtyła, trans. Andrzej Potocki (Dordrecht: D. Reidel, 1979), xxii–xxiii.

8. In her introduction to *The Acting Person*, Tymieniecka attempts to undermine the 1969 Polish edition of *Person and Act*, claiming that it was merely an unedited draft published before the author "had the opportunity to give it more careful attention and to edit it himself for publication" (p. xxii). This outrageous claim contradicts the fact that Wojtyła had already begun publishing fragments of *Person and Act* in 1966, as we indicated above, and that he did revise his draft of the book before it was published in 1969, as is evident from such a revision stored in the Kraków archive (AKKW CII 13/127).

abling the reader to easily identify and decide the significance of these changes.

Finally, a brief word is in order regarding the quality of the translation of the first English edition (1979). This edition took liberties in translation through frequent imprecisions, omissions and additions, and inconsistencies in translating the same terms with different English words.[9]

The reader must wonder how Wojtyła responded to all these editorial interventions, especially concerning the first English edition. We know that not all the changes introduced to the text by Tymieniecka met with the approval of the author. In fact, documents in the Kraków archive indicate that Wojtyła protested the removal of explicit references to St. Thomas from the text and footnotes. This removal was not a simple elimination of extraneous material but a weakening of the metaphysical underpinnings of Wojtyła's work. Commenting on the progress of the translation efforts in 1977, Wojtyła noted: "The elimination of the references to St. Thomas Aquinas. What do I think of it? I think that it is right to show the author's own thought. However, I think that it is wrong to efface all traces of dependence."[10] Similarly, Wojtyła disagreed with the removal of all Latin terms and their replacement with English words.[11] We also know that he attempted to correct the English translation so that it conformed to the Polish text of his book. Overall, he was not fully satisfied with the English translation and could not understand why the corrections prepared by his "Kraków Commission" were not incorporated into the English text.[12]

---

9. Two key terms provide examples of such inconsistent translation. The word *ogląd* (vision) has been rendered variously in the first English edition (1979) as "apprehension," "exfoliating," "revealing," "approach," "intuition," "perception," "insight," and "vision." The word *suppositum* has been translated as "autonomous individual being," "basic ontological structure," "ontological basis/foundation of action," "structural ontological nucleus/foundation/basis," "ontological basis for existence," "ontological groundwork," "basic structure," "structural support/nucleus," "ontological support," "structural core of a being," and "factor."

10. Wojtyła to unknown recipient, "Sprawy związane z tłumaczeniem *Osoby i czynu*" [Matters concerning the translation of *Person and Act*], March 1977, catalogued in the Archive of the Metropolitan Curia in Kraków under AKKW CII 17/136a.

11. Wojtyła to unknown recipient, "Notatki JP2 Styczeń 1981" [Notes concerning the translation of *Person and Act*], January 1981, catalogued in the Archive of the Center for Documentation and Research of the Pontificate of John Paul II in Rome under AODiSP - EE/X (Sr. Emilia Ehrlich materials). This correspondence was accessed with the help of Fr. Andrzej Dobrzyński, director of the archive.

12. Wojtyła to unknown recipient, "Notatki JP2 Styczeń 1981," January 1981.

Textual basis for the current translation

This volume presents a completely new translation of *Person and Act*. Its fundamental strength is the underlying Polish text, which has been derived exclusively from original sources found in the Cardinal Karol Wojtyła Archive of the Metropolitan Curia in Kraków, Poland. This archive contains the world's most complete collection of Wojtyła's writings, including various manuscripts and typescripts of *Person and Act*, manuscripts and typescripts of Wojtyła's revisions to the 1969 introduction and first chapter, his new headings for the book, and an abundance of related materials. After extensive research, it became clear that the only Polish edition of *Person and Act* that the author thoroughly reviewed and approved for publication was the first edition from 1969. This fact is confirmed by multiple manuscript versions of *Person and Act* and by typescripts of this work that bear Wojtyła's handwritten corrections. The fact that in 1966 and 1968 Wojtyła published fragments of an earlier version of *Person and Act* also affirms that the 1969 edition had been well thought through by the author. Because these fragments are reproduced in the present volume, the reader will be able to compare them to the later text of *Person and Act*.

Despite the maturity of the first Polish edition, Wojtyła made multiple changes to it after its publication in 1969. Only changes found in manuscript form, that is, in Wojtyła's own handwriting, have been accepted as authentic. Therefore, the 1969 Polish text of *Person and Act* used for our translation has been updated in accord with Wojtyła's own revisions to the introduction and chapter 1, his new title headings within the text, new footnotes, and his afterword. Changes not made by Wojtyła himself are marked by the critical apparatus and placed in the endnotes. In order to accomplish this task, all three Polish editions were compared not only with one another but also with the original manuscripts and typescripts of *Person and Act* that reside in the Kraków archives. This course of action included footnotes, because some of the original footnotes appended to the archival manuscripts and typescripts were truncated in the 1979/1985 and 1994/2000 editions. The comparative study ensured the most authentic text of *Person and Act*, which was rendered into English and is presented in this volume.

As a result, many passages and phrases that its editors excised from the first Polish edition have found their way back into the present English text, title headings, and footnotes. For example, the following two passages removed from the 1969 edition by the 1985 and 1994 Polish editions have been reintroduced to the main text: "After all, we indirectly owe to the philosophy of consciousness a more thorough cognition of man in the context of consciousness—and this certainly enriches the vision of person and act. Remaining on the basis of the philosophy of being, we would like to take advantage of this enrichment" (from introduction); and "We not only record in the beginning the philosophical interpretation of act proper to Aristotelianism and Thomism but also intend to continue developing and elucidating it in a number of aspects" (from chapter 1). Both passages confirm that in his method Wojtyła never abandons the metaphysics of Aristotle and St. Thomas and that he is not limited to it. Hence, such passages are essential for a correct understanding of the thought presented in *Person and Act*.

Similarly, many footnotes have been restored to their original state. These changes include bringing back references and quotations—especially those from the renowned Polish phenomenologist Roman Ingarden—that were truncated or removed in the second and third Polish editions and in the first English edition. In particular, some of these truncated notes initially contained citations in original languages (such as Greek and German) that are now included in the present edition and accompanied by English translations.

Lastly, the original text emphasis and paragraph divisions have been restored. In particular, the text emphasis introduced by the author helps the reader note the critical points of the author's thought. Several printing mistakes present in the Polish editions have also been corrected in light of the original manuscript or typescript.

In addition to presenting the new translation of *Person and Act*, this first volume of the ECE offers new translations of all other included works. They have been produced with the same careful review and approval as that given to the text of *Person and Act*. The original manuscripts and typescripts stored in the Kraków archives were compared to the published editions in order to ensure the most authentic texts and footnotes for translation into English. This task was at times challenging due to multiple editions of the same work having been delivered or published with differences in the text (as in the article "Participation or Alienation") and footnotes (as in the article "The Transcendence of the Person in the Act and the Auto-teleology of Man").

Additional remarks regarding translation

Translating *Person and Act*, as well as other texts in this and forthcoming volumes of the ECE, requires familiarity with Karol Wojtyła's work as a whole and with certain philosophical traditions presupposed in Wojtyła's own reflection. Especially important in this regard are the figures of Plato, Aristotle, St. Thomas, Kant, and Scheler. Producing a high-quality English translation also requires, in addition to proficiency in Polish and English, knowledge of ancient and modern languages, especially Latin and German.

Alongside such scholarly qualifications, however, translating any of Wojtyła's texts requires a sincere reverence for the author and his work, especially considering that the author is a man of God—a prophet and witness of the triune God's love in the world. Like his other works, *Person and Act* is not only a result of Wojtyła's thought but also a fruit of his profound faith and prayer. His prayer life is especially visible on the pages of his manuscripts, each of them always bearing the inscriptions AMDG (*Ad majorem Dei gloriam*), J+M (Jesus and Mary), and ☧ (Chi Rho) in the top left-hand corner as well as verses of prayers in Latin (such as *Totus tuus ego sum*, *Veni Sancte Spiritus*, *Ave Maris Stella*, and *Jesu Redemptor omnium*) in the top right-hand corner. Also for this reason, the ECE translation—the fruit of seven years of research, translation, and redaction—strives for fidelity and consistency in rendering the Polish text into English, so as to present Wojtyła's thought in all its original depth and eloquent splendor. Faithfulness to the text required our English translation to retain all non-Polish terms used by Wojtyła (especially those in Latin) and to not shy away from reproducing his technical language, whether metaphysical or phenomenological. The reader can be assured that any terms or passages in languages other than English appear as such in the original text. Translations of such passages and of less common terms have been provided using published translations wherever possible. Any ambiguities present in Polish are retained in our English translation whenever possible, and significant alternative readings are provided in editorial notes.

Finally, several persons should be acknowledged for their valuable contributions to this volume of the ECE. The excellent work of Caitlin Jolly, Katarzyna Ignatik, Emily Lyon, and David Henderson, the copyeditors of this volume, was indispensable for greatly improving the translation's accuracy and readability. A special recognition should be given to Mrs. Jolly, whose painstaking work with the truly challenging text and bibliography of *Person and Act* proved to be more than that of a copyeditor. Last but not least, Michael Camacho deserves recognition for his masterful translation of French passages into English.

On Editorial Interventions and the Critical Apparatus

In order to let Wojtyła speak, this English Critical Edition keeps editorial interventions to a minimum. In addition to correcting printing errors and obvious misspellings by the author (e.g., *fisico*, changed to *physico*), the only alterations to the text concern editorial notes and the critical apparatus. Relatively few editorial notes have been added. The goal of these is to explain the intricacies of the Polish text, point out some of its ambiguities, and provide pertinent publication information. All editorial notes are clearly marked and separated from the original text and footnotes. Editorial notes are employed in three ways. First, they can appear as endnotes collected at the end of the volume and marked in the text by roman numerals in superscript. Second, these notes can appear within original footnotes. Third, they can be found within the texts reproduced by the critical apparatus at the end of the volume. When appearing in both original footnotes and the critical apparatus, they are enclosed within brackets and introduced with the phrase "Editorial note."

In order to maintain the text's legibility, only essential textual alterations are marked by the critical apparatus. The criterion for distinguishing essential from nonessential changes is that the former do and the latter do not substantially alter the meaning of the text. Nonessential changes include altering punctuation and word order, using synonyms, removing dashes from within words, removing or adding quotes, changing paragraph divisions, and introducing changes in number (from singular to plural and vice versa). Wherever possible, nonessential changes made by Polish editors were reversed to reflect the original text.

Lastly, the editorial interventions include a revised general organization (ordering, numbering, and capitalization) of headings and subheadings throughout the volume. Although this revised organization streamlines all the headings for compilation into a single volume, it relies closely on the original manuscripts, typescripts, and published editions.

Critical apparatus for *Person and Act*

The critical apparatus marks changes to the text and footnotes between various editions of the same work by alphanumeric characters (1a, 2a, 2b, etc.) and records these changes at the end of the volume (in contrast to the original footnotes, which are marked by arabic numerals only, and editorial endotes, which are marked by roman numerals). The changes are presented at the end of the volume, where the source in which the change appeared is also indicated in brackets.

There are slight differences between the critical apparatus as it is employed in text and in footnotes. Both series of markings use alphanumeric numbers. However, the text markings appear in superscript (e.g., $^{1a\ 1b}$), whereas the footnote markings appear in brackets (e.g., [1a] [1b]). The critical apparatus numbering for the main text restarts with each work (except in regard to the fragments of *Person and Act* presented in part 1 of this volume), whereas the numbering for footnotes is continuous.

The critical apparatus marks four categories of changes made to *Person and Act* and other texts: additions, removals, substitutions, and marginal notes. The following are made-up examples to help the reader understand the markings of the apparatus.

1) Additions
example: the transcendence formed in the person through freedom and ^{1a} efficacy
endnote: ^{1a} [1979/1985] conscious
explanation: The word "conscious" was added in the 1985 Polish edition.

example: [13a]An attempt to render the subjectivity of man[13b]
endnote: [13a] [13b] [1969: added]
explanation: The text marked between [13a] and [13b] was added to the text of the 1969 edition.

2) Removals
example: it is fitting to [2a]fully[2b] approve the vision of human reality
endnote: [2a] [2b] [1979/1985: removed]
explanation: The word "fully" was removed in the 1985 Polish edition.

3) Substitutions
example: [3a]The emotivity of the subject and the efficacy of the person[3b]
endnote: [3a] [3b] [1969] Integration: emotivity and efficacy
explanation: The phrase "Integration: emotivity and efficacy" that appeared in the 1969 Polish edition was subsequently replaced with the phrase "The emotivity of the subject and the efficacy of the person."

4) Marginal notes
example: [7a] Every act in a sense finds consciousness already present
endnote: [7a] [1969 marginal note] The problem of the identity of consciousness, like that of its continuity, runs through the entirety of Western philosophical reflection.
explanation: A source document (a manuscript or typescript) contains a marginal note that reads, "The problem of the identity of consciousness, like that of its continuity, runs through the entirety of Western philosophical reflection," and that has not been incorporated into the main text.

Please note that only modifications marked with "1969" indicate changes made by Wojtyła himself to the text of the 1969 Polish edition. Thus, the 1969 removals indicate what Wojtyła removed from the 1969 edition; the 1969 additions mark what he added to the 1969 edition; and the 1969 substitutions note the text that he removed and replaced with some other text. The 1969 marginal notes are taken from the document that introduces changes to the 1969 edition. Because the changes marked with "1979/1985" and "1994/2000" are those made by Polish editors, all of them are placed in the endnotes without modifying the main translated text in any way. To sum up, the 1969 notes show what Wojtyła himself did to his 1969 edition, whereas the 1979/1985 and 1994/2000 notes show what others did to his 1969 edition and when.

It is worth noting that the changes marked with "1979/1985" are also retained in the 1994/2000 edition of *Person and Act*, because, as we indicated above, the 1994/2000 (3rd) edition is based on the 1979/1985 (2nd) edition. Thus, the critical apparatus uses "1979/1985" label for changes that appeared in that edition and subsequently in the 1994/2000 edition. However, the changes marked with "1994/2000" belong only to that edition and do not appear in the previous ones.

Critical apparatus for other texts

The critical apparatus markings to all other texts in this volume follow the same system as that used for *Person and Act*. Because some of the articles included in this volume were also published in Polish in the same volume as *Person and Act*, the reader will occasionally encounter the same year designations as those found in *Person and Act* (e.g., [1994/2000]). Lastly, when needed, the critical apparatus is made more expressive for the sake of clarity, for example, [the 1978 edition places the following footnote here] or [here begins the marginal note].

Critical apparatus for footnotes

The critical apparatus for footnotes functions in the same way as that for *Person and Act* and other texts, with the slight differences in numbering indicated above. This apparatus marks changes to the corresponding footnotes in various editions of the same work (normally in Polish, though original typescripts in other languages are also consulted whenever relevant). In some cases, the apparatus indicates the removal of the entire footnote. However, changes in footnote placement and indications of footnotes found in other versions of a given text but excluded here are marked by the critical apparatus for texts.

ACKNOWLEDGMENTS

The charitable support of Cardinal Stanisław Dziwisz, former archbishop of Kraków, in granting access to the Kraków and Rome archives was essential. Likewise, we must note the kind permission extended to us by His Excellency Marek Jędraszewski, current archbishop of Kraków, to continue this archival research. We are grateful for the assistance of Fr. Jacek Urban, director of the Archive of the Metropolitan Curia and professor at the Pontifical University of John Paul II, both in Kraków, and we extend our thanks to the other archivists, especially Sr. Maria Teresa Sawicka, SSCJ; Sr. Karola Lidia Zaborska, SSCJ; Ms. Delfina Kościółek; and Ms. Alicja Kędra. A special gratitude is owed to Sr. Maria Teresa Sawicka, who devoted hours to assisting with research and lent her expertise in reading Wojtyła's handwriting. The support of Fr. Jarosław Kupczak, OP, professor at the Pontifical University of John Paul II in Kraków, also deserves appreciation. Finally, we express our gratitude to Mr. Peter Veracka, director of library services at the Pontifical College Josephinum in Columbus, Ohio, for his reliable help in obtaining copies of previously published texts.

I

PRE-1969 SYNOPSIS AND FRAGMENTS

1 ❖ *Person and Act*

A Synopsis

Introduction

Our reflections on person and act were born *from the experience of morality*.[i] It inheres in these reflections as their root, as their realistic context. Of course, these reflections could be derived from some other experience as, for example, the concept [1a]*homo aeconomicus*[1b]—from the context of economic life. By drawing our knowledge of person and act from the experience of morality, we *thereby position it within the philosophy of morality and ethics*. We do so consciously and with premeditation, accepting in advance that such a grasp of the problem of person and act will be simply a part (*pars integrans*) of the philosophy of morality or a presupposition of ethics. We also think that this grasp laden with the aforementioned implications *is not at all detrimental to the very conception of man as such.* "Ethical" anthropology might be the truest, the most humanistic anthropology. *It will manifest man to us in what is most essentially human.*

However, I would not *gratis asserere* this. Thus, if at this point I do not resort to various arguments that would aim at proving this proposition *stricto sensu, I wish at least to explain it.* For the sake of explanation, we ought above all to define more closely the meaning of the experience of morality.

In my opinion, this experience constitutes the basis and root of the entire philosophy of morality and ethics, two fields of knowledge that differ by their formal object. They converge, however, in the area of their

3

material object. Explaining all this is a separate task—and should be the subject matter of a treatise entitled *The Conception and Methodology of Ethics*, which I would also like to prepare. At this point, our concern is rather to ascertain that the experience of morality exists—*for morality exists as a reality grounded in the man-person* and his acts. Morality—reality.

This means that morality contains in a particular way the man-*person and his acts as a reality* given experientially, which we can thus *correctly and thoroughly read* from the experience of morality. The center, the central point of this experience, is the moral value, which in the reality known to us exists only in conjunction with the man-person and his acts. The philosophy of morality is concerned above all with this value, with its internal specificity, but also with the conditions of its *fieri* in the person through acts—it attempts to explain this. An occasion or opportunity thus arises for a *specific and thorough cognition of the person as such*—an opportunity to study the problem of "person and act."

This study does not promise to be aspectual. The experience of morality does not reveal the person to us in an accidental, collateral, or secondary way—but, properly, in a most essential way. Man as such, *as a person in his proper essence*, *actualizes* and expresses *himself in morality*— that which is most proper, most essential to him. We can ask how we know this. This is *a conviction formed precisely on the basis of the experience of morality, constituting one element of its content*—a *fundamental* element at that. As soon as this element is excluded from the interpretation of the experience of morality, the interpretation falls into heterogeneity. [2a] A certain proof of this is the so-called sociology of morality—and even the psychology of morality. Thus, since the correct interpretation of the experience of morality, that is, the accurate understanding of the essence of the moral value and of its *fieri* in the person, demands a grasp of that which is essential to the person, within this interpretation we can also build *an anthropology that is as essential and integral as possible*.

At the same time, this will *be a specific anthropology*. Its specificity results from the fact that the experience of morality introduces us into the world of the man-*person not only as a being but also as a consciousness*. This experience introduces us into the acts of the man-person in a parallel manner: *not only into the acts* (actus), in accord with the tradition of *philosophiae perennis*, but also into the lived-experiences linked to consciousness. There is, then, a certain novelty or freshness in the philosophical anthropology built along these lines. This anthropology holds out the possibility of unifying what has been a sphere of division throughout the history of science, and especially of philosophy, and has formed, as it were, an impassable *"hiatus" in the method*—that is, in the very principle of philosophizing, in the cognition of reality in general, especially human reality. The present study is—at least collaterally—a certain *attempt to resolve this difficult situation, at least concerning the conception of man*.

It seems that this resolution is possible *when we employ simultaneously the so-called phenomenological method and the method proper to the philosophy of being*. Right away a question arises as to whether such a linking of methods is not a linking of mutually exclusive things or at least *eorum quae in se sunt inconciliabilia* (non-linkable). This is an important question because it determines not only the methodological but also indirectly the substantive value of the entire attempt. Thus, we have to answer it at the beginning.

What seems possible is *at least a systematic confrontation of these two methods* and of what we can say about the man-person and his acts with the help of these methods. Of course, such a confrontation requires constant vigilance so as not to blur the boundaries between them. Indeed, we must constantly *attend to the line of demarcation* that divides these two methods and their effects in the field of cognition and knowledge about man. A systematic confrontation will convince us that the two fields approach each other very closely and, indeed, meet in the cognition and knowledge about the object, that is, the man-person and his acts. Our knowledge of him in light of one method does not in the least oppose the knowledge attained in light of the other. Rather, *the one complements and explains the other*. This is a coherentia *rather than a collision* of two general epistemological aspects. The one does not in the least contradict the other, as long as we do not posit collision and contradiction in advance. We do not need to fear a diversity of epistemological positions but rather their absolutization, which generates an a priori divergence.

In light of our chosen method, there emerge *two stages in relation to the chosen problem*. The first stage *is, in a sense, an in-depth reading of the experiential fact*: the contents of the experiential data need to be in a sense thoroughly and penetratingly decoded and explicated. This is the *intuitive function of intellect* (*intus-legere*). The second stage is *interpretation*, which is linked with the second *function of intellect*, namely, *with reasoning*. This is not the classic *ratiocinatio*; it is not concerned with demonstrating the truthfulness of a proposition (thesis). The interpretation or explanation of experiential data that have been read as thoroughly as possible has in itself *nothing of deduction—it requires a reduction*. We mean the reduction to a proper foundation, that is, a cause or reason.

This effort holds out the *possibility of bringing both methods of investigating reality*, the phenomenological and the metaphysical (i.e., in a certain sense meta-phenomenological), *closer together*—indeed, we see their inevitable encounter. To reduce what is contained in the experience investigated by the method of phenomenology to what constitutes the object of metaphysics *is not an unjustified "jump"* but a "discovery." The discovered content is contained in experience no less than what we discover with the method of phenomenology. Thus, for example, the statement that man is a being is revealed through all facts of consciousness, and it is revealed in them as their root and basis, which we do not "build into" the content of experience (this is neither an interpretation nor a result of introducing a form a priori). [3a] [4a] This statement is revealed to us *on the basis of the same experience* as that in which we grasp all facts of consciousness proper to man. Thus, experience is the basis here as well. The distinctness of the phenomenological and metaphysical methods does not in the least cancel this. These methods grasp their proper contents in one and the same object given in experience. *These contents contain each other*—and, for the intellect investigating the object in light of the data of experience, *explain each other*. This is the correct sense of reduction.

We will continue to return to methodological remarks in a more detailed manner when we analyze particular problems.

1. Consciousness

1.1. Morality as the content of consciousness

According to what has been said in the introduction, the starting point in our cognition of man (of person and act) is to be the experience of morality. *This experience is shaped in a twofold manner:* (1) *as a specific objective totality* connected with the conscious action of man (with his acts), which contains the *fieri* of the moral value, and (2) *as a subjective content of consciousness* connected with this objective totality. (In this form, morality stands vis-à-vis so-called interior experience.) It is often suggested that (2) completely obscures (1). Whoever accepts morality as a content of consciousness will never escape all the *consequences of subjectivism*. However, no one can deny that morality occurs experientially *also* (!) as a content of consciousness. Subjectivism is a consequence of presupposing morality as *exclusively* (!) a content of consciousness. We do not accept this presupposition here, as is clearly evident from the introduction. But we accept the aspect of experience in which morality occurs as a content of consciousness, confidant that this *will not impede or negate our knowledge about the man-person in the objective order.*

Consciousness mirrors to us not only the moral value as an isolated content (and even the content located *in iuxtapositione* to the person-act content) but *also the* fieri *of the moral value in the subject.* This is of fundamental significance for our position (and for our knowledge about man). The moral value [5a]not simply "is" but "becomes" (*fit*) in the subject[5b] under the appropriate conditions. Consciousness is the fundamental condition. These conditions ought to be grasped in a twofold manner: *the moral value in the person "becomes"* (1) in the case of conscious efficacy, and (2) when this conscious efficacy is realized in relation to the so-called norm.

(In the above understanding, per [1] and [2] there exists *in nucleo*, as it were, in the experiential germ, both what can be defined as the objective content of morality, especially [2], and what constitutes its subject, i.e., the person and the act, especially [1].) In order to explicate this (1) most fully, we will attempt to analyze consciousness and its role in the structure of the person and the act.

1.2. An introductory analysis of consciousness

According to what was stated above, consciousness *mirrors* the *fieri* of the moral value in the subject. This statement already indirectly shows that *consciousness itself is not the proper subject of that* fieri, *which does not take place in it but is merely mirrored by it.* This *fieri* is accomplished in the person through acts. Consciousness is the subject of mirroring, that is, a cognition that accompanies the person and his action (acts). Already, this indicates that consciousness does not possess its own subsistence.

Our aim is to characterize precisely this cognition. This task is important because *certo constat et quidam experimentaliter* (the experience of morality) that only that which is conscious, the conscious act, possesses the moral value. [6a]However, we must state right away that "conscious" [*świadomy*] is not the same as "made conscious" [*uświadomiony*] (mirrored in consciousness). Here, there emerges already a distinction that will have to be thoroughly studied.[6b]

Thus, consciousness possesses a cognitive character, is a kind of cognition. This is *mental cognition*—judgments based on concepts. We ascertain this without prejudice concerning so-called sensual consciousness. [7a] Mental consciousness is not identified with the totality of mental cognition, with the totality of our intellectual knowledge. Indeed, *consciousness differs essentially from knowledge*. As cognition, it possesses a *reflective character* but is not *ex toto* equivalent to reflection itself. Reflective acts do not have to be *eo ipso* acts of consciousness. What seems to be characteristic of acts of consciousness besides reflectivity is a *specific connection to the subjective acting "I."* However, consciousness is not simple self-cognition or self-knowledge. "To know oneself" or "to know about oneself" differs from "to be conscious" or "to be conscious of oneself" (the latter refers to so-called self-consciousness).

All this indicates a *completely specific character of consciousness* (*and so-called self-consciousness*). It is linked with the totality of human cognitive capabilities through a common root (*in potentia*) but differs from them *in se* by the separate character of its acts. This is a *specific character: consciousness-related,* which all other cognitive acts do not possess.[ii]

1.3. Consciousness and the subject (*suppositum*) (and the subjectivity of the human person)

Our introductory analysis of consciousness adequately indicates its *functional—not its substantial—character.* The latter is not negated by everything that we can say about the so-called "state of consciousness": *nota bene*, consciousness is not a state; man, however, is in a state of consciousness when consciousness functions, in contradistinction to when it does not function. [8a] *Amplius*: consciousness not only "mirrors" but truly "reveals" man as a *substantial subject of existence and action* (suppositum), a subject that resides outside consciousness—or rather *at its foundations.* Indeed—precisely at its foundations. Consciousness is not a mechanical mirror of a "being" (matter) but remains with this being in an *organic, vital connection*. This is particularly evident in the human act. *The being ("I") is both the object and the subject of consciousness*—this also determines the specific character of consciousness as cognition. (The subject of action, that which acts, etc., is something different from that in which the action of the subject and the subject himself are mirrored.)

[9a] Nonetheless, *consciousness is "quasi-subiectum"* insofar as in it the person and the act are mirrored "as if" in the subject ("as if" because consciousness possesses a fundamentally functional character, thus *in se* it is not a subject). *However, thanks to consciousness the subjectivity of the human person* (namely, his experiencing himself as a subject) *is shaped and manifested*—which, in my opinion, is absent in animals (?).

Corrolarium. How the *method of* (interior) *experience* (*empiria*), unilaterally applied together with the "*substantialization*" *of consciousness*, can lead to subjectivism and idealism (the person as pure consciousness?). And how this is contradicted by experience—by, among other things, interior experience. How interior experience inheres in integral experience.

1.4. Consciousness (and self-consciousness) and self-knowledge

Man has the consciousness of the *fieri* of the moral value in the person—that is, in accord with the previous discourse: *consciousness mirrors the fieri of the moral value in the person* (*suppositum*). Because this is accomplished in and through acts, *a fortiori consciousness mirrors these acts* of the person and thereby constitutes an introduction, as it were, to our knowledge on that topic. The acts of the person are *in suo esse physico*, each for itself a specific, deeply complex reality. Consciousness mirrors this complexity insofar as in it various elements of the dynamic reality "man" (the person-*suppositum*) find their place, elements that not only individually possess their own dynamic but also participate in acts, each of which in a particular (essential) way contains and expresses the dynamic of the entire person (*suppositum*). Objectively, all this is the object of integral experience and of intellectual intuition—though at this point, in order to more fully elucidate the matter, let us take a look at this in the subjective reflection of consciousness.

It is now fitting to present *the extent to which the "body" and the main functions of the interior life of the person—namely, cognition, striving, desire*, and also *affection and drive (instinct)—are the object of consciousness.* At the same time, however, we ought to very clearly separate that which is the object of consciousness from that which is already the *object and achievement of a certain knowledge*. This can be a descriptive (experiential-descriptive) knowledge or a fuller knowledge that contains a certain interpretation, that is, *per causas viciniores vel etiam ultimas*.[10a] *This knowledge differs from self-knowledge,* though at the same time it somehow relies on it (how much does it differ and how much does it rely?). Self-knowledge possesses a personal, experiential—*ergo* an individual—character, whereas knowledge *ex definitione* has a general character.

What connection does each have with consciousness? Knowledge and especially self-knowledge draw from consciousness, which does not yet contain any reasoning, does not strive for any explanation. Knowledge—even self-knowledge—is built up by way of reasoning for the sake of explaining. In turn, a problem arises: *to what extent is consciousness enriched thanks to the knowledge about man?* And *to what extent is it identified with self-knowledge?* It seems to me that this never occurs on the side of the character of acts.

All this ought to be sketched while considering particular elements of the person that are parts of acts—*for the time being, in the reflection of consciousness*. Later we shall try to transition from this reflection to the elements that are parts of the act of the person *in se*.

Particular attention should be devoted to various *manifestations of emotional life*. This issue is separate insofar as they not only are mirrored in consciousness but also (1) *form a specific "consciousness"*: man is not only "conscious of himself," but also "feels himself," etc. (the superiority of "consciousness" over "sensation"); (2) in a particular way penetrate consciousness, contributing to the *"emotionalization of consciousness."* We are still concerned with the mirroring consciousness (!).

1.5. The human act in the reflection of consciousness

Consciousness mirrors not only the various elements that participate in acts but also the act itself—and *not only as a whole composed of various (diverse) elements, but also as a whole homogeneous in itself,* irreducible to those ("material," but possessing *their own internal essence*) elements. We shall try to gradually bring this to light.

(a) First, consciousness clearly *distinguishes that which merely "happens" in man* (in the subject, in the "I," in the *suppositum*) *from that which this subject does*. In the latter case, consciousness reveals to us *the "efficacy" of the subject*, which definitely does not occur when something merely "happens" in the subject. This efficacy is an indispensable condition of the *fieri* of the moral value. What is concealed behind it—and consciousness mirrors this—is either *"volition"* ("I will") or *consent*. Neither of them, as the content of consciousness (i.e., as lived-experience), is completely identified with the efficacy of the human "I." *"Efficacy" is something fuller*: in a sense it contains volition or consent, but at the same time it also contains a relation to everything else that inheres in that "I" (here originates the problem of the immanence of the person in the act).

(b) This mirroring of the subject's efficacy in the human act is connected with *a certain mirroring of freedom* linked to volition or consent. Both contain the *lived-experience "I can—I do not have to"*—which means that (1) *I am the master* of my action *in potentia et in actu*, and (2) *I myself decide* about my action with respect to both its existence and essence, that is, with respect to the fact that it will be and what kind it will be.

This lived-experience of freedom contained in the human act, mirrored in consciousness, is an *indispensable implication of the* fieri *of the moral value*. It is mirrored in consciousness always with this implication and never without it. (It is fitting to add that we are always conscious of a "conscious act" as a "free" act—but this is a problem for the subsequent analysis: consciousness not only accompanies human acts but also co-creates them.)

1.6. The *"fieri"* of the moral value in the reflection of consciousness

Efficacy and freedom constitute in the reflection of consciousness an *indispensable implication of the particular process* that we have called the *"fieri"* of the moral value. The consciousness of "I can—I do not have to" in this process occurs as the *consciousness of the potency to act "in this or that way."* Consciousness mirrors this potency as a real implication of every act in which the moral value is born, *as a real ability of the human will*. We thereby discover that consciousness itself does not produce the moral value but finds it in the will—yet we shall speak of this later (on account of the characteristic *subjectivistic deviation, which the experience of morality* ex se *opposes*, and which deserves a separate discussion).

Consciousness of the potency to act "in this or that way" *transitions into consciousness of duty*. This transition possesses a fundamental significance for the *fieri* of the moral value. Between its two ends, the entire "interior world" of the person exists—the world that we call "morality" (*moralitas*) and that constitutes the foundation of so-called moral personhood. The transition itself—as mirrored by consciousness—is an effect of the coming to be of a new and *completely specific factor: the norm*. In the ultimate phase of its influence over freedom toward duty, this norm *assumes the form of the conscience*: it is an interior mandate. However, the norm is something fuller and more extensive, which—also in the mirror of consciousness—*progresses through specific stages*. A series of these stages can be identified, but two seem the most important: the "*ideality stage*" and the "*duty stage*." Others are more indirect. Values occur at every stage of the norm's formation, and duty is gradually specified at each of them (hence the *problem of the relation between so-called value ethics and so-called duty ethics* can be easily explained). The most important element of the norm, however, is the *element of the truth about the good*.

(The structure of the norm should be the subject matter of a separate analysis—though not in this book. It is fitting to state that the norm and the norming definitely do not take on the character of consciousness-related acts. Such acts are *mental, cognitive acts, which have a particular content and dynamic*, and which are merely mirrored in consciousness.)

At this point, we shall devote some attention to the *problem of the so-called subjectivistic deviation*, which, even though it is *in se* an interpretative problem (the interpretation of the experience of morality), is already based on one's very manner of reading this experience and, of course, on certain a priori presuppositions. In its *principal outline, this deviation is formed as follows: consciousness produces morality* (the moral value); however, in order to produce it, consciousness uses the *idea of freedom* (*the will*), which it also produces. The subjectivistic deviation is also utterly idealistic. It grasps the relation of consciousness to morality, but *not in conformity* with experience. For, on the one hand, consciousness mirrors moral facts (the *fieri* of moral values), and, on the other hand, it co-creates them. The first function of consciousness has been discussed thus far; the second will be covered later.

From a historical viewpoint, we can outline this process of the subjectivistic and idealistic deviation concerning the *fieri* of morality in the following three stages: (1) *Hume*—the negation of freedom of the will and its reduction to a specific combination of ("consciousness-related") acts: ideas and impressions; (2) *Kant*—the freedom of the will as a postulate (idea?); and (3) *Sartre*—freedom (the idea of freedom) as the end and norm of action. We see that whatever constitutes the necessary realistic implication of every moral fact and of the entire *fieri* of the moral value in light of the experience of morality transitions to "ideal" positions. For a *certain idealness (ideality)* belongs to the *essence of the norm* and does not hinder its concreteness, especially at the last stage of appearing in consciousness.

2. Efficacy and Freedom

2.1. From the consciousness of efficacy to conscious efficacy

In turn, it is fitting in a sense *"to place outside the parentheses of consciousness"* what, according to the very witness of consciousness, constitutes an indispensable implication of morality—namely, *efficacy and freedom—and to examine it as an objective reality*. Therefore, we shall not examine efficacy and freedom as they are mirrored in consciousness, but rather according to what they are and how they are shaped in themselves. Perhaps this will have to be accomplished gradually, *successive*. Nonetheless, the *terrain of experience changes*: we transition from the field of consciousness, in which interior experience is based, to the field of exterior experience (observation), though still keeping in view the fundamental unity of all experience, from which proceeds our knowledge about man as an acting being.

The problem of efficacy in light of integral experience possesses a *fundamental significance for our knowledge about the act* (the person-act), and this, after all, is attested to by our consciousness, as was stated. What is very clearly delineated in the field of consciousness is that which, according to the view of *N. Ach, distinguishes the so-called simple act of the will from all remaining manifestations of man's interior life* (or processes?, since Ach calls this simple act of the will the *phenomenological moment of the will*). Thus, according to Ach, the simple act of the will (i.e., its phenomenological moment) is a completely homogeneous moment in which *man experiences himself as the cause of action.*

It is fitting to *analyze* this statement. Does Ach speak of the act of the will as an objective reality or rather of the consciousness-related reflection of this reality? In my opinion, he speaks of both, and this also follows from further studies on the will. The *meaning of the term "lived-experience"* is very important here. Ach's statement not only requires us to understand this term, but also helps us to do so. (The term "lived-experience" will be explained later.) At any rate, this simple act of the will—*volition*—as an objective reality is *first manifested as an act of the efficacy* of the subject "I" (the person) *rather than as an intentional act* (the latter comes out only within the so-called process of the will).

It is due precisely to the clear contribution of the efficacy of the person (the "I") contained in it that this act is *clearly distinguished from other acts* that occur in the subject and that consciousness possibly mirrors as what *merely "happens"* in man. It does so "possibly" because not everything that happens in man is mirrored by consciousness in a parallel way. For this reason, it is fitting to divide the totality of "acts" into three groups: (a) the *not-made-conscious* [*nieuświadamiane*] (and the not-able-to-be-made-conscious [*nieuświadamialne*]); (b) the *made-conscious* [*uświadamiane*] (and the able-to-be-made-conscious [*uświadamialne*]) but non-conscious [*nie-świadome*]); and (c) the *conscious* [*świadome*], that is, more than made-conscious, though also made-conscious.[iii]

The consciousness of efficacy—that is, the consciousness that the subject-"I" is the efficient cause—*is connected only and exclusively with* (c). (What still remains is the problem of interpretation in this case, i.e., of understanding and explaining the essence of this efficacy.) The consciousness of efficacy is *not a content "produced" by consciousness, for this is contradicted by the "experientiality" of ascertaining it.* In the cases of (a) and (b)—in contradistinction to (c)—there is no consciousness of efficacy, that is, we are conscious that the subject-"I" is not the efficient cause.

Although in (a) and (b) the subject-"I" is not mirrored in consciousness as the efficient cause (for these two cases only "happen" in the subject), *consciousness does mirror the fact that both (a) and (b) proceed from the subjective "I,"* that above all they are *his own "acts(?)-processes(?)."* And it does not suffice to say that they proceed only "from the substratum" (*causa materialis*)—or that they proceed on the basis of *causa formalis*. They would then be flanked by mere "properties" of the subject ("I") and not his "powers." As we see, the problem has great significance for the integral understanding of the subject (the I-person). Taking interior experience, that is, the "state of consciousness" as a basis, we must state the following:

(1) *Both (a) and (b) certainly have their beginning in the subject "I," not outside him.* Is this "beginning" the same as efficacy?
(2) At any rate, *conscious efficacy is out of the question in (a) and (b)*, for it occurs only in (c).

Does this, however, exclude the existence of an efficacious relation between the subject "I" and these "acts-processes" (a) and (b)? We merely state the lack of conscious efficacy. The fact that consciousness itself does not grasp another efficacy apart from the conscious one (which *per se* is capable of being made conscious) [11a] *does not exclude the possibility of grasping that efficacy in another way*, that is, by means of observation "from without." Of course, this efficacy of the subject ("I") will not have the same experiential value as that in the case of (a).[iv]

(It is fitting to include a certain explanation of the word "act" [*akt*] at the end of these reflections.)

2.2. The meaning of the word "act" [*akt*] and its place in the framework of our investigation

This word has already been used several times. We must now explain its meaning. It is derived from the Aristotelian-Thomistic philosophical tradition. *We shall attempt to "discover" it anew, as it were.* On the one hand, our analyses demand that the word "act" [*akt*] be explained, while on the other hand, they have now arrived at the point at which it can be "discovered anew."

What appears very clearly before us is the *difference between the "act of the will"* (whose study has barely begun) *and other "acts"* (which for now are encompassed under [a] and [b]). Concerning the "act" of the will, we have so far discovered only its homogeneous germ: the conscious moment of efficacy. However, we also mentioned "volition," which possesses an "intentional" character: volition is a clear intentional act. This cannot be said—either on the basis of the witness of consciousness (introspection) or on the basis of integral experience and observation—about any of the "acts" that fall under (a) and (b). (A separate problem concerns so-called feelings, e.g., the feeling of value, which possess the character of intentional acts.) *Nota bene*, the *concept of intentionality* and the attribute "intentional" also require explanation.

The reason to speak of the "act" in the cases of (a) and (b) and in the case of (c) seems to be as follows: both (a) and (b), as well as (c), [12a] *reveal the dynamic (the immanent dynamic) of the subject (the "I"-person-man-suppositum)*. They reveal the diverse dynamic of that same subject. However, *we do not find* in the history of thought or in philosophical terminology any other concept that would adequately capture the becoming (*fieri*), the accomplishment of anything in a being, [13a] *except the concept and word "act."* This word first and foremost indicates both the integral dynamic (of the substantial being) and the particular dynamic (of accidents in the substantial being). This is not indicated by words such as "process" or especially "function." "Process" takes into account merely the phenomenal side of the becoming, of the dynamic belonging to substantial or accidental being.

However, *not only (c) (conscious efficacy) but also (a) and (b) (that which happens) appear in the reflection of consciousness as something dynamic*, something that becomes (*fit*). [14a] The subject "man" as a concrete "I" possesses his proper dynamic, which is also not-able-to-be-made-conscious and non-conscious. Consciousness to some extent mirrors this dynamic, although it is not consciousness's own dynamic (consciousness-related acts have their own dynamic, similar to cognitive acts—which is why, by the way, we use the word "acts"). *"Actualization," that is, the transition from potency to act (fullness, state, etc.) is most essential for "acts."* This is the function of a being (thus the "act" of consciousness indicates that consciousness is also a being).

In summary: *with the help of its acts, consciousness mirrors and dis-*

tinguishes "happening" from "action" in the subject—though in both cases some actualization takes place (thus actualization [*actu*] is common to "happening" and "action"). At this point, it is worthwhile to analyze the extent to which *acts of mental cognition* are "happenings" and the extent to which they are "actions." The actualizations "happening" and "action" take place in the subject, proceed from him (from the "I") as from their source—and in this sense *we can say that this subject is their cause.* [15a] However, it is only about the acts of the will that we can say—above all on the basis of interior experience, that is, relying on the witness of consciousness (here another experience cannot come into play) [16a]—that this subject "I" is their self-conscious efficient cause. *The very concept of "act-actualization" does not yet contain efficacy, especially conscious efficacy.* Efficacy is certainly more than "cause" (causality), but conscious efficacy is again more than efficacy. We can speak of the cause if acts (actualizations) occur in the subject. [17a] We can speak of efficacy if they proceed from the subject. We can speak of conscious efficacy if the subject causes them. In relation to the actualizations (a) and (b), phenomenology accepts only the first. However, I think that on the basis of experience (the experience of morality, among other things) we can maintain the second (i.e., efficacy), *for we have the intuition of the actualizations (a) and (b) also proceeding from the subject*. Concerning (c), we have the intuition not only of its proceeding from the subject "I" but *also of its being caused by the subject, that is, of its being actively evoked by the subject* who is conscious of both himself and his efficacy.

Precisely this is our experiential basis—we must admit, quite an extensive and rich one—for knowing and interpreting the act of the will.

2.3. The analysis of the act of the will (I)

The title "The analysis of the act [*akt*] of the will" proposes a very extensive and multilateral task, at whose threshold we have arrived and which is *the central issue for our knowledge of the act* [czyn].[v] We must state at once that this task—i.e., the analysis of the act of the will—cannot be exhausted in one paragraph but must be carried out successively, in a sense up to the end of this book (*ad intra* of the analysis of the act).

Our starting point is the fundamental experience—*the experience of the efficacy of the personal "I."* We deal with the act of the will when this

"I" is the efficient cause. *Nota bene*, the act is then accomplished. The act [*akt*] of the will is, so to speak, the backbone of the act [*czyn*], its most essential element. We cannot grasp the act without grasping the act of the will—but, on the other hand, *the understanding and analysis of the act* [czyn] *greatly contribute to the understanding of the act of the will*. For the time being, we will follow this path instead: we do not construct the act on the basis of the act of the will, but rather we attempt to understand the act of the will on the basis of the experiential material provided to us by acts. This methodological remark clearly underscores the *empirical and inductive character of our study*.

The efficacy of the personal "I" is not simply the starting point in the analysis of the act of the will. We must *constantly keep it before our eyes* in order to adequately grasp particular elements or aspects of this act. We should also note that *the object of our analysis is the "act of the will," not the will itself*. The act of the will is visual, for it is manifested and hence allows itself to be described and investigated by methods of experiential psychology. The will itself is a reality that stands outside the acts of the will. *The transition from the investigation of the will's acts to that of the conception of the will itself is, of course, justified and legitimate*. It is the fruit of the question about the sufficient reason of particular acts or about their cause. We will try to formulate this question at the end of particular inquiries concerning the act of the will. This question constitutes the starting point for an interpretative attempt.

The well-known school of psychologists of the will, whose founder was Narziss Ach, followed three stages in its analysis of the act of the will: (1) the analysis of the phenomenological moment (discussed above) (Ach), (2) the analysis of the process of the will (Michotte), and (3) the analysis of the will (Dybowski). These are not three stages of the act of the will, but *three stages of investigating the act of the will*. The act itself can be *simple* (the phenomenological moment itself, i.e., simple volition) *or developed* (the phenomenological moment, i.e., volition enriched by motivation and possibly by a struggle of motives in whose context the moment of choice is all the more fully manifested). Somehow this can be a *purely internal act* or an internal act that transitions into an *external act and is manifested in some action*. All this can be investigated separately, but we must never lose sight of the *organic unity* of particular elements and their *reciprocal permeation in the dynamic and vital order.*

2.4. The analysis of the act of the will (II)

While keeping the efficacy of the personal "I" ever in view, we must in turn investigate *the specific correlation and coordination of two aspects* that we easily discern in the act of the will. We shall call one of them *dynamic* and the other *dialectic*, or simply cognitive.

Concerning the first aspect, experience bids us state that every act of the will *in se* is *some concrete "volition"*: this is confirmed by both the simple "I will" and the choice that is a consequence of motivation or even a struggle of motives. [18a] At the same time, the same experience bids us state that this concrete volition developing and maturing through motivation takes its form from its first moment *thanks to some presentation of value*—motivation and especially the struggle of motives introduce the *whole expanded dialectic theme* into the process of volition. This and nothing else explains the character of the entire act of the will *as a conscious act*—not only made conscious, but precisely conscious. *We are concerned here with co-creating consciousness*, which differs functionally from mirroring consciousness. Its acts have a different character—not the consciousness-related character, but the character of ordinary cognitive acts, though in a special orientation (which we will address presently).

Volition is an "intentional act." Its intentionality differs from the intentionality of cognitive acts (also the so-called feeling of value). Aristotle and St. Thomas observed this eloquently. The intention of volition turns *toward an end* (good, value): this is essential for every volition from the first moment (simple volition). The whole of so-called *motivation presupposes precisely this intentionality and adapts to it* (at the same time thoroughly manifesting the nature of the will). For motivation consists not merely in a simple presentation of the good (the object of the will), but in such a presentation of it that the will turns to it as an end—that is, a presentation that *evokes volition. Aliter*: a presentation of the good that brings the potency of volition to the act of volition. Motivation thus has a character that is not so much directly "practical" as directly "teleological." The will's dynamic inheres at the root of motivation and stimulates it. In turn, thanks to motivation, this dynamic is actualized and developed.

This view is most closely correlated with what was said above concerning the act and actualization, *but it opposes the intellectualistic approach (formalism and Kant)*. Conclusion: How ought one to understand and interpret the whole of so-called practical (teleological) thinking? Differently from theoretical thinking. Because every practical judgment enters the structure of motivation, such judgment must be analyzed in this context. The same applies to value judgments—inasmuch as they are components of motivation.

Furthermore, however, we cannot treat (practical) thinking as something "of utility," something that is completely subordinated to teleology in acts of the will (volition). Nothing of the sort. *Thinking brings to these acts its most essential orientation, that is, the orientation toward truth.* Thanks to this, every (mature) volition, every act of the will *most fully manifests its nature in the moment of choice. In its essence, choice indicates the moment (element) of truth in the object of the will. Ex definitione*, that is, by the nature of things, "to choose" means "to prefer the true good over the not-true good," that is, "to contrast (beforehand) the true good with the not-true good." Without the moment (element) of truth, the very concept of choice does not make sense, *obiective sumendo*—choice does not make sense in the structure of the acts of the will. Thus, precisely through choice—and not through motivation alone—the will manifests itself in its acts as *appetitus rationalis* (Thomas).

Everything said above concerning the act of the will as the intentional act (volition) ought to be constantly grasped in connection with the fundamental fact of the efficacy of the personal "I." This efficacy is actualized in the act of the will from the first moment of simple volition unto the moment of choice. *Motivation and choice in particular not only manifest this efficacy (sensu phenomenologico) but also enable it (sensu realistico).* The *suppositum* ("I") is the cause (the efficient cause) thanks to the fact that it can choose while presupposing the entire process of the will, that is, a motivation and a struggle of motives.

At this point, we also see the sense of the *connection between efficacy and morality (the moral value)*. The act of the will (volition) is the subject of the moral value not because it contains the striving for the good, but because this striving passes in a sense through the moment of truth: the act of the will is oriented toward the good but under the aspect of truth.

Therefore, *the norm is possible within the framework of this act* (this will be treated in more detail elsewhere).

Concluding these reflections (remarks) about the act of the will, we need to formulate *a question about the basis of this act, that is, about the will itself*. This question could be *ut sequitur*: what must lie behind every volition that contains the efficacy of the personal "I" and that develops from the simple "I will" through motivation unto the moment of choice? According to St. Thomas, behind such volition lies the power (*potentia*) that is at the same time the property (*proprium*) of the human soul.

2.5. The discovery and interpretation of freedom

We discover the freedom of the will in the efficacy of the personal "I." It is thus *given experientially and contained in the same experience as efficacy*. Namely, it is freedom in the sense of auto-determination. The fact that the "I" is the agent of the acts of the will—volition and especially choice—means that *from this "I" proceeds an impulse* that is decisive for the striving toward a value as an end. Thus, this is a system *contrary to the deterministic system* in which the striving impulse proceeds from values themselves that act as stimuli and move directly ("motivation" in the deterministic sense). This is out of the question in relation to the will: *motivation prepares and conditions choice but does not determine it*. [19a] This is linked with a *specific governance of the personal "I"* in the act of the will over its object (value, end), which occurs both before the moment of choice and in it, and also after its completion. For the subject preserves the consciousness of auto-determination even when he chooses.

The erroneous explanations of the freedom of the will are *materialistic determinism* (which results from a certain preconception that does not take into account the entire experience of efficacy and choice) and *specific intellectualistic determinism* (Kant), in light of which practical reason by its judgments (i.e., intellectual forms) in a sense *elicits freedom from the will*, which is otherwise blind and can be subordinated to the senses. This conception, too, does not fully consider the experience of man and especially the experience of morality and the act of choice, which pertains to striving-willing, not to (practical) cognition alone. *Freedom inheres in the entire act of the will from its first moment and is most fully revealed in the moment of choice*—it is revealed as the culminating point of conscious efficacy (the element of the truth about the good). However, *"volition"* itself *ex definitione* indicates some freedom of action: I can—I do not have to (*libertas contrarictatis*), without which we cannot understand the lived-experience of the efficacy of the personal "I."

Later in the course of the process of the will (especially in the struggle of motives) this fundamental freedom of action turns out to be *freedom in relation to goods, to values* (*libertas contradictionis, libertas specificationis*). Here, the teaching of Aristotle and Thomas concerning the teleology of the act of the will deserves to be recalled and pondered. *Auto-determination presupposes at the origin, at the foundations, some indetermination, which, however, denotes not merely an indifference to the good but also a readiness for volition and choice*—all of this following a certain order. According to Aristotle, this is the order of means-ends, that is, the chain of goods. Only on a rational basis (*"rationalitas" appetitus*) can we think of striving for one good on account of another.

The final good-end following this order (according to Aristotle) is happiness. However, in speaking of determining the will by the final end, we must not forget *about "organic" auto-determination and its basis, which is the moment of truth*. Even with respect to the final end the will must remain itself—otherwise, even the *lived-experience of happiness will not take place*. Understanding this is of great significance for the philosophical conception of morality. What is hidden at the basis of volition, that is, at the basis of the conscious striving for the good, is not only and above all indetermination but also a specific transcendence: *the relation to the good as such* (*bonum per se*) *inheres in the will by nature* and governs not only every act-process of the will but also the lifelong process of the will.

3. The Structure of the Act

Introductory remarks

The preceding part was almost completely devoted to an analysis of conscious efficacy. In light of that analysis, there opens a possibility to *grasp even more deeply the relation between person and act*. The person is the efficient cause of the act, which remains *essentially and exclusively correlated* with him (*only the person is capable of the act*).

What does "efficient cause" mean? We refer to Aristotle's conception, according to which four causes determine every being: two external (the final and the efficient) and two internal (the material and the formal). *The efficient cause determines the being according to the way in which this cause influit esse (gives existence).* The person, then, gives existence to the act.

Accordingly, *the act in its existence and essence simultaneously differs from the person and depends on him most closely.* For the effect bears in itself, in a sense, the essence of the cause. The act as an effect of the person bears in itself and expresses his essence. It does not extend this essence but in a particular way expresses and actualizes it. In the same way, it does not obscure the existence of the person but expresses and in a particular way actualizes it. At this point we ought to *oppose the conception* according to which the act is understood *merely as a manifestation of the existence of the person*. On the other hand, we should also oppose the conception in which an *excessive "essentialization" of the act* takes place: the act is considered only as a separate being. In reality *operari sequitur esse*: the act has its own essence and its own existence while remaining most closely linked to the essence and existence of the person.

On the one hand, the act *is in a sense the person* (persona) *in actu, and, on the other hand, it is the* actus *of the person* (personae). This is not a mere play on words but expresses two different aspects of the act, each of which deeply defines the structure of the act in its connection with the person. Each of these aspects is *closely connected with the dynamic of the will and with the structure of its acts,* which was previously analyzed; for we observed that in every stage of the act of the will, the efficacy of the personal "I" and its proper intentionality overlap. Hand in hand with this bi-aspectual structure of the act of the will goes the *bi-aspectuality of the act,* namely, that it is (1) *persona in actu,* and (2) *actus personae*.

In the first aspect it is fitting to speak of a *specific immanence* of the person in the act. The person is considered here as a physical whole in *his diverse dynamic*—that is, *his potentialities and capacities for actualization.* These various capacities for actualization deserve a separate—at least general—discussion. All of them can enter into the structure of the act, although a *concrete configuration of these capacities and their actualization always enters* the structure of *every concrete act separately.* In this sense the act is not, physically speaking, *persona in actu.* These various actualizations belong to the act *insofar as they are integrated by the act of the will* (i.e., the act of conscious efficacy). Thanks to this integration we can say that the act is *persona in actu*.

The first aspect, however, does not exhaust the structure of the act in its essential connection with the person. Hence, it is fitting to grasp it in turn *in the second aspect, speaking of a specific transcendence of the person that is contained in every act*. For the act of the will not only integrates various actualizations that compose every act, but also contributes to them *its own relation to the good and to truth* (to the good in truth), *that is, its own transcendence*. Precisely this transcendence of the act of the will is the basis of the transcendence of the person in every act. Thanks to it—more than to the integration through the act of the will—*the person is the efficient cause of the act in a way proper to him, that is, connatural*.

※

In conclusion, let us offer *a few words on the relation of the act to lived-experience*. This relation is parallel to that *between a being and consciousness. It is not only the relation "whole—part" but also the relation "the whole in the understanding of integral experience—the whole in the understanding of interior experience alone."* They occur in parallel—and they should be studied in parallel. In a certain sense, we have already done this by means of the entire *status quaestionis* concerning consciousness (the accompanying consciousness). This should all be kept in view during subsequent inquiries into the structure of the act. For the act and the *fieri* of the moral value contained in this act *are accomplished in being* (*in ordine essendi*) and at the same time—*in another way*—*in consciousness*: not only through the contribution of the co-creating consciousness in the act of the will, but also through the contribution of the mirroring consciousness.

We will study the very structure of the act in its connection with the person in these two aspects: (1) the immanence of the person in the act, and (2) the transcendence of the person through the act.

3.1. The first aspect of the structure of the act: The immanence of the person in the act

[20a] What we must keep constantly in view within this aspect of the structure of the act is *the person as a concrete objective whole*, one that we already know *to be mirrored in consciousness in a non-uniform and irregular way*. Consequently, this whole is not perceivable in the same measure

within interior experience (introspection), but this does not mean that what is not provided by interior experience fails to be supplemented by observation ("exterior experience"). On this basis, we can distinguish in the person as in a concrete physical whole *two spheres that are actualized in different ways—and that in different ways enter the structure of the act*. The latter is accomplished thanks to the integrative power of the will. The two spheres are (1) *the somatic-reactive sphere*, and (2) *the psycho-emotive sphere*. These phrases (despite sounding phenomenological) indicate the contribution of both spheres to, on the one hand, the *structure of the very being* (esse) *of the person* and, on the other, *the structure of his action* (age-re, operari). Here, we wish above all to analyze the latter.

In terms of the integrative power of the will, we will address at least briefly (without entering into details) *the extent to which the aforementioned spheres create difficulties and obstacles in this work*. Thus, we will also address the extent to which they are the source and *cause of a certain disintegration* due to which the human act cannot be constituted, or at least cannot be constituted in its proper perfection (*voluntarium perfectum*).

A separate problem along this line of inquiry is *the problem of drives*. Drives also belong to the internal structure of the person; they are manifested in the particular spheres of his *esse et operari*. It is particularly necessary to examine *the coordination between, on the one hand, the act of the will and the conscious efficacy of the personal "I" connected with this act and, on the other hand, the activity of drives*.

The somatic-reactive sphere

21a *The human body* participates in the act. *By saying "body,"* we have in mind that which is given to us in integral experience—especially in observation—*and which we shall describe as* "soma." We also have in mind, however, that which does not constitute an object of observation—though it can become the object of scientific study and of the knowledge thus acquired—*and which we call "organism."* From the cognitive point of view, we must state that the "body" has not only its external shape (*figura*) but also *its proper "inwardness."* In the analysis of human *operari*, we must take into account both the one (*soma*) and the other (organism).

22a For what is characteristic of the body both as "*soma*" and as "organism" is *reactivity*. The actualizations of the body possess the character of vital, organic—not mechanistic—reactions. This is an important distinction (i.e., mechanism *contra* organism) and deserves a certain explanation. The reactions of the body (of the organism-*soma*) demonstrate a *feature of adaptiveness*. They are *linked with a separate sphere (field) of stimuli* that evoke these reactions. *Values suitable for the body*—that which corresponds to its nature and needs—are hidden in these stimuli. However, these values *are not experienced as values*. The reason is that the entire somatic-reactive sphere is fundamentally not-able-to-be-made-conscious. The reactions of this sphere are identified at least to a large extent with the *acts and processes of the vegetative life in man*.

We must take into account the fact that *the body (soma-organism), with its reactivity, enters in some way into every human act*—including the so-called *actus interni*—either in the form of distinct components ascertainable by observation or in the form of the "internal," invisible components that condition internal acts. *The reactivity of the body certainly conditions the emotivity of the psyche and enters into the conscious efficacy of the will.*

What influence does the latter have on somatic reactivity? Or in other words, *how does the integration of somatic reactivity in the act of the will take place? Teste experientia*, this occurs *instinctively, as it were*, or intuitively—without the commitment of reflection and in many cases without the commitment of consciousness.[23a] *In this way, the will uses somatic reactivity for its own act*, which contains conscious efficacy. Efficacy is conscious, but the use of somatic reactivity does not have to be—*and most often is not—conscious*. This does not mean, however, that it cannot become conscious to some extent.

This is linked with another problem that is important for the structure of the act: *to what extent can somatic reactivity limit conscious efficacy?* Fundamentally, it can do so *directly only in the physical and not the ethical sense*. "In the physical sense" means that the will cannot want what the body cannot accomplish. "Not in the moral (ethical) sense" means that (moral) evil cannot be ascribed to the will in this case because here only physical evil comes into play. The limitation of the will's conscious efficacy by reactivity of the body can occur only in the indirect sense, namely, inasmuch as this reactivity conditions certain inclinations in the psyche that possess significance for morality.

The psycho-emotive sphere (the concept of emotivity)

The second sphere that deserves a thorough analysis concerning the structure of the act is the sphere that we call here "*psycho-emotive.*" This very name requires an explanation. Whereas somaticity is fundamentally reactive in man (the person)—just as in the animal—the psyche is *fundamentally emotive.* Emotivity denotes a capacity for emotions (*wzruszenia* in Polish) and the actualization of that capacity. Emotivity differs from reactivity by the entire structure and course of actualization. According to the content of the word "*emovere,*" in such actualization there occurs in a sense an elicitation of a given "*motus*" from the subjective psychical potency with the help of an objective factor that constitutes the "*movens*" (not a motive, or at most a "quasi-motive") of that movement. The movement itself (*motus*) does not possess a physical character and, unlike the reaction of the body, *is not located in the body* (the *soma*-organism). Hence the word "*motus*" is used here *sensu analogico*.

Furthermore, this emotion (*motus*—emotion) not only constitutes the object of consciousness (which cannot be said of the majority of the organism's reactions) but also *allows itself to be cognitively isolated on account of its varied content.* After all, we cognize our affections and distinguish them; for example, the affection of anger differs from the affections of joy, sorrow, desire, love, hatred, etc. This subjective content contained in emotion determines *its psychical specificity* to a still higher degree. [24a] Such content does not occur in the entire somatic sphere, which is incapable of it.

Emotions (affections) possess a strong *subjective character and rootedness in the subject on account of their nature.* However, their *objective relation* is also clear: they arise from an objective cause. This cause lies either in the subject—more concretely, in the body (the organism-*soma*)—or outside it. The *problem of emotions is closely linked with cognition. However, this specific kind of cognition occurs in a very different way,* and this to a certain degree is reflected in the character of affection itself. Thus, so-called *bodily affections,* such as the affection of physical pain or strength—which ought not to be confused with the sensation of the body (besides, the sensation of affection itself also exists)—differ from affections that have their basis neither in a state of the body nor in a bodily sensation, though these, too, are accompanied by the sensation of affection that in turn possesses a significance for the consciousness of affection (and, in the second case, for the consciousness of the body). Sensation itself is of a sensual nature: we sense with the senses—and this indirectly indicates the sensual character of affection, even when it is so-called higher affection.

The superiority of affections has been linked with the nature of cognition: an affection (an emotional fact) that arises on the basis of an act of *mental* cognition (judgment) is higher than one that arises on the basis of an act of *sensual* cognition (impression). [25a] This matter requires a more thorough analysis. At any rate, the ability to evoke affections by judgments about values indirectly indicates a spiritual—and not a merely sensual—character of affections. As is evident, *emotivity as a dynamic property* of the psyche is linked just as firmly to the body as it is to the mind and will (the problem of so-called directed affections). Nonetheless, it is a specific property that is marked by a proper *gradation of intensity* (weaker affections—stronger affections)—and this is perhaps particularly connected with the reactivity of the organism (*temperaments*). The rootedness of emotivity in the spiritual structure of the person (thought-reflection), which is manifested as *a specific depth of emotional life*, a depth of affections, deserves separate attention.

The psycho-emotive sphere (the relation to values)

We have said that (1) every emotional fact (the actualization of human psycho-emotivity) *occurs in some objective relation*, and that (2) *it is connected with some cognition*. It is fitting to add that the nature of every affection contains a certain *qualificative element. Affection is positive* (+) *or negative* (−). Furthermore, it is a response to a good or an evil (e.g., sorrow to an evil, joy to a good), a fact to which St. Thomas drew attention in particular—this is what he primarily emphasized. *Thus, the "+" and the "−" belong to the nature of affection* (i.e., affection is positive or negative) *in connection with the objective correlate to which affection is a response*. This qualificative character of emotions or affections indicates their *close connection with values*.

In what way does this connection take place? (a) An opinion according to which emotion possesses an appetitive character (*Thomists*). [26a] At this point, one ought to thoroughly analyze *the significance of Thomas's* "passio." (b) An opinion according to which emotion (affection) possesses a cognitive character or at least enables the cognition of values (*Scheler*)—only emotion provides cognitive access to value. Neither of these opinions can be accepted (the emotive fact is completely specific), though each possesses a *significant amount of truth*.

[27a] Let us begin with (b). *The psycho-emotive fact (affection) is not cognitive per se*. However, because it creates real contact with values (purely emotive contact), *it creates an occasion for cognizing them*. This occasion is "subjective": values *are* contained in emotional facts *as their objective correlate, though they are not yet recognized as values in them*. This is the task of a separate act. According to emotionalists, this act is *feeling*. Certainly, feeling exists in the interior life of man and possesses a cognitive character, but it certainly is not an act of psycho-emotivity itself, being instead a reflex of an emotional fact (affection is an actualization of emotivity) in the cognitive powers (in the cognitive acts).

Here exists an opportunity to compare *the three forms: sensation, affection, and feeling*, defining their distinctness and function in the formation of personhood (the person-act).

[28a] Let us now consider (a). *Emotion-affection is not in itself desire or striving*, although it possesses a great significance for them precisely on account of its qualificative feature, whence originates its *appulsive or repulsive function* (joy, longing *contra* sorrow, fear). Affection. Passion.

Because emotivity—although *in se* irreducible to *appetition*—*possesses a great significance for appetition* in the interior life of the person, we ought to pay particular attention to the function of emotivity, or rather of emotional life, as the *"concentrator" in the interior life of the person*. What does this mean? (1) In the psycho-emotive sphere, the values of the experienced *values of the body (the* soma-*organism) connected with reactivity*, which in the sphere of reactivity itself are not experienced, acquire significance. *Nota bene*, thanks to this, their cognition becomes more possible (e.g., through the affection of physical pain or the opposite affection). (2) In the emotive (psycho-emotive) sphere, *there occurs a quasi-*redundantia *of spiritual (higher) values*, which are connected with mental cognition. Left to themselves, these values *demonstrate a certain weakness despite their superiority*. Hence, a spiritual struggle, as it were, ensues in the subject (in man)—not only against the psycho-emotive sphere, but also and above all for the sake of overcoming and mastering this sphere. Every educational process contains this struggle.

The psycho-emotive sphere (the problem of temperament and disposition)

The psycho-emotive element occurs in the interior life of the person and plays a role in his acts not only through particular affections (emotional facts) *but also through a certain totality that is called "temperament" or "disposition."* It is a totality because it somehow captures the entirety of psycho-emotive facts in a given subject and attempts to bring out *their resultant or rather their chief feature*. Although a given resultant or chief feature is repeated in different people—of course, *secundum quandam analogiam*—we can nevertheless grasp it as a certain generality. We call it a temperament or disposition. *It confers on every subject a specific concreteness, different from that conferred by "soma" (figura) or somatic reactivity*, though nonetheless important. Man is *individualized* physically through his "body" and psychically through his temperament or disposition.

By "temperament" we usually (Aristotle-Kretschmer) mean a specific resultant with its proper chief feature of psycho-emotivity in connection with the reactive-somatic sphere (pyknic—cyclothymic, leptosomic—schizothymic, etc.). By "disposition" we mean instead psycho-emotivity itself in its individual (average) concretization. *The traditional teaching on temperaments always brought out the characteristic*, strictly "psycho-emotive" *principal feature* (e.g., in the choleric person, emotive reactions progress quickly, intensely, and are long-lived, etc.). Temperament indicates *a certain characteristic "modality" of psycho-emotivity.*

Hence typologies ensue. I do not list all of them. Perhaps an opportunity will present itself to mention *the possibility of a Thomistic typology* based on the distinction between *appetitus concupiscibilis* and *appetitus irascibilis*, with which St. Thomas links separate groups of affections.

The psycho-emotive sphere (the relation to conscious efficacy)

The relation of the psycho-emotive sphere to conscious efficacy in the act of the will is *fundamentally different from that of the reactive-somatic sphere*. We ascertain this on the basis of both interior experience and observation, but especially interior experience. Thus, what follows first and foremost from previous examination is that *the psycho-emotive sphere possesses its own specific intentionality*, which appears as a cognitive act in a feeling. Second, this sphere possesses *its proper rootedness in the subject, its own subjectivity*. Both the one and the other are of great significance in the formation of the act—perhaps more so as *"persona in actu"* than as *"actus personae"* (because this is conscious efficacy *simpliciter*). But this is not without significance for *"actus personae"* as well.

For, as is well-known, emotional facts emphasize certain values—the values that *hic et nunc* are important for the subject in his specific subjectivity. *What appears with values is also significance*. These values are given through an emotional fact not only for cognitive reading but also and even more so as an object of striving, that is, an end. Here, we should pay particular attention to the link between material (vital) values and sensual desire (*appetitus sensitivus*) based on sensual cognition (the impression of value). Thus, emotional facts influence the acts of the will in both cognitive and appetitive ways. *They can undoubtedly stimulate efficacy* without hindering freedom. However, they *can also hinder it* by imposing their direction or their intentionality, and by limiting the possibility of conscious auto-determination (affection, passion). A firm rootedness in the subject also helps with this. In addition, the emotional fact *imposes its subjective truthfulness*, which can hinder the objective truth that is important for acts of conscious choice.

The role of temperament and disposition, which, as we know, form a specific totality in the interior life of the person, *deserves a separate discussion*. What we must take into account is the fact that temperament and disposition, which, as we stated, designate a certain modality of the entire psycho-emotivity of the person, also designate a certain modality of acts. Here is a problem: to what extent is this modality significant for their moral value? This problem is at least partly identified with *the problem of so-called* habitus innati.

Drives and integration [29a]

At the end of these reflections on the immanence of acts in the person, it is fitting to reflect on *the problem of drives*. First, what does *the word "drive"* mean? It is often used interchangeably with *the word "in-*

stinct," though I oppose this. (1) Drive is connected with *a certain determination of the being "man" by his nature,* and in the order of action this corresponds to *natures of various powers.* Each of these powers is in its proper way determined with respect to its own object (*obiectum formale et materiale*).

(2) Besides, the entire being "man" possesses certain *a priori-natural tendencies connected with his own (individual) existence and the* (collective) *existence of his species: the drive for self-preservation and the reproductive drive.* These tendencies are based on the nature of man and his powers. The realization of these tendencies progresses *through particular spheres of the human being*—and is manifested in each of them in the way proper to it (differently in the reactive-somatic sphere than in the psycho-emotive sphere). In these spheres, drives are the source of what "happens" in man, though not only in man, but also in the animal.

Drives are also a source of action. This action *in the animal originates from an instinct* that orients the entire subject with respect to what "happens" in it toward a proper self-preserving or reproductive end. *Man also sometimes acts "by instinct"*—but such actions are merely *actus hominis*. The proper way of acting for man is *action by choice*: an act of the will in which the object toward which the drive inclines also becomes an object of volition and choice. *Integration through choice in the act of the will— not integration through instinct—is proper to man*. Only thanks to such integration is *the essence of self-determination* preserved in human action. Self-determination constitutes the basis of the transcendence of the person in the act. This is the second aspect of the structure of the human act.

3.2. The second aspect of the structure of the act: The transcendence of the person in the human act

Self-determination as the basis of the transcendence of the person

It is fitting to analyze first the *sense of the expression "self-determination."* This expression denotes an ability that inheres in the person, *an ability to manage oneself, one's acts,* with respect to both their physical and moral "*fieri*." Thus, the person is, on the one hand, *a managing subject* and, on the other hand, *a managed object*. This is what the Scholastic adage *sui iuris* expresses. It is linked to the fact of governing over oneself (as to the fact of managing oneself), the fact given experientially—of course, in "phenomenological" experience. The fact of governing over oneself is expressed in the Scholastic phrase *alteri incommunicabilis*.

The self-determination of the person is closely connected with the dynamic of the will spoken of in section 2, "Efficacy and freedom," and also in aspect 3.1. *The characteristic "duality" perceivable in the analysis of self-determination refers to the known juxtaposition "persona in actu— actus personae." Moral values have their source in this self-determination of the person*: the person determines his acts (efficacy—freedom) and their moral value. Therefore, he can determine moral values, which are the values of the person himself, the person as such, because he can determine his acts. However, self-determination *sensu physico* constitutes only a basis for self-determination *sensu morali*. The latter is achieved because the transcendence of the person is manifested in self-determination.

What is this transcendence? It denotes not only "access to the transcendentals" (truth, good, and beauty) and the ability to experience them, the ability to experience all of reality under their aspect (this would be the case in the Platonic conception), but also—in our case— *an ability to direct oneself by truth in striving for the good*. In this respect, it is fitting to analyze the Aristotelian teleology of human action: (a) the cognition of good, that is, the truth about the good, as the first condition of the transcendence of the person in the act; and (b) the problem of the highest good.

The transcendence of the person in the act as the fruit of the ability to direct oneself by truth in striving for the good *is expressed through the norm, that is, the mental principle of action and especially of striving for the good in action*. The norm is a judgment. However, this judgment—just as every value judgment—is only an instrument of the striving for truth (of knowing truth) in striving for the good. This striving conditions the transcendence of the person in acts.[vi]

Conscience as a condition of the efficacy of the person in the moral order

At this point the problem of conscience emerges. First, it is fitting to describe its structure. *Conscience is not identified with so-called moral consciousness,* for the acts of conscience do not possess a consciousness-related character. At most we can say that moral consciousness is born as a result of the acts of conscience. *These acts are cognitive acts that have for their object the person's moral good*—in contradistinction to evil—as obligatory in a given act. Hence the *normative character* of conscience is more than practical, though at the same time it is *strictly concrete*. Constituting the so-called subjective norm, conscience *in se* is not an expression of subjectivism but—quite the contrary—has an *objective character* (in this it differs from consciousness-related acts). However, it possesses a *consciousness-related reflex*. We mean not merely a simple mirroring but a *lived-experience* that is usually quite strong. This explains various *conceptions of conscience*, such as the voluntaristic and emotionalistic as well as the intellectualistic. We must add that the *emotional facts* that accompany conscience possess a *specific depth and varied intensity* (Scheler).

What is most important in our analysis is the fact that conscience constitutes a *manifestation of the transcendence of the person in the act, for it brings into every act an element of truth in striving for the good*. In this it directly meets the need of the will in the moment of choice. *The essence of choice* and its proper dynamic require not only a value judgment or the entire nexus of such judgments, but also *the norm*. (The great problem of the norm will be the object of a separate study.) It is a fact (in a sense, a central fact) known from the experience of morality that the lived-experience of moral good and evil (moral good and evil) *is a consequence of the relation of the norm to conscience*. Thus, the integral fact of conscience itself impinges on that consequence: hence its character is all the more personal.

In the act of the will, conscience with its structure *enters into the entire process of the efficacy of the person* and decides the definitive form of the human act. Namely, it determines that the act of the will in the human act is the agent of moral value (good—evil). This particular efficacy, whose effect is the whole of moral personhood, has its basis in the transcendence of the person. Moral values themselves as real properties of the person have their proper and direct subject in this transcendence. Without it, we do not find a place for them in the person.

We can say that this is a "place" in the phenomenological sense, insofar as the transcendence of the person is a "phenomenon." In the *ontological structure of the person*, this place is the spiritual soul. The cognition of the ontological structure of the person is accomplished to a large extent by way of integrating the experience of morality.

The self-determination of the person and collective life (?)

We will distinguish here two systems of reference in which human acts are realized: (1) the "society" system of reference; and (2) the "neighbor" system of reference. We shall analyze separately whether and to what extent each of these systems helps or hinders the transcendence of the person in the act.

What is characteristic of the "society" system of reference is the striving of many toward one common end and in this context various possibilities of "acting together" or "co-operating." All of this can play a negative role for the self-determination of the person, though it does not have to. A personal relation in the act of conscience to the truth about the good, especially the good that constitutes the common end, is always a condition. On this substratum, various possible attitudes arise—for example, positive attitudes such as those of solidarity and rightful opposition, and negative attitudes such as those of conformism and avoidance. Self-determination must take into account that which is located at the opposite pole, with which so-called crowd psychology concerns itself.

What is characteristic of the "neighbor" system of reference is not so much a striving for a common end, and thus action "together with," as action "with respect to." This is the basis of all actions having an interhuman character. Self-determination does not have to be harmed by this as long as the truth about the good, that is, humanity in every man, dominates in the act of the will.

When analyzing both systems of reference, we must ponder whether we find ourselves still within pre-normative reflections or whether we somehow enter the sphere of reflections about the norm (ethics).

Finally, it is fitting to state that there exists a separate field of actions "with respect to" that is closely connected with the lived-experience of the transcendentals. This is the field of religion and the religious act. Let us, however, allow its relation to self-determination and morality to be a topic of separate inquiries.

NOVEMBER 16, 1965

2 ❦ Person and Act

The Introductory and Fundamental Reflections

1. The Significance of the Topic

In the study of "the person and the act," we proceed from one of the most ordinary and most frequent facts—from the fact that man performs acts.[vii] This fact occurs exceedingly often in the life of every man. If we multiply it by the number of all people, we obtain quite a countless number of facts. We should not wonder that because of their frequency these facts can seem ordinary and can fail to evoke the interest they deserve. And yet, we are faced here with one of the most important and most interesting fragments of all of reality. This fragment must be known in a manner that is thorough and as accurate as possible, above all for its own sake but also on account of its effects and especially its particular properties. The human act introduces us into a new world, as it were, or, at any rate, into a new order, which within the reality accessible to us exists neither outside this act nor without it.

Namely, we mean the world of morality, or, more strictly speaking, the world of moral values. We also mean the moral order, which is a separate totality that we find in the reality that surrounds us. The expressions "world of morality" and "moral order" actually indicate the same totality, though in somewhat different ways and under different aspects. The world of morality and moral order differ from the world and the order that we are accustomed to call physical. Human acts introduce us precisely into this world of morality and this moral order. This constitutes their deepest specificity in a functional sense: if acts did not exist, there also would be no morality nor the moral order within the reality accessible to us. We must express ourselves with even more precision here:

if the particular relation that occurs between the act and the person did not exist, there also would be no morality as the fragment of reality accessible to us. For the act occurs—that is, exists—only and exclusively in relation to the person. Only man performs acts. The beings that surround us and that are not people act in various ways, but none of them performs acts.

This is not merely a matter of the precision of language that distinguishes any "action" from "act." Behind the difference of words, there resides an intellectual ability to differentiate, which commands us to give various names to various objects and various realities. Undoubtedly, the act is action; however, it contains something more and something different from any other action. Grasping the matter in the categories of logic, we can say that action is a kind, and the act is a species within it. We can also say that the relation that occurs between the act and any other action in the world that surrounds us is precisely the same as the relation between the man-person and other acting beings. From this analogy we conclude that what distinguishes "act" from "action" originates precisely from the relation of the act to the person—or even more, of the person to the act. This relation ought to be examined as thoroughly as possible in order to discover and determine that by which the act differs from any other action in the reality that surrounds us. This is precisely the intention and task of this study.

In beginning this work, we are aware of the apparent ordinariness of the subject matter as well as its objective depth and a cognitive difficulty linked to it. It is not only in relation to this point that reality has seemed and constantly seems to man as something more given to him than entrusted as a task. Man pays almost no attention to the act as the action that he performs because he governs it to such an extent in the existential and practical order. Consequently, he does not pose many fundamental questions to himself and does not search for answers to them. At the beginning of this work, it is fitting to break this—so to speak—"commonplace" atmosphere right away and attempt a different attitude. Let the above statement help us with that—namely, the statement that with the analysis of the relation between person and act we run up against the border between two orders and even two worlds. Here the physical order meets the moral order: thanks to human acts, a new world appears in the reality accessible to us—the world of morality.

2. The Problem of Experience

All that was said thus far possesses the character of an announcement that needs to be realized gradually. This realization first requires addressing a method or at least certain methodological remarks. The word "method" is etymologically linked with "way" (*he hodos*). A method is the consciousness of the way that one ought to follow in order to reach a given end—and it is also the choice of this way. In our case, this is the way of cognition and the presentation of its results. We ought to state that this way possesses above all an empirical, that is, an experiential, character. After all, our starting point is the fact, or rather the countless number of facts, that every man performs acts; he performs them when he acts consciously—every man is capable of conscious action, is capable of performing acts. All that we stated in the previous sentence already bears the character of empirical knowledge. Experience stands at the root of this knowledge; it creates and in a certain sense already is this knowledge. At the beginning of our work, which is based so fundamentally and so generally on facts, it is fitting to examine in what the relation between experience and understanding consists.

Beforehand, however, it is fitting to pose the very problem of experience. Is the statement that man's conscious action is a fact equivalent to the statement that our knowledge about this action possesses an experiential character—that is, that the experience of the act exists as the basis of this knowledge? In other words: is that which we call an act—and calling is already a certain act of knowledge—given to us directly and immediately in experience? Is conscious action and its relation to the man-person given to us in this way? Is all this given already in experience or only shaped—on the basis of the empirical data of experience—in the mind? These are questions with a noetic, that is, an epistemological, character—questions that pertain not only to the relation of experience to understanding but also to the contribution of the sensual and mental powers in the cognitive act. At the beginning of our work, the object of which has already been defined, we ought to become aware of these questions—and also at least partially take a position with respect to them, of course without getting into details, since this work in itself is not a study of the theory of cognition.

By stating that our knowledge about the act and its relation to the man-person possesses an empirical, that is, an experiential, character, we wish to exclude a purely phenomenalistic sense of experience and also the linking of this experience with merely sensual powers. Experience in accord with phenomenalistic understanding encompasses only in a sense a thin layer of cognitive contents—something like their surface or epidermis—namely, a layer of purely sensual contents. Even if it is true that only the senses remain in direct contact with the objects of the reality that surrounds us, it is difficult to accept that the cognitive act that directly apprehends these objects is only a sensual act. We see the same directness in apprehending them by a mental act, and this does not in the least ruin the mental act's otherness with regard to content, nor its separate genesis. At this point, we concern ourselves with the cognitive act as a concrete whole to which we owe both contact with an object and knowledge about it. It is always by means of such an act that we grasp the concrete act, that is, the conscious action in its relation to the man-person. In no way can we agree that, in this case, experience is limited to a group of sensory contents, which are always unique and unrepeatable, and that the mind simply combines this group into a conceptual totality to which it gives the name "act." The mind does not wait for the data of experience, for the group of sensory contents, in order to "make" them its object. The mind is already engaged in experience itself, thanks to which it establishes contact with the object, a contact that is equally, though in a different way, direct.

In human cognition (regardless of whether scientific or pre-scientific cognition), there is no experience that does not already include some understanding. Therefore, we cannot look at the problem of experience in the way that phenomenalists do. They differ from phenomenologists, who, in fact, take into account the concrete cognitive act as a vital totality without separating that which is purely sensual in it and is the work of the sensual powers from that which is mental and is the work of reason. "Not to separate," however, does not mean "to deny the difference" or even "not to perceive it." Concerning that which interests us here, the human act and its relation to the person is the object of experience in the sense that the concrete cognitive act [*akt*] directly grasps this act [*czyn*], that is, grasps conscious action in its relation to the man-person.[viii] We do not have to reach this object only by way of intellectual conclusion from the data of experience; we find it in these data themselves. The relation of cognitive forms—the sensual to the mental—is another matter, namely, to what extent the mental presupposes the sensual and in what way it originates from it. These are already problems of pure epistemology, which we do not intend to discuss here. At any rate, the process that occurs between cognitive forms and even between the entire sensual and mental grasp of the object already occurs within one and the same cognitive act that allows us to establish direct contact with the object that interests us: with the human act, that is, with conscious action in its relation to the person.

So, when we say that in the study of the person-act we proceed from a fact, or rather from a countless number of facts, we point to experience as the basis of our study. This experience, however, needs to be characterized more closely. It is a fact that man performs acts (that is, acts consciously)—that I perform them, and that others around me also perform them. It is also a fact that the acts performed by me and by other people possess diverse moral values, are good or evil. Thus, it is fitting to speak of the experience of acts and of the experience of morality in connection with them. In this study we can either separate the experience of acts from the experience of morality or in some way join them. This is a problem that must be solved at the beginning of this work. The experience of morality in itself is similar to the experience of acts. Within the boundaries of the purely sensual contact with reality, namely, with man and his conscious action, we do not grasp morality, the moral values, as we grasp the act in its relations to the person. However, the act and its relation to the person are given to us directly as a specific reality—this means that we do not have to arrive at them by way of reasoning, of conclusion. It is similar in the case of morality, that is, the moral values connected with the act and with the person. They *are also given to us together with the act, and more strictly speaking, together with the relation that occurs between the act and the person performing this act.* All this is given to us directly; we grasp it by the cognitive act as one living totality. The question arises as to whether for the study of the act in its relation to the person it would be more proper to separate this totality, which in itself is enormously rich and complex, or to keep it together. We will try to answer this question next, noting right away that it is not the last problem that we must posit to ourselves at the beginning of this work.

3. Anthropology and Ethics

The fact that the human act is given to us in experience together with its moral value has contributed to the very close connection between anthropology and ethics, the connection that for a long time has existed in philosophy and in moral theology. Not only the experience of the act but also in a sense the entire experience of man is linked with the experience of morality. The science that aims at a thorough knowledge of the problems of moral good and evil can never disregard the fact that this good and evil occur only in acts, through which man participates in them. This is why ethics, especially traditional ethics, has also been the terrain where people have occupied themselves with the act and the entire man. Both the *Nicomachean Ethics* and the *Summa theologiae* provide examples. And even though a tendency exists in modern and especially contemporary philosophy to separate these two fields of knowledge, the complete elimination of anthropological implications in ethics is impossible. The more integral a given system of philosophizing, the more recurrent the anthropological problems in ethics. Their presence is much more prevalent, for instance, in the phenomenological than in the positivistic approach, in Sartre's *L'être et le néant* than in the studies of Anglo-Saxon analysts.

Nonetheless, significant arguments support a certain separation of anthropology from ethics. These arguments proceed above all from the nature of ethics itself. This science attempts to answer the question most closely connected with the person and the act, namely, what makes human acts good or evil—and why. By this very question we can see that the problem of the act and its relation to the person constitutes an indispensable implication of strictly ethical subject matter, though it is only an implication. The task of ethics as such is not to examine the relation occurring between conscious action and the person. Ethics already presupposes this relation and a certain knowledge of the person and the act. The traditional way of joining anthropology with ethics, or at any rate the knowledge of the act as such with the knowledge of what is morally good and what is evil—and why—had its methodological merits, but also its shortcomings. The integration of knowledge was a merit, whereas a shortcoming was a lack of specialization. Science went in the direction of specializing knowledge even to the detriment of integration—sometimes too far, it seems. Perhaps the ideal is a development of science in which science grows in all its particular directions, so that science is perfected specialistically without, however, losing at least the foundations of integration. If the regard for specialization requires a separation of the objects of science, the bonds between what in reality is a unity can in no way disappear.

This is how human acts and moral values are linked with each other in reality. Thus, if the regard for specialization—that is, the regard for the separate problems and tasks of ethics as a science—supports not dealing with the anthropological issues within it also in a specialized way, and in particular not dealing with the reciprocal relation between person and act, then at any rate we must attempt to maintain the bonds that occur in reality between these fields. It is fitting to separate them in such a way that they could always meet and even mutually complement and affirm each other. Therefore, *we can treat* the study of the person and the act, whose subject matter is in principle anthropological, *as an attempt to "place factors outside parentheses"*—to borrow from methods employed in mathematics. We place outside the parentheses the elements of a mathematical operation that in some way inhere in all its other elements, that is, which in some way are common to all that remains within parentheses. This placement outside the parentheses aims to simplify the operation, though its purpose is neither to reject what is located outside the parentheses nor to break the ties between what stands outside the parentheses and what remains within them. Quite the contrary—this placement emphasizes all the more the presence of the given element in the operation. If this element were not placed outside the parentheses, it would be hidden in the other elements of the operation. Thanks to this placement, the element becomes overt and clearly visible.

This is more or less the sense in which we intend to treat a separate study of the person and acts in relation to the totality of the problems dealt with by ethics. This also means taking a certain position with respect to experience. The experience of acts in their relation to the person is connected with the experience of morality. Our point is not to separate one from the other—this would be an artificial procedure—but to emphasize one in a more particular way. However, this emphasis is nothing else than "placement outside the parentheses"—a procedure that is accomplished in a close connection with that which remains within the parentheses and in dependence on it. Only in this way can we act with respect to the acts and their relation to the person. If in this work we aim to thoroughly understand this relation, we are aware from the beginning that *the relation between person and act is most fully manifested thanks to moral values*. Thus, by concerning ourselves with the reciprocal relation between person and act, we do not have to concern ourselves with morality—because this is a separate task and in itself very far-reaching—but we may not lose sight of the bonds that link the act with morality. The problem of morality as such remains within the parentheses, whereas the person and the act stand outside the parentheses—and only this is what we wish to concern ourselves with, though in such a way that specialization does not hinder integration.

The experience of acts and the experience of morality are by nature integrated in the experience of man. The experience of man is the richest and most comprehensive among the experiences that man has at his disposal. It is also the most diverse experience, which we shall speak of in a moment. At any rate, the tradition of dealing with anthropology in ethics has solid empirical foundations. While analyzing morality, that is, while answering the question of what is good and what is evil in human acts, people rightly conduct an analysis of the acts themselves and their relation to the person. However, this is done in the way and to the extent that is needed for understanding morality. In this work, by consistently employing the model of "placement outside the parentheses," we wish to go in a certain sense in the opposite direction. Namely, we intend to use morality for understanding the person, the act, and their reciprocal relation. The element placed outside the parentheses becomes overt and transparent thanks to the fact that it was singled out, but at the same time it is explained fully thanks to that which remained within the parentheses. This also helps in understanding it.

4. The Experience of Man: His Simplicity and Complexity

The study of the person and the act should have an empirical character because its object is given in experience. The experience of human acts is linked almost organically with the experience of morality and *is integrated in the experience of man*. Indeed, morality does not exist outside man, and man does not exist (at least in a certain sense) outside morality. As we said a moment ago, the experience of man is the richest and also most diverse of the experiences that man has at his disposal. The experience of every thing that exists outside man is always linked with some experience of man himself, and man never experiences something outside himself without in some way experiencing himself in this experience. The experience of morality, which to a certain degree (as a particular order, as a group of objective norms) is also something outside man, is linked with the experience of man himself more than is the experience of any other thing: here man experiences himself more than in any other experience.

When speaking of the experience of man, however, it must be understood in the way in which we generally understand it here. Man encounters, that is, establishes cognitive contact with, himself. This contact has an experiential character both continuously, as it were, and every time it is established. For this contact does not last without interruption even when one's "I" is concerned—it breaks off at the very least during sleep. Nonetheless, man as his own "I" is constantly with himself, that is, he is constantly given to himself as the object of experiential cognition while being the subject of this cognition as well. As a result of the continuity, the ceaselessness of this "subject-object" relation of experience, which everyone bears in himself, the consciousness or the lived-experience of oneself can sometimes fade away, although the experience itself lasts. When its moments happen to be more distinct, we become aware—usually *post actum*—of the fact of experience. However, there exists independently of this an entire sequence of experiential moments that are made conscious to a lesser degree and that constitute a great totality of the experience of the man I am myself. This experience consists of a multitude of experiences and constitutes in a sense their sum, or rather their resultant.

Such a grasp of the problem is possible only with a previously established understanding of experience itself. The phenomenalistic position excludes this unity of many experiences, seeing in the individual's experience only a group of impressions or emotional stirrings that are in turn ordered by the mind. Certainly, experience is something individual and is, every time, unique and unrepeatable, but there still exists something that can be called the experience of man, precisely on the basis of the entire continuity of empirical moments. The object of experience is not only a moment, but also man, who emerges from all moments and at the same time inheres in each of them (we leave out other objects at this time). Moreover, we cannot say that experience is itself only in that moment, after which what remains is only the work of the mind forming "man" as its object on the basis of an individual empirical moment or of a series of such moments. The experience of man—the man I myself am—lasts as long as does the direct cognitive contact in which I am the subject, on the one hand, and the object, on the other. The process of understanding, which likewise has its moments and its continuity, progresses in closest connection with this contact. Ultimately, the understanding of oneself consists of many understandings, just as experience consists of many experiences.

The foregoing referred properly to one man only—the one I myself am. However, other people outside me are also the object of experience. The experience of man consists of the experience of oneself and of all other people who remain for the subject in the position of the object of experience, that is, in direct cognitive contact. Of course, no individual man's experience reaches all people, not even all his contemporaries; it is instead necessarily limited to a smaller or greater number of them. The quantitative aspect plays a certain role in this experience. The greater number of people that enter the sphere of someone's experience, the greater the experience. Interrupting the course of these reflections on experience, the course that is important not for its own sake but on account of the whole problem of the knowledge of man, we must at once say that various people communicate to one another the results of their experiences concerning man even without direct contact. These results already constitute a certain knowledge and contribute to the increase not of the experience but of the knowledge of man—either scientific knowledge of various scopes and directions or pre-scientific knowledge. However, experience always stands at the basis of this knowledge, and therefore the knowledge of man communicated reciprocally by people can in a sense coincide with everybody's own experiences. Knowledge not only proceeds from them but also somehow influences them. Does it deform them? In light of what we said about the connection between experience and understanding, there is no reason to think so. Rather, we ought to state that knowledge is a means of multiplying and supplementing experiences.

But it suffices to briefly note this aspect. What is much more important for the present and especially for the further reflections in this book is the fact that other people who are the object of experience are this object in a different way than I am for myself, that is, the way every man is for himself. We could even hesitate here as to whether both cases are rightly considered as the experience of man—or whether what occurs are two experiences irreducible to each other. In one of them we would experience only "man," whereas in the other only and exclusively one's own "I." It is difficult to deny, however, that in the latter case we also encounter man and experience him while having the lived-experience of our own "I." Although these are two separate and different experiences, they are not irreducible to each other. The fundamental unity of the experiential object exists despite the considerable difference that occurs in both cases between the subject and the object of experience. *Even though indubitable reasons exist for speaking about the incommensurability of experience, its fundamental sameness cannot be denied.*

The incommensurability occurs because man is more greatly and more differently given to himself, that is, as his own "I," than any other man that is not him. Even if we grant maximum closeness to this other man, the difference nevertheless remains. It happens that when we draw very near to the other man, it is easier for us to objectivize what is in him or who he is; however, objectivization is not the same as experience. Everyone is for himself the object of experience in a unique and unrepeatable way, and no external relation to any other man can be substituted in the place of this experiential relation shared by one's own subject. Perhaps this external experiential relation contributes to a number of cognitive attainments, which the experience on the part of one's own subject does not provide. These attainments will vary depending on the degree of closeness and on the manner of involvement in the experience of another man, which is, in a sense, involvement in the experience of another "I." All this, however, cannot obscure the fundamental incommensurability between the one unique experience of the man I myself am and any other experience of man.

The experience of oneself, however, does not cease to be the experience of man; it does not go beyond the boundaries of the experience that encompasses all people or, in general, man. This happens certainly as a result of the human mind's participation in the acts of human experience. It is difficult to say what stabilization the senses alone can ensure regarding the object of experience, for no man knows from his own human experience what the purely sensory experience that belongs to animals looks like and to what it is limited. Yet some stabilization must occur even there, though at the most it happens through individuals, that is, through *individua* in which given groups of sensory qualities concentrate (in this way, for instance, a dog or a horse can distinguish its owner from a stranger). The stabilization of experiential objects that is proper to human experience is fundamentally different—it proceeds through mental differentiations and classifications. By virtue of this stabilization in particular, the experience of the subject's own "I" remains within the boundaries of the experience of "man," thus allowing these experiences to overlap each other. As a consequence of the "specific" stabilization of the object, this interference of experiences constitutes in turn the foundation of forming the knowledge of man on the basis of what is provided by both the experience of the man I myself am and the experience of every other man who is not myself. It is proper to note that the very stabilization of the object of experience by reason is by no means a proof of cognitive apriorism but only a proof of the contribution of the mental, intellectual element—indispensable for the entire human cognition—in the formation of experiential acts, namely, these direct cognitive encounters with objective reality. It is to this element in particular that we owe the fundamental sameness of the object of the experience of man in both cases, that is, when the subject of this experience identifies himself with the object and when he differs from it.

The sameness should not obscure the incommensurability. The reason for the incommensurability is the fact that the experience from within (the interior experience), which does not take place in relation to any other man outside me, takes place only in relation to the one particular man who I myself am. All other people are encompassed only by the experience from without (the exterior experience). Of course, in addition to experience alone, another communication with others is possible, one that somehow makes accessible the object of their exclusive experience from within. However, the interior experience itself is untransferable outside one's own "I." Nonetheless, in the totality of our cognition of man, this circumstance does not cause a split, whereby the "interior man," who experientially is only one's own "I," would differ from the "exterior man," that is, any other man outside myself. *Other people do not remain for me merely some "outwardness" opposite my own "inwardness,"* but in the totality of cognition these aspects complement and equalize each other; also, experience itself in its two forms, that is, as interior and exterior, works toward this complementing and equalizing, not against it. Therefore, remaining the object of both experiences—from within and from without—I myself am first and foremost for myself not only "inwardness" but also "outwardness." Although being for me only an object of experience from without, every other man outside myself does not stand in relation to the totality of my cognition as a mere "outwardness" but has an interiority proper to him. Even though I do not experience this interiority directly, I know of it—I know of it in general concerning people and sometimes a great deal concerning particular individuals. Sometimes this knowledge, on the basis of a given contact, passes in a sense into a sort of experience of the other's interiority, which is not the same as the experience of my own "I" from within, though it also has its proper empirical characteristics.

All this must be taken into account when we speak about the experience of man. In no way can we artificially isolate this experience from the totality of the cognitive acts that have man in particular as their object. Also, in no way can we artificially sever it from the intellectual factor. The entire group of cognitive acts directed at man, both at the man I myself am and at every other man outside me, has both an empirical and an intellectual character. Each is in the other, each affects the other, and each profits from the other. In this work, we should constantly have the integral experience of man before our eyes. The experience of acts as well as the experience of morality inheres in him organically. The one and the other do not exist outside the experience of man and without it. If in grasping the relations that occur between person and act we intend to take advantage of the experience of morality that is contained in the acts, then we must constantly keep before our eyes the full experiential context, that is, man. As we have stated previously, the experience of morality introduces us particularly deeply into this man, especially when the person-act relation is concerned.

We must remember that this experience, as well as the experience of the acts that is most directly connected with it, is subject to the same incommensurability and the same complexity as the experience of man. I experience my own acts differently from the acts of any other man, for they are given to me not only from without but also from within. Also, the moral values connected with my own acts are given to me in the same way, in contradistinction to the moral values demonstrated by the acts of all other people. However, this incommensurability does not entail at this point any cognitive split or [1a]irreducibility[1b]. We can cognitively venture very deeply into the structure of man without fostering a fear that the particular aspects of experience lead us into error. It can be said, however, that *the fundamental simplicity of the experience of man prevails over its complexity*. The very "complexity" of that experience simply indicates that the totality of the experience and consequently of the cognition of man "is composed of" both the experience that every one of us has with respect to oneself and the experience of other people—the experience both from within and from without. In cognition, all this "composes" one whole rather than causing "complexity." The conviction of the fundamental simplicity of the experience of man constitutes a rather optimistic feature for the whole of the cognitive task that we undertake in this study.

5. The Ways of Understanding and Conception

In this study, we aim to understand—as fully as possible—the relation between person and act. What does it mean that man performs acts when he acts consciously? What does "conscious action" contain that makes it fundamentally different from all other actions in the surrounding world and deserving of the name "act"? The problem is defined in detail; we see its objective boundaries, but at this point we do not see its full content, which remains to be explicated gradually. We already said that the fragment of reality that is the relation between person and act is both given and entrusted to us as a task. It is here that we touch upon the relation between experience and understanding. For the conscious action of the person, that is, the act, is given to us in experience and at the same time entrusted to our understanding as a task. Therefore, at the end of the introductory and fundamental reflections, it is fitting to at least briefly outline the ways of this understanding and the ways of conception. For a conception is an expression of an understanding. A conception is shaped together with the understanding of an object and acquires the forms needed for the understanding—as full and comprehensive as possible—to be expressed and eventually find its way to others. After all, human knowledge as a social fact is formed through the reciprocal communication of understandings.

We have said previously that no experience exists without at least some understanding. The fundamental and simple bond between the one and the other inheres in the cognitive act proper to man. By experience we understand the direct cognitive contact with the object, the contact that entails a cognitive effect proper to man. This effect is of a mental and not only of a sensual nature—and therefore at least some understanding is contained in experience. If (at least some) understanding is lacking, we cannot speak of experience, for it does not occur when a cognitive effect is lacking. After all, "experience" always denotes some "cognition"—the contact having a cognitive character. Nonetheless, understanding is something different from experience. It develops in man's intellectual powers in a way proper to them. It develops and is shaped in connection with experience in a sense from the materials provided by the latter, though according to its own regularity and a dynamic proper only to it; it is the dynamic of intellectual acts and processes, a dynamic of human thinking.

In a certain sense, in its acts and processes, thinking is immanent to experience—it does not part ways with it, but is constantly faithful to it, even in the most abstract apprehensions and far-reaching conclusions. On the other hand, however, already from the very first understandings it is transcendent with respect to experience. However, the transcendence of the acts and the processes of understanding with respect to experience do not mean in the least a departure from it, from its objective content. Quite the contrary: understanding means a deeper and deeper entry into experience, into the object experientially given to us. Thanks to understanding, this object becomes in a sense brought out from darkness. Understanding is in a sense the light of human experiences, since their cognitive character—as was stated, this is the proper character of experience—would not be achieved without understanding. Thus, understanding helps experience to fulfill itself in its proper, that is, cognitive, character. In other words, we can say that understanding constitutes in a sense an exploration of experience. By this we emphasize the "material" role of the latter in human cognition and the "formal" role of understanding.

The first and elementary understanding of the relation that occurs between person and act in the case of conscious action is similar to the first and elementary understandings of other objects of our cognition. Such an understanding possesses a spontaneous and intuitive character. When we say that it is "first," we do not indicate above all the chronology of human life, but this understanding's position in the entire process of understanding, the mature expression of which is a particular conception. Therefore, this understanding is "elementary." We must here distinguish the understanding that suffices man in practice, that is, that suffices for him to be and act consciously, from theoretical understanding. In this work, of course, we are concerned with the latter; the entire process of understanding and conception tends in the theoretical direction. We are concerned with a theoretical apprehension of the person-act relation and not merely with the ability to enact it.

In order to arrive at this apprehension, we cannot be content with spontaneous understanding alone—even though its intuitive content has for us a fundamental significance—but we must originate a certain conscious cognitive process. It is a process of a deeper and deeper understanding. Because the source from which we draw here is experience, *the condition of a cognitive process, correctly conducted, is the conscious relation to experience*—that is, becoming conscious of (understanding) its simplicity and complexity, its aspects and contexts, namely, all that constituted the topic of our reflections in our previous point. Of course, experience as such is both spontaneously simple and complex, interior and exterior, integral and partial. However, it is indispensable for the cognitive process *to transition from spontaneity to reflectivity*, and this first and foremost means the understanding of experience itself. The object, that is, "man consciously acting," and the very relation between person and act as an object are given in experience, and become better understood by understanding the experience itself in its simplicity and complexity. This is particularly important in relation to man as an object of cognition more than in relation to any other object outside him. The preceding remarks on the experience of man had to convince us of this. It is fitting to add that the understanding of experience (or experiences) means much more for the conception of the object, constitutes in a sense its origin.

The cognitive process consists in the fact that we move from elementary understandings, which have not only a spontaneous but also an intuitive character, to the discursive way. We posit questions linked with the object of our interests and answer them, or possibly we search for answers. The basis for both, that is, the questions and the answers, is, speaking most generally, experience. Within experience and relying on it, the basis of the questions is already always some understanding either first and intuitive or—with further questions—the understanding contained in the answers to previous questions. We must add that the cognitive process in the discursive stage very often evokes new intuitive understandings, which thanks to the entire traversed discourse are more mature than the previous ones. They thereby constitute in a sense a deeper penetration into the object and its fuller reading or a fuller exploration by the intellect. We can even say that these understandings of the intuitive type are the proper end of discursive attempts, for the cognitive discourse itself is only a means, and the cognitive process as a process of understanding progresses together with the essential delving into the object.

In order to understand our object, that is, the relation between person and act, intellectual discourse must progress in close connection with experience, because the object is given in it and not outside it. We do not have to reach this object by way of reasoning, by proving its existence. *We only must understand it most fully, that is, explain it* (to oneself and others). Reasoning, which constitutes a cognitive procedure that leads to a full understanding of the object of inquiries that is given in experience, thus really existing in its sphere, has *above all a reductive* sense and character. Its end is an interpretation of the object—and in our case, an interpretation of the person-act relation. Precisely this sort of understanding in a sense takes control of all our understandings by discursive means, by way of questions and answers whose starting point is the first intuition of the object. In order to "understand" it fully, especially in order to create a proper conception of it, we also must "reason"—and reason reductively at that, namely, "interpret." The interpretation of the relation between person and act is the same as its full "explanation," which is achieved by explaining.

Nonetheless, the reductive direction of our work indicates yet something else. The word "reduction" [*redukcja*] has its Polish equivalent in the noun derived from the verb "to reduce" [*sprowadzać*] (reduction [*sprowadzanie*]). For an explanation of a thing is the same as a mental reduction to proper reasons or foundations. Our understanding of the person-act relation can and should go precisely in this direction, and consequently its proper conception will emerge. What is perhaps most evident here is the need for understanding, that is, for becoming conscious of what and what sort is the experience of an object—for the sake of understanding the object itself. We stated previously that this experience is marked by a countless number of facts that compose it. Hence, its first "complexity" is quantitative. Besides, the experience in which our object (the relation between person and act) inheres constitutes in a sense a part of a greater whole, which is the experience of man taken most broadly. This part is linked with its whole by most organic bonds and does not allow itself to be grasped or—above all—be understood without and outside it. In order to understand the person-act relation correctly, one must at least in a certain measure understand man in general, must also understand morality as a group of facts most closely connected with man. Here we find another complexity of experience—this is rather a "qualitative complexity." For man is given to us both as his own "I" and as everyone outside me; thus he is given to us both from within and from without. Before it becomes reductive, the mental function of cognition must first be inductive, though we understand induction as did Aristotle and not as did nineteenth century positivists such as Mill.

Thus from a plurality of facts we must first *arrive at their qualitative sameness, and only then can we begin to explain them*. Of course, this procedure could be omitted (then we would be explaining to ourselves what the relation between my own act and my own person consists in). In fact, we do not omit it and we do attempt to explain the relation between person and act "in general." This, however, presupposes a generalization, that is, a fruit of induction in the Aristotelian sense. Knowledge pertains to objects "in general," and therefore the mental processes that have a reductive and inductive character penetrate and condition each other.

Induction is by nature anterior. First, from the plurality of experiential objects we must arrive at ascertaining their sameness—that is, at ascertaining that every fact of man's conscious action contains "the same" person-act relation. Only then can this relation be explained, that is, interpreted in the general sense. Sameness is nothing but a given semantic unity. Reaching this semantic unity is the work of the intellect and the result of induction, for experience by itself leaves us, in a sense, with a plurality of facts. The statement that in every one of the facts where man acts consciously there occurs "the same" person-act relation is given to us intuitively in an original and elementary way. The verifying reflection must take the incommensurability of experience into account: the person-act relation is given to me differently in my own experience than in the experience of other people—it is given in my own experience also from within, whereas it is given only from without in the experience of others. Nonetheless, I find no basis for doubting the fundamental "sameness" of this relation. Although I know it differently in myself than in others, I do not doubt that it is fundamentally the same. We can say that the simplicity of experience is stronger than its complexity here. Besides, intellectual moments act in experience itself, the moments that attest to the sameness not only intuitively, but also reflectively. Since in every particular case there is "the same" man who acts consciously, then "the same" relation between him as a person and his act should occur.

As we see, the inductive factor is a fundamental way of understanding here. Experience quantitatively surpasses its possibilities. There are immensely more facts in which man acts consciously than the individual mind can encompass and register. Therefore, it has to limit itself to ascertaining the "fundamental sameness," abstracting from individual particulars. Experience will remain with particulars, whereas reason will take on that which is fundamental, that which is repeated in various particular contexts as "the same." Nevertheless, *an entire wealth of facts, their multiplicity and diversity, will remain with experience; reason will take on the semantic unity.* By taking on this unity, it allows itself, in a sense, to be surpassed by experience. At the same time, however, the mind does not cease to understand its wealth and diversity. By this understanding—and not only by the "semantic unity" that it discovers and through which it grasps that which is essential in the multiplicity—the mind dominates experience. In this consists the function of induction in the totality of the cognitive process, at least the process that in our case is to lead to understanding the relation between person and act.

6. The Ways of Understanding and Conception (Conclusion)

Reduction presupposes the semantic unity to which induction leads, and on the basis of this unity it attempts to explain the object, that is, to deepen the understanding of the person-act relation that we possess thanks to the original and elementary intuition. Thanks to induction we possess understanding in a general and fundamental sense; we are free from particular and individual contexts in which this relation occurs. In a sense, we are free even from the contexts in which it occurs experientially and most directly in ourselves. We look at this relation as at an object, even despite the fact that our own subject (and *per analogiam* all other people as subjects) is engaged in it directly. To induction we owe the objectivization and the inter-objectivization of the process: the "person-act" relation stands as a cognitive object and problem that all can see objectively, freeing themselves from a subjective engagement in which this object is *de facto* involved. (After all, the person-act relation does not occur *de facto* in any other way but in subjective involvement.) At the same time, thanks to induction, in a sense a new mobilization of experience takes place for the sake of understanding, although experience is in a sense nothing other than a subjective involvement, which is the lot of every man as far as the person-act relation is concerned. This relation is for everyone first a fact, that is, a lived-experience, and only afterward does it become a problem. We said that the inductive process leads us out of the "quantitative complexity" of experience but does not separate us from it. Indeed, it allows us to keep our finger on its pulse, as it were. In human cognition there is no fracture between experience and understanding. Instead, there is a continuity, an organic continuity that, of course, does not obscure the otherness or even distinctness of one from the other.

This also refers to the reductive process. Explanation, that is, interpretation, is not interpolation. By explaining, we follow the object as deeply as possible, according to how it is given to us in experience. Explanation is oriented toward a real object, not toward an abstraction but toward what exists or "occurs" in reality (we can say that the person-act relation occurs and in this way exists). Nonetheless, explanation penetrates into this really existing or occurring object under the aspect of essence. This sufficiently indicates the necessity of explaining "from within," that is, *finding the reasons by which the object is explained in itself*. All these reasons inhere in the object itself, thus, they are contained in experience. The goal for the intellectual image of the object is to be adequate, to "live up to" the object or, in other words, to grasp all the reasons explaining this object and to grasp them correctly. Precisely this is the task of reduction. In our case it is to correctly grasp all reasons that explain the relation between person and act (conscious action of man) and to give them an expression in the appropriate conception. This is the task of reduction. We must add that also in this direction experience in a certain way surpasses understanding. Although the first spontaneous intuition to some extent already captures the essence of the person-act relation, nonetheless this essence is still concealed to a great degree in experience. Elementary knowledge suffices but does not satisfy. The mind is left with an important task consisting in bringing out many—or all if possible—reasons that explain the object. Precisely this is the task of this study. A full—as full as possible—understanding, as well as a conception as its expression, is precisely the understanding that will live up to experience by proportionally taking into account all its aspects.

This last problem emerges with a thorough and scientific study of the object. Pre-scientific knowledge and especially practical knowledge, that is, knowledge suitable for acting, for enacting the person-act relation, does not manifest this problem. Here experience dominates in its fundamental simplicity—although we know from elsewhere what difficulties can occur in particular people when the person-act relation is enacted correctly. As is evident, in this study we are interested in the theoretical grasp of this relation. Precisely here the proportional relation of the aspects of experience is a problem. However, we already stated that a condition for correct understanding (in the inductive and the reductive sense) is the understanding of experience—including experience in its complexity. Once we understand this incommensurability that inheres in the experience of man as well as in the experience of the person-act relation, the incommensurability of the experience of one's own "I" in comparison with the experience of other people, the incommensurability of the interior experience in relation to the exterior relation, *the problem of correctly unifying these experiences in understanding and conception must arise*. This problem does not arise by way of spontaneous understanding, but must arise during reflection that has a scientific character.

For it seems that what we call subjectivism or idealism in philosophy resulted precisely from a disproportional understanding of experiences—and above all *from a disproportional understanding of the experiences of man*: for the experience of every other thing outside man is always indirectly linked with some experience of man. Mental attitudes such as subjectivism or idealism are a consequence of the absolutization of one of the aspects of the experience of man at the expense of another. Concretely speaking, the interior experience, thus also the experience of one's "I" (of the man who is myself), is here elevated to an absolute position at the expense of just the experience of man, in which the exterior experience is correlated with the interior one. At the basis of objectivism and realism stands precisely the understanding of the correlation of the experiences of man—the correlative role that the experience of oneself fulfills in relation to the experience of every other man and the aspectual sense of interior and exterior experience. The absolutization of one of them is precisely a denial of the correlation: that which is absolute has meaning only from itself and for itself without a reference to anything outside it.

Such an understanding of the experience of one's own "I" as well as of interior experience must in turn generate a unilateral understanding of the object of this experience, above all man himself and then every other object, since—as we said—the experience of every other thing outside man is linked with some experience of man. It is difficult to resist the conviction that fundamental mental attitudes and their opposition, such as the opposition between objectivism and subjectivism, between realism and idealism, somehow are rooted in a contrary or incorrect understanding and conception of man—of the very experience of man at that. Thus *not only is the philosophy of man* (anthropology) *an implication of many branches of philosophy, and perhaps especially ethics,* as we noted in the beginning, but also through the understanding of the experience of man *it somehow lies at the root of the main mental attitudes that have found their expression in philosophy.*

Conversely, all this is significant for the problem of reduction, thus, for the full interpretation of the object, namely, the relation between person and act. For not only does the—proper or improper—experience of the very experience of man contribute to the formation of the mental attitudes noted above, but also—in turn—these attitudes are reflected in the understanding of reality, and above all in the understanding of man, in the interpretation and conception of man. The reductive reasoning basically consists in searching for the reasons that explain the object as comprehensively and deeply as possible. However, in searching for and finding these reasons, it must constantly be conscious of the opposition of the mental or philosophical attitudes by which this object can be grasped and explained. For usually interpretation—as the history of human knowledge teaches—is *not only an indication of the reasons that explain the object, but also an application of a particular mental attitude.* Therefore, following the way of reduction to understand the object—the object that, as we know, is the relation between person and act—we must constantly demonstrate the understanding of the experience of man in its simplicity and complexity and the understanding of fundamental mental foundations in their possible opposition.

3 ❋ Person and Act in the Aspect of Consciousness

A Fragment of the Study *Person and Act*

1. "Conscious Action" and "*Actus humanus*"

At the beginning of proper reflections on the relation between person and act, it is fitting, if only briefly, to highlight what appears to be a merely terminological problem.[ix] What we call act [*czyn*] is exclusively man's conscious action. No other action deserves this name. The equivalent of our "act" [*czyn*] in the Western philosophical tradition is *actus humanus*. Hence, even in our terminology we sometimes find the phrase "human act" [*akt ludzki*]. Perhaps this Latinism is not needed since we have the native and beautiful expression "act" [*czyn*], although the Latin term's presence in the literature, especially in the manuals, is very remarkable. The phrase *actus humanus* not only derives from *agere*, which directly establishes its kinship to act and action, for *agere* means precisely "to do" or "to act." In the philosophical tradition of the West, the phrase *actus humanus* also presupposes a certain interpretation of act, namely, one that was developed on the basis of the philosophy of Aristotle in antiquity and of St. Thomas Aquinas in the Middle Ages. This interpretation is realistic and objectivistic as well as metaphysical. It stems from the entire conception of being, and directly from the conception of *potentia-actus*, by means of which the Aristotelians and Thomists explain the changeable and dynamic character of being.

In this case, we refer to the concrete being that is man together with the action proper only to him. Therefore, "act" [*czyn*] in Scholastic terminology is defined as *actus humanus* or, more specifically, as *actus volun-*

tarius. It is a concretization of the dynamic proper to the human person because it is accomplished in the way proper to free will. The property indicated by the attribute *voluntarius* determines the very essence of the act and its distinctness with respect to the action of other subjects that are not persons. A close link with the corresponding *potentia*, which indicates a potential substratum of actualization, is always characteristic of expressing *actus* in light of the entire Aristotelian or Thomistic conception of being. Therefore, *actus humanus* not only captures the entire subject that acts but also in a certain way already specifies the relation between him and action. The expression *actus voluntarius* accomplishes this in an even more particular way by indicating not only the way of realizing the action proper to man but also the power to which we owe this action. This way of which the attribute *voluntarius* speaks is possible only because precisely such a power as the free will acts.

The interpretation whose fruit is the philosophical term *actus humanus* and *actus voluntarius*, is perfect in its own way. It coincides with the entirety of existential facts and grasps as deeply as possible what is essential in them. In a certain sense, there can be no other interpretation of the human act; at any rate, we know of no other equally accurate attempt to grasp the act's utterly dynamic character and its union with man as a person. All attempts to take on this subject matter must in some way presuppose this philosophical interpretation hidden in the expressions *actus humanus* and *actus voluntarius*. Most frequently, these attempts clarify and specify different variations of *voluntarium* that occur in human action, as we can observe in many manuals. However, yet another possibility exists, namely, *the possibility of elaborating integral aspects of the act*, that is, the possibility of refreshing, so to speak, the fundamental conception of *actus humanus*. [2a] Since the crystallization of the metaphysical concept of *actus humanus*, philosophy and science have progressed through many phases of development. Precisely this provokes us to undertake anew the perennial problem of the act in its relation to the person.

In the present chapter we intend to analyze the act and its relation to the person under the aspect of consciousness. It is precisely one of the integral aspects that greatly developed and matured in the course of centuries-old scientific and philosophical reflection. In our language—because we are interested first in terminological inquiries—the word "act" [*czyn*] denotes action proper only and exclusively to the human person, that is, "conscious action." Referencing what we said earlier, the "act" [*czyn*] is the same as "*actus humanus*," but the very word "act" [*czyn*] does not reach so clearly into the philosophical interpretation as does *actus humanus*. We understand the act as action proper to man, though "action" [*działanie*] does not denote all that *actus* does in its philosophical sense. *Actus* is always correlative to possibility (*potentia*), thus it indicates a potential substratum from which it proceeds. Furthermore, "*actus*" indicates that action is a kind of becoming organically linked with this substratum and subject. The very word "action" does not indicate this. It pertains much more to the phenomenon or manifestation than the metaphysical structure that stands behind it. The phrase "human action" very closely defines its object in the phenomenal and experiential order—but in no way explains it, this explanation being in some sense accomplished by the expression "*actus humanus*," as we noted a moment ago. However—and we ought to emphasize this—perhaps the word "action" renders the phenomenological specificity of its designation better than the word "*actus*" does. "*Actus*" explains "action"; however, wishing to state that it denotes action and nothing else, we must use a certain interpretation. The phenomenological specificity of the object is closer to us than the metaphysical one.

The act is conscious action. When speaking of "conscious action" we mean that this action is accomplished in a way proper to the will and characteristic of it (as is immediately and directly expressed by the phrase *actus voluntarius*). The action proper to the will is conscious. However, if the reduction of "action" to *actus* demands a certain path of thought, a passage through a certain interpretation, then the reduction of "conscious action" to *actus voluntarius* demands a yet longer path, a passage through many more interpretative details. Before we reach this point—and we will do so primarily in the next chapter—we must observe that the phrase "conscious action" leads us directly to the aspect of consciousness in the act and its relation to the person. This is the aspect that we shall consider first.

2. Conscious Action and the Consciousness of Action

The expression "conscious action" directs us to the aspect of consciousness in the act and its relation to the person, without, however, manifesting this aspect. We should make the distinction between "conscious action" and the "consciousness of action" in order to reveal the aspect of consciousness. This is a fundamental distinction because thanks to it we gain access to consciousness, and we can examine its proper role in the existence and action of the person. Man not only acts consciously but also has the consciousness that he acts and, moreover, that he acts consciously. Although in both applications we find the same word (consciously—consciousness), only one of them concerns consciousness as such. The fact that man acts consciously in itself tells us nothing about the consciousness of action, though as a rule the consciousness of action accompanies conscious action. However, action is "conscious" not because consciousness accompanies it—at any rate, not only because of that and not properly because of that. When we speak of conscious action, we mean the internal property of action, the constitutive property—that is, the property that constitutes the essential character of the human act. To this property the act also owes the fact that it is "*voluntarius*," that is, that it is performed in a way proper to the will. As we see, both properties condition and penetrate each other. Thus, the act is conscious and "voluntary" action—although this latter attribute neither accurately renders what the term "*voluntarium*" contains nor is necessary for knowing that conscious action is also "*voluntarium*," that is, performed in a way proper to the will.

We must add that the traditional interpretation of the act as *actus humanus* followed this sense of "consciousness," a sense that can be called attributive and that completely enters the realism of human *voluntarium*. As a result of this, the aspect of consciousness as such has not been developed in this interpretation. However, consciousness in the nounal sense, consciousness as such, is by all means present in action, and especially in the relation between person and act. It itself constitutes an important aspect of this relation. The act—*actus humanus*—is not complete in itself, but always appears in a greater whole, namely, in correlation to the person. Against the background of this greater whole, consciousness as a separate aspect is revealed anew, an aspect in which the being and acting of the person is not only mirrored but also in a certain way shaped. The conception *actus humanus* did not so much ignore this aspect as conceal it; this aspect was contained in this conception only *implicite*. For, as was noted, the conception *actus humanus* was not only realistic and objectivistic but also metaphysical. It concerned itself with consciousness as something incorporated into man's being and his action. According to this conception, man exists and acts consciously, but he does not exist and act also through consciousness. We do not mean an absolutization of this consciousness. [3a] *Our goal is only to open an aspect that was too confined and* remained only an implication *in the traditional conception.* This was an implication contained in man's rationality (referring to the definition *homo—animal rationale*); concerning the act, this was an implication of *voluntarium*. Our task in this study is a certain "explication" of consciousness (the Latin term very clearly indicates the opposite of implication).

For man not only acts consciously but also is conscious of his action and of the being that acts—thus, he is conscious of the relation between person and act. This consciousness occurs simultaneously with conscious action; in a sense, it accompanies that action. It also occurs before and after that action. It possesses its continuity and its identity separately from the [4a]consistency[4b] and identity of every individual act. Every act in a sense finds consciousness already present; it is formed and fades away in relation to consciousness, leaving behind a trace of its presence, so to speak. Consciousness accompanies the act and mirrors it when the act is born and when it is performed—once it has been performed, consciousness still mirrors it, though, of course, not accompanying it any longer. However, the act is not merely conscious action because consciousness accompanies or mirrors it—which perhaps was sufficiently stated already. The attributive usage ("conscious action") differs essentially from the nounal usage of the word "consciousness." In the first case, only action is conscious, whereas in the second case man is conscious of his action. This also causes man to act as a person and—in this the aspect of consciousness plays its most proper role—to experience his action as an act.

The proper function of consciousness is cognitive. However, we characterize this function in this way only in the most general terms. Consciousness is a reflection, or rather a mirroring, of what "happens" in man and of what man "does" (this distinction is very important for our further study of act, but for the time being we shall not deal with it). Consciousness is also a reflection, or rather a mirroring, of everything with which man comes into objective contact by means of any (including cognitive) action (for instance, by means of acts of knowledge) and on occasion of everything that "happens" in him. Consciousness mirrors all of this. In some sense, the entire man and also the entire world accessible to this concrete man (that is, to the man "I myself am") are in consciousness. In what way is all that "in consciousness"? In reply to this important question, we must say that all this—we already know what—is in consciousness in a way proper only to it; we can call it *a consciousness-related way*. The thinkers who absolutized consciousness by making it in their conceptions a single subject of all contents—here inheres the common foundation of idealistic thinking—perhaps did not adequately take into consideration the way in which everything that inheres in consciousness inheres in it. For this way—"consciousness-related," as we said—indicates that consciousness neither fulfills the cognitive function in the proper sense of the word nor possesses its own subjectivity—it is not a *suppositum* or a power from which this function could develop organically.

The essence of cognitive acts performed by man consists in penetrating the object, objectivizing it intellectually, and in this way "understanding" it (let us rather refer to the cursory analysis of "understanding" that was conducted in the introductory chapter). Therefore, cognitive acts have an intentional character; they are clearly turned toward the cognized object. Properly speaking, the intentionality characteristic of, for example, acts of knowledge is foreign to consciousness. However, the cognitive role of consciousness (that the role is cognitive is difficult to question) is quite different. It does not consist in the penetration of the object, in the objectivization for the sake of understanding. Consciousness is understanding—for its intellectual character is beyond doubt—but it is always an understanding of something already understood, of course, in accord with the degree and manner of understanding. The acts of consciousness do not possess an intentional character, although what is the object of our cognition exists in consciousness in an intentional way. Thus, that which exists in consciousness exists just as it does in the entire human cognition, namely, through an image—but the intellectual formation of this image is neither a task nor a work of consciousness. For only mirroring belongs to consciousness. In this consists the consciousness-related character of cognition, when both particular acts of consciousness and their totality—hence either a sum or a resultant—are concerned.

It must be added that the sum or resultant of the acts of consciousness determines the actual state of consciousness. However, the subject of this state is not consciousness but man, who we rightly say remains in or outside the state of consciousness, who possesses full or diminished consciousness, etc. Consciousness itself does not exist as a "substantial" subject of acts of consciousness; it exists neither as a separate *suppositum* nor as a power. It is difficult to fully substantiate this thesis here, as this belongs to psychology or integral anthropology. Nonetheless, what follows from what has already been said concerning consciousness is that it wholly inheres in its acts and in their "consciousness-related" specificity, which is connected with mirroring as something different from cognitive objectivization. Man not only cognitively enters the world of objects and even finds himself in that world as one of these objects but also possesses all of this world in the mirroring of consciousness, by which he lives most interiorly and personally. For consciousness not only mirrors but also in a particular way "interiorizes" what it mirrors, giving to it all a place in the person's own "I." Here, however, we already touch upon a further and perhaps deeper function of consciousness, which we shall discuss separately.

In any case, in light of what we have already said, the consciousness of the act, which is always the consciousness of the person-act relation, appears somewhat more fully. We stated that it is something different from what determines the act as conscious action. The consciousness of the act is a mirroring, one of many mirrorings that compose the totality, in terms of content, of the person's consciousness. This mirroring in itself has a consciousness-related character; it does not consist in the objectivization of the act (or rather the person-act relation), though it retains the image of this act and of the person-act relation.

3. Consciousness and Self-Knowledge

It was stated previously that consciousness mirrors human acts in a way proper only to it, namely, in the consciousness-related way. However, consciousness cognitively objectivizes neither the acts nor the person who performs them, nor finally the entire "world of the person" that is linked in some way with his existence and action. Nonetheless, the acts of consciousness, as well as their sum or resultant, remain distinctly related to all that exists outside of them, particularly the acts performed by a concrete person. This relation is established thanks to the content proper to consciousness, a content that consists of the meanings of individual elements of reality and their mutual connections. When we consider this semantic side of consciousness and state that by itself it does not reach these meanings, for it does not objectivize cognitively, then we conclude that some knowledge very closely cooperates with consciousness.

Knowledge possesses a different cognitive character than consciousness does. Knowledge contains an intellectual direction toward an object, the consequence of which is cognitive objectivization and active understanding. Thanks to knowledge, we discover the meaning of particular things and advance in the understanding of these things themselves and of the connections that take place between them. For to understand is nothing else but to intellectually grasp the meaning of things or the connections between things. All this is alien to consciousness; the whole process of active understanding occurs neither in nor thanks to it. The meanings of things and of their interrelations are given to consciousness by way of the knowledge that man acquires and possesses in different ways and to different degrees. Hence, the different degrees of knowledge determine the different levels of consciousness, although between knowledge and consciousness a thorough difference exists with respect to the intellectual formation of both individual acts and cognitive totalities.

What ought to be distinguished from all forms of knowledge possessed by man, and what indirectly shapes his consciousness with respect to content, that is, from the semantic side, is so-called self-knowledge. It is more coherent with consciousness than with any other knowledge, for its object is one's own "I," with which consciousness remains in the closest subjective union, as further analysis will more fully demonstrate. At this point, self-knowledge most closely meets consciousness while remaining in a sense separate from it, for consciousness, with its subjective union with that "I," is not cognitively oriented to that "I" as to an object. We may even say that consciousness is in a sense cognitively indifferent to one's own "I" as an object. No intentional acts of consciousness exist that would objectivize this "I" with respect to existence or action. This function is performed by acts of self-knowledge. It is to them that every man owes the objectivizing contact with himself and with his acts. Thanks to self-knowledge, consciousness mirrors acts and their relation to one's own "I." Without self-knowledge, consciousness would be deprived of semantic contents concerning both the world of objects and man's own "I" as an object; it would find itself in a vacuum, as it were. The idealists postulate a state like this, for in it consciousness can be considered a subject that produces its contents with no regard for any factor located outside consciousness itself. A valid question in this line of thought arises—namely, whether consciousness itself can be considered a real subject or whether it is only its own product. At this point this remark is merely marginal.

Thanks to self-knowledge, the acting subject's own "I" is cognitively grasped as an object. As a result, both the person and the act connected with him have an objective meaning in consciousness. The consciousness-related mirroring, which is subjective throughout, removes neither the objective meaning of one's own "I" nor that of its acts, for it constantly draws this meaning from self-knowledge. The coherence of self-knowledge with consciousness should be considered the basic factor of the equilibrium of the person's interior life, especially concerning its intellectual content. Man is an object as a subject, is an object for himself as for a subject, and even in the consciousness-related mirroring he does not lose an objective meaning. *In this regard, self-knowledge is in a sense anterior to consciousness,* for it brings into it the semantic relation to one's own "I" and to its acts, though consciousness in itself is not intentionally directed to them.

Moreover, the objectivizing turn of self-knowledge toward one's own "I" and toward the acts connected with it also concerns consciousness itself. Consciousness becomes an object of self-knowledge. This explains the fact that when man "possesses the consciousness" of his action, he at the same time "knows that he acts" and "knows that he acts consciously." He knows that he is conscious, and he knows that he acts consciously. Self-knowledge has for its object not only the person and his acts but also consciousness—here we mean consciousness in the nounal sense. Consciousness in the attributive sense, as a property of being and acting of the person, is anterior to self-knowledge. Self-knowledge objectivizes the consciousness of being and acting of the person and, in a sense, passes this onto the mirroring consciousness. Hence, in the consciousness-related reflection, the objective sense is possessed not by any being and acting of the person who is my own "I," but by conscious being and acting, that is, the person and acts. In this way, man is conscious of his conscious action, just as he is conscious that he consciously exists. Thus, he is conscious of the consciousness of his being and his acting in acts. Consciousness in the nounal sense—consciousness as such—presupposes consciousness as a property of human being and acting, consciousness in the attributive sense. Self-knowledge has the one and the other for its object: I know that I act consciously, and I know that I have the consciousness of my (conscious) action. Consciousness in the attributive sense (I know that I act consciously) is merely the object of self-knowledge. However, self-knowledge not only shapes consciousness in the nounal sense (being anterior to consciousness)—namely, it shapes the relation of consciousness to objects—but also objectivizes it, that is, has it for its object (I know that I have consciousness of my action).

The making conscious of not only one's own "I" and the acts connected with it but also the very consciousness of these acts in their relation to the "I" is a work of self-knowledge. Self-knowledge makes consciousness as a property of the being and acting of one's own "I"—in fact, being and acting themselves—become *in a sense an object of consciousness in mirroring, though the latter does not in itself objectivize anything but only subjectivizes*. In itself, it merely constitutes the plane of subjectivization, and the world of objects as well as its own "I" as an object and consciousness as an objective property of actions, that is, acts, are cognitively indifferent to it. When we speak as follows: "I become conscious of my act" or "I become conscious of something else," then, by indicating the actualization of consciousness, we in fact indicate the actualization of self-knowledge. For an act (or anything else) can be "made conscious" not in a consciousness-related manner but only intentionally, thus by an act of self-knowledge. Speaking this way, however, we express ourselves correctly because consciousness is most closely united with self-knowledge. As long as mirroring is concerned, the consciousness-related actualization suffices; however, if "making something conscious" is concerned, then the actualization of consciousness must in a sense include the act of self-knowledge.

It is very remarkable and very fortunate that our language has at its disposal both these expressions. Thanks to this fact, many noetic and ontological problems are sorted out. On the one hand, the objectivity of the subject becomes more intelligible, as does, on the other hand, the subjectivity of the object, namely, the complex object that is the person in his relation to his act. We shall in turn analyze this subjectivity of the object. However, before we undertake such analysis, we must state once more that *when we speak of the consciousness of act, we mean not only the consciousness-related mirroring itself but also intentional self-knowledge*. I have consciousness of the act—this in fact means that by the act of self-knowledge I objectivize my act in relation to my person. I objectivize the fact that my act is a true action of my person and not something that only happens in my person; that this action is conscious (internally, that is, constitutively conscious, which is indirectly equivalent to *voluntarium*); that this action, as performed in the way proper to the will (which is directly equivalent to *voluntarium*), has a positive or negative moral value, is good or evil. All this, the entire content of the act, objectivized by an act of self-knowledge, becomes the content of consciousness. Thanks to this objectivization, we can speak of consciousness in the objective sense—of the relation of consciousness to the objective world—in contradistinction to subjective consciousness, consciousness as a property of being and acting. We speak of consciousness in the objective sense on account of the meaning of various objects that it contains due to various forms of knowledge. But we speak in a particular way of consciousness in the objective sense on account of the meaning in consciousness of one's own "I," its *esse* and *operari*, and all that is in any way connected with it. Consciousness owes this meaning, or rather this group of meanings, to self-knowledge. Thanks precisely to this group of meanings, consciousness merits in a particular way to be called self-consciousness. *It is self-knowledge that contributes to the formation of self-consciousness.*

Since we have already outlined the reciprocal relation between consciousness and self-knowledge—before we move ahead in the analysis of the function of consciousness—let us take a brief look at self-knowledge regardless of its functional connections with consciousness. Among various forms and varieties of human knowledge (pre-scientific or scientific), self-knowledge is a particular knowledge. As follows from the above analysis, every man's own "I" is the object of this knowledge. It is the knowledge of one's own "I" that at the point of one's own "I" meets all that in whatever way is connected with or refers to that "I." Thus, for example, there is moral self-knowledge—something fundamentally different from knowledge about morality, let alone from ethics; religious self-knowledge—existing independently from all forms of knowledge about religion, religious knowledge, or theology; social self-knowledge—existing independently from any knowledge about society; and so on. For self-knowledge, concentrated on its own "I" as its proper object, enters with the "I" all the areas into which this "I" expands. Self-knowledge, however, does not objectivize any of these areas for their own sake but only in connection with and because of the "I."

We should stress again that self-knowledge has nothing to do with a philosophy whose object is the "I." In that case, it would concern an abstracted and generalized "I." In self-knowledge, the object is the "I," concrete and "one's own." Self-knowledge can have a philosophical character—just as it can possess a character that is more biological or psychological depending on the specialized tendencies of its concrete object—but never becomes a philosophy, physiology, or psychology. It is something completely different from these. The distinction—which is so important when knowledge is concerned—between pre-scientific and scientific knowledge does not properly apply to it. We might have certain reservations in applying to self-knowledge even the concept of knowledge, which, strictly speaking, has a general object. Yet, self-knowledge not only has one's individual "I" for its object but also is constantly entangled in the particulars connected with that "I." It is a knowledge of one's own "I" as a fact in its whole particularity. After all, it is a true knowledge, for it is not content with registering the particulars connected with one's own "I," but constantly arrives at generalizations. Such generalizations are, for example, all view or assessments of oneself, proper only to self-knowledge and created by it. We must add that these views—some integral vision of one's own "I"—become mirrored in consciousness: thus, they are mirrored not only as the particular facts connected with one's "I" but also as the constantly increasing and developing integral fact that is my own "I." Views on that fact have not only the character of a self-knowing theory of one's own "I" but also the character of assessment, because the aspect of value is no less essential for self-knowledge.

Self-knowledge does not constitute merely a particular case of the knowledge of man in general, even though the "I" that it attempts to objectivize as comprehensively as possible is man. The "I," as the object of self-knowledge, is man in the ontological and intentional sense. Yet, all the cognitive work proper to self-knowledge proceeds exclusively from self-experience to self-understanding without passing into generalizations about man as such. Here runs *a boundary distinctly drawn by the object of knowledge about man and self-knowledge, that is, the knowledge of one's own "I."* If there is a shift to be seen, it is rather in the direction of the knowledge of oneself. For self-knowledge uses knowledge about man in general, that is, the various views on the human being; it also uses experiential knowledge about people in order to better understand one's own "I." In this sense, comparison is not alien to it. Nonetheless, self-knowledge does not use the knowledge of its own "I" in order to better understand other people or man in general. The latter belongs to the knowledge of man, which readily takes advantage of self-knowledge in order to better understand its own object. Self-knowledge, however, stops at one's own "I" and remains in the individual cognitive intention, for in its own "I" it constantly finds new resources of content. The old adage says, "*individuum est ineffabile.*"

Person and Act in the Aspect of Psychological Consciousness (Résumé)

The article presented here constitutes one of the introductory chapters of a more comprehensive study in ethics entitled *Person and Act*.[x]

The author examines the reciprocal relation between person and act from the perspective of consciousness. In his analysis he appeals to the traditional idea of conscious activity, which constitutes one of the basic elements of the concept *actus humanus*. This analysis leads him to highlight new aspects of the consciousness of action in relation to the person, aspects that in truth are implicitly contained in the traditional idea of the person's rationality: that of the subject of action, on the one hand, and the concept of voluntary action, on the other. These aspects have not yet been sufficiently emphasized, and thus call for more detailed examination. Such is the precise purpose of the analysis presented here. A convenient starting point is provided by the common linguistic distinction between conscious action, on the one hand, and consciousness of acting, on the other. There corresponds to this distinction, objectively, genuinely distinct aspects of consciousness; for we not only act consciously, but also are conscious of being and acting (consciously). Classical philosophy studied only the first of these different aspects of consciousness, leaving aside the second. Yet the latter aspect takes on particular importance when it is a question of carefully defining the relation between person and act in moral action. Consciousness, in fact, when viewed from this perspective, not only is concomitant with the moral act, but also precedes and follows it, constituting an integral, subjective background that serves as the image and reflection of the "I" that acts, of the act itself, of what takes place within the self, and of the object with which it enters into contact as a result of this act. For precisely this reason, the analysis of this aspect of consciousness constitutes a necessary dimension of any adequate conception of the relation between person and act (from which follows the need for this analysis in a study whose object is precisely this relation). A full, intelligible perception of this relation, however, is not possible by way of consciousness alone, but rather by virtue of consciousness's own cognitive function, which is to "reflect" the content that is provided it, in collaboration with the cognitive function par excellence of self-knowledge. This collaboration is indispensable, given the fact that consciousness as such can only "reflect" what appears in its field, without organizing it or relating it to an appropriate object; consciousness, that is, does not objectivize. Objectivization is rather the proper task of knowledge—in this case, self-knowledge—which is intentional by nature, relating the contents of consciousness to the objects to which they correspond. It is by virtue of self-knowledge's objectivizing function that the subjective content of consciousness is transformed into full consciousness, in which the being grasps its own existence and the activity of its own "I." The final considerations of the article aim to define more precisely the concept of self-knowledge.

4 ❦ *Person and Act*

The Reflexive Functioning of Consciousness and Its Emotionalization

Contents: Introduction; 1. Person and Act in the Aspect of Consciousness; 2. The Reflexive Feature of Consciousness and Lived-Experience of the Act; 3. The Problem of the Emotionalization of Consciousness[xi]

Introduction

The present article presents the second fragment of a more extensive study entitled *Person and Act*. In this study the author analyzes the person and the act in their reciprocal relation, proceeding from the conviction justified *in via* that the rich and specific content located in that relation most decisively distinguishes *human* action from all other action. The author is convinced that the person-act relation constitutes the original and direct *datum* of experience understood in a sufficiently broad way. This *datum* is revealed above all in the moment when people, and first of all I myself, perform acts. Colloquial expressions such as "I am performing an act" or "I am acting" are most often a linguistic expression of that *datum*. However, the fact that the person-act relation is given in experience does not mean in the least that we "see" in it right away clearly and distinctly all specific elements of this relation together with their structural implications. Quite the contrary: making these elements distinct and bringing out their necessary (noncontradictory) implications are precisely the tasks to be performed. This starting point, namely, the *object*—the experientially given person-act relation—and the end—the manifestation of its full structure together with its implications, that is, the full understanding of the said *datum* of experience—defines in turn the author's *method* of analysis. He first briefly shows the specific elements of the person-act relation (description), and then immediately proceeds to bring to light all that is not always given directly but that, nonetheless, enables the very occurrence of the analyzed "fact" and of its structural "quality" manifested in the description. A rejection of these—at times deeply hidden—"implications" would have to lead to canceling the specificity of the perceived fact and thereby the fact itself. The analysis thus conducted aims—and this constitutes its *result*, that is, its point of arrival—at formulating necessary propositions about the examined object, which provide knowledge of the highest methodological rank, that is, at formulating *philosophical* propositions concerning the examined object. The study oriented in this way is located within the subject matter of the philosophy of man, that is, philosophical *anthropology*. At the same time, however, the analyses conducted in this study continuously indicate the constantly co-present—though placed in parentheses for methodical reasons—normative-axiological "implication" as the *sine qua non* condition of the occurrence and intelligibility of the fact of performing an act by the person as a person. Thanks to that, this study shows anew—though incidentally—the reciprocal relation of philosophical anthropology and ethics. In place of the universally accepted one-sided methodological dependence of ethics on the philosophy of man (consciousness and freedom as the indispensable condition of morality) we ought to accept a two-sided, reciprocal interpenetration of both disciplines, since—as it turns out—it is ethics (the experience of morality) that provides a sufficiently broad context within which the "anthropological" fact of performing the act by the person (the experience of the act) can be understood "in full."

1. Person and Act in the Aspect of Consciousness

The first fragment of the study *Person and Act* was published in the commemorative book entitled *Pastori et magistro* and dedicated to His Excellency Bp. Piotr Kałwa in 1966 in Lublin as part of a series published by the Learned Society of the Catholic University of Lublin [Towarzystwo Naukowe KUL]. The relation between "The Person and the Act in the Aspect of Consciousness" was analyzed in it. The main point there was to show two specific—both distinct and mutually inseparable—functions of consciousness. The first is the function of "reflecting." As a result of this function, consciousness becomes in a sense identical (*quodammodo omnia*) to the reflected contents, though as yet in a complete suspension as to whether these are the contents of "my world" or "the world outside me," thus without introducing any duality into the subject and the object. Only the second function of consciousness, in fact inseparably linked with the first one, causes the reflected contents to take on the character of something objective and at the same time "meaningful." Here there arises the subject-object duality and the corresponding distance of the subject from the object. As a result of precisely this function we are able to look at ourselves "from a distance," that is, at our own objectivized person-act relation. In other words, we are able to possess self-knowledge. However, the functions described thus far, namely, the reflecting (mirroring) and the objectivizing, do not exhaust the role of consciousness, at least in relation to its one-of-a-kind object, which is the person-act relation. In the present fragment of his work, the author analyzes yet another function of consciousness, one that is particularly important for "the person and the act in the aspect of consciousness." This function, called reflexive (in contradistinction to the reflective function!), resembles in a certain respect the first function analyzed thus far on account of "identifying" the subject with the object, except for an important difference, namely, (1) that it exclusively pertains to what is contained in the field of the person-act relation; (2) that it is accomplished not *prius*—as was the case concerning the first—but *posterius* in relation to the function of objectivizing, thus presupposing the result of the latter: the objectivization of the person-act relation (self-knowledge); and (3) that the direction of "identifying" the subject with the object is here exactly opposite than that of the first function. For the specificity of the reflexive function consists in the "subjectivization" of the objectively given person-act relation and of its very elements (thanks to the functions of reflecting and objectivizing) and especially of the person himself as a *suppositum*—he is *experienced as an "I,"* that is, what he objectively is becomes also "from within," subjective. Only in this way does the person-*suppositum* arrive at his full culmination and definitive completion.

This completion is possible thanks to the "constitution of the I" through the reflexive-experiential function of consciousness. It would be an error, however, to think that the reflexive function by itself creates the entire "I" (idealism); it merely activates the appropriate energies that inhere in the person-*suppositum*. It is in the proper perception of all these functions of consciousness, and in consideration of their reciprocal connection and cooperation, that the author sees the only way out of the impasse posed by earlier pseudo-solutions to the problem of man as both person and subject (idealistic or idealizing subjectivism, on the one hand, or extreme objectivism leading to the "reification" of the person, on the other), solutions that are characterized by a greater or lesser degree of one-sidedness.

Directly referencing the reflective function of consciousness, the author in turn analyzes the problem of the emotionalization of consciousness and then, against the backdrop of the latter and the preceding reflections, he addresses the issue of subjectivity as an element of the objective reality of man and subjectivism as a defective and the most widespread theory of that subjectivity.

2. The Reflexive Feature of Consciousness and the Lived-Experience of the Act

The analysis of self-knowledge allows us to better understand consciousness in its mirroring function, that is, consciousness as reflection. However, as we have already mentioned several times, the mirroring function is neither the sole nor the complete function of consciousness. In addition to reflection, lived-experience is also linked to consciousness—both are proper to man, both are extremely important for understanding the person in his relation to the act and the act in its relation to the person. The aspect of consciousness is not exhausted in the role of a mirror placed next to acts in order to reflect them to one's own "I"—a mirror placed from without, as it were. The mirror of consciousness introduces us certainly into the interiority of acts and into the interiority of their relation to one's own "I," while the role of consciousness itself does not change as much as finds a complement. It allows us not only to interiorly see our acts and their connection with our own "I," but also to experience them as acts and as our own acts at that. *We owe to conscious-*

ness the full subjectivization of what is objective. In it, person and act in their reciprocal relation (which is a close correlation), as well as all that constitutes the intentional "world of the person," are subjectivized. We are fully justified in analyzing this world in its objective content—at this point, however, we undertake a study of subjectivization.

A feature that we can call reflexive is proper to consciousness. This feature is characteristic of both the particular acts of consciousness and the sum of these acts (or possibly their resultant in man), which compose the actual state of consciousness. The reflexivity of consciousness denotes its natural turning toward an object as such. Reflexivity is something other than the reflectivity proper to the human mind and its acts. For reflectivity presupposes the intentionality of acts of thinking, that is, their turning toward an object. Thinking becomes reflective when we turn to the act previously performed in order to more fully grasp its objective content or possibly also its character or structure. Reflective thinking is an important element in the coming to be of all knowledge—including knowledge about oneself, that is, self-knowledge. This thinking [5a]indirectly[5b] serves consciousness and its development in man, a fact that is completely clear in light of reflections from the previous point—however, this thinking does not constitute consciousness itself. *What is constitutive of consciousness is its turning toward the subject as such—consciousness is reflexive, not reflective.*

This turning is different from reflection itself. In reflection, the subject still appears as an object. The reflexive turning of consciousness causes this object, which ontologically is a subject, to experience himself as a subject—that is, to experience his own "I." This is something new and different from all previous categories: being a subject differs from being known (objectivized) as a subject, even being mirrored in this way, which is still different from subjective lived-experience itself. Man is the subject of his being and acting; he is this subject as a being of a given nature, and this fact has its consequence in action. This subject of being and acting, which is man, is denoted in ontology by the word *suppositum*. The word *suppositum* is used to denote the subject in an utterly objective manner while abstracting from the aspect of lived-experience, in which this subject is given to himself as his own "I." The word *suppositum* abstracts from the aspect of consciousness, the consciousness thanks to which the object, which is a subject, experiences himself as a subject—and objectivizes this lived-experience with the help of the word "I." In fact, the word "I" contains more than *suppositum*, for it contains the subjective lived-experience of subjectivity and implicates the object that is a subject (that is, subjectivity in the objective and ontological sense—precisely that which *suppositum* denotes). However, the word "I" can denote less than *suppositum* if we severed this word from its implication. In that case, it would merely denote the consciousness-related aspect or, in other words, the psychological aspect of subjectivity.

In the present reflections—in accord with the cognitive presuppositions made in the introductory chapter—*we do not intend to sever the "I" from its ontological implications*. Every man is given in integral, that is, simple, experience as a *suppositum*—as a being that is the subject of existence and action. At the same time, however, he is given to himself as an "I"—and not only in a consciousness-related way but also in self-knowing objectivization. Self-knowledge reveals this: the suppositum that is me is my own "I," since in it I experience myself as a subject. Consciousness is an aspect but not only an aspect—it is also a real factor that constitutes subjectivity in a psychological way. Thus, in a sense, consciousness constitutes one's own "I."

It is worthwhile to consider the path that leads from reflection to lived-experience. This is precisely the path of consciousness. Consciousness is linked with a being, that is, with a concrete man "who is myself," who objectively is some "I." Consciousness neither obscures this being nor absorbs it into itself, as would follow from the basic premise of idealistic thinking, according to which *esse* is *percipi* ("to be" is the same as "to be the content of consciousness," while no being outside consciousness is accepted). Quite the contrary; consciousness *inwardly, as it were, reveals* this being, the human being—the person, to speak concretely. Its reflexive function consists in this, provided we understand this function integrally. Thanks to this function, man exists in full conformity with his mental essence and exists "inwardly." This existence is identified with lived-experience. Lived-experience is not a reflex that appears on the surface of man's being and acting. Quite the contrary—it is *the mode of the actualization of being and acting that man owes to consciousness*. It is, in a sense, a final and definitive mode in which the real and objective energies contained in man as a being are actualized not only objectively but also in the profile of his subjectivity, *finding their subjective completion in lived-experience.*

Inasmuch as it mirrors, inasmuch as it is a reflection, consciousness still remains, so to speak, at an objective distance from its own "I." However, inasmuch as consciousness constitutes the basis of lived-experience, inasmuch as it constitutes this lived-experience thanks to its reflexivity, it already goes beyond this distance, enters the subject, and experientially constitutes this subject together with every lived-experience. Of course, consciousness mirrors the subject in one way and constitutes it in another: thanks to self-knowledge, it mirrors by retaining the subject's objective meaning, its objective position, as it were; whereas it constitutes in the pure subjectivity of lived-experience. This is very important. Thanks to the duality of the function of consciousness, we do not lose the sense of our own being in its real objectivity while we remain within our subjectivity. The fact that our lived-experiences are formed thanks to consciousness, that without consciousness there is no human lived-experience—though there exist various manifestations of life or various actualizations—in its way confirms and verifies the definition of man, namely, the attribute *rationale* contained in it. This fact also indirectly confirms and verifies the spirituality of man. The spirituality of man is manifested in consciousness, thanks to which it forms in lived-experience the experiential inwardness of his existence and action. Although the foundations of man's spirituality, in a sense, its roots, reside outside the direct sphere of experience—we reach them by way of reasoning—spirituality itself has its experiential manifestations in man. This is proven by the close, so to speak, constitutive connection of the lived-experiences proper to man with the reflexive function of consciousness. Man experiences himself and all that is in him, his entire "world," mentally, for the nature of consciousness is mental, intellectual. It determines the nature of lived-experiences and, so to speak, their level in man.

In what way does man experience his acts? We know already what his being conscious of them means—that is, we know how we ought to understand the consciousness-related reflection of the act. Apart from this, however, man experiences his acts, and he owes this lived-experience, just as any other, to consciousness in its reflexive function. Man experiences his act as "action" that is causally linked with his own "I." Man accurately differentiates his action from everything that merely "happens" in his own "I." Here, the distinction between *actio* and *passio* finds its first experiential basis. The distinction itself is a work of self-knowledge; it belongs to the semantic side of consciousness-related mirroring. However, it goes hand in hand with lived-experience: man experiences his action as something utterly different from anything that "happens" in him. Only in connection with action (that is, the act) does man experience his morality, moral values, good and evil ("morality" or "immorality," as is commonly though erroneously said). Again, man not only is conscious of the morality of his acts but also experiences it authentically. The act and morality, moral values, function not only objectively in the meaning mirrored by consciousness, but also in an utterly subjective manner in the lived-experience that consciousness directly conditions. Because it constantly turns to the subject as a subject, consciousness evokes the lived-experience of the subjectivity of every act and its moral value. At the same time—thanks to its mirroring function, closely linked with self-knowledge—it allows us to both become objectively conscious of and to experience the act (i.e., the action causally connected with our own "I") and its moral value (which is also the moral value of this "I," that is, of a person, by virtue of the causal connection). As we already stated, lived-experience is not an additional and "superficial" reflex of the act but constitutes a reflexive reduction inward, thanks to which the act becomes a fully subjective reality in man. In a sense, it gains its completion in his subjectivity.

Together with this completion, it acquires an experiential expression through which it becomes an object of understanding—a more and more thorough understanding, as was outlined in the introductory chapter. This experience is different from self-experience, and understanding is different from self-understanding, which remains exclusively within self-knowledge and consciousness in both its functions. Here we already cross the boundaries toward a knowledge about man, a knowledge about the act and the person-act relation. Already at the starting point we position ourselves—as is evident—differently; we position ourselves, in a sense, outside of our own "I" since this understanding's object is not one's own "I" but man, who is also myself.

3. The Problem of the Emotionalization of Consciousness

Consciousness mirrors man's own "I" and his acts while at the same time allowing him to experience himself and his acts. Both cases in some way involve one's own body. Man has consciousness of his body and also experiences it; he also experiences his own "bodiliness," just as he does his own sensuality and affectivity. These lived-experiences go hand in hand with consciousness-related mirroring, and therefore self-knowledge directs them as well. We easily discover its contribution on account of a certain abstractness of the contents made conscious and experienced. After all, to experience one's own body is one thing and to experience one's own bodiliness is another. What occurs here is a difference in the degree of intellectual abstraction, which is from knowledge and, in relation to one's own "I," from self-knowledge. Self-knowledge creates the semantic side of the consciousness-related reflection, the side that, together with the reflexive function of consciousness, passes into lived-experience and determines its character as regards content. In acts of self-knowledge and relying on self-experience, man understands his own "I" both particularly and as a whole. Concerning the understanding of the body, self-knowledge, as well as consciousness, owes a great deal to particular bodily sensations. We know that neither the organism in all its particular internal structure nor the particular vegetative processes that occur in it constitute, generally speaking, the object of self-knowledge or of consciousness. Self-knowledge, and consciousness with it, reaches as far or, rather, as deep into the organism and its life as sensations allow. It happens very often, for instance, only due to an illness, that man becomes conscious of this or that organ or of a vegetative process within himself. In general, the human body, and all that is more or less directly connected with it, constitutes first the object of sensations and only later the object of self-knowledge and consciousness. We do not take "first" and "later" in a chronological sense, but only in the sense of a natural adequation of the object and subjective acts.

The world of sensations has its objective richness in man, who is a sensing being and not only a thinking one. This richness corresponds to the material structure of man and of the world outside him. Sensations

Consciousness and Its Emotionalization | 83

are diversified not only quantitatively but also qualitatively—in this respect they form a certain hierarchy. Qualitatively higher sensations correspond to man's psyche and even indirectly reflect his spiritual life. What is proper to the human psyche is emotivity, which will be analyzed in more detail in one of the subsequent chapters of this study on account of the significance that particular emotions and the entire emotional life possess for human acts and their relation to the person. It is known, and numerous manuals of ethics state this fact, that affections in some respect intensify our action, although in another respect they have a limiting or at times even paralyzing influence on what is essential in that action, namely, on *voluntarium*. We stated previously that *voluntarium* denotes the way proper to the will, the way in which human acts should be performed. We properly designate this way by referring to the act as "conscious action." Thus, consciousness as a property of acts—consciousness understood attributively—is at times limited by emotive facts. Sometimes these facts can even bring about a paralysis of the constitutive consciousness of action. Then they destroy *voluntarium*—action is not performed in the way proper to the will; it is not an act.

In the present chapter, however, we concern ourselves with consciousness in a different sense, as is evident thus far from our entire course of reflections. We mean consciousness in the proper sense—not only consciousness as a property of human action, but also human action, that is, acts and their relations to the person, in the aspect of consciousness. Therefore, we pose ourselves a slightly different problem. It lies very close to the aforementioned problem: the relation of emotions to *voluntarium*, that is, to conscious action. One could even think that this is the same problem. However, in light of the current analysis we must accept the fact that the problem of the emotionalization of consciousness—for this is what we have decided to call it—possesses a certain distinctness of its own. Consciousness possesses such distinctness in the nounal sense—that is, consciousness as such, proper consciousness—in relation to consciousness in the attributive sense—that is, consciousness as a property of man's being and acting (sometimes we also call it "constitutive" or "internal" because it constitutes acts from within in the same sense as the will to which the human act owes its *voluntarium*).

The gist of the problem consists in the fact that emotions, emotive facts in the various forms in which they occur ("happen") in man as a subject, not only are reflected in consciousness but also influence in a uniquely proper way the consciousness-related mirroring of various objects, beginning with one's own "I" and acts. Hence: emotionalization. Various sensations emotionalize consciousness—which means that they enter its functions, namely, the mirroring and the reflexive, and slightly modify their character. This is manifested first of all in the consciousness-related reflection, which in a sense loses its distance from emotion. As we know from the previous analysis, consciousness owes this distance to self-knowledge. Self-knowledge has the ability to objectivize emotions and sensations. In that case, consciousness has at its disposal the meanings of the facts occurring in the subject, and precisely thanks to this it preserves an objective distance from these facts. Although emotions themselves "happen" in man, the same man is conscious of them and in a sense governs them through consciousness. This governance is very important for interior integration. Only on the basis of this governance can moral value be formed. In this consciousness-related point, reflection manifests its significance for conscious action, that is, for *voluntarium*. The consciousness-related governance over emotional life not only is an effect of the will and virtue, but also influences *voluntarium*, that is, the will and virtue.

The emotionalization of consciousness starts when, in the mirroring, the meaning of particular affective facts vanishes, when sensations in a sense grow beyond actual comprehension by man. [6a]Properly speaking, this is a collapse[6b] of self-knowledge. For consciousness does not cease to mirror these affective facts but loses its superior, that is, its objective, relation to them. It is known that objectivization is not its proper function, but a function of self-knowledge. The collapse of the objective relation of consciousness into sensations and affections that "happen" in man originates from the fact that self-knowledge ceases to objectivize. It does not establish meanings and thereby does not keep emotions in intellectual dependence. Why does this happen? Reasons for that can differ. What is most often indicated as the reason is the strength, that is, the intensity, of affections, their changeability, the quickness in which one follows the other. This explains the problem unilaterally. For, on the other hand, *we also need to take into consideration the smaller or greater efficiency of self-knowledge.* Just like any other knowledge, self-knowledge is, after all, subject to the laws of efficiency and therefore can handle better or worse its own object (by which we mean here the "objective material" that for self-knowledge is all facts connected with one's own "I"—emotive facts being precisely such facts). Let us stress again that our point concerns not a mere effective "mastery over affections," which is the task of the will and of corresponding virtue, but only a "governance over sensations," which is a task of self-knowledge and self-consciousness.

Self-knowledge has here a fundamental task to perform, and therefore its efficiency is very important. It seems that consciousness itself is not subject to the laws of efficiency. We do not think that it can be more or less efficient, although it can be more or less developed or mature. Self-knowledge takes on the whole efficient side of consciousness. It is self-knowledge that should work to prevent the emotionalization of consciousness, so that consciousness is not deprived of the objectivizing relation to emotive facts. Sensations in the subject that is man undergo undulation. Sometimes they surge, that is, they multiply and, above all, gain strength. For in every man a specific emotive dynamic exists as an objective psychical fact. This dynamic is expressed by the degree of intensity of particular sensations or of their entire groups or resultants. *A certain degree of this intensity of emotion conditions the normal or even correct functioning of consciousness;* however, at the moment of exceeding the mentioned threshold, the emotionalization of consciousness begins. Due to either an excessive quantity or strength of affections—excessive in relation to the threshold—or an insufficient efficiency of self-knowledge, self-knowledge is unable to identify affections intellectually. Thus, the semantic side of sensations is lost. At first, consciousness still mirrors emotional facts as "something that happens in me." However, with a yet greater intensity, or a greater helplessness of actual self-knowledge, consciousness still mirrors the facts as "something that happens," as if losing their connection with the "I." The fundamental content of consciousness—one's own "I"—is in a sense pushed to the background, and the intensified sensations behave as if they were severed from the basis whence both their unity and their semantic plurality and distinctness originate. For in the normal course of events, self-knowledge objectivizes both this unity in one's own "I" and the semantic distinctness of particular emotions. In moments of emotionalization, however, especially extreme emotionalization, they in a sense fall directly into consciousness. It does not cease to mirror them, but this mirroring lacks the element of any objectivization and understanding, for self-knowledge has not provided it.

Hand in hand with the emotionalization of reflection goes the emotionalization of lived-experience. As we said, consciousness does not cease to mirror—even in the greatest intensity of emotions and sensations, we still discover a consciousness-related reflection, although this reflection no longer possesses the proper significance for the emotional sphere of interior life. The reflexive function of consciousness, the one that shapes lived-experience, also loses its decisive influence. It is worth noting that with a significant intensification of affections or passions, man, properly speaking, ceases to experience them and instead only lives by them. For sensations, though very subjective in themselves—that is, closely connected with the subject, with the concrete "I"—do not possess the reflexivity, the ability to subjectivize, that is at the disposal of consciousness. In a certain sense, affective lived-experience is [7a]posterior[7b] to the actualization of emotions and the invasion of [8a]sensations[8b] in consciousness. Faced with this invasion, the reflexive function of consciousness is also in a sense hindered, and man *lives by his affections objectively rather than experiencing them subjectively*. The truly human lived-experience of affections, indeed, emotional lived-experience itself, again demands the threshold of consciousness that we mentioned earlier. At a certain degree of intensity of sensations, consciousness functions normally with respect to both mirroring and reflexivity. What can then be formed are authentic, affective lived-experiences in all their subjective completion and not merely the objective, emotive facts onto which consciousness cannot confer a subjective completion, even though they undoubtedly reside in the subject. For the emotionalization of consciousness impedes or even prevents the actualization proper to it.

By writing all this, we did not intend in the least to prejudge the value of sensations and emotions for man's interior life and morality. We shall devote a separate chapter to this matter. [xii]

5 ❦ *Person and Act*

Subjectivity and Subjectivism

The analyses conducted thus far enable us to pose this problem, and indirectly they even demand posing it.[xiii] Our aim is to clearly distinguish the two mental attitudes mentioned in the previous chapter, or rather to apply this distinction in the study of person and act. To ascertain the man-person's subjectivity has a fundamental significance for the realism and, indeed, the objectivism of our study. For in reality man is a subject and experiences himself as a subject. The relation between person and act fully originates from this fact. Without ascertaining the subjectivity of man, no plane exists on which we could derive this relation in an integral manner. The aspect of consciousness has a great significance for ascertaining the subjectivity of man, for this aspect confers on this ascertainment a comprehensively experiential character, in a sense making this ascertainment manifest. It is thanks to consciousness that man experiences himself as a subject—it is difficult to get a closer empirical instance than that. He experiences, thus, he is a subject in the most strictly experiential sense. Here, understanding grows directly from experience without any intermediary stages, without reasoning. Man experiences his acts as the action of which he—the person—is the agent. The experientiality of this efficacy, the experientiality of the relation between person and act, occurs again in the aspect of consciousness; it becomes evident thanks to lived-experience. We must fully grasp the subjectivity of man in order to draw near to this relation in this way. By grasping subjectivity only in the metaphysical way, by stating that man as an objective being is a true subject of existence and action—that is, a *suppositum*—we abstract ourselves in a sense from all that is for us a source of visualizations, a source of experience. Therefore, it is better to attempt some coordination and union of both aspects, namely, the aspect of being and the aspect of consciousness, the aspect of the "act" and the aspect of lived-experience.

This is important due not only to methodological considerations (of which we already spoke in the introductory chapter) but also to objective ones. We indicated this a moment ago by stating that without a possibly complete delineation of man's subjectivity, there can be no full delineation of the dynamic relation between person and act. For this relation is not only mirrored in consciousness, as if in the [9a]external[9b] mirror of man's existence and action, but also thanks to this consciousness—we continue to mean the consciousness as such, in the nounal sense—the relation's definitive, subjective form is also determined in its own way. It is thus the form of lived-experience, the lived-experience of the act, the efficacious lived-experience of the relation of person to act, and the lived-experience of the moral value that germinates from this relation. *All these are objective facts, which nonetheless possess their objectivity and realness only and exclusively in the subjectivity of man.* Without the full revelation of this subjectivity there is no way of reaching and explicating the full and objectively comprehensive content of these facts. Let us add that subjectivism can also develop due to a too narrow and unilateral objectivism. What protects us from this is a possibly comprehensive analysis of the object in all its [10a]aspects[10b].

Subjectivism in the given case would consist in reducing acts exclusively to lived-experience and in reducing moral values—which germinate (as we figuratively stated) in precisely these acts, and also in the person through their efficacious dependence on the person—to the very contents of consciousness. We ought to emphasize the adverb "exclusively" used in the previous sentence—for it indicates what was described in the introductory reflections as the absolutization of an aspect. Intellectual reduction connected with the absolutization of the experiential aspect characterizes precisely this mental attitude, namely, subjectivism, and, in a further perspective, idealism. The experiential aspect is undoubtedly consciousness, which under the subjectivistic mental attitude undergoes an absolutization and thus ceases to be an aspect. As long as consciousness is understood as an aspect—an understanding that we attempted to follow throughout this entire chapter—it simply helps us to understand more fully the subjectivity of man, especially in his interior relation to his own acts. However, once consciousness ceases to be understood as an aspect, thus in relation and correlation to the being that is a concrete man, it also ceases to explain subjectivity, that is, the subjectivity of man and of his acts, and it itself becomes a subject. Subjectivism understands consciousness as an integral and exclusive subject—the subject of lived-experiences and values if the sphere of moral lived-experiences is concerned. Regrettably, under this assumption, with this mental attitude, both these lived-experiences and their objective equivalents, that is, values, cease to be something real. They remain only as contents of consciousness: *esse* = *percipi*. Finally, consciousness itself ceases to be something real and becomes merely a thought subject of contents. The path to subjectivism ends in idealism.

This path has a certain basis in the purely consciousness-related character of the acts of consciousness. We stated previously that these acts and the consciousness wholly contained within them are in themselves, so to speak, indifferent to real objects, even to their own "I" as a real object. They do not objectivize anything but only mirror. Everything in them is only content, and they owe an objective relation to self-knowledge. Self-knowledge creates the semantic side of consciousness. Idealism consists in a complete canceling of the semantic side of consciousness, whereas subjectivism leads to it. We can say that—with respect to an analysis of the subjective aspect of being and action—both these mental attitudes are identified with the conception of a complete separation of consciousness from self-knowledge. One's own "I" ceases to be an object for consciousness, as do one's acts—they remain mere contents of consciousness. Thus, the boundary of objectivity and realism in the conception of man—and in our case we mean the "person-act" relation—is marked by the acknowledgment of self-knowledge. Despite its consciousness-related character, the consciousness integrated by self-knowledge retains the objective sense and the objective status in the internal structure of man. In this sense and with this status, it is only the key to subjectivity—that is, the basis for a full understanding of the subjectivity of the person in his relation to his own acts—and is not the basis for subjectivism.

6 ❧ Person and Act in Light of Man's Dynamism

1. The Fundamental Directions of Man's Dynamism

Turning now to the interpretation of human action,[xiv] which is conscious action, we already know that this action together with *the entire dynamic linking of the act with the person is accomplished in the field of consciousness, though it is by no means identified with consciousness.* Action is not conscious only by being made conscious. It is already clear in what way it is made conscious. The point still concerns understanding: in what way and through what it is conscious. The interior consciousness of action—thanks to which it is conscious, and not only made conscious—remains organically connected with *voluntarium*, that is, with the fact that human action is performed in a way proper to the will. Hence, the problem of the will and its freedom shall constitute in a sense a lodestar of our reflections in the next stage.

However, the freedom of the will, and even its very existence, is not the starting point for our inquiries but rather the point of arrival. This follows from the empirical presuppositions that we posed at the beginning of these inquiries, that is, in chapter 1. Presently, we face the elementary experiential fact that is expressed most simply in the statement "man acts," and we attempt to understand and interpret this fact in the deepest possible way. The analysis of the aspect of consciousness conducted in the previous chapter bids us to acknowledge in the elementary fact "man acts" not only the moment of becoming conscious, but also the moment of lived-experience. Thanks to the latter we reside primarily, as it were, inside the fact: lived-experience is always linked with a concrete "I" that acts and at the same time experiences action. The lived-experience "I act" contains in a sense the fullness of experience, from which generalization and analogy lead toward the fact "man acts." For the "I" is a man, and every man is an "I"—a second "I," a third "I," etc. Hence, this action—when "you act," "he acts," or "whoever acts"—can also be understood and interpreted on the basis of the experience contained in "I act." The lived-experience of action is subjective; however, it does not sever us from the intersubjectivity needed for understanding and interpreting human action.

The very lived-experience of action, namely, the lived-experience "I act," is different from action in itself, that is, from the objective reality that is action—it is different from the dynamic linking of the person with the act. We also know this from the analysis of the aspect of consciousness. Nevertheless, this linking of the person with the act, that is, conscious action in itself, is experientially given to us above all thanks to lived-experience. It is then given as an objective reality, not merely as a content of consciousness—even of reflexive consciousness, which constitutes lived-experience. Lived-experience introduces us in a sense inside this reality, and thereby it allows us to know this reality as such more deeply. Lived-experience itself subjectivizes the objective reality of conscious action, of the dynamic linking of the person with the act. However, this subjectivization neither separates us from objective reality nor places us outside the circle of intersubjectivity. It only commands the analysis of the objective reality of action to observe the demands resulting from the full subjectivity of man.

Continuing to identify the starting point for the interpretation of conscious action, we ought to emphasize—again in conformity with the presuppositions indicated in chapter 1—that the experiential fact expressed in the statement "man acts" stands before us not in separation from the particular content that is its "morality," but together with it. The lived-experience of action together with the lived-experience of morality constitutes the experiential starting point in the interpretation of conscious action. For the time being, as was said, we do not intend to interpret morality itself, creating a theory of it—this is a separate task to be undertaken later. However, we do not see the possibility of a full interpretation of conscious action itself without taking into account morality as a fact that is most closely linked with this action, is contained in it. *Linking the act with the person culminates in the fact of morality; mor-*

al values, good or evil, give particular witness to the very dynamics of that linking. Without yet interpreting moral good and evil themselves, we must constantly keep them in view when interpreting human action. The starting point here is lived-experience as a specific fullness of experience: the lived-experience of morality and the lived-experience of values that is contained in it. Without considering these lived-experiences, it is impossible to adequately interpret conscious action, that is, to thoroughly and fully understand the structure of the dynamic linking of the act with the person.

The lived-experience of morality, like the lived-experience of values contained in it, in itself is not yet the same as the objective structure of morality or the objective relation to the good. Nevertheless, the one and the other are given to us in lived-experience, just like conscious action itself. They are given to us through the aspect of consciousness and its specific reflexivity. However, lived-experience does not keep our attention on itself, but introduces us into the objective reality that is morality or the relation to values—and indirectly into the very reality of conscious action. Through it, the dynamic linking itself of the act with the person stands before us not only in the fullness of its subjectivity, but also in its objective fullness. It stands as the full object of cognitive exploration.

These are the starting points of the present chapter, of the new stage of inquiries. We already know these starting points from chapter 1. Now, however, after analyzing the aspect of consciousness, they have taken on a specific verification and, with it, new significance. Thus, it was fitting to define them more closely once again. Through this we have grasped a connection with the aspect of consciousness and at the same time, in a sense, have disengaged ourselves from it.

II

PERSON AND ACT

> The Church, by reason of her role and competence, is not identified in any way with the political community nor bound to any political system. She is at once a sign and a safeguard of the transcendent character of the human person.
>
> —Pastoral Constitution on the Church in the Modern World, *Gaudium et spes*, no. 76.[xv]

✺ Introduction

1. The Experience of Man
How do we understand this experience?

This study arises from the need for objectivization in the area of the great cognitive process that may be defined as the experience of man. It is the richest of experiences available to man and, at the same time, perhaps the most complex. The experience of every thing located outside man is always connected with some experience of man himself. Man never experiences anything outside of himself without in some way experiencing himself in this experience. When speaking of the experience of man, however, we mean above all the fact that man encounters, that is, establishes cognitive contact with, himself. This contact has an experiential character both continuously, as it were, and every time it is established. For this contact does not last without interruption even when one's "I" is concerned—[1a] it breaks off at the very least during sleep. Nonetheless, man [2a] as his own "I"[2b] is constantly with himself, and therefore the experience of himself still continues in some way. What takes place in it are more vivid moments along with an entire sequence of less vivid moments, all of them together constituting a specific totality of the experience of the man I myself am. This experience consists of a multitude of experiences and constitutes in a sense their sum, or rather their resultant.

The phenomenalistic position seems to exclude this unity of many experiences, seeing in the individual's experience only a group of impressions or emotional stirrings that are in turn ordered by the mind. Certainly, experience is something individual and is, every time, unique and unrepeatable, but there still exists something that can be called the experience of man, precisely on the basis of the entire continuity of empirical [3a]moments[3b]. The object of experience is not only a [4a]moment, but also man, who emerges from all moments[4b] and at the same time inheres in each of them (we leave out other objects at this time). Moreover, we cannot say that experience is itself only [5a]in that moment[5b], after which what remains is only the work of the mind forming "man" as its object on the basis of [6a]an individual empirical moment or a series of such moments[6b]. The experience of man—the man I myself am—lasts as long as does the direct cognitive contact in which I am the subject, on the one hand, and the object, on the other. The process of understanding, which likewise has its moments and its continuity, progresses in closest connection with this contact. Ultimately, the understanding of oneself consists of many understandings, just as experience consists of many experiences. It seems that every experience is also some understanding.

Experience at the basis of the knowledge of man

The foregoing referred properly to one man only—the one I myself am. However, other people outside me are also the object of experience. The experience of man consists of the experience of oneself and of all other people who remain for the subject in the position of the object of experience, that is, in direct cognitive contact. Of course, no individual man's experience reaches all people, not even all his contemporaries; it is instead necessarily limited to a smaller or greater number of them. The quantitative aspect plays a certain role in this experience. The greater number of people that enter the sphere of someone's experience, the greater [7a] the experience. Interrupting the course of these reflections on experience, the course that is important not for its own sake but on account of the whole problem of the knowledge of man, we must at once say that various people communicate to one another the results of their experiences concerning man even without direct contact. These results already constitute a certain knowledge and contribute to the increase not of the experience but of the knowledge of man—either pre-scientific knowledge or scientific knowledge of various scopes and directions. However, experience always stands at the basis of this knowledge, and therefore the knowledge of man communicated reciprocally by people can in a sense coincide with everybody's own experiences. Knowledge not only proceeds from them but also somehow influences them. Does it deform them? In light of what we said about the connection between experience and understanding, there is no reason to think so. Rather, we ought to state that [8a] knowledge is a means of multiplying and supplementing experiences.

One's own "I" and "man" in the field of experience

We must yet return to this, for what becomes more and more evident is the need to explain the meaning of experience in general and, particularly, of the experience of man. For the time being, however, we do not explain this fundamental concept. Instead, we attempt to describe roughly this rich and complex cognitive process that we called the "experience of man." What has enormous significance for the present and especially for the further reflections in this book is the fact that other people who are the object of experience are this object in a different way than I am for myself, that is, the way every man is for himself. We could even hesitate here as to whether both cases are rightly considered as the experience of man—or whether what occurs are two experiences irreducible to each other. In one of them we would experience only "man," whereas in the other only and exclusively one's own "I." It is difficult to deny, however, that in the latter case we also encounter man and experience him while having the lived-experience of our own "I." Although these are two separate and different experiences, they are not irreducible to each other. The fundamental unity of the experiential object exists despite the considerable difference that occurs in both cases between the subject and the object of experience. *Even though indubitable reasons exist for speaking about the incommensurability of experience, its fundamental sameness cannot be denied.*

The incommensurability occurs because man is more greatly and more differently given to himself, that is, as his own "I," than any other man that is not him. Even if we grant maximum closeness to this other man, the difference nevertheless remains. It happens that when we draw very near to the other man, it is easier for us to objectivize what is in him or who he is; however, objectivization is not the same as experience. Everyone is for himself the object of experience in a unique and unrepeatable way, and no external relation to any other man can be substituted in the place of this experiential relation shared by one's own subject. Perhaps this external experiential relation contributes to a number of cognitive attainments, which the experience on the part of one's own subject does not provide. These attainments will vary depending on the degree of closeness and on the manner of involvement in the experience of another man, which is, in a sense, involvement in the experience of another "I." All this, however, cannot obscure the fundamental incommensurability between the one unique experience of the man I myself am and any other experience of man.

Experience and understanding

The experience of oneself, however, does not cease to be the experience of man; it does not go beyond the boundaries of the experience that encompasses all people or, in general, man. This happens certainly as a result of the human mind's participation in the acts of human experience. It is difficult to say what stabilization the senses alone can ensure regarding the object of experience, for no man knows from his own human experience what the purely sensory experience that belongs to animals looks like and to what it is limited. Yet some stabilization must occur even there, though at the most it happens through individuals, that is, through *individua* in which given groups of sensory qualities concentrate (in this way, for instance, a dog or a horse can distinguish its owner from a stranger). The stabilization of experiential objects that is proper to human experience is fundamentally different—it proceeds through mental differentiations and classifications. By virtue of this stabilization in particular, the experience of the subject's own "I" remains within the boundaries of the experience of "man," thus allowing these experiences to overlap each other. As a consequence of the "specific" stabilization of the object, this interference of experiences constitutes in turn the foundation of forming the knowledge of man on the basis of what is provided by both the experience of the man I myself am and the experience of every other man who is not myself. It is proper to note that the very stabilization of the object of experience by reason is by no means a proof of cognitive apriorism but only a proof of the contribution of the mental, intellectual element—indispensable for the entire human cognition—in the formation of experiential acts, namely, these direct cognitive encounters with objective reality. It is to this element in particular that we owe the fundamental sameness of the object of the experience of man in both cases, that is, when the subject of this experience identifies himself with the object and when he differs from it.

The totality of the experience of man is realized simultaneously in the interior and exterior aspects (in the aspects of man's interiority and outwardness)

The sameness should not obscure the incommensurability. The reason for the incommensurability is the fact that the experience from within (the interior experience), which does not take place in relation to any other man outside me, takes place only in relation to the one particular man who I myself am. All other people are encompassed only by the experience from without (the exterior experience). Of course, in addition to experience alone, another communication with others is possible, one that somehow makes accessible the object of their exclusive experience from within. However, the interior experience itself is untransferable outside one's own "I." Nonetheless, in the totality of our cognition of man, this circumstance does not cause a split whereby the "interior man," who experientially is only one's own "I," would differ from the "exterior man," that is, any other man outside myself. *Other people do not remain for me merely some "outwardness" opposite my own "inwardness,"* but in the totality of cognition these aspects complement and equalize each other; also, experience itself in its two forms, that is, as interior and exterior, works toward this complementing and equalizing, not against it. Therefore, remaining the object of both experiences—from within and from without—I myself am first and foremost for myself not only "inwardness" but also "outwardness." Although being for me only an object of experience from without, every other man outside myself does not stand in relation to the totality of my cognition as a mere "outwardness" but has an interiority proper to him. Even though I do not experience this interiority directly, I know of it—I know of it in general concerning people and sometimes a great deal concerning particular individuals. Sometimes this knowledge, on the basis of a given contact, passes in a sense into a sort of experience of the other's interiority, which is not the same as the experience of my own "I" from within, though it also has its proper empirical characteristics.

All this must be taken into account when we speak about the experience of man. In no way can we artificially isolate this experience from the totality of the cognitive acts that have man in particular as their object. Also, in no way can we artificially sever it from the intellectual factor. The entire group of cognitive acts directed at man, both at the man I myself am and at every other man outside me, has both an empirical and an intellectual character. Each is in the other, each affects the other, and each profits from the other. In this work, we should constantly have the integral experience of man before our eyes. The aforementioned incommensurability of the experience of man does not entail any cognitive split or irreducibility. We can cognitively venture very deeply into the structure of man without fostering a fear that the particular aspects of experience lead us into error. It can be said, however, that *the fundamental simplicity of the experience of man prevails over its complexity*. The very "complexity" of that experience simply indicates that the totality of the experience and consequently of the cognition of man "is composed of" both the experience that every one of us has with respect to oneself and the experience of other people—the experience both from within and from without. In cognition, all this "composes" one whole rather than causing "complexity." The conviction of the fundamental simplicity of the experience of man constitutes a rather optimistic feature for the whole of the cognitive task that we undertake in this study.

2. [9a] The Cognition of the Person on the Basis of the Experience of Man

The empirical position is not identified with phenomenalism

What certainly emerged in the course of our previous reflections was the need to explain more closely how we understand "experience" in general when speaking about the experience of man. Clearly, we do not comprehend experience in a purely phenomenalistic sense, as has been and remains the case within the broad circle of empiricist thinking.

The empirical position that we adopt here does not in the least have to, and in fact cannot, be identified with the phenomenalistic conception of experience. Reducing the sphere of experience to the functions and contents of the senses alone generates profound contradictions and misunderstandings. This can be illustrated by using the example of the object of cognition that interests us in this study. For if we adopt the phenomenalistic position, we must pose the question to ourselves: what is given to me in an indirect way? Is it only a "surface" of the being I call man that falls under the senses, or is it man himself? Is it, and to what extent, my own "I" as man? It would be somewhat difficult to accept that what is directly given in man—or rather of man—is some unspecified group of sensory qualities, whereas man himself is not given, that is, man and his conscious action (his act) are not given.

We start from the fact "man acts," which is given in phenomenological experience

Experience is undoubtedly *linked to a sphere of facts given to us.*[1] The dynamic totality "man acts" is certainly such a fact. In this study we start from precisely this fact, which occurs exceedingly often in the life of every man [10a]. If we multiply it by the number of all people, we obtain quite a countless number of facts and thus an enormous wealth of experiences.

---

1. [1a] Roman Ingarden opposes an overly narrow understanding of experience. See, for example, *Z badań nad filozofią współczesną* (Warsaw: Państwowe Wydawnictwo Naukowe, 1963).

"We said that experience is the source and basis of all knowledge about objects. However, we have not said that *one* and only one kind of experience exists and that this experience is 'sensory' perception, either 'external or internal'" (Ingarden, *Z badań nad filozofią współczesną*, 291). "By 'direct experience' phenomenologists understand every cognitive act in which the object itself is given, in the original (*'personally'*), that is—as Husserl states—as 'bodily self-present' (*leibhafte selbstgegebenheit*). A particular case of experience thus understood is what scientists call experience, and also internal experience, that is, internal perception. However, many varieties of experience exist in which individual objects are given, for example, the experience of somebody else's individual psychical facts, the aesthetic experience in which works of art, etc., are given to us" (Ingarden, *Z badań nad filozofią współczesną*, 292).[1b]

The problem of experience, together with the totality of methodological problems, found an extensive response among Polish philosophers in the discussion on *Person and Act*. See the statements of Jerzy Kalinowski, Fr. Marian Jaworski, Fr. Stanisław Kamiński, Fr. Tadeusz Styczeń, and Fr. Kazimierz Kłósak in *Analecta Cracoviensia* 5–6 (1973–74). Taking a different position from that of Jerzy Kalinowski, Fr. Marian Jaworski stresses the specificity of the experience of man, which inheres at the foundation of understanding him. [Editorial note: The concluding clause of this sentence can be read either as "understanding him," i.e., man, or as "his understanding," i.e., Fr. Jaworski's understanding.]

Experience also indicates the directness of cognition itself, *the direct cognitive contact with the object*. It is true that the senses remain in direct contact with the objects of the reality that surrounds us—precisely with these various "facts." Nevertheless, it is difficult to accept that only the sensory act grasps these objects or facts in a direct way. We must state that a mental act at least participates in this directness of grasping the object. This directness, as a feature experienceable in cognition, does not in the least ruin the mental act's otherness with regard to content nor its separate genesis in relation to the purely sensory act. These are particular problems in the theory of cognition that will not be investigated here. At this point, we concern ourselves with the cognitive act as a concrete whole to which we owe, for example, the grasp of the fact "man acts." In no way can we grant that, in grasping this fact, experience is limited to the mere "surface"—to a group of sensory contents, which every time are unique and unrepeatable—and that the mind in a sense waits to "make" of these contents its object, naming this object "act" or "person and act." It seems instead that the mind is engaged already in experience itself, thanks to which it establishes contact with the object, a contact that is equally, though in a different way, direct.

In this experience, the act is given as a particular moment of the vision of the person (the insight into the person)

For this reason, *every human experience is at the same time some understanding of what I experience*. It seems that this position opposes phenomenalism and is proper to phenomenology, which emphasizes above all the unity of the act of human cognition. Presenting the matter this way bears a key significance for the study of person and act. For we hold that *the act* is *a particular moment of the vision*—that is, the experience—*of the person*. Of course, this experience is at the same time a closely specified understanding. It is the intellectual vision given on the basis of the fact "man acts" in all its countless frequencies, as mentioned above. *In its full, experiential content, the fact "man acts"* can be understood in this way, namely, it *can be understood as an act of the person*. The entire content of experience reveals the fact to us in precisely this and not another way, that is, with the evidentness proper to it. What does "evidentness" denote in this case? First, it seems to indicate the essential property of revelation or manifestation of the object, the cognitive feature characteristic of it. At the same time, however, evidentness means that the understanding of the fact "man acts" as the act of the person—or, perhaps *better, as the "person-act" totality*—finds complete confirmation in the content of experience, that is, in the content of the fact "man acts," with its enormous frequency.

We stated, however, that the act is a particular moment of the vision of the person. This statement more closely defines both a relation to the facts on which we ground this study and the very direction of the experiences and understandings that find their expression in this study. The understanding of the fact "man acts" as the dynamic conjunction "person-act" finds full justification in experience. No opposition is voiced by it when we objectivize the fact "man acts" as an "act of the person." However, that which remains within this conjunction, expressible in so many ways, is the problem of the proper relation between the "person" and the "act." Their close correlativity, their semantic correspondence and interdependence, are made manifest in experience. The act is undoubtedly action. Action corresponds to various agents. However, *we definitely cannot ascribe the action that is the act to any other agent except the person*. According to this understanding, *the act presupposes the person*. This understanding was adopted in various areas of knowledge that had human action as their object; in particular, however, this understanding was adopted in ethics. Ethics was and is a science about the act that presupposes the person: man as a person.

In this study, however, we intend to turn this understanding around. Although it bears the title *Person and Act*, the study nevertheless will not be of the act that presupposes the person. We adopt a different direction of experience and understanding. Namely, *this study will concern the act that reveals the person; it will be a study of the person through the act*.[2] For

---

2. [2a] This direction of investigation concurs with that expressed by Roman Ingarden and in another way by Maurice Blondel. See Ingarden's statement: "Wie er in seiner tiefsten eigenen Natur ist, die sich sozusagen hinter seiner Erlebnissphäre birgt (obwohl sie nicht notwendig verborgen sein muss), so verhält er sich auch im Leben, und das wirkt sich entsprechend in seinen Taten und Erlebnissen aus, indem er dabei im grösseren oder keineren Masse das Selbstbewusstsein erlangt und sich selbst auf entsprechende Weise weitergestaltet." [How he *is* in his own deepest nature—which is so-to-speak concealed *behind his sphere of experiences* (though it need not necessarily be concealed)—is how *he also behaves in life; and this is correspondingly discharged* in his deeds and experiences, by achieving in them in greater or lesser measure a self-awareness, and molding himself further in a

such is the nature of the correlation inhering in experience, in the fact "man acts": the act constitutes a particular moment of revealing the person. The act allows us to have the most proper insight into his essence and to understand it most fully. We experience that man is a person, and we are convinced of this because he performs acts.

Morality is the property of human acts

That is not all, however. Experience and the intellectual vision of the person in and through acts are derived in a particular way from the fact that these acts possess a moral value. They are morally good or morally evil. Morality constitutes their interior property, their particular profile, as it were, unknown in the action that presupposes agents other than the person. *Only the action that presupposes the person as the agent*—and we stated that only such action deserves to bear the name *"act"* [*czyn*]— *is characterized by morality*. And therefore the history of philosophy is the stage for the perennial meeting of anthropology and ethics. The science—and this science is ethics—whose end is to thoroughly examine the problem of moral good and evil can never disregard the fact that this good and evil occur only in acts, through which man participates in them. This is why ethics, especially traditional ethics, has occupied itself very earnestly with the act and with man. Both the *Nicomachean Ethics* and the *Summa theologiae* provide examples. And even though what can be observed in modern and especially in contemporary philosophy is a tendency to treat ethical issues in a certain isolation from anthropology (this is the case more accurately with psychology and moral sociology), the complete elimination of anthropological implications in ethics is not possible. The more integral a given system of philosophizing, the more recurrent the anthropological problems in ethics. Their presence seems to be much more prevalent, for instance, in the phenomenological than in the positivistic approach, in Sartre's *L'être et le néant* than in the studies of Anglo-Saxon analysts.[3]

---

corresponding manner (Wojtyła's emphasis)]. Roman Ingarden, *Formalontologie*, vol. 2 of *Der Streit um die Existenz der Welt* (Tübingen: Max Niemeyer, 1965), pt. 2, p. 323; translated by Arthur Szylewicz as *Controversy over the Existence of the World* (Frankfurt am Main: Peter Lang, 2016), 2:699.[2b]

3. It is peculiar that the deliberations of authors representing the so-called school of common language analysis in ethics, especially its Anglo-American representatives, are almost completely devoid of the anthropological character or are limited to marginally treated reflections on the freedom

The moral value of the act reveals the person more deeply than the act itself does

We did state above that ethics fundamentally presupposes the person on account of the acts, which directly entail a moral value. In this study, however, we wish to go in the opposite direction. The acts are a particular moment of vision—thus a moment of the experiential cognition of the person. In a sense, they constitute the most proper starting point for understanding his dynamic essence. *Morality as the internal property of these acts leads to understanding this essence in an even more particular way.* Moral values do not interest us here for their own sake, as that is the particular subject matter of ethics. Rather, what interests us the most is the fact of their becoming in the acts, their dynamic *fieri*. For this *fieri reveals the person to us even more deeply and thoroughly than the act itself.*[xvi] Thanks to this aspect of morality—one that we can also call dynamic or existential—we are able to more deeply understand man precisely as a person. This is the proper end of our inquiries in this study. Therefore, when consciously drawing from the integral experience of man, by no means can we sever ourselves in it from the experience of morality. The experience of morality in its dynamic, that is, existential, aspect is, after all, an integral part of the experience of man, the experience that, as we stated, constitutes for us the broad basis for understanding the person. The experience of morality must interest us in a particular way, for the moral values—good and evil—not only constitute the internal property of human acts but also are such that *man, precisely as a person, himself becomes good or evil through these morally good or evil acts.* Hence, dynamically or existentially speaking, we can say that the person is revealed both at the starting point of these values and at their point of arrival. The person is thus revealed even more, revealed even more fully than through the "pure" act itself. In fact, it seems artificial to abstract the human act from moral values, for doing so separates us from its full dynamic.

---

of the will and determinism. See, for instance, Charles Leslie Stevenson's *Ethics and Language* (New Haven: Yale University Press, 1944) and the work of his main critic, Richard Booker Brandt, *Ethical Theory: The Problems of Normative and Critical Ethics* (Englewood Cliffs, N.J.: Prentice Hall, 1959).

The union of the experience of man with the experience of morality at the foundation of anthropology and ethics

This study, therefore, will not be a work in the area of ethics. It does not presuppose the person, does not implicate him. Quite the contrary—this study aims *in the broadest sense to explicate the reality that the person is*. The act will be the source from which we shall draw cognition about the reality that the person is, whereas the yet more particular source will be morality in its dynamic, that is, existential, aspect. In this approach, we shall try to respect not so much the traditional bond between anthropology and ethics as the real, objective unity of experiences: the cohesion of the experience of morality with the experience of man. This is the fundamental condition for the vision of the person and for understanding him progressively.

On the basis of this union, we place the ethical subject matter outside the parentheses, as it were[xvii]

The relation between anthropology and ethics can be grasped *in a manner similar to placing factors outside the parentheses*, to borrow from methods employed in mathematics. We place outside the parentheses the elements of a mathematical operation that in some way inhere in all the other elements, that is, are common to all that remains within parentheses. This placement outside the parentheses aims to simplify the operation, though its purpose is neither to reject what is located outside the parentheses nor to break the ties between what stands outside the parentheses and what remains within them. Quite the contrary—this placement emphasizes all the more the presence and significance of the factored element in the entire operation. If this element were not placed outside the parentheses, it would be hidden in the other elements of the operation. Thanks to this placement, the element becomes overt and clearly visible.[4]

---

4. This appeal to the methodical operation employed in mathematics seems to demonstrate well in what sense and to what extent we intend to use the "placement outside parentheses" in this study. We mean to exclude essentially ethical issues in favor of essentially anthropological issues. However, by no means do we exclude essence from actual existence (*epoché*), an exclusion characteristic of Edmund Husserl's phenomenological method. The study is not designed according to the presuppositions of a strict eidetic method. At the same time, from beginning to end, the author aims at understanding man as a person, thus he also aims at a certain "eidos."

Similarly, by [11a]a specific placement[11b] outside the parentheses, the "person-act" problem, which traditionally inhered in ethics, can reveal itself more fully not only in its own reality, but also in the rich reality that is human morality.

3. The Stages of Understanding and the Direction of Interpretation
The process of induction and the grasp of semantic unity

We stated that the grasp of the "person-act" relation, or, more strictly speaking, the vision of the person through the act, is accomplished on the basis of the experience of man. The experience of man "consists" of innumerable facts, among which the many instances of the fact "man acts" are particularly important for us, for in them a specific discovery of the person through the act takes place. Apart from plurality, that is, quantitative complexity, all these facts demonstrate the complexity of which we spoke previously, namely, that they are given from without in all other people outside of me and that they are also given from within on the basis of my own "I." *The passage from this plurality of facts and their complexity to the grasp of their fundamental sameness*—previously defined as the stabilization of the object of experience—*is the work of induction*. At least, this is how Aristotle seems to understand the inductive function of the mind.[5] The modern positivists, such as John Stuart Mill, differ from him, for they already see in induction a form of demonstration, whereas for Aristotle, induction is not any form of demonstration or reasoning at all. It is a mental grasp of semantic unity in phenomenal plurality and complexity. In reference to the previous statement on the experience of man, we can say that induction leads to the simplicity of the experience of man that we ascertain along with all its complexity.

The moment the experience of man is formed as a vision of the per-

---

5. Phenomenologists speak of the cognition of what is essential (in our case, they would speak of the cognition of what is essential in the fact "man acts"). [3a]However, in their opinion, cognition of this kind is attained not in an inductive but in an a priori way. Ingarden writes: "Although... a phenomenologist fundamentally does not renounce the examination of facts, his proper field of work lies elsewhere. His main task is *an a priori cognition of the essence of objects*" (see Ingarden, *Z badań nad filozofią współczesną*, 318). However, on account of this, it seems all the more indispensable to stress the function that is fulfilled by induction according to Aristotle in contrast to positivists.[3b]

son through the act, this vision concentrates in itself all the simplicity of experience, becoming the expression of that experience. So now, with regard to the vision of the person, we proceed from the plurality of experiential facts and arrive at their sameness—at the statement that every fact "man acts" contains "the same" relation "person-act," that the person becomes manifest through the act in the same way. *The sameness is nothing but a semantic unity*. Reaching that unity is the work of induction, for experience by itself leaves us, in a sense, with a plurality of facts. The whole wealth of facts, their diversity, which is determined by individual particulars, remains with experience, whereas the mind grasps in them all simply the semantic unity. While grasping this unity, it allows itself, in a sense, to be surpassed by experience. At the same time, however, the mind does not cease to understand its wealth and diversity. Grasping the semantic unity is not equivalent to canceling this experiential wealth and diversity (this is how the function of abstraction is at times erroneously interpreted). Grasping the person and the act—for instance, on the basis of the experience of man, on the basis of all instances of the fact "man acts"—the mind in this fundamental understanding still remains open to the full wealth and diversity of the data of experience.

The process of reduction is, so to speak, an "exploration" of the experience of man

Perhaps this explains the fact that what arises together with the understanding of the relation "person-act" is the need to interpret this relation, the need to explain it. Induction paves the way for reduction. The present study comes into being precisely as an expression of the need to explain or interpret the rich reality of the person given to us together with acts—and through acts—in the experience of man. It seems that *there is no need to demonstrate or prove to anyone that man is a person, that man's action is an act*. This is rather already given in the experience of man: the reality of the person and act is included in every fact "man acts." However, *there exists the need for a more comprehensive explanation of the reality of the person and act*, a need based on some fundamental understanding of the person and act. The experience of man not only reveals that reality to us but also generates the need to explain it and at the same time creates the basis for this explanation. The wealth and diversity of experience, so to speak, provoke the mind, so that it tries to grasp the already-understood reality of the person and act in the most comprehensive way and to explain this reality most fully. This, however, can be accomplished only by way of an increasingly deep entry into experience, into its content. Thanks to this, the person and act are in a sense brought out of darkness. Standing before the mind that cognizes them, they appear more and more fully and more and more comprehensively. Interpretation, or reductive understanding, constitutes, *so to speak, an exploration of experience.* The very word "reduction" ought not to be erroneously understood. It does not in the least mean a reduction in the sense of diminishing or limiting the wealth of the experienced object. The aim is to consistently bring out this object. The exploration of the experience of man must be a cognitive process in which the constant and homogeneous development of the original vision of the person in the act and through the act is accomplished. During the entire process, this vision must be consistently deepened and enriched.

Reduction and interpretation proceed toward a theory growing from human *praxis*

This is how we see the direction of the interpretation of the person and act in this study. To induction we owe perhaps not so much the objectivization as the inter-subjectivization so fundamental for this study: the person and act appear as the object that can be seen by everyone independently from the at least partial subjective involvement of this object. "At least partial"—because the experience of one's own "I" constitutes a part, and an enormously important part at that, of the experience of man. We can say that the person-act relation is for everyone first and foremost a lived-experience, a subjective fact. Thanks to induction, it becomes a topic and a problem. Then it enters the area of theoretical inquiry. For as a lived-experience, that is, as an experiential fact, the person-act relation at the same time constitutes that which the philosophical tradition called "praxis." It is accompanied by "practical" understanding, namely, the understanding that is sufficient and required for man to live and act consciously. Our chosen *direction of understanding and interpretation leads through the theorization of this praxis.* The point here is not how to act consciously, but to ascertain what conscious action, or the act, is and how this act reveals the person to us and helps us fully and comprehensively understand him. This direction of interpretation is evident in this study from the very beginning. Nonetheless, it was also worth taking into account the moment of the relation to praxis, to the so-called practical cognition with which ethics has been traditionally linked. We emphasized previously that ethics only presupposes the person, whereas in this study the point is to show and interpret him.[6]

Our aim is to properly grasp the reasons that explain the object

This is why this study has a reductive character. As we have already noted, the word "reduction" does not in the least indicate limitation or diminishment. *Reducere* means "to lead back"—to lead back to proper reasons or foundations, that is, precisely, to explain, to clarify, to interpret. By explaining, we continue to follow the object that is given to us in experience and the manner in which it is given to us. All the wealth and diversity of experience together with its complexity lie open to us. Induction and the inter-subjectivization of the person and act, linked to induction, in no way obscure the wealth and complexity that for the mind seeking the proper reasons—reasons that comprehensively and thoroughly explain the reality of the person and act—constitute in a sense an inexhaustible source and constant help. For *we are not concerned with the abstract but with a penetration into the actually existing reality. The reasons that explain this reality* [12a]*are contained in*[12b] *experience*. Thus reduction, and not only induction, is also immanent to experience without ceasing to be transcendent to it, though in a different way from induction. In general, understanding is immanent to human experience and at the same time transcendent in relation to it. This is not because experience is the sensual act and process whereas understanding and explanation are the intellectual ones but because of the essential character of the one and the

---

6. The problem of practical cognition according to Aristotelian-Thomistic presuppositions (taking into account the achievements of Kant and contemporary philosophy) is the object of Jerzy Kalinowski's study entitled *Teoria poznania praktycznego* (Lublin: Towarzystwo Naukowe Katolickiego Uniwersytetu Lubelskiego, 1960). In this study, we do not intend to concern ourselves with practical cognition as a particular source and basis of human praxis. Rather, we intend to explore praxis itself as a source of knowing the man-person.

other. "To experience" is something different from "to understand" or "to explain" (which already presupposes understanding).

The aim of explanation, or interpretation, is that the intellectual *image of the object is adequate*, that it "lives up to" the object, in other words, *that the image grasps all the reasons explaining this object and grasps them correctly, preserving the proper proportions between them*. The accuracy of interpretation depends on this to an enormous degree. In this also lies its difficulty.

A conception is an expression of the understanding and interpretation of the object

This is also the difficulty of *a conception, through which, in this case, we comprehend the very expression of an understanding* maturing from the initial vision of the person in the act into a comprehensive interpretation. The point is not only the interior conviction that the man who acts is a person; it is also that this conviction takes on a mental and linguistic shape, is formed "on the outside" (i.e., in this study), so as to be fully communicative. This conception is shaped together with the understanding of the object and takes the forms needed for this understanding, which is as full and comprehensive as possible, to be expressed, to be communicated to other people and received by them. After all, human knowledge as a social fact is formed through reciprocal communication of understandings.

The difficulty of the interpretation and conception of man is linked to the aforementioned incommensurability inhering in the experience of man and thereby indirectly in the grasp of the person-act relation, the grasp that takes place on the basis of this experience. It is clear that this relation must manifest itself differently on the basis of one's "I," in the sphere of interior experience, than it does in the sphere of exterior experience that encompasses other people outside the man I myself am. What, then, appears in the interpretation and conception of the person and act is *the problem of the correct unification of the understandings that emerge from this incommensurability of experience*. Solving this problem—attempting to correctly unify both aspects of the experience of man in the conception of the person—is one of the main tasks posited by us in this study.

[13a]This task is all the more difficult because we find ourselves in the current of the philosophical tradition that for ages has demonstrated a characteristic division. We can even speak of two philosophies, or at least of two fundamental methods of philosophizing. One of them can be defined as the philosophy of being and the other as the philosophy of consciousness. Neither at this point nor in the remaining course of the work will we enter into the gnoseological problem that lies at the foundation of the aforementioned division. On the side, we can ask ourselves whether and to what extent the bi-aspectuality of the experience of man, and especially a certain absolutization of each of these two aspects, also influences this division (in particular, we can ask to what extent the absolutization of interior experience inheres at the root of the philosophy of consciousness). In this work, instead, we undertake an attempt to overcome this division—not at its crucial point, of course, since we are not concerning ourselves here with the epistemological subject matter, but in the very conception of man. After all, we indirectly owe to the philosophy of consciousness a more thorough cognition of man in the context of consciousness—and this certainly enriches the vision of person and act.

Remaining on the basis of the philosophy of being, we would like to take advantage of this enrichment. An attempt to correctly unify in the conception of the person and act the understandings that emerge from the experience of man in both its aspects *must in some measure become an attempt to unify two philosophical orientations, in a sense, two philosophies.* Everyone who is aware of the depth of the division that occurs between them, and consequently of the distinctiveness that characterizes their styles of thinking and of language, must admit that this task is not easy.

Therefore, one ought to look at the attempt undertaken here with great forbearance.[13b]

[14a]4. The Conception of Person and Act That We Intend to Present in This Study
An attempt to render the subjectivity of man

If this incommensurability of the experience of man, the incommensurability we have noted from the beginning, constitutes a difficulty for the interpretation and conception of man, we ought to admit that at the same time it creates a particular possibility in this area and opens rich vistas. The person is revealed to us through the act on the basis of the integral experience of man precisely because in this experience man is given not only from without but also from within. Since he is given not only as a man-subject but also as the "I" in the entire experiential subjectivity, there opens before us the possibility of *such an interpretation of man as the object of our experience that will at the same time reproduce the subjectivity of man* in the proper measure. This has a fundamental significance for the conception of the person and act that we intend to present in this study.

I venture to say at this point that the experience of man together with its division into the aspects of interiority and outwardness, so characteristic of this experience (and only of it),[xviii] seems to stand at the root of the powerful divisions in the main currents of philosophical thought: the objective and subjective currents, the philosophy of being and the philosophy of consciousness. To reduce these great divisions to the bi-aspectuality of the experience of man, to the duality in the data of that experience, would obviously be an oversimplification of the matter. However, in this study, which has a strictly defined subject matter, we do not intend to undertake reflection in that direction. Nonetheless, from the viewpoint of precisely this subject matter, from the viewpoint of the person and act, which we try to understand and interpret on the basis of the experience of man ("man acts"), a conviction must be born that *absolutizing either of the two aspects of the experience of man must yield to the need for their reciprocal relativization*. If somebody asks why this is so, we shall reply that it results from the very essence of this experience, namely, of the experience of man. We understand man thanks to the reciprocal relation of both aspects of experience. Relying on this relation, we build a conception of the person and act on the basis of the experience of man ("man acts").

The aspect of consciousness

Positing the matter in this way at once indicates that we intend to conduct the analyses foreseen for this study not on the plane of consciousness alone but according to a clearly delineated aspect of consciousness. If, as was said earlier, the act is a particular moment of the vision of the person, it is clear that the point is not the act as the content constituted in consciousness but the dynamic reality itself, which at the same time reveals the person as its efficacious subject. In this sense we intend to concern ourselves with the act in all the analyses of this study, and in this sense we intend to reveal the person through the act. At the same time, we are fully aware that this act as a moment of a particular vision of the person—and the *person* whom it essentially reveals in a particular way *on the basis of the experience of man, especially of the interior experience—appears always* through consciousness. Accordingly, the person and act must be considered *in the aspect of consciousness*. It is obvious, however, that the reason for which the act—the *actus personae*—is conscious action is not reduced in the least only to the fact that the act appears to us in the aspect of consciousness.

Thus, we think that what should be undertaken as the first task in this study is the examination of the reciprocal relation between consciousness and the efficacy of the person, that is, of that which essentially determines the dynamism proper to the human act (chapters 1 and 2). Penetrating the depth of this rich experiential whole in which the person more and more fully reveals himself through the act, we discover the specific transcendence that the person discloses precisely in his act, and which we attempt to analyze quite thoroughly (chapters 3 and 4).

Transcendence and integration

The vision of the transcendence of the person in the act constitutes in a sense the main framework of the experience to which we appeal in our entire conception, for in that experience we also find the fundamental source of the conviction that the man who acts is indeed a person and that his action constitutes a true *actus personae*. Of course, the theory of the person himself as a being can be elaborated more fully and more thoroughly. The aim of this study, however, is above all *to explicate from the experience of the act* ("man acts") *everything that bears witness to man as a person*, that in a sense makes this person manifest.

The fundamental intuition of the transcendence of the person in the act allows us at the same time to perceive the moment of his integration in the act as complementary to transcendence. For integration essentially conditions transcendence in the whole psychosomatic complexity of the human subject. We devote a further part of our study (chapters 5 and 6) to analyzing that complexity under the aspect of the person's integration in act. We are concerned not so much with exhausting the vast subject matter as with confirming a fundamental intuition. Integration as a complementary aspect of the transcendence of the person in the act strengthens in us the conviction that the category person-and-act is the proper expression of man's dynamic unity, the unity whose basis must be his ontic unity. However, we do not intend to analyze the latter in this entire study, being content with drawing as near as possible to the elements and problems essential to that unity. It is this *drawing near, which will allow us to take full advantage of experience and the phenomenological vision of man, that we consider as the specificity of the intended conception of person and act in this study.* The last chapter of the book, entitled "An Outline of the Theory of Participation," introduces us into another dimension of the "man acts" experience, one which we must note here but which we shall not fully analyze in this study.[14b]

The significance of personalistic issues

[15a]The entirety of the inquiries and analyses contained in this work reflects above all the enormous relevance of personalistic issues. It is difficult to deny that these issues have a fundamental significance for every man and for the entire, ever-growing human family.[15b] Constant reflection on various directions of that family's development in the quantitative aspect and on the development of culture and civilization—with all the inequalities and drama of this development—generates a living need to practice the philosophy of the person. It is difficult not to have an impression that the multitude of cognitive efforts directed beyond man surpasses all the efforts and achievements concentrated on man himself. Perhaps this, after all, is not the problem of cognitive efforts and achievements themselves, which, as is well-known, are very numerous and more and more particular. Perhaps it is simply man who continues to expect a new and penetrating analysis and, above all, an ever-new synthesis, which is not easy to attain. As the discoverer of so many secrets of nature [*przyroda*], he himself must be constantly discovered anew. While remaining to a degree an "unknown being," he still demands a new and increasingly mature expression of this being.

Furthermore, because, as we stated above, he is the first, most proximate, and most frequent object of experience, man is exposed to the danger of becoming commonplace. He is threatened to become overly ordinary to himself. It is this threat that must be overcome. This study also originates from the need to overcome this temptation. It originates from "wonder" at the human being, wonder that constitutes the very first cognitive impulse. It seems that this "wonder"—which is not the same as admiration, though wonder also has something of it—stands at the origin of this study as well. Wonder as a function of the mind becomes a system of questions and, in turn, a system of answers or solutions. Thanks to this, not only does the train of thought about man develop but also a certain need of human existence is satisfied. *Man may not lose his proper place among this world* that he himself shaped[16a].[7]

Our aim is to touch upon human reality at its most proper point—the point indicated by the experience of man and from which man cannot withdraw without the sense that he has lost himself. In undertaking this work, we are aware that it has already been undertaken many times and that it will certainly be undertaken many times again. The reader will easily identify in this study all dependencies and borrowings, all the continuation of the great heritage of the philosophy of man, into which every new study on the subject of man must enter out of necessity, as it were.[17a] [18a]In undertaking this work, the author is certain that in it the effects of a long-standing interaction with the Aristotelian tradition, primarily through St. Thomas Aquinas, and simultaneously with contemporary phenomenology, especially with the work of Max Scheler, will be heard. (An interaction with Kant took place through the Schelerian critique.)[8] These currents, which have been extremely active in Poland,

---

7. It seems that this formulation not only explains the issue of the ends that, in accord with the author's intention, this study is meant to serve, but also touches on the aforementioned problem of priorities concerning the reciprocal relations of "theory and practice." What is also at stake is the very sense of philosophical and scientific cognition, in which this study also desires to participate.

8. The author devoted much time to the analysis of Max Scheler's philosophy, especially of his *Der Formalismus in der Ethik und die materiale Wertethik: Neuer Versuch der Grundlegung eines ethischen Personalismus*, 5th ed. (Bern: Francke, 1966; first published 1913–16). In turn, the critique of Kant as contained in this work of Scheler's, central to our inquiries, became for the author an occasion to think over and partially accept some elements of Kantian personalism. What is meant here in particular is his "ethical" personalism, which finds its expression in his *Grundlegung zur Metaphysik der Sitten* (Riga, 1785), appearing in a collective publication of the Berlin Academy of Sciences: *Kants*

found a particularly full expression in the philosophical achievements of Roman Ingarden, who, however, only partially occupied himself with the philosophy of man.[18b]

This work is undertaken in neither a commentarial nor even a "systematic" way. It is the author's own attempt to understand the object, an attempt of analyses aiming to find a synthetic expression in the conception of the person and act. What seems essential to this conception is above all the fact that *we strive to understand the human person for his own sake* in order to answer the challenge brought by the experience of man in all its wealth and by the existential problems of man in the contemporary world.[9]

---

gesammelte Schriften, herausgegeben von der Königlich Preussischen Akademie der Wissenschaft, vol. 4 (Berlin: G. Reimer, 1903), 385–463.

The author considers the discussion between the views of Scheler (*die materiale Wertethik*) and the views of Kant (*der Formalismus in der Ethik*) as a sui generis "launch site" for the reflections formed in this study on the theme of "person and act." For although it directly concerns the conception of ethics, this discussion at the same time works in the depth of the conception of man and especially of the conception of the person, which philosophy (together with theology) inherits from Boethius. And it provoked and even in a sense compelled a new grasp and a new presentation of these conceptions.

[4a] This also concerns the totality of the achievements of Ingarden, who greatly influenced philosophical environments in Poland. It was after the publication of *Person and Act* that Ingarden's work *Über die Verantwortung: Ihre ontischen Fundamente* was published (Stuttgart: Philipp Reclam Jun., 1970); translated by Adam Węgrzecki as *O odpowiedzialności i jej podstawach ontycznych*, in *Książeczka o człowieku*, 75–184 (Kraków: Wydawnictwo Literackie, 1972). This was perhaps the last work written by the renowned professor of the Lviv and Kraków universities.

Ingarden was a student and critic of Husserl. Ingarden's philosophical writings appeared many times in the Analecta Husserliana series. See especially vol. 4, *Ingardeniana* (Dordrecht: D. Reidel, 1976), which includes the discourse by A.-T. Tymieniecka entitled "Beyond Ingarden's Idealism/Realism Controversy with Husserl: The New Contextual Phase of Phenomenology," 241–418. [4b]

9. In the course of writing this study, the author participated in the work of the Second Vatican Council, and that also provoked an impulse to reflect on the theme of the person. It suffices to mention that one of the council's main documents, the pastoral constitution *Gaudium et spes*, not only foregrounds the issue of the person and his vocation but also expresses a conviction of his transcendental character. (See the following: "The Church, by reason of her role and competence, is not identified in any way with the political community nor bound to any political system. She is at once *a sign and a safeguard of the transcendent character of the human person* [*Gaudium et spes*, Vatican translation, Wojtyła's emphasis].")

PART 1 ❦ CONSCIOUSNESS AND EFFICACY

CHAPTER 1 ❦ **Person and Act in the Aspect of Consciousness**

1. [1a]The Philosophical Richness of the Expression *Actus humanus*[1b]

The traditional interpretation of act

At the beginning of our reflections on the relation between act and person, it is fitting, if only briefly, to highlight what appears to be a merely terminological problem. What we call act [*czyn*] is exclusively man's conscious action. No other action deserves this name. The equivalent of our "act" [*czyn*] in the Western philosophical tradition is *actus humanus*. Hence, even in our terminology we sometimes find the phrase "human act" [*akt ludzki*].[xix] Perhaps this Latinism is not needed since we have the native and beautiful expression "act" [*czyn*], although the Latin term's presence in the literature, especially in the manuals, is very remarkable. This presence indicates that *actus humanus* is in a sense untranslatable by "act" [*czyn*]—for example, when we say "act" [*czyn*], we do not have to add "human," for only human action is an act [*czyn*]. The very term *actus humanus* not only derives from *agere*, which directly establishes its kinship to act and action, for *agere* means precisely "to do" or "to act." In the philosophical tradition of the West, the phrase *actus humanus* also presupposes a certain interpretation of act, namely, one that was developed on the basis of the philosophy of Aristotle in antiquity and of St. Thomas Aquinas in the Middle Ages. This interpretation is realistic and objectivistic as well as metaphysical. It stems from the entire conception of being, and directly from the conception of *potentia-actus*, by means of which the Aristotelians and Thomists explain the changeable and dynamic character of being.[1]

---

1. See Thomas Aquinas, *Summa theologiae* I-II (*De actibus humanis*, q. 6 and the following) and, before this, *Summa theologiae* I, q. 77, a. 3. See also Joseph de Finance, *Être et agir dans la philosophie*

In this case, we refer to the concrete being that is man together with the action proper only to him. Therefore, "act" [*czyn*] in Scholastic terminology is defined as *actus humanus* or, more specifically, as *actus voluntarius*. It is a concretization of the dynamism proper to the human person because it is accomplished in the way proper to free will. The property indicated by the attribute *voluntarius* determines the very essence of the act and its distinctness with respect to the action of other subjects that are not persons. A close link with the corresponding *potentia*, which indicates a potential substratum of actualization, is always characteristic of expressing *actus* in light of the entire Aristotelian or Thomistic conception of being. Therefore, *actus humanus* captures man as a subject that acts, and it indirectly encompasses his potentiality as a source of action. The expression *actus voluntarius* accomplishes this in an even more particular way by directly indicating the power that is the dynamic basis of conscious action, the basis of act. This power is the free will. The attribute *voluntarius* also speaks about the way the act is realized. What corresponds to this in some measure is the Polish expression "*dobrowolny*" [voluntary]. By saying "*dobrowolny*" [voluntary], we want to state that nothing prevents the actualization of the free will.

The act as *actus personae*

Nonetheless, the term *actus humanus* already constitutes a certain interpretation of act as conscious action, an interpretation that is closely connected with the philosophy of being. This interpretation is perfect in its own way. It coincides with the entirety of existential facts and grasps as deeply as possible what is essential in them. In a certain sense, there can be no other interpretation of the human act; at any rate, we know of no other equally accurate attempt to grasp the act's utterly dynamic character and its union with man as a person. [2a] All attempts to take on this subject matter must in some way presuppose this philosophical interpretation hidden in the expressions *actus humanus* and *actus voluntarius*. Our present attempt does so. We not only record in the beginning the philosophi-

---

de Saint Thomas (Rome: Presses de l'Université Grégorienne, 1965). [Editorial note: Wojtyła most likely used S. *Thomae Aquinatis Summa theologica* (Paris: Firmin-Didot, 1891–1900). Unless otherwise indicated, all English translations of quotations from the *Summa* are taken from Thomas Aquinas, *Summa theologica*, 5 vols., trans. Fathers of the English Dominican Province (Notre Dame, Ind.: Christian Classics, 1981; originally published in English in 1911).]

cal interpretation of act proper to Aristotelianism and Thomism but also intend to continue developing and elucidating it in a number of aspects. The starting point adopted in this study, according to which act is a moment of the specific manifestation and vision of the person, does not in the least contradict the conception of *actus humanus*. We can only state that this conception[2b] presupposes the man-person as the source of the act, whereas our point, in line with the inquiries we adopted, is rather to bring to light what the conception *actus humanus* presupposes, for act is at the same time the source of knowing the person.[2] In itself, act as *actus humanus* should help bring about the mental and cognitive actualization of the potentiality it presupposes, the potentiality present at its root. This potentiality is that of a personal being, and the act itself is explained not only as *actus humanus* but also as *actus personae*. [3a]Thus, at the beginning of our inquiries directed at the cognition of the person through act, we must state that we do not in the least abandon this capital philosophical intuition, which is irreplaceable for objectivizing all dynamism, including the dynamism of act, that is, conscious action. Our aim is to objectivize this dynamism as fully and comprehensively as possible, because only in this way can we bring to light the whole reality of the person.[3b]

Although the act is the same as *actus humanus*, the very word "act" [*czyn*] does not seem to refer to the same metaphysical configuration as *actus*; thus, it does not contain in itself the ready-made interpretation inhering in the traditional Latin term. The noun "act" is connected with the verb "to do," "to act." The act is the same as the action proper to man as a person. While the expression *actus humanus* manifests this action to us as a certain "becoming" on the basis of the potentiality of the personal

2. It was sometimes said that through acts, through action, man reveals himself; however, the point there was not necessarily the structure of man as a person. For example, see the (in fact, very general) statement of Maurice Blondel: "Le corps de l'action n'est pas seulement un système de mouvements manifestés par la vie organique dans le milieu des phénomènes; il est constitué par la synthèse réelle et plus ou moins harmonisée des tendances multiples où s'expriment notre nature, notre spontanéité, nos habitudes, notre caractère." [The body of action is not only a system of movements manifested by organic life in the realm of phenomena; it is constituted by the real and more or less harmonized synthesis of multiple tendencies in which are expressed our nature, our spontaneity, our habits, our character.] Maurice Blondel, *L'action humaine et les conditions de son aboutissement*, vol. 2 of *L'action*, new ed. (Paris: Presses Universitaires de France, 1963), 192–93. What is proper to the present study is the perspective of the person, who reveals himself through the act. In this sense, the point of this study is also the ontological grasp of the person through the act as act. The "ontological grasp" ought to be understood above all as the presentation of the reality that the person is.

subject, the expression "act," or "action," speaks nothing of this. It seems that the latter expression describes the same dynamic reality, but in a sense more as a phenomenon or manifestation than as an ontic structure. This does not mean, of course, that it cuts off our access to that structure. Quite the contrary. The expression "act," just like "conscious action," tells us about the dynamism proper to man as a person. And by this essential content it contains in itself all that is hidden in the term *actus humanus*, for, [4a]as we stated, philosophy knows no other term that would express dynamism apart from the term *actus* (of course, in its correlation to the corresponding potency—*potentia*)[4b].[3]

Voluntarium indicates consciousness

The act is conscious action. When speaking of "conscious action" we also mean that this action is accomplished in a way proper to the will and characteristic of it. Thus, in a sense, the expression "conscious action" corresponds to the term *actus voluntarius*, for the action proper to the human will is conscious. In this way, the semantic wealth concealed in the word "act" and its colloquial equivalent, "conscious action," becomes much more evident. Condensed in this word are the ontological contents proper to the term *actus humanus* and the psychological contents indicated by the Latin *voluntarium* and the Polish "conscious" [*świadome*]. The word "act" contains in itself rich semantic implications that ought to be gradually explicated (*ex-plicare*). This explication will also be a gradual unveiling of the reality that is the human person. Therefore, this study is conceived precisely as such a gradual bringing out or "explicating" of the act under the aspect of unveiling the reality of the person. We intend to achieve this end through an analysis of particular aspects while constantly regarding the organic integrality of the act in relation to the person. This, by the way, belongs to the concept of an aspect. An aspect can neither replace the whole nor displace it from our field of vision. If that took place, we would deal with the absolutization of an aspect, which is always an error in the cognition of a complex reality. The person and act is such a complex reality. Consciousness of this complexity and of the principles

---

3. The proper philosophical interpretation of the term "dynamism" used in this study will emerge gradually from further reflections.

that follow from it in the area of cognitive work must constantly accompany us when we analyze the person and act in the aspect of consciousness, in the aspect of efficacy, and in other aspects.

2. [5a]The Attempt (Proposal) to Reveal Consciousness in the Structure of Conscious Action[5b]

The possibility of and need for undertaking this particular attempt (proposal)

The expression "conscious action" directs us to the aspect of consciousness in the act, without, however, distinguishing this aspect. We should make the distinction between "conscious action" and the "consciousness of action"—then the aspect of consciousness will be revealed in a sense for its own sake. Thanks to this distinction, we gain in a sense a direct access to consciousness, which we can examine while, of course, constantly taking into consideration the function that consciousness fulfills in action and in the person's entire existence. *Man not only acts consciously but also has the consciousness that he acts and, moreover, that he acts consciously.* As is evident, the same expression occurs here in two different applications, namely, as an attribute when we speak of conscious action and as a noun or subject when we speak of the consciousness of action. We intend to concentrate our further reflections precisely around the consciousness of action, thus consistently around the consciousness of the acting person; that is, we intend to bind our reflections to the person and act. Only within this scope will we concern ourselves with consciousness as such. However, when we speak of conscious action (without distinguishing the consciousness of action), we indicate only the act, its constitutive property linked with cognition. We mean the cognition to which the act also owes the fact of being *voluntarius*, that is, of being performed in a way proper to the will. For the correct operation of the will presupposes cognitive objectivization. Hence, it is clear that the expression "conscious action" does not speak directly about the consciousness of action. However, a possibility exists of revealing consciousness as such in this dynamic totality and examining it as a special aspect. It also seems that there is a need to reveal this aspect. We shall deal with conscious action in this entire study. *The examination of the very consciousness of action*, to which we devote the first chapter, *can shed new light on the full dynamic configuration of the person and act.*

A question can and perhaps even must arise as to why it is the first chapter and *why* the study of the consciousness of action precedes the study of efficacy, since it is precisely efficacy that constitutes conscious action as an act of the person. Why is it, then, that our analysis first undertakes what is secondary in action and not what is fundamental? This question cannot be answered in advance; a fairly full answer should become apparent in the course of our inquiries. In any case, by first conducting the (consciousness-related, see A.T.)[xx] analysis of the consciousness of action we expect to better prepare the analysis of efficacy—in a sense, to widen its field—and at the same time to bring out a fuller image of the act as the dynamism that most properly expresses the human person as such. It is clear, however, that the analysis of consciousness, though preceding the analysis of efficacy, at the same time refers to that efficacy (and to the entire human dynamism) and constantly presupposes it. *We intend to deal here with consciousness not in separation from dynamism and efficacy but in close union with them*—just as in reality and human experience the consciousness of action is closely united with conscious action. The temporary exclusion of consciousness as a separate aspect is a methodical measure; it is, in a sense, a placement outside the parentheses that at the same time helps us to better understand what remains within the parentheses. Therefore, the title of this chapter does not speak of consciousness alone but of the person and act in the aspect of consciousness.

In what way does "*actus humanus*" implicate (conceal in itself) consciousness?

The traditional interpretation of the act as *actus humanus* takes into account the sense of consciousness that we described as attributive: *actus humanus* is the same as "conscious action." In this sense, "consciousness" blends, so to speak, completely into *voluntarium*, into the dynamism of the human will. In this interpretation, the aspect of consciousness has been neither distinguished nor developed. Yet, consciousness as such, consciousness in the nounal and subjective sense, allows itself to be distinguished in conscious action, for it deeply permeates the entire "person-act" relation and constitutes in itself an important aspect of that relation. This is the aspect in which the existence and action of the person are not only reflected but also shaped in a specific way. The traditional conception *actus humanus* did not so much ignore this aspect as conceal it; this aspect was contained in this conception only *implicite*.[4]

For, as was noted, the conception *actus humanus* was not only realistic and objectivistic but also metaphysical. [6a]It concerned itself with consciousness as something "incorporated" or in a sense "blended" into man's action and his being, which is a being of a rational nature. According to this conception, man exists and acts "consciously," yet his existence and action do not have a specific source in consciousness. Let us not forget here that in our presentation we are as far as possible from the tendency to "absolutize" consciousness. *Our point is only to explicate* (to open, as it were) *the* sui generis *aspect of consciousness that is contained in* actus humanus. When the traditional approach concerned man as a person, the aspect of consciousness was, on the one hand, contained (hidden, as it were) in "rationality" (referring to the definition *homo est animal rationale* or *persona est rationalis naturae individua substantia*) and, on the other hand, contained in the will (understood as *appetitus rationalis*) and expressed in *voluntarium*. Our task in this study, however, is the "explication" of aspects of consciousness, the exposition of consciousness as the essential and constitutive aspect of the entire dynamic structure that is the person and act.[6b]

For man not only acts consciously but also is conscious of his action and of who acts—thus, he is conscious of the act and the person in their dynamic correlation. This consciousness occurs simultaneously with conscious action; in a sense, it accompanies that action. It also occurs before and after that action. It possesses its *continuity* and its *identity* sepa-

---

4. The conviction that the traditional conception *actus humanus* contained *implicite*, i.e., concealed, the aspect of consciousness, which we attempt to discover and unveil in this study, is grounded in an even deeper conviction of the fundamental continuity and homogeneity of the entire philosophy of man—regardless of whether this philosophy is practiced "from the position" of the so-called philosophy of being or the so-called philosophy of consciousness. The act, as the fundamental key to understanding and presenting the reality that the person is, constitutes at the same time a guarantee, as it were, that we touch reality itself, that we do not remain merely on the plane of (somehow absolutized) consciousness.

rately from the constitution and identity of every individual act.[5] [7a] Every act in a sense finds consciousness already present; it is formed and fades away in relation to consciousness, leaving behind a trace of its presence, so to speak. Consciousness accompanies the act and mirrors it when the act is born and when it is performed—once it has been performed, consciousness still mirrors it, though, of course, not accompanying it any longer. This accompaniment of consciousness determines not that action is conscious but rather that man is conscious of his action. *This also causes man to act as a person and—in this the aspect of consciousness plays its most proper role—to experience his action as an act*, which is what we wish to gradually explain here.

What do we primarily mean when we use the term "consciousness"?

Although the function of consciousness can be described in the final analysis as cognitive, this description characterizes it only in the most general terms. For consciousness in this function seems to be only a reflection, or rather a mirroring, of, on the one hand, that which "happens" in man, and, on the other, of both the fact that man "acts" and what it is he does (this distinction between happening and acting is very important for our further study of act; we shall deal with it thoroughly in the next chapter). Consciousness is also a reflection, or rather a mirroring, of everything with which man comes into objective contact by means of any (including cognitive) action and on occasion of everything that "happens" in him. Consciousness mirrors all of this. In some sense, the entire man and the entire world accessible to this concrete man (i.e., to the man I myself am) are "in consciousness." In what way is all of this "in consciousness"? [8a]In reply to this important question, we must say that it is so in a way proper only to consciousness. Let us in turn describe this way.[8b]

---

5. The problem of the identity and continuity of consciousness recurs in Western philosophical thought—from Plato through Descartes and from Kant to Ingarden. By acknowledging in the context of this study the continuity and identity of consciousness, we thereby state (as previously said) that consciousness itself determines the reality of man as a person. The person is constituted in some sense through consciousness ([5a]not only "in consciousness"[5b]). The continuity and identity of consciousness mirror but also condition the continuity and identity of the person. [6a]"*Die Dieselbigkeit unseres Ichs die letzte Grundlage der Einheit unseres Bewusstseinsstromes ist.*" [The selfsameness of our ego is the ultimate basis of the unity of our stream of consciousness.] Ingarden, *Formalontologie*, 285; translated by Szylewicz as *Controversy over the Existence of the World*, 2:666–67.[6b]

The essence of cognitive acts performed by man consists in penetrating the object, objectivizing it intellectually, and in this way "understanding" it. [9a] In this sense cognitive acts have an intentional character; they are turned toward the cognized object, for in it they find their reason for being as acts of understanding or of knowledge. It seems that we cannot assert this about consciousness. [10a] The cognitive reason for the existence of consciousness and its proper acts does not consist in the penetration of the object, in the objectivization that brings with it the understanding [11a] of this object.[6] Therefore, the intentionality that is characteristic of cognitive acts, thanks to which we acquire understanding of objective reality in any of its dimensions, does not seem to belong to acts of consciousness. These acts do not have an intentional character, although the object of our cognition, understanding, and knowledge is also the object of consciousness. However, while understanding and knowledge help form the object intentionally—and such forming is the essential dynamism of cognizing—*consciousness is limited to mirroring what was already cognized in this way*. In a sense, it is an understanding of what has already been understood. Here we express the view that the essential cognitive dynamism, the very activity of cognizing, does not belong to consciousness. If this activity consists in a specific constitution of meanings with respect

---

6. As is evident above, by refusing the intentional character to consciousness and its acts, the author does not intend to deny that consciousness is always *the consciousness of something*, as Brentano emphasized and as we read in Husserl and phenomenologists in general. For example, Husserl writes: "We understood under intentionality the unique peculiarity of lived-experiences to be 'the consciousness *of something* (*von etwas*).'" Edmund Husserl, *Allgmeine Einführung in die reine Phänomenologie*, vol. 1 of *Ideen zu einer reinen Phänomenologie und phänomenologischen Philosophie* (Halle: Max Niemeyer, 1913), 168; translated by W. R. Boyce Gibson as *Ideas: General Introduction to Pure Phenomenology* (London: Allen and Unwin, 1931), 242, and by Danuta Gierulanka as *Idee czystej fenomenologii i fenomenologicznej filozofii* (Warsaw: Państwowe Wydawnictwo Naukowe, 1967), 280. However, by grasping consciousness on a broader basis (for he considers person and act in the aspect of consciousness), the author asks the question *by which principle* (*qua ratione*) and *in what way* (*quo modo*) consciousness is always the consciousness of something. Accordingly, it seems to us proper to adopt another, dynamic concept of the act [*akt*], one connected with the Aristotelian tradition, and consequently another concept of intentionality. Thus, we consider *acts* [*akty*] in the proper sense to be merely actualizations of the person's real potentialities. So when—following a quite common way of speaking in phenomenology—we mention acts of consciousness [*akty świadomości*], the reader should remember that in our understanding this use of the term is only improper and figurative. Also, we understand *intention* as an active orientation toward the object; therefore, in our conception, intentionality does not properly belong to consciousness, which has it only in a derivative, secondary sense, thanks to the intentionality of acts of knowledge or of self-knowledge as real potentialities of the person.

to objects being cognized, it is not consciousness that constitutes these meanings, though certainly they are constituted also in consciousness.[9b]

Thus, although it is difficult to doubt that the cognitive character and even the cognitive function belong to consciousness, both are, nevertheless, distinctive. This character—let us call it "consciousness-related" [*świadomościowy*][xxi]—marks both the particular acts of consciousness and their actual totality, which can be defined as a sum of the acts of consciousness or as their "resultant," and which is most often simply called consciousness. If the "mirroring" consciousness (i.e., consciousness in its mirroring function) is pictured here as, so to speak, a derivative of the entire process of active cognition and of the cognitive relation to objective reality—if it is pictured as, so to speak, the process's last "reflection" in the cognizing subject[xxii]—then we must also assume that this mirroring or reflection is possible only when *we grant consciousness a specific ability to "transilluminate" all* that is cognitively "given" to man, in whatever way. However, this "transillumination" is not the same as the active understanding of objects and the constitution of their meanings that results from it. If we are to continue applying the same comparison, this "transillumination" is rather "maintaining the light" needed for objects and their cognitive meanings to be mirrored in consciousness. For what is proper to consciousness is the same intellectual light to which man owes his traditional definition as *animal rationale* and the human soul its description as *anima rationalis*.

Consciousness is not a subsisting subject

Of course, these reflections do not claim to have developed a complete theory of consciousness. To deny the intentional character of acts of consciousness seems to contradict what the majority of contemporary thinkers maintains on that topic. However, we still regard consciousness not as a separated reality but only as the subjective content of the existence and action that are conscious, that is, the existence and action proper to man. While revealing consciousness in the totality of human dynamisms as a constitutive property of act, we still try to understand it in connection with act, with the dynamism and efficacy of the person. This way of understanding and interpreting consciousness—in the nounal and subjective sense (as we say)—protects us from considering this consciousness to be an autonomous subject. Considering consciousness as an autonomous subject could pave the way to its absolutization and, consequently, to idealism, once the consciousness-absolute is taken to be the only subject of all contents of consciousness, which are ultimately reduced to this subject alone (hence, *esse* = *percipi*). However, here we leave reflections of this kind completely aside. What interests us is consciousness on account of the person and his efficacy. It is this consciousness that we attempt to characterize by speaking of the function of mirroring and transilluminating, which is proper to particular acts of consciousness and to the entire sum or resultant of these acts.

It must be added that the sum or resultant of acts of consciousness determines the actual state of consciousness. However, the subject of this state is not consciousness but man, who we rightly say remains in or outside the state of consciousness, who possesses full or diminished consciousness, etc. Consciousness itself does not exist as a "substantial" subject of acts of consciousness; it exists neither as a separate [12a]*suppositum*[12b] nor as a power. [13a]It is difficult to fully substantiate this thesis here, as this belongs to psychology or integral anthropology.[13b] Nonetheless, what follows from what has already been said concerning consciousness is that it wholly inheres in its acts and in their "consciousness-related" specificity, which is connected with mirroring as something different from cognitive objectivization. *Man not only cognitively enters the world of objects* and even finds himself in that world as one of these objects *but also possesses all of this world in the mirroring of consciousness,* by which he lives most interiorly and personally. For consciousness not only mirrors but also in a particular way "interiorizes" what it mirrors, giving to it all a place in the person's own "I." Here, however, we already touch upon a further and perhaps deeper function of consciousness, which we shall discuss separately. Then we will have to answer how this "interiorization" arises from consciousness—from the function that is both mirroring and transilluminating, which we ascribed to consciousness in our previous analysis. In any case, in light of what we have already said, the consciousness of the act, as well as the consciousness of the person, appears somewhat more fully. We stated that it is something different from what determines the act as conscious action. The consciousness of the act is a mirroring, one of many mirrorings that compose the totality, in terms of content, of the person's consciousness. This mirroring in itself has a consciousness-related character; it consists in the objectivization of neither the act nor the person, though the image of both is most faithfully contained in it.

3. Consciousness and Self-Knowledge
Consciousness is conditioned in the function of mirroring (transilluminating)

It was stated previously that consciousness mirrors human acts in a way proper only to it, namely, in the consciousness-related way. However, consciousness cognitively objectivizes neither the acts, nor the person who performs them, nor finally the entire "world of the person" that is linked in some way with his existence and action. Nonetheless, the acts of consciousness, as well as their sum or resultant, remain distinctly related to all that exists outside of them, particularly the acts performed by one's personal "I." This relation is established through the content of consciousness, which consists of the meanings of individual elements of reality and their mutual connections. When *we consider this semantic side of consciousness* and state that by itself it does not reach these meanings, for it does not objectivize cognitively, then we conclude that the entire human cognition—the ability and habit of active understanding—closely cooperates with consciousness. *Consciousness* is conditioned by that ability and habit—it *is conditioned*, we can say, *by* the entire *cognitive potentiality* that we grasp together with the whole philosophical tradition as the fundamental property of the man-person[14a]: *rationalis naturae individua substantia*[14b].

Thanks to the ability and habit of active understanding, we discover the meaning of particular things and advance in the intellectual comprehension of these things and of the connections that take place between them. For to understand is nothing else but to intellectually grasp the meaning of things or the connections between things. All this is alien to consciousness inasmuch as the whole process of active understanding occurs neither by it nor thanks to it. The meanings of things or of their interrelations are given to consciousness in a sense "from without" as a fruit of knowledge resulting from the active understanding of objective reality, the knowledge that man acquires and possesses in different ways and to different degrees. Hence, the different degrees of knowledge determine the different levels of consciousness, although between knowledge and consciousness a thorough difference exists with respect to the intellectual formation of both individual acts and the cognitive totality.

What ought to be distinguished from all forms and kinds of knowledge acquired and possessed by man, and what indirectly shapes his consciousness with respect to content—that is, from the semantic side—is so-called *self-knowledge*. As the name itself indicates, it is about understanding oneself; it is a kind of cognitive permeation of the object that I am for myself. We may add that this permeation introduces a specific continuity among the most diverse moments or states of the existence of one's own "I,"[7] reaching that which determines their original unity through being rooted in this "I." It is not surprising, then, that self-knowledge, more than any other knowledge, must be coherent with consciousness, for its object is one's own "I," with which consciousness remains in the closest subjective union, as further analysis will show even more fully. At this point, self-knowledge most closely meets consciousness while remaining in a sense separate from it, for consciousness, *with its subjective union with that "I," is not cognitively oriented to that "I" as to an object*. We may even say that consciousness is in a sense cognitively indifferent to one's own "I" as an object. No intentional acts of consciousness exist that would objectivize this "I" with respect to existence or action. This function is performed by acts of self-knowledge. It is to them that every man owes the objectivizing contact with himself and with his

---

7. Here, the "I" denotes a subject experiencing his subjectivity; thus it also denotes a person in this aspect. The structure of the human person will be analyzed more broadly in the reflections devoted to the personal structure of self-governance.

[7a]At this point, we ought to add that the way of understanding self-knowledge in this study differs from that of Ingarden, who considers self-knowledge to be a knowledge of forms (or "moments") of consciousness. This difference of positions is only an exponent of the integral conception represented in this study, where we constantly aim to show the reality of the person in the aspect of consciousness, not to analyze consciousness for its own sake.[7b]

Thanks to self-knowledge, the person—that is, the "I" subjectively constituted through consciousness (self-consciousness) in the sense of experiencing his proper subjectivity—is at the same time given to himself as an object and cognized objectively by himself. Therefore, we shall in turn speak, among other things, of the "coherence of self-knowledge with consciousness."

Writing from the position of existential Thomism, Mieczysław Albert Krąpiec understands self-knowledge as the cognition of the existence of the "I." See Krąpiec, *Ja—człowiek: Zarys antropologii filozoficznej* (Lublin: Towarzystwo Naukowe Katolickiego Uniwersytetu Lubelskiego, 1974), 109.

acts. Thanks to self-knowledge, consciousness mirrors acts and their relation to one's own "I." Without self-knowledge, consciousness would be deprived of semantic contents [15a]concerning both the world of objects and man's own "I" as an object[15b]; it would find itself in a vacuum, as it were. The idealists postulate a state like this, for in it consciousness can be considered a subject that produces its contents with no regard for any factor located outside consciousness itself. A valid question in this line of thought arises—namely, whether consciousness itself can be considered a real subject or whether it is only its own product. However, as previously said, this question is merely marginal in our study.

Self-knowledge opens consciousness to its own "I" as a concrete object

Thanks to self-knowledge, the acting subject's own "I" is cognitively grasped as an object. As a result, both the person and the act connected with him have an objective meaning in consciousness. Consciousness-related mirroring, which not only is something subjective but also constitutes the basis for subjectivization (we shall speak of this more extensively later), removes neither the objective meaning of one's own "I" nor that of its acts, for it constantly draws this meaning from self-knowledge. *The coherence of self-knowledge with consciousness* should be considered the basic factor of the equilibrium of the person's interior life, especially concerning its intellectual structure. Man is an object for himself as a subject, and even in consciousness-related mirroring he does not lose an objective meaning. *In this regard, self-knowledge is in a sense anterior to consciousness*, for it brings into it the semantic relation to one's own "I" and to its acts, though consciousness in itself is not intentionally directed to them [16a]. At the same time, self-knowledge constitutes a boundary, as it were, for consciousness—a boundary beyond which the process of consciousness-related subjectivization cannot proceed.

Moreover, the objectivizing turn of self-knowledge toward one's own "I" and toward the acts connected with it also concerns consciousness itself. Consciousness, too, becomes an object of self-knowledge. This explains the fact that when man "possesses the consciousness" of his action, he at the same time "knows that he acts" and "knows that he acts consciously." He knows that he is conscious, and he knows that he acts consciously. Self-knowledge has for its object not only the person and his acts but also the consciousness of both. Self-knowledge objectivizes this consciousness; hence, in the consciousness-related reflection, it is not just any being and action of the person who is my own "I" but rather the being and action connected with consciousness, that is, both conscious and made conscious, that possesses objective meaning. Man possesses self-knowledge of his consciousness, and in this way he is conscious of the consciousness of his being and of his action in acts. After all, this process does not progress ad infinitum; it is precisely self-knowledge that circumscribes the boundary of mirroring. *Inasmuch as, on the one hand, self-knowledge constitutes the basis of mirroring by forming the semantic side of consciousness, it marks out, on the other hand, the boundary* thanks to which consciousness ultimately "holds on to" being and affirms itself as grounded in it, instead of being doomed to some unending process of "self-grounding." [17a]

We said previously that consciousness itself is neither a separate subject nor a power. Further analyses display more fully that what is present at the foundation of consciousness is the same cognitive potentiality to which man owes all processes of understanding and objectivizing knowledge. Consciousness grows from that very potentiality as, so to speak, from a common root. It appears, as it were, "in the background" of the processes of understanding and objectivizing knowledge. At the same time, it appears, as it were, even more "inside" the personal subject. Therefore, its work is all "interiorization" and "subjectivization," of which we shall speak later.

Self-knowledge lies at the foundation of self-consciousness

The making conscious of not only one's own "I" and the acts connected with it but also the very consciousness of these acts in their relation to the "I" is a work of self-knowledge. When we speak as follows: "I become conscious of my act" or "I become conscious of something else," then, by indicating the actualization of consciousness, we in fact indicate the actualization of self-knowledge. For an act (or anything else) can be "made conscious" not in a consciousness-related manner but only intentionally, thus by an act of self-knowledge [18a]. Speaking this way, however, we express ourselves correctly because consciousness is most closely united with [19a]self-knowledge[19b]. [20a]As long as mirroring is concerned, the consciousness-related actualization suffices; however, if "making something conscious" is concerned, then the actualization of consciousness must in a sense include the act of self-knowledge.[20b]

It is very remarkable and very fortunate that our language has at its disposal both these expressions. Thanks to this fact, many noetic and ontological problems are sorted out. On the one hand, the objectivity of the subject becomes more intelligible, as does, on the other hand, the subjectivity of the complex object that is one's own "I." We shall in turn analyze this subjectivity of the object. However, before we undertake such analysis, we must state once more that *when we speak of the consciousness of act, we mean not only the consciousness-related mirroring itself but also intentional self-knowledge.* I have consciousness of the act—this in fact means that by the act of self-knowledge I objectivize my act in relation to my person. I objectivize the fact that my act is a true action of my person and not something that only happens in my person; that this action is conscious (which is indirectly equivalent to *voluntarium*); that this action, as performed in the way proper to the will (which is directly equivalent to *voluntarium*), has a positive or negative moral value, is good or evil. All this, the entire content of the act, objectivized by an act of self-knowledge, becomes the content of consciousness. Thanks to this objectivization, we can speak of consciousness in the objective sense, that is, of the relation of consciousness to the objective world. We speak of consciousness in the objective sense on account of the meaning of various objects that it contains due to various understandings. But we speak in a particular way of consciousness in the objective sense on account of the meaning in consciousness of one's own "I," its [21a]*esse* and *operari*[21b], and all that is in any way connected with it. Consciousness owes this meaning, or rather this group of meanings, to self-knowledge. Thanks precisely to this group of meanings, consciousness merits in a particular way to be called "self-consciousness." *It is self-knowledge that contributes to the formation of self-consciousness.*

On the specificity of self-knowledge in the totality of human cognition

Since we have already outlined the reciprocal relation between consciousness and self-knowledge, and before we move ahead in the analysis of the function of consciousness, especially of self-consciousness, *let us take a brief look at self-knowledge for its own sake*. Let us attempt to do so by, in a sense, forgetting momentarily the functions of consciousness, *as if the concrete human "I" were the exclusive object of one's own cognition, that is, of self-knowledge.*

As follows from the analysis above, every man's own "I" constitutes, so to speak, the rallying point of all intentional acts of self-knowledge. It is the knowledge that meets everything in whatever way connected with or referring to the "I" at that point—namely, the objectivized "I." Thus, for example, there is moral self-knowledge—something fundamentally different from knowledge about morality, let alone from ethics; religious self-knowledge—existing independently from all forms of knowledge about religion, religious knowledge, or theology; social self-knowledge—existing independently from any knowledge about society; and so on. For self-knowledge, concentrated on its own "I" as its proper object, enters with the "I" all the areas into which this "I" expands. Self-knowledge, however, does not objectivize any of these areas for their own sake but only in connection with and because of the "I."

The analyses conducted here display quite clearly that the function of self-knowledge opposes the egotistic grasp of consciousness, in which the latter would appear (if only substitutively) in the character of a "pure I"-subject. Moreover, self-knowledge has nothing to do with the objectivizing cognition that would concern an abstracted and generalized "I"; it is not some "ego-logy." *In self-knowledge, the object is the "I," concrete and "one's own."* We might have certain reservations in applying to self-knowledge even the concept of knowledge, which, strictly speaking, has a general object.[8] Yet, self-knowledge not only has one's individual "I" for

---

8. The view that knowledge has a general object originates in the Aristotelian tradition.

[8a]In the context of these reflections on self-knowledge, the author also wishes to note the position of Roman Ingarden. He has always stressed the plurality of senses of the term "I" and the corresponding difference between the acts of cognition that come into play each time. "We ought to distinguish the so-called 'pure I'—the subject performing acts of pure consciousness—and the 'I' *in*

its object but also is constantly entangled in the particulars connected with that "I." This is [22a]an objectivizing permeation of one's own "I" in the fact of its entire concreteness[22b] and, at the same time, its entire particularity, which escapes any generalizations. In addition, however, this is also true "knowledge of oneself" as an integral whole, for it is not content to register the particulars connected with one's "I" but constantly strives for generalizations. Such generalizations are, for example, all views or assessments of oneself, proper only to self-knowledge and created by it. We must add that these views—some integral vision of one's own "I"— become mirrored in consciousness: thus, they are mirrored not only as the particular facts connected with one's "I" but also as the constantly increasing and developing integral fact that is this "I." Views on that fact have not only the character of a self-knowing theory of one's own "I" but also the character of assessment, because the aspect of value is no less essential for self-knowledge.

Self-knowledge does not constitute merely a particular case of the knowledge of man in general, even though the "I" that it attempts to objectivize as comprehensively as possible is man. The "I," as the object of self-knowledge, is man in the ontological and intentional sense. Yet, all the cognitive work proper to self-knowledge proceeds exclusively from self-experience to self-understanding without passing into generalizations about man as such. In our cognition, a discrete, though nonetheless distinctly drawn, *boundary runs between the knowledge of man in general and self-knowledge, that is, the knowledge of one's own "I."* If there is a shift to be seen, it is rather in the direction of the knowledge of oneself. For

---

the sense of a certain real psycho-physical individuum, of the human person endowed with this or that real character, etc. The 'I' in the sense of the real human person is as 'transcendent' in relation to the given stream of consciousness and the 'pure I' that performs acts of this consciousness as are all the objects of the external world" (Ingarden, *Z badań nad filozofią współczesną*, 373–74).[8b]

The following statement of Joseph Nuttin also seems to draw close to the position expressed in the analysis of self-knowledge conducted here: "Cette *présence cognitive* de l'objet en face du moi implique, pour le moi, une certaine possession cognitive de soi-même, et une possibilité de prendre possession de l'objet comme tel. Une telle perception de l'objet crée la 'distance' nécessaire qui permet à la personnalité de *se percevoir* comme sujet percevant le monde, sans coïncider avec cet acte." [This *cognitive presence* of the object vis-à-vis the 'I' implies, for the 'I,' a certain cognitive possession of itself, as well as the possibility of taking possession of the object as such. Such a perception of the object creates the necessary 'distance' that allows the person to *perceive himself* as a subject perceiving the world, without simply coinciding with this act.] See Joseph Nuttin, *La structure de la personnalité* (Paris: Presses Universitaires de France, 1971), 219.

self-knowledge uses knowledge about man in general, that is, the various views on the human being; it also uses experiential knowledge about people in order to better understand one's own "I." In this sense, comparison is not alien to it. Nonetheless, self-knowledge does not use the knowledge of its own "I" in order to better understand other people or man in general. The latter belongs to the knowledge of man, which readily takes advantage of self-knowledge in order to better understand its own object. Self-knowledge, however, stops at one's own "I" and remains in the individual cognitive intention, for in its own "I" it constantly finds new wealth of content. The old adage says, "*individuum est ineffabile.*"

4. [23a]The Twofold Function of Consciousness and the Lived-Experience of One's Own Subjectivity[23b]
Mirroring (reflection) and lived-experience

[24a]The analysis of self-knowledge allows us to better understand consciousness in the function previously ascribed to it. This is the function of mirroring: consciousness is not limited here to simple reflection of all that simultaneously constitutes the object of understanding and knowledge—and, in particular, of self-understanding and self-knowledge. Rather, it specifically transilluminates all of this, and it mirrors precisely in this transillumination. We are far from depriving consciousness of its proper (i.e., consciousness-related) cognitive vitality.[9] Nonetheless,

---

9. Since the times of James and Bergson people have spoken of the stream of consciousness. In his philosophy of man, Ingarden treats the stream of consciousness as belonging to the "I": "Als ein reines Geschehen hat er die Form eines Vorgangs und ist somit kein 'System'. Als solcher braucht er [der Bewusstseinsstrom] ein Seinsfundament und findet es tatsächlich einerseits im Leibe, andererseits in der menschlichen Seele. Er ist sozusagen die Berührungsfläche zwischen dem Leib und der Seele des Menschen." [As a pure occurrence it has the form of a process and is therefore not a "system." As such, the stream of consciousness needs an ontic foundation, and finds it in fact in the body on the one hand and in the human psyche on the other. It is, so to speak, a surface of contact between the body and the psyche of man.] See Ingarden, *Über die Verantwortung: Ihre ontischen Fundamente*, 91–92; translated by Węgrzecki as *O odpowiedzialności i jej podstawach ontycznych*, 155, and by Arthur Szylewicz as *On Responsibility: Its Ontic Foundations*, in *Man and Value* (Washington, D.C.: The Catholic University of America Press, 1983), 97. Ingarden applies the term "soul" to what we describe as the psyche.

By speaking here of the vitality characteristic of consciousness and proper to it, we do not merely mean the vitality manifested in the form of the stream of consciousness; rather, we attempt to reach the sources of that stream.

Within the discussion published in *Analecta Cracoviensia*, it is Andrzej Półtawski in particular

what was said here about self-knowledge can lead to the conclusion that the mirroring function of consciousness "gets lost," as it were, in self-knowledge, in the objectivizing processes of self-understanding, which are directed to one's own "I" as their object. In that case (i.e., in light of the role of self-knowledge presented here), does consciousness have its own reason for being? This question is linked to another of a methodological nature: how do we arrive at precisely this conception of consciousness, and, in particular, at this conception of the relation of consciousness to self-knowledge? As we see, these are fundamental questions with regard to the entirety of our previous analyses and their continuation.

In order to answer these questions, we ought to recall once more that in this study we consider consciousness on the basis of experience, which allows the objectivization of man's full dynamism—in particular, the dynamism expressed by the very title of the study: *Person and Act*. Thus, the conception of consciousness and the grasping of its relation to self-knowledge precede but also presuppose the integral conception of the man-person that we intend to continue developing in this study. What seems decisive for deciphering the "consciousness-self-knowledge" problem in this approach is the issue of *the simultaneous objectivity and subjectivity of man*. Consciousness is the "terrain" on which one's own "I," while appearing in all its proper objectivity (precisely as the object of self-knowledge), at the same time fully experiences its proper subjectivity. In this way, the second function, or feature, of consciousness emerges before us, which in the living structure of the person complements its transilluminating-mirroring function and in a sense confers on consciousness its definitive reason for being in the specific structure of person and act.[24b]

[25a]As we have mentioned a few times, *consciousness is not exhausted in its transilluminating-mirroring function*. This is only a partial, even though in a sense original, function of consciousness. *The principal function of*

---

who deals with the problem of consciousness, and who undertook a very interesting attempt to compare the conception of consciousness contained in *Person and Act* with the analyses of Henri Ey, the renowned French psychiatrist. See Andrzej Półtawski, "Czyn a świadomość," in *Logos i ethos: Rozprawy filozoficzne*, 83–113 (Kraków: Polskie Towarzystwo Teologiczne, 1971). Also, see the reviewed and expanded version of this article in English: "Ethical Action and Consciousness," in *The Human Being in Action*, ed. Anna-Teresa Tymieniecka, 115–50, Analecta Husserliana 7 (Dordrecht: D. Reidel, 1978).

consciousness is the fact that it forms lived-experience, which allows man to experience his own subjectivity in a particular way. Therefore, it seems that what is indispensable for understanding the acting person and for understanding the act proceeding from him as lived-experience—thus, proceeding in the experiential dimension of one's own subjectivity—is an analysis of consciousness that goes beyond its original mirroring function. Consciousness is not exhausted in that function, in mirroring the act in its relation to one's own "I," which still occurs, so to speak, from without, though it takes place in the interior dimension. However, the mirror of consciousness introduces us all the more into the interiority of acts and their relation to one's "I"—only here does the role of consciousness appear in its fullness. *Consciousness allows us not only to view our acts interiorly* (introspection), including their dynamic dependence on one's own "I," *but also to experience these acts as acts and as our own.*

In this sense, we assert that *it is precisely to consciousness that man owes the subjectivization of what is objective.* Subjectivization *is in a sense identified with lived-experience; at any rate, subjectivization is experientially manifested in it.* As long as the person and act constitute a certain reality that appears as the object of self-knowledge in its proper objectivity, then the same person and act are simultaneously "subjectivized" thanks to consciousness, inasmuch as consciousness conditions the lived-experience of the act performed by the person and thereby conditions the lived-experience of the person in his dynamic-efficacious relation to the act. Together with this and in this very way, all that constitutes the intentional "world of the person" is also "subjectivized." We can analyze this "world" in its objective content and on the basis of consciousness-related mirroring. At the same time, however, this world, inasmuch as it becomes the content of lived-experience, definitively enters the sphere of every human "I's" own subjectivity. In this way, for example, a mountain landscape cognitively mirrored in our consciousness and the same landscape experienced by us on the basis of this mirroring simultaneously overlap and differ discretely from each other.[25b]

The reflexive function of consciousness conditions the lived-experience of one's own "I"

[26a]In reference to all that was said above, there is a need to indicate a new feature of consciousness. We mean here a feature in the constitutive sense, because what clearly corresponds to it is a new function, different from the transilluminating-mirroring function previously characterized. We shall describe this feature as reflexive, while assuming that it characterizes both consciousness, taken simply, and what consists of the so-called state of consciousness, the specific sum or resultant of the acts of consciousness. This state of consciousness indicates not only the mirroring and all that is mirrored in a given moment but also the lived-experience, in which the subjectivity of man as the experiencing subject is manifested in a particular (because experiential) way. It is in this sense that the reflexive feature, that is, *the "reflexivity" of consciousness, denotes, so to speak, a natural turning of consciousness toward the subject, inasmuch as it makes his subjectivity manifest in lived-experience.*

The reflexivity of consciousness ought to be distinguished from "reflectivity," which is proper to the human mind in its cognitive acts [*akty*]. Reflectivity presupposes the intentionality of these acts, that is, their cognitive turning toward the object. If we describe the activity of the mind as thinking, then thinking becomes reflective once we turn to the act previously accomplished in order to grasp more fully its objective content (*noema*?) and possibly its character, course, or structure (*noesis*?). In this way reflective thinking becomes an important element in the coming to be of all understanding, all knowledge—including the knowledge of oneself, which we called self-knowledge. Thus, reflection goes hand in hand with consciousness and serves it, which is completely evident in light of our remarks on the transilluminating-mirroring function of consciousness. However, reflection and reflectivity alone do not suffice as far as the constitution of lived-experience is concerned. A special turning toward the subject takes place, a turning to which we owe, together with lived-experience, the particular manifestation of the subjectivity of the experiencing "I." It is *this constitutive function of consciousness* that we describe as reflexive, that is, as *turning everything toward the subject*. In this sense, *consciousness is "reflexive" and not merely "reflective."*[26b]

[27a]This turning toward the subject as a function of consciousness is something different from the mirroring. In the mirroring (thanks to self-knowledge), this man, who is a subject and his own "I," is still present as an object. The reflexive turning of consciousness causes this object, precisely because it is ontologically a subject, to experience himself as a subject while experiencing his own "I." By this statement, we simultaneously define reflexivity as an essential and a completely specific moment of consciousness. Let us add at once that this moment allows itself to be perceived only when we follow consciousness in close, organic connection with "being": with man, and especially with man who acts. We then clearly distinguish that *being a subject* differs from *being known* (objectivized) *as a subject* (which also still occurs in the consciousness-related mirroring) and from *experiencing oneself as the subject of one's actions and lived-experiences* (we owe the latter to consciousness in its reflexive function). This distinction is of enormous significance for all our further analyses, through which we shall attempt to approach the entire dynamic reality of the person and act while also taking into account the subjectivity given to us in lived-experience.

Undoubtedly, man is above all the subject of his existence and action; he is this subject as a being of a given nature, and this has consequences precisely in action. Traditional ontology describes this subject of existence and action, which is man, by the term *suppositum*. We can say that the word *suppositum* denotes the subject in an utterly objective way, abstracting from the aspect of lived-experience, and especially from the lived-experience of the subjectivity in which the subject is given to himself as his own "I." The word *suppositum*, then, abstracts from the aspect of consciousness, thanks to which a concrete man—*the object that is the subject*—experiences himself as a subject and thus *experiences his subjectivity; this lived-experience gives him the basis on which to describe himself with the pronoun "I."* We know that this is a personal pronoun: "I" always indicates a concrete person. We draw attention to the fact that the term "I" contains more than the term *suppositum*, for it joins the moment of experienced subjectivity with ontic subjectivity, whereas *suppositum* speaks only of the latter: of the being as the subjective basis of existence and action.[10] [28a] Of course, this interpretation of the term "I" presup-

---

10. Of course, the question may arise whether outside experience—that is, outside the lived-

poses a particular conception of consciousness and its relation to man as a real subject. In fact, we can say that it presupposes the reflexivity of consciousness. For if we separated the lived-experience of one's own subjectivity, which provides the basis for describing oneself as an "I," from the real subject, which is precisely that "I," then this experienced "I" would represent nothing else but the content of consciousness. Therefore, *the reflexive turning of consciousness toward the real subject in order to co-constitute it through its own dimension* is of fundamental importance. In this way, the "I" is a real subject that experiences its subjectivity, that is to say, is at the same time constituted in the dimension of consciousness.

---

experience of one's subjectivity, which was linked here with the reflexive function of consciousness—we can know anything about the fact that the "I" is a subject. In light of previous statements on the topic of experience (see the introduction to this study), we should answer this question as follows: although the experience of man (as exterior experience) allows us to establish (to some extent) that he is the subject of existence and action (*suppositum*), it is nonetheless the experience of one's own "I" (and also interior experience) that confers on this conviction a particular evidentness and at the same time establishes its new dimension. This is the dimension of experienced subjectivity.

[9a]Another problem is that of the link between the lived-experience of subjectivity and consciousness in its "reflexive" function.[9b] According to Emmanuel Lévinas, a certain "enjoyment" (*jouissance*) belongs to the essence of lived-experience: "Le monde dont je vis ne se constitue pas simplement au deuxième degré après que la représentation aura tendu devant nous toile de fond d'une réalité simplement donnée et que des intentions 'axiologiques' aient prêté à ce monde une valeur qui le rende apte à l'habitation. *Le 'revirement' du constitué en condition s'accomplit dès que j'*ouvre les yeux: je n'ouvre les yeux qu'en jouissant déjà du spectacle." [The world I live from is not simply constituted at a second level after representation would have spread before us a backdrop of a reality simply given, and after 'axiological' intentions would have ascribed to this world a value that renders it apt for habitation. *The 'turning' of the constituted into a condition is accomplished* as soon as I open my eyes: I but open my eyes and already enjoy the spectacle (Wojtyła's emphasis).] Emmanuel Lévinas, *Totalité et infini: Essai sur l'extériorité*, 4th ed. (The Hague: Martinus Nijhoff, 1971), 103; translated by Alphonso Lingis as *Totality and Infinity: An Essay on Exteriority* (Dordrecht: Kluwer Academic Publishers, 1991), 130. Further on: "La sensibilité met en rapport avec une pure qualité sans support, avec l'*élément. La sensibilité est jouissance. L'être sensible, le corps, concrétise cette façon d'être qui consiste à trouver une condition en ce qui, par ailleurs, peut apparaître comme objet de pensée, comme simplement constitué.*" [Sensibility establishes a relation with a pure quality without support, with the element. Sensibility is enjoyment. *The sensitive being, the body, concretizes this way of being, which consists in finding a condition in what, in other respects, can appear as an object of thought, as simply constituted* (Wojtyła's emphasis).] Lévinas, *Totalité et Infini*, 109 (136). [10a]If we consider Lévinas's opinion, then we could understand the function of consciousness only and exclusively as one that conditions lived-experience and not as one that essentially constitutes it.[10b]

The "I" is constituted as a subject existing through the lived-experience of its own subjectivity

It follows clearly from what has already been said that, in accord with the cognitive presuppositions made in the introductory chapter, the separation of the experienced "I" from its ontological foundations in no way comes into play. Our consciousness-related analysis can even serve to embed that "I" more thoroughly in its own ontic basis. Every man, including the one who is myself, is given in integral, or simple, experience as an individual real being, as a subject of existence and action (that is, as *suppositum*). At the same time, everyone is given to himself as a concrete "I," both through self-consciousness and self-knowledge. Self-knowledge states that the being that is objectively myself is at the same time subjectively my "I," since I experience my subjectivity in my "I." Thus, I not only possess the consciousness of my own "I" (on the basis of self-knowledge); I also, thanks to (reflexive) consciousness, experience my "I," that is, I experience myself as a concrete subject in its very subjectivity. *Consciousness is not only an aspect but also an essential dimension or real moment of the being that "I" am, since it constitutes the being's subjectivity in an experiential sense.* If this being, a real individual object in its fundamental ontic structure, corresponds to what in traditional philosophy was called *suppositum*, then without consciousness this *suppositum* could in no way be constituted as an "I." It seems that in this way consciousness belongs to the real constitution of this being, which is man, inasmuch as we want to emphasize proportionately its subjectivity—in particular, the subjectivity thanks to which every concrete man is the one and unrepeatable "I."[27b]

[29a]Perhaps it is worthwhile to consider in yet another sense the path that leads us from mirroring to lived-experience in these reflections on consciousness. Consciousness appears to us here as a specific dimension of the individual real being that is the concrete man. Consciousness neither obscures this being nor absorbs it into itself. This would be the case according to the basic premise of idealistic thinking, which presupposes that *esse = percipi*—that is, that "to be" is the same as "to be the content of consciousness"—and which does not accept any mode

of existence outside consciousness.[11] We, however, take the opposite view: consciousness united with the existence and action of the concrete man-person *neither absorbs nor obscures* this being, this dynamic reality, *but rather unveils it "inwardly,"* thereby unveiling it *in its* specific distinctness and *unrepeatable concreteness.* The reflexive function of consciousness consists in such unveiling. We can say, thanks to this function of consciousness, that man exists "inwardly," as it were, and at the same time exists in the full dimension of his intellectual (rational!) being. This "inward" existence goes, so to speak, hand in hand with lived-experience and is in some sense identified with it. According to our understanding, lived-experience does not constitute a reflex appearing in a sense on the surface of man's existence and action. Quite the contrary—it constitutes *the proper form of the human subject's actualization, which man owes precisely to consciousness.* Thanks to consciousness, the real and the "objective" energies contained in man as a being—the energies that compose the manifold and diversified richness of potentiality—are actualized in a real and objective way (as will be discussed in detail in subsequent chapters). At the same time, they are actualized *in the profile of the subjectivity proper to man as a person.* Moreover, being actualized in this way, they find in lived-experience their, in a sense, subjective completion.[12] [30a] (We will see that this does not correspond to all energies of human potentiality in equal measure.)[29b]

The experiential expression of man's spirituality

Inasmuch as it mirrors, inasmuch as it is a reflection, consciousness still remains, so to speak, at an objective distance from its own "I." However, inasmuch as consciousness constitutes the basis of lived-experience, inasmuch as it constitutes this lived-experience thanks to its reflexivity, it already goes beyond this distance, enters the subject, and experientially constitutes this subject together with every lived-experience. Of

---

11. This approach has remained in modern philosophy, in subtle variations, from Berkeley through Kant to Husserl.
12. We could also note that, according to this understanding, consciousness as the direct condition of experiencing the subjectivity of one's own "I" becomes a fundamental factor of realism in the conception of man. "Realism" here means not only ascertaining man's objective "beingness" but also bringing the analysis to the very edge of the possibility of grasping this man in his unrepeatable concreteness.

course, consciousness mirrors the subject in one way and constitutes it in another: thanks to self-knowledge, it mirrors by retaining the subject's objective meaning, its objective position, as it were; whereas it constitutes in the pure subjectivity of lived-experience. This is very important. Thanks to the duality of the function of consciousness, we do not lose the sense of our own being in its real objectivity while we remain within our subjectivity. The fact that our lived-experiences are formed thanks to consciousness, that without consciousness there is no human lived-experience—though there exist various manifestations of life or various actualizations of man's potentiality—*is explained in its own way by the attribute* rationale *in the Aristotelian conception* and definition of man, [31a]or by the formulation *rationalis naturae individua substantia* in the Boethian conception and definition of the person. *Consciousness gives access to the spirituality of man; it gives us a certain insight into that spirituality.*[31b] The spirituality of man is manifested in consciousness, thanks to which it forms in lived-experience the experiential inwardness of his existence and action. Although the foundations of man's spirituality, in a sense, its roots, reside outside the direct sphere of experience—we reach them by way of reasoning—spirituality itself has an experiential expression, becoming in a sense a sum of manifestations. This is proven by the close, so to speak, constitutive connection of the lived-experiences proper to man with the reflexive function of consciousness. Man experiences himself and all that is in him, his entire "world," mentally, for the nature of consciousness is mental, intellectual. It determines the nature of lived-experiences and, so to speak, their level in man.

The consciousness of the act and the lived-experience of the act in the dimension of moral values

[32a]In what way does man experience himself in the act? We know already that he is conscious of himself as "acting," that is, as the subjective agent of action. Understanding the consciousness-related mirroring of the act, inasmuch as this act goes beyond the subjective sphere of man to occur, in a sense, in the external world, poses a separate problem.[32b] Apart from this, however, man experiences his acts within his own subject, and he owes this lived-experience, just as any other, to consciousness in its reflexive function. [33a]Man experiences his act as the "action" of

which he is the subjective agent and which is also a profound expression and revelation of what composes his own "I," of what this "I" simply is.[33b] Man accurately differentiates his action from everything that merely "happens" in his own "I." Here, the distinction between *actio* and *passio* finds its experiential basis. The distinction itself is a work of self-knowledge; it belongs to the semantic side of consciousness-related mirroring. However, it goes hand in hand with lived-experience: man *experiences his action as something utterly different from anything that "happens" in him.*

[34a]Only in connection with action (that is, act) does man experience as "his" values the moral values of "good" and "evil" (of "morality" or "immorality," as is commonly though erroneously said). He experiences them on the basis of a relation that is both feeling and assessment. At any rate, man not only is conscious of the "morality" of his acts, but also experiences it authentically (and at times very deeply).

The act and moral values belong objectively to the real subject, which is man as their agent. This objective belonging is equally real and existential: they are a reality in a particular way connected with and dependent on this subject. *At the same time*, both the act and its corresponding moral values—good and evil—*function* (if we can say so) *in an utterly subjective way in lived-experience.* Consciousness in its reflexive function conditions this lived-experience rather than simply mirroring it on the basis of self-knowledge, for such mirroring would still consist only in becoming objectively conscious of both the act and its moral value.[13] As

---

13. Scheler presents moral values as appearing *"auf dem Rücken"* (on the occasion) of volitions directed to various objective values (*materiale Werte*). See Scheler, *Formalismus*, 45–51, and especially: "Der Wert 'gut' erscheint ... *an* dem Willensakte. Eben darum kann er *nie* die Materie dieses Willensaktes sein. Er befindet sich gleichsam 'auf dem Rücken' dieses Aktes, und zwar wesensnotwendig; er kann daher nie *in* diesem Akte intendiert sein" (49). [The value "good" appears ... *on* the act of willing. It is for this reason that it can *never* be the content of an act of willing. It is located, so to speak, on the occasion of this act, and this by way of essential necessity; it can therefore *never* be intended in this act.] Translated by Manfred S. Frings and Roger L. Funk as *Formalism in Ethics and Non-Formal Ethics of Values: A New Attempt toward the Foundation of an Ethical Personalism* (Evanston, Ill.: Northwestern University Press, 1973), 27 (translation slightly modified). Appreciating all the subtlety of the Schelerian analysis, it is difficult not to have the conviction that what is relaxed or perhaps even lost in this analysis is the bond between the subject—that is, one's own "I" given in lived-experience as the agent—and precisely the values whose agent, and not merely whose subject, he is. Consequently, the moment of a certain "identification" of the subject with the good or evil performed by him—the essential moment for the experience of morality—seems to be lost as well. It is precisely this moment that makes these values utterly personal.

The author of this study critically examined this problem several times. See, among others,

we can see, both functions of consciousness take part in this particular "drama" of human interiority, which is the "drama of good and evil" that occurs in acts and, through the acts, in the person. Thus, thanks to its mirroring function closely connected with self-knowledge, consciousness allows us to become objectively conscious of the good or evil of which we are the agents in a given act. At the same time, thanks to its reflexivity, consciousness allows us to experience this good or evil together with our own efficacy. As we stated previously, this lived-experience is not an additional and "superficial" reflex of the act and of good or evil as its moral qualification. Quite the contrary—the point here is the *reflexive reduction "inward,"* as a result of which both the act and *the moral good or evil become a full subjective reality in man*. They acquire, in a sense, their proper completion in human subjectivity. It is precisely then that man experiences good or evil simply in himself—in his own "I." At the same time, he experiences himself as the one who is good or evil. This is the full dimension of morality as a subjective and personal reality.

To what extent does one's own "I" help us to understand "man"?

This "full dimension," that is, the dimension of lived-experience, is also the dimension of experience through which good and evil as the person's moral values, as well as the very person and act with them, become the object of a more and more thorough understanding, as we indicated in the introductory reflections of our study. There we spoke about the experience of man and morality as the basis and source of understanding man and morality. This experience and understanding are certainly broader than self-experience and the self-understanding developed with it and contained in the lived-experience of one's own "I." We asked ourselves in the introductory reflections *whether* this self-experience (i.e., the lived-experience of one's own "I") and the self-understanding (i.e., the consciousness of self, based on self-knowledge) that increases with it could be at all transferred into the ever-expanding circle of man's experience outside his own "I." Of course, a problem like this exists. We

---

Karol Wojtyła, "The Intentional Act and the Human Act, That Is, Act and Experience," in *The Crisis of Culture*, ed. Anna-Teresa Tymieniecka, 269–80, Analecta Husserliana 5 (Dordrecht: D. Reidel, 1976).

returned to it in the reflections on self-knowledge, and here we return to it once more. For there is no way to deny that, while remaining in the sphere of self-experience and self-understanding, we remain *in a particularly privileged and particularly fruitful point in the experience and understanding of man*. Therefore, retaining all the unrepeatable specificity of self-knowledge (we spoke of that at the end of the previous paragraph) and of the lived-experience of one's own "I," we attempt in our cognition of man to draw in some way from the source of self-experience and self-understanding. This happens perhaps in this way: already from the very start we have positioned ourselves, so to speak, in a twofold manner—namely, by proceeding "from within" oneself toward "man" outside of one's own "I" and, at the same time, by proceeding from this "man" and returning to one's own "I," that is, "inward." In this way, our cognition of man has, so to speak, a cyclic character. This is fully substantiated, since the object of cognition is to be not only one's own "I" but also man—and at the same time, this man is, among other things, also "myself," is also my own "I."[34b]

5. The Problem of the Emotionalization of Consciousness

The consciousness-related element and the emotive element in man

[35a]In this paragraph we intend to consider a certain concrete problem, although we cannot do so without at least indicating the broader context. And because this broader context will be the object of detailed analyses in further chapters of this study, here we partially anticipate, as we did in the entire analysis of consciousness, what will later be discussed more extensively. This time we are concerned with the particular sphere of man's vitality originating from the emotive element of his psyche. It is known that the conscious action of man, or precisely, acts are linked in various ways with the influence of this element or bind it in themselves. Because of this, *voluntarium,* as the activity of the will that is essential to these acts, undergoes various modifications. This, of course, interests us immensely in our entire study of person and act. However,

we first wish to examine these modifications in the aspect or dimension of consciousness in the same way consciousness was revealed here, in a sense distinguished and moved to the foreground in all our inquiries.

Consciousness mirrors man's own "I" and his acts while at the same time allowing him to experience this "I," to experience himself and his acts.[35b] Both cases in some way involve one's own body. Man has consciousness of his body and also experiences it; he also experiences his own "bodiliness," just as he does his own sensuality and affectivity. These lived-experiences go hand in hand with consciousness-related mirroring, and therefore self-knowledge directs them as well. We easily discover its contribution on account of a certain abstractness of the contents made conscious and experienced. After all, to experience one's own body is one thing and to experience one's own bodiliness is another. What occurs here is a difference in the degree of intellectual abstraction that belongs to the process of understanding and, in relation to one's own "I," to the process of self-knowledge. Self-knowledge creates the semantic side of the consciousness-related reflection, the side that, together with the reflexive function of consciousness, passes into lived-experience and determines its character as regards content. In acts of self-knowledge and relying on self-experience, man understands his own "I" both particularly and as a whole. Concerning the understanding of the body, *self-knowledge, as well as consciousness, owes a great deal to particular bodily sensations.* We know that neither the organism in all its particular internal structure nor the particular vegetative processes that occur in it constitute, generally speaking, the object of self-knowledge or of consciousness. Self-knowledge, and consciousness with it, reaches as far or, rather, as deep into the organism and its life as sensations allow. It happens very often, for instance, due to an illness that evokes corresponding bodily sensations, that man becomes conscious of this or that organ or of a vegetative process within himself. In general, the human body, and all that is more or less directly connected with it, constitutes first the object of sensations and only later the object of self-knowledge and consciousness. [36a]We take "first" and "later" not necessarily in a chronological sense, but only in the sense of a natural adequation of the object and subjective acts. The sensory acts correspond to the lived-experience of the body more closely than do the acts of understanding from which consciousness is in some way built. Nonetheless, man experiences not only sensation of his body but also consciousness of it.[36b]

The world of sensations[xxiii] has its objective richness in man, who is a sensing being and not only a thinking one. This richness corresponds in some degree to the structure of man and of the world outside him. Sensations are diversified not only quantitatively but also qualitatively—in this respect they form a certain hierarchy. Qualitatively higher sensations participate in the spiritual life of man. In one of the subsequent chapters of this book we will conduct a separate analysis of human emotivity as a particular property of the psyche. It is known that man's entire emotional life bears a great importance in the formation of human acts. It is known, and numerous manuals of ethics state this fact, that affections in some respect intensify our action, although in another respect they have a limiting or at times even paralyzing influence on what is essential in that action, namely, on *voluntarium*. We stated previously that *voluntarium* denotes a participation of the free will in action, which is at the same time conscious action. As is evident, in this chapter we concern ourselves with conscious action (thus also *voluntarium*) in the aspect of consciousness.

In what does the essence of the emotionalization of consciousness consist? (An attempted analysis)

Only in that aspect do we want to analyze the influence of the emotive element. However, *this analysis will be aspectual*, not integral. *We are concerned with the emotionalization of consciousness,* for this is what we have decided to call this particular influence of the emotive element on the consciousness of action (which, of course, is not without significance for the entire dynamism of the person, for conscious action, that is, act).[14]

---

14. Thereby, we ascribe to consciousness, and especially to self-consciousness, in the structure of the person a certain function of possessing oneself, which other authors also note. See Nuttin, for instance: "Cette perception et connaissance, ou *conscience*, de soi est une forme de *possession de soi*, qui constitue un élément essentiel d'un psychisme personnalisé." [This perception and knowledge, or *consciousness*, of self is a form of *self-possession*, which constitutes an essential element of a personalized psyche.] Nuttin, *La structure de la personnalité*, 22. (It is another matter whether self-consciousness in Nuttin's understanding means the same as in this study.)

The problem of the emotionalization of consciousness is analyzed here precisely with the presupposition that consciousness conditions a certain possession and governance of oneself in the structure of the human person. If in the subsequent chapter the author links self-possession

The gist of the problem consists in the fact that emotions, emotive facts in the various forms in which they occur ("happen") in man as a subject, not only are reflected in consciousness but also influence in a uniquely proper way the consciousness-related mirroring of various objects, beginning with one's own "I" and acts. Various sensations emotionalize consciousness—which means that they enter its functions, namely, the mirroring and the reflexive, and slightly modify their character. This is manifested first of all in consciousness-related reflection, which in a sense loses its distance from emotion and the objects encompassed by this emotion. As we know from the previous analysis, consciousness owes this distance to self-knowledge. Self-knowledge also has a certain ability to objectivize emotions and sensations. In that case, consciousness has at its disposal the meanings of the emotive facts occurring in the subject, and precisely thanks to this it preserves an objectivizing distance from these facts and the objects encompassed by them. Although emotions themselves "happen" in man, the same man is conscious of them and in a sense governs them through consciousness. This governance of consciousness over emotion is very important for interior integration. "Consciousness-related" governance over emotion certainly does not take place outside the will, without its participation. Therefore, only on the basis of that governance can a moral value be formed. We are faced with the reciprocal permeation of consciousness and the will; *consciousness-related governance over the spontaneous emotive dynamism that conditions* voluntarium—*that is, the action proper to the will—is at the same time conditioned by the will.*

Emotionalization of consciousness starts when, in the mirroring, the meaning of particular emotive facts and of the objects encompassed by them vanishes, when sensations in a sense grow beyond actual comprehension by man. Properly speaking, this is a collapse of self-knowledge. For consciousness does not cease to mirror these emotive facts the way they "happen" in man but loses its superior, that is, its objective, relation to them. It is known that objectivization is in this case the proper function of self-knowledge. The collapse of the objective relation of

---

and self-governance directly with self-determination, that is, with the will, then this position will manifest all the more the joint and in a sense homogeneous function of consciousness and self-determination, that is, of the will in the integral structure of the person and act.

consciousness to sensations and affections that "happen" in man, and to the objects encompassed by them, originates from the fact that self-knowledge in a sense ceases to objectivize. It does not establish meanings and thereby does not keep emotions in intellectual dependence. Why does this happen? Reasons for that can differ. What is most often indicated as the reason is the strength, that is, the intensity, of affections, their changeability, the quickness in which one follows the other. This explains the problem unilaterally. For, on the other hand, *we also need to take into consideration the smaller or greater efficiency of self-knowledge.* Just like any other knowledge, self-knowledge is, after all, subject to the laws of efficiency and therefore can handle better or worse its own object (by which we mean here the "objective material" that for self-knowledge is all facts connected with one's own "I"—emotive facts being precisely such facts). Let us stress again that our point concerns not an effective "mastery over affections," which is the task of the will (and of the corresponding virtues as moral habits, in accord with the Aristotelian conception), but only a particular "governance over sensations," namely, the governance that is a task of self-knowledge and self-consciousness. (Let us defer an attempt to explain the relation of sensations to affections until a separate chapter, one that will cover issues concerning emotivity.)

Self-knowledge has here a fundamental task to perform, and therefore its efficiency is very important. It seems that consciousness itself is not subject to the laws of efficiency. We do not think that it can be more or less efficient, although it can be more or less developed or mature. Self-knowledge in a sense takes on the whole efficient side of consciousness. It is self-knowledge that should work to prevent the emotionalization of consciousness, so that consciousness is not deprived of the objectivizing relation to the totality of emotive facts. Sensations in the subject that is man undergo undulation, as it were. Sometimes they surge, that is, they multiply and, above all, gain strength. For in every man a specific emotive dynamic exists as an objective psychical fact. This dynamic is expressed by the degree of intensity of particular sensations or of their entire groups or "resultants." (It seems that we can also speak of certain "resultants" of emotional lived-experiences in man.)

Emotionalization in relation to the twofold function of consciousness: Mirroring and lived-experience

A certain degree of this intensity of emotion conditions the normal or even correct functioning of consciousness; however, at the moment of exceeding this degree—like a threshold—the emotionalization of consciousness begins. Due to either an excessive quantity or strength of affections—excessive in relation to the threshold—or an insufficient efficiency of self-knowledge, this knowledge is unable to objectivize affections, that is, to identify them intellectually. Thus, the semantic side of the facts possessing an emotive character is lost, as it were. At first, consciousness still mirrors these facts as "something that happens in me." However, with their greater intensity or a greater helplessness of actual self-knowledge, consciousness, while continuing to mirror the facts, does so only as "something that happens," as if losing their connection with the "I." The fundamental content of consciousness—one's own "I"—is in a sense pushed to the background, and the intensified sensations behave as if they were severed from the basis whence both their unity and their semantic plurality and distinctness originate. For in the normal course of events, self-knowledge objectivizes both this unity in one's own "I" and the semantic distinctness of particular emotions. In moments of emotionalization, however, especially extreme emotionalization, they in a sense fall directly into consciousness. It does not cease to mirror them, but this mirroring lacks the element of any objectivization and understanding, for self-knowledge has not provided it. [37a]Man is then conscious of his emotions but does not govern them by his consciousness.

Hand in hand with emotionalization in the sphere of consciousness-related mirroring goes the emotionalization of lived-experience. As we said, consciousness does not cease to mirror—even in the greatest intensity of emotions and sensations we still discover this consciousness-related mirroring, although it no longer possesses the proper significance for forming lived-experiences in the emotional sphere of the whole interior life. The reflexive function of consciousness, the one that shapes lived-experience, then loses its decisive influence. It is worth noting that with a significant intensification of affections or passions, man, properly speaking, ceases to "experience" them and only "lives by" them;

rather, he allows them to live in him and off him in an original, or, so to speak, "impersonal," way. For a lived-experience is personal when the lived-experience of the subjectivity of one's own "I" is also manifested. However, *the emotive facts* as passions (*passiones*), even though they possess their own original subjectivity, *do not contribute in themselves to the lived-experience of subjectivity in which the personal "I" is manifested as the source of lived-experiences, as the center governing emotion*. All this is connected to the reflexive influence of consciousness. What sometimes impedes this influence is the very movement or invasion of sensations, with respect to which the reflexive function of consciousness is, so to speak, inhibited. Man then simply "lives by" his affections—he allows them "to live" in him according to the measure of their original subjectivity—but he does not "experience" them subjectively such that the personal "I" is manifested in this lived-experience as its authentic center.

As we see, the problem of the emotionalization of consciousness is very complex and—each time—very individual, that is, unrepeatable. It happens sometimes that, even with maximum intensity of emotion, consciousness does not yield to "emotionalization" in the sense described here—it does not cease "to govern over emotion." However, the opposite also happens; namely, the "emotionalization of consciousness" occurs with an (objectively) weaker movement of emotion. We do not intend to analyze such issues here. What interests us is the very essence of the problem—precisely *from the viewpoint of consciousness and the co-constitution of the personal subjectivity of the human "I" in which consciousness participates*, as we attempted to show in the previous paragraph. The truly human—personal—lived-experience of affections, and in this sense the emotional lived-experience itself, seems to demand the threshold of consciousness that we mentioned earlier. Up to a certain intensity of sensations, consciousness functions normally with respect to both mirroring and reflexivity. What can be formed then are authentic, affective lived-experiences in all their subjective completion and not merely the original emotive facts onto which consciousness cannot confer the subjective profile proper to the personal "I," even though these facts undoubtedly reside in the subject. For the emotionalization of consciousness impedes or even prevents its proper actualization.[37b]

By writing all this, we did not intend in the least to prejudge the value of sensations and emotions for man's interior life and morality. We shall devote a separate chapter to this matter.

6. Subjectivity and Subjectivism
Subjectivity closely belongs to the reality of the person and act

The analyses conducted thus far enable us to pose this problem, and indirectly they even demand posing it. Our aim is to clearly distinguish man's subjectivity—which we consider here together with the analysis of consciousness—from subjectivism as a certain mental attitude, which we definitely want to avoid. To ascertain the man-person's subjectivity has a fundamental significance for the realism and, indeed, the objectivism of our study. *For in reality man is a subject and experiences himself as a subject.* The dynamic relation—or correlation—between person and act is realized on this basis. Without ascertaining the subjectivity of man, no plane exists on which we could comprehensively grasp this relation. The aspect of consciousness has a fundamental significance for ascertaining the subjectivity of man. It is thanks to consciousness that man experiences himself as a subject. He experiences, thus, he is a subject in the most strictly experiential sense. Here, understanding grows directly from experience without any intermediary stages, without reasoning. Man experiences his acts as the action of which he—the person—is the agent. This efficacy, which we shall consider in the next chapter, becomes evident thanks to lived-experience and appears as such to us in the aspect of consciousness. Thus, we must draw closer to lived-experience—and to its proper basis, the subjectivity of man—in order to grasp efficacy as a fact that is fully experiential. By grasping subjectivity only in the metaphysical way, by stating that man as an objective being is a true subject of existence and action—that is, a *suppositum*—we abstract ourselves to a considerable extent from what is for us a source of visualizations, a source of experience. Therefore, it is better to attempt some coordination and union of both aspects, namely, the aspect of being (of man, person) and the aspect of consciousness, the aspect of "act" (action and the act) and the aspect of lived-experience.

This is important due not only to methodological considerations (of which we already spoke in the introductory chapter) but also to objective ones. We indicated this a moment ago by stating that without a possibly complete delineation of man's subjectivity, there can be no full delineation of the dynamic relation between person and act. For this relation is not only mirrored in consciousness, as if in the interior mirror of man's existence and action; rather, thanks to this consciousness, the relation's definitive, subjective form is also determined in its own way. It is thus the form of lived-experience, of the lived-experience of the act, of the efficacious lived-experience of the relation of person to act, and of the lived-experience of the moral value that germinates in this dynamic configuration. *All these are objective facts, which nonetheless possess their objectivity and realness only and exclusively in the subjectivity of man.* Without the full revelation of this subjectivity there is no way of reaching and explicating the full and objectively comprehensive content of these facts. Let us add that subjectivism can also develop due to a too narrow and unilateral objectivism. What protects us from this is a possibly comprehensive analysis of the object in all its aspects.

> By what does subjectivity differ from subjectivism (and where does the boundary pass between them)?

Subjectivism in the given case would consist in [38a]completely separating lived-experience from act[38b] and in reducing moral values—which germinate (as we figuratively stated) in precisely these acts, as well as in the person through their efficacious dependence on him—to the very contents of consciousness. [39a]What we speak of at present was described previously as the absolutization of an aspect.[39b] Intellectual reduction connected with the absolutization of the experiential aspect characterizes precisely this mental attitude, namely, subjectivism, and, in a further perspective, idealism. The experiential aspect is undoubtedly consciousness, which under the subjectivistic mental attitude undergoes an absolutization and thus ceases to be an aspect. As long as consciousness is understood as an aspect—an understanding that we attempted to follow throughout this entire chapter—it simply helps us to understand more fully the subjectivity of man, especially in his interior relation to his own acts. *However, once consciousness ceases to be understood as an aspect, it also ceases to explain subjectivity, that is, the subjectivity of* man and of his acts, and it itself becomes [40a]an ersatz subject[40b]. *Subjectivism understands consciousness as an integral and exclusive subject*—the subject of lived-experiences and values if the field of moral lived-experiences is concerned. Regrettably, under this assumption, with this mental attitude, both lived-experiences and [41a] values cease to be something real. They remain only as contents of consciousness: *esse = percipi*.[15] Finally, consciousness itself ceases to be something real and becomes merely a thought subject of contents. The path to subjectivism ends in idealism.

We can say that this path has a certain basis in the purely consciousness-related character of the acts of consciousness. We stated previously that these acts and the consciousness wholly contained within them are in themselves, so to speak, indifferent to real objects, even to their own "I" as a real object. They do not objectivize anything but only mirror. Everything in them is only content, and they owe their objectivity and realness to self-knowledge. [42a]Self-knowledge creates the semantic side of consciousness. Idealism consists in a complete canceling of the semantic side of consciousness, whereas subjectivism leads to it. We can say that—with respect to an analysis of the subjective aspect of being and action—both these mental attitudes are identified with the conception of a complete separation of consciousness from self-knowledge. One's own "I" ceases to be an object for consciousness, as do one's acts—they remain mere contents of consciousness.[42b] *Thus, the boundary of objectivity and realism in the conception of man—and in our case we mean the "person-act" totality—is marked by the acknowledgment of self-knowledge.* Despite its consciousness-related character, the consciousness integrated by self-knowledge retains the objective sense and with it the objective status in the subjective structure of man. [43a]In this sense and with this status, it is only the key to the subjectivity of man, not the basis for subjectivism. Consciousness is the key to the subjectivity of man by the

---

15. Berkeley distinguishes two ways of existing: the *esse* of things is equivalent to *percipi*, whereas the *esse* of spiritual beings is equivalent to *percipere et velle*. Considering the views of various philosophers, we must note the meaning of the term "consciousness" adopted each time, for it can simply denote "a conscious being." [11a]Hence, for example, in Ingarden, "it [i.e., consciousness] is a being that exists for the sake of itself, and in its pure existence it possesses a certain 'knowledge' about itself. This knowledge is that consciousness knows about itself. 'Experiencing' (*erlebt*) other objects, namely, having them 'given,' it experiences (*durchlebt*) itself and is nothing else than this experiencing itself." Roman Ingarden, *U podstaw teorii poznania* (Warsaw: Państwowe Wydawnictwo Naukowe, 1971), 368–69.[11b]

fact that it conditions lived-experience in which the human "I" manifests itself directly (experientially) as a subject.[43b]

At the threshold of the analysis of human efficacy

It seems that, having explained all of this, we can finally disengage ourselves from the aspect of consciousness in order to move on to the analysis of efficacy. At the same time, however, we take with us the entire outcome of the previous analysis and bring it into our further inquiries on the dynamism proper to the human person. This dynamism, and, in particular, efficacy as an essential moment of the dynamic procession of the act from the person, is not only realized in the field of consciousness but also thoroughly permeated by consciousness, as we have attempted to demonstrate in this chapter. A certain exclusion of the aspect of consciousness—as if we were placing it outside the parentheses—manifested perhaps even more profoundly the presence of consciousness in the acts of the person and the specific function performed by consciousness in forming the particular subjectivity of the person—the subjectivity from which the act emerges, also by virtue of efficacy.

Efficacy has a different specificity. It is clear, however, that in no way can the specificity of human efficacy be grasped in isolation from consciousness. Each of them specifically determines the person and act.

CHAPTER 2 ✺ The Analysis of Efficacy in Relation to the Dynamism of Man

1. [1a]Fundamental Visualizations and Concepts concerning the Dynamism of Man[1b]

An introductory note concerning the relation of dynamism to consciousness

Having better understood the function of consciousness, we disengage ourselves from the aspect of consciousness in order to analyze the fact "man acts." This fact is given to us first in the lived-experience "I act." Thanks to lived-experience, we reside mostly, as it were, inside this fact. Lived-experience contains the fullness of experience, on the basis of which the fact "man acts" is formed by way of analogy and generalization. For the "I" is a man, and every man is an "I"—a second "I," a third "I," etc. Hence, this action—when "you act," "he acts," or "whoever acts"—*can also be understood and interpreted on the basis of the experience contained in "I act."* The lived-experience of action is subjective in the sense that it keeps us within the concrete subjectivity of the human "I," without, however, obscuring the intersubjectivity needed for the understanding and interpretation of human action.

The objectivization of the fact "man acts" also requires grasping the integral dynamism of man in an objective way.[1] For this experiential fact

---

1. Further analysis will gradually show in what sense the author uses the term "dynamism." It is known that this term is connected to the Greek *dýnamis*, having both Platonic and Aristotelian genealogy; from there it was passed on to medieval philosophy (*potentia*). In modern philosophy, dynamism (Leibniz) is opposed to mechanism (Descartes). "Dynamics," which we most often understand—also in the context of this study—as the opposite of statics, is very closely linked to dynamism.

appears not in isolation from but in relation to the entire dynamism of man and in a strict organic connection with it. We mean here the integral dynamism that is given to us in the integral experience of man. Not everything that composes it is mirrored in consciousness. So, for instance, almost the entire vegetative dynamism proper to the human body is not mirrored in consciousness. Additionally, not all facts that compose the integral dynamism of man are consciously experienced by him. We have already had a chance to briefly consider the incommensurability that exists between the whole of life in man and the scope or range of his lived-experiences. The cursory remark previously made on that topic will yet be expanded and complemented in our further inquiries. At any rate, the necessity to disengage from the aspect of consciousness and also from the scope of lived-experiences themselves when grasping the dynamism proper to man seems to be dictated precisely by the demands of experience. Not without reason did we distinguish in the introductory chapter the integral experience of man from its aspects, although then the interior aspect already appeared to be particularly linked to consciousness.

Nonetheless, not only does the dynamism proper to man find its fundamental mirroring in consciousness, but also man is conscious of the principal directions of this dynamism, and this is connected with experiencing them. *After all, man experiences action as something fundamentally different from what happens*, that is, from what only takes place in man and in which man as man is not active. This lived-experience—as well as the diversification in the field of lived-experiences—of two objectively different structures, namely, "man acts" and "something happens in man," attests, on the one hand, to the fundamental adherence of consciousness to the being in man. On the other hand, this diversification of lived-experience confers on each of these structures the interiorization and subjectivization that we generally owe to consciousness. However, at present we are interested not in lived-experiences [2a] *but precisely in the structures* whose objective diversification is based on the integral experience of man and not merely on the exclusive witness of consciousness. The interior experience—concerning all that happens inside the human body, what belongs to the life of the organism—must constantly reach beyond the spontaneous and provisional witness of consciousness alone and of the lived-experiences connected with it; it must constantly supplement them [3a]from without[3b], so that the cognition of man in this field is as integral as possible.

The distinction between "man acts" (action) and "something happens in man" (happening) as the experiential basis of the category *agere-pati*

The two objective structures, namely, "man acts" and "something happens in man," determine two fundamental directions of the dynamism proper to man. These directions are opposite inasmuch as the activity of the subject "man" in the one and his passivity in the other are manifested—and also realized. In each of these elementary directions of the dynamism proper to man, the phenomenon, that is, the content of visualization, corresponds to the real structure, and, conversely, each of the structures appears as a phenomenon. *The activity and passivity—* agere *and* pati—*are made manifest in them as the* constitutivum *of the structures and the objective basis of their diversification.* The *agere* contained in the structure "man acts" is something different from the *pati* in the structure "something happens in man"; it is something opposite to *pati*. The entire structure, the one and the other, participates in this opposition. It is known that both *agere* and *pati* constitute two separate categories in Aristotle's metaphysics. [4a]The experience of human action and of what happens in man certainly greatly helped[4b] in distinguishing these categories.[2]

---

2. By starting the analysis of the dynamism proper to man by distinguishing "man acts" and "something happens in man" as its fundamental structures, we touch upon what seems to be most original in experience. This diversification, to which, according to Aristotelian metaphysics, two separate categories seem to correspond, namely, ποιεῖν and πάσχειν or παθεῖν, is also given in experience: thus, it appears as directly evident in man's cognition. See Aristotle, *Metaphysics* 9.1.1046a19–22: φανερὸν οὖν ὅτι ἔστι μὲν ὡς μία δύναμις τοῦ ποιεῖν καὶ πάσχειν (δυνατὸν γάρ ἐστι καὶ τῷ ἔχειν αὐτὸ δύναμιν τοῦ παθεῖν καὶ τῷ ἄλλο ὑπ' αὐτοῦ), ἔστι δὲ ὡς ἄλλη [Obviously, then, in a sense the potency of acting and of being acted on is one (for a thing may be "capable" either because it can itself be acted on or because something else can be acted on by it), but in a sense the potencies are different.] [Editorial note: For all of Aristotle's works, Wojtyła most likely used *Aristotelis opera omnia: graece et latine* (Paris: Firmin Didot, 1848–83) or *Aristotelis opera*, 5 vols. (Berlin: Academia Regia Borussica, 1831–70). Unless otherwise indicated, all English translations of Aristotle's works are taken from *The Basic Works of Aristotle*, ed. Richard McKeon (New York: Modern Library, 2001)].

The author asks himself about the relation of the starting point for the analyses intended in this study to Paul Ricoeur's *Le volontaire et l'involontaire*, vol. 1 of *Philosophie de la volonté* (Paris: Aubier, 1967).

These two categories—*agere* and *pati*—not only oppose but also condition and explain each other in man just as they do in metaphysics. Every one of us can draw in himself a line of demarcation, as it were, that separates action from what happens, although the one not only differs from but also is explained by the other. This is very important for understanding the structure "man acts" and, in turn, for interpreting it fairly thoroughly. We can say that what takes place between the action of man and all that happens in him is not only an opposition, but also a clear correlation [5a]resulting from a fundamental equivalence[5b] of both facts or both structures. [6a]This equivalence has its basis precisely in the dynamism of man,[6b] for when we ascertain action by saying that "man acts," and when we ascertain a happening taking place in man by saying that "something happens in man," *then in both cases man appears as a dynamic subject*. Both action and what happens in man reveal and at the same time—each in its own way—*realize the dynamism proper to man*. [7a]Both have their source in man, precisely in his dynamism. Thus we cannot speak of two different directions of the dynamism of man. There is one direction, namely, "from within"; this direction belongs to the essence of every dynamism. If previously we spoke of two different directions of the dynamism proper to man, it was only in the sense of the differentiation that is conferred on this dynamism by *agere* and *pati*—activity and passivity. The former (activity) distinguishes action, that is, act, from the other manifestations and realizations of the dynamism proper to man.[7b]

From this point of view, perhaps we should also take notice of two different forms of passivity that are expressed in the statements "something happens *in man*" and "something happens *to man*." These statements are used interchangeably in colloquial speech, and so sometimes when we say that something happens to man we wish to indicate what happens in him. Strictly speaking, what happens "to man" indicates suffering from without. Such passivity is different. Man is then not the dynamic subject of the happening that has its source in him but rather an object to which some other subject or even some other power does something while he merely suffers. Suffering in itself speaks of the passivity of the subject "man," but it does not speak—at least not directly—of the interior dynamism of that subject, in particular of the dynamism that the statement "something happens in man" indicates.

The Coupling *Potentia–Actus* as Conceptually Corresponding to Dynamism Is in a Sense Irreplaceable

In the traditional conception of person and act, the dynamism proper to man was grasped by an analogy to the dynamism of every being. Metaphysics concerns itself with the dynamism of being, and it is to metaphysics—and in particular to its great creator, Aristotle—that we owe the conception that expresses being's dynamic character in philosophical language. This conception consists not in the sole concept of *actus* *but in the pair of concepts* potentia–actus, *which are linked into one mental whole*. The linking is so essential for them that by using one of them we at the same time indicate the other. For the one always contains correlated content without the grasp of which the other remains unintelligible, and vice versa. Thus *actus* cannot be understood without *potentia*, nor *potentia* without *actus*.[3] Concerning the terms themselves, they are in a sense untranslatable into Polish, especially the term *actus*. The term *potentia* would have "potency" [*możność*] as its corresponding noun in Polish. Potency denotes what in some way already is and at the same time is not: it is in preparedness, in disposition, and even in readiness, but not, however, in reality[8a]. *Actus*, which is present in philosophical manuals in the polonized form as "act" [*akt*], is the same as the realization of potency, its fulfillment.

As we see, the meaning of both concepts is closely correlative; it

---

3. See, for example, Aristotle, *Metaphysics* 9.1.1045b34–35: ἐπεὶ δὲ λέγεται τὸ ὂν τὸ μὲν τὸ τὶ ἢ ποιὸν ἢ ποσόν, τὸ δὲ κατὰ δύναμιν καὶ ἐντελέχειαν καὶ κατὰ τὸ ἔργον ["Being" is in one way divided into individual thing, quality, and quantity, and is in another way distinguished in respect of potency and complete reality]; and 1046a1–2: ἐπὶ πλέον γάρ ἐστιν ἡ δύναμις καὶ ἡ ἐνέργεια τῶν μόνον λεγομένων κατὰ κίνησιν [For potency and actuality extend beyond the cases that involve a reference to motion]. Also see, among many other places, *Metaphysics* 12.5.1071a4–5.
See also Thomas Aquinas: "In uno et eodem quod exit de potentia in actum, prius sit potentia quam actus tempore, simpliciter tamen actus prior est potentia: quia quod est in potentia, non reducitur in actum nisi per ens actu." [For although in any single thing that passes from potentiality to actuality, the potentiality is prior in time to the actuality; nevertheless, absolutely speaking, actuality is prior to potentiality; for whatever is in potentiality can be reduced into actuality only by some being in actuality.] *Summa theologiae* I, q. 3, a. 1; see also q. 3, a. 8. Additionally, "Potentia, secundum illud quod est potentia, ordinatur ad actum. Unde oportet rationem potentiae accipi ex actu ad quem ordinatur." [A power as such is directed to an act. Wherefore we seek to know the nature of a power from the act to which it is directed.] *Summa theologiae* I, q. 77, a. 3.

inheres not so much in each of them separately as in their linking. This linking indicates not only two states of being, simultaneously diversified from and adhering to each other, but also the transition from one of them into the other. This transition objectivizes the structure of every dynamism that inheres in being—in being as such (for being constitutes the proper object of metaphysics) and, at the same time, in every being and any being, regardless of the field of human knowledge that considers that being specifically. We can say that at this point metaphysics turns out to be the soil of thought in which the roots of all the sciences inhere. So far we do not know another conception or language that would render the dynamic essence of change and *all changes taking place in any being, except for this one conception and this one language with which we were endowed by the philosophy of* potentia–actus. *Every dynamism* taking place in any being *can be adequately grasped on the basis of this conception and with the help of this language.* We must use these when we grasp the dynamism proper to man.

The concept of actus—this is what we can call it for short, knowing what sort of correlativity it entails—*has above all an existential sense.* The two terms essential for this conception (potency and act) do not merely indicate two different states of being to which correspond two different kinds of existence (*existentia*). For the transition from potency to act, that is, the so-called actualization, is also a transition in the order of existence; it indicates a certain *fieri*, that is, a becoming—not in the absolute sense, for such belongs only to the *fieri*-becoming out of nothing, but in the relative sense, namely, that of the *fieri* relying on a being that already exists, the *fieri* within a being's own internal structure. A being's dynamism is joined with its very existence and at the same time constitutes the basis and source of all structures that we can find in this being. Every actualization contains potency and *actus* as its real fulfillment, thus not as two essences but as [9a]two existences[9b] correlative to each other. Actualization always implicates the following configuration of existences: that which exists in potency, by the fact that it exists in potency, can exist *in actu*; and that which already exists *in actu* exists due to the potency in which it earlier existed. In actualization, potency and *actus* are, so to speak, two moments or two phases of a concrete existence, joined in a dynamic unity. *Actus*, however, denotes not only the completed state of fulfilled potency but also the very transition from potency to this state, the being-fulfilled itself.[10a]

A certain ambiguity of the concept of *actus* in relation to the diversified experiences of "action" and "happening"

By relating the concept *actus* to the dynamism that is proper to man and that also constitutes the vital core of the dynamic linking of act and person, we must state at this stage in our reflections that *this concept coincides with both of the fundamental forms of man's dynamism known from experience* and, to a large extent, from lived-experience. The structure "man acts" and the structure "something happens in man" both constitute the concretization of his proper dynamism. Their equivalence consists in the fact that man appears as a dynamic subject in both of them. This equivalence is from the viewpoint of man's dynamism itself. From this point of view, having presumed the analogy of being, *we can grasp both man's action and what happens in him as the fulfillment of a certain potency. Both of them are actualization, the dynamic unity of potency and act.* The general dynamism of man entitles us to grasp them this way. It also entitles us to seek and define the potencies that inhere in man at the origin of both various actions and various "happenings" (if we may express "that which happens" in the nounal form).

The difference between man's action and what happens "in man," the difference of the *agere–pati* type, the difference between dynamic activity and passivity, does not obscure or eliminate man's dynamism, which inheres in both forms. It does not obscure this dynamism with respect to phenomenological experience, and it does not eliminate it with respect to the need for a realistic interpretation. The concept *actus* fundamentally explains the dynamism of man. In this sense, the word *actus*—and we should remember that this word belongs to precisely defined philosophical language—adequately renders the dynamic content of both structures, namely, "man acts" and "something happens in man." The question is whether it fully renders the specificity of the act as well. To pose the problem more properly, let us ask how the word *actus*, while rendering the dynamism of every being as well as any dynamism of man—both *agere* and *pati*—can fully render the specificity of the act.

2. [11a]The Specificity of Efficacy[11b]

The basis for the diversification of the experiences of "action" and "happening" is the lived-experience of efficacy

In the manuals we usually encounter the distinction between *actus humanus* and *actus hominis*. In this way, act is distinguished by means of the attribute *humanus* from all the other actualizations that occur in man (*actus hominis*). It seems, however, that the sense of this distinction is technical rather than substantive; it also indicates a difference rather than explaining it. After all, *actus humanus* (which can be translated as "human action") is at the same time the action of man, that is, *actus hominis* in the literal translation. Thus we first need to explain when and why the action of man is not human action, in order to understand that only human action is the proper action of man, that is, to understand the content of the structure "man acts." [12a]We can find such an explanation in every manual. Thus, we shall not repeat it here. However, in our own explanation, we shall try to keep to the starting points that have already been established—at least in the previous analysis.[12b]

Our starting point is the ascertainment of the experiential difference that occurs in the totality of man's dynamism between "man acts" and "something happens in man." By investigating the facts, we ascertain that *this fundamental difference is determined by the moment of efficacy*. What we understand by the moment of efficacy in this case is the lived-experience "I am the agent." This lived-experience distinguishes human action from everything that merely happens in him. It also explains the opposition of facts and structures in which activity and passivity are clearly manifested. When I act, then I experience myself as the agent of this form of dynamizing my own subject. When something happens in me, then the dynamization has occurred without the efficacious contribution of my "I." It is in order to indicate dynamism without efficacy, without the efficacious contribution of man, that we describe this type of fact as something that happens in me. Thus, in the dynamism of man there appears an essential difference resulting from the lived-experience of efficacy. The first form of man's dynamism is the one in which he himself appears as the agent, that is, as the cause conscious of his causation—and this form we describe by the statement "man acts." The second form of man's dynamism is the one in which man is not conscious of his efficacy, in which he does not experience it—and this form we describe by the statement "something happens in man."

The opposition of action and happening, of activity and passivity, makes evident yet another *opposition that results from the lived-experience of efficacy or its lack*. Objective efficacy corresponds to the lived-experience of efficacy, for this lived-experience introduces us into the structure of the efficacious "I." The lack of the lived-experience of efficacy, the lack of the commitment of the efficacious "I" to what merely happens in man, cannot mean the objective lack of [13a]this efficacy[13b]. If something happens, if some internal change takes place in man, then the cause of this change must exist. Experience, in which the interior aspect is particularly manifested, attests only that one's own "I" is not that cause in the same way as is the case in the act, in action.

The lived-experience of efficacy reveals the causal connection between person and act

Thus, although the moment of efficacy—the efficacy present in action and absent in happening—does not at first explain this cause, it does indicate the particular dynamic structure of human action and of the one who acts. He who in acting experiences himself as the agent thereby [14a]stands in a sense above his action[14b]. Action as such depends on him for its existence—he gives it its beginning, and he sustains its existence. To be a cause means to evoke the coming into existence and the existence of an effect, its *fieri* and *esse*. Man is the cause of his action in a most fully experiential way. The clearly experienced causal connection between person and act takes place. This connection causes the person, that is, every concrete human "I," to have to consider the act not only as the effect of his efficacy and as his possession but also—due to the moral character of the act—as the field of his responsibility. Responsibility and a sense of possession in a particular way qualify the causation itself and the very efficacy of the person in the act. Those who concern themselves with issues of causality, on the one hand, and psychologists, on the other hand, often state that human action is actually the only full experience of efficient causality. [15a]Without investigating the rightness of this thesis, we must nonetheless accept the part of it that ascertains in action a particular evidentness of man's efficacy, of the person in the act.[15b]

The lived-experience of efficacy manifests man's transcendence in relation to his own action

Efficacy itself as the relation between cause and effect introduces us into the objective order of existence; it is thus of an existential nature. In our case, efficacy is at the same time a lived-experience. Hence originates the particular empirical expression of human efficacy connected to action. As noted above, on the one hand this efficacy draws man into the form of his own dynamism, which is action, and on the other hand it sustains him above that dynamism. What also takes place in the structure "man acts" is *something that should be described as the immanence of man in his own action and, at the same time, something that we shall describe as his transcendence with respect to this action.* The moment of efficacy—the lived-experience of efficacy—manifests above all the transcendence of man with respect to his own action. However, the transcendence proper to the lived-experience "I am the agent of action" passes into the immanence of the lived-experience of action itself: when "I act," I am already wholly in my action, in this dynamization of my "I," to which I contributed efficaciously. One would not be fulfilled without the other. The "efficacious I" and the "acting I" form a dynamic synthesis and a dynamic unity every time in every act. This is precisely the synthesis and unity of the person with the act.

However, this unity neither blurs nor destroys difference. It is precisely this that characterizes the structure "man acts" and differentiates it from the structure "something happens in man." Man is clearly the subject in action because he is the agent. In happening, it is not man but "something" that manifests itself as efficacious; man is only the passive subject. He passively experiences his own dynamism. In keeping with experience, in no way can we describe what happens in him as action, even though happening is always some actualization. The term *actus* is not as phenomenologically determined as "action" or, even more so, "act" is. The latter concerns not just any actualization, any dynamization of the subject "man," but only the dynamization in which man as the "I" is active, that is, experiences himself as the agent. According to the witness of integral experience, then and only then does man perform an act.

The lived-experience of efficacy allows us to differentiate "act" from various kinds of actuation

Every *other dynamization of man in which he as the concrete "I" is not active, that is, does not as the "I" experience his efficacy, could be called*—in keeping with the spirit of our language—*"actuation"* [*uczynnienie*]. Actuation occurs when something only happens in man, though this happening originates from the interior dynamism of man himself. It is evoked from within, yet differently from what man does, from what is his act. The word "actuation" seems to link perfectly the moment of passivity with the moment of certain activity, or, in any case, with that of actualization. This word is sometimes used in the natural sciences but, strictly speaking, is not applied in the science of man, even though it seems to render perfectly and even in a sense explain the experiential difference taking place between the fact "man acts" and the fact "something happens in man." However, *it perfectly expresses the opposition to "act"* (*act–actuation*) by referring to colloquial language and the semantic differences that inhere in it.

At this point, it seems that the dynamism proper to man is at first glance adequately characterized. This first glance is connected with the experiential diversification of this dynamism through the facts of action and the facts of happening that take place in man. [16a]We can say that it itself is above all experiential.[16b] At this first experiential glance, all the specificity of linking person and act already emerges from the structure "man acts." We see it through the moment of efficacy, which is at the same time the moment of the transcendence of the person with respect to action. *The linking of person and act is accomplished precisely through this moment of transcendence*, and therefore we must yet subject it to a special, thorough analysis.

Man "creates himself" through the act: At the foundation of human ethos

A particular dependence of action on the person accompanies efficacy and transcendence. Man *is* not only the agent of his action but *also its creator*. The task of evoking the coming to existence and the existence of the effect belongs to the essence of efficacy. However, the task of forming a work belongs to the essence of creativity. Action is also, in a sense, the work of man. What particularly attests to action's character is morality as a property of action, to which we constantly appeal in this study. Morality is something essentially different from human action, though at the same time the two are united such that morality does not really exist without human action. This essential distinctness does not blur the existential connection of action and morality. Both are linked most closely with the efficacy of the person, indeed, with a phenomenon, with the lived-experience of efficacy. (At this point, phenomenology seems to enter most boldly into metaphysics and to most need metaphysics, for the phenomena themselves adequately make a thing manifest but are not adequately explained.)

If man forms his moral value in action—and herein lies the element of particularly human creativity—then in this also inheres the fact of forming action itself, the act itself, by the man-agent. The old Aristotelian problem[4] of whether acts are also the products of the acting man or whether the product is only the external effect of action—as is, for instance, a written sheet of paper or a strategic plan elaborated by

---

4. Concerning this topic, Roman Ingarden writes: "In dem Bereich seiner möglichen Verwandlungen ist das Subjekt der Schöpfer seines Selbst. Es gäbe diejenige Gestalt seines Wesens nicht, die sich letzten Endes in seinem Leben realisiert, wenn es seine Taten und Verhaltensweisen in den Beziehungen zu seiner Umwelt nicht gegeben hätte. Unter den Menschen unseres Jahrhunderts hat das zuerst und am konkretesten R. M. Rilke gesehen, nach ihm erst Max Scheler, dann Heidegger und die Existentialisten." [In the realm of its possible transformations, the subject is the creator of its own self. There would not be that Gestalt of its essence which is ultimately realized in its living were it not for its deeds and modes of conduct in the relations to the world surrounding it. Among the personalities of this century, it was Rainer Maria Rilke who saw this first—and most concretely—followed by Max Scheler, then Heidegger and the existentialists.] Ingarden, *Formalontologie*, 299n30; translated by Szylewicz as *Controversy over the Existence of the World*, 2:679n2299. The conception of forming oneself through the act, as expressed here, provides an opportunity to ask more general questions concerning so-called auto-creationism in the philosophy of man. In a more proximate context (represented directly by Analecta Husserliana), it provides an opportunity to ask comparative questions concerning the analyses conducted by Anna-Teresa Tymieniecka in her works such as "Beyond Ingarden's Idealism/Realism Controversy with Husserl: The New Contextual Phase of Phenomenology," in *Ingardeniana*, ed. Anna-Teresa Tymieniecka, 241–418, Analecta Husserliana 4 (Dordrecht: D. Reidel, 1976), esp. part 4, "The Contextual Phase of Phenomenology and Its Program: Creativity; Cosmos and Eros"; and "Initial Spontaneity and the Modalities of Human Life," in *The Crisis of Culture*, ed. Anna-Teresa Tymieniecka, 15–37, Analecta Husserliana 5 (Dordrecht: D. Reidel, 1976).

thought—already indicates adequately that which we now discuss. Human efficacy seems to be some creativity. *This is the creativity for which man himself is the first material. Man first of all shapes himself by action.* In the opposition of "man-maker" and "man-material" we find a new form, or rather a new aspect, of the opposition between activity and passivity, *agere–pati*, which we have traced from the beginning. This is rather a new aspect than a new form. [17a]For the identification of the "man-maker" with human action and the "man-material" with what happens in the human subject would perhaps be an oversimplification of the experiential whole.[17b]

At any rate, the moment of creativity, which goes hand in hand with the moment of efficacy, with the lived-experience of efficacy that constitutes the objective structure "man acts," manifests all the more the superiority of efficacy over the integral dynamism of man. Efficacy itself is something dynamic; indeed, it is so to speak the peak of man's dynamism. At the same time, it is clearly differentiated from the whole of this dynamism. We must properly emphasize this difference in the interpretation.

3. The Synthesis of Efficacy and Subjectivity: Man as *Suppositum*

The diversification of "action" and "happening" reveals the opposition of man's efficacy and subjectivity

The analysis of the dynamic totality "man acts" must consider equally "man" and "action," for this totality consists of these two elements. What is man who acts, and what is man when he acts? We ought to pose these questions at this point in our inquiry. Man is the subject of his action—this formulation is heard at times and is generally taken for granted. However, what is the meaning of "the subject"?

Following the course of our previous analysis, we ought to state that *what appears* in the integral experience of man—taking its interior aspect into particular consideration—*is the diversification and even, so to speak, the opposition of subjectivity and efficacy*. Man experiences himself as a subject when something happens in him. When man acts, however, he experiences himself as the agent, as was indicated earlier. The fullest experiential reality corresponds to lived-experiences. Subjectivity shows itself to be structurally connected with happening, whereas efficacy is structurally bound with man's action. When I act, my own "I" is the cause of the subject's dynamization. The position of this "I" is then superior, whereas subjectivity seems to indicate the opposite, namely, the "I" that is present "under" the fact of its dynamization. This is exactly what takes place when something happens in that "I." Efficacy and subjectivity seem to divide the field of human lived-experiences into two areas irreducible to each other. Together with lived-experiences come structures. The structure "man acts" and the structure "something happens in man" seem to divide man, so to speak, into two worlds. We will return to these worlds in further analyses.

Despite so evident—especially in the interior aspect of experience—a diversification and opposition, in no way can we deny that the one who acts is at the same time the one in whom this or that happens. In no way can we question the unity and identity of "man" at the basis of action and happening. *In no way can we question his unity and identity at the foundations of efficacy and subjectivity*, structurally contained in action and in what happens in man. This man is, as we stated earlier, a dynamic unity or, as we called him in previous analyses, a dynamic subject. We uphold this description here. Action together with man's efficacy, which constitutes it experientially, and all that happens in man meet, so to speak, in one common root. Man as a dynamic subject is this root. By saying "subject" we simultaneously indicate subjectivity. This subjectivity differs somewhat in meaning from the subjectivity found in the lived-experience "something happens in man," a subjectivity that we discover by contrasting this lived-experience (and the structure with it) with action and the efficacy contained in action. On this latter plane subjectivity and efficacy seem to be mutually irreducible, *whereas both are reduced to the former subjectivity*. They in fact proceed from it, as experience teaches us at every step.

In what sense is *suppositum* a subject?

The subjectivity of man that is common to both structures—to action and happening—found its expression in the concept of *sup-positum* in the philosophy practiced according to the principles of Aristotle and

Thomas Aquinas. Etymologically, this word indicates something that lies under (*sub-ponere*). Accordingly, man "lies under" all action and "under" all that happens in him. *Suppositum indicates* either the very being of the subject or *the subject as a being*. This subject as a being inheres at the basis of every dynamic structure, of every action and happening, of every efficacy and subjectivity. This being is real, the being-"man" really existing, and consequently really acting. There is a close connection between existence and action, a connection that is the subject matter of one of the most fundamental human understandings. Man conveyed this understanding in the statement *operari sequitur esse*, which should be expressed in our language perhaps as follows: something must first exist before it can act. *Esse* itself is present at the beginning of action and also at the origin of all that happens in man; *it is present at the beginning of all dynamism proper to man*.

This *esse* is not the same as *suppositum* but only its constitutive aspect. For if this "something" did not exist, then it would not be the origin and subject of all dynamism proper to it, of action and happening. If man did not exist, neither would he act, nor would anything happen in him. Taking into consideration this fundamental, constitutive aspect of every being, it is sometimes said that *suppositum* is a being as a subject of existence and action.[18a] With this definition, we descend very deeply into the structure of the being; we descend to the real difference between essence and existence.[18b] In St. Thomas's conception, existence is the first act (*actus*) of every being, that is, *the first and fundamental factor of its dynamization*.[5] All the dynamism that consists in action and happening, which occur in a dynamic subject, is secondary in relation to that other dynamism: *operari sequitur esse*. By *operari* we ought to understand precisely all this secondary dynamism, not only action but also everything that happens in the subject.

In what sense is man a *suppositum*?

The man-person ought to be identified as a *suppositum* at the first and fundamental view. The person is a concrete man—the *individua sub-*

---

5. See Joseph de Finance, *Être et agir dans la philosophie de Saint Thomas* (Rome: Presses de l'Université Grégorienne, 1965).

stantia, as Boethius declares in the first part of his classical definition.[6] Concreteness is in a sense both uniqueness and unrepeatability; it is, at any rate, individualization. However, something more is contained in the concept of the person than in the concept of *individuum*; the person is something more than an individualized nature. The person is always an individual of a rational nature, as Boethius's definition declares: *persona est rationalis naturae individua substantia*. Nonetheless, neither the concept of (rational) nature nor its individualization seems to render the specific fullness that corresponds to the concept of the person. This fullness is not merely concreteness, but rather uniqueness and unrepeatability. Colloquial language uses here a concise and emphatic pronominal expression: *the person is "somebody."* This pronoun is a capital semantic sign, for it immediately evokes an association in which a comparison and contradistinction to "something" take place. The identification of the person as a *suppositum* demands taking into consideration the difference between "somebody" and "something."

The person is a *suppositum*, but one very different from all those that surround man in the visible world. This otherness, this proportion, or, rather, disproportion, indicated by the pronouns "somebody" and "something" penetrates to the very root of the being that is a subject. According to St. Thomas, the fundamental dynamization of this being through existence (*esse*) and consequently its entire secondary dynamism expressed in *operari* (action and happening) demonstrate the same otherness, the same proportion, in which the disproportion inheres. The existence and action of the person are subject to the principle of metaphysical analogy (the analogy of being), but at the same time they are also explained and distinguished by that principle. The person, man as a person, is a *suppositum*, is a subject of existence and action—although the existence (*esse*) is personal and not only individual in the sense of the individualization of nature. Consequently, *operari*, by which we understand the entire dynamism of man—both action and what happens in him—is also personal. *The person allows himself to be identified as a* suppositum *when the proper analogy is applied*: the *suppositum* "somebody" demonstrates not only the

---

6. See Boethius, *Liber de persona et duabus naturis*, in Patrologiae cursus completus, series latina, vol. 64, ed. J.-P. Migne (Paris, Migne: 1860), 1343C–D: "Persona proprie dicitur naturae rationalis individua substantia" [Person, properly speaking, is an individual substance of a rational nature].

similarity but also the difference and distance with respect to every *suppositum* "something."

The synthesis of efficacy and subjectivity does not obscure the difference that exists between them

The identification of the man-person as a *suppositum* allows us to see in him, so to speak, a synthesis of the lived-experiences and dynamic structures that have been distinguished since the beginning of this chapter. The structures "man acts" and "something happens in man" run through the phenomenological field of experience so as to divide it, whereas they join and unite in the metaphysical field. The man-person is their synthesis, and the ultimate subject of this synthesis is described as *suppositum*. The *suppositum* not only statically dwells ("lies") under the entire dynamism of the man-person *but also constitutes the dynamic source itself of this dynamism*. The dynamism that originates from existence, from *esse*, entails the dynamism proper to *operari*.

The synthesis of action and happening, which takes place through the *suppositum*, is at the same time indirectly the synthesis of the efficacy proper to action and the subjectivity proper to all that happens "in man." This synthesis ultimately takes place in the *suppositum*, that is, in the ontic subject. Therefore, man, being the agent of action, does not cease to be its subject. He is simultaneously the agent and the subject, and he experiences himself as the agent and the subject, though the lived-experience of efficacy moves the lived-experience of subjectivity to the background, as it were. But when something only happens in man, the very lived-experience of subjectivity is manifested. Efficacy is not experienced, for then man as a person is not the agent.

The difference of these lived-experiences and structures does not lose anything in the synthesis of efficacy and subjectivity, in the reduction of both these elements to the *suppositum*. Indeed, this difference must constantly return in our subsequent inquiries, for without it the dynamism proper to man cannot be fully understood and explained. Man as a person, as a "somebody," is—if we retain the metaphysical analogy—identifiable with *suppositum*. The *suppositum* is a subject, that is, simultaneously the basis and source of the two very different forms of dynamism. What is rooted in it and ultimately proceeds from it is the dynamism of all that happens in man and also the complete dynamism of action with conscious efficacy as constitutive of it. The unity of the human *suppositum* can by no means obscure the profound differences that determine the real richness of man's dynamism.

4. Person and Nature: From Opposition to Integration

Why do we pose this problem to ourselves?

Along with reflecting on *suppositum*, we decisively began to analyze the subject of action. We wish to carry this analysis even further in order, so to speak, to unveil the deepest roots of man's dynamism, especially his efficacy, which constitutes the key to understanding the person-act relation. Man as the subject of action and the action of the subject are two correlated components of our study, one of which must be constantly cognized and cognitively deepened by means of the other. It could seem that the identification of the person with *suppositum*—of course, while applying the analogy of proportion—already prejudges *the meaning that we intend to confer on nature in the analysis of the subject of action*. However, the person as well as the *suppositum* was understood not only as a metaphysical subject of existence and of man's dynamism, but also as, in a sense, a phenomenological synthesis of efficacy and subjectivity. Accordingly, *the meaning of "nature" must also acquire a certain duality, which we now intend to elucidate.*

"Nature" defines the subject (the basis) of action

As is well known, the word "nature" is derived from the Latin verb *nascor* ("to be born"), hence *natus* ("born") and *naturus* ("about to be born"). Thus, "nature" literally signifies all that is to be born or that is contained in the very fact of birth as its possible consequence. Hence, the Polish words corresponding to the adjective "natural" are "innate" [*wrodzony*] and "inborn" [*przyrodzony*]. As a noun, "nature" has many meanings. We know that it signifies all of nature [*przyroda*], animate and inanimate, although in the latter case we go, so to speak, beyond the framework determined by the etymology of "being born," for birth occurs only in animate beings: "inanimate nature" is in a sense a contradiction. Besides, the word "nature" accompanied by an appropriate attribute has a narrower meaning. Thus, for example, we speak of human nature, animal nature, or vegetative nature; we even speak of the nature of a concrete man: "This is his nature." In all these applications, the noun "nature" seems to indicate the fundamental property of the given subject, that is, that which we also render with the noun "essence." In some cases, these two nouns are used almost interchangeably—for instance, "animal nature" and "animal essence"—even though a certain semantic hiatus always remains between them. Something different is indicated by "essence" than by "nature."

Nature does not signify a real, concrete subject of existence and action; it is not identified with *suppositum*. It can only be a separated subject (*in abstracto*). For example, when we speak of human nature, we indicate something that really exists only in a concrete man, who is a *suppositum*, and that has no real existence outside of him. However, by in a sense separating nature from every man, in whom it really exists, we can understand this nature as a separated being that remains in relation to all people. In this way, human nature directly indicates what is common to all people on account of the fact that they are people, and it indirectly indicates its own possessors, that is, the people themselves. Here, "nature" semantically approaches "essence" most closely, for *it indicates what is proper to man as man*, what is essentially human, that by which man is man and not somebody or something else.

"Nature" defines the way of action

In accord with its etymology, the meaning of "nature" extends to yet another sphere. *Not only does the sphere of the subject of action* stand open before it, as we have partially presented, *but also the sphere of the way of action*. For the time being, we leave aside the problem of the specific way of action proper to nature itself. *At this time, let us consider only the orientation of nature toward action, or, more broadly, toward dynamism*. This is indicated in a sense by the literal meaning of the participle: "nature" denotes that which is to be born, that which is contained in the fact of birth as its possible consequence. The fact of birth is itself something dynamic; it is the beginning of the dynamism proper to the subject that is being born. Birth is the same as coming to existence, for it contains in a sense the first and fundamental dynamization by *esse*, by existence, from which the entire secondary dynamism of *operari* will result. Thus, as far as man is concerned, the whole synthesis of action and happening, which we have followed from the beginning of this chapter, will result from birth. Does nature stand at the foundation of this whole synthesis? If so, then it would be either identical with the *suppositum* "man" or integrated in him. Or does nature indicate only a certain sphere of man's dynamism, a given form of actualization? In this case, not all action but only a certain way of action could be ascribed to it and deduced from it.

What inclines us to oppose nature to the person?

It seems that *phenomenological reduction* would lead to the latter understanding of nature. By this reduction I understand [19a]*a moment of*[19b] *the fullest and at the same time the most essential visualization of the given content.* By accepting man as a specific dynamic whole, it is not the moment when "man acts" but precisely when "something happens in man," not the moment of the act but of actuation (as we termed it previously), not the moment of efficacy but of subjectivity that can rightly pass for the moment of the fullest and most essential manifestation of "nature." Why? Because the concept of nature implicates the dynamism that is the direct and exclusive effect of birth itself, the dynamism that is exclusively innate or inborn, exclusively immanent in a given subject of action, the dynamism that is in a sense determined in advance by the subject's properties.[xxiv] Nature indicates the dynamism of the subject and thereby indicates his activity, but this activity is fully contained in the subject's dynamic readiness. *This activity is given to the subject, so to speak, in advance; it is, in a sense, fully prepared in the subject's subjective and dynamic structure.* This activity does not require efficacy in the sense in which efficacy takes place in every act, in the structure "man acts," in the form of the certain superiority or transcendence of the acting subject, of the acting "I," with respect to this dynamized subject itself.

According to this understanding, nature is presented not as the basis of the entire dynamism proper to man but as a certain, specified defined moment of this dynamism. Nature is made manifest exclusively in actuations of the subject "man," whereas acts reveal this man as a person. Acts contain efficacy, the efficacy that manifests the concrete "I" as the self-conscious cause of action. And the person is precisely this. The person thus understood differs in man from nature; he is even, in a sense, opposite to nature. As we see, this diversification and opposition follow the first experiential diversification, namely, the diversification and opposition of the lived-experiences and structures "man acts" and "something happens in man." *This division of lived-experiences and structures would separate man, in a sense, into two worlds: the world of the person and the world of nature.* By emphasizing certain experiential moments, we might fail to perceive and accept in man the transition between nature and person, their integration. Let us observe that person and nature would then each indicate almost exclusively a certain way of action (*modus*) and, together with it, a certain form of the dynamism proper to man; they would almost completely fail to signify the subject of this dynamism and action, to indicate this subject.

What advocates the integration of nature in the person?

What lies behind this is a transfer of aspects of experience beyond its integral expression. The integral experience, which is also the simple and fundamental grasp of man, whether in the pre- and extra-scientific sphere or in the field of science—above all, that of philosophy—testifies to the unity and identity of the subject "man." This is accompanied by the synthesis of action and happening, the synthesis of acts and actuations, the synthesis of efficacy and subjectivity on the basis of one and the same *suppositum*. *This makes the basis for opposing person and nature in man disappear and imposes the necessity of their integration.* We must pass from moments or aspects of experience to the whole, and from moments or aspects of man as the subject of experience to the integral grasp of man. (In the course of real cognition, such passing and its direction do not occur—for there the moments and aspects always inhere above all in the cognitive whole. Nonetheless, here we accept this passing and direction for the sake of a certain thoroughness of cognition. The point is also to show how phenomenology and metaphysics penetrate the same object, and that the phenomenological and metaphysical reductions do not cancel each other.)

5. Nature as the Basis for the Dynamic Coherence of the Person

The efficacy of the person and the causality of nature

In what way is the integration of nature in the person accomplished? The previous analysis of the relation between man's interiorly diversified dynamism and the *suppositum* already indicated this way. On the basis of the *suppositum*, the difference and opposition between action and happening, between the efficacy proper to action and the subjectivity proper to what happens in man yield, in a sense, to the obvious unity and identity of man. He is the one who acts. And although he—the personal "somebody"—does not act when something happens in him, nonetheless the entire dynamism of "actuations" is as much his possession as the dynamism of acts. He—this personal "somebody"—inheres at the origin of actuations that happen in him, just as he inheres at the origin of acts that he performs as their agent.

The experience of man culminates, so to speak, in the experience of his own "I." This "I" is the agent of the acts. When man acts, this "I" experiences its efficacy in action. However, when something happens in man, the "I" does not experience efficacy and *is not the agent, but it experiences the interior identity between itself and what happens and at the same time the dependence of what happens exclusively on itself.* What happens in the form of various "actuations" belongs to my "I" and, moreover, proceeds from it as from the only proper substratum and cause, although the "I" does not experience here its causation, its efficacious commitment, the way it does in acts. If, however, one would attempt to educe these happenings, these actuations, from another cause outside my own "I," one would encounter an absolute protest of experience. In this culminating point, which is the experience of one's own "I," the experience of man definitely holds that all that happens in man belongs to the "I" as to the dynamic subject. *This belonging also implies the causal dependency* which is different in actuations than in acts, though it is nonetheless experiential and real. If someone would doubt this belonging and this causal dependency, he would explicitly collide with the experience of his own "I," of its unity and dynamic identity not only with all that man does but also with all that happens in him.

In this way, we find ourselves already on the path to integration [20a]. Even if "nature" is identified only with the moment of actuations as opposed to the moment of acts, which manifests the person in man, then, at any rate, the former moment is not located outside the unity and identity of one's own "I." The experience of the unity and identity of one's own "I" is at the same time objectively anterior to and more fundamental than the experiential diversification of action and happening, of the efficacy and non-efficacy of this "I." The experience of unity and identity permeates the other experience, thereby creating an experiential basis for the integration of nature in the person-*suppositum*. Nature does not cease to designate another form of dynamism as its derivative, a form that is different from the person. Integration does not annul differences in the way the subject is dynamized but only cancels the possibility of understanding person and nature as two separate subjects of action. *According to this understanding, nature, integrated in the one and only* suppositum *"man," which is the person, also indicates yet another causation of this* suppositum. Is this causation non-personal? Personal causation is contained in the lived-experience of the efficacy of the concrete "I"—then and only then "man acts." However, when anything "happens in man," then there is a lack of both the lived-experience of efficacy and, together with this, the causation proper to the person. Nonetheless, we cannot seek the cause of this form of the dynamization of the subjective "I" outside this "I" but only in it. This cause would be nature in particular. Thus, nature integrated in the unity of the subject "man" would signify a basis of this subject's causation different from the person.

According to this understanding, we follow the phenomenological distinction of nature in the person as far as possible.

How do we understand the statement
operari sequitur esse?

Metaphysical reduction, however, aims at the full integration of nature in the person. In doing so, it sets aside "nature" as a specific moment of the subject's dynamization and takes nature into account as the fundamental property of the acting subject—of the subject "man" in our case. Nature in the metaphysical approach is, in a sense, the same as essence; thus nature in man means the entirety of "humanity." It is not, however, static but dynamic "humanity": *humanity as the basis of the entire dynamism proper to man*. This displays a fundamental difference with respect to the previous, the rather phenomenological, understanding of nature. Nature in the metaphysical sense means the essence of any being, grasped as the real basis of this being's entire dynamism.

The first, elementary understanding of the relation between action and the acting being is expressed in the statement already quoted: *operari sequitur esse*. Let us investigate the content of this sentence more thoroughly. *It manifests existential content above all*; it speaks of the fact that in order to act, one must first exist. It also speaks of the fact that action as such is different from existence as such, is not identified with it, does not merely constitute its homogeneous continuation or prolongation, as it were. The two totalities, namely, "man exists" and "man acts," really differ from each other, even though it is the same man who exists and acts. When man acts, his action also somehow exists. The existence of action depends on the existence of man—it is precisely here that the fundamental moment of causality and causation inheres. The existence of action is ordered and at the same time subordinated to the existence of man in an accidental way, as *accidens*.

However, our capital sentence, *operari sequitur esse*, allows us not merely to grasp and define these relations in the order of existence. It also allows us to perceive and determine the connection that exists between action and the acting subject—which in our case is the subject "man"—*in the order of essence*. This is indicated above all by the word *sequitur*. This word affirms that *a specific coherence occurs between action and the agent. This coherence cannot be grasped and expressed differently than it is precisely through the concept of nature. Nature is nothing else but the basis of the essential coherence between the one who acts* (or something that acts, if the agent is not man) *and his action*. Speaking more broadly and more strictly, nature is the basis of the essential coherence between the subject of dynamism and the entire dynamism of this subject. The attribute "entire" is important here because through it we definitively avoid understanding nature as only a certain moment or one mode (*modus*) of the subject's dynamization.

Personal existence at the basis of the dynamic coherence of man

This coherence is an experiential fact. When man is considered as the subject of dynamism, this coherence encompasses both his action and what happens in him, both every act and every actuation. This coherence includes both the efficacy experienced by the concrete "I" in the act and the very subjectivity of this "I" in the case of actuations when the lived-experience of efficacy is absent. The coherence occurs always and everywhere when any *operari* follows (*sequitur*) from the human *esse*. The basis for this coherence is human nature, that is, humanity permeating the entire dynamism of man and dynamically shaping it as human.

The experience of man's coherence with his entire dynamism, both with action and with what happens in man, allows us to understand how the integration of nature occurs in the person. This integration cannot consist only in the individualization of nature by the person, as someone might think by latching on to the words of the Boethian definition: *Persona est rationalis naturae* individua *substantia*. The person is not merely an "individual humanity" but the manner of individual existence that is proper (among the beings of the visible world) only to humanity. This way of being originates from the fact that *the existence as an individual proper to humanity is personal*. The first and fundamental dynamization of any being originates from existence, from *esse*.

The dynamization by personal *esse* must inhere at the root of the integration of humanity by the person. In any case, when grasping the experiential coherence of the entire human *operari* with that *esse*, there seems to be no difficulty in accepting the Thomistic basis of this coherence. Human nature is the more proximate basis for the coherence between the subject "man" dynamized in any way from within and any dynamization of this subject. As the basis of this dynamic coherence, nature does really inhere in the subject. This subject itself is the person, for it possesses personal existence (*esse*). Accordingly, since any form of the dynamization of this subject, any *operari*—whether action or happening, that is, actuation—is really connected with humanity, with nature, it will also really be personal. The integration of human nature, of humanity, in the person and by the person entails the integration of the entire dynamism proper to man in the human person.[7]

Human nature exists really as a person

At the same time, however, this integration is possible only in man precisely because of his nature, his humanity. Humanity, human nature, is equipped with the properties that enable a concrete man to be a person: to be and to act as a person. [21a] We postpone a more proximate description of these properties until later, for at present we are content with a general mention of them. However, it is already adequately evident that the integration of nature by the person in man not only presupposes this nature, this humanity, but also [22a]relies on it, in a sense depends on it[22b]. No other nature exists really (i.e., individually) as a person—this is proper only to humanity.

---

7. Although accepting with traditional philosophy that nature is the basis of the coherence of the person, it is nonetheless difficult not to perceive the "paradox of freedom and nature" of which Ricoeur writes: "Derrière ces structures est le paradoxe qui culmine comme paradoxe de la liberté et de la nature. Le paradoxe est, au niveau même de l'existence, le gage du dualisme au niveau de l'objectivité. Il n'y a pas de procédé logique par lequel la nature procède de la liberté (l'involontaire du volontaire), ou la liberté de la nature. Il n'y a pas de système de la nature et de la liberté.

"Mais comment le paradoxe ne serait-il ruineux, comment la liberté ne serait-elle pas annulée par son excès même, si elle ne réussissait pas à récupérer ses liaisons avec une situation en quelque sorte nourricière? Une ontologie paradoxale n'est possible que secrètement réconciliée. La jointure de l'être est aperçue dans une intuition aveuglée qui se réfléchit en paradoxes; elle n'est jamais ce que je regarde, mais cela à partir de quoi s'articulent les grands contrastes de la liberté et de la nature." [Behind these structures lies the paradox which culminates in the paradox of freedom and nature. Even on the level of existence, the paradox is a measure of the dualism of the objective level. There is no logical procedure by which nature could be derived from freedom (the involuntary from the voluntary), or freedom from nature. There is no *system* of nature and freedom.

But then what prevents the paradox from being destructive? How can freedom help being annulled by its very excess if it does not succeed in recovering its connection with a situation which would in some sense sustain it? A paradoxical ontology is possible only if it is covertly reconciled. The juncture of being appears in a blind intuition reflected in paradoxes; it is never what I observe, but rather what serves as occasion for the articulation of the great contrasts of freedom and nature.] Ricoeur, *Le volontaire et l'involontaire*, 22; translated by Erazim V. Kohák as *Freedom and Nature: The Voluntary and the Involuntary* (Evanston, Ill.: Northwestern University Press, 1966), 19.

The integration of human nature in the person and by the person brings to mind this *ontologie paradoxale* of which Ricoeur writes: "[Elle] n'est pas possible que secrètement réconciliée" [(It) is possible only if it is covertly reconciled], precisely on account of the moment of freedom, which is essential and constitutive for the act. And the act reveals the person in a particular way.

In the discussion published in *Analecta Cracoviensia*, the problem of the relation of person to nature in *Person and Act* is the object of Jerzy Kalinowski's critique.

Our understanding of the person as a *suppositum*—and at the same time as a living, constantly growing synthesis of the dynamism proper to man, a synthesis of acts and actuations, and, with them, a synthesis of efficacy and subjectivity—was cognitively enriched in the preceding analysis by the introduction of the element of nature, of humanity. In light of this element, the entire grasp of the "person-act" relation confirms this relation's "human" mark. In the person, the fact that action and happening are human originates from nature, from humanity. After all, the person himself is human, and so is his act. The efficacy of the human "I," which is proper to act and reveals the transcendence of the person to us, does not, however, detach the person from nature. It only indicates the particular properties of this nature[23a].

6. Potentiality and Consciousness

The relation of nature to the person interests us on account of the potentiality of the subject "man"

The integration of nature in the person, accomplished by means of metaphysical reduction, manifests the unity and identity of man as a subjective being, as *suppositum*. The integration of humanity by the person, which is also the integration of the person by humanity, *does not in the least remove the difference between person and nature*, the difference delineated in the integral experience of man and manifested more particularly in the interior aspect. The fact of the unity and identity of man as the subject of the entire dynamism proper to him does not in the least remove the difference that occurs between man's action and what merely happens in man, between act and various actuations. The integration of nature in the person by no means removes or obscures the fact that we ascertain man's personhood thanks to his actions, that is, conscious actions, while everything else is contained in the person on the basis of the identity and unity of the subject—in particular, the subject who consciously acts, who performs acts. By "personhood" we understand here only and exclusively the fact that man is a person. The fact that man is a person is manifested in conscious action; it is also manifested in consciousness itself—we analyzed this in the previous chapter. We owe to consciousness, and in particular to its reflexive function, the fact that man—a subjective being (*suppositum*)—experiences himself as the subject and thus exists in a fully subjective way.

The difference between person and nature within the same *suppositum* is beyond doubt even when we consider metaphysical integration: if this difference did not exist, there would be no need for integration. Humanity is different from personhood (the fact of being a person). However, in this study, in which we attempt to understand as deeply as possible the structure "man acts," nature as humanity can constitute only a further basis for analysis, in a sense, its background. Nature as the foundation of the causation of the human *suppositum* is moved into the foreground, and this is followed by a certain form of the dynamization of this *suppositum*. In other words, *we are interested in nature and the relation of nature to the person on account of the potentiality of the subject "man."* We can say that the entire previous analysis was an analysis of his potentiality.

Potentiality always indicates the very source of the actual dynamization of the subject

We ascertain the potentiality of the subject "man" by ascertaining his dynamism. Both forms of this dynamism—man's action, i.e., act, and all that happens in man, which we called "actuation"—originate from within; they have their beginning in the subject, which for that reason was rightly described as dynamic. The dynamism of the subject proceeds from the subject's potentiality, for it consists in using certain forces that inhere in the subject. At this point, however, we need first of all *to clarify the meaning of terms*. The term "dynamism" is of Greek etymology: *dýnamis* means "force" or "power." The term "potentiality" is of Latin etymology: *potentia* means "power" or "faculty." We see that the two terms are etymologically very close to each other; they are almost identical. Applying them in our present inquiries, however, demonstrates a clear distinction. Thus, *dynamism*, as we can see, *indicates above all the actual dynamization of the subject "man,"* which originates from within and acquires the form of either action or happening. On the other hand, *potentiality indicates the very source of this actual dynamization of the subject*: this source inheres inside the subject, in a sense constantly pulsating in the subject, manifesting itself through this or that form of dynamization. The traditional conception of man, which stems from metaphysical presuppositions, calls this source a power (*potentia*). A power is the center of a certain force, the center of possessing and wielding this force.

We ascertain the potentiality of the subject "man" along with his dynamism. Thus, we ascertain it experientially in principle: what is contained in the experience of any form of man's dynamism, whether action or happening, is also potentiality as the basis and source of actual dynamization. However, this basis is not manifested in experience in the same way as the very dynamization of the subject, as its actual form. In understanding, the grasping of this basis, that is, of the dynamic source of this or that form of actual dynamization, relies on certain reasoning. This reasoning is accomplished in close connection with the integral object of experience, without being separated from it, but instead penetrating it deeper than when ascertaining any form of dynamism. When man acts or when anything happens in him, then first of all the concrete form of the dynamization of the subject "man" is experientially given, although its basis and source are given only indirectly and secondarily. *For experience clearly demonstrates that this form of dynamism proceeds from within. But if it demonstrates the proceeding from within, then it also indicates that from which it proceeds within the subject*: not only the whole subject (*suppositum*), but also the more particular and proximate dynamic source of this or that dynamization of the subject. Without these more proximate and different sources, it would be difficult to understand why the subject is dynamized in such different ways.

Agere and *pati* have different foundations in the potentiality of man

The difference in the dynamization of the subject, the difference that takes place between "man acts" and "something happens in man," is extremely striking. Apart from this difference in the dynamization of man there must exist a difference in the potentiality of the *suppositum* "man." To grasp the distinctness of the structure "man acts" from precisely the perspective of the subject's potentiality is one of the main tasks of this study. We gradually realize this task by analyzing the distinct content of both structures. The structure "something happens in man" indicates a different basis in the potentiality of the subject "man" than the structure "man acts." We can grasp the matter in the categories of the traditional (metaphysical) philosophy of man: since there occurs such a distinct difference in the forms of the dynamism itself, there must exist a corresponding difference in potentialities; that is, different powers (*potentia*) must constitute the dynamic roots of action and happening, of act and actuations. This was very extensively examined by traditional philosophical anthropology (psychology).[8] However, in this study, in which we attempt to keep before our eyes the person in all his dynamic specificity, we shall not follow this traditional path of distinguishing the powers themselves in man. We shall leave this path, which is well-known and thoroughly trodden. *We shall follow, however, the fundamental intuition of the person*, the way he reveals himself in and through act.[xxv] [24a]It is clear that this intuition of the person, this vision of him, contains an experience of man's potentiality. As we already indicated, potentiality itself is an implication of all dynamism.[24b] At the end of the analysis of this dynamism, the analysis that already manifested all the specificity of the personal "I's" efficacy in every act, let us attempt to refer once more to the previously conducted analysis of consciousness. We shall attempt to do so in order to more precisely describe the very relation of consciousness to the potentiality in man.

The relation of consciousness to psycho-emotive potentiality

We choose for this purpose to consider the *two distinct variants of dynamism and potentiality*. We could also describe these two variants *as two structural layers* of the dynamic subject "man." Furthermore, these are the two layers of the subjectivity of every concrete "I"—of subjectivity because the "I" experiences itself in them as subject and not merely as agent, the latter being the case in conscious actions, that is, in acts. One of these layers of the dynamism and potentiality of man is the somatic-vegetative layer, and the other is the psycho-emotive layer.

---

8. Both the concept *actus* and the conviction of man's potentiality—the conviction closely connected with this concept—belong to the Aristotelian philosophical heritage. A certain systematization of the powers at man's disposal was accomplished on the basis of these concepts. See Aristotle, *De Anima* 3.8.432 and especially 3.9.432b, 433a, and Thomas Aquinas, *Summa theologiae* I, qq. 77–83. In this study we pass over this systematization. For it seems that, in order to reveal and consequently to understand the reality of the person, his transcendence in the act, and his integration, a fundamental significance belongs to what is given in the most original way, namely, to the difference between the experience "man acts" and the experience "something happens in man."

We should note that it is the connection of dynamism and potentiality that remains the object of this study—principally, *the way that this connection is made manifest to us in the experience* of man when we take into particular consideration the aspect of his interiority. Accordingly, precisely in this aspect, vegetative dynamism and, indirectly, vegetative potentiality differ in man from emotive dynamism and, indirectly, emotive potentiality *by different relations to consciousness*. We are concerned here with the mirroring consciousness and, consequently, the reflexive consciousness as the condition of subjective lived-experience, and, in this case, the lived-experience of what happens in man. Thus, at present, we are not concerned with the objective difference between the acts (*actus*) and powers (*potentia*) that belong to the two aforementioned layers (the somatic-vegetative and the psycho-emotive). In a sense, we are concerned with their place in the mirroring of consciousness and in lived-experience, and also *with the scope of consciousness in these spheres of man's potentiality*. All of this is not without significance for the full image of the man-person, who interests us not only as an objective being that is a subject (*suppositum*), but also as one that has lived-experience; thus, we are interested in man from the perspective of the very subjectivity of his being and action. This is also not without significance for understanding the very forms of vegetative and emotive dynamism and potentiality.

The difference between these two forms of the dynamism and, at the same time, between the two layers of man's potentiality is manifested also by the fact that only one of them has a conscious character. The point above all is the character of the dynamism itself, that is, of the corresponding actualizations (*actus*). The acts of the emotive sphere—that is, *the form of man's dynamism whose basis and source in the subject is the psycho-emotive potentiality*—find their distinct mirroring in consciousness. They enter into the sphere of consciousness, if we may say so, and function in the subject as a more or less vivid lived-experience. We can maintain not only that they are made conscious and [25a]even must be made so, that is,[25b] that consciousness must mirror and introduce them as lived-experience into the interior profile of subjectivity.

The relation of consciousness to somatic-vegetative potentiality

The acts (*actus*) of the vegetative sphere—that is, the entire field and *form of man's dynamism whose basis and source in the subject is the somatic-vegetative potentiality*—are not generally made conscious and even seem unable to be made so. We ought to underscore that the somatic-vegetative dynamism and the potentiality that corresponds to it in the subject "man" are connected with the human body as an organism. Here we understand vegetativeness itself more broadly than, for instance, the vegetative system is understood in medicine. This concept corresponds in scope more or less to what was expressed by the old Aristotelian concept of *anima vegetativa*. The somatic-vegetative dynamism is the form of the dynamism proper to man that determines the life of the human body as a concrete organism—insofar as this organism conditions various psychical functions.

The totality of this dynamism as well as its corresponding potentiality seems to have in man a completely different consciousness-related scope, much more modest and indirect, than the psycho-emotive dynamism. Man is conscious of his body—but as of something that lives its proper life. The consciousness of the body is also the indirect consciousness of the organism. Man, however, does not possess a direct and particular consciousness of his organism; he is not conscious of the individual dynamic facts (*actus*) that compose the entirety of the vegetative dynamism. Consciousness does not reach these *actus*, these forms of the dynamism of the human subject. They take place spontaneously outside the scope of consciousness, thus without the mirroring of consciousness to accompany them. Moreover, these dynamic facts, the *actus* of the somatic-vegetative nature, do not enter the interior profile of human subjectivity as lived-experience. If we experience anything of this structural layer of our human subject, it occurs by means of sensations. We spoke of this in the previous chapter. Thus, for example, when we experience physical pain or feel physically well, then this lived-experience is in itself psychical and not vegetative, though the objective basis of the lived-experience inheres in the somatic-vegetative layer, in its potentiality.

It seems that both the integral lived-experience of the body and the consciousness of the body find their extensive basis in the sphere of sensations, of so-called bodily sensations. We defer a more thorough and penetrating analysis of vegetativeness and somaticity, as well as emotivity and the psyche, to another chapter. Their great significance for the entire study of person and act cannot be questioned.

7. The Subconscious as the Expression of the Relation between Potentiality and Consciousness
The "priority" of potentiality with respect to consciousness

The one who acts, who performs acts—man—is at the same time the dynamic subject of all that happens in him, in both the emotive and vegetative layers, in the ways that both can and cannot be made conscious.[9] He is one and the same subject—the subject that is wholly a person, a "somebody," and does not cease to be so even within all the causation of nature, which, as we have already noted, differs from the causation of the person. The subject "man" does not cease to be a person on account of the actuations that shape the dynamism proper to the emotive sphere and the dynamism proper to the vegetative sphere of his integral being. The unity and identity of the being that is the subject (*suppositum*) testify to the potential unity, and thus to the dynamic unity, of this subject. *This unity is not abolished by structural differences, for example, those manifested by the relation of potentiality to consciousness, and vice versa.* We stated that consciousness does not equally mirror the entire potentiality of man and the resulting dynamizations (*actus*). The vegetative potenti-

---

9. [12a] The need to distinguish the unconscious from the subconscious is stressed, for instance, by Tresmontant: "Dans l'inconscient de l'homme, il n'y a donc pas seulement ni même d'abord ce que j'ai 'refoulé,' des souvenirs que je me dissimule à moi-même. Il y a d'abord l'inconscient biologique, organisateur, qui opère en moi, dans l'organisme que je suis, sans que je sache comment. C'est un premier niveau de l'inconscient, un premier ordre ou domaine de l'inconscient." [In man's unconscious there is thus not only or even first of all something I have 'repressed,' memories that I conceal from myself. First is the biological unconscious, an organizing principle operating within me, in the organism that I am, without my knowing how. It is a first level of the unconscious, a first order or domain of the unconscious.] Claude Tresmontant, *Le problème de l'âme* (Paris: Seuil, 1971), 186. [12b] However, we should note that we can speak sensibly about the unconscious as a structural element of man only inasmuch as we presume the potentiality of man and consider the relation between this potentiality and consciousness. Without this, the unconscious does not seem to signify anything that belongs to the real structure of the human subject; it is merely a simple negation of consciousness.

ality and dynamism of man reside, properly speaking, outside the reach of consciousness; they remain not being made conscious. Nonetheless, they belong to the structure of the dynamic subject that is a person. This potentiality constitutes an indisputable cofactor of so many conscious human actions, of so many acts (of course, we ought not to understand that the vegetative potentiality itself is their source).

Hence we see that the dynamic unity of the subject "man" in the vegetative layer is not realized through consciousness. It is realized without consciousness and, in a sense, outside it. Consciousness in its mirroring function is not needed for this. The dynamic unity is, as we see, anterior to and more original than consciousness in both its mirroring and reflexive functions. The dynamic unity of the subject "man"—at least in the somatic layer—*is first of all the unity of life, and only secondarily and in a sense collaterally the unity of lived-experience.* This statement testifies to the priority of potentiality in relation to consciousness. Any analysis of man—any analysis of the person and act—that would proceed from consciousness alone is doomed in advance to be inadequate.

To what extent does the relation to consciousness mark the boundary between the psyche and somaticity?

The order *potentiality before consciousness* should also be taken into consideration in the emotive layer, though consciousness reaches this layer of the human dynamism very clearly and very effectively. Man not only becomes spontaneously conscious of but also very intensively experiences what belongs to the emotive sphere of man's dynamism, namely, various sensations or affections. The boundary of these lived-experiences in relation to the facts of the somatic-vegetative life—which are not experienced by man, despite being very rich and diversified in themselves—coincides in a sense *with the boundary between the psyche and somaticity.* Although the latter boundary is determined by other criteria, for it pertains to the objective structures themselves, it is the criteria of this latter division that in a sense appropriate the criteria of the former distinction. This is correct in principle as long as it is accomplished on the proper plane, for what often results is a certain confusion of the aspects of experience and consequently a confusion in the understanding of man, something that we wish to avoid here. If man is a particular field of experiences and understandings, then consciousness and lived-experience, which help in grasping this field above all in the interior aspect, cannot be used interchangeably with what determines the relation between objective structures themselves. An example of such determination seems to be the division into psyche and somaticity, not to mention the distinction between soul and body in man. Each of these distinctions has a different meaning and proceeds from different presuppositions, though we can say that they meet in a common root.

Introducing the subconscious into the current analysis

We shall attempt to look for a moment at the relation of consciousness to potentiality in man from the perspective of the so-called subconscious. Our analysis has allowed us thus far to designate within the totality of the human dynamism the sphere that can be made conscious and the sphere that cannot be made conscious. The dynamism made conscious is differentiated from the dynamism not made conscious on the basis of the same subject—man who is a person. In a sense, the former opposes the latter if the relation to consciousness is made the criterion of the division. The concept of the subconscious, however, contains something more than the mere inability to make conscious the facts of dynamic actuations that occur in the subject "man," particularly in the somatic-vegetative layer. *The subconscious*—the way we know it from psychoanalysts' studies—*designates a source of content experienced by man different from the one encompassed by consciousness*. This is the case, for instance, with sexual content in Freud's understanding or other content in Adler's or Jung's understanding. The genesis of this content is linked with instinct, with the sexual instinct or that of self-importance.

We leave the problem of instinct and the problem of drive in the integral structure of human dynamism to be examined later. At this point, we can—and must—state that *the subconscious indicates the potentiality of the human subject*. Moreover, it indicates a specific priority of potentiality with respect to consciousness. By no means do we mean "superiority" when we say "priority." We mean a structural priority and, consequently, a priority concerning interpretation and hence understanding: it would be impossible to understand and explain man, his dynamism, and his conscious action—that is, the act—if we relied on consciousness alone.

In this area, potentiality is something first, anterior, and more indispensable for the interpretation of human dynamism—and for the interpretation of conscious actions. Consciousness manifests the subjective aspect of these actions and, in part, of what happens in man; it does not, however, determine the [26a]integral[26b] structure of human dynamism.

The subconscious attests to the dynamism and potentiality of man

The subconscious confirms all of this in a specific way—specific inasmuch as the subconscious itself is connected above all with the interior aspect of the experience of man. What is understood by "the subconscious" is, in a sense, the interior space into which some content is pushed or in which it is detained before the threshold of consciousness. Both the pushing and the detaining indicate the fact that the subconscious is also governed by the laws of a specific dynamism. This is attested by the threshold of consciousness through which some content must break in order to be made conscious and to be experienced. For such content remains outside the scope of lived-experience as long as it inheres in the subconscious—*it inheres in sub-lived-experience,* to be more precise. Is the threshold of consciousness guarded by consciousness itself, or does this task belong to yet another, superior factor in man, namely, the will? After all, the threshold of consciousness does not always seem to be guarded; control or censorship by the superior factor in man does not always work here. The ordinary transition to consciousness, that is, becoming conscious, is accomplished in a spontaneous and uncontrolled way—for example, when man feels pain in some organ and thus becomes conscious of the existence of this organ and its (in this case defective) functioning. In this example, however, what takes place is merely a transition from unconsciousness to consciousness. The subconscious, in contrast, was reserved by psychoanalysts exclusively for the content whose transition across the threshold of consciousness is linked with the action of the superior factor in man, with its particular watchfulness.

But in this case, the subconscious attests even more to the dynamism and potentiality of man. For on the one hand, *it indicates this superior dynamism* and the superior potentiality standing at its basis [27a]; on the other hand, however, it indicates the potentiality that resides in the subject "man" below the boundary of consciousness or, at any rate, under the actual threshold of consciousness. After all, the content pushed into the subconscious—sometimes we even speak of its suppression—or not admitted to consciousness does not inhere in a vacuum but evidently remains in the subject. It remains there in a dynamic state, for it is always ready to cross the threshold of consciousness. We learn from psychoanalysts that this content seeks suitable circumstances to do so, for example, when consciousness is weakened or inhibited, during fatigue or, especially, sleep. Should we not infer from this that the lower layers of human potentiality—namely, the vegetative and, in a certain way, the emotive—*not only shelter this content but also, so to speak, aid it with their own respective dynamisms?* [28a]Indeed, the dynamism of the vegetative layer resides almost completely outside the scope of consciousness. However, emotive dynamism—which we shall later attempt to examine more closely—seems greatly to facilitate the psychical representation and manifestation of certain content, including that from which consciousness and the will have severed themselves.[28b]

The subconscious indicates consciousness as the sphere (dimension) of the human person's proper realization

This section devoted to the subconscious has particular significance for that part of our study in which we primarily concentrated on man as the subject of action and of dynamism in general.

First: This section better manifests the potentiality of the subject in the interior aspect.

Second: It helps us perceive—at least to some extent—the interior continuity and coherence of the subject, for thanks to the subconscious, we see the transitions between that which merely happens in man by way of natural, vegetative (or possibly emotive) actuations and that which man consciously experiences and considers as his act. This continuity and coherence take place both within the subconscious itself and between the subconscious and consciousness. The threshold of consciousness not only separates the one from the other but also joins them together.[10]

---

10. The statement that the threshold of consciousness not only divides consciousness and the subconscious but also joins them together may be accepted as long as we consider consciousness

Third: In its continuous relation with consciousness, the subconscious shows us man as a being that is subject to time from within, a being that has its own interior history. This history is fundamentally determined and shaped by the very cofactors of man's dynamic structure. Consciousness has at times been compared to a stream of content that constantly flows in the subject "man." The subconscious allows us to better understand how this stream is connected with the potentiality of the subject; it thus indirectly shows us where to seek the springs of the human individual's history.[11]

Finally, fourth (and this point only complements the third): The subconscious distinctly delineates the hierarchy of man's potentiality. This pressing toward consciousness, this striving to become conscious, to have conscious lived-experience, that constantly emanates from the subconscious is very remarkable. The existence of the subconscious and the function it fulfills indubitably indicate consciousness as the sphere within which man most properly realizes himself. The subconscious is shaped through consciousness to a considerable extent; apart from that,

---

and the subconscious on the basis of their relation to man's potentiality. We ask whether this would make sense in Sigmund Freud's conception. He writes: "Es gibt zwei Wege, auf denen der Inhalt des Es ins Ich eindringen kann. Der eine ist der direkte, der andere führt über das Ichideal, und es mag für manche seelische Tätigkeiten entscheidend sein, auf welchem der beiden Wege sie erfolgen. Das Ich entwickelt sich von der Triebwahrnehmung zur Triebbeherrschung, vom Triebgehorsam zur Triebhemmung. An dieser Leistung hat das Ichideal, das ja zum Teil eine Reaktionsbildung gegen die Triebvorgänge des Es ist, seinen starken Anteil." [There are two paths by which the content of the id can penetrate into the ego. The one is direct, the other leads by way of the ego ideal; which of these two paths they take may, for some mental activities, be of decisive importance. The ego develops from perceiving instincts to controlling them, from obeying instincts to inhibiting them. In this achievement a large share is taken by the ego ideal, which indeed is partly a reaction-formation against the instinctual processes of the id.] Sigmund Freud, *Das Ich und das Es und andere metapsychologische Schriften* (Frankfurt: Fischer Taschenbuch Verlag, 1960), 205; translated by Joan Riviere as *The Ego and the Id*, ed. James Strachey (New York: W. W. Norton, 1960), 74–75.

11. The problem of linking man to time, of subjecting him to time, is a particularly familiar and important problem for phenomenologists and existentialists. See, for example, Jean-Paul Sartre, "La temporalité," in *L'être et le néant: Essai d'ontologie phénoménologique*, 150–218 (Paris: Gallimard, 1943); Dietrich von Hildebrand, *Wahre Sittlichkeit und Situationsethik* (Düsseldorf: Patmos-Verlag, 1957), 103–4; Emmanuel Lévinas, "La relation éthique et le temps," in *Totalité et infini: Essai sur l'extériorité*, 195–225; Roman Ingarden, "Człowiek i czas," in *Książeczka o człowieku*, 41–74. The traditional philosophy of man, built on the basis of the philosophy of being, did not concern itself with this problem directly and *explicite*. This problem was contained *implicite* in the conception of the contingency of being (*contingentia entis*), which referred to the human being and similarly to other derivative (i.e., created) beings.

The author must note that, unfortunately, neither the aspect of man's contingency nor even that of his historicity is adequately elaborated in this study.

it is only a reserve, as it were, or a repository, in which resides what in the subject "man" waits to become conscious. For it will then acquire a fully human significance.

Let us add that bringing into consciousness the content suppressed in the subconscious and, especially, thoroughly objectivizing this content is one of the important tasks of education and morality. This, however, is not our immediate concern in the present study.

8. Man *in fieri*: The [29a]Revelation[29b] of Freedom in the Dynamism of the Human Subject

Esse-operari-fieri: Their reciprocal relations in the *suppositum humanum*

In the preceding analysis of man's proper dynamism, we attempted, first, to grasp the differences manifested in this dynamism and, second, to indicate the necessary connection between the dynamism and the potentiality of the subject "man." We should note one more thing, namely, that every form of the dynamism ascertained in man—both action, that is, act, and happening in various forms, which was described as "actuation"—*is at the same time linked with a certain becoming of this subject "man." Becoming is what we grasp with the Latin word* fieri. By *fieri* we can understand, in a sense, an aspect of man's dynamism (of his actions or of what happens in him)—an aspect directed to man himself as the subject of this dynamism. Amidst all its dynamizations, this subject does not behave indifferently: it not only takes part in them, as was already shown to a certain degree, but also through each of them is in some way shaped or transformed in itself. (Here we also touch upon the interior structure of life.)

Thus, in the analysis of human dynamism we descend again to the deepest plane—the one spoken of by the word *suppositum*. The *suppositum* is not the static substratum but the first, fundamental plane of the dynamization of the being that is a personal subject: dynamization by *esse* itself, by existence. *It is existence to which, in the ultimate analysis, we ought to refer every becoming, every* fieri *that takes place within the already existing subject "man."* For "to become" is the same as "to begin to exist." The first dynamization through existence, by *esse*, is simultaneously the first *fieri* of the human being, his coming into existence. Any further dynamization through *operari* no longer brings this fundamental coming into existence. Nonetheless, with every such dynamization, something begins to exist in the already existing subject "man." In metaphysical categories, such coming into existence is accidental in relation to the original coming into existence that constitutes the substance itself. Man, who at one time substantially came into existence, *simultaneously becomes more and more "of some sort"* [*jakimś*] *and even, in a sense, more and more "somebody"* [*kimś*] *through everything that he does and everything that happens in him*—*through both forms of the dynamism proper to him*. The analysis of man's dynamism should manifest this becoming, this *fieri*. If the analysis is metaphysical, it manifests this becoming above all. This is precisely the case in Aristotle's, and later in Thomas's, conception of *actus*. *Actus* only secondarily indicates man's action or what happens in man, for it primarily indicates a change, the *fieri*, of the very subject "man" or of his particular powers.

Various spheres of the becoming and development of man correspond to the diversified potentiality of the subject

In this analysis we cannot disregard the becoming—the *fieri* of man —connected with the entire dynamism of man. It is easy to observe that *every form of this dynamism is linked to a different form of* fieri—that man's becoming is interiorly diversified depending on which form of the dynamism contributes to the integral process of becoming and on which potentiality this dynamism is based. If previous analyses distinguished the somatic-vegetative dynamism from the psycho-emotive, and together with this the two layers of the potentiality proper to the human subject, then we can state that what corresponds to these two layers of potentiality and the dynamisms connected with them are two different, so to speak, layers of becoming. The first is man *in fieri* with respect to the somatic-vegetative aspect. In the course of its entire life, the human organism undergoes continuous transformations: first it grows and develops, then it is spent and, so to speak, gradually dies away. These changes can be observed with the naked eye. Knowledge about the organism much more accurately presents its *fieri*, which is connected with potentiality and dynamism *in the somatic-vegetative layer*. For example, it is known that, in the course of several years, the physical-chemical composition of all cells is completely replaced. The natural activity of the organism consists not only in the organism's self-conservation but also in its constant rebuilding. It is difficult to go into details here, for this is the proper task of particular, appropriate sciences. In this study, we are interested not in how the human organism is shaped (which in itself is most interesting) but in how this organism is integrated in the person and how its proper dynamism is integrated in the person's acts, in man's conscious action.[12]

The case is similar concerning *the psycho-emotive dynamism* and the layer of human potentiality on which this dynamism grows in the subject "man." This layer also has its corresponding *fieri*, namely, man's becoming as his psychical development. We can think and speak of it in analogy to man's becoming with respect to his organism. In a separate chapter, we shall attempt to analyze in more detail the ways of man's psycho-emotive becoming—his *fieri*. Both kinds of becoming—that connected with the vegetative potentiality and dynamism of the organism as well as that connected with the psycho-emotive potentiality and the dynamism proper to it—progress in man on the basis of a certain passivity. This is the passivity proper to all that merely happens in man; in this we perceive the causation of nature but not conscious efficacy, which contains the causation of the person. However, we should note immediately that the vegetative dynamism *remains susceptible to conscious efficacy* and penetrable to it *in a completely different measure* than the emotive dynamism. The human organism almost exclusively shapes itself; man only creates the conditions for its development. It is a different matter with the psycho-emotive sphere, which by itself provides conditions—the material, as it were—for its own development, while the formation of this sphere depends on man to a fundamental degree.

---

12. Faced with the fact of change in both man's body and his psyche, philosophers occasionally thought about the problem of man's identity in time. Of course, their answers differed depending on the presupposed metaphysical position. We can offer Shoemaker's reflection as an example. Among other topics, this author wonders on what basis we speak of the identity of man in time. In this matter, we presuppose knowledge (significant only for persons and not for things) that does not have to use any criteria: "There is noncritical knowledge of the identity (or persistence) of persons, namely that expressed in memory statements." Sydney Shoemaker, *Self-Knowledge and Self-Identity* (Ithaca: Cornell University Press, 1963), 258. "Persons are spatiotemporally continuous entities that can know their own pasts without using spatiotemporal continuity (or anything else) as a criterion of identity" (Shoemaker, *Self-Knowledge and Self-Identity*, 259).

Through his acts, man becomes good or evil as man

The formation of the psycho-emotive sphere already falls within the scope of human *fieri*, which in turn we shall analyze most thoroughly. Man becomes "somebody" and "of some sort" first and foremost through his acts, through conscious action. This form of human *fieri* thus presupposes efficacy, that is, the causation proper to the person. The fruit of this causation, the homogeneous *effect of the efficacy of the personal "I," is morality*—not as an abstraction, but as the strictest existential reality connected with the person as its proper subject. Through his acts, through conscious action, man becomes good or evil, good or evil in the moral sense. To be morally good means to be a good man, to be good as man. To be morally evil means to be an evil man, to be evil as man. Through his acts, man becomes morally good or morally evil—depending on what kind of acts they are. The quality of acts, which depends on the norm of morality, [30a] passes into man, the agent of acts. Efficacy alone is not yet the source of man becoming morally good or evil—for this is determined by the relation to the norm of morality. Nonetheless, such becoming, such *fieri*, is not possible without efficacy.

This becoming, the *fieri* of man in the moral sense, the *fieri* most closely connected with the person, *determines the realistic character of good and evil, of the moral values themselves*. By no means are they contents of consciousness alone; they are contents of human, personal *fieri*. Man not only experiences them but also thanks to them becomes really good or really evil as man. Morality is the reality that belongs to the reality of human acts as a specific *fieri* of the subject—the deepest *fieri*, most essentially connected with both his nature, that is, his humanity, and the fact that he is a person.

Freedom is the root of man's becoming good or evil as man

When we investigate the integral structure of this *fieri*, of man's becoming morally good or morally evil thanks to his acts, that is, conscious actions, *we discover in this integral structure the proper moment of freedom*. We speak of this moment in a phenomenological sense, for freedom is manifested most properly in the structure of man becoming morally good or evil through his acts. However, freedom not only is a moment of this structure but also really belongs to it, determining it in a structural way: *freedom is the root of man becoming good or evil through acts*; it is the root of the very *fieri* of human morality. Freedom enters into efficacy; thus it determines man's action as the structure fundamentally separate from every other form of dynamism, from all that merely happens in man. Together with efficacy—through being really contained in it—freedom determines not only action, the act, whose personal "I" is the agent itself, but also moral good and evil, that is, man becoming good or evil as man.

The discovery of the moment of freedom at the conclusion of the analyses of the human subject's dynamism: Freedom and the efficacy of the person

Through morality, through the moral value that the act really introduces into man, we reduce this act, that is, conscious action, to the moment of freedom. This freedom is most properly made manifest to every man *in the lived-experience that can be summarized as "I can but do not have to."* This is not only a content of consciousness but also a manifestation and concretization of the dynamism proper to man. This dynamism lies along the line of action, and in this line it belongs to the efficacy of the personal "I" while being distinguished from all that merely happens in man. This manifestation and concretization of man's proper dynamism must correspond to something in the potentiality of the subject "man." *We call this something the will.* For the human "I will" is formed between "I can" and "I have to," thus constituting the dynamization proper to the will. The will in man is what allows man to want.

The discovery of freedom as the moment that is decisive for the lived-experience of efficacy, and, at the same time, as the factor that really constitutes the structure "man acts" in its structural distinction from all that merely happens in man (the structure "something happens in man"), in a sense *concludes the analysis of the human person's dynamism, the analysis conducted thus far.* For the person is the real subject of this dynamism, and in the case of action, he is not only the subject but also the agent. The discovery of freedom at the root of personal efficacy allows us all the more thoroughly to understand man as a dynamic subject. According to basic experience, the totality of the dynamism proper to this subject can be divided into action and happening (i.e., acts and "actuations"). This difference can be reduced to the real participation of freedom, which occurs in conscious action, in acts, or to the lack of freedom. What merely happens in man lacks at its root the dynamic element of freedom—what is absent is the lived-experience "I can but do not have to." From the perspective of the person and of his proper dynamization, that is, his dynamization in act, all that merely happens in man proceeds *as dynamization by interior necessity, without the participation of man's free efficacy.* This lacks the moment of dynamic transcendence; only the immanence connected with the causation of nature is present. However, the act—in relation to the causation of the person—contains the transcendence that passes into the immanence of action itself, for action also consists in the dynamization of the subject. The dynamic transcendence of the person is based on freedom, which is absent in the causation of nature.

PART 2 ❖ THE TRANSCENDENCE OF THE PERSON IN THE ACT

CHAPTER 3 ❧ The Personal Structure of Self-Determination

1. [1a]The Fundamentals concerning the Personal Structure of Self-Determination[1b]

In self-determination, the will manifests itself as a property of the person

The full discovery of the will is not reduced to the moment of volition alone, to the lived-experience "I will," which contains the moment of freedom, the moment identifiable with the lived-experience "I can but do not have to." Although these lived-experiences are essential for the act and for morality, man's will (as well as his interior freedom) has yet another experiential dimension. In this dimension, the will is made manifest not so much as an interior property of the act performed by the person but as a property of the person who is able to perform acts because he possesses this property. We can also reverse this relation and say that it is the person that is made manifest through the will, and not merely the will through and in the person. Every act confirms and concretizes this relation, in which the will is revealed as a property of the person; the person is revealed as the reality constituted properly by the will with respect to his dynamism. We shall describe this relation as self-determination.

Self-determination is connected with the *fieri* of which we spoke at the end of the previous chapter. [2a]This is the *fieri* of the person that possesses its own phenomenological distinctness and its own ontic content[2b]—however, morality is manifested in both as an existential fact characteristic of man. Therefore, it is morality to which we turned our attention at the end of the previous chapter. *Self-determination, which is the proper dynamic basis of this* fieri *of the person, presupposes in him a par-*

ticular complexity, as it were. For the person is someone who possesses himself and who at the same time is possessed only and exclusively by himself. (In another order, on account of his creatureliness, the person is possessed by God; however, this dependence by no means annihilates [3a] the interior relation of self-possession or "self-ownership" that is essential for the person.) Medieval thinkers expressed this relation by the sentence *Persona est sui iuris*.

Self-determination reveals the structure of self-possession and self-governance as essential for the person

Self-possession as a specific structural property of the person is revealed and at the same time confirmed in action through the will. The simple lived-experience "I will" cannot be correctly read in the dynamic totality of man without considering that specific complexity in it, proper only to the person, contributed by self-possession. Self-determination is possible only on the basis of self-possession; every [4a] "I will" is precisely such self-determination, not as the content of lived-experience isolated from the dynamic [5a]whole[5b] but as the content deeply rooted in this totality. "I will" as actual self-determination structurally presupposes self-possession. For one can determine only what he really possesses. And only the one who possesses can determine. Man determines himself by the will because he possesses himself. At the same time, the will, every real "I will," [6a] confirms and realizes the self-possession proper only to the person—the fact that he is *sui iuris*.

Another relation, taking place in the very structure of man as a person and being most closely connected with the will, follows in the wake of self-possession. This is the relation of self-governance, without which it is also impossible to understand and explain self-determination. *Self-governance* can also be expressed as a specific complexity: on the one hand, the person is the one who governs, who governs himself, and, on the other hand, he himself is the one whom he governs. We understand self-governance here as something different from what is indicated by the colloquial phrase "mastery over oneself." This phrase refers only to a certain function of the dynamism proper to the person; it concerns a certain habit-virtue or a group of such habits. In that case we should rather speak of self-mastery. Self-governance, however, is something more fundamental, something connected with the interior structure of the person, who is distinguished from other structures and beings by the fact that he governs himself. Hence, we should speak of "governance of oneself" rather than "mastery over oneself."

Self-governance presupposes self-possession

This *governance of oneself, as a property that distinguishes the person, presupposes self-possession* and constitutes, in a sense, an aspect of it or its more proximate concretization. The self-governance that we ascertain in the person can occur only when the self-possession proper to him takes place. Both condition self-determination. Both are realized in the act of self-determination, which is every true human "I will." Every man actually governs himself by self-determination; he actually exercises the specific power over himself that no one else can exercise or perform. Medieval thinkers expressed this by the statement *Persona est alteri incommunicabilis.* This statement's content is even richer than that on which we concentrate here. Man owes his structural "in-communicability" (*incommunicabilitas*) to the will inasmuch as self-governance is realized [7a]in[7b] it, and this is manifested and expressed in action as self-determination. Without grasping this structural feature of the entire person, it is impossible to thoroughly grasp and understand the will.

In general, we can in no way grasp and understand it unless within the personal structure. Only there does the will occur and only there is the will itself. The will has no reason for existing in non-personal beings, whose dynamism [8a]proceeds from a given nature and[8b] is realized on the level of nature alone. But self-determination is proper to the person. It is self-determination in particular that *binds and integrates various manifestations of man's dynamism on the level of the person.* It also unceasingly constitutes, determines, and manifests this level. It is through self-determination that man is given in experience (above all in self-experience) as a person. *In self-determination the will appears above all as a property of the person,* and only secondarily as a power.[1] We shall re-

---

1. Here we ought to note a certain (possible!) duality of the meaning of "self-determination." For we can understand this term in the sense "I myself determine," and then the discovery of self- determination would be identified with the discovery of the freedom of volition: "I can but do not have to" (of which we spoke in the previous paragraph). We can also understand the term "self-determination" in the sense "I determine myself" (of which we shall speak in the next

turn to this distinction and then better explain its meaning. The relation of person to nature will also be gradually and more fully manifested—in the way that the experience of freedom contained in self-determination bids us to understand this relation.

2. [9a]An Attempt to Characterize the Integral Dynamic of the Will[9b]
The relation to one's own "I" as an object (the "objectivization" of the subject of the will) is essential for self-determination

Self-determination—that is, the will as a property of the person—is rooted in self-governance and self-possession, and it reveals in the dynamic order the objectivity of this person, that is, of every concrete "I" that acts consciously. The point here is not mere ontological objectivity, a mere statement that the person is objectively and really a being, an existing "somebody," as we have already said in the previous chapter's analyses. The point, rather, is that through self-determination in the act the person himself is an object for himself, and, in a sense, the first, or most proximate, object.

Every actual self-determination realizes the subjectivity of self-governance and self-possession; [10a]for each of these structural, intrapersonal relations contains this objectivity. It constitutes an essential correlate of complexity:[10b] the person as the object (the one who is governed and possessed) is given to the person as the subject (the one who governs and possesses). As we see, objectivity corresponds to the subjectivity of the person, and in a particular way it seems to manifest this subjectivity.[11a]

The objectivity of which we speak is realized and at the same time revealed through self-determination. *In this sense, we can speak of the "objectivization"* that is brought by self-determination into the specific dynamism of the person. This objectivization means that in every ac-

---

paragraph). In the former sense, the will is manifested above all as a power, whereas in the latter sense, as a property of the person.

It seems that at the basis of these two senses (and, in turn, of two ways of shaping the philosophy of the will) stand not so much two different experiences as two dimensions and two "moments" of the same experience.

tual self-determination (that is, in every "I will"), one's own "I" is the object—and the original and most proximate object at that. This is expressed in the very concept and word, for "self-determination" indicates that *somebody determines himself by himself*. The subject and the object are at the same time and correlatively contained in this concept and word. One's own "I" is both the one and the other.

However, the objectivization of the subject *does not have an intentional character* in the sense of intentionality found in every human volition. When I "will," I always will something. Volition demonstrates a turning toward an object, and this turning determines its intentional character. In order to intentionally turn to an object, we place this object, so to speak, in relation to ourselves (or we receive it in this position). Of course, we can also posit our own "I" as an object in relation to ourselves and turn toward it by a similar intentional act, an act of volition. Such intentionality, however, is not proper to self-determination. In self-determination we do not turn toward our "I" as toward an object, but *we only actualize the, so to speak, ready-made objectivity of this "I" contained in the intrapersonal relation of self-governance and self-possession*. This actualization has a fundamental significance for morality [12a]. The entire realness of morality, of moral value, is rooted here.

This "objectivization" is more fundamental than the intentionality of particular volitions

The objectivization essential for self-determination takes place together with the intentionality of particular volitions. *When I will anything, then at the same time I determine myself.* Although one's own "I" is not the intentional object of volition, the objectivity of the "I" is, after all, contained in this volition. Precisely thanks to this, volition is self-determination. Self-determination does not merely signify the going out from one's own "I" as the source of volition or choice. At the same time, it signifies a specific penetration into the identity of the "I" as into the first and fundamental object, in relation to which any intentional objects—all that man wills—are in a sense external and more indirect. The most proximate, the most direct and interior is the objectivity of one's own "I," and thus of one's own subject. It is precisely this subject that man makes "of some sort" by willing this or that object, this or that value.

We touch in this place upon the deepest personal realness of the act. For while making his own "I" of some sort—this or that sort—man becomes somebody. All of this shows how deeply the "objectivization" reaches, that is, the objectivity of self-determination: the objectivity of one's own "I" in self-determination.[2]

The objectivization that is meant here is contained in the dynamic of the will as self-determination but is rooted in the very structure of the person, in the self-possession and self-governance proper to the person. As we have demonstrated, it is impossible to accurately understand and interpret the will without grasping its rootedness in the person, in the specifically personal structure of man. *Thus, we do not render the dynamism proper to the will by grasping only the intentionality of particular volitions.* Here we should make a very essential distinction. Volition as an [13a] intentional act, that is, the lived-experience directed to the appropriate object (we can define this object as an end and value), differs from the lived-experience "I will" in its full content. For the lived-experience "I will" contains self-determination and not merely intentionality. Orienting oneself toward any external object as a value and as an end presupposes a fundamental orientation toward one's own "I" as an object.

We ought to distinguish the lived-experience "I will" from the lived-experience "I feel like" on the basis of self-determination

Volition as an intentional act inheres in the dynamic of the will only inasmuch as it contains self-determination. Introspection tells us of an entire series of volitions that appear in man's interiority as authentic intentional acts and that do not inhere in the dynamic of the will. We can say that some volition then "happens" in the subject, though man does not will—we do not ascertain the lived-experience "I will." *Nota bene*: what belongs to the essence of this lived-experience, to the essence of the will, is that this lived-experience never occurs in man as "happening" but is always "action"—and the very core of every action at that. It is the person as a person who is then active. According to the terminology used

---

2. "Liberum arbitrium est causa sui motus, quia homo per liberum arbitrium seipsum movet ad agendum." [Free-will is the cause of its own movement, because by his free-will man moves himself to act.] Thomas Aquinas, *Summa theologiae* I, q. 83, a. 1, ad 3. It seems that the will for St. Thomas is above all a power, by which man himself determines his act.

by phenomenologists, volitions that do not inhere in self-determination are nonetheless intentional acts. We discover in them a direction toward a value as an end, a direction that is sometimes very intense in lived-experience; then their appetitive character is particularly manifested. All this, however, does not suffice to ascertain the will. Our language in its great precision *accurately distinguishes between the lived-experiences "I will" and "I feel like."* A volition takes place in both. But only the former contains the true dynamic of the will.

The lived-experience "I will" as an expression of self-determination is the basis for revealing the transcendence of the person in the act (*actus personae*)

This dynamic cannot be completely reduced to volition with its corresponding intentionality. What is essential to this dynamic is that it engages the person in the structure of self-possession and self-governance specific to him. In this way, every authentic *"I will" reveals the specific transcendence of the person in the act.* The meaning of this transcendence, the transcendence mentioned in the previous chapter's analyses, shall be more thoroughly examined in this chapter. At any rate, this transcendence is connected with self-determination and the "objectivization" proper to it, not simply with the subjectivity of the human "I" or the intentionality of volitions taking place in this "I" and tending outside it toward various values as ends.

As we see from previous reflections, the term "objectivization" indicates the objectivity of the "I" itself, which is manifested together with every human "I will." In the philosophical and psychological tradition, this "I will" was perhaps considered too much under the aspect of an external object, thus considered too exclusively as "I will something" and not sufficiently under the aspect of interior objectivity, as self-determination, as simply "I will." In this latter aspect it has significance above all for the philosophy of the person; in our study, for the conception of person and act; and, in a further perspective, for personalistic ethics. Sometimes a thought comes to mind that the act, which is traditionally defined as *actus humanus*, was presented *more as* persona in actu *than as* actus personae. This distinction is not at all a play on words [14a].

[15a]The very statement that man possesses a rational nature—and that the

individual of a rational nature is a person—does not yet determine how we will grasp and interpret the person's participation in the act: the way in which he himself performs it and, at the same time, fulfills himself in and through it.

As we can see, this pertains to the problem of interpreting the act. We previously said that the concept *actus humanus* does not raise concerns.[15b] The point is simply to see how the act is the true *actus personae*: not only is an individual rational nature actualized in it, but also—as experience attests—the one and unrepeatable person performs it. He performs it and at the same time fulfills himself in it. The word "fulfillment," as we said earlier, can be considered as corresponding semantically to actualization, thus to the metaphysical term *actus*. [16a]Nonetheless, vision itself and the phenomenological analysis connected with it somehow stand in the way of reducing the person to nature,[16b] and therefore they can play an important role in the interpretation of the act precisely as *actus personae*.

In the lived-experience "I will" (in self-determination), the relation to one's own "I" as an object is at the same time subjectively shaped by consciousness

Metaphysically speaking, the person is both an object and a subject. He is both an objective being, that is, a somebody (a being that exists as "somebody" in contrast to all the other beings that exist as "something"), and a *suppositum*, that is, he exists as a subject. When, in the previous chapter, we examined person and act on the basis of man's general dynamism, we stated that we encounter in the person, so to speak, a synthesis of efficacy and subjectivity. This chapter serves, in a sense, to deepen our understanding of efficacy by entering into the integral dynamic of the will. [17a]In the course of this deepening, a new synthesis, as it were, emerges: *the synthesis of objectivity*. Objectivity is proper to action insofar as its dynamic core is self-determination identifiable with the lived-experience "I will."[17b] Self-determination places one's own "I," that is, the subject, in the position of an object. It then realizes the objectivity of one's own "I" in subjectivity.

[18a]In the integral dynamic and specific structure of the person, subjectivization corresponds to this "objectivization." The former—as we

know from the analysis of chapter 2—is in a particular way conditioned by consciousness.[18b] The person as a specific structure possessing consciousness lives in a way proper only to himself (we understand life here as broadly as possible, approaching the formula *Vivere est viventibus esse*): he lives not only in his own reflection or mirroring but also in the specific self-lived-experience that is conditioned by consciousness in its reflexive function. Thanks to it, the man-person experiences himself as a subject, as the subjective "I." Thus, the lived-experience of one's own subjectivity, so to speak, overlaps the metaphysical subjectivity of the human *suppositum*. In this sense, consciousness conditions "subjectivization."

If the will as self-determination brings *objectivization*, this *is accomplished within and, so to speak, in the bedrock of the simultaneous and actual subjectivization through consciousness*. For man experiences every "I will," every self-determination, [19a]as a subjective fact. This is, in a sense, a constant discovery of the subject in his profound objectivity—and an objective construction of this subject. Consciousness subjectivizes all of this, that is, introduces it into the orbit of lived-experience and the psychological subjectivity connected with it. Man therefore experiences the fact[19b] that he determines himself and that, as a result of self-determination, he becomes somebody and also of some sort (good or evil); ultimately, he experiences the very fact that he is somebody.

In its objectivizing function, cognition directs the will (*nihil volitum nisi praecognitum*)

However, inasmuch as this self-lived-experience of self-determination is conditioned by consciousness, *we cannot say that it is governed by consciousness*. The cognitive governing function, which is indispensable for the will's dynamization, for self-determination (this is attested to by experience and the philosophical tradition no less than by empirical psychology), ought not to be confused with the mirroring or the reflexive function of consciousness. These functions are important for the subjectivization that is so essential for man. The cognitive governing function, however, has an objectivizing character. Thus, if anything governs self-determination and the entire dynamism of the will (including the sphere of its intentionality, that is, its willing values-ends), it is above all and directly self-knowledge. Indirectly, it is all knowledge of reality, especially the cognition of values as possible ends and as the basis for various norms, the norms by which man governs himself in action.

Only the objectivity of cognition can correspond to the objectivity of self-determination and of volition. *Only in its objectivizing function does cognition lead the will (nihil volitum nisi praecognitum)*. However, in the subjectivizing function, cognition as consciousness accompanies the will and complements it within the specific structure that is the person, yet without leading or governing it. Overlooking this fundamental difference cannot but generate solipsism, subjectivism, and idealism—thus self-loss of the subject in his completely specific reality, that is, his objectivity. This statement also has a fundamental significance for the interpretation of act, that is, of conscious action. By speaking of "conscious action," we indicate above all and fundamentally the governing function of cognition in this action, and not only the becoming conscious that accompanies it or the consciousness-related aspect.[xxvi]

The unity of self-determination and consciousness contains a specific synthesis of the personal "I" as object and subject (the dialectic of "objectivization" and "subjectivization" is proper to the integral dynamic of the will)

In this way, the person in act, in conscious action, appears to us as a specific unity of self-determination and consciousness, and thus as a specific synthesis of objectivity and subjectivity. Considering the integral experience of man in both its aspects (interior and exterior), while paying particular attention to the experience of morality, we observe that *objectivization and subjectivization complement and in a sense counterbalance each other*. Consciousness counterbalances and complements self-determination, and vice versa. Inasmuch as consciousness—as stated in chapter 2—brings a certain interiorization in addition to subjectivization, self-determination evokes a certain exteriorization. This exteriorization differs from objectivization, just as interiorization does from subjectivization.

Actus internus is also an exteriorization of the person

Every *act is an exteriorization of the person, even if it is accomplished in a way that is merely interior* and thus merits for it the name *actus internus*. We should note that in the manuals this name is applied to acts that are accomplished without the commitment of all that in man confers on action a mark of visibility, as it were. Thanks to this mark, acts traditionally deserve to be called *actus externus*. Nonetheless, visibility is neither the only nor even the proper criterion of the exteriorization that we ascertain in the act relative to the person. For the person not only objectivizes himself in his every act but also exteriorizes himself—even if, in light of the criterion of visibility, the act is completely interior. On the other hand, *together with the subjectivization by consciousness*, every act, no matter how exterior in light of that criterion, *undergoes interiorization as well*. In this way, the synthesis of objectivity and subjectivity in the dynamic image of the person is projected in the direction of the synthesis of exteriorization and interiorization.

3. [20a]The Freedom of the Will as the Basis for the Transcendence of the Person in Action[20b]
Self-determination reveals freedom as a real attribute of the person

The previous reflections lead us *to grasp the freedom of the will in its fundamental meaning*. Freedom is identified with self-determination—with the self-determination in which we discover the will as a property of the person. Hence, freedom appears as the property of the person connected with the will, with the concrete "I will," which contains, as previously ascertained, the lived-experience "I can but do not have to." In the analysis of self-determination, we descend to the very roots of both this "I will" and this "I can but do not have to." The freedom proper to man, the freedom of the person through the will, is identified with self-determination as the existential, fullest, and most fundamental reality.

We are, then, concerned with freedom as a reality, with *the freedom that is a real property of man and a real attribute of his will*. This is a very essential presupposition, for in reflecting on freedom it is easy to yield to a certain idealism by proceeding from the concept of freedom "as such," and not from the reality that man constitutes and that freedom constitutes in man.[3] The key to this reality is the fact of self-determination

---

3. In a certain sense, Kant expresses this "a priori of freedom." The entire concept of the categorical imperative is built so that "pure freedom" (autonomy) is manifested in the act of man, be-

along with everything that thoroughly conditions self-determination in the very structure of the person, namely, self-governance and self-possession. Thanks to this, self-determination appears as that which binds and integrates the dynamism proper to man on the level of the person. Self-determination allows us to distinguish the dynamism on the level of the person from the dynamism on the level of nature alone. In the latter we ascertain a lack of self-determination. Consequently, we ascertain a lack of "action" in the sense established by the previous chapter's inquiries.

The dynamism of self-determination fundamentally differs from the dynamisms of instinct

There is no action, there are no acts, on the level of nature alone, for there are only, strictly speaking, "actuations"; at any rate, there is a specific sum of what "happens" in the subject—and this forms a separate whole of the subject's life and dynamism. *This whole is formed along a certain directional,* bio-existential *line,* as it were, which depends on the natural endowment of particular individuals, on their potentiality. In this way, nature is in a sense identified with the potentiality that inheres at the origin of actuations themselves. However, the meaning of "nature" goes beyond the sphere of actuations and encompasses simultaneously—and even above all—the direction of their integration. According to this direction, everything that happens in a given individual has a mark of some finality. *The subjective basis of* both *the integration and the finality on the level of the dynamism of nature alone is called instinct* (especially in animals). Despite

---

cause "pure morality" can be realized only in this freedom. At the same time, it is difficult to resist the conviction that Kant contributed to the discovery of the personal sense (and, indirectly, the personal structure) of self-determination. In fact, what played a fundamental role in this case was perhaps not so much his theory of a priori freedom as the second imperative: "*Handle so, dass du die Menschheit sowohl in deiner Person, als in der Person eines jeden anderen jederzeit zugleich als Zweck, niemals bloss als Mittel brauchest.*" [*So act that you use humanity, whether in your own person or in the person of any other, always at the same time as an end, never merely as a means.*] Immanuel Kant, *Grundlegung zur Metaphysik der Sitten* (Leipzig: Philipp Reclam Jun., 1904), 65; translated and edited by Mary Gregor as *Groundwork of the Metaphysics of Morals,* Cambridge Texts in the History of Philosophy (Cambridge: Cambridge University Press, 1997), 38 (emphasis original). Above all, it indicates self-determination as the right of the person. A right, however, cannot hang in a vacuum—a real structure must correspond to it. By virtue of this structure, the person, i.e., that which is subjective in itself, becomes for itself the first object. It is this relation that we call self-determination. We think that this relation cannot be expressed only in the categories of the intentionality of the will's act ("I will something").

their being almost etymologically identical, "instinct" ought not to be confused with "drive," which we shall discuss in further reflections.

Individual instinct in an animal unifies and orients everything that, strictly speaking, only happens in it into a totality that can give the impression of action, although it is merely a coordination of actuations, which is magnificent in its own way. Only in the case of self-determination can we speak of action (i.e., act) in the strict sense of the word, that is, in the sense based in the integral experience of man. In the case of being governed by instinct, a certain external analogy of action takes place: the given dynamism looks like action, though the essence of the action-act is not realized in this dynamism.

In all this comparative discourse, we reach outside the experience of man; as is easy to see, we reach the animal world before all else. Even though, of course, the problem is rich in itself, we shall not explore it here. The comparative sense of the discourse is this: the dynamism on the level of the person opposes the dynamism on the level of nature precisely through the fact of self-determination. Dynamism on the level of nature does not know the fact of self-determination as the basis from which action proceeds with its direction and finality. The dynamism on the level of nature lacks the particular dependence on one's own "I" that marks the dynamism of the person. *It is precisely this dependence on one's own "I" that is the basis of freedom, whereas its lack places the entire dynamism proper to a given individual (an animal, for example) outside the sphere of freedom.* A lack of freedom corresponds conceptually to "necessity." Hence, what is ascribed to the dynamism on the level of nature alone, the dynamism whose integrative factor is instinct, is necessity as the opposite of freedom, the latter being proper to the person thanks to self-determination. The person is then dynamized in a way proper to him when he depends on his own "I" in this dynamization. Precisely this is contained in the experiential fact of self-determination; this also conditions the lived-experience of efficacy. Efficacy is in this case a derivative of freedom.

Freedom of the will denotes the self-dependence of the person—the dependence of actions on the personal "I"

We should particularly underscore the fact that the fundamental meaning of man's freedom—the freedom of the will, based on experience—requires us to call attention to dependence, namely, the dependence in dynamism on one's own "I." It is precisely here that *the realism of experience contradicts the idealism of pure abstraction*. For taking the matter abstractly, freedom is the same as independence, a lack of dependence. However, the converse is true: a lack of dependence on one's own "I" in the dynamization of the given subject is equivalent to a lack of freedom, or, at any rate, to the lack of a real basis of freedom. Hence progresses the most visual boundary—that is, the boundary most grounded in simple experience—between "person" and "nature," between the world of persons and the world of "individuals" (to use Scholastic terminology): individuals, or specimens, for example, animal specimens, whose entire dynamism is limited to the level of nature. A non-dependence on one's own "I" in their dynamization, a lack of this dependence, is proper to the latter. This lack results from the lack of the structure itself. The structure of the specimen-individual differs from the structure of the person. We do not perceive in it the complexity that structurally conditions self-determination, the complexity that we defined at the beginning as self-possession and self-governance. In the dynamism on the level of nature, however, *the individual is possessed by the potentiality of its own subject; potentiality governs this individual and shapes the direction of dynamizations*. Instinct is both a manifestation and an actualization of this governance of nature over the individual.

Within this structure, a dependence of dynamism on one's own "I" is out of the question, simply because this "I" does not exist. In the natural species, there exist only individuals and no constituted "I's." In order for this "I"—that is, the person in his strictly experiential profile and content—to be constituted, consciousness, as well as self-determination, is indispensable, as we indicated in chapter 2. *The transcendence of the person in the act is explained by self-determination*, and the act itself is constituted as *actus personae*, which we have already clearly distinguished from *persona in actu*. Such an act contains the ever-experiential moment of becoming dependent and of dependence on one's own "I." It is precisely this moment that conceals in itself the very basis of freedom and, with it, the basis of the transcendence of the person in the act.

How do we understand the transcendence of the person in this context?

Here we should briefly explain this philosophical term, and especially its application in this study. The word *transcendence* etymologically indicates crossing a threshold or boundary (*trans-scendere*). This can mean crossing the boundary of a subject toward an object—a crossing that takes place in various ways in so-called intentional acts. Crossing the boundary of the subject occurs one way in acts of cognition and another way in acts of volition, which have the character of strivings. We shall find an opportunity to better draw out the specificity of given intentional acts. Crossing the boundary of the subject toward an object, that is, intentionality, *can be called horizontal transcendence*. However, this transcendence is not primarily what we mean (although we will explore it later on) when we speak of the transcendence of the person in the act. What we mean is the transcendence that we owe to self-determination, the transcendence by the very fact of freedom, the fact of being free in action, and not merely by the intentional orientation of volitions toward an object, a value-end that is proper to them.[4] *We can call this transcendence vertical*, in contradistinction to the one we described as horizontal.

Transcendence thus understood *as a property of the dynamism of the person* is explained precisely by comparing it to the dynamism of nature. Here, self-determination contributes this comparative superiority of one's own "I." This superiority, proceeding from self-determination, forms a vertical, as it were. An individual that is merely the subject of actuations coordinated by instinct lacks this superiority. By analogy to the formula *persona in actu*, we can call each of them *individuum in actu*. This particular formula is here the proper and fundamental formula, whereas in the case of act, the proper and fundamental formula is *actus personae*, which can be transferred only by analogy to the non-personal individual

---

4. This is not transcendence "toward something," directed transcendence, which we ascertain together with an object (a value or an end). It is, however, the transcendence within which the subject confirms himself by surpassing himself (in a sense, by rising above himself). Kant seems to express this transcendence more than Scheler.

as *actus individui*. Properly speaking, however, the latter lacks a basis for such a formula. Action *sensu stricto* cannot take place where there is no capacity for making one's own dynamizations dependent on one's "I."

What role in the structure of freedom does the "objectivization" of one's own "I" play?

The fundamental meaning of man's freedom, the freedom of the will, enjoins us to see in it above all *this particular self-dependence that goes hand in hand with self-determination*. Man is free, which means that he depends on himself in the dynamization of his subject. The fundamental meaning of freedom presupposes the "objectivization" analyzed previously. In order to be free, one must constitute a concrete "I" that [21a]is an object for itself[21b]. The dynamism on the level of nature alone, the dynamism to which we comparatively refer here, does not demonstrate this objectivity of the subject. We encountered this lack when in the previous chapter we distinguished subjectivity and efficacy. When something merely happens in it, the *suppositum* demonstrates only subjectivity; when it acts, then it demonstrates efficacy together with subjectivity. Because this efficacy stands on the basis of self-determination, [22a]the subject is an object for himself. This objectivity ("objectivization") is contained in the fundamental meaning of freedom. *Only he who is an object of action for himself can be free:*[22b] "objectivization" conditions self-dependence, which contains the fundamental meaning of freedom.

4. [23a]The Will as the Power of the Person's Self-Determination[23b]

Self-dependence (auto-determinism) conditions independence in the sphere of intentional objects of volition (indeterminism)

Only from the fundamental meaning of freedom can we move to its developed meaning. We discover this meaning in volitions as intentional acts turned to a certain value as an end. Then we take into consideration not only the "I will" but the whole "I will something." It is precisely here that we ascertain a specific independence. For when I want this or that, x or y, then I experience the intentional orientation to this object as an orientation free from coercion or necessity—"I can" and thus "I do not have to" will that which I will. Of course, when I already actually will the object x or y presented to my will, then I find myself in a sense beyond the threshold of decision or choice. Volition is defined with respect to its object (the value-end); that is, it is determined. If it were not determined, it would not be volition but hesitation. Nonetheless, the lived-experience "I can—I do not have to" persists in a certain way even in this determination. Designating a value as the end of striving does not remove the interior independence in relation to this end, that is, to the object of volition.

This matter requires further examination, that is, an analysis of the developed meaning of freedom, which we intend to undertake in turn. Already here, however, keeping fresh in mind what seems to be the very basis of freedom, that is, self-dependence, we should state that *independence in the sphere of intentional objects of volition* (i.e., values as ends) *is explained precisely by self-dependence*. Man experiences his independence in relation to these objects only because he constantly carries his fundamental dependence on himself at the root of his actions. Thus the realistic interpretation of the freedom of the will is an interpretation according to the formula of auto-determinism, and not of indeterminism alone. Experience indicates that [24a]in the interpretation of freedom[24b] indeterminism is something secondary, whereas auto-determinism is something original and fundamental. This position remains closely connected with the course of our prior reflections, in which the will was manifested above all as self-determination. It is thus first and foremost a property of the person, firmly rooted in the structure of self-governance and self-possession.

The dynamism of self-determination consists in the fact of man "using" the will

Experience, however, allows us to see the will *not only as a property of the person but also as a power*.[5] This is, so to speak, a second experi-

---

5. See "Quamvis liberum arbitrium nominet quandam actum secundum propriam significationem vocabuli; secundum tamen communem usum loquendi, liberum arbitrium dicimus id quod est huius actus principium, scilicet quo homo libere iudicat. Principium autem actus in nobis est et potentia et habitus.... Oportet ergo quod liberum arbitrium vel sit potentia, vel sit habitus.... Quod autem non sit habitus." [Although free-will in its proper sense denotes an act, in the common manner of speaking we call free-will, that which is the principle of the act by which man judges

ential aspect of the same reality. For after all, the will signifies not only what simultaneously reveals and actualizes the structure of self-possession and self-governance, but also *what man employs, what in a sense he uses,* to achieve certain ends. In this case, the will does not so much determine the person as depend on him, being subordinate to him. It is thus also something different from and lower than the person. The experience of the will's dependence on the person is also important for understanding its freedom. The freedom of the will is not, in any case, some independence of this will from the person. If its freedom is manifested in the lived-experience "I can—I do not have to," then this lived-experience is contained above all in the dependence on the person who "can" but at the same time "does not have to" use freedom as a power. Therefore, the first crystallization of the freedom of the will is the first and elementary fact that the will as a power depends on the person. This fact is expressed colloquially by the sentence *"I can will or not will."* The elementary manifestation of freedom of the will is at the same time an acknowledgment of the complete and exclusive power of the person over the will. Independence is constituted and formed by self-dependence, indeterminism by auto-determinism. Thanks precisely to this complete and exclusive power of the person over the will, *the will is the power of the freedom of the person.*

The grasp of the will as a power, as that which the person uses in realizing self-determination and which is at the same time a striving for some end-value, allows a reference to the previous chapter's reflections on the connection between dynamism and potentiality. The person owes to the will his proper dynamism, the dynamism of self-determination, of act. Proper potentiality must correspond to this dynamism. When we speak of the will as a power in the language of traditional philosophical anthropology, we have precisely this potentiality in mind. This potentiality is contained, to use the same language, in rational nature. However, "rational nature" really exists only and exclusively as a person. Dynamization of the will occurs in the manner proper only to the person and not to nature itself. Freedom denotes precisely this manner of the dynamization of the person, whereas the manner of the dynamization of nature was called instinct.

---

freely. Now in us the principle of an act is both power and habit.... Therefore free-will must be either a power or a habit.... It is not a habit.] Thomas Aquinas, *Summa theologiae* I, q. 83, a. 2.

What does "instinct of freedom" mean?

When we think about the dynamism proper to the person, about his action, we can also ascribe to him the "instinct of freedom." This expression, however, has a merely analogical and, in a sense, even metaphorical sense. It indicates that self-determination is something proper and innate to the person—something natural to him (for we can, after all, speak of the nature of the person). When a person acts, when he is dynamized in the way proper to him, then *self-determination, that is, freedom*, in both the fundamental and developed meanings of the word, *appears in this action spontaneously, as a reflex, so to speak*. However, instinctive action is not proper to the person as such: instinct neither governs his dynamism nor integrates it. The dynamism corresponding to the nature of the person, that is, action, is not in this sense dynamism on the level of nature, dynamism integrated by instinct.

In what sense do we speak of the "instinctive action" of man?

The dynamism corresponding to the nature of the person is not the dynamism on the level of nature, even, perhaps, when man himself describes his action as instinctive. Man, for example, "instinctively" turns away from danger, distress, and pain; he "instinctively" reaches for food in order to satisfy hunger, etc. The analysis of drive as it occurs in man will be important for explaining this instinctiveness. We have stated from the beginning that man not only acts but also is the subject of what happens in him. The drives connected with the potentiality of the body and with man's natural emotivity (both of which we shall analyze in further chapters) explain much in this area. However, neither this potentiality nor these drives are identified with instinct as the factor that unifies the individual's dynamism and determines its direction. Therefore, it seems that when man's instinctive action is concerned, we very often mean *a certain increase of its spontaneity and even its intensity, with a simultaneous attenuation of the vividness of self-determination*. Self-determination is identified with conscious decision. On the other hand, spontaneity—or even the reflex of action—can be explained by the orientation of the drive joined with the potentiality of the body or even with some effortlessness of emotion.[6] Then conscious decision is reduced, sometimes almost to naught.

For the potentiality of the will is manifested in conscious decision; it is the power of conscious decision. We shall in turn consider it from this point of view. In addition to the previous remarks concerning man's "instinctive action," we must state that, although self-determination is something proper, something natural to the person, *a certain tension occurs in man between, on the one hand, the will as the power of self-determination, the power of conscious decision, and, on the other hand, drives, emotivity, and the potentiality of the body.* But in light of experience, we ought to state that it is not simple and pure self-determination but precisely this tension that constitutes a property of man. The entire specificity of the dynamism of the human person emerges from this tension.

5. [25a]Decision—The Very Center of the Activity of Free Will[25b]

Transcendence or *appetitus*?

This chapter's subsequent analyses will be completely devoted to the developed meaning of freedom. At the same time, they will continue shaping the image of the person. For this image emerges as we [26a]objectivize[26b] the transcendence in the act, the transcendence that belongs to the person thanks precisely to freedom, that is, to self-determination. We called this transcendence "vertical," taking into particular account the fact of being free, of self-determination, and the superiority connected with this, namely, superiority over one's own dynamism. Freedom's

---

6. According to Anna-Teresa Tymieniecka, "The initial spontaneity makes itself ascertain, within the complete phenomenological framework of inquiry, as the authentic counterpart of the ordering systems in which it represents the *elemental* ground of the primitive forces and the *subliminal* source of man's passion, drives, strivings, and nostalgias." Anna-Teresa Tymieniecka, "Initial Spontaneity and the Modalities of Human Life," in *The Crisis of Culture*, ed. Anna-Teresa Tymieniecka, Analecta Husserliana 5 (Dordrecht: D. Reidel, 1976), 24. See also: "'Brute' Nature could hardly by itself explain in its universally designed progress the *differentiation* of the initial spontaneity as it flows into the act of human experience.... Once bound into the orchestration of human functions these blind energies of Nature may stir from below its apparatus and supply it with 'forces.' However, it is the intermediate 'territory' of *spontaneity, differentiating, differentiated, and endowed with specific virtualities*—territory which we call 'subliminal'—that is postulated in order that the functional progress and its articulation may come about" (Tymieniecka, "Initial Spontaneity and the Modalities of Human Life," 34).

very spontaneity does not hinder the lived-experience of this superiority, although it is perhaps more manifest in a greater reflectivity of self-determination, in the mental maturation of decisions. At any rate, with the quite clearly delineated profile of vertical transcendence we enter already into a more precise analysis of the will. The particular stages of this analysis will constitute, so to speak, the *unveiling of deeper and deeper layers of this transcendence*, [27a]which is in a sense identified with the experiential fact of the person[27b]. The deeper layers condition the shallower ones—that is, the ones we discover and objectivize earlier—and at the same time tell us more and more about the person and his specific structure. They allow us to define more and more fully his proper distinctness, his spiritual nature.

This method of analyzing the will and delving into the interior structure of the person seems to differ slightly from the traditional method. For it seems that within the framework of the latter method, *the will was considered rather in the dimension of "horizontal" transcendence*. For example, it was considered and analyzed by philosophers and psychologists as *appetitus*. This analysis, not without reason, moved to the foreground the will's characteristic drive for the good as an object, that is, an end. In this way, the most essential part of the analysis of the will was the analysis of its intentionality, of intentional acts or volitions, in which the will is undoubtedly manifested and actualized. It seems, however, that through the exclusive analysis of volitions in their variations and modifications, we do not yet reach the root of the will. For it is rooted in the very structure of the person, as we have attempted to demonstrate, and it does not have its proper reason for being outside this structure. Further, the intentionality of volitions with their turning toward a value-end does not fully explain the will; it does not give adequate insight into the will's proper dynamism and potentiality.

Appetition and intentionality

A separate consideration should be devoted to the expression *appetitus* (and to this expression's occurrence with the attribute *rationalis*). The Polish language perhaps lacks a word that would faithfully render the essential content of *appetitus*. In a certain sense, the word "striving" corresponds to it, for to strive means to tend toward an end—thus subordination to an end is an essential mark of *appetitus*. Yet in a different sense, the Polish word "appetite" corresponds to the word *appetitus*. Concerning the will, however, this rendering contains a certain semantic convergence as well as a divergence. For according to our linguistic sense, the word "appetite" seems to indicate exclusively what "happens" in man, as opposed to what resides in the sphere of his conscious decisions. Therefore, the linguistic construction "rational appetite" sounds a bit strange, almost like an intrinsic contradiction, which does not seem to occur in the Latin *appetitus rationalis* precisely on account of the more neutral meaning of *appetitus*.

Thus, concerning meanings and especially the semantic variations proper to our language, *it will be difficult to ascribe appetition to the will*, for appetition is associated almost exclusively with sensuality and seems to lack the capacity for conscious decisions. The problem of language, the terminological problem, is not trivial in the least, for we aim to indicate accurately in every respect what is really contained in every human "I will," and, more broadly, in every "I will something": x or y. We take the will into consideration with all its proper intentionality. *This intentionality is, in a sense, diametrically different from the intentionality of cognition*, of cognitive acts. Thomas Aquinas noted this emphatically, stating that what takes place in cognition is, so to speak, the introduction of an object into the subject, such that the object begins to exist in the subject in a new way—in precisely an intentional way.[7] In willing, by contrast, there occurs, so to speak, a going out toward an object, such that the subject begins in a sense to exist through volition in the object—again, of course, not really but intentionally. The word *intentio* signifies for St. Thomas one of the key moments of the will's actualization. However, we ought not to confuse this word in its nounal meaning with the adjective *intentionalis*; we find the trace of this in the expression "intentional act," used widely by contemporary philosophy.

The intentional act consists in the directing, the turning oneself toward an object, the turning that is experienced by man. It is a specific going out toward the object, for in this going out the boundaries of the subject are in a sense crossed. This takes place both in the act of volition and in the

---

7. It seems right and accurate to distinguish between "intentional" and "intentive" in the way applied by Ingarden, *Z badań nad filozofią współczesną*, 364n1.

act of cognition, of thinking. As intentional acts, thinking and willing resemble each other through the turning toward the object, and each of them crosses the boundaries of the subject in this turning. They differ, however, in all their specificity. In this respect, "to know," or "to understand," and "to will" are completely irreducible to each other. The turning toward the object, the turning experienced in the one and the other, has a completely different effect in and for the subject. As we stated above, Thomas pointed this out in particular. In this study we will consider willing and thinking as "intentional acts," without forgetting, however, the meaning St. Thomas ascribed to intentionality. At present, we analyze the act of volition.

Decision is an essential and constitutive moment of the lived-experience "I will"

We must state that the moment of decision always enters volition as an intentional act that is directed to an object proper to the will in a way proper to the will. This moment is essential for volition because it determines its internal structure and dynamic distinctness. This moment is contained both in what the psychologists (such as Ach [28a]) call a simple act of the will and in what is called a complex or developed act.[8] As we continue, we shall attempt in a separate analysis to explain this distinction in more detail. At present, it suffices to state that both when *I simply will* something and when *I choose*, that is, when I will as a result of a certain motivating process, *decision as an essential and constitutive moment is always contained in this volition*. Decision denotes the very essence of volition ("I will"), especially when its intentional subordination to an object ("I will something": *x* or *y*) is concerned.

Never does a passive directing of the subject toward an object take place in authentic volition. Never does this object—a good or a value (the meaning of these concepts requires a separate differentiating analysis)—lead this subject toward itself by in a sense imposing its reality on

---

8. See Narziss Ach, Über den Willensakt und das Temperament (Leipzig: Quelle and Meyer, 1910); Albert Michotte and Emile Prüm, "Étude expérimentale sur le choix volontaire et ses antécédents immédiats," *Archives de psychologie* 10 (1911): 113–320. In Poland, analyses of the will were developed in a similar direction, for instance, by Fr. Mieczysław Dybowski, *Zależność wykonania od cech procesu woli* (Warsaw: Drukarnia Instytutu Głuchoniemych i Ociemniałych, 1926), and *O typach woli: Badania eksperymentalne* (Lwów-Warszawa: Książnica-Atlas, 1928).

the subject and thus determining the subject from without. We would, in fact, call this type of subject-object relationship determinism. In such a case, a certain absorption of the subject by the object, absorption of inwardness by outwardness, would take place. The human will excludes a relationship of this kind precisely by the moment of decision. Thanks to this moment, when "I will something," I go out on my own toward an object, toward what I will. As we said earlier, what is proper to volition is not the very direction toward values but the *"directing of oneself."* The reflexive mode brings out perfectly the distinctness that results from the subject's active commitment. Here, we touch in a sense the very core of the experiential difference between action and what happens in man. The will is the core of action, of act. Here is the remarkable thing: this fact is determined precisely by the moment of decision proper to the will. In this moment, the person manifests himself in both his efficacy and his transcendence—furthermore, he manifests himself simply as a person.

The will's readiness to go out toward the good lies at the basis of its every decision

Of course, decision does not replace this drive for the good, which is proper to the will and which determines the multilateral dynamism of the human person. The greater this good, the greater the possibilities that inhere in it for drawing the will and thus also the person. The fact that the person allows himself to be pulled by true values, to be completely drawn in and, in a sense, absorbed by them, fundamentally determines his maturity, his perfection. However, we ought to stress all the more that *all forms and degrees of this* [29a]*commitment*[29b] *assume their personal character through the moment of decision.*[9] Decision is, in a sense, a threshold through which the person as such goes out toward the good. And this personal going out must remain in every absorption by the good, even when it could rightly seem that a good—some great end—literally en-

---

9. For Thomas Aquinas, "proprium liberi arbitrii est electio" [the proper act of free-will is choice]. See *Summa theologiae* I, q. 83, a. 3.

We indicate the moment of decision in this study in virtue of the presuppositions previously accepted. For we concern ourselves with the will above all as self-determination (the personal structure of self-determination) and only secondarily, in a sense, as a power. It is remarkable that Ricoeur also includes the problem of choice ("le choix et les motifs") in the analysis of decision: *décider*, and even more so *se décider*. See Ricoeur, *Le volontaire et l'involontaire*, 37ff.

grosses man. Precisely the more man is engrossed, the more thoroughly he decides, and vice versa. After all, we can also understand this as follows: the effects of the first decision expand in proximity to the good itself, in the interaction or union with it. In any case, in no way can we speak of these effects without an autonomous crossing of the threshold of the person.

On account of its proper ability to decide, the will is not in the least doomed to a cold distance from its objects, its goods. We ought not to think that some neutrality in relation to all goods, some indifference (*indifferentia*) to their attractive power that manifests itself in the world of hierarchy, inheres at the innermost of the human person, at the origin of all dynamizations proper to the will. On the contrary: constant readiness to go out toward the good belongs to the essence of every "I will," which is always objective, which is an "I want something." In a certain sense, *this readiness is for the dynamic essence of the will something more original and fundamental than the ability to decide.* For the ability to decide presupposes the dynamic readiness of striving for the good. If, however, we were to understand the will, the human "I will," only and exclusively or even above all as this readiness, we would not grasp that which is most personal in this dynamic—that which most closely binds this dynamic of the will to the structure of the person and only through this structure allows us to understand and fully read him.

6. The Originality of the Act of the Will (between Motivation and the Response to Values)

In what does motivation consist?

We should not only continue the analysis of decision but also take it up from the beginning, for it seems that our previous reflection outlined the meaning of decision rather than introducing us into its structure. [30a] In order to do so, however, we need to consider more broadly the problem of motivation. By motivation, we mean the influence of motives on the will, and this closely corresponds to its intentionality. When "I will something," I go out toward the presented object—or perhaps, rather, toward the object presenting itself to me as a good, manifesting its value to me. The presentation to which corresponds man's specific cognition is essential for motivation. Speaking most generally, this cognition is the cognition of values. However, the concept of motive contains something more, as attested by the very word "motive," which is derived from the Latin *movere*—to move. It is to motivation that we owe *movement, that is, the movement of the will toward a presented object*. Thus, not merely a turning, but a full movement. To will means to strive for a certain good, which thereby becomes an end. When Aristotle equated the good and the end, he thus followed the eloquence of elementary experience.

The subjective complexity of man requires us to accurately distinguish this "movement" of the will, which we owe to motivation, from "emotional stirring" [*wzruszenie*]. In this way, we encounter a very subtle boundary that passes inside man and that can easily be blurred when our insight fails to penetrate deeply enough. We shall return to this boundary when we analyze human emotivity, the emotional life. *Fundamentally speaking, motives move but do not stir emotionally.* They move, that is, they evoke the fact that man "wills something": x or y. If he "wills something," then he thereby also simply "wills"—even if our previous reflections led us to a certain difference between these two facts. It is easy to establish that "I will" is simultaneously something more original and durable in man and something that occurs in intentional orientation toward various objects—this latter being in a sense secondary and changeable. Motivation meets the intentional changeability of the human "I will," the possibility of subordinating this "I will" to various objects presented as values.

Motivation of simple volition differs from motivation of choice

If psychologists distinguish the simple act of the will from the complex or developed act, they take into consideration above all *two different forms of motivation, and, with this, two different forms of decision* proper to the will. The simple act of the will indicates the motivation in which only and exclusively one object is presented to the will; only one value that moves the will is indicated. And so, man simply wills this one object on account of this one value shown in it. He experiences no division; he does not hesitate and does not have to choose, as this is always connected with a suspension of volition. We can, then, speak of an unambiguous motivation and an unambiguous decision. For although there is no need to choose, a decision is nonetheless made. The simple "I will something," "I will x," is an authentic decision.

In no way can we deny that decision is far better expressed and made manifest in choice, which is usually preceded by a more complex and developed motivating process than is simple volition. This process takes place when more than one object of possible striving is presented to the will, when more values are shown and, so to speak, compete with or even combat one another. Each of them in its own way attempts, in a sense, to acquire the will for itself, to draw to itself the human "I will." In this case, there is no unequivocal decision; instead, what must first take place is *a separate process that precedes and conditions this decision*. This process is called the discussion of motives. In itself this process deserves an extensive analysis, which we do not intend to fully conduct here, though we shall touch upon some of its most essential moments. The object of such an analysis should be, on the one hand, the object of motivation—that is, the world of values that is broadly manifested precisely on the basis of the discussion of motives—and, on the other hand, volition itself in its specific complexity and potentiality. For during the discussion of motives, in a sense many potential volitions arise at the same time; the will can turn to each of the presented values, and, moreover, it is ready to turn to them. This indirectly attests that the comprehensive and multidirectional readiness to strive for good is something original and fundamental to the dynamic essence of the will.

The ability to decide is manifested more fully in choice than in simple volition

At the same time, however, during the discussion of motives we ascertain, in a sense, a suspension of volition. None of the potential volitions becomes actual until the moment of decision, which in this case is identified with choice. A simple decision is not a choice, for there is no need to choose in the face of unambiguous motivation. But in the case of complex motivation, decision must also be choice. Man must decide not only the dynamization of his own subject in which he orients himself toward an object, toward this x or that y, but also the object to which he will turn. It is precisely this *decision regarding the object of volition that we call choice*. Choice always means leaving other possible objects or values in favor of one object or value. Choice also dismisses other potential volitions in favor of an actual one. This volition and this chosen value form a whole in which the dynamic essence of the will, that is, the nature of the will, and, indirectly, the person in his transcendence are made manifest in a particular way.

The one is accomplished through the other, thus once again confirming the thesis emphasized from the beginning of this chapter, namely, that the will is firmly rooted in the specific structure of the person. By taking into account the whole process of the will, the discussion of motives, and the suspension of volition, we must reach the conviction that what we call the will is not first and foremost connected with horizontal transcendence, with the ability to pass beyond the subject toward objects, which are various values as ends of volition. What we call the will is above all linked to the ability to decide, which also contains the power to suspend volitions for the sake of making a choice. In this way, the will inheres in vertical transcendence, which is connected with self-governance and self-possession as a specific structural property of the person. [31a] *The ability to decide is more fully manifested in choice than in simple volition*, though every "I choose" is at the same time a given "I will." What is confirmed in this way is the homogeneity of the will, the will's fundamental homogeneity despite the multiplicity of objects of volition and despite the evolution of the forms assumed by volition itself in connection with simple or complex motivation.

Taking into consideration the very property of decision, which occurs in every act of the will, both simple and complex, we can say, on the one hand, that choosing is the volition developed and enhanced by the richness of motivation, and, on the other hand, that every simple volition, on account of the unambiguousness of motivation, is in a sense a reduced or simplified choice. For when I decide, I also somehow choose.

Freedom of will is expressed in the autonomous determination of an object

The latter remark introduces us anew to the problem of freedom, the problem that, as we noted, remains the subject matter of our analysis in this chapter. Freedom seems to occur and to be manifest precisely, and more than anywhere else, in the ability to choose. For this ability confirms the will's independence in the intentional order of volition: here the will is not restricted by the object, by the value as an end. *The determination of this object belongs exclusively to the will itself.* In this way, indeterminism enters the formula of auto-determinism. For its part, independence from the object, from the value as an end of volition, confirms self-determination, which, concerning the manifestation of the will, seems to be the fullest and most elementary experience. For self-determination as an experiential fact would not be possible if an already-existing determination by the object in the intentional order took place in man—in the field of all the experience accessible to us. Such determination would have to eliminate within the person the experience of efficacy and of self-determination, the experience of decision, that is, simply speaking, of volition. It would be, in a sense, the elimination of the person himself—inasmuch as through all these experiences he manifests himself and confirms his own existence. The existence of the person is identified with the existence of a concrete center of freedom.

This *freedom*—that is, a specific independence from objects in the intentional order, the ability to choose among them, the ability to decide about them—*does not in the least remove a conditioning, most broadly understood*, by the world of objects, and especially by the world of values. For this is not freedom "from" objects, "from" values, but, quite the contrary, freedom "to" them, or even better, freedom "for" them—for objects, for values. In a sense, we read this meaning of freedom in the very essence of the human "I will," in each of its forms. Volition is striving, and as such it contains a certain form of dependence on objects. Such dependence, however, does not in the least destroy or annihilate the independence whose expression we find in every simple "I will" and, even more so, in choice—and in both of them through the fact of decision.

The dynamic originality of the act of the will testifies against suggestions of determinism

There exist opinions that—lacking an adequate regard for the experiential fact of decision and choice—see in the very dependence on the world of objects the basis for determinism, that is, for canceling freedom and indirectly also the person, indeed, the entire reality that we call "person and act." *Determinism* possesses *a materialistic form*, in which a rather presupposed conception of matter enters the interpretation of the person's experience and does not allow this very experience to speak to its full extent. This passing remark cannot replace a discussion with various models of materialistic determinism, a discussion that we do not undertake here. For the point of this study is, above all, to allow the experience of the person to speak as fully as possible. Concerning the discussion with materialistic determinism, it suffices to consult appropriate studies or manuals.

Besides materialistic determinism, there exists an opinion that links *determinism—that is, the denial of the person's freedom*—with that which (in accord with the discourse conducted here) conditions freedom, or, speaking concretely, that which conditions the decision contained in every authentic "I will." Thus, there exists an opinion that perceives the inherent foundation of determinism in motivation, that is, in the presentation of objects to the will. This means restricting the will *not by the object itself but by the presentation of the object*. According to this form of determinism, man cannot will the object without its presentation. Hence, as many times as he "chooses," so many times he follows the presentation: he chooses what was presented to him, and he chooses in accord with how it was presented. And if it happens sometimes that, for instance, man chooses a lesser good over a greater one, this does not indicate the will's freedom, that is, its independence from objects, for between the object and the will stands presentation, that is, motivation, which determines by completely defining the direction of volition. [32a]

It seems, however, that this approach contains a far-reaching simplification—that is, a reduction of the experience of the person—in which what is essential is disregarded or even sacrificed to a certain schema. Here, the phenomenological method, as well as the connected skill of accurately exploring experiential data, can render a great service. For, in fact, in the case both of the simple "I will" and of choice, decision—which is essential to the will—has a dynamic specificity that excludes determination. Determination not only by the intentional object (value) but also by the object's presentation disagrees with the dynamic originality of decision. For decision contains and manifests a relation to the intentional object (value), a relation proper only and exclusively to the will. *It is this relation to the object itself that presentation merely makes pres-*

ent, thereby enabling and conditioning decision. The deterministic thesis, according to which presentation would fully determine this relation, confuses the proper reason with a condition.

The act of the will as the response of the person to values

This is linked with the entire dynamic structure of the "movement" essential to the will. The proper reason for this movement is the good, that is, the value of the object—on the condition of its presentation. The presentation is in no way the reason for the will's movement and thus is not the factor that essentially determines this movement or its direction; it is merely a condition for this movement. Decision refers to objects themselves, to presented values. It contains *not only a passive reception or assimilation of the presented value but also an authentic response to the value*. Every "I will" (this is evident particularly in every "I choose") is this specific and unrepeatable response.

If the analysis of the will is conducted *in abstracto*—that is, if the analysis is made as if the will constituted a certain autonomous reality and whole for itself—then this striking feature of its dynamism may not be manifested. If, however, we conduct the analysis of the will within the entire dynamic structure, which is the person, on the basis of self-governance and self-possession, then the will manifests itself as self-determination, and its relation to intentional objects is manifested as an active response. The ability to respond to presented values is characteristic of the will. When man decides, he always responds to values. This responding contains his independence in relation to objects, the independence that does not remove a certain subordination to and thus a dependence on them. However, it is not them, not objects, not values, that commit man and his will, but *he himself commits himself to them*. Again, the reflexive mode best expresses [33a]activity[33b]. The specific response to the presented values in motivation seems to indicate both the *agere* proper to the will and the reality that determines the *agere* of the person, that distinguishes action from all *pati*—which from the beginning denotes for us all that merely happens in the person.

7. [34a]The Moment of "Truth about the Good" as the Basis of Decision and the Transcendence of the Person in the Act[34b]

In what way do *volitum* and *praecognitum* form one dynamic structure?

In the present analysis, we attempt to reveal the deeper and deeper layers of the reality that is action by continuing to follow the original experience that allowed us to distinguish *agere* from *pati* in man. By stating that the ability to respond to presented values is characteristic of the will that shapes this action (*agere*), we enter, in a sense, a new layer of the analysis. We speak analogically about the ability to respond in connection with the will. For this ability belongs properly to the human person in the intellectual sphere. The most ordinary manifestation of the ability to respond is speech, which presupposes thought. However, ascertaining this active, dynamic ability to respond to values as characteristic of the will indicates not only a certain analogy of will and thought, but also the very nature of the will. Great medieval thinkers called this nature *appetitus rationalis*. In a sense, this description is classical due to its conciseness and clarity, for it grasps the organic bond between willing and thinking, the bond that has never ceased to be one of the most fascinating problems of philosophy and psychology.

For although no one is able to undermine the accuracy of the traditional adage *nihil volitum nisi praecognitum*, the problem nonetheless exists as to *how this* volitum *forms one dynamic structure with* praecognitum. This is configured differently in Thomas Aquinas's interpretation than it is in Kant's, for instance.[10] It would be most beneficial to at least compare these quite classic interpretations. We would then see the extent to which the solution to this particular problem posited by the adage *nihil volitum nisi praecognitum* decides the vision of the whole man-person, and, at the

---

10. See Karol Wojtyła, "Zagadnienie woli w analizie aktu etycznego," *Roczniki filozoficzne* 5, no. 1 (1955–57): 111–35; Wojtyła, "O kierowniczej lub służebnej roli rozumu w etyce: Na tle poglądów Tomasza z Akwinu, Hume'a i Kanta," *Roczniki filozoficzne* 6, no. 2 (1958): 13–31.

By performing this juxtaposition, we express the conviction that, despite the radical difference between metaphysical realism (Thomas) and rationalistic apriorism (Kant), some approximation and comparison on the basis of the conception of man is possible.

same time, how it is rooted in this vision of the whole. We find in a given solution all the traces of interpretative integration or disintegration, traces that must ultimately lead to experience as the first source of the cognition of man. Therefore, at the beginning of this study, we had to define this source and indicate a way of exploring it. For experience constitutes with understanding a certain whole, and it is on the basis of understanding that interpretation begins.

The relation to truth, proper to the will, is the interior principle of decision

The typical characteristic of the interpretation of action given in this study is the fact that it in a sense presupposes the person, so that through this interpretation, which is, so to speak, a deeper and deeper unveiling of the reality of act, we simultaneously unveil the person more and more deeply. His dynamic cohesion with act is, on the one hand, the first experiential fact and, on the other, the ultimate topic and task of interpretation, which we are gradually approaching. Can this topic and task be fully accomplished, *or is our study rather a collection of consecutive approximations* over the course of which a more and more mature cognition of the object "person and act" is achieved and the sentence *persona est ineffabilis* is confirmed [35a]? This sentence is a certain modification of another, namely, *individuum est ineffabile,* for the person, after all, is more than an *individuum*. This sentence retains its power, even though in this study we are concerned with the person as such—being convinced that this is possible—and not merely with some concrete person, a person-*individuum*.

After these more general remarks that refer to the introductory and fundamental reflections covered in chapter 1, we pick up our analysis where it left off. The ascertainment of the will's specificity connected with the ability to decide and choose allows us in turn to reveal the relation to truth characteristic of the will's dynamism. This relation belongs to the very essence of decision and manifests itself particularly in choice. The essential reason for choosing and for the very ability to choose cannot be anything but *a particular relation to truth—the relation that penetrates the intentionality of volition and forms its interior principle, as it were.* To choose does not merely mean to direct oneself to one value while disregarding the others (this would be a "purely material" understanding of choice).

To choose means above all to decide about the objects presented to the will in the intentional order on the basis of a certain truth. In no way can we understand choice without reducing the will's proper dynamism to truth as the principle of volition. This principle is something that inheres in the will itself; it is something that determines the essence of choosing. More broadly, it determines the essence of every decision, even in the case of unambiguous motivation when we deal with the so-called simple act of the will; however, it is manifested most fully in choice.

If the striving toward intentional objects on the basis of a certain truth about these objects did not belong to the dynamic essence of the will, then *both choice and decision in their proper dynamic originality would cease to be intelligible.* Insufficient for understanding them is the hypothesis that this relation to truth comes only from without, from thoughts, from the cognition of objects of choice or simply of volition. The cognition of objects conditions and enables choice or decision, thanks to which the relation to truth is actualized. However, this relation in all its originality proper to choice or decision originates in the will and belongs to its own dynamic. The dynamic of the will in itself is not cognitive: "to will" is in no measure "to cognize" or "to know." Instead, this dynamic is in a specific way subordinated to and dependent on truth. It is therefore open to cognition and specifically coherent with it: *volitum* presupposes *cognitum*. This explains *all the originality of choice and of decision in general.* Namely, what explains this originality is a certain subordination to truth and not simply a mere relation to objects. This in turn explains the fact that, by deciding and choosing, the will—and through the will the person—*responds to motives* and does not merely undergo some determination by them. The ability to respond in this way manifests the freedom of the will in its developed sense. Responding always presupposes a certain relation to truth, and not merely a relation to the objects of response.

"Dependence in truth" makes the will independent from objects and their presentations

In this discourse, we use the phrase "relation to truth" or possibly "subordination to truth." These phrases express the reality that is meant, for in the interior dynamic of the will we discover the relation to truth, which differs from the relation to objects of volition, is deeper than that

Personal Structure of Self-Determination | 241

relation. The relation to truth is not exhausted in the structure of volition considered as the intentional act, *but it does determine this act's rootedness in the person*. Because it is deciding or choosing, every volition demonstrates a specific dependence on the person. We can call this dependence the dependence in truth. What we describe in this way requires a thorough explanation. In any case, this "dependence in truth" seems to definitively explain the transcendence of the person in the act, his superiority with respect to his own dynamism.

We stated previously that we owe this transcendence to self-determination, that is, to the freedom of the will. The person is transcendent in his own action because he is free—and inasmuch as he is free. Freedom in the fundamental sense is the same as self-dependence. Freedom in the developed sense is independence in the intentional sphere. Orientation toward various possible objects of volition is determined neither by these objects nor by their presentation. In the intentional sphere, independence thus understood is explained precisely by the relation to truth—the relation that is interior and essential to the will itself—and by dependence on truth. *It is this dependence that makes the will independent from objects and their presentation* while giving the person superiority over his own dynamism, the superiority that we call transcendence in the act (vertical transcendence). The person is independent from the objects of his own action through the moment of truth contained in every authentic decision or choice.[11]

The moment of "truth about the good" is the basis for the moral qualification of acts

Let us stress once again that we ought to concern ourselves with describing this "moment of truth" more precisely. First of all, however, we must state that this moment, which is proper to the will and is the will's own, is not in the least identified with the truthfulness of particular choices or decisions. Quite the contrary. If at the beginning of our study we appealed to the integral experience of man, taking into particular account the experience of morality, then at this point we should take advantage of this experience. Thus, it is out of the question that particular

---

11. The transcendence of the person in the act is thus definitively constituted as "surpassing oneself" (see footnote 4 in this chapter) not so much "toward truth" as "in truth."

choices or decisions proper to the human will are always correct. Man often wills what is not a true good, and such a good he often chooses. Such a decision or choice is not merely an error, for an error is made in thought and not in the will. The decision and choice that have what is not a true good for their object—especially if this decision and choice are made against what has been cognized as a true good—bear the character of fault, of sin. But it is precisely this reality of fault, of sin, of moral evil, known from the experience of morality, that *reveals all the more fully the fact that the relation to truth and the interior dependence on it inheres in the human will.*[12]

If decision and choice did not contain the "moment of truth," if they were not accomplished by a specific relation to it, then morality as the reality most characteristic of the man-person would cease to be intelligible. For what is essential for this reality is the opposition of moral good and evil. This opposition not only presupposes a relation to truth, the relation proper to the will in its intentionality, but also [36a]very extensively expands this relation[36b]. In short, the opposition of good and evil, so essential for morality, presupposes the fact that the volition of any objects is realized *on the basis of the truth about the good* constituted by these objects.

8. [37a]The Cognitive Lived-Experience of Value as a Condition of Decision and Choice[37b]

Motivation serves to lead the will out of the state of initial indetermination

It seems that the previous analysis had a great significance for explaining how *volitum* and *praecognitum* form one dynamic whole proper to man as a person. By indicating the will's own relation to truth—a

---

12. See "En pervertissant l'involontaire et le volontaire, la faute altère notre rapport fondamental aux valeurs et ouvre le véritable drame de la morale qui est le drame de l'homme divisé. Un dualisme éthique déchire l'homme par delà tout dualisme d'entendement et d'existence. 'Je ne fais pas le bien que je veux, et je fais le mal que je ne veux pas.'" [In perverting the involuntary and the voluntary, the fault changes our fundamental relation to values and opens the true drama of morality which is the drama of a divided man. An ethical dualism rends man before any dualism of understanding or of existence. "The good that I would I do not, and the evil I would not I do."] Paul Ricoeur, *Le volontaire et l'involontaire*, 24; translated by Kohák as *Freedom and Nature: The Voluntary and the Involuntary*, 21.

relation that determines the dynamic originality of every decision or choice—*we thereby excluded the determinism that bases itself in the very fact of the cognitive presentation of objects of volition to the will.* According to this understanding, motivation would be identified with determination, canceling all the originality of choosing and deciding, and, indirectly, of self-determination. However, even though the relation to truth in action, while proper to the will and being the will's own, does not originate exclusively in the cognitive presentation of objects, it is nonetheless clearly conditioned by it. The will is not going to bring itself into its proper relation to objects in truth through a choice or a simple decision unless these objects are first presented to it. Motivation is not identified with determination, but motivation conditions auto-determination.

Auto-determination is the proper moment of freedom not only in the fundamental sense as the self-dependence of the person but also in the developed sense, that is, the sense concerning the intentionality of the will, the will's relation to possible objects of volition. A certain indetermination exists at the starting point of this relation. This indetermination, however, *does not in the least mean an indifference toward objects, toward values*; rather, we mean the as yet undetermined *in concreto* readiness to will one of them. Motivation serves to lead the will out of the state of this initial indetermination, not, however, by itself determining but by conditioning and enabling auto-determination. The personal originality of decision and choice consists precisely in the fact that they possess a distinct auto-determinative feature. They constitute a manifestation and concretization of self-determination, and in doing so they reach the structures proper only to the person himself, namely, self-governance and self-possession. These are also the structures of the transcendence that characterizes the person in the act.

Cognition, which conditions the act of the will, possesses a particular character

Cognition conditions choice, decision, and self-determination in general—it conditions the transcendence of the person in the act. We stated that this transcendence results from the relation to truth, *and the relation to truth constitutes the most essential property of cognition.* If, in its own way, the relation to truth constitutes a property of the will manifested in every choice or decision, then in the totality of the human person's dynamism this relation to truth as a property of the will is united in a particular way to the relation to truth as a property of cognition. Here we speak of the conditioning of the will by cognition. At the same time we should perceive yet another relation. Through the will's proper relation to the truth of all the objects to which it turns by virtue of its intentionality—and this is the intentionality of volition—the will influences cognition. This influence ought not to be understood as a sui generis reverse determination that would deform cognition or human thought. Only by the relation to objects, proper to its intentionality, does the will assign to cognition and thought specific tasks, so to speak. These are cognitive tasks; they belong to the sphere of "to know," not to the sphere of "to will." However, since "to will" is so essentially—through the very relation to truth—conditioned by "to cognize" and "to know," [38a]it is not difficult to accept also this influence on the "to cognize" and "to know" themselves that follows from this conditioning[38b].

The moment of truth about the good is essential for the lived-experience of value

In this way, we can explain the basis in man of the specific area of cognition and knowledge that we call the cognition of value. But there is more. It seems that we reach the vital core of what we call the lived-experience of value.[13] *The moment of truth is essential in the lived-experience of value.* This is the truth about this or that object as this or that good. If, for instance, we experience the nutritional value of food, then we also

---

13. See Scheler, *Formalismus*, especially chapter 2, "Das Apriori-Materiale in der Ethik," 101–30. In this context, the statement that in the lived-experience of value the moment of truth about a certain good is essential bears significance above all for manifesting the personal structure of self-determination and, at the same time, for emphasizing the transcendence of the person in the act. The author is aware that this statement must be considered against the extensive background of studies that have as their specific object the problems of value and cognition (or the cognitive lived-experience of value). See part 1 of Dietrich von Hildebrand's, *Ethik*, vol. 2 of *Gesammelte Werke* (Regensburg: J. Habbel, 1973), especially section 2, "Die Realität der Werte wider ihre Verächter," 83–134, and section 3, "Wesentliche Aspekte der Wertsphäre," 135–74; translated as *Christian Ethics* (New York: David McKay Company, 1953). See also Nicolai Hartmann, *Ethik*, 4th ed. (Berlin: Walter de Gruyter, 1962; first edition, 1926), part 1, section 5, "Vom Wesen der ethischen Werte," 107–53, especially chapter 16, "Vom idealen Ansichsein der Werte," section (a) "Gnoseologisches Ansichsein der Werte," 133–35.

cognize the good that this object, food, is. If we experience the educational value of this or that book, then we also cognize that this book as an object is a given good. Our cognition in both cases does not have to be directly evoked by a concrete volition, and it does not have to remain at the direct service of this volition (which would take place whenever "I cognize the value of food in order to eat it" or "I cognize the educational value of a book in order to take advantage of it"). The cognitive lived-experience of value—that is, the cognition of the good that this or that object is—does not depend directly on a concrete volition, although it fundamentally remains very closely connected with such a volition. For what then arises in cognition is the relation to truth that, in turn, can become the principle of volition in the case of decision or choice. We make a decision about an object of volition, or we choose one object among many possible objects on account of its given value. The cognitive lived-experience of value always forms the framework of motivation with regard to content.

The problem of the cognition of values and its relation to the will can be—and usually is—treated as its own problem, for this problem is very rich and multilateral. (In a further chapter, we shall consider separately the emotional component of the lived-experience of value.) In this study, we do not want to permit the problem of value to become its own problem. Perhaps we will have an occasion to do so in another study. *Here, however, this problem bears significance for understanding the person and his specific dynamic in the act*, and for the transcendence that is closely connected with the moment of truth in action. The lived-experience of value contains cognition of the truth about the objects to which the will turns in virtue of its specific intentionality. This is the intentionality of volition, and this volition, precisely due to the lived-experience of value—that is, through the moment of truth about the good that the given objects are—assumes the form of decision or choice. We already stated that it is not the intentionality of volition alone, that is, the directing toward the objects that are in some way valuable, but the directing through decision or choice that is characteristic of the will. This is always a "directing" of the person.[xxvii]

Axiological truth differs from so-called practical truth

The moment of truth contained in the very essence of deciding or choosing *determines in this way the dynamism proper to the person as such.* This is the dynamism of the act. The moment of truth evokes the very *agere* of the person and most deeply determines the differentiation of this *agere* from *pati*, action from happening, of which the person is in various ways a subject. It is precisely this moment that is directly conditioned by the cognitive lived-experience of value. Both decision and choice—but each in its own way—are realized through the relation to the truth about the object as a good. Thus they presuppose the cognitive lived-experience of value, for this lived-experience contains the truth about the object precisely as a good. This is the *axiological truth*, which differs from the ontological truth. By grasping the former, we ascertain not so much what the given object is as what value it constitutes. However, the axiological truth (or rather: the truth in the axiological sense) is not the so-called practical truth and does not directly belong to so-called practical cognition. Rather, it belongs to theoretical cognition; it is the essential element of the very vision of reality. Nonetheless, this is the element to which we owe the most in action and thanks to which "to know" passes into "to will."

9. [39a]The Judgment concerning Value and the Creative Meaning of Intuition[39b]
A glance at thinking from the perspective of the subject's efficacy

In our preceding analysis of cognition as a condition for the transcendence of the person in the act, we emphasized above all the content-related aspect of this cognition. Human cognition, however, is a very rich and complex function of the person, and for this reason it deserves yet another analysis that would explain its share in the act and in the transcendence of the person, which is connected with the act. The entirety of human cognition is also contained within the boundaries of the experience through which we attempt in this study to grasp the dynamism of man. Characteristic of this experience is the distinction between *agere* and *pati*. This distinction also applies in a specific way to cognition as a function of the person. Cognition is *fundamentally* given to us in experience *as* agere, *as* action. This is its proper moment: when I cognize, when I think, I act. [40a]However,[40b] in addition to the active lived-experience of cognition or thinking, we also ascertain in ourselves *the lived-experiences that have a passive character, and which have a cognitive significance*. We mean here not merely the lived-experience of the "it comes to mind" type, in which we encounter a certain flow of cognitive contents, and our human "I" behaves as a passive subject and not as an acting agent. The lived-experiences of this type constitute a certain analogy to the lived-experiences of "I feel like," in which the psychic form of volition does not in the least inhere in the personal-efficacious "I will." Therefore, we have stated a number of times that the intentionality proper to volitions does not yet determine the dynamism of the will.

Thinking differs from volition by its direction[41a]. This direction is "toward the subject"[41b]: inasmuch as a certain going out toward an object is linked to volition (in its essence, volition is striving), a certain introduction of an object into the subject is linked to thinking—or, more broadly speaking, to cognition. Thus, for instance, the introduction of an object into the subject is accomplished through [42a]impression[42b] or imagination, which is, in a sense, an interior reproduction of impressions; it is also accomplished by understanding. Through each of them, though in different ways, an object is cognitively introduced into the subject of cognition; this happens in a sensual way through [43a]impression[43b] or imagination, and in an intellectual way through understanding.

In the moment of judgment, man experiences himself as the "agent of thinking"

This direction "toward the subject," which is proper to thinking, also takes place in the aforementioned lived-experiences of the "it comes to mind" type. However, even when we deal not with lived-experiences of this type but with the normal "I think," we should ascertain within it *the characteristic struggle between a certain passivity and the proper activity of the personal "I."* Thinking—and more broadly speaking, cognition—happens in man up to a certain point, as it were, and from a certain point is his explicit action. It is clear that this cognitive "happening" is already a manifestation of man's cognitive dynamism, thereby presupposing a cognitive potentiality in all its proper complexity. Nonetheless, man experiences himself as the agent of thinking and cognition only at a definite moment. *This moment is certainly the moment of judgment.* The activity of judging is the most proper cognitive activity of man. It presupposes—as analysts of cognition have extensively noted—an even more original activity of the intellect, namely, conceptualization. Experientially, however, this activity inheres in the activity of judging, and through judgment it is manifested in consciousness as the action in which my own "I" is not only subject but also agent.

The mental activity of judging has its "external" structure thanks to the objects that constitute its material (*obiectum materiale*). This structure is manifested in sentences expressed in speech or writing. Thus, for example, in the sentence "This wall is white," the activity of judging consists in ascribing to the given thing (the wall) a property that it really possesses (whiteness), and this is expressed by a certain "external" structure, proper not only to speech but also to thought. For if we speak in sentences, it is because we think in judgments. Nonetheless, something more is essential to judgment, namely, the grasp of the truth about the objects that constitute the material of judgment. Thus, the sentence "The wall is white"—besides the external structure in which the activity of judging clothes itself on account of its objects (*obiectum materiale*)—conceals the "internal" structure that is the most essential for this activity: the grasp of truth (*obiectum formale*). *Grasping the truth is equivalent to introducing an object into the subject-person in accord with the essential property of this subject-person.* [44a]The realm of truth is identified with the realm of spirit proper only to it.[44b] Truth constitutes the essential reason for the existence of human cognition and is the basis of the transcendence of the person in action. For the act is itself through the moment of truth, [45a]which manifests it as an authentic *actus personae*[45b].

The correspondence between judgment and decision (*praecognitum* and *volitum*)

There exists a distinct correspondence and correlation between judgment and the decision or choice proper to the will. This correspondence is of *praecognitum* in relation to *volitum*. However, we gain a proper vision of the correspondence and correlation together with the vision of the person in his transcendence. *Through judgment, the person acquires his proper cognitive transcendence in relation to objects.* This is transcendence through the truth about cognitive objects—in this case, we mean the axiological truth contained in the judgment of such objects' values. It is precisely this cognitive transcendence (*prae-cognitum*) that conditions the proper transcendence of the will in the act (*volitum*). Decision and choice presuppose judgment of values, for this judgment not only is constituted in itself through the truth about objects, but also enables and conditions the will's proper relation to objects through the moment of truth, the fact that—as we stated—determines the originality of decision and choice. Where the person decides or chooses, there he has previously passed judgment on value.

It is worth pointing out that every decision—and choice is reduced to decision—constitutes the most proximate analogy of judgment, to the extent that judgment itself is sometimes considered to be decision. However, the essence of judging is cognitive—it belongs to the sphere of "to know"—whereas the essence of deciding is closely connected with "to will." "To will" means not only to strive for an end but also to strive by deciding. It is precisely for this reason that the will inheres so thoroughly in the structure of the person, and every authentic, fully mature "I will" actualizes the self-governance and self-possession proper to the person.

The creative role of intuition in relation to the discursive processes of cognition of value

By thus portraying the significance of judgment to the reciprocal relation between *volitum* and *praecognitum*, we do not intend in the least to depreciate *the creative role of cognitive intuition, especially concerning the lived-experience of value*. We already stated that we observe within human thinking a struggle, as it were, between a certain passivity and the proper activity of the personal "I." This "I" experiences itself in cognition as the agent—as the one who acts when he judges. Nonetheless, cognition is also sometimes *a sort of experiencing [doznawanie] of an object*, which at times reveals itself, and especially its value, in a particular way to the subject. The subject "I" is then more passive than active, more a subject than merely an agent, yet such moments are at times immensely important, creative, and enriching for cognition.

Although intuition may seem to be cognition, which "happens" in man to a much greater extent than he acts in it as agent, we nonetheless ought not to undermine [46a]action[46b]. Above all, judgment seems always to accompany the intuitive experiencing [*doznawanie*] of objects. This is the judgment of value, the judgment that states the existence of a given value, since value is the object of intuition. Judgment, in this case, does not have a discursive character. We do not arrive at a value by way of reasoning but rather find it in our cognition, so to speak, ready-made and not reasoned out. In this sense, we can speak of a certain cognitive experience [*doznanie*]. This experience [*doznanie*], however, is quite often the fruit of previous cognitive measures, the fruit of sometimes many attempts to [47a]mentally[47b] grasp the value, attempts that did not directly afford a vision of it. When the intuitive grasp of this value takes place *hic et nunc*, then we have the right to think that it is indirectly a result of discursive measures.

Intuition and discourse are entangled in different ways in the totality of cognitive processes; sometimes the intuitive moment lies at the origin of discursive thinking, and sometimes it constitutes its terminus and indirect result. What is important from the viewpoint of the transcendence of the person is not so much the more intuitive or more discursive look of the cognitive process as the moment of truth, for the relation to truth also explains all deciding or choosing. The intuition that inheres at the origin of the discursive process seems to indicate a need to be grounded in intuitive truth. But the intuition that constitutes the fruit of the discursive process seems to be the discovery of truth and a dwelling in it. The transcendence of the person [48a] is linked not so much with the intellectual function of judging as precisely with the truth about objective reality, with respect to which man must constantly decide and choose, that is, find proper responses to this reality in his acts.

CHAPTER 4 ❧ Self-Determination and Fulfillment

1. What Does the Statement "I perform an act" Mean?

The statement "I perform an act" pertains to the essential subject matter of our study

We have appealed several times in this study to the particular precision of our language, which conceals a specific depth of thought in colloquial expressions or phrases. Continuing the reflections of chapter 3, we should also refer at the beginning of this chapter to the phrase that holds an established position not only in literary but also in colloquial language. We mean here the phrase "to perform an act." In the course of our reflections, whose subject matter is the transcendence of the person in the act, we must consider in particular the fulfillment of which the above expression speaks. *The phrase "to perform an act" conceals in itself, in a sense, the entire subject matter of this study.* For, in fact, we concern ourselves here with person and act not as two realities separate from each other but—as we have emphasized from the beginning—as one deeply coherent reality. This coherence takes place in reality; thus it must also take place in understanding, that is, in interpretation. It therefore seems that the classic expression of this existential and essential coherence of person and act is, in the Polish language, the phrase "to perform an act" [*spełniać czyn*].[xxviii] Hence, we should refer to it in the philosophical interpretation of person and act. [1a]

We are concerned here above all with the internal and intransitive effect of the act

The very verb "to fulfill" [*spełniać*] speaks primarily with its stem and etymology. This stem is the same as the one found in the adjective "full" [*pełen, pełny*] or in the noun "fullness" [*pełnia*]. "To fulfill" means "to make full," or "to bring to fullness." Therefore, fulfilling seems to correspond most properly to the term *actus*, which particularly indicates the fullness corresponding to a given potency or potentiality. This is the perspective in which traditional philosophy analyzed the act. In our present inquiries, we try to respect this achievement while seeking a perhaps more adequate expression both for the person as subject and agent of the act and for the act as the authentic *actus personae*. When we speak of performing an act, the person appears as subject and agent [*sprawca*], whereas *the act itself is taken as the effect of this efficacy* [*sprawczość*].[xxix] This result is *both external in relation to the person and internal, immanent to him*. In addition, it is both *transitive and intransitive* in relation to him.[1] The one and the other are most closely connected with the will, which—as we ascertained in the previous chapter—is simultaneously self-determination and intentionality. Self-determination is something more fundamental to the will; it is also linked to the fundamental meaning of freedom. Intentionality is something in a sense secondary to and integrated by self-determination. This intentionality indicates the developed meaning of freedom.

---

1. It seems that a close connection exists between acknowledging the intransitive effect of the act and acknowledging the full realness of good and evil—the moral values—inside the personal subject that is man. On this depends, in turn, the sense of all our reflections concerning the relation between self-determination and fulfillment. When we continue to use the formula "man fulfills himself" (or "man does not fulfill himself"), we are aware that "fulfillment" has in itself, so to speak, an absolute sense. However, neither this chapter nor the entire study speaks of the absolute dimension of fulfilling oneself. No concrete act in the earthly experience of man realizes this dimension. At the same time, however, every act in some measure reveals the structures of personal fulfillment as well as the structures of personal self-determination. Therefore, because in the previous chapter we analyzed the structures of self-determination, we consider it indispensable to undertake in this chapter a certain analysis of the structures of personal fulfillment connected with the act.

The distinction between what is transitive and what is intransitive in the act remains in connection with the traditional philosophy of being and acting (*l'être et l'agir*).

Morality as an existential and personal reality presupposes the fulfillment of self through the act

[2a]Precisely this dynamic of the will explains the fact that acts[2b], which are the effect of the person's efficacy [3a](*operari sequitur esse*)[3b], *join in themselves outwardness and inwardness, transitiveness and intransitiveness.* For every act contains a certain intentional orientation; it is directed toward certain objects or objective groups; it is directed outside the person. At the same time, in virtue of self-determination, the act penetrates the subject, its own "I," which is its first and fundamental object. What goes hand in hand with this is the transitiveness and intransitiveness of the human act.

Every act is a reality that in some respect passes away—it has its beginning and end both in the external dimension in relation to man and in its internal dimension. The latter is of utmost importance for us here, for we are concerned mainly with the very connection of the act to the person and not with the formation of the world by man's action. It is in the internal dimension of the person that the human act both passes and does not pass away. The act's effect is more lasting than the act itself, for this effect is explained by efficacy and self-determination, that is, by the commitment of the person in freedom. In accord with the structure of self-determination, this commitment *is objectivized* not only in the act alone as a transitive effect but also *in the person, due to its intransitive effect. We witness such an objectivization particularly in morality*, where man himself as a person *becomes* morally good or morally evil through the morally good or morally evil act.

In this way the proper meaning of the phrase "to perform an act" becomes evident to us. Performance is not identified with efficacy. To perform an act does not mean merely to be its agent. Rather, *performance is something coordinate to self-determination*. It progresses in parallel to self-determination, but, in a sense, in the opposite direction. Indeed, *being the agent of the act, man at the same time fulfills himself in it.* He fulfills, that is, he realizes or, in a sense, brings to proper fullness the structure that is characteristic of him on account of his personhood, on account of the fact that he is somebody and not merely something. It is the structure of self-governance and self-possession. The intentionality of willing and acting, the going outside oneself toward objects presenting themselves to man as various goods—thus, toward values—constitutes at the same time the going into one's own "I" as the most proximate and most essential object of self-determination. Morality, that is, moral value as an existential fact, is based on this structure; thanks to this structure, morality enters the interior constitution of man as a person and there obtains its permanence. This permanence is connected with the intransitiveness of acts, and at the same time it determines this intransitiveness in a particular way. Human acts remain in man thanks to moral values, which are the objective reality most closely coherent with the person [4a]. Man as a person is somebody, and as somebody he is good or evil.

Of course, morality can be to some extent isolated from this nexus, from the existential totality that morality constitutes together with the person. In a sense, this is even indispensable, for this nexus is a reality that is too rich to allow us to interpret simultaneously and in equal measure both the person-act structure and morality, not to mention the entire normative profile in which the proper nature of ethics is expressed. Therefore, in ethics we usually meet with a more or less advanced separation of [5a] moral reality, with a sort of placing it outside the parentheses, as was described in part 1. *Nonetheless, morality as an existential reality always remains closely connected with man as a person.* Its vital root is in the person. In reality, it exists neither outside the performance of the act nor outside the fulfillment of oneself through the act. The fulfillment of oneself through the act is the same as the realization of self-governance and self-possession thanks to self-determination. Only in this dynamic cycle is morality possible as a fact, as a reality. Morality as an axiological reality consists in an utterly peculiar division, or even opposition, of good and evil—the moral values—inside man. The philosophy of morality examines this particular axiological reality while ethics presupposes it. However, this reality contains, in a sense, a deeper layer: the ontological reality, *the reality of fulfilling oneself through the act—which is proper only to the person.* Morality as an axiological reality is rooted in this ontological reality but at the same time explains it, helps us to understand it. Therefore, in this study we greatly emphasize the experience of morality.

2. [6a]Self-Fulfillment and Conscience[6b]
The fulfillment of the person in the act has an ethical dimension

The fact that the expression "to perform an act" indicates action not only as an external and transitive effect but also as an internal and intransitive effect has a fundamental significance for interpreting the person. At the same time, a path *toward an adequate interpretation of conscience* is opened to us, *a path that again seems to be possible only with the presupposition that performance of the act constitutes at the same time fulfillment of the person through the act.* No other path seems to render intelligible the specific vitality of conscience, of its strictly personalistic sense. Certainly, it does not constitute a more or less separated dialectic of values, of good and evil, but with its root reaches the ontological fact that is personal self-fulfillment through act. Man fulfills himself as a person, as somebody, and as somebody he can become good or evil—that is, he can fulfill himself or, in a sense, fail to fulfill himself.

In this contradistinction we already enter morality as an axiological reality, for every act is ontologically a fulfillment of the person. Axiologically, however, this fulfillment is a fulfillment only through good; through moral evil it is, in a sense, non-fulfillment. It seems that this view possesses a certain link to grasping all evil—including moral evil—as a lack. This lack exists in the moral order and, thus, in the axiological order (i.e., in the order of values), whence it permeates the ontological order. For moral values are so essential for the person that, on the one hand, *his true fulfillment is accomplished not so much through the act itself as through the moral goodness of this act.* On the other hand, moral evil determines non-fulfillment, even though the person is still performing an act. By performing the act, he ontologically fulfills himself in it. We can thus grasp the deepest reality of morality as the fulfillment of oneself in good or in evil—the latter being precisely non-fulfillment.

The possibility of the fulfillment or non-fulfillment of oneself manifests the contingency (*contingentia*) of the human person

Precisely the fulfillment of self (which is realized through every "I perform the act")—as regarded in the ontological sense—already allows us to think of the human person as a potential, not a fully actual, being. If the human person were so-called pure act, then no possibility of any actualization would exist in him. We were accustomed to such a way of thinking about person and act by traditional realist metaphysics and somewhat disaccustomed to it by the subsequent philosophy of consciousness. It is clear, however, that the person, the act, and their dynamic coherence constitute not only a certain content of consciousness but also a reality outside of consciousness. Since the person performs an act, fulfilling himself through it and in it, morality considered in the ontological perspective *testifies to what traditional metaphysics called the contingency* (contingentia) *of being: man is a contingent being*. Every being that must proceed toward its own fullness, that is, every being that is subject to actualization, is contingent. Morality as an axiological fact also seems to testify to this, though in a different way. The possibility of being good or evil—that is, of fulfilling oneself [7a]in moral good or evil (the latter is axiological non-fulfillment)[7b]—testifies to the particular contingency of the person. The fact that he can be good or evil results from freedom; it also manifests and confirms freedom. At the same time, it manifests that this freedom can be used well or badly. Man is neither absolutely rooted in good nor certain of his freedom. Precisely in this consists the ethical aspect of the person's contingency and, at the same time, the significance of conscience.

In a particular way, conscience reveals the moment of the dependence of acts on the true good

Conscience manifests the dependence on truth that inheres in man's freedom. As we stated previously, this dependence is the basis of the person's self-dependence, that is, of freedom in its fundamental meaning—freedom as auto-determination. In addition, it is also the basis of the transcendence of the person in the act. The transcendence of the person in the act is not merely self-dependence, dependence on one's own "I," for it also entails the moment of dependence on truth, and it is this moment that definitively shapes freedom. For freedom is not realized through the subordination of truth to oneself, but through the subordination of oneself to truth. The dependence on truth defines the boundaries of the human autonomy proper to the person.

Freedom belongs to the human person not as pure independence but as self-dependence, which entails dependence on truth. It determines, above all, the spiritual dynamism of the person.[xxx] At the same time, it indicates the dynamic of the fulfillment and non-fulfillment of the person in the ethical sense. The criterion of division and opposition is reduced to truth: the person as a "somebody" endowed with a spiritual dynamism fulfills himself through true good and does not fulfill himself through not-true good. The line of separation, the line of division and opposition between good and evil as moral value and moral anti-value, is reduced to truth. [8a] Dependence on this truth constitutes the person in his transcendence; the transcendence of freedom passes into the transcendence of morality.

The transcendence of the person can be considered with respect to various transcendentals: Truth, good, and beauty

The concept of the transcendence of the person can be extended and considered [9a]in metaphysical categories. It will then be identified with *the relation to transcendentals* such as being, truth, good, and beauty, *a relation that is proper to man as a person*. Man has access to them through thought, and, in the wake of thought, in the wake of the mind, also through act.[9b] According to this understanding, act contributes to the realization of truth, good, and beauty. Act was often examined from this viewpoint in traditional metaphysics. This was accomplished slightly differently in Platonic metaphysics than in Aristotelian metaphysics. Despite all the distinctness, however, certain themes remained the common property of these various metaphysics and the anthropologies based upon them. [10a]These anthropologies were also metaphysical; they constituted a part of special metaphysics.[10b] The significance of viewing the transcendence of the man-person through his relation to the transcendentals is not at all diminished [11a]. The transcendence of the person understood metaphysically is not in the least something merely abstract. For we ascertain experientially that *man's spiritual life concentrates and pulsates around truth, good, and beauty*. Thus, on the basis of the human person we can speak boldly of a certain experience of the transcendentals, which goes hand in hand with the experience of personal transcendence.

Conscience is the normative reality inside the person

In this study—without detaching ourselves from that experience—we wish to indicate the more proximate and more concrete meaning of the transcendence of the person in the act. As we stated, this is also the transcendence of freedom, which is realized in morality. [12a]This is a realization through act.[12b] By performing an act, man fulfills himself in it, for he becomes good or evil as man, as a person. This fulfillment is accomplished on the basis of self-determination, that is, of freedom. *Freedom contains dependence on truth, and this is manifested with full vividness in conscience.* For the function of conscience consists in designating the true good in the act and [13a], with this, in creating duty[13b]. Duty is the experiential form of dependence on truth, to which the freedom of the person is subject. The proper and complete function of conscience is not merely cognitive; it does not consist in indicating that "*x* is good—*x* is a true good" or that "*y* is evil—*y* is not a true good." The proper and complete function of conscience consists in subjecting the act to truth. This entails the subjection of self-determination, that is, of the freedom of the will, to the true good—or rather, the subjection of it to the good in truth.

It is this *subjection to the good in truth that creates, in a sense, a new reality within the person*. This is *a normative reality*, which is expressed by formulating norms and by their influence on human acts.[2] These norms take specific part in the performance of acts, which is simultaneously the fulfillment of oneself—that is, of the person—through the act. Normative reality is essential and proper to morality and ethics, though not to

---

2. Perhaps precisely at this point we should specifically recall that Max Scheler critiqued Kant's ethics as the ethics of "pure duty" (*Pflicht aus Pflicht tun*) and did not critique duty itself as a specific fact, i.e., as a specific lived-experience. In other words, this lived-experience should be correctly rooted in value. On the other hand, we must ask whether Kantian imperatives (especially the so-called second imperative) do not in some way presuppose a turning toward values at the foundation of duty, whether they do not even impel one to duty.

In the analysis undertaken here, the author attempts above all to show the roots from which the lived-experience of both value and duty grows, in a sense, organically. Values are normogenic.

them only. Next to the norms proper to morality, those we can call norms of ethics, we find in the integral experience of man also norms of logic, norms of aesthetics, and perhaps even others. Some are linked with the field of theoretical cognition and theoretical truth, others with the field of art and beauty. A sort of affiliation of the normative order comes into view, on the one hand, with respect to the world of the transcendentals and, on the other hand, with respect to the multidirectional action of man.

Conscience as the norm of acts conditions the fulfillment of the person in acts

The norms of ethics, however, differ from the norms of logic and aesthetics, as traditional philosophy indicated. Only the norms of ethics, which correspond to morality, refer to act and to man as a person. For man himself as a person becomes good or evil through them—through them, that is, depending on them, on the basis of conformity or non-conformity to them. Neither norms of logic nor norms of aesthetics influence man in this way, for they are not, as Aristotle rightly observes, norms of action, of act, but only norms of [14a] production. What stands in their field of vision is not man himself as a person but merely man's product, his work. This work can be considered in relation to the property of truth or of beauty—thus being true or false (erroneous), beautiful or ugly. However, this *qualification of the work, of the product that is distinct from the entire world of norms, is not the same as the qualification—or disqualification—of the person himself.*

This fulfillment that ontologically corresponds to the very structure of the person is realized only in the person. The person fulfills himself through his act; he achieves as a person his proper fullness or form—this is precisely the form of self-possession and self-governance. Through act, the person realizes and manifests himself as a "somebody." What goes hand in hand only with this fulfillment—indeed, in direct contact with it—is self-fulfillment in the axiological and ethical sense, the fulfillment through moral value. [15a]Fulfillment or non-fulfillment. This is where the function of conscience is shaped. This function is designated by the ontology of the person and the act and by the interior dependence of freedom on truth, a dependence that is proper only to the person in the spiritual order.[15b]

3. [16a]The Dependence of Conscience on Truth[16b]
Why is the normative power of truth rooted in the mind?

Our analysis has thus far allowed us to establish that fulfillment is linked to the internal and intransitive effect of the act. In this effect, man's action is, in a sense, retained and consolidated in his person. This is accomplished thanks to self-dependence, which constitutes the fundamental structure of the freedom of the human will, and which contains and manifests an ability to submit man [17a] and his acts to truth. This ability, which is manifested in conscience, points to [18a]*the deepest reality of the person's very being. This reality has long been called the mind.* The mind is commonly understood as an organ of thinking, although the very function of thinking is ascribed rather to reason.[18b] In fact, the mind denotes above all the property of the man-person, similarly to the freedom that is also his property. The mind as man's property [19a]entails the ability to think[19b]. What is essential to this ability is not merely the formation of thoughts but the grasp of truth, the differentiation of what is true from what is not true. [20a]The mind as a property of man allows him to remain in potentially comprehensive contact with reality, which becomes the content of cognition and acquires a specific mental form in the thinking subject. Thomas Aquinas expressed this in the formulation *intellectus est quodammodo omnia.*[20b]

At the same time, however, through the ability to grasp truth and distinguish it from non-truth, from error, the mind—and reason in particular—constitutes the basis of a specific superiority of man in relation to reality, to objects of cognition. [21a]This superiority belongs to the entire experience of the transcendence that we analyzed in the two previous chapters. *This is a superiority, a transcendence through truthfulness and not through consciousness alone.* We have already made several distinctions that indicate this. The sources of human consciousness ought to be sought in the mind, because consciousness has a mental character. However, its proper function does not consist in inquiring after truth but rather in mirroring and subjectivizing. Man owes to consciousness the interiorization of himself and of the world of objects with which he remains in contact. However, although both functions of consciousness point to the mind as their source, they seem to be, in a sense, only secondarily connected with its proper dynamism. The dynamism of the mind consists in grasping truth, and this is linked above all to objectivization. This dynamism consists in the active differentiation of truth from non-truth. In its mirroring or its reflexive function, consciousness does not take an active part in that. Rather, it only draws its semantic content from the activity of the mind directed toward truth.[21b]

But precisely the activity of the mind, the effort directed toward truth—and not consciousness alone—[22a]is[22b] the basis of the person's transcendence. [23a]Here we understand this effort as truthfulness. It indicates the essential dynamism of thinking. For grasping truth is not a static order of the mind but a specific striving that has truth for its end.[23b] Man strives for truth, and the mind joins in itself the ability to grasp truth (through differentiation from non-truth) and the need to inquire after it. This already manifests the mind's dynamic subordination with respect to truth, which is also, in a sense, the human mind's own world. This subordination conditions the superiority, that is, the transcendence, of the person. Man is not merely a passive mirror that reflects objects, but he retains in relation to them [24a]*a distance, as it were, through truth or the superiority of truth*. This distance or superiority is something essential for personhood[24b].[3] Therefore, the old Boethian definition accurately underscores rationality, that is, the mind, as the *distinctivum* of the person: *persona est individua substantia rationalis naturae.*

The truthfulness of conscience as the basis of the transcendence and fulfillment of the person in the act

We have indicated self-possession and self-governance as the structural feature of the person. These structures are fundamental for grasping the act in its essential dependence on the person, its transitiveness and simultaneous intransitiveness. The fact that the act remains in the person through its moral value has its source and basis in conscience. *And in man, conscience is linked with the mind not only through consciousness but also through truthfulness.* It has been stressed many times that conscience

---

3. The reflections on "truthfulness and consciousness" remain closely connected with the whole of chapter 1: "Person and Act in the Aspect of Consciousness." The entire process of the gradual unveiling of the person in his constitutive structures through the act bids us to concentrate on truthfulness. For only in the broad and, in a sense, "secondary" meaning of the word can conscience be identified with "moral consciousness."

is a judgment that determines the moral value of the act, the good or evil contained in it. This understanding is right, though perhaps partial. It seems that we can in no way grasp the integral specificity of conscience without first outlining the structure of the person, the structure of self-possession and self-governance. What is explained only on the basis of these structures is the dynamism of self-determination and its parallel dynamism of fulfillment. Conscience is rooted in it. Conscience is an indispensable condition for fulfilling oneself in the act. As we said, the man-person fulfills himself in both the ontological and the axiological, that is, the ethical, senses. In the latter case, fulfillment occurs through moral good and non-fulfillment through moral evil.

This in particular depends directly on conscience. [25a]Duty also belongs to its totality, but we shall analyze duty in turn.[25b] Truthfulness, on which duty depends, moves to the foreground. When we say that conscience is a judgment, we take into consideration its last stage, as it were, and at the same time—and very often—its formal aspect only (this is linked to the purely intellectualistic understanding of conscience). Conscience integrally understood is a completely specific effort of the person that aims at grasping truth in the sphere of values. Conscience is first of all seeking and inquiring after this truth before becoming certainty and judgment. After all, we know that conscience is not always certain and not always true, that is, in conformity with the reality of the good. Nonetheless, this also confirms that conscience ought to be linked to the order of truthfulness and not only to the order of consciousness [26a]. In light of this, speaking of the act as a merely "conscious" action seems to be afflicted with some inadequacy.[26b]

This effort of conscience as a task of the mind aiming at truth in the sphere of values does not possess the character of a theoretical inquiry. *Instead, it is linked most closely with the specific structure of the will as self-determination and, at the same time, with the structure of the person himself.* It proceeds from this structure and in a specific way tends toward it. As we know, the will is characterized by intentional orientation; it is always a volition of some object under the aspect of value. This volition, however, does not remain as a separated intentional act but has an intransitive significance in the person. By willing something outside myself, in some way I thereby relate to myself with the will. No volition as an intentional act can bypass its own "I," which is, in a sense, the first object of the will. Freedom as independence from possible objects of volition presupposes freedom as self-dependence. The effort of conscience is most closely connected with this reality of human [27a] freedom. If this is an effort of the mind aiming at truth in the sphere of values, then it concerns not merely separated values of the objects of volition, but also—together with the intransitiveness of the act—the fundamental value of the person as the subject of the will and, with this, as the agent of action.

The normative power manifests itself in conscience as the linking of truthfulness with duty

What is at stake is to be good and not to be evil, to become good through act and not to become evil.[4] *Through this content we touch the normative roots of truthfulness that inhere in conscience.* We thus touch the very essence of the fulfillment of oneself, the fulfillment of the person, which in his proper dynamism progresses, in a sense, in parallel to self-determination. Conscience brings into it the normative power of truth, which conditions not only the person's performance of the act but also his fulfillment of self. It is precisely in this fulfillment that the particular structure of self-possession and self-governance, proper to the person, both confirms and realizes (actualizes) itself. Truthfulness, the normative power of truth contained in conscience, constitutes, in a sense, the keystone of this structure. Outside it, in isolation from it, we can in no way properly understand and interpret conscience and, more broadly, the entire specificity of the normative order. What we mean here first of all are the norms of morality, for they serve the performance of acts, that is, the fulfillment of the personal "I" through acts, whereas the mere norms [28a]

---

4. The point here concerns the fundamental dynamic structure of self-determination. The fundamental striving to become good and not evil is connected with self-determination. The position of Scheler, who thinks that moral value cannot be the object of volition because it would then signify a pharisaical attitude, is understandable in light of his presuppositions. For "to will to be good" is different from "to will to experience that I am good." In the latter, we can see a certain pharisaism. On that topic, see also Karol Wojtyła, "The Intentional Act and the Human Act, That Is, Act and Experience," 272–73.

It is precisely on the basis of these comparative analyses that we find grounded the conviction that the will in the structure of person and act ought to be considered above all in the aspect of self-determination and not in that of "intentionality" (see chapter 3, "The Personal Structure of Self-Determination" [p. 207 in this edition.]).

of production serve only the values of human products, that is, works, as we recalled earlier. Therefore, in this study we consider above all *the normative power of truth that is proper to conscience.*

Here, contemporary analysts employ far-reaching abstraction by making the very truthfulness or non-truthfulness of normative sentences the object of their research. Besides, they hold that no logical value can be ascribed to these sentences: truthfulness or non-truthfulness can be predicated not in relation to sentences whose syntactic functor is expressed by the word "should," but only in relation to sentences whose syntactic functor is expressed by the word "is."[5] This position does not in any way change or diminish the fact of conscience as the fundamental experiential reality in which the person most fully manifests himself (or even "reveals himself") to himself and to other persons. The fact of conscience is not so subjective as not to be in a certain measure intersubjective. It is in conscience that the particular *linking of truthfulness with duty takes place, the linking that is manifested as the normative power of truth.* The human person in his every act is an eyewitness of the transition from "is" to "should": from "x is truly good" to "I should perform x." Faced with this reality, ethics as philosophy (i.e., wisdom) and as science (i.e., a certain method of systematic investigation of truth) cannot leave the person without a basis. Thus, ethics rightly sees its principal task as the need to substantiate the norms of morality and in this way to render service to the truthfulness of consciences.

This most recent digression concerns ethics. It seems, however, that it was fitting to express it particularly at this point in the analysis of the reality of person and act.

---

5. The view expressed here on the nature of ethical judgment is linked with the metaphysical conviction that values do not exist in a real way (*evaluational nihilism*) and, respectively, with the epistemological conviction that values are not the object of cognition (*acognitivism*). This conviction is common to the emotivism of Alfred Jules Ayer (*Language, Truth and Logic* [London: Victor Gollancz, 1936]) and the prescriptivism of Richard Mervyn Hare (*The Language of Morals* [Oxford: Clarendon Press, 1952]). Hare, however, attempts to attenuate the extremity of emotivism in the name of the objectivity of ethical judgment, maintaining that moral norms can be substantiated, though in his opinion their substantiation does not consist in demonstrating their truthfulness.

4. [29a]Duty as the Expression of the Call to Fulfill Oneself [29b]

We examine duty in the perspective of the fulfillment of the person in acts

The normative power of truth is explained by duty and, at the same time, explains duty. Truthfulness, the statement "*x* is truly good," evokes through conscience, in a sense, an interior compulsion or mandate in the form "I should perform the act by which I will realize this *x*." This fact is most closely connected with the specific dynamism of self-fulfillment, the fulfillment of the personal "I" in and through act. *It is from this viewpoint in particular that we intend to consider duty in this study.* For it is known that other viewpoints can be used to consider it. Duty can be considered as the consequence of a certain [30a] moral or legal principle. Such a principle is called a norm on account of its content, which is not merely declarative (i.e., expressed by the functor "is") but obligatory (i.e., expressed by the functor "should" or "ought to"). In this understanding, duty—moral or legal—can appear as something derived from outside the subject-person. Such duty establishes for man as a social individual his obligations with respect to others and with respect to the entire society to which he belongs. The sphere of the person's duty toward other persons constitutes yet another problem linked to the order of participation manifested as the interaction and cooperation of persons. We shall speak of this in a separate chapter.

The truthfulness of ethical norms—that is, their rightness in themselves

However, all these forms of duty toward somebody, determined by an entire group of moral or legal norms, presuppose *duty as a specific intrapersonal reality*. This is a dynamic reality that constitutes an integral component of performing the act, for, as we have stated many times, the performance of the act is at the same time the fulfillment of oneself as a person. The fact that by performing an act man simultaneously fulfills himself through truth is made manifest in conscience. *There exists a correlation between conscience as the intrapersonal source of duty and the objective order of moral or legal norms*—the order whose significance goes beyond one person and his concrete interiority. Nonetheless, the duty-creative force of these norms lies in the fact that they objectivize some true good [31a] in the social sphere—in some measure in its interpersonal dimension and in some measure in its suprapersonal dimension. *The fundamental value of norms lies in the truthfulness of the good objectivized* in them and not in duty itself, although the normative formulas used in the given cases emphasize [32a] duty by employing expressions such as "one should," "one ought to," "there is an obligation," etc. Nonetheless, the essence of normative statements, whether of morality or of law, inheres in the truthfulness of the good objectivized in them. Through this truthfulness they acquire contact with conscience, which in a sense turns this truthfulness into concrete and real duty. This takes place even when conscience in a sense only accepts duty on the basis of the objective norms of morality or law. We must remember that the truthfulness of the good contained in these norms can be directly evident, and this is linked to the direct assimilation of their normative contents by conscience and the conferral on them of its own normative power.[xxxi] Otherwise, when this evidentness is missing, conscience very clearly performs a specific verification of norms, in a sense making them true on its own ground.

For truthfulness is most closely bound with duty. The point here is not only the objective truthfulness of the norms *in abstracto* but also *the lived-experience of this truthfulness, which is expressed by the conviction, that is, by a subjective certitude,* that this or that norm indicates true good. The deeper this conviction, the stronger the obligation, that is, the duty, it evokes. The lived-experience of duty is most closely joined with the lived-experience of truthfulness. At times—and even almost as a rule—what is spoken of in this case is not so much truthfulness as rightness. Theoretical judgments are true or false, whereas norms are right or wrong. Etymology seems to indicate precisely duty as the consequence of norms. For *"rightness"* [*słuszność*] has the same root as *"to hear"* [*słuchać*], that is, *"to be obedient"* [*być posłusznym*]. Hence, a right norm is one that ought to be obeyed, for it contains the basis for obedience; it is the true source of the obedience of conscience[33a]. It is quite the opposite in the case of a wrong norm.

In what does the creative character of conscience consist?

Despite the great accuracy and suitability of the attributes "right" and "wrong" when applied to norms, it seems, however, that these terms somewhat obscure the very moment of truthfulness, the lived-experience of truthfulness, and the transcendence of the person in the act of conscience—the transcendence linked with that lived-experience. The point is not in the least to confer a legislative power on conscience, as was postulated by Kant, who identified this power with the concept of autonomy, that is, [34a]the freedom[34b] of the person. Conscience is not the legislator; it does not create norms by itself. Rather, it finds them in a sense ready-made in the objective order of morality or law. The view according to which the individual conscience of man would by itself determine this order overlooks the proper proportions that exist between the person and a society or community—also overlooking those that exist in another order between the created person and the Creator. Such a view must constitute the root of individualism and a threat to the ontic and ethical equilibrium of the person[35a]. At the same time, however, we ought to accept that, from the position of the integral experience of man as a person, the function of conscience is not reduced to some mechanism of deducing or applying norms, whose truthfulness would inhere in abstract formulas, possibly codified as far as the positive legal order is concerned.

Conscience is creative within the very truthfulness of norms, that is, of the principles of action that constitute the objective stem of morality or law. Its creativity is not limited to simple commending and commanding, that is, to evoking duty synonymous to obedience. The lived-experience of rightness is preceded and integrated by the lived-experience of truthfulness. The lived-experience of truthfulness is contained in the acknowledgment of the norm, with which is linked the force of subjective conviction. In all this, conscience is creative within the truthfulness of the norm. This creativity coincides with the dimension of the person; it is completely interior and subordinated to action, which is simultaneously the act of this person and the moment of his fulfilling himself. Conscience confers on norms *the unique and unrepeatable form that they have precisely in the person, in his lived-experience and fulfillment*. What follows this molding of conviction and certainty, this formation of the truthfulness of the norm in accord with the dimension of the person, is duty. Duty—that is, the normative power of truth in the person, most closely connected with conscience—attests to the fact that the person in action is free. For truth does not destroy freedom but evokes it. The tension that occurs between the objective order of norms and the interior freedom of the subject-person is defused by truth, by the conviction of the truthfulness of the good. It is not defused merely by pressure alone, by the force of command or coercion. St. Paul most rightly postulates *rationabile obsequium*, which is the personalistic synonym of duty.[6] The means of coercion obscure the transcendence proper to the person or attest to his immaturity.[xxxii] It is difficult to deny that such immaturity often occurs, but it is inhuman to reduce duty to the very pressure of external means.

In what way does value "transition" into duty?

Everything points to the fact that the transcendence of the person through freedom is realized in truth or *truthfulness*. *It is truth or truthfulness that is the ultimate source of the transcendence of the person*, and therefore the old definition of "person" accurately emphasizes the mind (*natura rationalis*) as [36a]his foundation—though perhaps this definition does not adequately indicate how the mind determines the person and his transcendence in action. Perhaps this definition excessively reduces the mental element of the person to nature—but we shall speak of this separately.[36b] Duty attests once more to what the previous chapter emphasized, namely, that the person's will and freedom have their own proper dynamic subordination to truth, their own dynamic relation to it. This relation determines the specific originality of every decision and choice, and in a particular way it determines the originality of obligation, that is, of duty. For duty is, so to speak, a particular degree of the dynamization of the will through truth.

As we mentioned, this is not truth in the theoretical sense, not even axiological truth connected with the cognitive lived-experience of values. The lived-experience of values does not necessarily evoke the volition of them, let alone the lived-experience of duty. In order for value to generate duty, it must stand in the path of the person's action in a particular way.

The transition of value into duty is a separate problem, which we only

---

6. See Romans 12:1.

note without fully analyzing here. This transition is quite often accomplished by way of the duty to some non-action on account of value. For the majority of moral norms have the character of prohibition (e.g., the commandments of the Decalogue). However, this character does not in the least exclude or obscure value—in a sense, it even manifests value all the more. For instance, the commandment "You shall not bear false witness" all the more strongly emphasizes the value of speaking the truth, whereas the commandment "You shall not commit adultery" emphasizes the entire group of values connected with marriage, the person, progeny, education, etc. This way of transitioning from value to duty—*the way that is, in a sense, negative* and so characteristic of morality and legislation—is neither the only nor the primary one. *The positive way* seems to be primary. The most perfect and most complete example of evoking duty by value in the positive way is and will certainly remain the evangelical commandment "You shall love." According to this way, value simply evokes duty by its essential content and the force of attraction connected with that content. [37a]This content and power, in a sense, come up to the threshold of the person, which is the threshold of the truthfulness of the good—the truthfulness whence duty begins.[37b]

Man is called to fulfill himself in acts

Following the positive path of attraction by and acceptance of values that have been spontaneously or reflectively acknowledged as true, this duty can become an exponent—even a central exponent—of the vocation of the person. It seems that contemporary philosophy of morality demonstrates a distinct inclination to juxtapose and even oppose these two ways: the negative way, which is at times identified (not quite rightly) [38a]with the system of norms, and the positive way, which is identified with the hierarchy of values[38b]. The latter is the way of the person's vocation. The very problem of vocation deserves a separate study, as does the problem of the proper relation of values to norms. We consider this problem here only under the aspect of performance of the act, that is, together with the fulfillment of oneself through act. For it is difficult not to perceive the objective *closeness, and perhaps even the partial identity, of fulfillment thus understood and the vocation of the person*. In addition, it seems that every duty—including that to which the transition from value occurs in the negative way—in some manner informs us about the person's vocation. For in every duty the fundamental "imperative" is heard: to be good and not evil, in which the ontology and axiology of man constitute a unity, as it were. All the more particular vocations—the callings or perhaps "challenges" put to man by value—are reduced to this principal and fundamental one.

The drama of value and duty attests to the transcendence of the person

The close connection of duty with value manifests the human person in a particular relation to reality understood comprehensively. This is not merely a cognitive relation, which in a sense concentrates this reality in the lens of the man-microcosmos. All cognition, so to speak, interiorizes extra-personal reality in the person-subject (consciousness in a particular way interiorizes this reality together with the subject himself). Duty, however, acts in the opposite direction: it leads man out into reality; it makes him the subject of a specific drama (*dramatis persona*) belonging to this reality. From man's perspective, this is the drama of value and duty. Outside of this drama, man does not fulfill himself as a person. Indeed, the deeper and more thorough the drama of value and duty, the more mature does his fulfillment seem. Duty—*both as a component of the integral vocation of man and as the concrete content of a particular act*—seems to speak a great deal about the transcendence of the person. What is manifested through duty is, on the one hand, the realness of this transcendence and, on the other, its no less real boundaries[39a]. The person as a specific structure of self-possession and self-governance most properly realizes himself through duty—not through the intentionality of volitions, and not even through self-determination, but through duty as a particular modification of self-determination and intentionality.

In duty, the person opens himself toward values and simultaneously retains in relation to them the measure of the transcendence that conditions the act, for transcendence allows him to distinguish action from what "merely happens in the subject-man."

5. [40a]Responsibility[40b]
Responsibility is linked with efficacy through duty

It seems that the analyses conducted thus far create an adequate basis for grasping and explaining the connection that exists in man's action between efficacy and responsibility, and especially a basis for interpreting responsibility itself. The relation between the person's efficacy and his responsibility grounds the fundamentals on which the entire moral and legal order in its interpersonal and social dimensions is based. Nonetheless, just like duty, this relation is above all a certain reality in the person, inside the person. Only thanks to this intrapersonal reality can we in turn speak of the social sense of responsibility and establish certain principles for responsibility in social life. The first glance at the concept of responsibility shows that man, his personal structure, and his specific transcendence in action are what ought to be analyzed first here, so that the social and interpersonal sense of responsibility can also be properly outlined.

The fact that we link responsibility directly with efficacy, that we state that "man is responsible *for x* because he is the agent of *x*," indicates a great complexity as well as a cohesiveness and condensation of the content inhering in the simple totality "man performs an act." We see in these analyses how much of this content composes the reality of performing the act from the perspective of self-determination and, in parallel, from the perspective of fulfillment, which speaks more of the performing person than of the performed act itself. Likewise, responsibility speaks above all of the person performing the act and simultaneously fulfilling himself through this act. *For even though we connect it directly with efficacy, responsibility occurs not so much through the person's efficacy alone but through duty.* Man is responsible for *x* only when he should have performed *x* or when he should not have performed *x*. The one can be contained in the other due to the fact that the transition from value to duty takes place not only in the positive way but also in the negative way. For instance, a man who lies is responsible for leading others into error, which he should not have done, because at the same time he should have been telling the truth. The connection between responsibility and efficacy implicates duty.

The ability to respond to values and the responsibility for values

At the same time, this connection indicates that duty always contains an opening of the person toward values. Responsibility as an intrapersonal fact, experienced by man in the closest contact with conscience, seems to presuppose the specific dynamic of the will noted in the previous chapter. It was through the analysis of choice and decision in the originality proper to them that we arrived at the conclusion that the will is not so much the ability to strive toward an object on account of its value as the ability to respond on its own to this value. This ability integrates man's action in a particular way, conferring on it the feature of personal transcendence. It is also followed by *responsibility*, which is *most closely connected with the act precisely because the act contains the responding to values characteristic of the will*. In this way the *"responding-responsibility" relationship* emerges. Man is responsible for his acts and he experiences responsibility because he has the ability to respond to values with his will.

This ability presupposes truthfulness—the relation to truth, [41a]from which duty as the normative power of truth proceeds[41b]. Duty is the fullest way of responding to values, one most closely connected with responsibility. Responsibility contains something of a deontic relation to value. What comes into view is the *"I should–I respond" relationship: duty-responsibility*. On account of duty, the responding proper to the will acquires in the person and his action *the form of a responsibility for values*. As is known, thanks to the intentionality proper to the will, human acts are oriented toward various objects on account of them constituting this or that good, that is, on account of values. This orientation should be true, should correspond to the proper value of its object. For instance, if an act of the person has another person for its object, then this orientation to him should correspond to the value of the person. [42a]As we can see, the moment of truth about the object to which the act relates enters into play here. Truthfulness evokes duty and generates a responsibility for the object with respect to its value, that is, to put it briefly, *a responsibility for value*. This responsibility in a sense precedes duty and is contained in its coming into existence. At the same time, however, responsibility in a sense creates a further perspective on duty: it indicates the consequences of duty in man.[42b]

The fundamental responsibility for good and evil as the moral value of one's own subject is shaped on the basis of self-determination

Responsibility for the value that is proper to the object of action is most closely linked with the subject's responsibility for himself, namely, for the value that belongs to a concrete person, to a concrete "I," and for fulfilling it in the act. For not only intentionality, that is, the relation to objects outside one's own "I," but also and above all the relation to this "I," the objectivization of the "I" in action, is proper to the will. [43a]This is the first and fundamental meaning of self-determination and self-dependence.[43b] What is born in action on the basis of the self-determination and self-dependence of the personal "I" is—together with responsibility for the value of intentional objects—the principal and fundamental *responsibility for the value of the subject,* for the moral value of one's own "I," the agent of the act. Thus integrated, the responsibility "for" constitutes a totality that approximately corresponds to what we call moral responsibility. Perhaps at this point—through the analysis of responsibility—it is most clearly evident that morality is not reduced to heterogeneous elements, external in relation to the person, but finds a basis in the person himself, in his ontology and axiology. The transcendence of morality as an objective order, which in a sense surpasses the person, remains at the same time in close correlation with the transcendence of the very person—which manifests itself as self-determination and fulfillment. The responsibility for the intentional object of action and above all for the subject and agent of this action manifests a close connection with the fulfillment of oneself, with the realization of the personal "I" through every act.

Responsibility is linked with personal authority (responsibility "to somebody")

Yet another essential aspect belongs to the whole reality of responsibility, the aspect that we call *"responsibility to."* Responsibility "to" presupposes responsibility "for." This new aspect, which is undoubtedly contained in the essence of responsibility, speaks a great deal about the subordination of man as a person to the entire world of persons. For what inheres in the essence of this aspect of responsibility is the fact that responsibility is always a responsibility "to somebody," thus to a person. The world of persons has its interpersonal structure and its social structure. Within this structure, the need for responsibility "to somebody" certainly constitutes one of the foundations for forming power, especially so-called judicial power. The world of persons also has its religious structure, which is especially distinct in the religion of the Old and New Testaments. Within this structure, the responsibility "to somebody" acquires the meaning of religious responsibility to God. This responsibility has both an eschatological and a temporal sense. In the latter sense, human conscience—not in the governing but in the judicial function, though both are proper to it—acquires a particular authority. This authority permits us to think and speak of conscience as the voice of God himself. From the viewpoint of the philosophy of religion, as well as that of (moral) theology, this fact possesses a key significance.

In the present reflections, the fact of responsibility in the latter aspect—that is, as responsibility "to"—*sheds new light on the structure of the person himself and his connection with act*. The intransitiveness of the act, its specific [44a]penetration into[44b] the person as a subject on the basis of efficacy and duty, is once more confirmed in this aspect. Truthfulness—the relation to truth, proper to the person—stands at the boundary not only of the act proceeding from the person but also of this act penetrating into the person. In the form of conscience, truthfulness safeguards the paths proper to both the act's transitiveness and its intransitiveness. Both duty and responsibility are born in this deepest and thus most essential relation of the person—the relation to truth (which here we often call "truthfulness"). The responsibility "to somebody," regardless of its further points of reference, finds a point of reference also in the personal subject himself. This "somebody," to whom I am and feel responsible, is also my own "I." If this elementary form of responsibility did not inhere in the entire dynamic of fulfillment, responsibility to somebody else would be difficult to comprehend. The world of persons finds its experiential starting point and its semantic basis in the experience of one's own personhood. It is from this personhood that a path—which we shall already call the path of participation—leads to other persons, both in a human community and in a religious relation. [45a]The responsibility "to somebody" is one of the fundamental cofactors of participation; without it, it is impossible to be in community with other persons.[45b]

Man is responsible to himself in conscience

The responsibility "to somebody," integrated in the voice of conscience, places my own "I" in the position of judge over my own "I." It is difficult to deny that the experience of conscience indeed contains this function. *The responsibility "to somebody" as self-responsibility* seems to correspond to the self-dependence and self-determination proper to man, in which the will and freedom of the person are both manifested and realized. However, his structure—constantly designated here by self-possession and self-governance—certainly contains self-responsibility. If man as a person possesses and governs himself, this structure also entails that he is both responsible for himself and, in a sense, to himself. As was noted earlier, this structure indicates the specific complexity of the man-person. For he is at the same time the one who possesses and the one who is possessed by himself, the one who governs and the one who is governed. He is also the one who is responsible—as well as the one to whom the one who bears responsibility is responsible.

Thus, the structure of responsibility—which is characteristic of the person and proper only to him—determines personhood.[7] Diminished

---

7. See Ricoeur: "En me réveillant de l'anonymat, je découvre que je n'ai pas d'autres moyens de m'affirmer que mes actes mêmes. 'Je' ne suis qu'un aspect de mes actes, le pôle-sujet de mes actes. (En ce sens Husserl dit que hors de son implication dans ses actes le moi n'est pas 'un objet propre de recherche': 'si l'on fait abstraction de sa façon de se rapporter [*Beziehungsweisen*] et de se comporter [*Verhaltungsweisen*], il est absolument dépourvu de composantes eidétiques et n'a même aucun contenu qu'on puisse expliciter; il est en soi et pour soi indescriptible, moi pur et rien de plus,' *Ideen*, I, 160). Je n'ai aucun moyen de m'affirmer en marge de mes actes. C'est ce que me révèle le sentiment de responsabilité." [Now in waking up from anonymity I discover that I have no means of self-affirmation other than my acts themselves. "I" am only an aspect of my acts, the subject pole of my acts. (In this sense Husserl says that apart from its implication in its acts the self is not "a proper object of research": "if we abstract away its ways of relating itself [*Beziehungsweisen*] and behaving [*Verhaltungsweisen*], it is absolutely destitute of eidetic components and has not even any content which we could make explicit; it is in itself and for itself indescribable, pure Ego and nothing else," *Ideas*, § 80.) I have no means of affirming myself on the fringes of my acts. This is what the feeling of responsibility reveals to me.] Ricoeur, *Le volontaire et l'involontaire*, 56; translation by Kohák, *Freedom and Nature*, 57. See above all Roman Ingarden, *Über die Verantwortung*.

responsibility is equivalent to a diminishment of personhood [46a](the significance of which requires clarification). The structure of responsibility is, in a sense, first proper to the person from within, whereas it acquires a relation to other persons—responsibility "to somebody"—on the basis of participation. The structure of responsibility is *most closely connected with man's action; it is not linked with what merely happens in man*—unless what happens is itself dependent on action or, possibly, on non-action as an effect of one or the other.[46b]

6. [47a]Felicity and the Transcendence of the Person in the Act[47b]

Self-fulfillment as synonymous with felicity

The analysis conducted in this chapter, the analysis of fulfillment as a reality progressing parallel to self-determination in the dynamic totality "person-act," must at least touch upon a classic theme in the philosophy of man, namely, happiness. The difference between the expressions "happiness" [*szczęście*] and "felicity" [*szczęśliwość*] conceals a very subtle semantic distance, which is at first difficult to determine.[xxxiii] We detect, however, that "felicity" corresponds more closely to the direction and content of our analysis than "happiness." We are undertaking this theme not only out of faithfulness to a certain philosophical tradition, but also, above all, because of its convergence with the totality of our reflections. *The concept of happiness-felicity contains something very close to fulfillment,* regarding not so much the performance of the act *as the fulfillment of oneself through the act*. To fulfill oneself and to be happy are almost identical. To fulfill oneself is to realize the good by which man as a person becomes good and is good. The connection between felicity and the axiology of the person clearly comes into view. This connection occurs in the performance of the act and is realized in it.

Truthfulness and freedom as the source of the person's felicity

This, however, does not mean that the act itself as the dynamism proper to the man-person is a beatifying reality, a source of making man happy. As is known, the phrase "to perform an act" indicates a twofold effect of the person's efficacy and self-determination—the effect that is external and internal, transitive and intransitive. The sphere of felicity ought to be sought in what is internal and intransitive in the act—in what is identified with the fulfillment of oneself as a person. It is known from the previous analyses that this self-fulfillment consists of several elements that we gradually attempted to bring to light. Among them, two are reciprocally connected with each other, namely, truthfulness and freedom. The fulfillment of the person in the act depends on the active and intra-creative *union of truth with freedom. This union is also beatifying*. Mere freedom itself as a simple "I can—I do not have to" does not seem to be beatifying. Freedom in this state is only a condition for felicity, although depriving man of this condition is equivalent to threatening felicity itself. Felicity, however, is not identified with having freedom at one's disposal but with fulfilling it through truth. Fulfilling freedom in truthfulness, that is, on the basis of the relation to truth, is equivalent to fulfilling the person. And precisely this is beatifying in the dimension of the person, in his magnitude.

Happiness that proceeds from the relation to other persons

Clearly, it is not easy to distinguish this dimension of the person and his own unique and unrepeatable magnitude first from the entire network of inter-personal and social relations and then in turn from the entire system of reference to the "world," that is, nature [*przyroda*] understood in a most general way, consisting of a number of beings that are lower than man and at the same time somehow subordinated to and needed by him. All of these relations also have some significance for man's happiness. It is the relation to other persons, which we will define as participation, that has a particular and fundamental significance. We shall yet attempt to analyze separately the problem of this *participation*, for participation brings human persons together and unites them *on the personal plane proper to them*. We know from experience that such participation is beatifying in a particular sense. It is on the analogous plane of personal participation that we should understand felicity in the religious sense—the felicity that proceeds from interaction and union with God. A thorough understanding of the person certainly has great significance for understanding and interpreting the revealed Christian truth about eternal felicity, which consists in union with God.

We are concerned here only with the intra-personal profile of felicity

However, within our present study we are concerned above all with the fact of felicity in the internal and intransitive dimension of person and act. We do not go beyond this profile of felicity in order to understand felicity better in other profiles, the ones just mentioned. For this *intra-personal profile of felicity* seems principal and fundamental even in relation to other profiles. If man in a sense goes beyond himself in his search for happiness, then the very fact of this search indicates a particular correlation between the person and felicity. This is a dynamic correlation that occurs and is realized through act. However, we should seek the basis for this correlation in the person himself, in his constitutive properties of freedom and truthfulness, that is, in the relation to truth in cognition and action, rooted in the mind. We can even say that *felicity indicates a particular correspondence to the person*, with respect to his proper structure of self-possession and self-governance. This correspondence is so vivid that we can speak in turn of the specific structure of felicity itself as a "personal" structure, that is, one that does not occur and makes no sense outside the person or in separation from him.

The "personal" structure closely corresponds to felicity and its opposite

It appears that here lies a limit to analogy. For it seems that we cannot predicate felicity of nonpersonal beings, even if they are endowed with a psyche, as are animals. Surely we ascertain in them both pain and natural contentment, something like good or bad self-feeling on the [48a]animal[48b] level. However, felicity—similarly to its opposite, which perhaps would be best characterized by the word "despair"—seems to be connected exclusively with the person, with his specific structure that is unrepeatable in the world of nature [*przyroda*]. The fulfillment of oneself through act, which we also cannot transfer outside the person by analogy, is realized only in this structure. As is known, the principle of analogy serves to de-

Self-Determination and Fulfillment | 279

termine not only similarity but also dissimilarity. Otherwise, it would be an unsuitable instrument for orienting us in diversified reality.

Felicity cannot be reduced to pleasure

It seems that in this way we find the basis for drawing a certain *boundary line between felicity and pleasure*. This line runs within the experiential distinction to which we have appealed from the beginning. This distinction is between the facts "man acts" and "something happens in man." The fact "man acts" contains not only the performance of an act on the basis of self-determination but also the fulfillment of the person on the same basis—for self-determination always consists in a concrete realization of freedom. The realization of freedom constitutes the dynamic essence itself of the fact "man acts." This action, or act, as the realization of freedom is either in conformity with conscience, that is, with truth in the normative sense, or lacks this conformity with truth. In the former case, man as a person fulfills himself, whereas in the latter case he does not. What remains closely connected with fulfillment we shall call felicity, and never pleasure. In this way felicity remains structurally linked with the experience of action[49a] in the full content of this experience. What is also linked with this experience is the opposite of felicity[49b], namely, the despair that corresponds to action contrary to conscience, contrary to normative truth.

The introduction of pleasure into this integral structure seems to be a misunderstanding[50a], because it does not correspond to the experience of man, especially in its interior aspect[50b]. It is difficult to speak of the pleasure of a "good conscience" or the pleasure of a fulfilled obligation. In this case we speak of joy. The fact that this joy can at the same time be something pleasant is already secondary, as is the pain that proceeds from the reproach of conscience. However, pleasure and pain in themselves *are not connected with the personal structure of fulfilling oneself through act.* [51a]Man undergoes pleasure as well as pain. The fact that pleasure is a content of this undergoing belongs to the essence of pleasure—and this also seems to differentiate pleasure from felicity, which is a content of personal fulfillment. As we mentioned, felicity exhibits a sort of "personal" structure, whereas the "natural" structure is proper to pleasure. We also observe pleasure and pain in the animal world. In man, they correspond to his nature understood most broadly and most comprehensively. Therefore, we make sense when we speak of spiritual—and not only sensual or bodily—pleasures or pains. Felicity, on the other hand, corresponds to man as a person and to his fulfillment.[51b]

Person and act cannot be placed outside the "pleasure–pain" sphere

Here the boundary line seems to progress between felicity and pleasure. It is not easy to draw it in lived-experience, for felicity and pleasure overlap—each one can easily be taken for or identified with the other. It seems that we witness this quite often, when felicity is considered only as a form of pleasure, and pleasure as a homogeneous component of felicity.[8] Often, the difference between them is grasped only as a difference of degree or, rather, as a difference of depth: pleasure is something shallower or more "superficial," whereas felicity is something deeper or more "profound" in man. This distinction is suggested by the emotional side of the lived-experience of felicity and pleasure. We see this, for instance, in Scheler. Felicity is considered elsewhere as something spiritual, whereas pleasure is considered as something merely sensual or "material." Perhaps this is too great a simplification.

It seems that the dividing line follows that between the fundamental experiences of "man acts" and "something happens in man," and that it concerns structures contained in these experiences. Felicity corresponds to the structure of the person and of fulfillment. However, we should not claim that pleasure is connected only with what happens in man, for we can ascertain the pleasure or pain that accompanies action. It is also known that action can be and is at times oriented toward ensuring

---

8. It seems that this conviction inheres at the basis of so-called felicific calculus, built according to the principle of maximizing pleasure while minimizing pain. See Jeremy Bentham, *Introduction to the Principles of Morals and Legislation* (London: T. Payne, 1789). One can never give sufficient attention to the evolution that the old Greek concept of *eudaimonia* has undergone and still undergoes. See Władysław Tatarkiewicz, *O szczęściu*, 6th ed. (Warsaw: Państwowe Wydawnictwo Naukowe, 1973); translated by Edward Rothert and Danuta Zielińska as *Analysis of Happiness*, Melbourne International Philosophy Series 3 (Warsaw: Państwowe Wydawnictwo Naukowe, 1976). The position taken here is the fruit of reflection prompted both by Kant's reaction to Bentham's utilitarianism and by Schelerian analysis of human emotionality. See Scheler, *Formalismus*, 256–67, 341–56.

pleasure for oneself or others and avoiding pain, which, by the way, is the basis for the entirety of so-called utilitarian ethics, not to mention simple hedonism. From the viewpoint of the integral experience of man, any placement of person and act outside the sphere of pleasure and pain would be unwarranted. Similarly unwarranted would be the placement of man as a person outside nature. The sense of the distinction made here consists not in separating person and act from pleasure or pain, but in indicating that *what corresponds to the performance of the act, or, properly speaking, to the personal fulfillment of oneself through the act, is felicity* (or its opposite) *as something very specific*—something that cannot be divided into the elements of pleasure and pain and reduced to them. It is precisely this specificity and irreducibility of felicity that seem to remain closely connected with the transcendence of the person.

7. The Transcendence of the Person and the Spirituality of Man

On various meanings of the concept "transcendence"

The concept of transcendence has been the lodestar of our reflections on person and act in the last two chapters. When introducing this concept in chapter 3, we attempted to explain the particular meaning conferred on it in this study. For it is known that the term *"transcendence" has several meanings*. One, which is connected with metaphysics, with the philosophy of being, is expressed in the so-called transcendentals, which provide the most general descriptions of reality, such as being, truth, good, and beauty. None of these descriptions allows itself to be grasped within the definition that indicates the most proximate genus and the specific difference of a given thing. For each of them transcends with its content all genera and kinds according to which we grasp and describe objects of the reality known to us. The second meaning of transcendence is connected above all with the theory of cognition, and, more broadly, with the so-called philosophy of consciousness. According to this meaning, transcendence indicates what is characteristic of acts of human cognition, namely, the passing beyond the subject, the going outside of the cognizing subject toward the object. In chapter 2 we called this "horizontal" transcendence and distinguished it from "vertical" transcendence.

The concept of transcendence serves to express and explain the essential content of the experience "man acts"

The concept of *vertical transcendence* allowed us to gather the most essential content of *the experience "man acts"* into a certain descriptive-analytical whole. In this experience, man is manifested as a person, that is, as the wholly specific structure of self-possession and self-governance. As this specific structure, man is manifested in and through action, in and through the act. Hence, person and act constitute a deeply coherent dynamic reality in which the person is manifested and interpreted through the act, and the act through the person. Interpretation goes hand in hand with manifestation—this is the property of the phenomenological method, which is also reductive.[9] The concept of transcendence, as it is meant

---

9. In his work *O odpowiedzialności*, Ingarden states (1) that responsibility presupposes a specific theory of the person, and not just any theory: "All theories which reduce the person to manifolds of pure experiences are insufficient for the clarification of the ontic foundations of responsibility. Fulfillment of the requisites of responsibility is possible only insofar as a human being, in particular his mind and his person, is regarded as a real object persisting in time, an object which has a special, characteristic form." Roman Ingarden, *O odpowiedzialności i jej podstawach ontycznych*, trans. Adam Węgrzecki, in *Książeczka o człowieku* (Kraków: Wydawnictwo Literackie, 1972), 132; translated by Arthur Szylewicz as *On Responsibility: Its Ontic Foundations*, in *Man and Value* (Washington, D.C.: The Catholic University of America Press, 1983), 84. "Alle Theorien, welche die Person auf Mannigfaltigkeiten reiner Erlebnissereduzieren, sind für die Klärung der ontischen Fundamente der Verantwortung unzureichend. Nur sofern man den Menschen und insbesondere seine Seele und seine Person für einen realen, in der Zeit verharrenden Gegenstand hält, der eine spezielle, charakteristische Form hat, ist es möglich, die Postulate der Verantwortung zu erfüllen." Ingarden, *Über die Verantwortung: Ihre ontischen Fundamente* (Stuttgart: Philipp Reclam Jun., 1970), 66.

(2) Ingarden emphasizes that the freedom of the person performing an act is one of the essential conditions of responsibility. In his opinion, freedom itself presupposes a definitive formal construction of the person and of the real world in which the person acts. Both must form a relatively isolated system. Ingarden writes that the concepts of such systems conceal the key to solving the so-called problem of freedom (Ingarden, *O odpowiedzialności*, 133–34; 67 in the German edition).

(3) We can find in Ingarden the link between responsibility and duty when he speaks of the ontic foundations of responsibility. For he regards one of these foundations to be constituted by values, which, after all, he elsewhere acknowledged as being characterized by relation to duty. "The existence of values and of the interconnections obtaining among them is the first condition for the possibility of both the idea of responsibility and of the meaningfulness of the requirement directed at the agent that he assume responsibility for his deed and fulfill its requisites" (Ingarden, *O odpowiedzialności*, 107; 70 in the English edition). "Die Existenz der Werte und der zwischen ihnen bestehenden Zusammenhänge ist die erste Bedingung der Möglichkeit sowohl der Idee der Verantwortung als auch des Sinnvollseins des an den Täter gerichteten Postulats, die Verantwortung für seine Tat zu übernehmen und ihre Forderungen zu erfüllen" (Ingarden, *O odpowiedzialności*, 38).

In the discussion concerning *Person and Act* (see *Analecta Cracoviensia* 5–6 [1973–74]: 49–272), some Polish philosophers noted certain methodological analogies to Roman Ingarden's work

in this study, participates in this method. For it is with the help of this concept that we attempt to express the most essential content of the experience "man acts"—we attempt to objectivize that in which the person is revealed and made manifest in action precisely as a person. Hand in hand with revelation goes interpretation: the concept of transcendence not only expresses the fundamental content of the phenomenological experience, as far as the person is concerned, but also interprets the very reality of the person in his dynamic coherence with the act. The phenomenological method does not in the least remain on the surface of this reality but allows us to reach into its depth. It provides not only vision but also insight.

On the basis of this method, the concept of transcendence helps us to understand the structure that is revealed within the experiential fact "man acts." This is the structure of the person. The one who acts is a person; he verifies himself as "somebody," while *all the more precisely and more thoroughly, he manifests in action, in act, why he is entitled to be called "somebody."* Indeed, he has the particular ability and power of self-determination, in which he himself experiences himself as a free being. Freedom is expressed in efficacy, and efficacy entails responsibility. Responsibility manifests the subordination of freedom to truth and the dependence on it: this is what constitutes the proper sense of conscience as the deciding factor of the transcendence of the person in his acts. In this way, transcendence defines the particular structural feature of man as a person: a specific superiority in relation to oneself and one's own dynamism. Self-governance and self-possession result from this superiority. Only the one who is characterized by the structure of self-possession and self-governance is entitled to be called "somebody." He is entitled to that insofar as he is characterized by this structure either actually or potentially. Thus, man is already somebody at the moment of conception. He is also somebody when certain factors impede self-fulfillment in acts, that is, the mature realization of self-governance and self-possession. Man is entitled to be called "somebody" not only as a result of the experience of transcendence, but also on the basis of the analysis of being. None-

---

O odpowiedzialności i jej podstawach ontycznych. See Marian Jaworski, "Koncepcja antropologii filozoficznej w ujęciu Kardynała Karola Wojtyły (Próba odczytania w oparciu o studium 'Osoba i czyn')," *Analecta Cracoviensia* 5–6 (1973–74): 103–4, and Tadeusz Styczeń, "Metoda antropologii filozoficznej w 'Osobie i czynie' Kardynała Karola Wojtyły," *Analecta Cracoviensia* 5–6 (1973–74): 113–15.

theless, the analysis of being, to which in the case of man we owe the metaphysical concept of the person, also proceeds from the experience of transcendence, finding its fundamental content in this experience.

The conviction of man's spirituality is based on the experience of the transcendence of the person in the act

Thus, it is above all *on the experience of the transcendence of the person in the act*—the experience that we have attempted to describe and analyze here—*that the conviction of the spirituality of man is based*. The concept of spirit or spirituality is at times somewhat unilateral, identified with the denial of materiality. The spiritual is what is immaterial—what is intrinsically irreducible to matter. However, the explanation of spirituality through the negation of materiality presupposes a positive vision of spirituality itself. We find this vision precisely in the transcendence of the person. All that which composes the transcendence of the person in the act, which constitutes this transcendence, [52a]is spiritual[52b]. Because all of this, as we saw, enters into the sphere of phenomenological experience, the conviction of man's spirituality in its authentic manifestations not only results from some abstraction but also—so to speak—has a visual form. Spirituality is open to vision and also to insight. This form, the form of transcendence, is the concrete form of man's existence; indeed, it is the form of his life. Man as a person lives and fulfills himself in this form. For freedom, duty, and responsibility, through which, in a sense, we can see truthfulness—that is, the subordination to truth not only in thinking but also in action—constitute the real and concrete fabric of man's personal life. Moreover, it is precisely in them that the entire phenomenological structure of self-possession and self-governance finds its basis, as we have attempted to demonstrate multiple times in our present analyses.

The real immanence of the spiritual element in man must correspond to manifestations of spirituality

In following this eloquent totality of the experience of man, we cannot be content with mere manifestations of spirituality without reaching to its roots. *The real immanence of the spirit, of the spiritual element, in man must correspond to all manifestations of man's spirituality*, which acquire such a distinct form—the form of the transcendence of the person in the act. Man cannot manifest spirituality if he is not a spirit in some way. This view is supported by the fundamental principles for understanding all of reality, namely, the principles of noncontradiction and sufficient reason. By pointing out these principles, we also indicate the path that in the interpretation of man—the dualistic interpretation—has been followed for ages by the philosophy of being. This path is known from other sources; thus, it is not our intention to repeat it in this work. It is sufficient for us to indicate it. However, we do not limit ourselves to indication alone, for it seems that in previous analyses we gathered enough arguments to advocate the spirituality of man not only in a phenomenological (and not in the least epiphenomenological) sense, but also, at least indirectly, in an ontological sense. When investigating the transcendence of the person, we also learn where the spirituality of the human being is manifested.

What is the proper succession of understandings in this field?

We should stress that the human being's spirituality is known through the transcendence of the person. Such is the succession of understandings in this area. First we learn that man is a person: his spirituality is manifested to us in the form of the transcendence of the person in action—only later can we transition to understanding a spiritual being. This is accomplished by way of a certain abstraction. When abstracting, however, we cannot forget that the form of existence proper to this being is the form of the person. Just as we cannot sever person from spirituality, *we also cannot sever spirituality from person.* This seems to be indicated by experience. Therefore, we can accept the concept of "spiritual nature" (*natura rationalis*) insofar as it indicates a certain stability or substantiality of the spiritual being.

In no way can the manifestations of spirituality in man be comprehended and explained without this stability and substantiality of the spiritual element in him. However, the very way of being and acting that is proper to this element—or, in other words, that evokes this element in man—is not the way of being and acting proper to nature alone, as we have already indicated, but the way of being and acting proper to the person. Analogy has its limit here. The person is only in part and in a certain respect (namely, with respect to substantiality) reducible to nature. As a whole—and concerning his deepest essence—the person remains irreducible to nature. For freedom, which is proper to the person, cannot be reduced to the necessity proper to nature. We can only indicate the necessary connection between, on the one hand, humanity, that is, human nature, and, on the other hand, personhood (being a person) and freedom. Then we state that *the freedom of the will necessarily belongs to human nature. However, freedom itself is the same as non-necessity.* Thus, we can only speak of the nature of the person in the sense of the necessity of acting in a non-necessary way.

8. The Problem of the Man-Person's Unity and Complexity

Phenomenological vision speaks above all of the unity of the man-person and leads to his complexity

Our previous remarks on the relation of the transcendence of the person to the spirituality of man incline us to make further remarks. They will concern the problem of man's complexity as a bodily-spiritual being, where the "body" is understood as "matter" not in a merely physical but above all in a metaphysical sense. Experience as *a phenomenological vision speaks principally of the unity of the man-person.* Man is some-one. As a unity, he manifests himself also in his dynamism, although in this sphere we ascertain the characteristic divergence of action (the experience "man acts") and happening (the experience "something happens in man"). This divergence has not been fully interpreted, but we shall attempt to do so in subsequent chapters. Although the divergence of the dynamism of actions and "happenings" does not hinder man's unity as a person, it nonetheless speaks of his certain complexity, a fact we noted in chapter 2. The unity of the person is most fully manifested in the act, for it is manifested though transcendence. However, the transcendence of the person in the act also indicates a certain complexity. Man is at the same time the one who possesses himself and the one who is possessed by himself on the basis of self-determination. On this basis, he is simultaneously the one who governs himself and the one who is governed by him who governs. Subordination corresponds to superiority. Both "compose" the unity of the person.

Phenomenological experience indicates a certain complexity. What is characteristic, however, is the structure of this complexity, which is manifested above all not as a nonintegrated plurality but as a unity. It is manifested in this way in the act. The fact that man by performing the act simultaneously fulfills himself in it indicates that the act serves the unity of the person, that the act not only manifests this unity but also evokes it in a real way. The analyses conducted in this chapter attest to the fact that we owe this manifesting and real evoking of the person's unity in the act to the spirituality of man. We mean spirituality here not only as a group of manifestations determining the transcendence of the person in the act, but also as the real source of all these manifestations—*the spiritual element of the human being*. The experience on which we rely and the analyses that we have conducted allow us to conclude *that this element determines the unity of man*. In this way, the phenomenologically understood transcendence of the person in the act works toward the ontological conception of man in which the spirit, the spiritual element, determines the unity of man's being.

The spiritual element at the basis of man's spiritual potentiality

This element is the source of the dynamism proper to the person, as previous analyses have already adequately demonstrated. This dynamism is expressed in efficacy and responsibility, in self-determination and conscience, and in freedom and the relation to truth, which impresses its specific "measure of good" on the person's acts and on his very being. By being the source of the dynamism proper to the person, the spiritual element itself must be dynamic. As was demonstrated in chapter 2, potentiality corresponds to dynamism. *Hence we infer the spiritual potentiality of man, the powers of the spiritual nature.* The dynamic relation to truth corresponds to these powers in the cognitive function, whereas freedom and the dynamic dependence of freedom on truth do so in the function of self-determination. We describe the former with the concept of reason and the latter with that of will. Hence reason and will are powers of the spiritual nature. We owe the essential dynamism of acts to these powers. They determine the dynamic linking of person and act. Their proper potentiality shapes—so to speak—the profile of the person that is manifested as his transcendence in the act. Hence, by creatively participating in the profile of the person, these powers bear a very distinct personal mark. They cannot be fully reduced to nature. By ascribing the "spiritual nature" to reason and will, we do not state in the least that the dynamism, the way of dynamization proper to them, remains on the level of nature alone. The "spiritual nature" means the same as spirituality in the real and substantial sense.

Spirituality determines the personal unity of man who is a "body"

This notion of spirituality is the key to understanding the complexity of man. For man appears to us as a person, and in this way he appears to us above all in action, in the act. *He then stands* in the scope of our integral experience *as "somebody" material, being a body, while at the same time the spirit,* spirituality, the spiritual life, *determines the personal unity of this material "somebody."* Precisely the fact that spirituality determines the personal—and also ontic—unity of man who is a "body" allows and commands us to see in this man the ontic composite of soul and body, of the spiritual and material elements. Phenomenological experience does not directly reveal this complexity; rather, it manifests the unity of man as a person. At the same time, however, as we stated, this experience does not obscure complexity but in fact leads to it. For by manifesting the transcendence of the person in the act through spirituality, this experience *awakens the need for a further understanding* of what this spirituality is, not only in its manifestations but also in its ontic basis, in its root, as it were, and furthermore in its relation to the "body"—that is, to that which is visible of man, to that which falls under the senses. For what is spiritual is in-visible; it does not fall under the senses, even though in its manifestations it constitutes a vivid content of intellectual vision. Neither efficacy nor duty, nor responsibility, nor freedom, nor truthfulness falls under the senses; therefore, none of these is in its essence anything material, any "body," though each indisputably belongs to the experience of man. They are objects of vision as evident facts that the mind comprehends, and whose understanding it can appropriately deepen and develop in itself.[xxxiv]

The experience of the unity of the person awakens the need to understand the complexity of the human being

In this way, *the experience of the unity of man as a person simultaneously awakens the need to understand his complexity as a being.* Such understanding is equivalent to knowing "fully" or "thoroughly." It is proper to first philosophy, namely, to metaphysics, which long ago developed the theory of man as a being composed of soul and body, that is, of spirit and matter. Particularly convincing in this area is the teaching of Aristotle, deepened in the Middle Ages by Thomas Aquinas. We shall not repeat here their reflections on man's complexity and on spirit's essential irreducibility to matter. We do not exclude the fact that the analyses conducted in this study thus far, as well as those intended for subsequent chapters, in their own way undertake and "illuminate" those reflections—or perhaps rather take advantage of their light.[xxxv] For there is no doubt that the concept of man as a person—though it emerges from the first intuition and allows itself to be mentally developed within phenomenological vision—requires for its fullness a metaphysical analysis of the human being. Thus, inasmuch as the experience of the personal unity of man leads to his complexity, the thorough understanding of this complexity allows us in turn to fully understand the *compositum humanum* as one, ontically unrepeatable person.

The problem of the "lived-experience of the soul"

The cognition of the human soul as the principle of the unity of a concrete person's being and life is the fruit of metaphysical analysis. We conclude from effects that demand a sufficient reason, that is, a commensurate cause, that the soul and its spiritual nature exist. In light of this cognitive method, it is clear that neither direct experience nor the "lived-experience of the soul" (which would be precisely that direct experience) exists.[10] Man possesses only the experience of effects, and he

---

10. [13a] Roman Ingarden's analyses also seem to indicate that we are given only an indirect "lived-experience of the soul." According to him, this lived-experience consists in the lived-experience of the "pure I." Here is the text that expresses Ingarden's thought: "Es [das reine Ich] bildet nur eine eigentümliche Gestalt…, welche die menschliche Seele mit Notwendigkeit annimmt, sobald sie zum Selbstbewusstsein und zur Auswirkung in der Mannigfaltigkeit der Erlebnisse und der bewussten Handlungen gelangt. In den Tiefen der Kräfte, der Eigenheiten und der ursprüngli-

seeks in his being their proper cause. Nonetheless, people at times think and speak of their soul as something they experience. The content of the

---

chen Natur der menschlichen Seele gegründet, und eben als so gegründet, bildet das reine Ich das *Zentrum*, die *Achse* ihres ganzes Wesens.... Dieses Zentrum ist sozusagen ein Dispositionszentrum, von dem aus—wie aus einer letzten Quelle—die Erlebnisse hervorschiessen und in einem Strom sich entfalten und um welches herum alle seelischen Kräfte und Eigenschaften gelagert sind.... Es ist gewissermassen der Kreuzpunkt, an dem letzten Endes alles, was in der Seele geschieht und irgendwie wach wird und zur Erscheinung gelangt, zusammenläuft und von wo aus—so sehr dabei die Tiefen, in denen es gegründet ist, von ausschlaggebender Bedeutung sein mögen—alle bewussten Taten und Handlungen letzten Endes ihren Anfang nehmen.... Die Seele wächst eben dadurch zu einer *Person* aus, weil dieser Kern, diese zentrale Achse, das reine Ich, sich in dem komplizierten Aufbau der Seele in den Vordergrund schiebt und in ihrer Verfassung die hierarchisch oberste Stelle einnimmt—eben weil es Subjekt des Selbstbewusstseins und der Quellpunkt der Erlebnisakte sowie der bewussten Handlungen ist—sowie die Rolle eines *herrschenden, ordnenden oder organisierenden* und damit auch verantwortlichen Faktors im Aufbau der zur bewussten Person gereiften Seele ausübt.... Nur vermöge dieser Gegründetheit in den Tiefen der Seele ist es der eigentliche Vollzieher der Akte und Taten des Menschen, der Träger und Vollzieher der Willensakte. Dem Prinzip nach wenigstens entscheidet es über alle Taten und die Lebensweise und die Gestaltung und Umgestaltung der Seele, und wenn es ihm nicht gelingt, diese Entscheidung zu vollziehen und das in ihr Beschlossene zu realisieren, wenn es irgendeiner Kraft in der Seele selbst oder eine von der Aussenwelt den Menschen bezwingenden Macht unterliegt, so ist es—das Ich—dafür verantwortlich, da es letzten Endes der Repräsentant, die Selbstverkörperung des Eigenwesens der menschlichen Person ist." [It (the pure ego) only comprises a peculiar Gestalt ... which the human soul necessarily adopts as soon as it achieves self-awareness, and discharges itself in the manifold of experiences and conscious transactions. Set in the depths of the powers, of the peculiarities, and of the primal nature of the human soul, and precisely as so set, the pure ego forms the *center*, the *axis*, of the soul's whole essence.... This center is so-to-speak a center of disposition from which—as from an ultimate source—the experiences emanate and unfold, and around which all spiritual powers and properties are congregated.... This center is, as it were, a point of intersection at which ultimately everything that happens in the soul, and somehow becomes wakeful and attains appearance, converges, and from which—irrespective of how crucially important the depths in which it is set might be—all conscious deeds and transactions make their start.... The soul grows out into a *person* precisely because this kernel, this central axis, the pure ego, thrusts itself into the foreground within the complicated structure of the soul and assumes the foremost spot in the hierarchy of its composition—precisely because it is the subject of self-consciousness and the point of origin of experiential acts and of conscious actions—and also exercises the role of a *dominant, ordering or organizing*, and therewith also responsible, factor within the structure of the soul ripened into an aware person.... Only by means of this rootedness in the depths of the soul is it the genuine agent of human acts and deeds, the bearer and executor of acts of volition. In principle at least, it decides on all deeds and the lifestyle and formation and transformation of the soul, and when it does not manage to make that decision and realize what is implicit in it, when it is itself subdued by some power within the soul or by a power subjugating human beings by the external world, then it—the ego—is responsible for this, for it is ultimately the representative, the self-embodiment, of the human person's very own essence.] Ingarden, *Formalontologie*, 320–22; translated by Szylewicz as *Controversy over the Existence of the World*, 2:696–97 (Wojtyła's emphasis in the German text).

It seems that this text expresses *in nucleo*, as it were, the experience of both the transcendence and the integration of the person in the act. At the basis of this experience, philosophical reflection makes a discovery of the soul. [13b]

lived-experience of the soul is, as seen in our previous analyses, all that which "composes" the transcendence of the person in the act—namely, duty, responsibility, truthfulness, self-determination, and consciousness—though what is manifested above all in the lived-experience of the soul is the inwardness of this content. This content constitutes the vital fabric of man's interior life and, being experienced in this way, is identified by him with the lived-experience of the soul. The lived-experience of the soul is not limited to this content and its interiorization but encompasses in and through it, in a sense, the entire spiritual "I" of man. The lived-experience of the soul as man's spiritual "I" seems in its own way to point toward metaphysical analysis.

PART 3 ❦ THE INTEGRATION OF THE PERSON IN THE ACT

CHAPTER 5 ❦ Integration and Somaticity

1. Fundamentals Concerning the Integration of the Person in the Act

Integration as an aspect complementary to the transcendence of the person in the act

The last two chapters presented the human person in his dynamic specificity. This specificity is revealed in and together with the act. For what is essential in the act is the moment of self-determination, which we attempted to analyze thoroughly in chapter 3. The performance of the act is based on self-determination, the fact that was in turn analyzed in chapter 4. The analysis of both self-determination and fulfillment manifests the person to us as a completely specific dynamic structure, namely, the structure of self-governance and self-possession. This structure differentiates the person from nature, to which the element of self-determination, that is, of conscious freedom, is foreign, just as is *transcendence in action*, the transcendence formed in the person through freedom and [1a] efficacy. The experience "man acts" reveals to us precisely this efficacy born of freedom *as something most essential to the dynamic reality of the person*. The lived-experience "I am the agent" determines action and differentiates this action as the act of the person from all the—very numerous—manifestations of man's dynamism that lack the moment of the [2a] efficacy of the personal "I." Everything that merely "happens" in man as a subject manifests all the more the dynamic specificity of the act, shaped by [3a] efficacy and freedom.

However, the concept of the transcendence of the person in the act does not completely exhaust this dynamic reality. What appears thanks above all to this concept is the structure of self-governance and

295

self-possession as specific to the human person and his acts, and this structure demonstrates, in a sense, a characteristic bi-aspectuality or bi-polarity. In order to discover this duality, it is sufficient to note the real content that corresponds to the concepts of self-possession and self-governance, which express the dynamic reality of the person that appears to us through and together with the act. The concept of self-possession contains the person as somebody who both possesses himself and is possessed by himself. Likewise, the concept of self-governance contains the person as somebody who both governs himself and is subjected and subordinated to himself. Thus, these structures that grasp and define the dynamic reality of the person indicate something else besides transcendence. For we give the name "transcendence" to the very aspect of actively governing and possessing oneself, both of which are connected to self-determination, that is, to the will.

There remains *the second aspect or pole of this structure*. He who governs himself is at the same time subjected and subordinated to himself. He who possesses himself is at the same time possessed by himself: "to be possessed" and "to be subordinated" are elements of the same structure, the same dynamic reality, constituted by person and act. These elements cohere most closely and correlate most deeply with transcendence while remaining different from it. Thanks precisely to these elements, a second aspect is manifested within the dynamic structure of self-governance and self-possession, and thereby also within the structure of the human act. It is this aspect that we wish to grasp and define in the concept of the *"integration of the person in the act." This aspect is complementary to the transcendence of the person in the act*. One ought to understand this not merely in the sense that integration completes transcendence—from this the dynamic whole "person-act" is formed. One ought to understand this in a deeper way, namely, that without integration transcendence is suspended in structural emptiness. This sense is illustrated in the context of our foregoing analysis of self-possession and self-governance. For there is no governance of oneself without subjection and subordination of oneself to that governance. Likewise, one cannot actively possess himself without a corresponding passive component in the dynamic structure of the person.

We understand integration as the realization and manifestation of wholeness (and unity) on the substratum of a given complexity

In these reflections, then, we derive the concept of "integration" from the fundamental vision that permeates all the particular analyses conducted thus far. We derive this concept in a sense from the concept of transcendence that is complementary to it, for integration allows us to grasp and define the second necessary aspect of the reality contained in the experience "man acts." It is necessary inasmuch as without it transcendence alone would be suspended, as we said, in structural emptiness. Reaching even further back to chapter 2, we derive the concept of integration from reflections on the efficacy and subjectivity of the human "I" in action. Man experiences himself as the agent of his act, and consequently he is its subject. He also experiences himself as a subject, although the lived-experience of subjectivity differs from the lived-experience of efficacy. Furthermore, man experiences himself as the subject of all that merely "happens" in him. The lived-experience of subjectivity also contains a certain passivity, whereas the lived-experience of efficacy is active to its core and therefore determines the human act. Nonetheless, every act contains a synthesis of the efficacy and subjectivity of the human "I." If efficacy is, in a sense, the field in which transcendence manifests itself, then subjectivity is such a field for integration.

By establishing in a preliminary way the meaning of the person's integration in the act, we do not start from a definition but attempt to derive this concept from previous analyses of the dynamic reality that is the person and act. The very noun "integration" [*integracja*] is semantically linked with the Latin adjective *integer*, which is rendered as "whole, complete, intact." Hence, integration indicates the wholeness or completeness of a given thing. Etymologically, the Polish equivalent of integration can be the word "unifying" [*scalanie*] or "unification" [*scalenie*]. The former indicates the process of forming the whole out of parts, whereas the latter indicates the effect of this process. It is worth noting that despite the existence of these etymologically Polish words, it is the term "integration" [*integracja*] that is retained and used in science and philosophy. Apparently, the native Polish words do not correspond semantically in every respect to what the term expresses. For "integration" seems to indicate not only the joining into one whole of what was separated before, *but also the realization and manifestation of wholeness and unity on the substratum of a certain complexity.*

In this sense, the integration of the person in the act takes place, as indicated at least by the analysis conducted thus far. Characteristic of the person is a certain complexity of the structures of self-possession and self-governance that is manifested in and thanks to the act, or, speaking more precisely, thanks to self-determination. Self-determination reveals the transcendence of the person in the act. However, transcendence by itself constitutes only one aspect of personal dynamism; it unveils, so to speak, only one pole of this dynamism. If together with transcendence the human act reveals a subjective unity and wholeness of the structure of self-possession and self-governance proper to the person, then we see in this precisely the fruit of integration. In chapter 2 of this study, which was devoted to characterizing man's dynamism in general, we stated among other things that the transcendence proper to the lived-experience "I am the agent of action" passes into the immanence of the lived-experience of action itself. *When "I act," then I am already wholly in my action*, in this dynamization of my own "I" to which I efficaciously contributed (see chapter 2, section 2, "The specificity of efficacy").

The fact that "I am wholly in my action" is explained not only by transcendence but also by the integration of the person in the act.

2. The Manifestation of the Integration of the Person in the Act through the Phenomenon of Disintegration

The varied usage of the term "disintegration"

As is evident, in applying the concept of "integration" to our inquiries we link its fundamental and first meaning with the vision of the structure that is proper to the person and by which he most essentially reveals his dynamic specificity. We mean the structures of self-possession and self-governance. It is in this context that another concept is explained, that by means of which science and philosophy express a lack of integration, its defect or deficiency. This is *the concept of "disintegration."* It is *fitting for us to consider this concept as being in a sense parallel to integration,* because this will help us to establish its fundamental meaning. Clearly, we are not concerned merely with an analysis of concepts but rather with indicating what most properly corresponds to these concepts in reality. In this way, we attempt to grasp and explain the very reality of person and act in a possibly thorough manner.

The term "disintegration" is used many times—and certainly with multiple meanings—in the sciences that concern themselves with man. They apply it to various areas of his social and cultural activity as well as to his own personhood. This is most often carried out by the sciences that concern themselves with man's psychological personhood, seeing the manifestations of disintegration in all that in some way diverges from the human measure of normality or does not live up to it. In this understanding, the integrated man is simply the normal man, whereas the disintegrated man is not normal or is not completely normal. The question arises as to what in these sciences is considered the norm, that is, the measure of human normality. It seems that this measure is to a considerable extent assumed intuitively: simply, sound reason immediately indicates to us which man is normal and which one is not or not completely.

The sciences concerned with human personhood and relying on this intuition of the norm have managed to examine very thoroughly the various particular manifestations of disintegration in the dimension proper to each. This dimension is defined in the concept of psychological personhood, in which the moral personhood of man inheres very deeply. As is known, the experience of morality is an indispensable element of the integral experience of man, and this element has a fundamental significance for understanding man as a person, [4a]both in a static and a dynamic understanding[4b]. The concept of disintegration—as used by the particular sciences about man and by medicine (psychiatry)—is very often derived from facts of an ethical nature, thus, from facts that compose the totality of the experience of morality, in order to seek their conditions in man's psyche and somaticity.

Disintegration as a particular deficiency of the personal structure of self-possession and self-governance

It seems, however, that *this common—as well as scientific*, due to its being used in various areas of particular knowledge—*meaning of disintegration presupposes a fundamental meaning*. In the entire science about man, the fundamental meaning of disintegration is formed in parallel to the fundamental meaning of integration. This fundamental meaning of integration—and integration is always in some way the "integration of the person in the act"—remains closely connected to the structure of self-possession and self-governance, which is essential for the person. This structure is essential for being a person, although it is actualized and manifested in the act. What we call psychological or moral (ethical) personhood is something derivative, secondary, and in a sense aspectual in relation to being a person. In its fundamental sense, we consider integration, as well as disintegration, in relation to the fundamental structure and not simply in relation to derivative structures, even though we apply these concepts to the latter as well. Indeed, when we apply them to the fundamental structure, we can explain the proper sense of applying them also to particular manifestations in the psycho-ethical or, on the other hand, psycho-somatic dimension of man.

Thus, by disintegration in its fundamental sense we understand that *which is manifested in the structures of self-possession and self-governance— the structure proper to the person—as a lack or deficiency of this structure*. The lower boundary of disintegration is constituted by all the facts that are, in a sense, completely devoid of self-possession and self-governance. The being that is man, and thus ontologically a person, is or at least seems then to be deprived of these structures, which are proper to the person and manifested in and together with the act. This is therefore the disintegration of the person in the act. The cases of deep and thorough disintegration are well-known and have their names in particular sciences; they also have their psycho-medical qualifications. We refer to these facts here, in a sense by way of example, for what we attempt is not a highly diversified phenomenal description but a grasp of the fundamental meaning of disintegration. As was said, this meaning is linked with the dynamic structure of the person, and because this structure is formed through self-determination, disintegration also concerns self-determination. Man possesses and governs himself thanks to self-determination. *Disintegration signifies* some—more or less profound—*inability to possess and govern oneself through self-determination.*

As is known from previous chapters, the ability to govern and possess oneself, which is closely connected to self-determination, determines the transcendent vertical of the human person. In a certain respect and in certain cases, disintegration seems to break down this vertical. However, disintegration is not first and foremost a denial and exclusion of the very transcendence of the person in the act. Rather, in accord with its name, it constitutes a limitation of the integration of the person in the act. A disintegrated person *is unable* not so much to govern or possess himself as *to subordinate himself to himself and to be fully possessed by himself.*[1] A disintegrated person is manifested above all as the "unsubordinatible" or "unpossessible" "I" (excuse the awkwardness of these expressions), not as a simple annihilation or limitation of the transcendent "I." However, the defects and deficiencies of integration become the defects and deficiencies of transcendence, which is easily understood from the fact that transcendence and integration constitute the mutually complementary aspects of the dynamic reality "person-act."

Disintegration helps in understanding the fundamental meaning of the integration of the person in the act

The disintegration of the person in the act not only demonstrates very different particular forms, which deserve description, classification, and qualification by particular sciences. With respect to the fundamental meaning that we constantly seek here, *it also demonstrates various degrees of intensity*. These degrees correspond to the dynamic vision of man that was to a great extent developed by Aristotelian-Thomistic philosophy. In reference to this philosophy, we can distinguish between actual, ha-

1. The concept of disintegration is applied in particular sciences concerning man. Thus, for instance, the notion of so-called positive disintegration indicates in Polish psychology an attempt to grasp the totality of psychical facts. See Kazimierz Dąbrowski, *La désintégration positive: Problèmes choisis* (Warsaw: Państwowe Wydawnictwo Naukowe, 1964); Dąbrowski, *Personnalité, psychonévroses et santé mentale d'après la théorie de la désintégration positive* (Warsaw: Państwowe Wydawnictwo Naukowe, 1965); Dąbrowski, *Psychothérapie des névroses et des psychonévroses: L'instinct de la mort d'après la théorie de la désintégration positive* (Warsaw: Państwowe Wydawnictwo Naukowe, 1965); and other works by the same author.

bitual, and "potential" disintegration (in the sense of disintegration referring to man's potentiality itself). To use an *example*, there certainly occurs a difference between the fact of a one-time non-association of someone's external appearance with his proper last name and the fact of a frequent non-association, almost as a rule, of the one with the other. The latter case can have various causes. If, however, we consider the very non-association of someone's last name with his appearance as a manifestation of disintegration, then the one-time actual non-association demonstrates a lower degree of disintegration than the habitual one. But the habitual non-association of someone's last name with his appearance (which, as we said, can have various causes) also differs in degree from the fundamental inability to correctly associate the one with the other, for here we already enter the very potentiality of man[5a].

Another example could be chosen in which the feature essential for disintegration, namely, the failure of the subjective "I" to be subordinated or possessed, would appear even more clearly. But we can also notice this in the inconspicuous example just given. The inability to associate correctly is a defect of cognition itself, which has consequences in action. A man who is not able to associate correctly finds it difficult to act, to correctly decide and choose. As a result, his self-determination is also somehow defective, and the more thorough this defect, the more it is imparted to the person himself, the more it impresses a negative mark on his proper structures of self-governance and self-possession. We know from observing mentally ill people what deep drama in the area of factually—and not merely ontologically—being a person results from a fundamental inability to associate correctly.

In this way, in its own right, *the concept of disintegration affords us a better understanding of the fundamental meaning of integration*, of the aspect of the person's dynamic reality that we wish to signify by that name. As we said above, we do not start here from a definition, but we attempt to explicate the fundamental meaning of both integration and disintegration (in a sense, the meaning of integration through disintegration) from the increasingly penetrating insight into the dynamic reality of person and act.

3. The Integration of the Person in the Act as the Key to Understanding (Defining) the Psycho-Somatic Unity of Man

Understanding psycho-somatic unity presupposes grasping the transcendence and integration of the person in the act

Determining the fundamental meaning of the integration and disintegration of the person in the act is immensely important for the correct understanding of the dynamic reality of man. For man is very often defined as a psycho-physical unity, and this definition is taken to adequately grasp and express the essence of man. Properly speaking, however, only that which can be encompassed by particular empirical sciences finds its expression in this concept. For in this understanding, that by which man is a person and by which as a person he realizes himself in the act undergoes a specific reduction. Therefore, in this study, where we attempt to follow step by step the experience of the dynamic reality of person and act, *it is fitting to make in this respect a fundamental change in viewing the object.*

Determining the fundamental meaning of the integration and disintegration of the person in the act is a key, as it were, to this change in view. In light of the full experience of man, grasping man as a psycho-physical being presupposes grasping the person who manifests himself especially in the act. Thus, it presupposes grasping transcendence and integration as complementary aspects in order to thoroughly interpret what is contained in the experience "man acts." Man as a psycho-physical unity appears only within or, in a sense, in the framework of the dynamic unity that is person and act. Therefore, the correct understanding of psycho-physical unity *presupposes the anterior grasp of the transcendence and* especially *of the integration of the person in the act.*

Person and act is a unity superior to psycho-somatic complexity (and unity)

The fundamental meaning of the integration and disintegration of the person in the act clearly indicates [6a]this[6b]. The subordination of the subjective "I" to the transcendent "I"—that is, the synthesis of efficacy and subjectivity, already considered in chapter 2—contains the unity and also the complexity of man as a psycho-physical being. Perhaps the term "psycho-somatic" is more proper than the term "psycho-physical," as further reflections will show. It is the subordination of the subjective "I" to the transcendent "I," that is, the integration contained in the structure of self-governance, that encompasses the psycho-somatic unity as well as the complexity of man. It happens similarly with the integration contained in the structure of self-possession. *The analysis of integration obligates one* not only to mentally presuppose these personal structures, as we already have, but also *to penetrate the psycho-somatic complexity of man*. Precisely this complexity—for man owes his psycho-somatic unity ultimately to the integration and transcendence of the person in the act, and this is not properly [7a]understood[7b] in the interpretation conducted exclusively according to the empirical-inductive thinking of particular sciences.

However, in virtue of the full experience of man, it is precisely in the act that the entire psycho-somatic complexity becomes every time a specific unity of person and act. *This unity is superior to both that complexity and the psycho-physical unity*, if we understand the latter as a certain sum of somaticity, the psyche, and their proper natural dynamisms. Therefore, it is necessary to speak of the integration of the person in the act. The human act contains the plurality and diversity of the dynamisms proper to somaticity and the psyche. And it is precisely in relation to them that the act is a superior dynamic unity. In this consists the integration of the person in the act—integration as complementary to transcendence. For the human act is not only a simple summation of those dynamisms, but also a new and superior dynamism in which they acquire new content and new quality: the content and quality that is properly personal. They do not possess this content and quality as natural dynamisms of the psyche and somaticity of man; they acquire it in the act of the person.

Therefore, the integration of the person in the act grants us insight into the elements of the natural dynamic plurality that is proper to the entire psycho-somaticity of man. Thanks to this insight, we can shape the image of man as a psycho-somatic unity. However, this image presupposes a more fundamental vision of the unity of person and act, and this is contained in the experience "man acts," from which this image of psycho-somatic unity must also draw its proper meaning. *The concept of the integration of the person in the act is key to obtaining precisely this meaning.* Various dynamisms proper to man in the somatic and psychical layers of his natural potentiality take part in the human act.[2] Every act is some "unification" of them, though the concept of unification would indicate merely the formation of the whole out of homogeneous parts, which does not take place in the case of the act. What does take place is something more. These dynamisms proper to man's somaticity and psyche take an active part in integration—not on their own level but on the level of the person. And precisely this is the integration of the person in the act, the integration through which, as through the aspect complementary to transcendence, the structure of self-governance and self-possession proper to the person is realized. Thus, in this case, integration also means *an introduction into a higher unity than that indicated by the term "psycho-somatic unity"* when it is understood literally.

Integration as a particular introduction of actuations proper to man's psycho-somaticity into the dynamic unity of the act of the person

In this higher unity of person and act, the dynamisms proper to man's somaticity and psyche in a sense disappear; they lose their distinctness. This does not mean that they cease to exist. They exist and in a real way co-create the dynamic reality of the act of the person. This takes place in every act in some different way, depending on its individual specificity. If, for example, a given act involves a specific movement of the body as the visible element of its individual specificity, then this act contains and is co-created by the somatic dynamism, without which this movement could not be accomplished. If an act is completely interior, consisting, for example, in making an ultimate decision concerning some important matter, then, as we know from experience, various psychical dynamisms of an emotional nature often manifest themselves in the act's individual specificity and determine the act's concrete form.

It is known from the analyses conducted above all in chapter 2 that

---

2. In the discussions on *Person and Act* that took place in Poland, the significance of the philosophical conception of man as a person who "possesses and governs himself" was noted for both psychiatric research and practice. See, e.g., Wanda Półtawska, "Koncepcja samoposiadania—podstawą psychoterapii obiektywizującej (w świetle książki Kardynała Karola Wojtyły, 'Osoba i czyn')," *Analecta Cracoviensia* 5–6 (1973–74): 223–41.

these dynamisms in themselves are not "action." They are identified not with the experience "man acts" but with the experience "something happens in man." Insight into the dynamic elements of man's psycho-somatic complexity leads to the analysis of precisely these various "happenings" or, as we called them then, various "actuations" (by both analogy and contradistinction to the act, which alone corresponds to the experience "man acts"). The integration of the person in the act constitutes simultaneously the dynamic *introduction of these various actuations proper to human psycho-somaticity into the act*, which alone is dynamically proper to the person. The act is the new and superior unity in which they take an active part, whereas when outside the act, as the dynamisms of somaticity or the psyche, they only "happen" in man as a subject. And precisely this crossing of the boundary between "happening" and "action" is a particular function of integration.

This function is indispensable for realizing the fundamental personal structure of self-governance and self-possession, which takes place in and through the act. [8a]For thanks to this function, man in his entire psycho-somatic complexity becomes capable of objectivization, without which efficacy and freedom are not possible (see chapter 3).[8b] If the integration of the person in the act—and, in this integration, the integration of the dynamisms proper to the psycho-somatic complexity of man—did not take place, then only subjectivity and not efficacy could be realized in his ontic *suppositum*. We know from experience, however, that efficacy does dominate in it. The efficacy and freedom that we discover in this experience, as elements constitutive of the act, *draw all psycho-physical dynamisms into the unity of objectivization* where my own "I" becomes for myself the first object in action.[xxxvi] Thanks to integration, these dynamisms take an active part in self-determination, that is, in realizing the freedom of the human person.

4. The Integration and Integrity of Man on the Substratum of Mutual Psycho-Somatic Conditionings

We aim only at grasping the fundamental characteristics of the dynamisms of man's somaticity and psyche

The need for insight into the psycho-somatic complexity of man and into the complexity of the dynamisms proper to his somaticity and psyche is closely connected with the analysis of person and act in the aspect of integration, as just stated. In this field, our study must closely approach the various particular sciences concerned with man, his body, and his psyche as separate objects of knowledge. In turn, this knowledge often serves various areas of practice, whose center is man as a psycho-physical being. Medicine with its many specialized branches is a particular manifestation of such practice. At the present stage, namely, when considering the integration of the person in the act, our study will have to *approach these various particular sciences without being identified with them*. The precise reason for this is the specificity of viewing the object of our study, the specificity of which we spoke above. For this reason, we must have before our eyes the dynamisms proper to man in his psycho-somatic complexity, indeed, the dynamisms proper to the psyche and somaticity in a sense taken separately, though, from this specific point of view, constantly determined by the fact of the integration of the person in the act.

Thus, the aim of further analysis is not and cannot be insight into these dynamisms as it is accomplished by particular sciences. This is so both on account of advanced particularity, which would, in a sense, detract us from seeing the wholeness of the object "person-act," and on account of the fact that particular sciences seem to examine the particular components of man's psycho-somatic unity as well as the particular psychical and somatic dynamisms for their own sake, as it were. In this they do not consider what is most essential for us, namely, the specificity of the personal whole. Therefore, this insight into the dynamisms proper to man's psyche and somaticity will consist rather *in providing a fundamental characterization of these dynamisms*—a characterization that they acquire thanks precisely to their integration in the act of the person (which is linked to the integration of the person in the act). Although such characterization cannot diverge from the understanding of particular sciences, cannot contradict them, it also cannot share the particularities and methods they use. This is the characterization of man's psycho-somatic dynamism that we intend to create, ascribing to this dynamism both reactivity and emotivity,[xxxvii] where reactivity corresponds more to somaticity and emotivity to the psyche.

The psychical and somatic dynamisms condition each other

However, before we arrive at this characterization by analyzing the psycho-somatic dynamism of man in its complexity, it is fitting first of all to emphasize a feature that in a particular way determines the interior cohesiveness of this dynamism, enabling unity—that is, integration. Man in his psycho-somatic complexity constitutes this plurality and diversity, the particular elements of which are closely linked with one another, *conditioning and becoming dependent on one another*. What we mean here above all is the conditioning of the psyche by somaticity, the dependence of the dynamism proper to the psyche on somaticity and its proper dynamism.

The human body in its outwardness and inwardness (that is, as an organism)

When we speak of somaticity, we mean *the human body—first of all in the common, that is, prescientific, and then in the scientific sense of this word*. The body is matter, a visible reality that falls under the senses and is accessible to them—above all from without. The external shape of the body first of all determines what is visible in man; it creates his particular appearance and entails a particular impression that this man evokes. The human body thus understood consists of various members, each of which has its proper place in the body and fulfills its proper function. At this point, we mean the function perceptible from without. Thanks to this, the human body is also shaped from without as a whole made of members in a particular way—the way proper only to man. Member organization includes not only the spatial distribution of bodily members but also their reciprocal coordination in the entire external shape of man. To the noun "shape" corresponds the adjective "shapely," which qualifies man with respect to the distribution and coordination of the members of his body.

However, this whole that is *perceptible from without does not in the least exhaust* the entire reality of the human body—just as it does not exhaust the reality of the bodies of animals and plants. *The body also possesses an inwardness proper to it.* It is by taking into consideration precisely this inwardness of the body that we speak of the human organism. "Organism" defines the body in the complexity proper to it from within. If this complexity is expressed from without in the diversity and reciprocal coordination of the members, then from within it is expressed in the diversity and reciprocal coordination of the organs of the body. Organs determine its vitality, that is, the bodily dynamism to which somatic potentiality corresponds. The word "somaticity" (from the Greek *sóma*) indicates the body in both the external and internal aspects of its constitution. Thus, when we speak of somatic dynamism, we have in mind both the external reality of the body with its proper member organization and the internal reality of the body, that is, the organism: the constitution and joint function of all bodily organs.

In what does the psycho-somatic integrality of man consist?

It is between man's somaticity thus understood and his psyche that a close connection and dependence takes place, consisting in the *conditioning of psychical functions by the whole of somatic functions, and especially by certain particular functions.* The very word "psyche" (from the Greek *psyché*) indicates the soul, not immediately in the metaphysical sense of the word but first in the "physical" and, in a way, phenomenal sense. What is meant here is the entire series of the manifestations of integral human life, which are not in themselves bodily, material, even though they demonstrate a certain dependence on the body, a certain somatic conditioning. Thus, for example, emotional stirring or vision by sight is not in itself bodily but demonstrates a certain dependence on the body and a connection with it. The rich sphere of psychical facts can be distinguished without difficulty within the dynamism proper to man. However, when distinguishing them in relation to somaticity, in relation to what in itself is bodily, it is difficult not to ascertain a simultaneous dependence on and conditioning by the *sóma*: by the body as an organism. The ascertainment of this simultaneous distinctness and dependence is as old as the science about man. Here we owe a great deal to the philosophy of Aristotle, with his realistic attitude to the physical world, the attitude that underpinned the metaphysics and anthropology of the Stagirite differently than Plato's attitude to the world of ideas alone.[xxxviii]

The integration of the person in the act is based on the conditioning of the psyche by somaticity. It is hence that man draws his integrality. *The integrality of man is not only the presence in him of all the components belonging to the spheres of somaticity and the psyche, but also the system of reciprocal conditionings that enable functions proper to man in both spheres.* Thus, this integrality is not static but dynamic. With respect to the direction of reciprocal conditionings, it runs, in a sense, from without inward concerning the conditionings of psychical functions by somatic ones, and from within outward concerning the somatic expression of psychical functions. With respect to the former direction, psychology, or, rather, Aristotelian-Thomistic anthropology, distinguishes the somatic conditioning of psychical functions "from within" (in this way, all sensory functions are somatically conditioned) from the merely "from without" conditioning (in this way, man's spiritual functions are somatically conditioned). Spiritual functions are interiorly independent from matter. The integrality of man in the empirical sense is verified dynamically, namely, through the regularity of the function dependent on the totality of the conditionings of the psyche by somaticity and—in the direction of expression—of somaticity by the psyche. The integration of the person in the act is based on this dynamic totality. The various deficiencies in this area are denoted by the term "disintegration."

5. The Person and the Body
A remark about hylomorphism

It seems that at this point the background for posing the problem has been adequately prepared. In a certain sense, even the problem of "the person and the body" has already been properly posed. It seems that we are not in danger of concealing some form of "absolutizing an aspect" as we consider the body and its dynamic contribution to the dynamic totality of person and act. It is clear that *we cannot examine the human body in separation from the totality that is man, that is, without understanding that he is a person.* Neither can we penetrate the dynamisms and potentiality proper to the human body without understanding the act and its personal specificity. In this respect it is fitting to fully approve the vision of human reality bestowed on us by traditional philosophy (Aristotle and Thomas Aquinas), which, besides the element of "matter–*hýle*," discovers in man just as in other beings of the visible world yet another element, namely, "form–*morphé*." Hence, the theory of hylomorphism and the analysis of the human being conducted within the framework of this theory. The fundamental acceptance of this vision, however, does not entail the intention to reproduce the very formulas proper to the concept of hylomorphism. Our previous reflections have perhaps already adequately indicated the effort of rediscovering the dynamic human reality as a reality of person and act, even though the grasp of this reality in traditional philosophical anthropology is perfect in its own way.

The somatic constitution as the basis of the concretization of the person

With respect to the body in its intimate belonging to the human person, we can at first consider, in a sense, the static grasp of this problem. The belonging of the body to the human person is so strictly necessary that the body enters the definition of man—at least indirectly, as it does in the most frequently used definition, *Homo est animal rationale*, for the concept *animal* contains the body and bodiliness. The body determines the concreteness of man, which in a sense has been expressed by the metaphysical thesis concerning the individualization of man by matter. This is so at least in external experience, which allows us to grasp what is visible in man. We can equate "the visible" and "the external." Man exteriorizes himself—already in a static sense—through the body and its specific and strictly individual structure. The term *"constitution"* is also used here, although this term, while identified with the externally visible structure of the body, also seems to include the internal system, which goes hand in hand with the external somatic totality—indeed, it determines this totality. In the concept of constitution we understand not only the external shape of the body but also the dynamic configuration of the internal organic and structural factors that contribute to this shape. Although it is manifested already in his "statics," this constitutional feature of man also very clearly penetrates the dynamics. Namely, it is manifested *in the mobility characteristic of every man*. We can perceive this mobility from without and, on the basis of these perceptions themselves, offer certain distinctions between people. For a long time now these distinctions have suggested to anthropologists an idea concerning certain constitutional approximations, concerning certain—in the somatic sense—types of people. Moreover, in accord with what was said previously concerning the conditioning of the human psyche by somaticity, these approximations and types are manifested in the psyche as well. Hence the entire problem of temperaments, which runs through the ages of our knowledge about man from Aristotle to our days.[3]

The human body as the sphere and means of expression of the person

In a sense, we have already moved from the static image of man shaped by the body to dynamics. Particular and ramified anthropological knowledge is very rich in this area. However, because our point is to grasp the relation between body and person, the essence of the problem—according to everyone, including materialists—lies in the correct subordination of the visible exteriority of the body to the invisible interiority. In this case, the point is not the "inwardness" of the body alone, the organism as the somatic underpinning of constitution. As everyone understands, *the human body* in its visible dynamic *is the terrain and, in a sense, even the means of expression for the person*. The strictly personal structure of self-governance and self-possession runs, in a sense, through the body and is expressed in it. As is known, this structure is manifested in the act and realized through the act. It is most closely linked with the capacity for self-determination that is proper to the person, and which in turn is expressed in the decision and choice that contain a dynamic subordination to truth. It is this entire dynamic transcendence of the person, which in itself is of a spiritual nature, that finds for itself the terrain and means of expression in the human body. This is confirmed at every step

---

3. See Ernst Kretschmer, *Körperbau und Charakter: Untersuchungen zum Konstitutionsproblem und zur Lehre von den Temperamenten*, 24th ed. (Berlin: Springer, 1961).

by acts, especially the so-called *actus externi*, in which the visible, as it were, (or, in any case, "visual") exteriorization of self-determination—that is, of the efficacy of the person—takes place in and through the body. The body in the most common sense of the word is thus the terrain and, in a sense, the means of performing the act—and, with this, the means of the person's fulfilling himself in and through the act.

This quite ordinary manifestation of the person's integration in the act, one that in a sense progresses through the body and is expressed in it, attests perhaps most simply to the way that the body belongs to the person. This problem was at times the object of inquiries and conceptions, starting with Plato, who understood man as a spiritual substance using the body-matter in his earthly existence, and with Aristotle, who held the substantial unity of soul and body (that is, of form and matter) in the individual human being. For the time being, we pose the problem only regarding expression—and only in this sense do we say that the body becomes the terrain and means of exteriorization for the efficacy and self-determination of the person. Thus, it also becomes the means and terrain of exteriorization for the soul, for the dynamism proper to its spirituality[9a]—in accord with what was said at the end of the analyses pertaining to the transcendence of the person in the act (chapter 4). By progressing through the body and being expressed in it, the integration of the person in the act *at the same time reveals the profound sense of the integrality of man as a person*. The soul—a spiritual soul at that—must be the ultimate principle of this integrality. The person is not identified with the body alone. Perhaps that is not held even by behaviorists—in fact, they concern themselves (in psychology) merely with the external manifestations of man's "behavior" without attempting to explain anything "from within." Behaviorism can be a method only of the description and not of the interpretation of man's actions.

The man-person possesses his body and uses it in action

The fact that the person is exteriorized in and through the body, a fact that takes place above all together with the act, entails the moment of objectivization of which we spoke in chapter 3. The person himself becomes for himself the object in action. The body takes particular part in this objectivization. Every time the externalization of the person in the act is accomplished through the body, the body becomes at the same time the object of action. The objectivization of the body is a particular aspect or rather an integral component of the objectivization of the personal subject to whom the body belongs and in whose subjectivity it structurally inheres. The belonging of the body to the subjective "I" does not consist in an identification with it. Man "is" not his body but "possesses" his body.[4]

    4. (1) Ingarden often considered the relation of the soul to the body from the position of man's psycho-physical unity. By no means did he reduce to one model the reciprocal dependencies that are at play here. Naturally, he was very interested in cases concerning this kind of relation of the human "I" to the body, cases in which in a particular way man feels himself to be a unity. See, for instance: "In allen Fällen meines Übergewichts über meinen Leib und zugleich meiner Solidarität mit ihm unterwirft er sich mir auf solche Weise, daß er nicht nur zum Teil meiner selbst, sondern auch die reale *Grundlage* wird, auf die ich mich in meinem konkreten leiblich-seelischen Leben stütze.... Ich—der Mensch—scheine dann nicht aus heterogenen, einander nur geheimnisvoll zugeordneten, aber im Grunde einander immer fremden Faktoren: aus dem 'Körper'... und der 'Seele'... zusammengesetzt zu sein, sondern ich bin eben 'Mensch,' das heißt dann: Ich bin ein ursprünglich kompaktes Ganzes, aus welchem mein geistiges bzw. seelisches 'Ich' über das Niveau des Leibes gleichsam hinauswächst, ohne jedoch die Einwurzelung in dem realen-leiblichen Grund zu verlieren, der mit einem... eine Einheit bildenden Empfindungsfeld meiner Leiblichkeit erfüllt ist." [In all cases of my predominance over my body and my simultaneous solidarity with it, it submits itself to me in such a way that it becomes not only part of myself but also the real foundation on which I lean in my concrete psycho-somatic life.... I—the human being—do not then appear to be *composed* out of heterogeneous factors, only mysteriously correlated but at bottom always alien to each other—the physical 'body'... and the 'soul'... but I am rather precisely a 'human being,' which then means: I am a primally compact whole out of which my intellectual or spiritual 'ego' grows out, as it were, beyond the level of the body, although without losing its rootedness in the base of the real body which is filled out with... a unity-forming sensation-field of my corporeality.] Ingarden, *Formalontologie*, pt. 2, 333–34; translated by Szylewicz as *Controversy over the Existence of the World*, 2:706–7 (Wojtyła's emphasis in German text).

    (2) Wilhelmus Antonius Luijpen protests against treating the body as an object of possession (of course, he means possession literally): "*My Body is Not the Object of 'Having.'*... I 'have' a car, a pen, a book. In this 'having' the object of the 'having' reveals itself as an exteriority. There is a distance between me and what I 'have.' What I 'have' is to a certain extent independent of me.... My body is not something external to me like my car. I cannot dispose of my body or give it away as I dispose of money.... All this stems from the fact that my body is not 'a' body but *my* body... in such a way that my body *embodies* me." Luijpen, *Existential Phenomenology*, 3rd ed. (Pittsburgh, Pa.: Duquesne University Press, 1963), 188. Luijpen presents the relation between the conscious subject and the body as follows: "In the supposition that I 'am' my body, I am a thing and wholly immersed in a world of mere things. But then the conscious self is reduced to nothing and, consequently, also my body as 'mine,' as well as the world as 'mine.' Accordingly, I neither 'am' my body nor 'have' it. My body is precisely mid-way between these two extremes. It constitutes the transition from the conscious self to the worldly object. It is the mysterious reality which grafts me on things, secures my being-in-the-world, involves me in the world, and gives me a standpoint in the world" (Luijpen, *Existential Phenomenology*, 189–90).

    (3) On the other hand, Henri Bergson is inclined to think that the spirit uses the body. See, for instance, the following sentence, though spoken in a different context: "C'est dire aussi que la vie de l'esprit ne peut pas être un effet de la vie du corps, que tout se passe au contraire comme si le corps

This possession of one's own body conditions the body's objectivization in acts and at the same time is expressed through this objectivization. Man in a particular way possesses his body and in a particular way becomes conscious of possessing the body when he uses it in action as an obedient means of expression for his self-determination.

Through this obedience of the body—which Thomists seem to call by the term *usus passivus*—the integration of the person in the act is also fulfilled. The ability to objectivize the body and use it in action is a significant element of the personal freedom of man. Through this somatic moment—and also cofactor—of personal objectivization, the structure of self-possession and self-governance proper to the person is realized and expressed. *Man as a person possesses himself particularly in the somatic aspect through the fact that he possesses his body, and he governs himself through the fact that he governs his body.* To this extent, the relation of the person to the body is revealed to us "from without" in the act of the person. Hence result various important consequences for the psychology of action and for ethics.

6. The Self-Determination of the Person and the Reactivity of the Body

The possibility of distinguishing the body's proper dynamism from the whole of the dynamism of man

The exterior experience, however, does not fully exhaust the relation between body and person, especially in action, that is, in the act. Through this experience, we must in a sense descend "inside" the body itself; we must touch its proper inwardness. Then this relation will appear more

---

était simplement utilisé par l'esprit, et que dès lors nous n'avons aucune raison de supposer que le corps et l'esprit soient inséparablement liés l'un à l'autre." [This also means that the life of the mind cannot be an effect of the life of the body; that, on the contrary, everything happens as if the body were simply used by the mind; and that, consequently, we have no reason to suppose that the body and the mind are inseparably joined to each other.] Henri Bergson, "L'âme et le corps," in *Oeuvres*, 2nd ed. (Paris: Presses Universitaires de France, 1963), 858.

In reference to the viewpoints presented here, the author wishes to note the following: when in this study we state that "man 'is' not his body but 'possesses' his body," we state this on the basis of the conviction that man "is" himself (a person)* inasmuch as he possesses himself—and inasmuch as he possesses his body. [*Editorial note: The Polish applies a pun here: "*być sobą*" (to be oneself) means "*być osobą*" (to be a person).]

fully and more maturely. The previous analyses have prepared us to see clearly the difference between penetrating the interiority of the person, that is, of man, and penetrating the interiority of the human body. For, as was said above, the body possesses its own purely somatic inwardness. It is always this inwardness of which we think and speak whenever we call the human body (as well as the animal body) an organism. For *the body in its inwardness possesses a purely somatic dynamism, and the external dynamism of the body, the body's purely natural "mobility," depends on the former dynamism*—this, however, does not in any way hinder the entire body together with its external mobility from being the terrain and means of expression for the person, especially in acts, as we stated previously. What is still needed is an insight into the purely somatic internal dynamism itself, simply in order to more thoroughly grasp and understand the integration of the person in the act. This integration depends—at least in the somatic aspect—on man's somatic integrality, whose important or even decisive element is the somatic dynamism itself. We can say that this dynamism belongs to the body precisely as body.

Can we distinguish this dynamism? That we can seems to be attested by the universally accepted distinction between body and soul or—even more so—between somaticity and the psyche. Nonetheless, distinguishing the somatic dynamism from the totality of the human dynamism is a task that requires high cognitive precision. This precision must characterize those who concern themselves, in a sense, with the "body itself" and those who use the methods of particular sciences to examine the human psyche. Finally, at yet another degree of abstraction, it must characterize those who attempt to more closely define the nature of the soul and its relation to the body. Clearly, the present study of the human person is not exempt from undertaking in its own way this latter problem—one of the most difficult problems in the history of thought—and from taking responsibility for it. [10a]

We characterize the body's own dynamism (the somatic dynamism) as "reactive"

As noted previously, we are not concerned at this stage of our inquiries with the cognition of the dynamism of the human body "as a body," which is proper to particular sciences, but *with a certain characterization of this dynamism*. The starting point for this characterization must be the ascertainment that *through his body the man-person is an authentic part of nature [przyroda]*. This denotes, on the one hand, a certain likeness to its other parts and, on the other hand, a close link with all the external conditions of being that we also call "nature" [*przyroda*]. With respect to likeness, man is posited in nature [*przyroda*] nearest to animals, especially the so-called higher animals—a fact that, by the way, found its expression in the definition denoting man as *animal* with the attribute *rationale*. This definition contains a fundamental statement concerning human nature. This statement is constantly verified in the natural sciences, providing an incentive for the known evolutionist hypothesis on the origin of man. In this study, we do not concern ourselves with these matters directly.

However, the close connection of the human body with nature [*przyroda*] as a group of external conditions of being and living helps us to characterize the proper dynamism of human somaticity. It seems that this dynamism can be grasped and expressed in the concept of "reactivity" and in the attribute "reactive." Thus, reactivity would belong to the human body as a body. The strictly somatic dynamism can be characterized as reactive, as can the potentiality inhering in its roots.

The substantiation of such a characterization

As with other bodies in nature [przyroda], the human body's proper potentiality is the ability to react. The concept of "reaction" is an analogical concept, very often used to denote a totality of human conduct. We mean precisely this when we say, for example, that *x* "reacted" in a certain way to a certain piece of news. However, in this case we mean not only the somatic reaction but also the psychical one expressed emotively in a certain emotional stirring, and thus an affective reaction. Moreover, by this common "he reacted" we also sometimes mean a certain decision or choice, and thus a certain response of the will to values. We must admit that the word "reaction" is in a way accurately applied to all these indeed varied components of human conduct. This proves the analogous character of the very concept "reaction" and indicates further that the somatic-reactive element inheres thoroughly in all human action.

The reason we restrict reactivity to somaticity alone, to the dynamism of the body, lies in the body's direct link with nature [*przyroda*]. The psychical, emotive factor is connected with nature [*przyroda*] only indirectly through somaticity and the dynamism proper to it. The concept of reaction, which we use to characterize the somatic dynamism of man, presupposes, of course, the understanding of an action whose source and cause inhere in nature [*przyroda*] as a group of conditions affecting the being of the human body and the body's proper activity (reactivity). Inanimate bodies already demonstrate the ability to react, such as the ability to expand in heat or to contract in the cold. We ascertain an analogous ability in living beings, though their reactivity is manifested on the level of life. Just as physics or chemistry is suited to examine this reactivity on the level of nonliving beings, so is biology on the level of living beings. On the latter level, we ascertain that *reactivity is a property of life and even in a sense its "law," that is, its principle of formation, preservation, and development*. Reactivity also characterizes man in the sphere of his somatic potentiality and the purely bodily vitality that hence results. It is within it that we should look for all manifestations of the somatic dynamism, that is, the human body's own reactions composing its proper vitality.

The connection between the reactivity and the vitality of the human body

This vitality has a vegetative character. The human body's proper life is vegetation. In this respect, conception constitutes the beginning of vegetation, whereas death is its end. The external conditions of the vegetation proper to the human body are similar to the conditions of the vegetation of other bodies. These conditions are determined by the biological environment, by climate, by atmosphere, and by food and drink as means of somatic regeneration. The body as an organism is by nature, that is, in virtue of its innate properties, disposed to vegetation and reproduction. The latter is served by the sexual diversification of the human body, by its organs that physically enable the conception of a new man, his development up to the moment of bringing him into the world, and then this very bringing into the world, that is, the birth to life that is independent in the biological sense. *The dynamic fabric of this entire vegetative vitality of the human body is constituted by the sequence of purely instinctive reactions, namely, those that occur "in the manner" of nature itself.* These reactions occur—that is, "happen"—in the person with no influence of the will, without the contribution of self-determination. Thus, although they happen in the person, they do not constitute his conscious act. The body "actuates" itself following the interior finality of either vegetation or reproduction. This "actuation" of the human body has a reactive character.

Reactivity in this case denotes the instinctive and dynamic connection with nature [przyroda] as a given biological "environment," as the group of external conditionings of vegetation and reproduction. This connection is end-directed, because particular somatic reactions have vegetation or reproduction as their end. At this point, we already partially enter the area of the so-called drives, of which we shall speak shortly. The ability to react to stimuli is a particular feature of man's somatic potentiality. This ability must be manifested in a particular way, because it confers a specifically active character on the reactivity of the human body. This active character of the body's reactivity to stimuli is manifested in comparison with the body's passive subjection to the influence of external factors within its physico-chemical structure. *In the constitution of the human organism, the ability to react to stimuli is directly connected with the nervous system, which "services" the entire body* and determines the particular directions of its reactive dynamism and of the somatic potentiality inhering at its roots.

7. The Act and Motion
In what sense can we speak of the body's proper "subjectivity"?

The characterization of the somatic dynamism conducted thus far, that is, the analysis of the human body's reactivity, indicates that *this dynamism in itself does not demonstrate dependence on the self-determination of the person*. It is instinctive, self-projecting—it is the body's own dynamism. The body itself as an organism constitutes not only its substratum but also its dynamic source, that is, its efficient cause. The will is not this cause, for the body's proper dynamism is not the effect of the self-determination of the person. Therefore, we do not discover it immediately and directly in the experience "man acts," which reveals the efficacy of the person, but only in the experience "something happens in man," where the efficacy of the person is absent. Reaction and reactivity in themselves do not contain the efficacy of the person. We can then speak of *the body's proper efficacy*, which inheres in the person on the basis of the ontic unity of man. The fact that this efficacy of the body differs experientially from the efficacy of the person at the same time testifies very clearly to man's ontic complexity. As we shall see later, this complexity will not be exhausted in the concept of the psycho-physical or the psycho-somatic being.

The fact of this specific independence of the body and of its instinctive dynamism from the self-determination of the person renders the body in the totality of man's personal structure a substratum, as it were, an underpinning, or a kind of substructure relative to what determines the structure of the person properly and essentially. It is clear that this underpinning belongs to the unity of the human being and thus to the unity of the person. Moreover, it determines the integrality of this being on the basis of internal bonds and conditionings. *The fact that the reactive dynamism and the vegetative vitality proper to the body "happen" in the person independently from his self-determination*, without the active engagement of the will, *in no way cancels this unity*. Similarly, this unity is not cancelled by the fact that the entire vegetative vitality and reactivity of the human body correctly function in man outside the sphere of consciousness. As we said, this fact does not in the least cancel the personal unity of man, though it characterizes this unity in its own way. For we ascertain that the structure that exists and is dynamized "in the manner" of nature—which is different from that of the person—is very thoroughly "built into" this unity of the personal structure. Of course, the human body is not a separate subject in relation to the subject that is the man-person. Its unity with man's ontic subjectivity, with the human *suppositum*, is beyond any doubt. However, the lived-experience of oneself as a subjective "I," the lived-experience of one's own subjectivity, is connected with the reflexive function of consciousness, which encompasses the body and its mobility only from without. And this seems to suffice for man to experience his own subjectivity. For this purpose he does not have to become conscious of the internal reactions of his organism or his vegetative vitality, as previously noted. Neither does he have to be their agent. (We know that the ascetic exercises of the yogis aim at consciously controlling the internal reactions of the organism, but this controlling is not in the least equivalent to evoking these reactions, something that always belongs to the efficacy of the body itself.)

How is the synthesis of act and motion brought about?

Thus it seems that within the integral subjectivity of the person—the consciousness-related subjectivity—the body possesses a somewhat separate "subjectivity" without, of course, violating the ontic unity of man. This could be considered subjectivity in the sense that *the body as a body is merely the proper subject of reactions: it is thus a subjectivity that is reactive, vegetative, and outside consciousness.* The integrality of the man-person consists in the normal—and indeed as perfect as possible—harmonization of this somatic "subjectivity" with the efficacious and transcendent subjectivity of the person. Such integrality is a condition of the integration of the person in the act. A lack of integrality impedes integration and evokes various forms of disintegration. Then, what is in a sense the body's own subjectivity, the reactive-vegetative subjectivity, ceases to be harmonized with the person as efficacious subject. It in a sense breaks away and becomes "independent," to the detriment of the person. We then witness a certain abnormality, something that seems to clash with nature. For the very harmonization of the reactive and vegetative subjectivity of the body with the person as the efficacious and self-conscious subject seems natural—in the sense that it corresponds to the nature of man, who is a person.

The formulation that speaks of the quasi-subjectivity of the body makes sense only with respect to the specific independence of man's somatic dynamism and of the vegetative vitality connected to this dynamism in relation to the self-determination of the person: in relation to conscious efficacy. On the basis of this specific independence, that is, this instinctive self-projectedness of the somatic dynamism, we see more clearly that every *act that joins to itself the self-projecting dynamism of the body—whether it does so in the visible ("external") or the purely "internal" way*—is realized by way of a specific integration. This integration is that of the person in the act; it presupposes the integrality of the body. We can say that in the moment of self-determination man "turns on" [*włącza*] the body's reactive dynamism and in this way employs it. We can also say that in the moment of self-determination man "joins himself" [*włącza się*] to this dynamism, that he consciously takes advantage of it. Both correspond to the concept of *usus*, which is applied by Thomists to describe this moment of the human act.

This is manifested *when we witness the dynamic synthesis of act and motion*. This is very frequent and quite ordinary, for there exist a great number of "external" acts, namely, acts involving concrete and visible exteriorization in movements of the body. Movement of the body is in itself something somatic, something closely connected to the reactive potentiality of the body, to the ability to react to stimuli. This ability deeply permeates the internal constitution of the human body and is manifested externally as a separate power or habit of this body, as the *vis motrix*—the motive power. Being a result of the reaction to a given stimulus, such a motion *can be strictly self-projecting, instinctive. In this case, we call it a reflex*. The fact that reflexes exist in man seems to attest "from without" to a certain independence of the body from the will, to the body's potential property and its dynamic specificity. This fact does not in the least hinder another fact, namely, the synthesis of act and motion constantly recurring in normal man. For even though in reflex we can see only the body's "actuation" that lacks the moment of personal efficacy, the synthesis of act and motion contains this moment. This synthesis can consist in the fact that the given movement is itself an act because it proceeds from the will or in the fact that it inheres in an act as in a greater dynamic whole [11a]. After all, the body is the terrain and means of expression for the person, as we said above.

The moment of habit in the synthesis of act and motion

These dynamic *syntheses of act and motion considerably demonstrate a habitual feature in man*. It seems that the word "habit" [*sprawność*] as corresponding to the Latin *habitus* is most properly chosen in this case. For *habitus* means habit and virtue. Virtue indicates the *habitus* of spiritual life, whereas habit—to follow the spirit of our language—refers to the body. Man has a body that is either functioning well [*sprawne*] or not functioning well [*niesprawne*], and this is always manifested in movements. The body's mobility is something innate; it is closely linked with somatic reactivity, that is, with the ability to react to stimuli, which are processed in the appropriate neural centers into motor impulses. This processing is also something instinctive and self-projecting. The sphere of the bodily movements is in man the terrain of his earliest skills; based on instinctive reactions and impulses, motor habits are the earliest formed. It is also early on that the entire process of movements being formed is joined by the will, which is the source of motor impulses proceeding from inside the person—impulses that bear the mark of self-determination. Thus is constituted the synthesis of act and motion, within which appropriate habits continue to form.

Thanks to the factor of habit, the entire dynamic of movements, the entirety of human mobility, becomes so self-projecting *that in an enormous majority of cases man is not aware of and does not sense the contribution of the will* efficaciously forming the synthesis of acts and movements. This awareness occurs only in some cases with particularly difficult or significant motions, for instance, during mountain climbing, surgery, or, for another reason, during liturgical functions. It is in such cases that every movement is performed with appropriate attention and specific precision, and thus with more or less complete commitment and the distinct lived-experience of conscious efficacy. Furthermore, in ordinary and everyday movements, the factor of habit reduces the contribution of attention, thereby reducing the lived-experience of conscious efficacy. The movements performed by wont are accomplished as if the will were not efficaciously committed in them. However, we cannot reduce them to reflexes, since the efficacious commitment of the will contributed to the creation of the given habit, that is, motor skill.

Man's mobility and the somatic constitution

Concerning the movements and mobility of man, we should also state that *they constitute in every concrete case a specific and in a sense phenomenological whole together with the structure of the body, that is, with constitution.* This dynamic whole is manifested externally, though we should seek its roots inside the body, in the body's reactivity, which is accompanied by every man's specific ability to process stimuli into motor impulses. As the external specificity of somatic reactivity, mobility, which is partially innate and partially acquired by means of very early skills, corresponds to the external specificity of the organism and proceeds from it. This conviction perhaps stood and still stands at the basis of any *attempt to classify people with respect to temperaments*. Of course, together with the somatic factor, the psychical factor is also taken into account here. Although particular temperaments attempt to grasp the psychical rather than the somatic specificity of man, they clearly seek a link between the one and the other.

Finally, we also witness in this area, namely, in the sphere of the dynamic synthesis of acts and movements, *various forms of disintegration, which we can describe as exclusively somatic*. This disintegration occurs in the form of a lack either of certain members or organs of the body (thus causing a lack of corresponding movements) or of certain strictly somatic reactions or habits; such deficiencies are also impediments to human action, *impedimenta actus humani*, as defined by the manuals. Although these impediments in a certain measure allow themselves to be known from without, their roots always inhere inside the human body. We should stress that the purely somatic impediments of action have in themselves merely a physical and not a moral character. A man who has lost an arm or a lung suffers strictly specific impediments and hindrances in his action. However, these impediments are external in the sense that by themselves they neither disturb consciousness nor impede self-determination. Even a man who is somatically very disintegrated often presents a personhood of high caliber.

8. Drives and the Integration of the Person in the Act

The complex character of drives

At the end of our reflections devoted to the integration of the person in the act from the perspective of human somaticity and reactivity, we should also broach the matter of drives. The word "drive" etymologically approaches the word "instinct," even though we have already introduced between them semantic distinctions that we continue to apply here. For although it seems that we can speak of the human body's instinctive reactivity or movements (reflexes), it is difficult in this case to speak of a drive. Instinct indicates the manner of dynamization proper to nature itself. *Drive, on the other hand, indicates a certain dynamic orientation of this nature in a given direction.* This is what we have in mind when we speak of the drive for self-preservation or the sexual or reproductive drive. We are not concerned in this case with characterizing particular reactions as the end-directed actuations of the somatic subject, for this is what we mean by calling them "instinctive." Rather, we are concerned with a certain resultant of many instinctive reactions of the body, and thereby with a characterization of nature itself in its clearly dynamic directedness toward an end. It is clear that here we mean "nature" not in an abstract sense but as a reality concretely existing, and thus as a certain reality in the person, as we attempted to present in chapter 2 (see section 4, "Person and nature: From opposition to integration"). Drives are proper to man on the basis of this reality, and there emerges the problem of their integration in the act of the person.

A drive is a certain form of the dynamism proper to man by nature, proper to him inasmuch as it constitutes a part of nature [*przyroda*] and remains in the closest connection with it. At the same time, however, *a drive is not a merely somatic dynamism in man.* Therefore, its interpretation on the basis of somaticity alone cannot be complete. For drives, as a given dynamic feature, are communicated also to the human psyche and find in it their proper vividness. This is the case concerning the drive for self-preservation; this is also the case—perhaps with greater vividness— concerning the sexual drive. *This psychical feature of the drive is expressed in a specific impelling of an emotive type, which assumes and in a sense even produces the orientation proper to the drive.* For the very lived-experience of the impelling and thus, in a sense, of the "urging"—that is, of the compulsion indicating a certain objective necessity—has a psychical-emotive character, whereas the reactions of the organism are only a somatic basis of this lived-experience. In this chapter, however, which has for its object man's somaticity and its contribution to the integration of the person in the act, we concern ourselves, in a sense, with the somatic layer of human drives, while keeping in mind that they are not a simple somatic dynamism.

Concerning the conditioning of drives on the basis of the body's reactivity

Nonetheless, *we find the fundamental conditioning of human drives in the human body, in the reactivity proper to this body.* The drive for self-preservation is a resultant, as it were, of many vegetative reactions and is also their common property. The instinctive finality of these reactions consists in the preservation and correct development of vegetative life. The support and development of vegetation are linked to the need to preserve it; hence, a means of self-defense against all that could destroy or harm this vegetation is necessary. The whole human organism is equipped for this purpose with necessary self-preservation "devices," which act spontaneously, and thus in the way proper to nature, without the contribution of the person's consciousness and efficacy. The human body's proper efficacy is self-sufficient in this area, and the drive for self-preservation maintains contact with consciousness with the help of so-called bodily sensations.[xxxix] Man expresses precisely these sensations in very frequently recurring statements such as "I feel good" or "I feel bad." Of course, these statements demonstrate analogous content because they very often refer also to man's spiritual state; above all, however, they serve to express physical self-feeling. The feelings of health or sickness, of strength or weakness have the significance of self-preservation. *Not only the body but also the drive for self-preservation, which is most closely connected with the vegetative vitality of the body, is expressed through these feelings.* The elementary feeling of hunger or thirst, as, on the other hand, the feeling of their satisfaction, also originates in the substratum of the drive for self-preservation. The enormous entirety of medical knowledge and art developed in relation to this drive. It is easy to ascertain that this drive is not limited to somaticity itself but constitutes a certain dynamic feature of human essence and existence as a whole.

The drive for self-preservation

This feature also presents a metaphysical meaning, and therefore the interpretation of the drive must take this meaning into account. For what is hidden at the root of the drive for self-preservation is a certain fundamental content and value. Existence itself is this content and value. *The drive for self-preservation is, in a sense, a compulsion of existence, a subjective necessity of existence, inscribed in the whole dynamic structure of man.* It is served by all the somatic dynamisms safeguarding vegetation; it is served in a given case by the feeling of emotive impelling that makes itself heard whenever this vegetation and the entire physical existence of man (existence "in the body") are threatened. This feeling meets the intellectual affirmation of existence, the consciousness that it is good to exist and to live and that it is bad to lose existence and life; furthermore, this intellectual affirmation of existence and life demonstrates the particular and fundamental value of existence. Thanks to this, the drive for self-preservation takes the form in man of a conscious attitude and at the same time of a fundamental striving that aims at a fundamental value. It is also known that man, precisely in the field of his thinking, can in a sense cancel the value of his own existence and replace affirmation with negation. Thus, the drive for self-preservation does not seem to govern the person absolutely. Nonetheless, in people who take their own lives the following problem always remains open: is their goal not to exist at all, or only not to exist in a way that seems unbearable to them?

The sexual and reproductive drive

A glance at the drive for self-preservation demonstrates its irreducibility to somaticity as well as the great power of both its psychical reflex and the contribution of consciousness in the formation of processes proceeding from it. The same *can be said*—perhaps *to an even greater degree—concerning the sexual drive.* Relying on the division into male and female individuals, which is characteristic of man, this drive is indeed *rooted in somatic ground but also reaches very deeply into the psyche with its proper emotivity and into the very spirituality of man.* Just as the drive for self-preservation is the basis for the natural striving to maintain one's being, so in turn the sexual drive is the basis for the striving to be with another human person on account of a deep likeness and of the difference resulting from the distinctness of sex. This natural striving constitutes the basis of marriage and, through conjugal intercourse, the basis of the family.[xl] For in its integral dynamic and finality, the sexual drive becomes a source of the transmission of life. Thus it is simultaneously *the drive for reproduction*, to which man owes the preservation of his species in nature [*przyroda*].

This reproductive, procreative feature is most clearly visible in the somatic layer of the dynamism related to the drive. This dynamism is manifested as a precisely determined sequence of bodily reactions, which to a certain degree "happen" spontaneously in man. With all their somatic specificity and spontaneity, however, they are made conscious insofar as man as a person can govern them. This governance consists fundamentally in the conscious accommodation of the body's sexual dynamism to its proper finality. Although it is possible to govern the sexual drive, doing so is sometimes connected with difficulties, especially when somebody's sexual excitability possesses a particular intensity. This consists not only in somatic reactions but also in a particular psychical impelling of the emotive type. In the book *Love and Responsibility*, we attempted to demonstrate extensively why directing the sexual drive is necessary from the viewpoint of ethics.[5] There, we described somewhat more extensively the purely somatic structures in which the drive is manifested. These structures penetrate very deeply into the human organism, marking out the characteristic somatic difference between a man and a woman. We should add that, due to the key significance of the sexual drive, research continues that aims to know in an even more penetrating way all the somatic reactivity connected to the drive.

Toward the proper interpretation of drives

As is evident from the foregoing remarks, issues concerning drives, which we limited here to the two mentioned, are not purely somatic, though both the drive for self-preservation and the sexual drive are

---

5. *Miłość i odpowiedzialność: Studium etyczne* (Lublin: Towarzystwo Naukowe Katolickiego Uniwersytetu Lubelskiego, 1960; 2nd ed., Kraków, 1962 [4th ed., Lublin, 1986]); *Amour et responsabilité: Étude de morale sexuelle*, with an introduction by Henri de Lubac, trans. Thérèse Sas (Paris: Société d'Éditions Internationales, 1965); *Amore e responsabilità: Studio di morale sessuale*, with an introduction by Giovanni Colombo, trans. Ambretta Berti Milanoli (Turin: Marietti, 1969); *Amor y responsabilidad: Estudio de moral sexual*, with an introduction by Henri de Lubac, trans. Juan Antonio Segarra (Madrid: Razón y Fe, 1969). [Editorial note: See also *Liebe und Verantwortung: Eine ethische Studie*, trans. August Berz (Munich: Kösel, 1979); *Liebe und Verantwortung: Eine ethische Studie*, trans. Josef Spindelböck (Kleinhain: Verlag St. Josef, 2007); *Amor e responsabilidade: Estudo ético*, trans. João Jarski and Lino Carrera (São Paulo: Loyola, 1982); *Love and Responsibility*, trans. H. T. Willetts (London: Fount, 1981); *Love and Responsibility*, trans. Grzegorz Ignatik (Boston: Pauline Books and Media, 2013)].

deeply rooted in the body and its natural reactivity. Is the significance of drives in the person derived above all *from the subjective force of the somatic reactions that these drives evoke—or rather from the objective value of the ends toward which drives direct man*? This is a separate problem. Due to the rational character of the human person, we ought to opt for the latter. In the current chapter of our study, in which we are considering the relation of somaticity to the integration of the person in the act, issues concerning drives have been portrayed above all from the perspective of the body's subjective reactivity, in which both the drive for self-preservation and the sexual drive are clearly manifested. From this perspective, the integration of drives in the acts of the person constitutes a particular element of a more general problem, namely, the integration of the natural dynamism of the body in the act. It is clear, however, that through this element the problem of the integration of drives is not fully solved. What must be taken into account to a considerable extent is the psycho-emotive factor.

CHAPTER 6 ❧ Integration and the Psyche

1. The Psyche and Somaticity
We are concerned only with a general characterization of the psyche (as in the previous chapter)

At the beginning of the previous chapter we attempted to determine the fundamental meaning of integration, for in the analysis of the personal dynamism of man, integration constitutes an aspect complementary to transcendence. The transcendence of the person in the act is manifested through self-determination and efficacy. Self-determination and efficacy [1a]determine[1b] the structure of self-possession and self-governance that is proper to the person, while they simultaneously result from this structure. Taking into account the complexity characteristic of the structure of self-possession and self-governance, we attempt with the concept of the integration of the person in the act to emphasize a second component or second aspect of this complexity. This aspect is indispensable due to the fact that every human act is fulfilled not only by the transcendence of self-determination and efficacy but also *through the dynamization of the subjective "I," the dynamization subordinated to self-determination and efficacy*. The dynamisms of human somaticity and of the psyche also partake in it and are actuated spontaneously; in the act, however, they place this self-projecting dynamism at the will's disposal, as it were. The integration of the person in the act is based precisely here; while complementing transcendence, this integration, for its part, also determines the personal totality of the structure of self-possession and self-governance.

The analysis of the human act conducted from this perspective entitles and even obligates us to look into the psycho-somatic dynamism of man. This dynamism constitutes a specific unity, as we noted in the previous chapter. However, it is a unity in which a complexity clearly emerges—it is the unity of plurality. The psyche differs from somaticity, although in man the two constitute one unity, mutually conditioning each other. The key to grasping and properly understanding this unity is the concept of integration. In the previous chapter, we attempted to demonstrate this in relation to somaticity itself. For man's complexity in this respect allows us to distinguish somaticity from the psyche and to define more closely the dynamisms proper to the one and the other. For these dynamisms possess the most essential significance for manifesting integration. Thus, in the previous chapter, we attempted to demonstrate how the reactivity proper to human somaticity and connected to the external mobility of the body *constitutes a specific material for acts. In this chapter, we intend to conduct a similar analysis in relation to the psyche.* Of course, although this analysis relates to particular sciences that examine man's body and psyche with their own methods, it adopts neither these methods nor their particularity. As we stated previously, our point is a general characterization of a given dynamism with regard to the integration of the person in the act.

What do we mean by the concept of "the psyche"?

Before we attempt this characterization, it is fitting to state that *the concept of the "psyche" is not identified with the concept of the soul*. Colloquially, the concept of the soul is always used in correlation with the concept of the body. However, the proper meaning of the concepts thus correlated is metaphysical and requires a metaphysical analysis of human reality. In the present study, we endeavor to remain within the boundaries of such an analysis, and therefore we intend to return to the concept of the soul at the end of this chapter. The term "psyche," however, is not equal to the concept of the soul, although it is derived etymologically from the Greek *psyche*, which in fact means "soul." The concept of the "psyche" denotes in man only what belongs to his integrality, indeed, what determines this integrality without being itself bodily, that is, somatic. Therefore, the concept of the "psyche" corresponds to the concept of "somaticity"—and we attempt to use it here in this correlation.

The concept of the "psyche" and the adjectival concept "psychical" include *the elements* of humanity and of every concrete man *that we dis-*

cover in the experience of man as being in a certain sense coherent and integrated with the body while—in themselves—not being this body. Further analyses will help to define more closely both these elements and their relation to the body, to "somaticity." What we just stated indicates the experiential-visual basis of the psyche and of the attributive description "psychical." This is a certain sphere of facts given in phenomenological experience: what is manifested in such experience is both the distinctness of these facts in relation to somaticity and their specific integration with it, their unification in man. For we still remain within the integral experience of man. The manifestation of both the distinctness of what is psychical and its [2a]integration[2b] with what is somatic in man constitutes the basis for inferring the relation of soul to body or, regarding a further stage, of spirit to matter. This too we leave for later, for at present we want to characterize more closely what is psychical in man—that is, the psyche—in relation to the integration of the person in the act. For integration is the key to grasping and understanding the human psyche, just as it was the key to grasping and understanding human somaticity.

We stated in the previous chapter that integration presupposes a certain integrality of somaticity and takes advantage of it. This occurred perhaps most properly in the analysis of the relation between act and motion. In this case, the integrating will not only evokes motion but also draws from the natural somatic dynamism, from the natural reactivity and mobility of the body. Thus, the concept of the body's integrality includes not only the static totality, as it were, of its mutually coordinated members and organs, but also their ability to react in a way that is correct, "normal," and properly efficient. All of this is contained in the concept of somatic integrality. As is evident, this integrality demonstrates the—by all means external and visible—element of bodily constitution with which we are inclined to link the entire statics and dynamics of the human body.

The justified tendency to grasp the psychical totality of man in connection with his somatic constitution

Psychical integrality is also the basis for the integration of the person in the act. However, the psychical integrality of man *is not manifested with the help of a visible and external element as is his somatic integrality.* The sense of the psychical constitution of man is not the same as that of the somatic constitution. This is the simplest confirmation of the conviction that the psyche is not the body. External properties of the body do not belong to the psyche; the psyche is not "matter," it is not "material" in the way the body is. Also, the entire inwardness of the human body, namely, that which we define as the "organism," differs essentially from the psyche. Psychical functions are internal and immaterial; even though they are [3a] conditioned by somaticity and its functions, psychical functions do not allow themselves to be reduced to them. When we speak of man's interiority, of his interior life, we mean [4a] the psyche—the totality of psychical functions. In themselves, they are devoid of the outwardness and visibility that belong to the body together with the somatic constitution, although the body—as was previously noted—also serves to indirectly externalize these functions, that is, to express them. Therefore, there exists a justified *tendency to grasp the totality of man's psychical function in connection with his somatic constitution*, and this has been reflected in various approaches to the problem of so-called temperaments. It seems that the very concept of temperament and various attempts to classify people in this respect have aimed at a closer definition of man's psychic integrality, taking this integrality as the basis for the integration of the person in the act.

2. The Characterization of the Psyche: Emotivity
Emotivity and emotion: Their meaning in light of etymology

In this study, however, we do not undertake so particular an aim. Our aim here is neither classification nor typology, which have so frequently resulted from inductive inquiries on the topic of man's psychical integrality. We aim for a more general and, at the same time, more fundamental characterization of the psychical dynamism while taking into account its connection to somaticity with its proper dynamism. By characterizing the dynamism in this way, we also characterize the psychical potentiality of man, for it is the source of this dynamism. In the previous chapter, we did this in relation to somaticity, stating that its proper dynamism has a reactive character. This is the body's proper capacity for reactions that in the dimension of the human body determine both its vegetative vitality from within and its mobility, visible from without.

We now wish to characterize by way of analogy the psychical dynamism—and, indirectly, man's psychical potentiality—*indicating emotivity as the feature most characteristic of this dynamism and potentiality.* The concept and expression "emotivity"—used rather infrequently in colloquial language, though employed in science especially in the adjectival form "emotive"—is associated with the quite commonly used noun "emotion." This case is quite similar to the association between reactivity and reaction. The association is accurate, though the word "emotion" in our language serves to describe a certain group of manifestations of psychical emotivity. It seems that emotional lived-experience means more or less the same as affective lived-experience.

However, neither the term "emotivity" nor the adjective "emotive" exclusively indicates affections or describes man's affectivity. This term has a broader meaning; namely, *it is linked with the whole rich and diversified world of human sensations* [5a]. The very number of expressions containing this stem already indicates wealth and diversity. For we speak not only about sensations [*czucia*] and affections [*uczucia*] but also about feeling [*odczucie, poczucie*], self-feeling [*samopoczucie*], sensing [*wyczucie*], and presentiment [*przeczucie*]; we use perhaps still other expressions in which the same linguistic stem occurs. We can observe that these expressions occur with various attributes; thus we speak, for instance, about artistic or moral feeling. It is also noteworthy that in almost the same meaning we use the noun "sense" [*zmysł*] (for instance, in the artistic or moral sense).[1]

This great wealth of expressions, which also indicates the great wealth and diversity of human sensations, directs us toward a broader and perhaps proper meaning of emotivity. The etymology of the words "emotion" and "emotivity" indicates motion or movement [6a](*movere* means "to move") that originates from within, and this is attested by the prefix *ex*[6b]. No Polish expression exists that would strictly render this content

---

1. We find this expression in David Hume (*A Treatise of Human Nature* [London: Printed for John Noon, 1739]) and in a number of later authors. The expression "the moral sense" is in fact commonly accepted in scientific and popular literature. This expression presupposes a certain anthropology. In this study we move in this particular direction through all the matters concerning "the integration and the psyche."

of emotion and emotivity. It may also seem that in the etymology of these expressions we find nothing that could be said of a purely somatic dynamism. In such a dynamism there also occurs a certain "movement," a certain change resulting from within. The previous chapter sufficiently indicated the inwardness of the body and the close dependence of what is external and visible in the reactive order on what is internal. However, it can be very helpful in manifesting the essential difference between the somatic and psychical dynamisms to compare the expressions "reaction–emotion" and "reactivity–emotivity." *Whereas in the first case there occurs a somatic movement that in no way transcends the potentiality of the body, this potentiality is fundamentally transcended in emotion and emotivity.* This seems to be indicated by the prefix *ex*: although this psychical movement depends in some way on the body, on somaticity, by which it is in some way conditioned, it nevertheless no longer belongs to the body; it is something different from the body.[7a]

Emotivity and reactivity

The above reflection, which has an etymological character, aims to show—and perhaps does show—both the fundamental distinctness of emotivity in relation to reactivity and their deep connection in man. The psyche is conditioned by somaticity. Emotivity, which seems to characterize man's psychical dynamism, is conditioned by reactivity, which characterizes his somatic dynamism. Perhaps we encounter here a major line of reflections in the fields of anthropology and psychology, both older and contemporary. Linking the psyche with somaticity in the dynamic aspect fundamentally characterizes the entire inquiry concerning temperaments. *Furthermore, we very often talk about psychical reactions—this shows how deeply emotivity is seated in reactivity and conditioned by it.* Not only do we talk about psychical reactions, but we also simply say "a man reacted," having in mind not only somatic reactivity but also the totality of his conduct in the act, which also contains a conscious response to a given value. For this response, as a decision or choice proper to the will, also contains something of somatic reactivity. Man constitutes the complex unity on whose basis the integration of the act in the person always contains in some way all the elements of the psycho-somatic complexity. Thus, expressions such as "a man reacted in this or that way" are true, though they seem to emphasize in particular one of the elements of this complexity.

What does emotivity as a sensibility to values contribute to the conscious response of the will?

The full image of the integration of the person in the act must always take into consideration the fact of complementarity: integration complements transcendence, which is realized through self-determination and efficacy. In this dimension, the human act is a conscious response to values through decision or choice. However, this response always in some way takes advantage of the dynamism of both somaticity and the psyche. The integration of the person in the act denotes the strictly concrete and always unrepeatable introduction of somatic reactivity and psychical emotivity into the unity of the act: into unity with the transcendence of the person, expressed in efficacious self-determination, which is at the same time a conscious response to values. This conscious response to values [8a]is not integrated in the human act in a merely somatic way[8b], as we attempted to show in the previous chapter by speaking especially about the synthesis of act and motion. *Rather, the conscious response to values* [9a]*is integrated in the human act through the entire psycho-emotivity of man*[9b].

Emotivity also denotes a specific sensibility to values. For the time being, we do not intend to analyze this; we simply note it in order to outline properly the problem of this integration. Sensibility to values on the emotive basis in man has a spontaneous, self-projecting character. In this the sensibility shares the characteristic of emotivity itself, which always indicates what happens in the person psychically (similarly, reactivity indicates what happens in the person somatically). Through the spontaneous sensibility to values, the emotive potentiality provides, in a sense, a particular material for the will. For by decision or choice the will is always a mentally defined response to values. This mental definition is absent in emotive lived-experiences. *This is the context in which a particular need for the integration of the person in the act arises, and in which at the same time a particular meaning of this integration emerges,* a meaning that is, in a sense, not comparable to somatic integration. [10a]

Determining the meaning of the integration of the person in the act from the side of human emotivity—through subsequent analyses in this chapter—should itself also help us to understand more deeply the transcendence of the person in the act. It is in transcendence and not in the integration of human emotivity that the deepest meaning of the spirituality [11a]of the person and the most proper basis for ascertaining the spirituality of the human soul are revealed[11b]. It is fitting for us to have this constantly before our eyes in order to know that the "spiritual" is not in the least equivalent to the "psychical." The psychical is also emotive and sensual.

3. Sensation and Consciousness in the Lived-Experience of One's Own Body
The emotive dynamism functions as the concentrator of lived-experiences

Psychology and anthropology usually distinguish between man's bodiliness, sensuality, and spirituality. Without in any way violating the firm legitimacy of this distinction, we emphasize in this study above all emotivity, and we do so because we attempt to create an image of human dynamism that is as integral as possible. It is emotivity that defines the specific form and, at the same time, the current of this dynamism that is joined in a particular way to the personal dynamism of human acts. This psychical theme of emotivity runs, in a sense, between bodiliness and spirituality, not distancing the two but in a particular way drawing them together and uniting them. [12a] As further analyses will demonstrate, *the emotive dynamism seems to perform, so to speak, the function of the concentrator of human lived-experiences*. Although a clear difference exists between the emotive dynamism and the reactive somatic dynamism, they closely condition each other. Further, as we mentioned previously, a drawing near to spirituality also takes place. All that determines the spiritual transcendence of the person—namely, the relation to truth, good, and beauty together with the capacity for self-determination—demonstrates a very deep emotive resonance in man. As something utterly individual, this resonance with its quality and strength also determines in turn the quality and strength of personal transcendence itself, or in any case, it creates a specific foundation for this transcendence in man. [13a] Thus, investigating the secrets of humanity from this side deepens our understanding of person and act. In any case, without an analysis of the emotivity proper to man, there can be no thorough understanding of the integration of the person in the act.

[14a]The sensorial stimulus (the psyche) and the motor stimulus (somaticity)[14b]

Let us attempt to begin this analysis at the point where the somatic dynamism in a sense breaks off and where emotivity most closely encounters the reactivity of the body. Just like reactivity, emotivity is closely associated with the action of stimuli. We know that somatic reactivity is the ability to react to stimuli, although in the previous chapter we were most interested in the ability to react to motor stimuli. Another ability exists alongside that one, namely, the ability to sense. This ability in the somatic layer also consists in taking up the stimuli that originate from material objects, from various bodies. However, their effect is not somatic; it does not consist in the reaction and motion of the body. Their effect is psychical; it is expressed in sensation. *And even though this psychical effect is conditioned in the somatic layer by some reaction, in itself it nevertheless transcends this reaction from beginning to end.*

Together with sensation, the "psychical subjectivity" of man emerges above the somatic subjectivity

[15a]The sensorial stimulus differs fundamentally from the motor stimulus[15b], though very often they go together (for instance, when somebody instinctively moves back his hand after touching a hot furnace). Sensation in itself is not a somatic movement or reaction. It demonstrates a relation to the body such as that which a subject has to an object: although this relation is not made conscious in sensation itself, through it the body becomes a certain content that simultaneously permeates the field of consciousness. Thus, through sensation we rise above what in the previous chapter was called the subjectivity of the body itself[16a]; we rise toward a new subjectivity[16b]. While the other "subjectivity" is in itself based on somatic reactivity and to a considerable extent not encompassed by consciousness, *the psychical "subjectivity," which together with sensation emerges on the substratum of the body, is encompassed by consciousness.*[2] For sensation in itself constitutes a sensory cognitive reflex

---

2. It seems that the problem of the construction—or rather the "constructing itself"—of the

thanks to which the body becomes an objective content, and this content reaches consciousness and is mirrored in it.

Sensing one's own body is at the foundation of the consciousness of one's own body

We wish to grasp as thoroughly as possible the relation of sensation to consciousness, because this relation has a fundamental significance for the personal dynamism. First of all, what we mean here is *the sensing of one's own body*. One's own body with its various states and movements becomes the source of [17a]sensorial stimuli[17b], which fundamentally enable man to have the lived-experience of his own body. In this lived-experience, sensation enters consciousness and forms with it, so to speak, one basis of lived-experience, though sensation differs from intellectual consciousness.

We have noted several times that the sphere of the consciousness of the body is determined, so to speak, in an ongoing way by the field of sensations. Thus, the entire internal dynamism of the body-organism, connected with its vegetative vitality, is located in a sense outside the reach of consciousness, insofar as nothing of this dynamism passes into the field of sensations. At this point, let us emphasize the phrase "in a sense," for, having consciousness of his body, man also has some general consciousness of its inwardness and internal dynamism. This consciousness is concretized with the help of given sensations, for instance, sensations of bodily pain, which make the inwardness of one's own body also enter the sphere of consciousness. *It is by means of sensation that this concretization of consciousness constitutes the full basis of the lived-experience of one's own body.*

Self-feeling

The habitual experiencing of one's own body is a resultant of many sensations [18a]and thus of many sensorial stimuli that proceed from this body[18b] and its reactive-motor dynamisms. These sensations reveal to every one of us not a separate "subjectivity of the body" but precisely

---

personal subject, a problem that is merely outlined in this study, deserves fuller examination. Distinguishing somatic and psychical "subjectivities" within integral personal subjectivity calls for the conception of "layers" in the philosophy of man. See Hartmann, *Ethik*, especially pt. 3, ch. 2, section 71, "Zur ontologischen Gesetzlichkeit als Basis der Freiheit," pp. 657–85.

the somatic structure of the entire subject "man," of the entire "I." They reveal the measure in which he is the body and in which the body-*sóma* takes active part in his being and acting. We can say that a bodily sensation—the direct reflex of the body, in a sense constantly formed and shaped by its reactivity and mobility—has in this sphere a fundamental significance for the lived-experience of one's own bodily "I." As we said above, this habitual lived-experience is the resultant of many sensations, which is expressed as a certain "self-feeling." Some self-feeling constantly accompanies man—it constantly forms, in a sense, a psychical fabric and reflex of his being and acting. The direct and proper object of self-feeling is the entire somatic "I," not distinguished from the personal "I" but most essentially coherent with it.

We ought to underscore that *self-feeling manifests a distinct qualificative feature*, and thus a feature of value; for it is known that self-feeling may be good or bad, and within this fundamental distinction it takes on various gradations. Thus, it can happen to be more or less good, more or less bad. Man expresses precisely this by saying "I feel well," "I feel ill," and many other similar things, as when he states, for example, that he feels tired, exhausted, sick, or, on the other hand, strong, healthy, etc. Man also feels that he is functioning well or not, which—through the psychical reflex—manifests the significance of efficiency for the reactive-motor dynamism of the body. At every step, we are also reminded of the extent to which this dynamism and its functionality condition the so-called higher psychical functions. Thus, for example, physical fatigue adversely influences our thinking processes, whereas the "rested head" increases clarity of thought, and so on. In this way, we become aware of how thoroughly coherent our somatic "I" is with the entire personal "I," how close a unity they constitute.

The superiority of consciousness over sensations as a condition of personal dynamism

The sensing of one's own body is an indispensable factor for the lived-experience of man's integral subjectivity. In this lived-experience, the body and consciousness are in a sense bound together through sensation, which constitutes the most elementary manifestation of the human psyche and at the same time the most proximate psychical reflex of human somaticity. This *sensorial psychical reflex differs fundamentally from the reflexive function of consciousness*, which—as we clarified above—has a fundamental significance for the personal lived-experience of the concrete human "I." The mutual permeation of sensation and consciousness in this lived-experience manifests the dependence between the senses and the mind that in general exists in the area of human cognition. This is a bilateral dependence, because sensing one's own body allows one to establish an objective contact with it and at the same time reveals the psychical subjectivity integrated with that body, or somatic subject. For sensation happens in a psychical way in the human "I," and what this "happening" reveals is precisely subjectivity. This revelation occurs, in a sense, with respect to consciousness, which—apart from the extreme case of the emotionalization of consciousness (see chapter 1)—retains its distinct superiority regarding sensations. For we in fact possess the consciousness of our own sensations, among other things, which means that in the normal course of lived-experiences they are subordinated to consciousness. However, we cannot state that the converse is true, namely, that we possess the sensation or feeling of our consciousness. Precisely *this superiority of consciousness involving a certain "ordination"* [*wporządkowanie*] *and, at the same time, subordination* [*podporządkowanie*] *of sensations—particularly the sensation of one's own body—constitutes a condition for self-determination*, and thus for self-governance and self-possession: a condition for realizing the act, the truly personal dynamism.

The sensing of one's own body manifests the psycho-somatic subjectivity of man. Because this occurs in relation to consciousness, which performs both the mirroring and reflexive functions, the becoming conscious occurs together with the consciousness-related subjectivization and interiorization—so characteristic of the personal "I"—which also encompass the body as one's own, as different from all the other bodies. The sensing of the body allows man to penetrate his own somaticity inasmuch as it is needed for self-determination in the act and, through this, for the transcendence of the person. Accordingly, we ought to establish the measure of the integration of the person in the act: in this case, integration is equivalent to the normal lived-experience of the body[19a]. Any defects or deficiencies of sensation, which impede such a lived-experience, should be considered in this respect as manifestations of disintegration.

4. Sensibility and Truthfulness
The permeation of sensations into consciousness forms man's individual sensibility

The lived-experience of one's own body is not the only terrain where sensations permeate into consciousness, just as bodily sensations are not the only variety of sensations. Man senses not only his own body but also himself more integrally—he senses what determines his own "I" and its dynamic. Besides, he senses the "world" as a complex and diversified group of beings, among which his own "I" exists and with which it remains in various relations. *The permeation of these various sensations into consciousness shapes the lived-experience of one's own "I" in the world; it also shapes a lived-experience of the world.* We are concerned here above all with the world remaining in the sphere of the senses and not with all of reality, all of the existence encompassed [20a]by the mind in an abstract way[20b]. Sensation in its proper specificity, sensation as an emotive fact, is more directly connected with that which lies in the sphere of the senses—though it is not completely severed from intellectual content—than with all that by which human thought lives on different levels and in different modes of abstraction. An accurate observation of man speaks against an overly simplified dichotomy; it also speaks against an exclusive reduction of emotivity to sensuality. If we ascertain in man not only the sensing of his own body or of bodies in general (which are accessed cognitively through the senses) but also some aesthetic, religious, or moral sense, then this is a sign that the emotive element is in some way also proper to man's spirituality, not only to his sensuality.

At this point, we touch upon very essential problems of psychology, anthropology, and the theory of cognition, which, however, we do not intend to analyze in detail insofar as they belong to these other sciences. We are interested here in the problem of emotivity and, directly, in the problem of the cognitive function performed by various sensations—and this only with regard to the integration of the person in the act. The fact that sensations arise, that they have cognitive intentionality, and that they permeate consciousness *shapes an individual sensibility in every man.* In colloquial language, the very word "sensibility" is perhaps not semantically determined in an adequate way, for at times, sensibility is confused with "irritability." Here we shall try to free the word "sensibility" from semantic admixtures so that it can denote *man's specific property of sensation and feeling*, which either constitute a certain cognitive function themselves or at least participate in such a function. By grasping the problem in this way, we wish to refrain from deciding important and complex psychological and epistemological problems. These problems occur throughout the entire history of philosophy and science. In particular, they are manifested in connection with conceptions such as that of the moral and religious senses, not to mention the social and aesthetic senses. These conceptions—or perhaps simply modes of expression—point out the emotive moment, the moment of feeling as a real component of man's relation to those areas of reality to which he cannot relate cognitively by means of the senses themselves. Clearly then, the concept of "sense" is used here analogously. Namely, this concept indicates the *concreteness* of the cognitive function in a given area and its *intuitiveness*; it thus also indicates the properties that belong to the senses in relation to [21a] that which comes directly to them in cognition, in relation to [21b] the so-called sensory qualities. These qualities vary with respect to the particular senses and their functions: one is for seeing, another for hearing, another for touching, etc.

The permeation of sensibility by truthfulness as a condition for the personal lived-experience of values

When we speak of sensibility in our study, it is evident that we do not mean sensual sensibility *sensu stricto*, the sensibility of sight, hearing, touch, and so on. We also mean various intentional directions of human sensation that are deeply rooted in the spirituality and spiritual life of man. Sensibility itself, however, does not indicate the transcendence of the person, self-determination and efficacy. Rather, it indicates that which "happens" in the person as a subject endowed with emotive potentiality and which in this respect requires integration. After all, "sensibility" [*wrażliwość*] is etymologically linked with "impression" [*wrażenie*], with which it has a common linguistic and, in a sense, semantic root. By "impression" we understand the sensory reception and the sensory image of objects. Impression participates in some way in this sensory ability of man. It also has above all a receptive and not active character. Precisely for this reason it requires integration.

We are concerned in this case not merely with consciousness-related integration, that is, the permeation of particular sensations with their proper intentional contents into consciousness—the fact whence emerges the authentic lived-experience of a value. For sensations or feelings are intentionally directed to values in particular, as could have been ascertained already in the analysis of bodily sensations when their qualificative feature was emphasized ("I feel well," "I feel ill," and so on). Every other sensation is also directed to a fact within or without its own subject, though always with this "inclination toward values," with this qualificative feature, which is so clearly manifested in feelings concerning one's own body. Therefore, sensations or feelings become in man a particular center crystallizing the lived-experiences of values. Emotionalists such as Max Scheler maintain that they are the only source of cognitive contact established by man with values, that apart from feelings there is no other authentic cognition of values.[3]

This, too, is an epistemological problem that we do not undertake in this sense. We wish to state only that the very lived-experience of values on the basis of the integration of sensations in consciousness does not suffice. For on account of the transcendence of the person in the act, *yet another integration is necessary—the integration of truthfulness*, as it were. The transcendence of the person in the act consists in the relation to truth, the relation that conditions the authentic freedom of self-determination. Therefore, the lived-experience of values, which is the function of man's sensibility itself—and thus the function of sensations—must also be subject in the dimension of person and act to the relation to truth. *The permeation of sensibility by truthfulness is a requirement of the personal lived-experience of values. Only on the basis of such a lived-experience can authentic decision and choice be shaped.* Authenticity in this case denotes the fulfillment of freedom that is always conditioned by a conviction, that is, a mature relation to truth. Our point in the given

---

3. See Scheler, *Formalismus*, 214; translated by Frings and Funk as *Formalism in Ethics and Non-Formal Ethics of Values*, 199: "'Wertgefühle'... (z.B. 'Achtungsgefühl' usw.) dürfen diese nur darum heißen, weil in der primären Gegebenheit des 'vollen Lebens' die *Werte selbst noch* unmittelbar gegeben waren, derentwegen allein sie ja den Namen 'Wertgefühle' führen." [Feelings may be called "value-feelings" (e.g., "feelings of respect") only because *values themselves* were immediately given in the primary givenness of this "full life," values without which the feelings could not be called value-feelings.]

case is [22a]value in cognition[22b]—thus, the truth about the good of this object to which the decision or choice refers.

This understanding of the concept of "authenticity"—an understanding on the basis of truthfulness—is at times opposed on the basis of sensibility alone. In this latter understanding, sensibility as a characteristic of human sensations would be the final and only criterion of values and the exclusive basis of experiencing them, as if the consciousness-related integration of felt sensations and values no longer admitted any integration on the basis of truthfulness, any reflection, any intellectual assessment and judgment about values. In reality, however, this latter integration has a decisive significance for person and act. It is this integration that measures the authentic transcendence of the person in the act. A man who would rely only and exclusively on the course of his sensations and feelings in his relation to values would leave himself somehow in the orbit of what merely happened in him and would not be fully capable of self-determination. Self-determination and the self-governance connected with it sometimes require action in the name of the "naked" truth about the good, action in the name of the value that is not felt. At times it even requires action against provisional feelings.

Sensibility is a particular richness of the psyche

However, this does not in the least attest to some depreciation of sensibility. Sensibility itself is a great endowment and richness of human nature. The ability to sense, the ability to spontaneously feel values constitutes a foundation of man's many talents. Emotionalists are right when they state that this ability can in no way be replaced in man. Even an intellectual recognition of value, an objectively accurate assessment of it, does not shape the quality of lived-experience the way feeling does. It also does not bring man closer to value or concentrate on value, as feeling does. But to say that man deprived of given sensations must thereby remain "blind to values" (as emotionalists maintain) is perhaps debatable. It seems clear, nonetheless, that he cannot in this way—that is, so dynamically—experience them. *Thus, in this sense, sensibility is certainly a particular richness of the human psyche. However, in order to evaluate this richness accurately, we must take into consideration the degree to which sensibility is permeated by truthfulness.* This, too, is the measure of the integration of the person who governs himself all the more fully and possesses himself all the more maturely the more truly he feels all values, the more thoroughly the order occurring among values in reality is reflected in his lived-experience of them.

5. Is Desire or Excitement the Root of Emotive Excitability?

Appetitus concupiscibilis–appetitus irascibilis

In this study, we have referred more than once to the traditional conception of man. By this, we have in mind above all the thorough conception built by St. Thomas Aquinas on the foundation of the philosophy of being. This conception contains a very clear demarcation *between man's sensuality and rationality* while at the same time manifesting a close connection between them. This connection occurs on the terrain of cognition, where the senses [23a]provide the mind with direct objects and at the same time with material, as it were[23b]; we can say this because man cognizes the visible world, the world accessible to the senses, with his mind, and he simultaneously grasps [24a]its object by way of abstraction[24b]. Therefore, what is accessible to the senses is not cognized by man in the same way as it is received by the senses. In addition, mental cognition reaches far beyond the data provided by sensual experience itself. The connection between sensuality and rationality also occurs in the area that St. Thomas describes with the term *appetitus*: in a certain respect, *appetitus sensitivus* also provides objects for the will, which is called *appetitus rationalis*, although in another respect, sensuality creates specific difficulties for the will. We already indicated in the analysis of self-determination that the term *appetitus* does not have an unequivocally corresponding term in the Polish language. We render *appetitus* as "striving" or as "desire," though neither term properly renders what *appetitus* contains.

A question has arisen as to whether the appetitive character can be ascribed to the will. It seems that this difficulty does not exist with respect to the senses. Sensual desire is a reality known from experience. In order to describe this experiential reality more closely, *St. Thomas distinguished between the concupiscent appetite* (appetitus concupiscibilis) *and the irascible appetite* (appetitus irascibilis), each of them being a specific—we can say typical—variation of *appetitus sensitivus*.[4] Thomas's distinction becomes so significant here that we could even perceive in it the germ of a certain typology. This would be an axiological rather than a psychological typology, for the difference between *appetitus concupiscibilis* and *appetitus irascibilis* is manifested above all with respect to the given good (sensual value), which for the concupiscent appetite is only an object to be desired and for the irascible appetite is a difficult good (*bonum arduum*) and therefore an object to be acquired after overcoming certain difficulties. Thomas Aquinas sees in these two variations of sensual desire the basis for the diversification of human affections and passions (*passiones animae*). It is, then, in this form that we find in him an integral interpretation of the human psyche and psychical dynamism from the side of the senses; as mentioned, we also find the germ of a certain typology. It also seems that we can verify this typology to a certain degree on the basis of observation, for in some people the concupiscible appetite dominates, and in others the irascible appetite.

Excitement as a separate emotive core (fact)

The inquiries conducted in this study emphasize above all the emotive character of the human psyche. These inquiries, however, must coincide with the understandings of traditional anthropology (psychology) *at one common experiential point* (the fact that this anthropology is metaphysical does not in the least cancel its experiential character). *This point is a given lived-experience of an emotive character, and the lived-experience of excitement seems to be such.* Excitement "happens" in the subject, revealing his specific psychical potentiality. It is an emotive fact different from sensation, to which we rightly ascribe a certain cognitive intentionality. Excitement does not demonstrate such an orientation of the psyche: it does not have a cognitive character. Does it have a concupiscible, appetitive character? Rather, we should state that it has a character that is [25a]di-

---

4. The distinction between the concupiscible (*concupiscibile*) and the irascible (*irascibile*) is also found in Ricoeur's analysis: "'Irascible' ne se révèle empiriquement qu'à travers les passions d'ambition, de domination, de violence, de même que le 'concupiscible' se révèle empiriquement à travers les passions du plaisir et de la facilité." [The 'irascible' reveals itself empirically only through the passions of ambition, domination, and violence, just as the 'concupiscible' reveals itself empirically through passions of pleasure and ease.] Ricoeur, *Philosophie de la volonté*, 112; translated by Kohák as *Freedom and Nature*, 117.

rectly[25b] emotive, though the emotivity of excitement demonstrates different varieties and variations. Certainly, excitements of the irascible type (*irascibilis*) and the concupiscent type (*concupiscibilis*) occur in man. Thus excitement indirectly has an appetitive character, although what we ascertain in it directly ought to be described precisely as excitement, not as desire. The intentional turning "toward something" or "away from something" describes the subsequent specificity of human excitements. In themselves they are a manifestation of emotivity; they are a typical emotive "actuation" of the human psyche.

This actuation usually has a very vivid somatic setting. Excitement always inheres in a specific reaction of the body and even in the whole chain of an organism's complex reactions (blood circulation, respiration, the work of the heart, etc.), which we feel distinctly. *Each time, a specific sensation of the body is contained in the feeling of excitement itself*: we feel and experience the emotive and reactive moments as one dynamic fact, which in a sense entitles us to call this fact a reaction. Excitement's somatic accompaniment can be understood as a specific communication to the body of the dynamism that is *in se* psychical. It is fitting to distinguish from this the "excitement" of the body itself: this fact is in itself reactive, having only an emotive resonance. This close and easily detectable connection with the body makes us consider excitement as something sensual, as a dynamic manifestation of sensuality. It is usually accompanied by a specific intensification of sensations, a rich sensorial reflex that further determines the vividness of lived-experience.

Excitement differs from elation

However, the unilateral reduction of excitements to sensuality would be a great simplification. A source of excitement, that is, the stimulus evoking excitement, does not in the least have to influence the senses directly. It can be a value inaccessible to the senses themselves, one that can proceed from content derived from ideals. In such cases, however, we tend to speak of *elation rather than excitement*. Excitement [*podniecenie*] in itself seems to indicate the sphere of more sensual stimuli [*podniety*], hence the name. More spiritual elation can in varying degrees be connected in the subject with sensual or even bodily excitement. It seems that the latter in a certain measure favors spiritual elation but after a certain point of intensification begins to hinder it. This observation attests to the need for integration.

Excitability as a constant capacity for certain excitements

What we mean is the integration of not only particular excitements but also the entirety of human excitability, for this is what we call the emotive property of the psyche. Excitability is a capacity for excitement. It demonstrates various directions and variations, as do excitements themselves. Thus excitability also denotes a certain sphere of man's potentiality that seems to be quite closely associated with sensibility. If a connection exists between them, so does a distinct boundary: excitability indicates the emotive facts that completely differ from sensibility [26a]. Excitability and excitement as its dynamic leaven and core constitute in man, in a sense, the area where an "explosion" of affections occurs. It seems, however, that we also consider here a certain quality and subjective strength of these affections. We have reasons for distinguishing excitability from affectivity, which we will consider in turn. In accord with its verbal stem, excitability [*pobudliwość*] seems to indicate above all the very awakening [*budzenie się*] of affections, which is quite vehement; a moment ago we called it their explosion. In this case, the source of affections is rather irrational; lived-experience is at times connected with a certain "blindness"—these are characteristics that, in addition to emotive intensity, we also ascribe to passions. At this point the word *pasja* is sometimes used in Polish in reference to the classic *passiones animae*. Even if *excitability,* and thus excitement, *shapes certain forms of human affections,* it *nonetheless certainly does not exhaust* all the wealth of their variations.

Excitability as a component of drives

It seems that sensual-affective excitability is in particular *quite strongly rooted in human drives*. The previous chapter has already shown the somatic-reactive layer of both the drive for self-preservation and the sexual drive. At the same time, however, we noted that drives are not reduced to the dynamism of this one layer. It also has its own psycho-emotive center. And this seems to inhere above all in a given excitability, and thus in sexual excitability and in various forms of excitability concerning self-preservation. In both cases, it is a particular capacity for receiving stimuli, that is, a capacity for excitement. However, the concept of drive is not exhausted by this capacity, that is, excitability, just as it is not exhausted by the clearly determined reactivity of the body, the capacity for distinct sexual reactions or reactions of self-preservation. Rather, both reactivity and excitability stand at the disposal of the powerful force of nature that determines the orientation toward the value of existence itself—and this is the most elementary and at the same time the most fundamental value.

We will try to consider the problem of integration in this area more extensively and in connection with man's affectivity.

6. The Specificity of Emotional Stirring and Man's Affectivity

Distinguishing emotional stirring from excitement

In the analysis of human emotivity, we arrive at a sphere that requires a particular distinction, although the reductive method could blur this distinctness. What we mean is the lived-experience of emotional stirring [*wzruszenie*], which differs from excitement not merely by a verbal expression. The two different expressions indicate two different lived-experiences[27a]. Although both have a fundamentally emotive character, emotional stirring is different from excitement because it has a different specificity as a psychical fact. It also seems that the concept of "emotion" corresponds most closely precisely to this fact, to this specificity of lived-experience and experience, although it is difficult to speak of a complete overlapping of the meanings of emotion and emotional stirring, just as it is difficult to speak of the semantic overlapping of man's emotivity and affectivity. *Emotional stirring "happens" in the man-subject similarly to excitement, though we can distinguish these two variations from each other without difficulty among the* passiones animae. At this point, it is worthwhile to observe that the term *passio*, which Thomists use in imitation of their master to describe various facts of affective life, literally indicates the "happening."

The specificity of emotional stirring differs from that of excitement.

Excitement seems to be closer to man's sensuality, whereas emotional stirring seems, in a sense, further from it. Although both are accompanied by some somatic reaction, excitement seems to inhere more in this reaction than emotional stirring does. Thus we experience emotional stirring as a manifestation of, in a sense, pure emotivity, as an "actuation" of the psyche itself, in which the somatic conditioning is more weakly manifested. Therefore, in the lived-experience of many emotional stirrings, bodily sensation in a sense gives way to spiritual feeling. This happens all the more due to the fact *that the content of emotional stirrings sometimes remains closely connected with the spirituality and the spiritual life of man.* Thus, for example, we experience aesthetic emotional stirrings connected with the contemplation of beauty, cognitive emotional stirrings connected with the discovery of some truth, and variations of emotional stirrings connected with the sphere of the good, moral good and evil in particular. The latter lived-experiences, which Scheler considers the deepest manifestations of man's emotive potentiality, progress in close connection with the processes of conscience. The reproach of conscience caused by a fault is not merely a judgment of oneself, but, as we know from experience, this lived-experience as related to truthfulness demonstrates a remarkable emotional component. The same applies to the process of purification, justification, or conversion, in which a deep emotional stirring is again linked with a real detachment from evil and passage into good, or at least with their beginning in man. The content of these emotional stirrings and its emotive shades can vary diametrically. Man progresses from the anxiety of conscience, from at times a deep despondency due to fault, almost from despair, to a tranquility and to a no less deep joy, to spiritual beatitude.

Emotional stirring as the core of human affectivity

To say this is already to speak about various affections, *about various manifestations of man's affectivity. An emotional stirring stands at the core of each of them. This emotive core in a sense radiates interiorly,* thus creating a different emotional lived-experience every time. We call this lived-experience an affection. Although it is different every time, that is, unique and unrepeatable, there arise various affections that are similar—indeed, in a sense the same—with respect to their emotional content. They very often differ by a particular variation or intensity, but their essential content is the same. The identity of emotional content always finds its source, its experiential origin, in an emotional stirring, which is already colored with this content. This content is later spread throughout man's psychical layer by way of interior radiation. This is the way in which affection appears in man, is intensified in him, and is sometimes consolidated in a particular way. It is then that we have a particular reason to speak of affective states. Although every affection, even one that quickly passes away, is a certain emotional state of the man-subject, it is most proper to speak of a state when an affection is consolidated. The degree to which affection, while being consolidated, remains emotion is another matter. Rather, it seems that *what we call an affective state has very often already departed from its original emotive core, which is the emotional stirring of a given content, and has somehow become shared by the will.* The problem of the permeation of affections into the will, and together with this the problem of the transition of emotional states into certain affective attitudes, is very important for the study of "integration and the psyche"—and this is the proper topic of the present chapter.

The world of affections is rich and diverse

Let us return to the specificity of affections. As we said a moment ago, this specificity is that of the emotional stirrings themselves, which in turn spread throughout the psyche. By characterizing affections, by bestowing various names on them, we distinguish these various emotional stirrings above all from one another. So, for instance, the affection of sorrow is marked by one emotional stirring and the affection of joy by another, the affection of anger by one and that of tenderness by another, the affection of love by one and that of hatred by another. The world of human affections is very rich and very diversified, a little like colors on a palette. Psychologists and to some extent moralists have often attempted to grasp the principal affections to which all the richness of man's emotional life can be reduced. They have partially succeeded, though *the area of human affections—a little like a painter's palette—demonstrates a great number of individual shades and hues.* In addition, various possibilities exist for affections to be mixed with one another, to overlap, to permeate one another, and to support or fight against one another. This constitutes a whole separate world in man, a separate layer of human subjectivity. We have distinguished here for some time the particular sense of this subjectivity, for affections "happen" in man. This happening is their coming into being, their growth, and their passing away. *The emotional dynamic is not subject—at least not to a considerable extent—to the efficacy of the person.* As the great Greek philosophers observed, affections are not dependent on reason; they are *"irrational"* in their essence. However, one can easily understand this term as pejorative.

On some criteria for differentiating affections

Perhaps this is why human affectivity has been too unilaterally and at times too simplistically reduced to sensuality. We have already addressed this topic. At this point, however, there is a need to state that, emotional stirring in all its specificity differs from excitement. This is not merely a difference of degree but of essence. Even the strongest emotional stirring is not excitement. Also, the component of somatic reactions that accompanies emotional stirring [28a]is different[28b]. However, it may seem that excitement initiates certain emotional lived-experiences for which emotional stirring alone, in a sense, does not suffice. This is not so much a function of the force of affection as it is a level at which the emotive potentiality "discharges" or "breaks out" in man. It is at least this difference of level that we have in mind when we speak of emotional stirring as something different from excitement and when we speak separately of man's excitability and affectivity. *And because we speak of different levels, affective life in itself bears the possibility of a certain sublimation, that is, a passing from level to level*—for instance, from the level of excitements to the level of emotional stirrings.[5] Human potentiality is in this respect sublimative. Psychologists commonly distinguish lower affections from higher ones. They also indicate different depths of human affections and their either more "peripheral" or more "central" character. This distinction presupposes the interiority of the man-person, in a sense, an immaterial space within which on the basis of feeling we can distinguish a center and periphery as well as various levels. We ought not to confuse these levels "inside" man with the levels of affections themselves, for, as we saw,

---

5. See Scheler, *Formalismus*, especially ch. 5, section 8: "Zur Schichtung des emotionalen Lebens," 331–45.

affections can be lower or higher. These levels "inside," however, already speak of a certain integration of emotional stirrings and affections in the man-subject and have a bearing on the efficacy of the person.

This last fragment of the analysis also shows that the dynamism of affections is specifically joined with the system of sensations and feelings, which, permeating into consciousness, form each time a concrete specificity of emotional lived-experience.

7. [29a]The Emotivity of the Subject and the Efficacy of the Person[29b]

Affections are differentiated by their emotive content

Our recent analyses do not exhaust the richness of the reality of man's emotional life but only provide a certain view and help in characterization. Emotivity characterizes most properly our affective life. Every affection has its emotive core in the form of an emotional stirring from which it specifically radiates. In addition, on the basis of this emotional stirring, every affection defines itself as a completely original psychical fact. If a certain content belongs to it (and it is known that such content belongs to emotional stirrings and affections) then it belongs also in an emotive way—not in a cognitive or appetitive way, but precisely in an emotive way. *Every affection is a content occurring in man in a way that is directly and immediately emotive*: one content is, for instance, "anger" and another is "love," one is "hatred" and another is "longing," one is "sorrow" and another is "joy," etc. Each of these contents is realized properly and authentically only as emotion. Each constitutes a manifestation and actualization of the psychical potentiality of man. Each reveals his subjectivity in a particular way. On the basis of affections, within human emotivity, a certain tension is most clearly manifested between man's efficacy and subjectivity. Therefore, the synthesis of efficacy and subjectivity, as well as the concrete significance of integration in this sphere, deserves a particularly penetrating analysis.

The relation between spontaneity and self-determination

The emotional lived-experiences—emotional stirrings or excitements and consequently particular affections or even passions—fundamentally "happen" in man as a subject. They happen in a self-projected, spontaneous way, which means that *they are not a consequence of personal efficacy and self-determination*. Accordingly, some specific efficacy of the psyche must be assumed at the root of the emotive dynamism, for without this, all that happens in the man-subject in an emotive way would remain inexplicable. *In a certain sense, emotivity denotes precisely this self-projected efficacy of the human psyche.* When we state that it is self-projected or spontaneous, we thereby also want to indicate its dynamic independence from the proper efficacy of the person, that is, from self-determination. When man experiences various affections or passions, he very often becomes vividly conscious that it is not he who is acting but that something is happening in him, and even more so, that something is happening to him: as if he were not master of himself, as if he had lost governance over himself and could not reestablish it. Thus, together with emotion, affection, or passion, [30a]the structure of self-possession and self-governance opens before man as a particular task to be accomplished. Here, the contribution of consciousness is clear and vivid.[30b]

Affectivity is not a source of disintegration of the person in the act

The fact that the appearance of affection or passion *confronts man with a need for a certain integration as a specific task does not mean in the least that affection or passion themselves cause disintegration*. Such a view arose in Stoic philosophy and in modern times was to a certain extent revived in Kant. Based on these conceptions, which in various ways advocate a severance from affections so that man's action results exclusively from reason (the conception of the categorical imperative in Kant), we would have to accept that the entire emotive potentiality is in itself the source of the disintegration of the person in the act. However, the broadly understood experience of man, with particular consideration for human morality, does not permit us to accept this view, which was not accepted, for example, in the anthropology and ethics of Aristotle in contrast to the Stoics, nor in Scheler in contrast to Kant.[xli] A specific ethical and anthropological apriorism appears in a view that understands human emotivity, and in particular human emotionality, as the source of disintegration. And apriorism by its essence does not take experience into account. *To exclusively indicate man's emotivity and emotionality as the source of the disintegration of the person in the act* in a certain way determines man as someone irrevocably doomed to disintegration. In this regard, the Stoic view can be characterized as pessimistic. Pessimism proceeds here—particularly in Kant—from a specific idealism.

The tension between the emotivity of the subject and personal efficacy in acts is creative

Based on realistic thinking, to which we attempt to be faithful here, no human affection or even passion by itself causes the disintegration of the person in the act. It is true, however, that it posits a particular task for man [31a]. If self-governance and self-possession are proper to the structure of the person, then the task of integrating human emotivity and emotionality in the self-determination of the person is fully justified. For a distinct *tension* is manifested *between this self-projected efficacy of the human psyche and the efficacy of the person*. This tension is multifaceted and constitutes, in a sense, a key moment of personhood and morality. In traditional anthropology, this tension was understood above all as the tension between the powers of the human soul, between *appetitus rationalis* (the will) and *appetitus sensitivus*. In light of this study's inquiries, *we will attempt to look at it as a tension between the subjectivity and efficacy of the person*. We stated earlier that the synthesis of efficacy and subjectivity in the act of the person is not realized without a specific effort, which can be described as the effort of human interiority most proper to man. It is this effort that, among other things, allowed us to liken the efficacy of the person in the act to creativity (chapter 2). To some extent, the present chapter's analysis of the relation between sensibility and truthfulness in cognition prepared us to understand this problem. [32a]

The tendency of affections to take root in the subjective "I"

The tension between self-determination (that is, the proper efficacy of the person) and emotivity (that is, the self-projected efficacy of the human psyche) can undoubtedly be traced back to the mutual relation of the will and affections. If we perceive in it a tension between man's subjectivity and efficacy, then we have in mind, of course, not the subject as *suppositum* but rather subjectivity as an experiential correlate of what in man merely "happens," in contrast to action, for which efficacy is essential. The transcendence of the person in the act is linked with efficacy. As we said previously, affections merely happen in man. *This emotive happening may be transient,* as if it simply passed over the surface of the soul, *though it also demonstrates a specific tendency to take root in the subjective "I."* It is then, that is, when affection turns into a durable psychical state, that a certain interior attitude of man emerges and is shaped together with it. For instance, a provisional and transient affection of anger is something different from a lasting anger: anger as an interior attitude of man. Also, a transient affection of love or hatred is something different from love or hatred as man's interiorly consolidated attitude. Such attitudes constitute an important motif of the psychical life; they constitute a particularly important fruit of man's emotive potentiality and dynamism. Here we find ourselves, in a sense, at a point of particular closeness between "happening" and self-determination.

Emotional attitudes, however, are formed to a considerable extent in a self-projected, spontaneous manner. Their becoming consolidated and rooted in the subject proceeds from the very same emotive dynamism as do the first emotional stirrings or excitements. The consolidation and rootedness of emotion in the subjective "I" attest to the scope of emotive energy. At the same time, they constitute a specific accumulation of subjectivity and immanence. *Efficacy and the transcendence of the personal "I" connected with it are, in a sense, pulled into the subject.* The influence of affections on the will is such that the latter does not so much create a certain attitude of man as appropriate it from emotion—it is this attitude that we shall call the affective attitude. This attitude is typically "subjective." *Affection is rightly considered a particular source of man's subjectivism.* Structurally, subjectivism denotes a predominance of subjectivity over efficacy—in a sense, a predominance of psychical immanence over personal transcendence in action.

The permeation of affections into the will can confer a greater vividness on the efficacy of the person

All of this, however, does not in the least attest that emotion amounts to disintegration. Although we previously considered the problem of the emotionalization of consciousness, and despite the fact that diminished responsibility in action is commonly known and acknowledged when this action is performed in passion, all of this nonetheless does not entitle one to ascribe a disintegrative function to emotions. Emotivity can contribute to the blurring of the distance between the subjective and the efficacious "I"; it can to a certain extent impose its world of values on the will, though it does not merely constitute an obstacle for the integration of the person in the act. Indeed, *this integration is possible, and in it emotion confers a particular vividness on efficacy* and, with efficacy, on the entire personal structure of self-governance and self-possession.

8. [33a]The Emotivity of the Subject and the Lived-Experience of Value[33b]

To what extent is emotivity the source of a limitation to conscious efficacy?

The relation of emotivity to man's efficacy requires further analysis, for that undertaken so far does not adequately bring to light all the elements concerning this relation. It is evident that *emotivity becomes in man the source of self-projected subjectivization and interiorization*, which differ from the subjectivization and interiorization in consciousness. The emotionalization of consciousness is a kind of boundary phenomenon where abundance of emotion in a sense destroys consciousness and with it the capacity for normal lived-experience. [34a]These effects in the order of consciousness are accompanied by effects in the order of the efficacy of the person.[34b] Thus, the boundary event of the self-projected subjectivization by emotions is, in a sense, a severance of human subjectivity from conscious efficacy. These are the situations in which man ceases to be capable of both conscious action and responsibility. In such situations, action ceases to be action and remains only a specific "happening": something happens in man and to man, something that he neither determines nor performs. He cannot bear responsibility for it, though we always have to ask to what extent he is responsible for the very situation in which he could no longer take responsibility.

Leaving aside these *boundary cases*, in which emotivity in a sense destroys the efficacy of the person, we ought to accept *an entire series of cases in which only a certain limitation of this efficacy takes place*. The degree of this limitation can vary depending on the intensity of emotion. When we speak of the intensity of emotion, we make a certain simplification that does not grasp the entire complexity of the fact, although it seems very accurate in itself. By making the degree of the limitation of conscious efficacy—and of responsibility—dependent on the intensity of emotion, we seem to oppose emotivity and efficacy merely as two forces. Their opposition, however, is much richer, and the very concept of psychical force cannot be understood in the likeness of physical force. *The force of affection proceeds to a considerable extent from the lived-experience of value.* But it is precisely in this area that the particular possibility of creative integration emerges.

The vividness of human lived-experiences also has an emotional nature

When we say that the force of affection proceeds to a considerable extent from the lived-experience of value, we touch upon what seems most characteristic of human emotivity and what distinguishes it from purely somatic reactivity. Although, objectively speaking, the somatic ability to react to stimuli, especially on the basis of human drives, is marked by a relation to values, nonetheless there is no proper lived-experience of value on this layer. Perhaps also because somatic dynamisms by themselves are not connected with consciousness, this connection—and consequently the lived-experience of the body—is formed by means of sensations. The case is different when *emotions* are concerned, for *they in themselves are made conscious; indeed, they demonstrate a specific ability, in a sense, to draw consciousness in.* Thus, it is the case not only that we become conscious of our emotions but also that consciousness and especially lived-experience acquire from them a particular vividness. The vividness of human lived-experiences seems to stem not so much from consciousness but precisely from emotion. We can say that in the normal course of lived-experiences—that is, excluding the extreme or nearly extreme cases—man owes to emotion [35a] a particular value of his lived-experiences, even when these are cognitive lived-experiences.[35b]

By their content, emotional stirrings and affections always indicate the world of values

At this point, however, we wish to speak not about the value of lived-experience but about the lived-experience of value. Our previous analyses, especially the analysis of sensibility, have already prepared us for this. Human emotional stirrings and affections always remain in relation to a value; they are born out of this relation. That is the case when we get angry and when we love, when we regret, when we rejoice or hate. In each of these cases, a relation to value takes place; in a sense, the whole emotion is this relation. However, this relation is neither cognitive nor "appetitive." *Emotion*—emotional stirring or affection—*indicates a value*, though in itself it does not cognize or "desire" this value. We can also say that *emotions "demonstrate"—in a particular, experiential way at that—the existence of values beyond themselves, beyond the subject encompassed by emotional lived-experience*. If this indication or "demonstration" of values is accompanied by some cognition of them, this cognition occurs thanks to sensations and feelings that constitute, so to speak, an emotive reflex of affections. The more thoroughly this reflex permeates consciousness, the fuller the lived-experience of value. The emotionalization of consciousness hinders this lived-experience and at times even prevents it. However, by pointing beyond itself with its emotive content—and, in particular, by pointing to a value—emotion itself (namely, emotional stirring, excitement, affection, or passion) creates only an occasion for such a lived-experience of value, for an experiential cognition of value.[6]

The spontaneous lived-experience of value grows out of the emotive resources of the psyche

In any case, by arising, spreading, and becoming rooted in the subject, affection spontaneously evokes a certain relation to value. The very *spontaneity* of this relation seems valuable in its own way. This spontaneity is a specific psychical value, that is, a value "for the psyche," which, on the basis of its proper emotive dynamism, demonstrates a natural in-

---

6. The view expressed here differs from Scheler's position (see his *Formalismus*, especially "Formalismus und Apriorismus," 82–84), for it seems that we should distinguish even the maximal "proximity" of the subject to values—which is a function of emotions—from the proper "cognition" of values.

clination to spontaneity. *Spontaneity and the spontaneous lived-experience of value correspond to the human psyche*—perhaps not so much due to their easiness, that is, to the fact that the value is in a sense "given" and "ready" without effort, but *due to the specific emotional fulfillment contained in such a lived-experience*. This emotional fulfillment is at the same time a particular fulfillment of the very subjectivity of the human "I"; it creates a sense of completely being in oneself and of maximum closeness to the object—precisely, that is, to the value with which contact is spontaneously established.

The proper path toward resolving tensions between spontaneous lived-experience of value and personal self-determination

If the tension between emotivity and efficacy, a tension of which we have spoken several times, is a tension of two forces or two powers in man, it is such on the basis of a twofold relation to value. Efficacy together with personal self-determination is shaped in decision and choice, which in turn presuppose a [36a]subordination to truth, a dynamic relation of the will itself to truth[36b]. In this way, however, a new transcendent factor enters the spontaneous lived-experience of value and the striving, connected with this lived-experience, for the emotional fulfillment of one's own subjectivity. This factor *directs the person to fulfill himself in the act not by way of emotional spontaneity alone but by way of a transcendent relation to truth and to the duty and responsibility connected with it*. In the traditional understanding, this dynamic factor of personal life was called "reason." This word finds its expression in the frequent and common statements opposing affection to reason in particular, where "reason" denotes more than just the capacity for mental cognition.

It denotes man's power and ability to direct himself in decision and choice by the very truth about the good, an ability that is superior to affections, to man's emotive spontaneity. This ability determines the authentic power of the spirit, which in a sense designates the vertical, as it were, of human action. However, if the very property of this power demands a certain distance from values spontaneously experienced (it is, so to speak, the "distance of truth"), it is not in the least expressed by canceling [37a] values themselves, by rejecting them in the name of a "pure transcendence," which the Stoics and Kant both seem to demand. Authentic subordination to truth as the principle of the human will's decisions and choices *requires, rather, a particular binding of transcendence with integration in the sphere of emotions.* For we have already stated that these are two complementary aspects through which the complexity of human action is interpreted. It seems to be enormously important, particularly in the area of human emotivity, for this to be an interpretation of complexity and not an oversimplifying reduction.

9. Act and Emotion: The Integrative Function of Habit

The spontaneous relation to value is characterized by attraction or repulsion

Precisely here the integrative function of efficacy deserves to be noted. We owe the classical science of habit to the philosophers Aristotle and Thomas Aquinas. It presupposes their entire anthropology and psychology, the concept of the human soul and the soul's powers. In the previous chapter of this study, we appealed to the concept of habit while examining the integration of the person in the act on the basis of the somatic dynamism. We ascertained how much every synthesis of act and motion owes to skills acquired by man at the beginning of life, long before he reaches the age of reason. Our previous analyses of the human psyche and emotivity have adequately revealed the tension between the self-projected dynamism of emotions and the efficacy of the person. We also just explained the sense in which this tension occurs between affection and [38a]reason[38b] on the basis of the relation to value. Proper integration in this sphere thus presupposes some use of reason and a relation to the objects of action on the basis of the truth about the good that these objects are. It is from this perspective that we need to grasp the integrative function of efficacy, as understood by the aforementioned great masters of philosophy.

The tension between emotivity and the efficacy of the person originates from the fact that the dynamic of emotions entails *a self-projected orientation toward certain values. This orientation has the character of an attraction or a repulsion*—only in the former case can we speak of an orientation "toward," whereas in the latter it is quite the contrary. While the emotive orientation "toward" indicates a certain value, repulsion, the orientation "away from," indicates an anti-value, that is, some evil. Thus, the entire emotive dynamism bears a certain spontaneous orientation, introduces man into the clearly opposed configuration of good and evil, which Thomas Aquinas strongly emphasized in his classification of affections. The fact that man is dynamized emotively and is oriented toward good and away from evil does not constitute the function of emotional stirrings or affections so much as reach in man to the deeper roots of his nature. Emotions in this sphere follow the orientation of nature, which—as we have already stated—is expressed in drives. We are not concerned in this case with the drive for self-preservation or the sexual drive referred to in the previous chapter. Certainly, some division of affections into attraction and repulsion does occur in a given area on the basis of these drives. However, we are concerned above all with *the urge "toward" good and "away from" evil,* the urge *proper to human nature,* though the attraction and repulsion mentioned here in the most general way are not immediately determined with respect to an object. Their determination remains a task and function proper to the person; thus it belongs to [39a]reason[39b], which cognitively shapes the relation of man to truth[40a].

The moral decision between good and evil penetrates the sphere of spontaneous attractions and repulsions

Here, particular affections contribute their own spontaneous relation, one of an emotive and emotional character. A sense of value or anti-value goes hand in hand with affection. In this way, a more or less vivid psychical fact is shaped—a fact whose vividness we understand to indicate the strength of consciousness-related lived-experience. Accordingly, for instance, the affection of love, joy, or longing is oriented attractively, toward a good, whereas the affection of fear, reluctance, or—in another case—sorrow is oriented repulsively. St. Thomas rightly notes a different specificity of those emotional stirrings and affections that manifest the element of irascibility. The most typical among these affections is anger—an emotion that is fundamentally repulsive, though in a specific sense. This is even more manifested, for instance, in the affective lived-experience of courage. We have already mentioned this twofold specificity of human emotions dominated by either concupiscence or irascibility. Nonetheless, the division according to attraction or repulsion dominating in emotional lived-experience seems to be particularly essential when the spontaneous orientation of human psychical subjectivity "toward" good or "away from" evil is concerned. *On the basis of precisely this orientation,* at whose root inheres a deep urge of nature itself, *lies the main tension between the spontaneous emotivity* of nature *and personal efficacy,* that is, self-determination.

It is precisely here that the proper function of habit is manifested—the integrative function. The frequently mentioned great masters of philosophy, and in particular the masters of ethics, explained this function in their rich teaching on virtues, that is, on moral habits. We have held from the beginning of this study that morality most essentially determines both humanity and the person. Therefore, the experience of morality is an integral component of the experience of man. Without this experience, it is impossible to build an adequate theory of person and act. The integration of the person in the act on the basis of the emotivity (emotionality and emotivity) proper to the human psyche is accomplished though habits, which from the viewpoint of ethics warrant the term "virtues." Essential to the concept of virtue are both the element of moral value and, with it, a relation to the norm. If in the present analysis, however, we exclude this relation proper to morality insofar as we do not analyze it in detail and leave this task to ethics alone (at the beginning of this book we called this the "placing outside the parentheses"), then *in any case, what remains before us as most strictly personalistic is the problem of integration, that is, the problem of properly resolving the tensions between spontaneous emotivity and personal efficacy* (self-determination). We rightly refer to this resolving as the problem of integration because it concerns the realization of the personal structure of self-governance and self-possession [41a].

> In what does the function of moral habits, that is, virtues, consist?

This structure is realized thanks to various habits. For by their essence, habits aim to subordinate the self-projected emotivity of the subjective "I" to the self-determination of this "I." Thus they aim to subordinate subjectivity with respect to the [42a] efficacy of the person. They do this, however, in such a way as to take maximum advantage of emotive energy instead of merely suppressing it.[7] Thus the will to some extent "inhibits" the self-projected explosion of this energy while to some extent assimilating it. Properly assimilated emotive energy considerably fortifies the energy of the will itself. Precisely this is the task and work of habit. Something further is thus gradually achieved: *thanks to skills in various areas, the will can safely appropriate and make its own the spontaneity proper to affections and, in general, to all of emotivity.* To a certain extent, spontaneity is also a feature of habit—not original spontaneity, however, but one transformed by a steadfast process of so-called work on oneself. If, however, the relation to value is concerned, then the integrative process of improving one's own psyche gradually leads to the situation in which the will—guided by the light of intellectual cognition—knows how to appropriate, in the spontaneous relation of emotion, in spontaneous attraction or repulsion, what is truly good and to choose it. It also knows how to reject what is truly evil.

In this sphere, the integration of the person in acts is a task that extends throughout the entire life of man. This task in a sense begins in human life later than the somatic-reactive integration, which is, in a way, already complete when the psycho-emotive integration is just commencing. [43a] We identify the latter integration with the work of forming one's character or psycho-moral personhood. In this integrative task there inheres some moment of "unification," though—as we said at the beginning of our reflections on integration—the point here is not literal unification in the sense of joining parts into a whole but the realization and simultaneous revelation of unity on the basis of the specific complexity of the human person.

---

7. It seems that precisely this conviction is also expressed in Aristotle's view that the power of reason and will over affections has a "political" (or "diplomatic") and not an absolute character (see *Politics* 1.3; *Nicomachean Ethics* 4.3–5). It also belongs to the "political" character of this power to know when it ought to be exercised in an "absolute" way.

10. Conduct and "Behavior"

What do these expressions mean?

When we attentively observe ourselves and other people, we can draw a subtle line of demarcation between what we will call "conduct" and something else in the same man that we will define as "behavior." It is not without reason that we devote these final reflections to this distinction, for it concentrates many of the issues raised when analyzing the integration of the person in the act, on the basis of both somaticity and the human psyche.

The word "conduct" [*postępowanie*] seems to indicate the action of man as an outcome or resultant of his efficacy. This word, however, is figurative. Its original and proper meaning is associated with the path on which someone "steps" [*stąpa*], progressing in a certain direction. Conduct presupposes a multiplicity of "steps." In order to describe each of them separately, we use not the word "conduct" [*postępowanie*] but "deed" [*postąpienie* or *postępek*]. For "conduct" indicates a certain continuity of deeds or their resultant. Due to its fundamental association with the path on which man walks or steps—of course, in a figurative sense— we can ascribe to conduct a normative property: conduct always consists in "keeping to" a certain path. This keeping to a path and to the direction connected with it is not something passive, a resultant of what "happens" in or to man, but something active throughout. It has its basis in efficacy and self-determination. In this way, "*conduct*" *indicates above all the acts,* the proper and integral content of the statement "man acts."

After a closer insight into its content, we see that the word "behavior" indicates something different. It usually describes a certain "way of being" of a given person, easily perceptible from without. This way of being is linked to man's action but not identified with it. Man's behavior does not grasp the same reality or at least the same profile of reality that we indicate when speaking of man's conduct. What comprises behavior, this particular way of being that accompanies conduct, is a number of elements that are not determined or at least not completely determined by man himself, of which he is not or at least not completely an agent. These elements together shape the external expression or even simply the "appearance" of action. In this aspect of external expression or "appearance," they determine how a given man acts. However, this "how" ought not to be related to the very essence of the act or to the essential linking of the act with the person. *The point is not how a given man acts but precisely only how he behaves while acting.*

Aspects of the integration of the person in the act highlighted by these expressions

It is easy to observe that, while performing analogous acts, different people behave in different ways. We have in mind here the "phenomenal" quality, as it were, that is determined by somatic-constitutional and psycho-emotive factors. They cause an act performed by a man endowed with, for instance, a tall and slim body structure to "appear" different from an analogous act performed by a man endowed with a broad and stocky build. Also, for instance, a lecture and the gestures connected with it assume a different expression when given by a man endowed with a lively and passionate temperament than they do when given by a man who is slow and phlegmatic. Even if each of them does the same thing, each nonetheless "does" it slightly differently, that is, behaves differently while acting.

Additionally, the distinction between "conduct" and "behavior" can shed light on the problem of the integration of the person in the act, the problem we have dealt with throughout the last two chapters.

11. The Integration of the Person in the Act and the Discovery of the Relation of the Soul to the Body

We discover the complexity of man through the transcendence and integration of the person in the act

In both chapters devoted to analyzing the integration of the person in the act, we understood by "integration" the revelation and realization of unity on the substratum of the manifold complexity of man. In this sense, integration is an aspect of the dynamism of the person—an aspect complementary to transcendence, as was explained in the beginning of chapter 5. Having presupposed this, we considered above all in the last two chapters how the unity of various dynamisms is manifested in the acts of the person. Of course, multiplicity and diversity inhere in this unity, and this was also indirectly manifested by at least an attempt to characterize the dynamisms of human somaticity and the human psyche. However, neither in the last two chapters nor in the entire study have we dealt fundamentally with the problem of man's complexity. We can even say that *the dynamic revelation of the person in the act serves our cognition of man's unity rather than of his complexity.*[8]

Therefore, at the end of these reflections it is fitting to state that *man's complexity inheres in his unity and allows itself to be discovered—perhaps particularly through the reality of integration.* If the reality of transcendence was the only reality proper to the human person in his action, then nothing could be concluded about the complexity of man. Integration, how-

---

8. The relation of the soul to the body has been a frequent topic in the history of philosophy, providing various answers to a number of questions. [14a]Without for the time being seeking a metaphysical solution, Ingarden examines—within the framework of ontology—only pure *possibilities* in this area. "Warum *fragen* wir aber überhaupt nach der formalen bzw. existentialen Beziehung zwischen dem Leibe und der Seele des Menschen? Wir tun es, weil uns die ursprüngliche unmittelbare Erfahrung von uns selbst als dem konkreten Menschen mit den weitverbreiteten Auffassungen, sowohl naturwissenschaftlicher als philosophischer Art..., im Widerstreit zu stehen scheint.... In dieser Erfahrung stossen wir auf einen ausserordentlich engen Seinszusammenhang zwischen dem, was man üblicherweise die 'Seele,' andererseits den 'Leib' nennt.... Wir sind früher auch auf das merkwürdige Phänomen der ursprünglichen Solidarität oder auch Einheit zwischen 'mir' als dem Bewusstseins-Ich, insbesondere dem Ich des sinnlichen Wahrnehmens, und 'meinem' Leibe gestossen. In der Folge scheint es mir, dass ich so weit reiche, wie sich 'mein' Leib erstreckt. Es sind dabei *verschiedene Weisen und ... Grade dieser meiner Solidarität mit meinem Leibe möglich.*... Ich vermag mich aber mit meinem Leibe so weit zu identifizieren, dass ich mich einfach als Leib (sogar nicht mehr 'mein Leib,' denn da bleibt noch die prinzipielle Unterschiedlichkeit des Leibes von mir selbst bestehen) fühle und nicht zugleich als etwas anderes als der Leib und etwas, was irgendwie bedeutender, wichtiger als der Leib ist. Andererseits vermag ich auch nicht, mich meinem Leibe *radikal* gegenüberzustellen, so dass jegliche von mir empfundene Gemeinsamkeit mit meinem Leibe zerrissen würde." [Why do we *ask* at all about the formal or existential relation between the human body and soul? We do it because the primal, direct experience of ourselves as a concrete human being appears to be in conflict with widespread conceptions of both a scientific and philosophical bent.... In this experience we encounter an extraordinarily tight existential connection between what we customarily call the 'soul' and the 'body.' ... We also stumbled earlier onto the remarkable phenomenon of the solidarity, or even unity, between the consciousness-ego, in particular the ego of sensory perceiving, and 'my' body. Consequently, it appears to me that I reach as far as 'my' body extends. In this connection, various modes and ... degrees of this solidarity of mine with my body are possible.... However, I am incapable of identifying myself with my body to such an extent that I simply feel myself as body (no longer even 'my body,' since there the fundamental distinctiveness of the body from myself still obtains) and not at the same time as something other than the body and something that is somehow more significant, more important than the latter. On the other hand, I am also incapable of so *radically* opposing my body that every commonality I sense with it would be ruptured.] Ingarden, *Formalontologie*, pt. 2, 328–29; translated by Szylewicz as *Controversy over the Existence of the World*, 2:702–3.[14b]

ever, not only allows us to perceive the unity of different dynamisms in the act of the person but also opens before us the structures and layers of the complexity proper to man. We spoke several times in the analysis of integration about these layers and the psycho-somatic complexity. It is known, however, that the discovery of the psycho-somatic complexity in man is not yet the discovery of the proper relation of the soul to the body.

On the connection between the soul-body relation and the transcendence and integration of the person in the act

Nonetheless, *the discovery of the relation of the soul to the body is accomplished on the basis of the integral experience of man.* The concept of integration, just as that of the transcendence of the person in the act, serves to grasp—aspectually—the data of this experience. Speaking of the integration of the person in the act, we find ourselves on the terrain of the experience of man and achieve its fundamental [44a]description[44b] in the phenomenological sense, for the totality of the data of this experience, so to speak, "fits in" this concept of integration, just as in another aspect it "fits in" the concept of transcendence. This is what we attempted to demonstrate above all in the previous analyses. We ascertain all the richness of particular dynamisms on the level of somaticity and of the psyche—integration, however, is what "makes" these dynamisms personal and subordinates them to the transcendence of the person in the act. Thanks to this, they find their place in the integral structure of self-possession and self-governance that is proper to the person. In the beginning of chapter 5, we ascertained that this structure clearly indicates a certain complexity inherent in the personal unity of man, for he is both the one who possesses and governs himself and the one who is possessed by and subordinated to himself. The analysis of the integration of the person in the act on the basis of both the psyche and somaticity of man confirmed this complexity.

We cannot say that the ascertainment of this complexity is equivalent to the discovery of the relation of the soul to the body in man. This complexity is of a phenomenological and experiential type. We can accept that the lived-experience of transcendence and integration corresponds more or less to what was at times described as the "higher" and "lower" man, thereby manifesting the difference that originates from experience and human self-consciousness.[9]

At this point, however, we should recall the note on the "lived-experience of the soul" that was added to the end of the reflections devoted to the transcendence of the person in the act. We stated there that man does not directly experience his soul. Further, the lived-experience of the transcendence of the person in the act with all the elements and aspects of this lived-experience (see chapters 3 and 4) is not equivalent to a direct lived-experience of the soul. In the same way, we ought to state that the lived-experience of integration in connection with the transcendence of the person in the act is not equivalent to the lived-experience—that is, to the direct discovery and experience—of the relation of the soul to the body. Both the very reality of the soul and the reality of its relation to the body are in this sense trans-phenomenal and extra-experiential realities. *At the same time, however, the integral and comprehensive experience of man leads us to* these realities, both to *the reality of the soul and to its relation to the body*. It was exclusively by way of the experience of man—and by no other way—that the one and the other reality were discovered and are constantly being discovered by the method of philosophical reflection proper to the philosophy of being, that is, metaphysics.

We can say that although neither the soul in itself nor its relation to the body is directly given in the experience of man and his lived-experience, although they do not constitute the content of vision alone, it is nonetheless this visual content that indicates them, and thereby somehow contains *implicite* each of these realities: both the reality of the soul and its relation to the body. In this respect, the subordination of integration to the transcendence of the person in the act is very eloquent. [45a]It speaks of the fact that man must constantly complement his personal transcendence by integration; in addition, by integration the transcendence of the person in the act is constantly realized and in a sense confirmed.[45b]

---

9. This distinction, which we often encounter in the history of Christian ethics and ascetics, refers to the Epistles of St. Paul (see Romans 7:15–24 and additionally Romans 6:6 and 1 Corinthians 15:47–49).

In the context of the present book, the "higher man" denotes the subject that reveals himself in the experience of both transcendence and integration. Thus, the "lower man" must denote the same subject inasmuch as he reveals himself as one who needs this integration on account of the transcendence proper to the acts of the person.

The colloquial and hylomorphic understandings of the relation of the soul to the body

It seems that both these categories of phenomenological vision prepare a very proximate ground for grasping the relation of the soul to the body in man [46a]. This grasp is achieved through metaphysical categories, and such is the proper meaning of the concepts of "soul" and "body," though at the same time their colloquial meaning has also developed. In the metaphysical sense, *the soul is a "form," and its relation to the body, according to Aristotle or Thomas Aquinas, is the same as the relation of "form" to "matter"* (we must add that what is meant here is, properly speaking, so-called first matter, *materia prima*). [47a]We spoke of this at the end of chapter 4. Perhaps we should repeat once more what was stated there, namely, that the present inquiries lead indirectly to these classical understandings. At the same time, they attempt to show the entire richness of the experience of man that resides on the path to the metaphysical conception of the human soul and its relation to the body. They also attempt to grasp, in a sense, the boundary of this experience, the boundary of vision, and thus to better reveal the path of understanding along which the human mind progresses in grasping the realities that ultimately explain man and his entire dynamic. We must add that this method helps us to concretize what is contained in the colloquial understanding of the soul and its relation to the body in man. It seems that in this regard the concepts of the transcendence and integration of the person in the act are explained in a particular way.[47b] The *colloquial understanding of the soul and its relation to the body* [48a]*is certainly*[48b] *quite close to experience.* Precisely this closeness to experience, the grounding of the metaphysical content of the concepts of "soul" and "body" in experience, determines their meaning for people [49a]who know nothing of the relation of form to matter yet are convinced of the existence of the soul and its relation to the body[49b]. [50a]

The boundary of human dynamisms that is grasped in experience is not in itself the basis for the "demarcation" between soul and body in man (the human soul must be the principle of both the transcendence and the integration of the person in the act)

In order to grasp this relation, it is helpful to characterize the somatic and psycho-emotive dynamisms and to *bring to light a certain boundary* that they reach within the integral dynamism of the man-person. For at the same time, it is evident that this integral and adequate dynamism of the person—that is, the act—is transcendent in relation to those other dynamisms. Neither of them is identified with the act, even though they are contained in it in different ways. If the somatic dynamism and, indirectly, the psycho-emotive dynamism both have their source in the body-matter, then this source is neither sufficient nor adequate for the act in its essential transcendence. This was ascertained at the end of the analyses devoted to the transcendence of the person in the act [51a]. But we must now further that ascertainment at the end of the analyses devoted to the integration of the person in the act. For if the reactive dynamism proper to human somaticity [52a] and the emotive dynamism proper to the human psyche are integrated in the acts of the person, *then the ultimate source of these dynamisms should be sought in the same soul that is the principle of the transcendence of the person in the act.* After all, we stated that the integration of the person in the act is an aspect complementary to this transcendence.[52b]

On the one hand, our analyses indicate a certain boundary, as it were, in man, a boundary reached by the dynamism and thus also by the potentiality of the body-matter. On the other hand, they also indicate a potentiality of a spiritual nature, which is located at the root of both the transcendence and the integration of the person in the act. However, it would be a great oversimplification to consider the boundary of the body-matter potentiality as equivalent to the boundary "between" body and soul in man. For precisely the experience of integration intervenes in the simplified image of this division. Precisely as the aspect complementary to the transcendence of the person in the act, integration tells us that the relation of the soul to the body permeates all these boundaries that we find in experience, that it is deeper and more fundamental than they are. Perhaps this verifies, if only indirectly, the statement that both the very reality of the soul and the reality of its relation to the body can be correctly expressed only in metaphysical categories.

PART 4 ✻ PARTICIPATION

CHAPTER 7 ✣ (*Supplementum*): An Outline of the Theory of Participation

1. Introducing the Concept of "Participation"

Human acts are performed "together with others"

The starting point for the reflections conducted in previous chapters was the conviction that the act is a moment of the specific revelation of the person, a conviction expressed from the very beginning. In turn, later chapters served to develop particular aspects of the person's dynamism in the act. The path to knowing the person led through the act and was simultaneously the path to knowing the act. For the act not only constitutes the center or a particular basis of the vision of the person but also reveals itself proportionally to the person. The whole *path of cognition* we have followed thus far *was based on the close "co-relation" of the act with the person*—the correlation in which person and act constitute two components or, in a sense, two poles. These components correspond closely to each other; they mutually manifest and interpret each other. The fundamental line of the interpretation of person and act gradually emerges from their mutual correspondence and co-relation.

This final[1] chapter is meant *to add one more aspect to this totality*. We

---

1. The last chapter of the book *Person and Act* can and must be regarded only as a complement. It seems, however, that this complement is necessary and indispensable for the book. For proceeding in the beginning from the fact (of experience) "man acts," we must in the end at least mention that most often (if not always) in some way "man acts together with others." From the perspective of the person, this fact has manifold implications that we will not explicate here. We wish to focus on only one of them, namely, the one that seems to be particularly important from a historical point of view.

Above all, the cognitive dimension of intersubjectivity is emphasized in the sense that Husserl gave to the term "*Intersubjektivität*." In the fifth Cartesian meditation he successively analyzes—by way of "*Fremderfahrung*"—the problem of the constitution of the consciousness of the community understood as the *intermonadologische Gemeinschaft*, though it seems that the constitution of the

can say that this aspect was contained in all previous aspects, but that it has not yet been manifested. In the present chapter, we intend to manifest this aspect, namely, the aspect of the dynamic correlation of act and person, *an aspect proceeding from the fact that acts are performed by people "together with other"* people. The expression "together with others" is neither precise nor sufficient. However, it seems at this point to be most proper with respect to the various relations of a communal or social character in which human acts most often take place. This is a simple and natural consequence of the fact that man exists "together with others." The feature of community—the social feature—is impressed upon human existence itself.

Only a thorough understanding of human action can lead to a correct interpretation of co-operation[xlii]

Both this fundamental fact in the sphere of existence and the consequences of this fact in the field of action, the field of the act, bring us closer to the reality that we ordinarily define as "society." In this chapter, however, we do not intend to concern ourselves with society; we do not even want to begin with the statement that human acts have a social character, because this would bring us onto a new plane of reflection, creating a shift in both content and method *relative to the plane on which we have moved thus far*. We wish to remain on this plane. Person and act remain the object of our inquires through the end of this book. In this final chapter, we merely intend to emphasize the aspect of the dynamic correlation of act and person that results from the fact of existing "together with others" and acting "together with others." We could also describe this as a fact of co-operation, although a semantic difference can be seen between the two expressions: "to act together with others" means something dif-

---

intersubjective nature (*die intersubjektive Natur*) is the decisive step there. See Edmund Husserl, "Vergemeinschaftung der Monaden und die erste Form der Objektivität: Die intersubjektive Natur," in *Cartesianische Meditationen und Pariser Vorträge* (The Hague: Nijhoff, 1963), § 55, p. 149.

In this study, the fundamental source of knowing man as a person is the act. Because man *de facto* "acts together with others," there emerges a need to know man in his intersubjectivity on the same basis. In this way, "intersubjectivity" as a purely cognitive category is here, so to speak, exchanged for "participation." So, by *acting "together with others,"* that is, by *"participating,"* man reveals a new dimension of himself as a person. It is this dimension, which we call here "participation," that we wish to analyze at least in a cursory way. It seems that this approach affords us a fuller (or, in any case, a complementary) grasp of human intersubjectivity.

ferent from "to co-operate." At the beginning, however, it is better to keep using the expression "together with others," for this expression seems to be adequately open to further distinctions and clarifications, which this area needs.

We know that human acts are performed in various inter-personal and social relations. When we say that they are performed "together with others," we keep all these possible relations in mind without examining any of them in detail. All of them form the aspect—namely, that of the act and its dynamic "co-relation" with the person—that did not concern us in previous analyses. This is not a result of overlooking but simply of *the inner logic of the whole problem*. For it seems that *only an earnest understanding of human action can lead to a correct interpretation of co-operation*, and not vice versa. The dynamic co-relation of act and person is in itself a fundamental reality and remains such within any action performed "together with others." Only on the basis of this fundamental correlation does every fact of acting "together with others" acquire a proper, human meaning. This fundamental order can be neither reversed nor neglected. Thus we position our inquiries in this order.

The feature of participation marks the acts of the person when he acts "together with others"

It is obvious that the fact of acting "together with others" in all these various relations and systems of reference creates new problems. The extensivity and richness of sociology is well known, for this science concerns itself with society and social life and indirectly presents man as a member of various societies, social groups, or communities—a fact that in turn bears on his action. In this study, however, *we do not intend to undertake the problem of action* in all its social richness and breadth. *Above all*, we do not intend to undertake it *in its sociological specificity*. For this would be equivalent to shifting to a different plane. The plane of person and act will remain the proper plane for this study through the end. Here we follow the conviction that the dynamic co-relation of act and person also remains the principal and fundamental reality for the entire wealth of actions having a social, communal, or interpersonal character. For the acts that man performs as a member of various societies, social groups, or communities are simultaneously acts of the person. Their social or communal character is rooted in their personal character, not vice versa. However, it seems that in order to explain the personal character of human acts, it is indispensable to understand what results from the fact that they are performed *"together with others."* How is this performing manifested in the dynamic co-relation itself of the act with the person? The answer to this question seems all the more necessary because acting "together with others" is so common, so frequent, and so ordinary.

We want to answer this question within the reflections in this part of the study. We called this part "Participation" in order, first, to indicate the problem that we intend to undertake, and, second, to point out by the very title the solution to this problem. For it seems that precisely the feature of participation corresponds to the dynamic correlation of act and person, to the reality of acting "together with others." This feature, however, requires gradual explanation.

2. The "Personalistic" Value of the Act
The very fact of a person performing an act constitutes a value

By way of explanation, we must glance at the totality of the analyses conducted thus far, which show us the strictly personal content of the act. At the same time, these analyses show that *the very performance of the act by the person constitutes a fundamental value*. We can call this value the *"personalistic"* value of the act—personalistic *or personal*. This value differs from all moral values, which are always values of the act being performed and which result from a relation to the norm. The personalistic value inheres in the very performance of the act by the person, in the very fact that "man acts" in the way proper to him—that is, that this action is characterized by authentic self-determination, that the transcendence of the person is realized in it. This, as we ascertained in the last two chapters, entails integration in the fields of both human somaticity and the psyche. The personalistic value, which fundamentally inheres in the person's performance of the act, *contains a whole series of values* belonging to the profile of either transcendence or integration, for all such values in their own way determine the performance of the act, while each of them is simultaneously a value in itself. Thus, for example, every synthesis of act and motion (analyzed in chapter 5) brings a specific value that is different from that brought by, for example, the synthesis of act and emotion (chapter 6), though both inhere in the dynamic totality of the performance of the act. Each in its own way conditions and realizes self-determination.

The "personalistic" value of the human act—that is, the personal value—is a particular and, at the same time, perhaps the most fundamental expression of the value of the person himself. We do not intend here to enter principally into the axiology of the person, for ours is rather a study of his ontology. It seems, however—precisely through its specific character—that *this study can contribute to a fuller cognition of the axiology of the person*, both with respect to defining the value of the person in himself and with respect to defining various values in the person, to determining their proper hierarchy. For although *operari sequitur esse*—such that the person with his value is prior and fundamental to the value of the act—it is the person who simultaneously reveals himself through acts, as we have stated from the beginning. Accordingly, the "personalistic" value of the act, most closely connected with the very performance of the act by the person, constitutes a particular source and basis for knowing both the value of the person and the values that inhere in the person according to their proper hierarchy. The fundamental "co-relation" of act and person also operates in the sphere of axiology, as it does in that of the ontology of the person. However, we do not intend to study this axiology in detail.

The "personalistic" value of the act precedes and conditions the ethical value

The personalistic value of the act—that is, the one consisting in the very "performance" of the act according to the meaning conferred on this concept in chapter 4—*fundamentally differs from moral values* stricto sensu, *that is, the values of the performed act that result from relation to the norm*. The difference between the one and the other is evident. For the "personalistic" value of the act precedes and conditions all moral values. It is clear that this or that moral value, good or evil, presupposes the very performance of the act—one that is "fully-mature" at that.[xliii] If the act is not really performed, if it demonstrates deficiencies in the sphere of authentic self-determination concerning its various aspects, then its moral value also loses, so to speak, the ground under its feet, at least to a certain degree. Hence, any judgment about moral values, any ascription of merit or fault to man, must begin by ascertaining efficacy, self-determination, and responsibility. In other words, we must begin from ascertaining *whether a given man-person really performed the act*. All inquiries and distinctions concerning *voluntarium* refer to this, particularly in traditional studies of this problem. It is well-known that these inquiries and distinctions can be very penetrating.

We do not treat the performance of the act by the person as having merely an ontological sense. We also ascribe to it an axiological sense: *the performance of the act by the person in itself constitutes a value*. This is precisely a "personalistic value," for the person fulfills himself in the act when he performs it. We attempted to explain this in chapter 4 by analyzing the particular elements of this "self-fulfillment." We also ascertained there that fulfillment of oneself in the act is closely connected with ethical value—so closely that moral evil constitutes, in a sense, the opposite of fulfillment, that it is a particular "non-fulfillment" of oneself in action. However, this close connection between the ethical value and the personalistic value is not one of identity, as was also portrayed in chapter 4. *The personalistic value consists in the fact that the person actualizes himself in the act; his proper fundamental structure of self-possession and self-governance is expressed in this fact*. The ethical value is rooted on the basis of this actualization, which we call here "performance." The ethical value develops on the substratum of the personalistic value and permeates it, though without being identified with it.

What is the relation between the fact of acting "together with others" and the personalistic value of the act?

In this entire study, we remain in direct proximity to ethical values, also stepping indirectly onto their terrain. Our study's proper terrain, however, is the personalistic value itself. It is this value that—concerning human acts—allows us to speak of the fully-mature performance or of various deficiencies in this performance. What comes to mind is a comparison with the traditional approach, which in the teaching on human acts (*de actibus humanis*) distinguishes *voluntarium perfectum* from *voluntarium imperfectum*. The term *voluntarium* indicated the will as a power on which acts depend. This study ties the act and its performance to the person. This does not denote a rejection of the other approach but only an attempt to complement it or even to think through it fully. After all, the will as a power inheres in the person; it inheres in the self-determination by which the person reveals the structure proper to him. Therefore, reducing the meaning of *voluntarium* to the will as a power can entail a certain impoverishment of the reality that is the act.

Furthermore, it seems that *the revelation of the dynamic co-relation of act and person* and the attempt to interpret it *lead us immediately and directly to the personalistic value of the act*. The analysis of human action conducted on the level of [1a]powers seems in a sense to limit the meaning of the act to ontology, from which only an "ethical axiology" originates—that is, moral values as a result of relating the act to the norm[1b]. For at times it can almost seem that the act has a merely instrumental significance in relation to the entire ethical order. The personalistic conception of the act that we attempted to sketch in a number of aspects throughout this study convinces us of the [2a]authentic personalistic value, which itself is not yet an ethical value *stricto sensu* but *confers on the human act its proper fullness*. This fullness proceeds from the dynamic depth of the person, which in turn allows us to better understand ethical values in their close correspondence to the person, to the entire "world of persons."[2b]

All of this is extremely important with regard to the fact noted at the beginning of this chapter: man acts "together with others." What does this fact mean for the dynamic correlation of act and person? This is the question we previously asked ourselves. However, we now ask another question, which clarifies the first: what is the relation between acting "together with others" and the personalistic value of the act?

3. A More Precise Definition of the Concept of "Participation"
The transition "toward the position of the person" in the philosophy of man

By asking the question in this way, *we indirectly ask a whole series of questions* that are implicated in previous analyses. Thus we ask: In what way does man fulfill himself by acting together with others in various inter-personal and social relations? In what way does his act then preserve the proper coherence with the person that we called the transcendence of the person in the act and the coherence that we called the integration of the person in the act? In what way, within the fact of acting "together with others," will his acts preserve the hierarchy of values that results from both transcendence and integration?

We ask "in what way?"—and in this formulation our question does not seem to involve any doubt; we merely posit a problem that emerges along with the fact of acting "together with others." However, there is no need to conceal doubt, which, in any case, has *the character of methodical doubt*. This doubt clearly permeates modern thinking and the contemporary mentality. Perhaps *it is linked in the philosophy of man with a shift "toward the position of the person."* For the traditional philosophy of man—even in its conception of the person—clearly assumed "the position of nature": man is an individual of a rational nature, and as such he is a person. At the same time, his nature is "social." The reflection on man progressed and constantly progresses in relation to these approaches, not so much to fundamentally question them as to seek more proximate explanations, that is, a fuller picture. No one doubts that man is an individual of a rational nature and that at the same time he has a "social nature." However, we ask what this means. In this study, we ask concretely what this means in light of the dynamic correlation of act and person.

Such a question leads toward a certain unfolding or ex-plication of what is implied in affirming the social nature of man. In a sense, we are concerned with advancing our vision of the person. At the same time we move back, as it were, to the starting point. After all, *nothing could reside in the starting point of affirming man's social nature except precisely the experience that man exists and acts "together with others,"* the experience we also consult in this study. The "social nature" seems to denote above all the reality of existing and acting "together with others" that is ascribed to every man in a way that is, so to speak, incidental. Of course, the ascribing itself is an effect of this reality and not vice versa.

Participation as a property of acting "together with others"

In relation to this conception, the questions compiled in the beginning do not have a secondary character but precisely a fundamental one.

They do not question the social character of human nature but only aim to explain this character on the level of the person and to take into account his entire dynamic image that emerged from previous analyses. Now is the proper time to define more closely the concept of *"participation,"* which we introduced at the beginning in connection with the whole problem of cooperation (acting "together with others"). This concept *has a certain colloquial sense*, which is the most broadly known and used. It also has a philosophical sense. In the colloquial sense, "participation" is more or less the same as "taking part." Thus, we say, for instance, that somebody participated in a meeting, that is, that he took part in it. We state the fact in a most general and in a sense statistical way, without reaching the foundations of this partaking. *The philosophical sense of "participation," however, requires us to seek these foundations.* In this meaning, the term "participation," as corresponding to the Latin *participatio*, has a long and rich history in the language of both philosophy and theology. Of course, in the present study we follow the philosophical sense of the term and concept "participation," for we are concerned not only with externally stating the fact—the partaking of a concrete man in some action "together with others"—but also with reaching the foundations of this partaking.

Our point is *to reach the foundations that inhere in the person*. (Hence, the concept of "participation" used here will perhaps differ from the traditional philosophical sense that referred to nature itself.) By "participation" we understand that which corresponds to the transcendence of the person in the act when this act is performed "together with others," in various social or inter-human relations. Of course, if it corresponds to transcendence, it also corresponds to the integration of the person in the act, for, as we stated, integration constitutes an aspect complementary to transcendence. *Thus the feature of participation indicates that* by acting together with others man preserves in this acting the personalistic value of his own act, and at the same time he realizes what results from the community of action. Reversing this sequence, we can also say that thanks to participation, by acting together with others, *man preserves all that results from the community of action and at the same time—precisely by this means—realizes the personalistic value of his own act.*

Participation as a property of the person himself acting "together with others"

The expression "precisely by this means" is very important in the second, fuller formulation. For this expression indicates the proper character of participation. Thus, it is clear first of all that we use the concept of "participation" here in order to reach the very foundations of action "together with others"—the foundations that in fact inhere in the person and are proper to the person himself. In turn, we can see that everything that determines the personalistic value of the act—and thus the very performance of the act and the realization of the person's transcendence and integration contained in it—is not only preserved but also even realized precisely thanks to participation.

Thus, participation denotes a property of the person himself, an interior and homogeneous property that determines the fact that by existing and acting "together with others" the person exists and acts as a person.[2] Concerning action itself, participation as a property of the person determines the fact that by acting "together with others" the person performs the act and fulfills himself in it. Thus, participation determines the personalistic value of all cooperation. Cooperation—or, more specifically, action "together with others"—without participation deprives the acts of the person of their "personalistic" value. Experience convinces us that

---

2. We ought to underscore the semantic specificity of "participation" in this study. This is very important on account of the meaning or, rather, on account of various semantic variations that belong to this term in traditional and contemporary philosophy. In this study, "participation" emerges in a sense already at the starting point of the analysis of the fact "man acts together with others" as a fundamental experience through which we attempt to understand man as a person. The person as "man who acts together with others" is constituted in a certain way through participation in his very *esse*.* Thus participation is a specific property of the person. [*Editorial note: There are two ways of reading this sentence: (a) the person is constituted through participating in his own *esse*; and (b) the person is constituted in his own *esse* through participation.]

In the discussion published in *Analecta Cracoviensia* 5–6 (1973–74): 49–272, this semantic specificity of "participation" met with both understanding and polemics (see Leszek Kuc, "Uczestnictwo w człowieczeństwie 'innych?'" 183–90). These polemics offered both a substantive and a methodological counterproposal to *Person and Act*. According to this counterproposal, the fundamental cognition of man as a person is one that emerges in his relation to other persons. The author himself appreciates the significance of such cognition. However, after thinking over the counterarguments, he still maintains that a thorough knowledge of the subject in himself (of the person through the act) opens the way to a more thorough understanding of human intersubjectivity. Without such categories as "self-possession" or "self-governance" we will never be able to properly understand the person in relation to other persons.

action "together with others" also creates an occasion for various limitations of self-determination and, thus, limitations of the personal transcendence and integration of action. Indeed, the limitation of the personalistic value sometimes goes so far as to make it difficult to speak of action "together with others" in the sense of authentic acts of the person. Action—the synonym of the act—can in certain conditions turn into *passio*: the "happening" that occurs in some people under the influence of others. So-called crowd psychology provides us with extreme examples of this "happening" engulfing the human collective in a particularly [3a]thorough and[3b] uncontrolled way.

Participation as a manifold ability for the person to relate to "others"

We take all of this into consideration here as we develop the concept of "participation" in its proper sense. *Participation in diverse relationships of acting "together with others" appears as a form of the person's relation to "others," a form that is adapted to these relationships and is thus itself diverse.* In order to explain at least generally this form and this content of participation, we shall conduct an analysis of the community of action in the objective and subjective senses, along with some other analyses. In this, however, the meaning and content of participation are not fundamentally exhausted. Participation means not only the diverse forms of the relation of the person to "others," of the individual to society, but also, in this study, the very basis of such forms that inheres in the person and is proper to him. What corresponds to the transcendence and integration of the person in the act is participation as the property thanks to which man by acting "together with others" at the same time realizes the authentic personalistic value: he performs the act and fulfills himself in it. Action "together with others" therefore corresponds to the transcendence and integration of the person in the act when man *chooses what others choose* or even when he *chooses because others choose, seeing in this object of choice the value that is in some way homogeneous and his own*. Self-determination is linked to this—and in the case of acting "together with others," self-determination includes and expresses participation.

When we state that "participation" is a property of the person, we constantly keep in mind, of course, not the person as an abstraction, but the person in his dynamic co-relation with the act. It is in this co-relation that participation means, *first, the capacity* for acting "together with others" in which everything that results from the community of action is realized, while at the same time—precisely by that means—the agent realizes the personalistic value of his act. *What follows the capacity is its actualization. We apply the concept of "participation" to the one and the other.*

4. [4a]The Systems Limiting Participation[4b]
The concept of participation has a theoretical and normative sense

The concept of participation developed in this study has a theoretical sense. As we have already stated, it is an attempt to explain—on the basis of the dynamic correlation of act and person—what the social nature of man is in reality. *The concept is theoretical* and at the same time empirical in the sense that the theory of participation explains the experiential fact of acting and existing together with others. At the same time, however, we must perceive that this theory *indirectly possesses a normative sense.* It not only indicates how the person realizes himself by acting together with others, that is, realizes the personalistic value of the act, but also indirectly shows a certain duty resulting from the principle of participation. Because man by acting together with others can realize himself on the basis of this principle, *on the one hand, everyone* should strive for the participation that in action "together with others" will allow him to realize the personalistic value of his own act, and, *on the other hand, every community of action* or every human co-operation should be shaped so that the person who remains in its orbit can realize himself by participation.

This is the normative content that has emerged from the analysis thus far. It is this content that seems to determine the normative—and not merely the theoretical—sense of participation. Together with the personalistic value, to which it closely corresponds and on which it is based, this sense penetrates various systems of acting "together with others." If the personalistic value of the act is a fundamental value that conditions, as we said, the ethical value and the ethical order, then this norm of action that directly results from it also has a fundamental sense. This norm is not ethical in the strict sense of the word, according to which it would be the norm of the performed act on account of the act's objective content; rather, it is the norm of the very performance of the act, that is, *the norm of its personal subjectivity*, the "interior" norm *whose purpose is to safeguard the person's self-determination* and thus his efficacy, as well as his transcendence and integration in the act. We spoke quite extensively on this topic earlier, so the boundary between the strictly ethical and personalistic orders seems to be established and perhaps made sufficiently distinct.

Individualism and totalism as two forms of limiting participation

At the same time, however, the personalistic value not only conditions but also determines the entire ethical order in action and co-operation. The act should be performed not only so that it can have an ethical value—and so that this value can be ascribed to it—but also because the person possesses the fundamental and "natural" (i.e., resulting from the fact that he is a person) right to perform acts and to fulfill himself in these acts. This right acquires the proper sense of a right on the basis of acting "together with others." Here the normative sense of participation is confirmed. For precisely on the basis of acting together with others, the performance of acts in the sense previously defined—*the performance of acts that is simultaneously the fulfillment of the person in the act*, as its personalistic value consists in this—*can be limited or even annihilated in a twofold way*. This can happen, first, through a lack of participation originating in the person as the subject and agent of action, and, second, through a prevention of participation originating outside the person and resulting from an erroneous organization of the very community of action.

At this point in our analysis we touch upon the implications of the two systems, one of which is called individualism, and the other of which has borne different names in the past and in modern times is called "objective totalism." We could instead call this system anti-individualism. We concern ourselves not with these entire systems but with their implications, for we do not intend to present the entire systems here, as doing so would mean abandoning the plane of reflections that we have chosen. Besides, these systems have both an axiological and an indirectly ethical sense: *individualism* advances the good of the individual as the principal and fundamental good to which every community and society must be subordinated, whereas *objective totalism* proposes a quite contrary principle—it fully subordinates the individual and his good to the community and society. As is evident, each of these systems sees the principal good and the basis for norming in something different.[xliv] Additionally, each of them exists in a number of varieties and variations, a fact that also calls for the knowledge of the sociologist and the historian. Thus, in bypassing all of this wealth and in a sense simplifying the problem to the fundamental frameworks of the two orientations in accord with the names by which we call them here, *we wish to touch upon their implications from the perspective of the analyzed problem.* The point is the person and act in all possible variations of action "together with others."

In action "together with others" we discover the principle of participation as the essential feature of and, at the same time, as a particular source of the right and duty to perform acts. It is on account of the personalistic value contained in this performance that both this right—one to which the person is entitled—and this duty exist. Both of the aforementioned orientations limit participation in different ways—directly, by limiting participation as the possibility or ability that is actualized in acting "together with others," and indirectly, by limiting participation as the property of the person that corresponds to existing "together with others," to existing in the community.

The denial of participation as an essential implication of individualism

Individualism limits participation by isolating the person understood merely as an individual concentrated on himself and his own good, which is also understood in isolation from the goods of others and from the common good. In this approach, the good of the individual is opposed to every other individual and his good or, in any case, has a "self-preserving" and defensive character. According to individualism, acting together with others as well as existing with them is a necessity to which the individual must submit, a necessity to which no positive property of the individual corresponds; likewise, the acting and existing together with others serve and develop no such property. "Others" are for the individual only a source of limitations and even a pole of manifold oppositions. If a community comes into existence, this happens for the purpose of protecting the good of the individual among these "others." This is a terse outline of the individualistic position, the particular varieties and variations of which we shall not develop here. *This position implicates the denial of participation* in the sense previously imparted to this concept: no property exists that would enable the person to fulfill himself in action "together with others."

Totalism, that is, "individualism *à rebours*"

The denial of participation is also implicated in the opposite position. *Totalism or anti-individualism is, so to speak, "individualism à rebours."* What dominates in it is the need for protection against the individual, who is basically considered an enemy of the community and of the common good. Because it is presupposed that in the individual there is only the striving for his own good and no disposition to fulfill himself in acting and existing "together with others"—no property of participation—the common good can be achieved only by limiting the individual. Only this sense of the common good is presumed in advance. This good cannot be one that corresponds to the individual, one that he is capable of choosing on the basis of participation, but can only be one that must hinder and limit the individual. Accordingly, the realization of the common good must consist in coercion. This is again a very cursory presentation of the thought and conduct in accord with the anti-individualistic orientation, in which we can easily perceive the presuppositions of individualism, which proceed in a sense from the opposite side and aim at opposite ends. The point in individualism is the protection of the good of the individual against the community, whereas in totalism—as various experiences in history confirm—it is the protection of oneself against the individual in the name of [5a]some common good[5b]. However, *at the root of both orientations, of both systems of thought and conduct, we find an identical way of thinking about man.*

What way of thinking about man do we find
at the root of these systems?

This way can be called a-personalistic or anti-personalistic. For what is characteristic of the personalistic way of thinking is the conviction of the capacity for participation, which is proper to the person. Of course, this capacity needs to be actualized, needs to be shaped and cultivated so that it matures. For not only does man exist "by nature" together with others and must act together with them, but also in acting and existing "together with others" he can achieve his proper maturity, which is at the same time the essential maturity of the person. Therefore, every man must be granted *the fundamental right to act, that is, the freedom of the act*, through whose performance the person also fulfills himself. The sense of this right and this freedom inheres in the conviction of the personalistic value of the human act. On the basis of and because of this value, man is entitled to complete freedom of action. Individualism, anti-individualism, and their erroneous implications must be excluded here. Because of the personalistic value of the act, this complete freedom of act conditions the ethical order and at the same time fundamentally determines it. The ethical order in turn brings into human acts—especially in the orbit of action "together with others"—the determinations, and thus also the limitations, that result from strictly ethical values and norms. *These determinations and limitations, however, are not opposed to the personalistic value*: the person fulfills himself only in moral good, whereas evil is always some non-fulfillment. It is clear, of course, that man has freedom of action, the right to act, but has no right to do evil. The determination that both results from this right and corresponds to the personalistic order points in this direction.

5. [6a]Participation and the Community[6b]
Participation is also a specific *constitutivum*
of the community

Thus, as we stated, individualism and totalism (anti-individualism) proceed from the same substratum. Their common root is the conception of man as an individual more or less deprived of the property of participation. This thinking is also reflected in the conception of social life, in the axiology of community, and in the social ethics—or rather in different axiologies of community and in different social ethics—that proceed from the same substratum. In this study, we are not set to investigate the varieties of individualism and anti-individualism, for these have already been studied. We should only state that on the basis of this thinking about man, which is proper to both of these orientations, perhaps we do not find foundations for authentic human community. The concept of "community" expresses the reality to which we have attended from the beginning of this chapter, in which we have spoken many times of acting and existing "together with others." *However, the community remains closely connected with the experience of the person that we have attempted to follow from the beginning, and especially in this chapter.* We discover in it the reality of participation as the property of the person thanks to which he can exist and act "together with others," thereby fulfilling himself.[xlv] Participation as a property of the person is at the same time a specific *constitutivum* of the community. Thanks to this property, the person and the community in a sense adhere to each other and are not foreign or opposed to each other, which is the case on the basis of the individualistic or anti-individualistic way of thinking about man.

The community is not the proper (substantial) subject of action

Thus, in order to define more fully the meaning of participation—which is our main task in this chapter—*we shall attempt to consider it under the aspect of community.* In fact, we have done this from the very beginning, for from the beginning the phrase "together with others," which is linked with the analysis of the person's act and being, speaks about the community. As was said, the concept of community corresponds to this phrase while at the same time introducing a new attitude or, in a sense, a new "subjectivity." For as long as we speak about existing or acting "together with others," the man-person is clearly seen to be the subject of this existing and acting. Once we start to speak about "community," we can indicate in a nounal and abstract way what we previously designated by an adverbial phrase. However, we can also indicate a new quasi-subjectivity, which is determined by all existing and acting together. A certain community, society, or—speaking most generally—group shares in this new subjectivity. It is a "quasi-subjectivity" because *the proper (substantial) subject of existing and acting, even when existing and acting are realized together with others, is always the man-person.* The expression "community," just like "social group" or "society," indicates *an accidental order*. Existing and acting "together with others" does not constitute a new subject of action but only introduces new relations between people, who are the real subjects of action. This qualification must be made concerning all reflections on community. It seems that the concept of community [*wspólnota*], including its nounal and abstract sense, stands in particularly close relation to the dynamic reality of person and participation—perhaps even closer than the concept of the "social group" [*społeczność*] or "society" [*społeczeństwo*], although the semantic stem of both expressions is almost the same (*wspólnie* means *społem*).[xlvi]

Social belonging and community membership

Just as the analysis of person and act was based on numerous or even countless facts, so the analysis of community can and ought to be, as we indicated in the introductory chapter. In relation to the latter analysis, we should adopt methodological directives analogous to those used in relation to the former. This remark confirms that we remain located on the same plane of inquiry as that chosen from the beginning of this study. Thus, it is on this plane that we shall *analyze the relation between participation and community membership*.

For man with his proper dynamism appears to us within the community as its member. Different expressions speak about this membership in relation to different communities. For example, the expressions "kin" and "in-law" speak of man as a member of a familial community. The expression "compatriot" speaks of him as a member of a national community. The expression "citizen" indicates his membership in the community of his country, whereas the expression "believer" indicates membership in a religious community, etc. At the same time, each of these expressions designates man's social belonging. Sociologists rightly point out the semantic difference that divides society from community. Society or even a social group (the latter expression seems to indicate a less established social bond) is an objectivization of the community or of a number of mutually complementary communities. Because in the present study we look rather for the foundations themselves, we focus our attention *not so much on social belonging as on community membership*. For example, the aforementioned expressions (and there are many more such expressions) speak about this membership. They designate not only community membership *but also the diverse bonds that occur between people on account of diverse communities*. Thus, for example, the expressions "brother" and "sister" indicate the familial bond much more deeply than membership in the familial community, which is emphasized by the expression "kin."

Additionally, in the riches of language we find expressions that focus on the very community of being and the bond formed between people through this community. Such are all the expressions cited above. But there are also expressions that emphasize above all the very community of acting while, in a sense, setting aside the community of being. Thus, for example, when we say "assistant," "apprentice," or "foreman," each of these expressions emphasizes above all the community of acting and the bond resulting from it—the community of being can be inferred only indirectly.

Community membership is not the same as participation

All of the expressions cited here tell us that man is a member of different communities, which consist in the fact that man exists or acts together with others. In the present study, we are even more interested in the community of acting, for we are concerned with the dynamic co-relation of act and person as the foundation and source of knowledge. However, a community of being always conditions a community of acting, and therefore we cannot consider the latter in separation from the former. For a serious problem resides in the fact that *membership in these communities is still not the same as participation*. At this point, we shall use an example. In a group of laborers working at the same excavation or in a group of students listening to the same lecture, there certainly occurs the fact of acting together with others. Each of these laborers or students is a member of a certain community of acting. We can look at the community itself under the aspect of the end for which they strive together. In the first case, the end will be the completion of an excavation, which in turn can serve a further end such as construction. In the second case, the end will be familiarity with the problem that constitutes the topic of the lecture, which in turn belongs to a certain subject matter and the totality of studies in a certain field. We can also state that in the first case each of the laborers and in the second case each of the students strives for the same end. This objective oneness of the end helps to objectivize the very community of acting. *In the objective sense, the community of acting can be defined according to the end* for which people act together with one another. Each of them is a member of this objective community.

From the viewpoint of person and act, however, what is important is not only this objective community of acting *but also its subjective moment, which here we call participation.* The question is whether man, who is a member of a community of acting—such as those just used as examples—through action performs true acts and fulfills himself in these acts. For this is what is determined by participation. In acting "together with others," however, man can remain outside the community determined by participation. Here we face a problem that cannot be solved without glancing at the issue of the so-called common good. For it is known that the moment of participation resides, though not exclusively, in choice: man chooses what others choose—sometimes even choosing because others choose—while at the same time choosing it as his own good and the end of his own striving. What he then chooses is his own good in the sense that he as a person fulfills himself in it. Participation renders man capable of such choices and such action together with others. *Perhaps only then does this action deserve to be called "cooperation,"* for action together with others does not have to be cooperation, just as it does not have to evoke the moment of participation. The objective community can occur without the subjective on the basis of both acting and being.

6. Participation and the Common Good
The resolution of the problem of participation and community vis-à-vis the meaning of the common good

As we see, *solving the problem of the community and participation depends not on the very reality of acting or existing "together with others," but*—as was stated—on the common good. Speaking more precisely, it *depends on the meaning that we confer on the concept of the common good.*

When by "common good" we understand the "good of the community," then this meaning is proper, though it can contain a serious unilaterality. This unilaterality is in the field of axiology similar to that suggested in anthropology by the conceptions of individualism and anti-individualism. The common good is certainly the good of the community (or, to go further toward objectivization, the good of a social group, of society). However, this good must be more closely characterized on the basis of previous reflections.[3]

The objective community of acting can be ascertained on the basis of the fact that people act together—as, for instance, the laborers working at the same excavation or the students listening to the same lecture. In this context, the common good as the good of a given community of acting—and this is always linked to some community of being—*can very easily be identified with the end for which this community strives.* Thus, for example, what might seem to be the common good is in the first case the completion of the excavation and in the second case the familiarity with the subject matter that is the content of the lecture. In turn, we can look at each of the common goods thus understood through the teleological chain. So, for example, the excavation completed by the laborers will be used for laying the foundation for a building, and the lecture heard by the students will become a link in the long and complex process of acquiring knowledge, which will be formally verified by an examination on the lecture's subject matter.

Teleological and personalistic conceptions of the common good

However, the identification of the common good with the end of actions performed together is evidently too provisional and too superficial. In reference to the examples presented above, we can state that *the end of acting together understood in a purely objective and "material" way contains something of the common good but does not fully constitute this good.* Such a diagnosis clearly emerges in light of the analyses conducted thus far. The common good can in no way be defined without also taking into

---

3. The present reflections, preserving exclusively the character of an outline or sketch, attempt a certain reinterpretation of the concept of the common good. The analysis of authentic and non-authentic attitudes, which is subsequently sketched, carries in a given historical context a specific significance for the critical character of this interpretation.

consideration the subjective moment, that is, the moment of action in relation to the acting persons. Considering this moment, we ought to state that the common good is not only the end of action performed in a community and understood purely objectively; at the same time, and even *above all, the common good is also what conditions participation and, in a sense, evokes it in the persons acting together*, thereby shaping in them the subjective community of acting. If we can understand the common good as an end, it is only in this twofold meaning: objective as well as subjective. The subjective meaning of the common good is closely linked with participation as a property of person and act. This understanding enables us to maintain that the common good corresponds to the social nature of man.

In the present study, we tend to pass over the rich axiological and ethical issues that concern the concept of the common good and determine its full meaning. We are investigating the common good above all as the principle of correct participation, thanks to which the person by acting together with others can perform authentic acts and can fulfill himself through these acts. Thus our point concerns the truly personalistic structure of human existence in community—in every community to which man belongs. The common good is the good of the community precisely because it creates in an axiological sense the conditions of existing together, and action follows this. We can say that *in the axiological order, the common good determines the community*, the society, or the social group. Each of them is defined on the basis of the common good proper to it. We then take action (*operari*) together with existence (*esse*).[xlvii] However, the common good extends above all to the sphere of existing "together with others." Action "together with others" does not manifest to such a full extent the reality of the common good, though this good must also occur there. Even groups connected by some common action much more than by social community—such as the group of laborers working at an excavation or the group of students attending the same lecture—not only strive together for an end in their common action but also, in different ways, manifest the participation proper to particular members of the community of acting.

To what extent is the common good the foundation of authentic human community?

However, in groups connected by a provisional community of acting, this participation is not manifested and realized in the same measure as in communities enjoying stability on the basis of existence itself, as, for instance, the family, nation, religious group, or state. The axiology of such communities, which is expressed in the common good, is much deeper. Consequently, *the basis of participation is much stronger, and the need for participation is greater*. Every man expects from these communities of being (which earned the name "natural societies" on account of the fact that they thoroughly correspond to man's social nature) that in them he will be able to choose what others choose and because they choose—that he will be able to choose that as his own good serving the fulfillment of his person. At the same time, however, on the basis of the same capacity for participation, which is the basis for existing and acting together with others, man expects that in communities grounded on the common good his own acts will serve, sustain, and enrich the community. In this axiological system, man is even ready to relinquish various individual goods, sacrificing them for the community. This sacrifice is not "against nature," for it corresponds in every man to the property of participation and, on the basis of this property, opens to him the path toward fulfillment.

Therefore, the primacy of the common good, its superiority in relation to partial and particular goods, does not result merely from the quantitative aspect of society—according to which the common good would be that of many or of a greater number, whereas the partial or particular good would be that of an individual or of a smaller number. *It is not number or even quantitative totality but thoroughness* [gruntowność] *that determines the proper character of the common good*.[xlviii] This understanding is a continuation of the critique of individualism and anti-individualism. It proceeds from previous reflections on participation and also serves to confirm it. In the depth of the reality that is "acting together" and "existing together," participation as at once both a property of person and act and a basis for authentic human community is more and more clearly manifested.

7. The Analysis of Attitudes: Authentic Attitudes
The present analysis has a largely pre-ethical sense

On the basis of our reflections on the proper meaning of the common good, that is, on the relation that should occur between participation as a property of persons and the good of communities, we need to analyze certain attitudes characteristic of acting and existing "together with others." First, we shall look at *the attitudes of solidarity and opposition*. Both of these words, namely, "solidarity" and "opposition," acquire their proper sense on the basis of a community of acting or of being and through their relation to the common good, a relation specific to each of them, as we shall attempt to demonstrate below. A certain *qualification* is connected with this sense, one that is ultimately ethical. In the present analysis, however, we shall attempt rather to explicate the personalistic meaning of each of these attitudes, such that their qualification will have not so much an ethical *as a pre-ethical meaning*. For our point is to sketch the very structures of human action and, consequently, to emphasize the value of the very performance of the act and not the value of the performed act, which results from its relation to an ethical norm. Clearly, this entire reflection can easily be changed into an ethical analysis by assuming that the very performance of the act, in light of its immanent value, is a good that obligates. This, in fact, is beyond doubt. The very performance of the act is a good that obligates both the one who performs this act as well as others. The latter obligation constitutes a fundamental component of social ethics.

Thus, were we to pass into the field of ethics, we would have to treat the value of performing the act as an object of performed acts and also as the basis for norming them. This, however, we will not do here. *We still wish to concern ourselves with the subjective performance of acts and its immanent value as a "personalistic" value.* For in this approach we find the key to explaining the dynamism proper to the person, even when this dynamism is realized within various communities of acting and being. Hence, the qualification of the attitudes that we intend to analyze now will be above all "personalistic" and somehow in this sense "pre-ethical." At the same time, however, in the entire study and especially in this part, we are aware of the fact that we are constantly moving on the boundary of ontology and ethics on account of the axiological aspect, that is, the richness of values that cannot be excluded from the ontology of person and act.

The attitude of solidarity

We shall analyze the attitudes of solidarity and opposition together, for each is strictly necessary in understanding the other. The attitude of solidarity is a "natural" consequence of the fact that man exists and acts together with others. It is also the basis of the community in which the common good correctly conditions and evokes participation, and in which participation correctly serves the common good, supporting and realizing it. Solidarity denotes a constant readiness to accept and realize the share that falls to each due to the fact that he is a member of a given community. A man who lives in solidarity performs what belongs to him not only on account of his membership in a community but also "for the good of the whole," that is, for the common good. Consciousness of the common good commands him to surpass the part that falls to him as a share, though in this intentional relation he fundamentally realizes his part. In a sense, solidarity even prevents him from trespassing on someone else's obligation and appropriating as his own a part that belongs to another. Such an attitude is in conformity with the principle of participation, for participation *taken objectively and "materially" indicates certain parts in the communal structure of human action and existence.* The attitude of solidarity takes into consideration the parts that fall to every member of the community. Appropriating the part of the obligation that does not belong to oneself is fundamentally contradictory to community and participation.

However, in certain cases, solidarity also requires this. In such cases, keeping only to one's part would be proof of a lack of solidarity. This indirectly demonstrates that in the attitude of solidarity the relation to the common good must be constantly kept alive, that it must be dominant enough for man to know when he should assume more than his ordinary part in action and responsibility. A particular intuition concerning the needs of the community, one that is proper to the attitude of solidarity, elicits a certain complementarity in this attitude above every partialness or particularism: *a readiness to "complement" by the act that I perform* what others perform in the community. This complementarity belongs, in a sense, to the very nature of participation—participation that here we understand subjectively, as a property of the person, and not only objectively, as a division into parts that fall to everyone in the communal structure of action and existence. Therefore, we can say that the fundamental expression of participation as a property of the person is the attitude of solidarity. In virtue of this attitude, man finds his own fulfillment in complementing others.

The attitude of opposition

The attitude of solidarity, however, does not exclude the attitude of opposition. *Fundamentally, opposition does not clash with solidarity.* He who expresses opposition does not cease to contribute to the community; he does not withdraw his readiness to act for the common good. Of course, a different understanding of opposition can be presumed. Here, however, we understand opposition as an attitude that is fundamentally in accord with solidarity—and thus not as a negation of the common good and of the need for participation, but precisely as a confirmation of both. The content of opposition is only a way of understanding and, above all, of realizing the common good, especially regarding the possibility of participation. The experience of various instances of opposition, which had and have their place on the basis of human existence and action "together with others," teaches us that people who oppose do not want to withdraw from the community. Quite the contrary: they seek their own place in this community—*thus, they seek participation and an understanding of the common good by which they can better, more fully, and more effectively participate in the community.* There are numerous examples of people who contend with one another—that is, they assume the attitude of opposition—precisely because they are concerned about the common good. For example, parents contend with each other because they are concerned about how best to educate their children, and statesmen remain in opposition to one another because they intend the good of their nation and state.

Even if these examples do not comprehensively illustrate the essence of opposition, they in any case direct us to it. The attitude of opposition is a function of one's vision of the community, of its good, and of the living need to participate in existing together and especially in acting together. We must deem such opposition constructive. This is a condition of the correct structuring of communities, a condition of their correct constitution. We should define this condition more accurately. The point is such a structuring or constitution of communities *that the opposition that grows within them on the basis of fundamental solidarity can not only be expressed but also fulfill its function for the good of the community*—that it can become constructive. The human community possesses its correct structure when rightful opposition has not only the right of citizenship in it, but also the effectiveness demanded by the common good together with the right to participation.

The sense of dialogue

Hence, we can see, somewhat in accord with what we said previously, that the common good can be understood not statically but dynamically. It must fundamentally evoke the attitude of solidarity without closing itself to and severing itself from opposition. *The principle of dialogue seems, therefore, very fitting for this structure of human community and of participation.* The concept of "dialogue" has different meanings. At this point we mean to emphasize one of them, namely, the one that can be applied to the shaping and deepening of human solidarity even through opposition. For opposition can make the interaction and cooperation of people more difficult, although it should neither damage nor prevent them. Dialogue seems to help us bring out from the situation of opposition that which is true and right while leaving aside purely subjective attitudes or dispositions. These attitudes and dispositions are at times a hotbed of tensions, conflicts, and struggles between people. However, that which is true and right always deepens the person and enriches the community. The principle of dialogue is fitting because *it does not avoid tensions, conflicts, and struggles*, which are present in the lives of different human communities, *and because it addresses precisely that which is true and right in them, that which can be a source of good for the people*. We ought to accept the principle of dialogue regardless of the difficulties that emerge in the course of its realization.

8. The Analysis of Attitudes: Non-Authentic Attitudes
In what sense are we speaking of authentic and non-authentic attitudes?

All that we have said so far about solidarity and opposition and in general approval of the principle of dialogue (a detailed approval would require a separate discourse) is constantly subject to verification on the basis of the truth about person and act, the truth that we have so laboriously pursued throughout this entire study. *The attitudes of solidarity and opposition seem to be fundamentally authentic.* For not only participation but also the transcendence of the person in the act can be realized in each of them. We have conducted a multilateral analysis of this transcendence, an analysis of self-determination, and an analysis of fulfillment. It seems that these functions of transcendence can be correctly manifested in both aforementioned attitudes. In this sense, then, they are authentic attitudes, as each of them respects the "personalistic" value of the act.

Of course, presupposing a general and fundamental approval, each of them must be constantly tested in its particular elements and concrete manifestations. *For in this respect it is easy to distort both the attitude of solidarity and the attitude of opposition* by making them *in concreto* non-authentic attitudes, devoid of true "personalistic" value. What is decisive here is the dynamic subordination to truth (see chapter 3), so essential for the transcendence of the person in the act. This subordination is reflected in a right conscience. It is the definitive measure of the authenticity of human attitudes with regard to existing and acting "together with others." Also, the common good must seek its expression in this conscience, which ensures for it the dynamic and vitality of participation.

Speaking of a possible loss of authenticity, which threatens the attitudes of solidarity and opposition—each in a different way and for a different reason—*we should present here certain non-authentic attitudes.* We shall define these attitudes by terms used frequently today, ones that are perhaps popular rather than academic. One is the attitude of "conformism," and the other is "avoidance." We can arrive at each of them by taking the authentic attitudes of solidarity and opposition as starting points and then depriving them of the essential elements that determine both their personalistic value and the participation associated with them.

Gradually, through the loss of these elements, we can change solidarity into conformism and opposition into avoidance. This, then, would be an accidental distortion. It seems, however, that conformism and avoidance are non-authentic due to fundamental reasons and not merely because they are a distortion of the attitudes of solidarity and opposition. It is in this aspect that we will attempt to briefly analyze or at least characterize them here.

Why do we describe conformism as a non-authentic attitude?

The name "*conformism*" speaks of likeness and of becoming like others, which in itself is a natural process and, under certain conditions, is positive as well as creative and constructive. This creative and constructive becoming like others in the community is both a confirmation of solidarity and its efflorescence. Despite these positive connotations, however, the term "conformism" indicates something negative. *For it indicates a lack of fundamental solidarity and at the same an avoidance of opposition.* If it speaks of becoming like others in the community, it does so only in an external and superficial sense, devoid of the personal basis of conviction and choice. The attitude of conformism contains above all a certain submission, a specific variation of the *pati* in which the man-person is only a subject of "happening" and not an agent of his own attitude and his own commitment in the community. Man in this case does not form the community but in a sense "allows himself to be carried" by the collective. The attitude of conformism conceals if not a denial or limitation then at least some weakness of personal transcendence—of self-determination and choice. In this consists the personalistic deficiency of this attitude. Of course, the point here is not one's submission to others in the community. In many cases this can have a positive meaning. The point is something else, namely, the fundamental *relinquishing of one's fulfillment in and through action "together with others."* The man-person in a sense agrees to the fact that the community deprives him of himself.

At the same time, he deprives the community of himself. *Conformism is a denial of participation in the proper sense of the word.* True participation is replaced by a pretense of participation, a superficial adjustment to others, without conviction and without authentic commitment. In this way, the ability proper to man to creatively shape the community is in a sense suspended or even falsified. This must have negative consequences for the common good, whose dynamism flows from true participation. Conformism denotes the opposite, for it creates instead a situation of indifference toward the common good. In conformism we perceive a specific variation of individualism: a flight from the community, which threatens the good of the individual, and at the same time a need to hide from the community through external pretense. Conformism is "uniformity" rather than unity. What inheres under the surface of uniformity is in fact diverseness, and the task of the community is to create for this diverseness conditions for participation. We must not be content with the conformistic situation. For when people only externally adjust themselves to the demands of the community—which they do above all for their advantage or to spare themselves distress—both the person and the community incur irreparable losses.

What is the attitude we call "avoidance"—and why is it a non-authentic attitude?

The attitude called "avoidance" seems not to be concerned with the appearances of relating to the common good that belong to conformism. In a certain sense, this attitude is more authentic, but it too suffers essentially from a lack of authenticity. Conformism avoids opposition, whereas avoidance shirks conformism, and in this way does not become authentic opposition. Opposition consists in taking up the common good and participation. Avoidance, on the other hand, is merely a withdrawal, perhaps as a sign of protest, though without an attempt [7a]at taking up[7b]. Hence, avoidance is a lack of participation; it is an absence in the community. As the saying goes, "Those who are absent are not right." In many cases, avoidance confirms the validity of this saying, though in certain cases it counts on the fact that absence, too, has its significance—that absence creates a particular rightness. In such cases, avoidance can constitute, in a sense, a substitutive attitude for a man who cannot muster solidarity and does not believe in the possibility of opposition. It is also difficult to deny that this attitude can be consciously chosen, and, consequently, it is difficult not to grant it a fundamental personalistic value. If, however, there exist *reasons that justify the attitude of "avoidance," then the same reasons must constitute an accusation of the community*, for the possibility of participation is a fundamental good of the community. Because "avoidance," as the attitude justified in a given case, attests to the impossibility of participation, the community does not live correctly. It must be lacking the true common good since "avoidance" has become the only option for members of this community.

For despite all these reasons that can justify avoidance as a sui generis substitutive attitude, we can in no way grant it a character of authenticity within existence and action "together with others." At many points, the attitude of "avoidance" coincides with the attitude of "conformism," not to mention the fact that sometimes there can occur something of a "conformistic avoidance." Above all, however, in both attitudes man relinquishes the fulfillment of himself in action "together with others." He is convinced that *the community deprives him of himself, and therefore he attempts to deprive the community of himself.* In the case of conformism, he tries to do this while keeping up appearances, whereas in the attitude of avoidance, he does not seem concerned with pretense. In both cases, something quite essential is severed from man—it is the dynamic feature of participation as a property of the person, which allows him to perform acts and authentically fulfill himself through these acts in the community of being and acting with others.

9. The "Member of the Community" and the "Neighbor"[xlix]

Two different systems of reference that permeate each other

On the basis of the analysis of participation conducted in this chapter, we must discover, in a sense, a still deeper layer of the reality that is the person when we look at his existence and action under the aspect of community "with others." It seems we have already adequately considered the problem of participation in connection with the fact that man is a member of different communities. Membership in a community constitutes, in a sense, a specific system of reference: one that is very rich and complex owing to the possibility of participation by each person. This system is closely related to another system of reference, which is important for participation and which we call by the name "neighbor." Despite the closeness, despite the mutual permeation, as it were, of these systems of reference, they are not identified with each other. What we express in the concept "neighbor" differs fundamentally from what we express in the concept "member of the community." *Each of these concepts indicates different possibilities and different forms of personal participation.* In each of them the [8a] social nature of man is expressed differently.

We consider here what the concepts "neighbor" and "member of the community" express as two different types or even systems of reference, for it is generally known that existence and action "together with others" places every man in the sphere of various relations. The concepts "neighbor" and "member of the community" (of society) in a sense aid in [9a]ordering[9b] these relations, and in this way they help us understand participation itself more accurately and more comprehensively. For participation expresses something different when it occurs in relation to a member of the community than when it occurs in relation to a neighbor.

To some extent, a convergence takes place here. Every man is a neighbor to another man as a member of the community. Membership in the same community draws men closer to one another, that is, it makes each of them, in a sense, more a neighbor to the others. Hence, on the basis of membership in the same community, the circle of neighbors either draws closer to every man or moves away from him. Members of the same family or nation are "by nature" closer to one another than they are to members of other families or nations. In this system of reference, closeness constantly displaces the state of being strangers, although we cannot deny that this state also exists between people. *The concept "neighbor," however, indicates something deeper* than people's closeness or their being strangers to one another. Therefore, *it is much more fundamental than the concept "member of the community."* However, membership in a community presupposes the fact that people are "neighbors"—and it neither creates nor destroys this fact. People are or become members of different communities, and in these communities they are or become close or estranged to one another—the latter case indicating, in a sense, a lack of community. Nevertheless, all are neighbors and do not cease to be so.

The concept "neighbor" manifests the subordination of all people to one another in humanity itself

This is accompanied by an axiological moment, which is essential for those reflections in which we emphasized the "personalistic" value in the community of being and acting. For the concept "neighbor" requires us not only to perceive but also to value in man that which is independent from membership in any community. It requires us to perceive and value in him something much more absolute. *The concept "neighbor" is connected with man as such and with the very value of the person regardless of any relation to this or that community* or society. The concept "neighbor" considers, that is, it *takes into account, humanity itself*, which is possessed by every "other" man just as "I" myself possess it. Thus, the concept "neighbor" creates the broadest plane of community, a plane reaching further than any "otherness," including that which results from membership in various human communities. The concept "member of the society-community" in a sense presupposes the reality of which the concept "neighbor" speaks, while both limiting it and shifting it to the background or even obscuring it. What is thus brought to the foreground is the subordination to a given community, whereas the concept "neighbor" manifests only the fundamental subordination of all people to one another in humanity itself. The concept "neighbor" thus indicates the most common reality and the most common basis of community between people. *The community in humanity itself is, after all, the basis for every other community.* If any community is severed from this fundamental community, it loses its "human" character.

Under this aspect we must fully consider the problem of participation. We have attempted thus far to elucidate the meaning of participation with respect to the belonging of every man-person to different communities, the fact that manifests and confirms his "social nature." However, the capacity for participation reaches further, namely, as far as does the concept "neighbor." The man-person is capable not only of participation in the community, in existing and acting "together with others," but also of participation in the very humanity of "others." All participation in the community is based on this latter and at the same time *finds its personal sense through this capacity for participating in the humanity of every man. This is what the concept "neighbor" indicates.*

Participation in the very humanity of every man is the core of all participation

Together with the analysis of the concept "neighbor," we arrive at a specific fullness of the meaning of the reality that from this chapter's beginning we have called "participation." At this point, we should reject the suggestion that the concepts "neighbor" and "member of the community" have separable or contradictory meanings. We have already indicated their partial convergence, which we intend to develop more deeply further on. Man's "social nature" speaks of this fundamental convergence, even though it is on the basis of this nature that the difference between neighbor and member of the community is fully explained. In addition, one ought not to think that the "neighbor" system of reference constitutes the basis of all inter-human relations, whereas "member of the community" is the basis of social relations. Such an understanding would be too superficial and insufficient. For both systems of reference permeate each other, and not merely in the objective order where every neighbor is a member of some community and the members of various communities are at the same time neighbors.

The point here is *reciprocal permeation in the subjective dimension of participation*. We understood participation as a dynamic property of the person. This property is expressed in the performance of acts "together with others," in the co-operation and co-existence that also serve the fulfillment of this person. Participation goes hand in hand with both the community and the "personalistic" value. For this reason in particular, it cannot be expressed only by membership in different communities but must reach through them to the humanity of every man. Only through this subordination in humanity itself, the subordination meant by the concept "neighbor," does the dynamic property of participation gain its personal depth and its universalistic dimension. Only then can we maintain that participation serves the fulfillment not only of this or that person but also of every person in the community, precisely though the community. We can also say that participation thus understood serves "simply" the fulfillment of persons in any community of their action or existence. *The ability to participate in the very humanity of every man constitutes the core of all participation* and conditions the personalistic value of all acting and existing "together with others."

10. The Meaning of the Commandment to Love
The commandment to love manifests that the "neighbor" system of reference has a fundamental significance

Therefore, let us devote the final pages in this book to the meaning of the evangelical commandment to love. We have underscored several times that we do not enter the ethical field; here, too, we wish to stop, in a sense, at the threshold of the strictly ethical content of the commandment "You shall love." We will not analyze the entire objective content of this commandment; we will not inquire especially into the ethical meaning of love. We wish only to emphasize that this commandment, in a particularly vivid and consistent way, confirms that in any action and existence "together with others" the "neighbor" system of reference has a fundamental significance. This system manifests in a particularly consistent way the commandment "You shall love" by juxtaposing the neighbor to one's own "I": "your neighbor as yourself." *The "neighbor" system of reference has a fundamental significance* among all the systems proceeding from human community *because it surpasses them all in scope, simplicity, and depth.* At the same time, it indicates the fullness of participation, which is not yet evident in the membership of any community. The "neighbor" system of reference in a sense expresses completely what is contained in every system of community membership. In relation to the latter system (or, rather, systems), the former is marked by a fundamental superiority. This is the correct hierarchy of values, because the "neighbor" system of reference speaks of the subordination of all people to one another on the basis of humanity itself, whereas the "member of the community" system of reference does not directly reveal this subordination. We can also speak of a certain transcendence of the "neighbor" in relation to the "member of the community." All of this is indirectly contained in the evangelical commandment.

Of course, we ought not to understand this as a tendency to limit the communal values of human action and existence. This would be a distorted understanding. The commandment "You shall love" has an utterly communal character; it speaks of that which shapes the community, and above all it manifests that which makes the community fully human. It speaks of that which shapes the proper depth of participation. Therefore, we should see the two previously distinguished systems of reference—"neighbor" and "member of the community" (whose distinction is fully justified)—*as joined together, not as separated or even opposed to each other*. This is also contained in the "personalistic" content of the evangelical commandment. If we saw things differently, then some mutual limitation would have to emerge: man as a "member of society" would limit man as a "neighbor." A similar limitation would proceed in the opposite direction. Such a limitation would indicate a fundamental weakness of the person, a lack of the property we have called "participation," a lack of a social nature. After all, the social nature of man is rooted in a fundamental subordination that results from humanity itself.

The commandment to love reveals the very roots of alienation

Thus, from the viewpoint of participation, *we should reject the possibility of mutual limitation by these two systems*. In action and existence "together with others," both of these systems, "neighbor" and "member of the community," must permeate and complement each other. We cannot allow them to be separated, for this would conceal the danger of fundamental alienation. The philosophy of the nineteenth and twentieth centuries understood alienation as man's estrangement from his humanity, as a deprivation of the particular property that we have called "personalistic." In the sphere of action and existence "together with others," this can take place precisely once participation in a community obscures and limits participation in the humanity of "others"—once the fundamental subordination, which confers a human property on the community of people, is weakened. Perhaps somewhat unilaterally, at times some perceived the danger of dehumanizing people through the systems of things alone: nature [*przyroda*], relations of production, civilization. And even though it is impossible, at least to a considerable extent, to deny the rightness of this thesis, we also cannot accept it exclusively. Moreover, although man is not the creator of nature [*przyroda*], he is its master.

He is also the creator of the relations of production and the creator of civilization. Hence, he can fundamentally prevent them from having a "dehumanizing" character and thus from leading to alienation. *We must therefore presuppose that at the root of all alienation resulting from systems of reference based in things is an alienation resulting from man himself.* It seems that the commandment "You shall love" directs us to the essence of alienation. The root of the alienation of man by man lies in overlooking or neglecting the depth of participation indicated by the noun "neighbor" and, related to this, by the mutual subordination of people in humanity itself as a principle of the deepest community.[4]

The commandment to love makes suitable demands concerning existing and acting "together with others"

As we have stated several times, both systems of reference—"neighbor" and "member of the community"—permeate each other in the objective order. They permeate each other because they inhere in the same people. Man's social nature is expressed in both—in the fact that everyone is a member of a community and of various communities and in the fact that everyone is a "neighbor"—and this includes for everyone a particular relation to the person, to his own "I." However, in light of the hierarchy sketched above with regard to these systems, we must perceive—still in the "personalistic" layer of the great commandment of the Gospel—*the necessity of a coordination in action and existence "together with others" that will ensure the fundamental and also superior character of the "neighbor" system of reference.* In this way, we protect ourselves against the possibility of alienation. The point of shaping human interaction and cooperation on different levels and on the basis of the different bonds

---

4. The text "Participation or Alienation?" published in *The Self and the Other*, ed. Anna-Teresa Tymieniecka, 61–73, Analecta Husserliana 6 (Dordrecht: D. Reidel, 1977) [pp. 514–31 in this volume], is a particular attempt to more extensively study this problem.

We should state once more that all of chapter 7 is only a complement and a sketch. The analysis contained in it has led us to assert that participation as a property of man who exists and acts "together with others" remains at the basis of two different dimensions of human intersubjectivity. The first dimension is found in the "man-man" relation ("I-Thou," *soi-autrui*). We find the second in the "we" relation (community, *Gemeinschaft*). Each of these forms of intersubjectivity demands a separate analysis. For participation understood as a simple ability to participate in the humanity of another man (neighbor) differs from participation as a true membership of various communities (societies) in which man happens to exist and act "together with others."

that determine communities and societies is to make the "neighbor" system of reference ultimately decisive. If any human community impairs this system of reference, it dooms itself to a disappearance of the fullness of participation, to an abyss between person and community. This is not only an abyss of indifference but also an abyss of destruction, which can threaten the person more readily than the community—yet through the person it must affect the community as well. Perhaps this most reveals how closely person and community are joined together; here we see *the truth of affirming the "social nature" of man*. This truth also seems here to unveil its grave aspect.

This, however, is not its most proper aspect. The commandment "You shall love" manifests above all the bright side of the reality of human action and existence "together with others." This is the side that we have attempted to analyze in this final chapter of our study, a study that has person and act as its object. At the same time, the commandment to love defines the proper measure of the tasks and demands that all people—persons and communities—must posit for themselves so that all the good of acting and existing "together with others" can be truly realized.

✺ ¹ᵃAfterword

Before we conclude our reflections on person and act,[1] we feel a need to express certain thoughts that remain in this study as if unfinished or seemingly ignored. The last chapter of the book introduced us to a new dimension of the experience "man acts." In it, we focused on facts of the type "man acts together with others" while sketching the "outline of the theory of participation," which is linked with this new dimension of experience. We are aware that this attempt is incomplete, being only an "outline" and not a mature conception. By including this "outline" within the study, we wish at least to point out that the experience of man who "acts together with others" itself demands to be introduced into the conception of person and act. Accordingly, this whole conception waits to be studied anew. It is another matter whether it will be a conception of only person and act or a conception of the community or relation in which person and act reveal and confirm each other in some other dimension.

However, a question may arise: is not this experience of acting "together with others" fundamental, and, consequently, should not the conception of the community and relation be presupposed when studying that of the person? I think that the interpretation of the community and relation of persons can be correctly presupposed only if it is already based in some way on the conception of person and act—a conception in which the image of the transcendence of the person in the act has been adequately explicated from the experience "man acts." Otherwise, it is very easy in the interpretation of community and inter-personal relation not to manifest everything that is constitutive for the person and *that fundamentally conditions and defines community and relation precisely as the community and relation of persons*. Thus, what seems methodologically and substantively justified is the solution that grants primacy to the conception of person and act and that seeks on the basis of this conception an adequate interpretation of community and inter-human relation in all their richness and diverseness.

Lastly, we should perhaps put one more concern to rest before we complete our reflections on person and act. This concern pertains to the existential "status" of man, to the entire truth of his limitedness, that is, his ontic contingency (*esse contingens*). Is this truth adequately inscribed in our analyses of person and act? Is the ontic "status" of man sufficiently legible in them? This concern is justified if only due to the fact that the conception of person and act presented in this study proceeds from the experience "man acts" and wishes to correspond to its authentic content. Thus, the object of this study is the person who reveals himself in the act—he reveals himself through all the psycho-somatic conditionings that are both man's richness and his certain limitation. Therefore, the person reveals not only his transcendence in the act but also the integration proper to the act; the dynamic reality of the act is constituted in this integration and not outside or above it. The person, who reveals himself through the act, in a sense permeates and at the same time encompasses the entire psycho-somatic structure of his own subject.

If, as we admit, *the aspect of the integration of the person in the act does not in itself explain the ontic "status" of man*, it is certain that it *brings us closer to apprehending and understanding this status* inasmuch as the presuppositions of the entire study and the adopted method allow. In light of what we said in the introduction, the aim of this study was to explicate from the experience of the act that which attests to man as a person, that which, in a sense, makes the person manifest. The aim was not to build a theory of the person as a being, a metaphysical conception of man. Nonetheless, man, who reveals himself as a person in the way we attempted to present in the analyses conducted here, also seems to sufficiently confirm that *his ontic "status" does not go beyond the boundaries of contingency: esse contingens.*

It was fitting to explain these two matters in the afterword. Having done so, the author considers that for the time being he can conclude his reflections on person and act.[1b]

III

POST-1969 RELATED ESSAYS

1 ❧ Introductory Statement during the Discussion on *Person and Act* at the Catholic University of Lublin on December 16, 1970

I consider the discussion that is to take place today to be very beneficial, above all for myself.[li] I cordially thank Fr. Kazimierz Kłósak, chairman of the faculty of professors and lecturers of philosophy, for organizing the discussion within this faculty. I thank Fr. Albert Krąpiec, rector of the Catholic University of Lublin, for the hospitality he is extending to us, and the dean, Fr. Stanisław Kamiński, for his even earlier initiative to discuss my study within the philosophical faculty of the Learned Society of the Catholic University of Lublin[lii]—a discussion that did not happen in that form but is happening today in a still fuller dimension, since professors and lecturers of philosophy from all of Poland participate in it. Finally, I thank all who are participating in today's meeting, especially those who prepared presentations.

I wish first of all to speak *briefly about the motives* that induced me *to write Person and Act*. They are quite exhaustively compiled in the section of this book entitled "The significance of personalistic issues." I have been interested in the reality of the person for a long time and for many reasons—not only for strictly cognitive and academic reasons, but also in order to participate in the life of contemporary people through its various configurations and dimensions. In the aforementioned section, I note that the path to *Person and Act* led through my previous ethical study *Love and Responsibility*. *Person and Act* no longer bears such a description in the subtitle—it is not an ethical study. Nonetheless, it is developed on the foundation of the integral experience of man, whose central terrain is morality, the ethical reality, proper only to man as a person and closely connected with his act. I also recall in the aforementioned section the pastoral constitution of the Second Vatican Council, *Gaudium et spes*. This document manifests perhaps most fully the place that the reality of the person has and will continue to have in problems and dialogue concerning overall worldview. Hence the attempt to know this reality more deeply.

Although the study *Person and Act* does not possess a theological character, it nonetheless concerns a reality that possesses a central significance for theology. It is sufficient to mention the first centuries of the Church and its first councils. In turn, during our times, it suffices to read attentively not only *Gaudium et spes* but also another document of Vatican II—the Constitution on Divine Revelation *Dei verbum*. It very clearly contains a personalistic concept of revelation—hence, a personalistic concept of theology must follow suit. Perhaps we witness in theology a transition from a view that I would call more "cosmological" to one that is more "personalistic." I prefer expressing myself in this way over saying that what is happening is a transition from a theology of nature to a theology of the person—because that seems ambiguous and unsubstantiated to me. For theology has always been a theology of the person—and therefore it has also been a theology of nature.

As we see, the reality of the person in a sense presses in on us from all sides. This is attested not only by written sources but above all by the life, existence, and *situation of man in the contemporary world*, as well as by the processes of development and their proper sense.

Among my earlier works, which—as I think—opened the way to the understanding of the problem of person and act that we find in the study being discussed today, I wish to pay attention to a monographic lecture that I presented in the School of Ethics at the Catholic University of Lublin. The lecture is entitled "The Act and Ethical Lived-Experience." I also lectured—somewhat in connection with that topic—on the problem of "good and value." However, *the subject matter of the act and ethical lived-experience*, I think, was particularly decisive for the later undertaking of the topic "person and act." In the aforementioned lectures, I constantly moved on the boundary between, on the one hand, the classical philosophy of Aristotle and St. Thomas and, on the other, phenomenology, to which I was led from the side of ethics by my earlier studies on

Max Scheler. During my work in Lublin, these problems evoked ongoing friendly philosophical disputes, in which Professors Kalinowski and Świeżawski and Fathers Kamiński and Krąpiec were the most frequent participants. This was an invaluable professorial *seminarium* of philosophy, independent from those that I conducted on ethical topics for undergraduate students and separately for master's and doctoral students.

Finally, I must add that *Person and Act is not a scholarly work*. The lack of a scholarly apparatus, which must strike—or perhaps scandalize—the reader when he finds no reference or footnote in the book from the first page to the last,[liii] originates from the fact that with my current duties I simply cannot afford to introduce that entire apparatus, which always reveals so much about the erudition and diligence of a scholar, about his thorough relation to the thought of other scholars and authors. Although *Person and Act* is not a scholarly work but rather a collection of my own reflections on the topic indicated by the title, the reader introduced to the philosophical issues will easily establish from whom these reflections originate and to whom they refer.

While writing *Person and Act*, I showed certain fragments to Fr. Tadeusz Styczeń, my closest collaborator and successor as the chair of ethics at the Catholic University of Lublin. Once the entire text was in typescript form, I asked my friend Fr. Marian Jaworski to read it and tell me what to do with it next. After reading it, he recommended having it published. Thus, in some way *Person and Act* owes its seeing the light of day to his advice. The Polish Theological Society in Kraków undertook its publication.

I wish to briefly say once more *how I understand the sense of today's discussion* of my study. The fact that this discussion is taking place in the presence of the author surely will not prevent anyone from expressing his or her own opinion, because we are concerned here not so much about the man but about his work, and through this work about the fundamental end of science—the knowledge of the truth about man: the person and the act. I said in the beginning that I consider today's discussion to be particularly beneficial for myself. For it is known that the problems already broached continue to occupy us. Human knowledge, scientific knowledge, is creative because it is a search. And since it is a search, it is also a readiness to undertake anew the same problems. St. Augustine called this *retractationes*, and I think that with this term he captured a profound law of science. These wonderful Augustinian "*retractationes*" are an indicator for man who is deeply troubled by certain problems in life.

If, however, *retractatio* denotes first of all a readiness to undertake anew problems that have already been worked on, there thus occurs a need *to see these problems anew*. Problems once considered can be considered anew if they are seen anew. I count, then, on the fact that the sincere exchange of thoughts on the topic of my study can greatly contribute to that. Therefore, I earnestly ask for this exchange.

2 ❦ Symposium on *Person and Act*

(Lublin—Catholic University of Lublin, 1971)

Karol Cardinal Wojtyła:
Thank you very much, Father Rector, Your Magnificence, for the words directed to us all and, in particular, to me, who is, for the time being, the chairman of the Commission of the Episcopate for Catholic Education.[liv] I say "for the time being" because in a moment we will put this reality aside, even though we can never put it aside completely because it follows us everywhere. Thus, to use a certain expression from my study, we will only place it "outside the parentheses."

Let us move on from these partly substantive and partly playful introductory remarks to the essence of the problem. I appreciate the initiation of today's discussion. In fact, this is significantly different from the original initiative, which was as follows: After my study *Person and Act* was published, Father Rector Kamiński from the Learned Society of the Catholic University of Lublin proposed that I discuss the topic of my study with the philosophical faculty of this society—a discussion with a quite limited group. In all honesty, I expected this initiative to have a similar character from the beginning until almost the end.

Meanwhile, a group of professors and lecturers of philosophy at universities, philosophical faculties, and seminaries were planning their annual meeting for today and tomorrow. Thus, here in this place, we meet something of what lies outside the parentheses, that is, with my office of the chairman for the Commission of the Episcopate for Education, because all academic faculties are connected with that commission. The chairman of this faculty, if I remember correctly, is Fr. Kazimierz Kłósak, the dean of the philosophy department of the Academy of Catholic Theology. It was from Fr. Kłósak that I received a renewed invitation, or, properly speaking, the only formal invitation to the meeting of this faculty today and tomorrow, with a note on the schedule explaining that the first day of the conference—today—was to be devoted to a discussion of my study. Thus, a few days ago I found myself in a somewhat new situation, one that partially changes the "optics" of our discussion. For if we originally expected a working discussion in a relatively small group, now this discussion is to be conducted in a slightly larger group, a group of several dozen persons from all over Poland, who may not necessarily even know the study itself. The very style of the discussion must therefore be somehow crystallized as we progress.

I admit that interiorly I had to get somewhat accustomed to this new situation. However, in the course of a few days, I managed and I think that this discussion, as is finally taking place, can be beneficial for us and, above all, for me. Of course, we must somehow handle the internal situation of a certain awkwardness right from the outset. I think that we must anticipate such a situation on two sides. At any rate, I foresee it on my side, and perhaps it is for this reason I am speaking about this situation of a certain awkwardness right from the beginning. It is, of course, nothing unusual that there are evenings or meetings with the author—this is very popular nowadays. We can imagine this as an encounter with the author, a meeting that is to have the character of an exchange of thoughts, a critical character. I am prepared for this.

I was also told by someone outside that it would perhaps be better if I were not present, as this would allow the participants greater liberty. I am aware—and this is the reason for my awkwardness—that I may be a cause of awkwardness for others.

I am speaking sincerely about this at the beginning in order to help all of us—including myself—overcome this troublesome situation has undoubtedly arisen, and to help us all somehow recover our own "transcendence," to use, once again, terminology from my book.

I do not know what I should do, whether I should stay or leave. So, perhaps, let us agree that when I am not able to endure it, then I will leave. But for now, I will try to stay.

The suggestion that I should leave came from a friend, and, therefore, in turn, I do not know whether he will be glad that I did not leave. Thus, perhaps also respect for friendship will speak in favor of my leaving at a certain point. And so we will settle this matter by way of a "Kraków compromise," for I am from Kraków.[iv] If he would ask, "Why did you not leave? You hindered the discussion," then I would say, "Excuse me, I did leave." "Not in the beginning." "Right, but in the middle."

I am joking, but I think this must be said from the beginning.

Now, however, having finished with jokes—though I do not swear that I am finished completely—I will address how I envision the purpose of today's discussion. Indeed, I would like to first define this purpose from the perspective of what is to be discussed—namely, the study I authored that was published in Kraków by the Polish Theological Society at the end of last year. However, in order to exclude at once a certain number of grievances, I wish to personally present these grievances before myself and all of us here.

First, this edition of the study unfortunately contains many typographical errors. There are scores of them. Just before this discussion I read the book and made marks on the margin and became very dejected. Because, indeed, there are scores of these typographical errors, which are sometimes serious. Sometimes they are serious in a material sense, such as when printed lines are switched or there are omissions. Sometimes they are serious in a way surpassing this material sense: for instance, when a comma or a letter at the end of a word is missing, for although this is materially a minor error, it nonetheless quite seriously changes the thought. Of course, I must take responsibility for this matter because I did not review the book myself; it was quite a busy period—after an almost three-month absence, after the trip to America and the synod—and we know how it is here with printing: deadlines are pressing. But one day, Fr. Stanisław Grzybek, acting not so much as the president of the Society as the head editor, brought me the finished book, and in that I rejoiced. However, right away I became inwardly terrified because I accidentally opened the book and immediately noticed an error in a title. The title "Consciousness and efficacy [*sprawczość*]" was printed as "Consciousness and efficiency [*sprawność*]." A fiasco. But at least we saved this title in some copies, but only in some. This I wanted to say right from the beginning to make it clear for those who were planning to speak on that topic—and they would have the right to speak on that—and so create a certain atmosphere of simplicity around the whole issue.

I think that this atmosphere of simplicity consists in this: we have to deal with the problem before us and then with a certain understanding of it. We must strive to look at this problem and verify our understanding of it. At the same time, I am well disposed toward the *retractationes* and know that this still stands before me. This wonderful Augustinian word *"retractationes"* indicates a man who is troubled by certain problems in life. *Retractatio* means a need to return to the same topic. I therefore appreciate the need to return both to the topic of *Love and Responsibility* and to the topic of *Person and Act*, and precisely with a view to the potential return to these topics, I think our discussion today will help me a lot. I am even thinking that if this does not give me as much as I expect, then I myself will call for another discussion. I will organize it in Kraków, for I will be in a better situation there, I will, so to speak, have "home advantage."

Following these introductory remarks, which pertain to the meaning of today's discussion not only from the aspect of what we are to concern ourselves with here today, but also somewhat on the character of our approach—from which angle we are to deal with this and for what purpose—I would like to speak briefly about the reasons for the genesis of this book. I would like to speak about the motives that inclined me to write it. But I will speak rather about external motivations and not enter the structure of the book, its academic, philosophical fabric. For I think that the speakers scheduled for the discussion, who are to lead this discussion from its substantive aspect, will in turn touch on these matters. I admit to not arranging anything with any of today's speakers. Thus, greatly in conformity with the spirit of Advent, I myself am full of expectation, the expectation of what the speakers will say.

Among the speakers who are planned to present here is ... but perhaps I will postpone this until later, so as not to mix things up.

In any case, I want to speak about the reasons and motives for writing. To a certain degree, these motives are listed at the end of chapter 1, in the paragraph entitled "The significance of personalistic issues."[lvi] They are in fact quite exhaustively listed here. I would nonetheless like to return and slightly expand on this.

I will say that the reality that interests me the most is undoubtedly the reality of the person. I myself do not know how I became interested in this, but I admit that it is so. This is the reality that interests me the most.

Looking outside myself, I see that this is a reality that also—beyond myself, in the contemporary world, in the world of the contemporary thought—becomes, if not the central, then perhaps one of the central realities. Perhaps this is not especially revelatory, maybe it has always been this way, but perhaps not so completely, for the matter was somewhat different, which I will briefly mention in this motivation, namely, how I understand that this was different. In any case, I see and think that the reality of the person is a more and more central, a more and more important element when issues concerning the worldview, ethical issues, and finally theological issues are at stake. Although all these aspects are listed in the aforementioned chapter of my book, I nonetheless would still like to briefly draw our attention to them respectively.

I had my personal or, so to speak, my own access to the subject matter of *Person and Act*, which undeniably came through the previous study, namely, *Love and Responsibility*. Thus, this access came from the perspective of ethical problems. However, *Person and Act* is not suitable as an ethical study, and I do not consider it to be such.

However, while dealing with the ethical issues in *Love and Responsibility*, I saw that what lies at the root of these issues is a vision of the person, and that this person would have to be examined separately. Otherwise, the argumentation and substantiation of the ethical norms in the material covered by *Love and Responsibility* would not be complete and would not be sufficiently thorough. Nevertheless, the further development of matters in this field, among others, and all that preceded the publication of the encyclical *Humanae vitae* and all that followed it, confirms my conviction. Namely, this conviction is that in order to refer to the reality of the person in ethics—and not only in conjugal or family ethics, but also in general ethics in all its various subdivisions—we must see this reality more fully.

With respect to the scope of worldview-related issues, as I mentioned in the introduction, or rather in chapter 1 of the book, the work surrounding the council, especially the famous Schema XIII, which at present is the constitution *Gaudium et spes*, strongly confirmed my conviction of the importance of this topic. Of course, the council did not concern itself with the philosophical concept of the person, but, on the other hand, it in some way presupposed it. And this presupposition inclines the philosopher—let us admit, a poor philosopher—to undertake in his own workshop the problem, which is the reality of the person. (I think that concerns both the philosopher and theologian.) At any rate, the constitution *Gaudium et spes* is most certainly a declaration of the worldview of contemporary Christianity, of the contemporary Church, and indirectly indicates to us what place the reality of the person has, and gradually will have, in problems concerning this worldview and in dialogue about this worldview.

Lastly, I also think that this reality must somehow gain importance in theological matters.

The book *Person and Act* is no theological study. It is, let us say, a philosophical study, although Prof. Kalinowski, after having read this study, in his long letter to me finds issue with its philosophical character. He says that this study is psychological rather than philosophical. I leave this matter to those who will speak on this topic later. However, concerning the importance of the reality of the person in theological matters, we know that this was especially the case from the very beginning: that specifically theological disputes, moreover, disputes concerning the very doctrine of faith, the very teaching of the faith, greatly helped in clarifying the concept of the person at the very beginning of the history of the Church, in the first centuries, and in the time of the first councils. I think that today these matters return with new intensity. They return, of course, not only in one's worldview and in ethics, but also in all of theology—they return with new intensity and, in a sense, with a new position.

If I say this, then I have in mind the totality of the documents of Vatican II, and, above all, the Constitution on Divine Revelation *Dei Verbum*, which gives us, we can say, a personalistic conception of revelation itself. And what must follow this personalistic conception of revelation is, so to speak, the personalistic conception of theology. Has it been any other way? Has theology ever not been personalistic? I think that it has always been so. Nonetheless, some new vistas, new demands are opened here. I think that perhaps we are witnesses to a new process that is already taking place in theology. This is the process of shifting from the vision I would call "cosmological" to the vision I would call "personalistic"— or, as is promoted sometimes also in journalism, from the theology of nature to the theology of the person. And if we carefully read the documents, and especially the aforementioned *Dei Verbum*, then this change of orientation, the change of the profile of theology, is most justified. In fact, the council already in a certain way confirms it and at the same time opens it anew.

So, all these circumstances contributed to the motivation for my study of the person. Of course, only now am I more formally aware of these motives, for I was not aware of them to such an extent when I was beginning the work. Nonetheless, these motives were already then at play, perhaps in a way less conscious and certainly in a way less formalized than now.

When I look at my older work connected especially with the function of the professor of ethics at the University and of the professor of moral theology at the Kraków faculty, I see already in my older various interests, and even in publications, the stages, as it were, preparing me for precisely this topic.

I would pay particular attention to the work entitled "The Act and Lived-Experience." I do not know whether this was published as an article or whether it was presented as a lecture in a certain year. I know that I certainly presented it here as a monographic lecture at the philosophical faculty at the Catholic University of Lublin. However, I do not remember whether I published it anywhere. At any rate, I think that what began to be shaped precisely on the topic of the act and lived-experience was a certain relation to the philosophy of being and to the philosophy of consciousness, as well as a certain search based on matters concerning man, that is, on matters concerning the person. What I think on the very concept of *Person and Act* will be quite extensively manifested.

Once we go through all the exterior motives, the study itself can ultimately be thought of as a fruit of certain interests of my own, as I said in the beginning of my speech: a predilection for the reality of the person, which personally seems to me to be also a central reality.

Of course, this is a philosophical study of the person, and not so much an ethical one, as I said, and rather not a study in ethics at all; the ethical plane is presupposed in it rather than being the proper plane. This is rather simply a study in anthropology, in the philosophy of man. Of course, while being concerned with the topic of the person—of *Person and Act*—I was aware of the perennial relation between philosophy and theology, namely, that philosophy also provides tools for theology. While I was creating my own conception, my vision of the person, I also thought about this function. Namely, I thought about how this conception of the person, the reality of the person seen and presented this way, could be useful for practicing theology, especially in view of the personalistic orientation that gains importance in it, as I have said, on the basis of Vatican II and especially the constitution *Dei Verbum*.

This study can, of course, scandalize because it contains no footnotes, no references.[lvii] It is a collection of my own reflections; it is not a scholarly work in the way in which academic works are scholarly. It is the fruit of my own reflection, although what is evident in it, of course, is from whom these reflections originated, to whom they refer, to which sources, to which thinkers, to which personages of both philosophical and theological thought.

This whole scholarly apparatus was not introduced here. I will sincerely admit that it was not introduced, also somewhat because I cannot afford to do so with my present tasks. My present tasks still allow me to think, to entertain certain reflections of an academic character, but unfortunately they do not allow me to support academic efforts in a particularly detailed, technical sense.

This is what I wanted to say about the book. It is evident that these are basically introductory remarks that do not actually touch on the book's essence.

Concerning the meaning and implication of today's discussion, we already noted them. I think that if *Ecclesia est semper reformanda*, then so is all the more the *studium humanum*. I think that problems raised once can be raised again, but only under the condition that they are seen anew. In particular, a critique, that is, thinking about a problem or about grasping a problem, helps us in this seeing anew. Therefore, I think I approach both our meeting and the exchange of thoughts that is to take place here with all sincerity. I count on the elucidations that the discussion will bring, and I am very grateful to all who prepared their presentations for this discussion. I do not know on what particular topics they prepared their presentations, but among the participants in the discussion are Dr. Stanisław Grygiel from Kraków, Fr. Kłósak, Fr. Krąpiec, Fr. Kuc (whom unfortunately I do not see), Dr. Andrzej Półtawski, Prof. Antoni Stępień, and Prof. Tadeusz Styczeń.

It is added that the presentations will be given in an order determined by their content. But this is the task for our moderator, namely, in what way to order these presentations. At any rate, I am very grateful to all who prepared them and who in this way coauthored the discussion with myself and for all of us; they coauthored a *retractatio* of the problem at hand for the future. I personally entreated Fr. Professor[lviii] to add Dr. Grygiel to the list of opening speakers, because he occupied himself with these matters before the book was published, and for quite a long time he has had close contact with it. Thus, I wanted all his work connected to this study to find expression somewhere. I also asked to add Dr. Półtawski to the list of the opening speakers on account of his particular interests, which are actually on the periphery of *Person and Act*'s subject matter, and which the speaker himself will present at the right time. I also asked to add Fr. Kuc to the list because thus far he is the author of the only review, which appeared in *Tygodnik powszechny*, on the topic of this book.

Of course, leaving aside personal matters, I think that the meeting as it takes place today and eventual publications in the area of domestic literature are perhaps quite an important factor to create impulses and incentives, and to develop this domestic literature with respect to philosophy, theology, and all other fields.

I think that there exists... and here I return somewhat to the position that I left outside the parentheses, namely, the position of the chairman of the Episcopate for Education. So, I see from this position that, as far as our education, our philosophy, and our theology are concerned, there exists—let us sincerely admit this—quite a thorough ignorance of them in the dimension of the Universal Church. A thorough ignorance. I deal with this issue both in Poland and outside of Poland, I speak on these topics in the congregation with the chairman, with the prefect, with certain centers in Louvain, with the rector, and I see a need to introduce our academic achievements, our theological and philosophical achievements to a common market.

Of course, what is an obstacle here is our language, which is very little-known, and which dooms us somewhat to this Polish seclusion. This, however, is not an insurmountable obstacle, but is perhaps, from the viewpoint of the Church as a community most broadly understood, a lack—a lack of *communio*, if a community's thought, and a community as extensive as our Poland, is absent in the consciousness of the Christian *universitat*. And that is the case!—it is absent. It is absent, and the directories of literature in this field, for instance our neighbors' directories, German directories, show as our own achievements almost nothing—or at any rate very little.

And so, shifting from this common market in which we are so badly represented to our own market, I think that in our own market we remain undoubtedly under influence: the influence of the West. Additionally, there is a slight, not influence perhaps, but rather interest toward the East. This interest is perhaps fitting since we are here, in the borderland. However, being situated in this position, it is extremely important that we do not lose ourselves—that we do not lose ourselves. Therefore, we should treat our own achievements as important in their own way. Now I am speaking to us from myself, from a personal perspective, and I expose this problem. We should treat our achievements as important in their own way. We should concern ourselves with that. We should contribute by common effort so that what we create is more and more mature, more and more perfect.

That suffices for an opening. I apologize that it was too long and not completely to the point, but perhaps the broadening of horizons around a certain, concrete, and particular matter will also be beneficial for something. Thank you.

3 ❦ The Afterword to the Discussion on *Person and Act*

This afterword that follows the discussion on my study *Person and Act* is quite distant in time from the introductory statement given on December 16, 1970, during the meeting of the professors and lecturers of philosophy at the Catholic University of Lublin.[lix] I offer it after the conclusion of the discussion extended beyond that meeting on account of the decision to publish the entire discussion in *Analecta Cracoviensia*.[lx] This decision was made by Fr. Kazimierz Kłósak, dean and chairman of the faculty of philosophy. Because of the announcement to publish the discussion, individual participants saw a need to either adjust their own presentations or even formulate them anew. In addition, some other persons were asked to speak, persons who did not directly contribute to the Lublin discussion but, being interested in *Person and Act*, expressed a readiness to prepare their reflections in writing.

In this way, *a wealth of presentations resulted* over time, presentations that considerably surpassed what was included in the one-day Lublin discussion. Only a few of the presentations in the discussion (those of Fr. Kłósak and Prof. Stępień) correspond in volume and tenor to the discussion of December 16, 1970. The majority of presentations, even in the case of the in-person participants of that discussion, were very much expanded and deepened. This, of course, is greatly advantageous for the study *Person and Act* in view of the goal posited by our Lublin discussion. At the same time, however, by reading all the presentations published here, we should conclude that *Person and Act* was not only for them an object of analysis and of critical remarks based on it, but also became an occasion for further reflections, for integral and at times monographic approaches to the problems outlined or perhaps only occasionally mentioned in my study.

We can say that the discussion in its form today presents an entire cycle of *presentations deserving to be published for their own sake* on account of the objective problem they deal with, and not only because they creatively refer in various ways to the study *Person and Act*.

Therefore, I wish to thank, all the more, all the participants of the discussion for publishing it in its present form. I am thankful here for the effort of a thorough reading of my study *Person and Act* and for finding so much space for it in their own creative thought. Thanks to this, the study is better situated in the extensive background of philosophy and referred to its many *coryphaei*, both from the past and the present. Particularly valuable for me is manifesting certain essential connections between *Person and Act* and Professor Roman Ingarden's book *Książeczka o człowieku* [Little book on man], published after his death and mentioned by several participants of the discussion.[lxi] For, as it happened, the late professor read his study about man in its original language (it was written originally in German) during a number of evenings in my apartment in Kraków among a group of persons who also belong to the circle of authors of the present publication. That happened soon after the publication of *Person and Act*, whose author, while writing his study, knew nothing of the views of *Prof. Ingarden* that were to appear in *Książeczka o człowieku* [Little book on man]. Therefore, these evenings spent reading the work of Prof. Ingarden were an important event for us. While recalling this detail, I wish at the same time to thank all who, during the discussion, noted certain places of convergence between both works. Of course, there is more to be thankful for. I wish to express my thanks in the beginning, for it seems to me that the creative and benevolent thought of all the authors of this publication considerably developed the content of *Person and Act*. This development occurred both "inward," in the direction of my study's own content, and "outward," in the direction of its possible applications in life and in practice.

Speaking at the beginning of the discussion that took place in December 1970 in Lublin, I said that I saw its purpose as the possibility of a creative *retractatio* of the problems addressed in *Person and Act* and of the approaches and solutions contained in that study. Reading the presentations that are to be published in *Analecta Cracoviensia*, we can acknowledge that many of them took on the character of *creative retractationes* in relation to *Person and Act when written by their authors*. In this way, the publication by itself fulfills the end that the discussion was meant to serve. Thus, I think that the presentations of the discussion participants should, first of all, be manifested in their full spectrum, so they could thereby work for the presupposition adopted in the Lublin discussion.

Therefore, by speaking at last, I wish *above all to retain and accept* all that was covered by the entire discussion. At the same time, however, I would like to *perform a kind of concluding synthesis* for the sake of further reflections and examinations (not necessarily mine) of this problem. As was stated in the introduction, the discussion in the published presentations proceeds at times by way of several authors taking on the same problem and often corresponding to one another within their own presentations. Accordingly, a particular order was adopted in this publication so that these circles of reflections, namely, questions-reservations and responses-explanations, met before the eyes of the reader. This was attempted insofar as it was possible in the face of the complexity and many-sidedness of particular presentations. In this afterword, I shall attempt to follow these circles only inasmuch as I can assume the responses and solutions given by particular authors as my own. I think that this will make the work much easier.

Personally, it seems to me that the presentations of the discussion participants, which we publish in this volume of *Analecta Cracoviensia*, are concentrated:

> —*in the first circle*, around the problem of whether the study *Person and Act* has a philosophical character and in what sense it does;
> —*in the second circle*, around the problem of whether the concept of the person presented in this study corresponds to the reality of the person (as a whole and in particular parts or aspects);
> —and *in the third circle*, around the problem of how much this concept can become a basis for manifold practice.

In the following summary we shall attempt to move within these three circles.

1. The First Circle: The Problem of the Philosophical Character of the Study *Person and Act*

It seems that this problem received the most remarks in the discussion. This was certainly a consequence of two facts: first, the majority of the discussion participants were philosophers; second, methodological problems greatly absorb the attention of philosophers today. Therefore, we can observe that the majority of the presentations responded, above all, to the reflections of *Person and Act* included in its introduction.

Philosophical anthropology and experience

In his precise discourse, Prof. Kalinowski concludes that the study *Person and Act does not possess a philosophical character*, unless in the metonymical sense. Fr. Kłósak seems to concur with this position when he notes that we deal here with the phenomenology of the person rather than with the philosophy of the person. Other participants of the discussion, however, affirmed the philosophical character of the study. I am very grateful to Fr. Jaworski, who, relying on the teaching of St. Thomas and the fundamentals of his philosophy, attempted to prove that the study *Person and Act* has a philosophical character while manifesting all its philosophical specificity. He writes, "The author places his reflections on the human person in the perspective of the human being *itself*. He is concerned with the categories proper to the human person,"[lxii] and, as we read elsewhere, "with manifesting the structural moments themselves of the human being as a person."[lxiii]

Here we are immediately faced with the problem that perhaps found the most vibrant echo in the presentations of the discussion participants, namely, *the problem of experience as the source of philosophical cognition*. Fr. Jaworski also sees in this a characteristic feature of St. Thomas's philosophy, and in light of this reason, independently from substantive reasons, he assesses the rightness of the philosophical method adopted in *Person and Act*: "If we do not want to practice pure rationalism in the philosophy of man, then we first of all must indicate the reasons explaining his essence in experience itself.... The human person must ... be given visually in experience.... For whence could we know about this?"[lxiv] Prof. Kalinowski is of a different opinion when he writes, "According to the author [of *Person and Act*] 'it seems that *there is no need to demonstrate or prove to anyone that man is a person*, that man's action is an act.' This, unfortunately, does only seem so to him if, as everything suggests, he accepts with Boethius that the person is *rationalis naturae individua substantia*, because all the metaphysics contained in this formula clearly requires a proof, and what a complicated one at that."[lxv] Prof. Gogacz takes a similar position when he writes, "The act is not '*a particular moment of the vision ... of the person.*' The path to define the person leads through laborious analyses of metaphysics."[lxvi]

Hence the discussion brings, on the one hand, a certain *questioning* of the empirical starting point in the philosophy of the person and, on the other hand, a *confirmation* of this point. The questioning of experience by Prof. Kalinowski is, on the one hand, mitigated, although, on the other hand, it is all the more radical when he writes, "*Person and Act* is filled with the phenomenological analysis of the allegedly visual data—though in my opinion, with the phenomenological analysis of the metaphysical presuppositions confronted with experience."[lxvii] Perhaps the study *Person and Act* contains above all a confrontation of the metaphysical concept of the person with experience. However, would this confrontation be possible without some experience and some original understanding of the person already present in the starting point of the metaphysical concept of the person? For if the cognition of man as a person has no basis in experience, no starting point in vision, then one could think that the philosophical concept of the person is derived from other sources and imposed on experience by way of "laborious analyses."

Fr. Kłósak analyzes *the very theory of the experience of man* presented in *Person and Act* and sees a need for certain modifications of the text, which nonetheless do not, in his opinion, exert any essential influence on the conclusions of the work. Prof. Stępień also speaks on this topic. However, Fr. Kamiński approaches the problem in the most magisterial way. He thinks that *Person and Act* "extends too far the scope of what we call experience ... the acknowledgment of every experience as some understanding causes resistance ... as does especially the fact that in experience there are reasons interpreting experiential reality."[lxviii] This resistance arises on the basis of methodology, according to which "interpretation is considered an operation discursive by nature."[lxix] It seems to me, however, that *nowhere* in *Person and Act was experience identified with understanding* or let alone with the whole process of *interpretation*, but it was merely portrayed as its foundation and life-giving source. No discursive operation can be severed from this source if it is to preserve contact with reality, which we desire to understand and explain. Therefore, we constantly say that experience contains only "*some* understanding."

When Fr. Kamiński and elsewhere Prof. Kalinowski and Prof. Gogacz put forth their reservations against experience as the basis for knowing the person, for his creative understanding, they directly or indirectly indicate that this source ought to be sought in metaphysics. Only a general theory of being can constitute a basis for the theory of the person. However, let us say that first, the general theory of being also finds its root in experience, and second, no other way can be seen to apply the general theory of being to the theory of the person, unless on the basis of a specific experience of man. The point in *Person and Act* was not to deny the connection of the theory of the person with the general theory of being, but to manifest that the "proper categories of human being,"[lxx] to use Fr. Jaworski's expression, have their own basis in experience—we could say, in their own proper experience. Understanding the specificity of the human being as personal is, in this way, possible and at the same time less "theoretical"—that is, less threatened by the danger of pure rationalism. The person is a reality far more visual than it can seem through the prism of pure speculation. What can otherwise be a result of "laborious analyses" in the field of metaphysics has its realness in the experience of man. The path of philosophical anthropology itself proceeds from this experience, and it proceeds, as Fr. Jaworski states, "in the perspective of the philosophy of being."[lxxi]

I think that Fr. Styczeń approaches the difficulties advanced by Fr. Kamiński from a different angle, though at the same time in a very original way. This approach is even more interesting in light of the fact that both of them are guided by similar presuppositions. Fr. Styczeń, similarly to Fr. Kamiński, sees the need for "*methodologically and epistemologically perfect knowledge of [man]*"[lxxii] in the philosophical grasp of the subject matter concerning him. And so, conducting a methodological analysis of *Person and Act* in the name of this need, Fr. Styczeń sees in it "a model of the method that is able to ensure that the theory of man has a character of a ... philosophical discipline in the classical sense."[lxxiii] The author of *Person and Act* himself is not an "expert" methodologist, and therefore follows the opinions of philosophers-methodologists concerning his work with all the more attention. Fr. Styczeń's view seems to be here particularly revelatory while, at the same time, coinciding particularly accurately with the intentions of *Person and Act*.

It is *revelatory* especially due to the fact that Fr. Styczeń, by concentrating above all on what the study *Person and Act* says about the act as a way of the person to manifest himself, shows the fundamental feature of the applied method. He writes,

> The statements of the author, which methodologically express the only reasons not contradicting the occurrence of the dynamisms ascertained at the starting point, turn out with respect to content to be simply theses about what man is. They are theses of anthropology. The theses of anthropology of this type are thus necessary, apodictic theses while at the same time being really objective and validated experientially. For in their content they express what remains in a necessary connection with the content of the facts grasped at the starting point by descriptive statements. As a result of the portrayed reciprocal connection, as it were, between the starting point (the description of facts) and the arrival point (the statements expressing the only reasons not contradicting the facts), the statements about the fact are in a sense *"necessitated."* It has to be as it is and appears in experience. The statements about the reasons are *realized and empiricized*: the necessary reason of what is real cannot itself be non-real.[lxxiv]

Therefore, Fr. Styczeń does not even see an alternative to the model of the method applied in *Person and Act*, although he rightly adds that presenting this model "is not yet the same as developing it in detail."[lxxv] In this respect, he places discreet but firm demands on the author of *Person and Act* (and on others who will undertake this topic).

If the view of Fr. Styczeń is revelatory (revelatory above all for the author of *Person and Act* himself) because it shows in such a convincing way the link between the experience of man and philosophical anthropology, then at the same time *it coincides very accurately* with the philosophical intentions of that study. At this point, allow me once more to return to another valuable elaboration, namely, Fr. Kamiński's presentation. The very title "Jak filozofować o człowieku?" [How to philosophize about man?] indicates that Fr. Kamiński reflects on the problem of the method in philosophical anthropology in a somewhat more general way, for he attempts to show which necessary conditions should be met for any philosophizing about man—even though he does this apropos *Person and Act* and on the basis of that study. If, however, these reflections are in general correct and important also for *Person and Act*, then it seems to me that their author moved somewhat beyond the specificity of this study. It also seems to me that Fr. Styczeń concentrated more on that specificity, that he remained in a sense within the boundaries of *Person and Act*. Perhaps thanks to this, the assessment of the method in his approach fell closer to the essential property of the study.

The philosophy of being and consciousness

For, in fact, this study does not contain the "maximalistic project" that is perceived in it and analyzed by Fr. Kamiński from the general methodological position.[lxxvi] This "maximalistic project," which according to the reflections of our distinguished methodologist turns out to be "unfeasible," would indeed be unfeasible if the author of *Person and Act* saw it and applied it in his study in the way Fr. Kamiński considered it. But the project of unifying two philosophical orientations, namely, the Thomistic and the phenomenological orientations, the philosophy of being and the philosophy of consciousness, is in reality much more modest and does not have this "maximalistic" dimension, according to which Fr. Kamiński examines this project in his presentation. Here, I think that Fr. Jaworski grasped the proper intentions of the author of *Person and Act*, and, therefore, I wish simply to refer to his explanation of the problem. In any case, *there is no unifying* of these two philosophies in *Person and Act*, and there is, in particular, no unifying of *the philosophy of being and the philosophy of consciousness* as *reducing* the entire reality to the subject-consciousness and its content. All this has no place in *Person and Act*. Instead, I attempt to conduct in this study the "reflection on the proper data of consciousness," and this, as Fr. Jaworski writes, "can indicate both the transcendent reality in relation to it and a concrete, really existing subject, thus the transcendence of the real subject-person being the ontic source of consciousness."[lxxvii]

At this point we encounter the problem that was rightly undertak-

Afterword on *Person and Act* | 441

en by the participants of the discussion. This is *the problem of the duality of the experience of man*, which was presented in *Person and Act* under the name of the experience "from within" and "from without." Dr. Grygiel speaks on this topic extensively, and Fr. Kamiński refers to it in his methodological reflections. Of course, none of the participants question the fact of this duality of experience. The problem, however, is how to correctly introduce this duality in the unity of the concept, or theory, of the person. Fr. Kamiński sees here a fundamental difficulty, for "uniting the data from within and from without on the level of exterior experience" seems to him "almost completely impossible, if the interior data were to preserve their peculiarity."[lxxviii] And identifying the experience of man with self-consciousness (that is, with self-experience) denotes epistemological anthropocentrism, as a result of which "the cognition of the person is ultimately a vision of the person in the act ... and not a theory of the person."[lxxix]

We shall return in a moment to the issue of the theory of the person. Concerning the problem of the duality of experience, however, it seems to me that it is simply *unavoidable in the cognition of man*. The authors rightly consider whether this problem has been elaborated in *Person and Act* in a sufficiently comprehensive manner. At this point, Dr. Grygiel proposes an extension, he writes: "What should be distinguished and analyzed here are four kinds of experience, namely: the experience of one's own subjectivity, that is, one's own interiority; the experience of one's outwardness (the experience of the body); the experience of someone else's outwardness; and in special cases the experience of someone else's interiority."[lxxx] This suggestion deserves to be taken into consideration. The author of *Person and Act*, however, intended to posit, or even only to mention, the problem rather than to elaborate it in an exhaustive way.

It seems that if we agree to the experiential basis of philosophical anthropology, we must at the same time realize this duality of experience and the fact of its incommensurability, which was also underscored in *Person and Act*. We must realize all this if only because we use this dual experience *de facto* in the philosophical concept of man or in the theory of man. The author of *Person and Act* is all in favor of submitting the whole process of this use—this drawing from two experientially incommensurate sources—to a thorough methodological analysis in order to clarify all that is here to be clarified. Therefore, he fully appreciates the methodological clarifications pointed out by Fr. Kamiński, especially on the topics of induction, intersubjectivization, and reduction as well. At the same time, however, the author expresses a conviction that both the duality of experience and the precision of further stages of the philosophical cognition of man do not remove the fundamental unity of this cognition. For otherwise the philosophy of the person would have to remain a theory that does not meet experience. The study *Person and Act* was written to demonstrate, among others, that that is not the case.

The theory of the person or hermeneutics?

The problem of the theory of the person deserves a few more words. Fr. Kamiński expresses a view that "analytical-ostensive procedures neither lead to a fuller philosophical theory ... nor validate it."[lxxxi] Fr. Krąpiec writes that by emphasizing the existential moment and the factuality of the person, the work (i.e., *Person and Act*) gives too little consideration to the theory of the person and the role of the "nature of man."[lxxxii] I would be ready to agree with the latter opinion, though at the same time it should be said that in his penetrating discourse Prof. Kalinowski discovered under the phenomenological layer of *Person and Act* a more or less complete theory of the human person, a theory corresponding to the Thomistic (that is, as he says himself, the personalistic) concept of man. Moreover, he arranged its principal theses on the basis of *Person and Act*.

At this point, a thought suggests itself that *the theory of the person is one thing and the language* in which this theory is expressed *is another*. Assessing different attempts of philosophical anthropology and the methodology proper to it, all within the framework of St. Thomas's thought, Fr. Jaworski writes, "The attempts thus far were (1) too 'metaphysical' in the sense of interpreting the human being 'from above,' within general presuppositions of the system, and thus they did not tend to understand this being in its own specific categories." He then adds in parentheses an expressive remark: "Is this not why the modern philosophies of the subject grew outside the traditional direction of philosophy?"—that is, outside the philosophy that in discussion is often called "classical." In further assessing these attempts, Fr. Jaworski writes as follows: "(2) They did not adequately take into consideration the experience of man as the basis for building philosophical anthropology."[lxxxiii]

The remarks in points (1) and (2) relate to each other. In light of these remarks, we should say that the study *Person and Act* is not a metaphysical theory of the person, in the sense that it is neither constructed in the categories of metaphysics nor expressed in its traditional language. However, we do not have to argue whether this is a theory of the person or only "a vision of the person in the act." It is known that the Greek *theoria* expresses more or less the same as "seeing" or "vision." What seems essential for the author of *Person and Act* is that *the cognition of man*, and *philosophical cognition at that, has at its disposal the possibility of a "vision,"* that is, the intellectual "seeing" that, and by which, he is a person. It is this seeing that also confirms the metaphysical theory of the person. This is closely connected with the process called by Fr. Jaworski a successive "healing" of experience (initiated by phenomenology), which has a great significance for the thinkers who represent a realistic position in philosophy.[lxxxiv]

In order to complete the first circle of reflection, within which the particular participants of the discussion on *Person and Act* thought about the problem of whether this study has a philosophical character and in what sense, we should add that Dr. Grygiel and Prof. Gogacz try to define the *philosophical specificity of the study in the categories of hermeneutics*. Dr. Grygiel's suggestion goes in the direction of demonstrating the kinship between the concept of *Person and Act* and the philosophy of the symbol including the interpretation of the latter. In this case, the symbol would be the act in which the person is made present. Dr. Grygiel sees the entire study as "a formal hermeneutics of the act, within which one should arrive at the philosophical explication of the act that makes the person present."[lxxxv]

Inasmuch as this hermeneutical proposition seems to the author of *Person and Act* not only very interesting but also sufficiently coherent with the real content of his study, it is somewhat more difficult for him to accept the suggestions of Prof. Gogacz, who, recalling the "multiplicity of etymological analyses" in that study, perceives in it "a tendency of linguistic philosophies."[lxxxvi] Thus, by grasping *Person and Act* through the categories of hermeneutics because this study attempts "to make" the person and the act "something intelligible to us," Prof. Gogacz finds in it above all a "hermeneutics of meanings"; "phenomenology itself appears here ... as an analysis of language."[lxxxvii] In his presentation, Prof. Gogacz devotes much space to accurately qualifying the study *Person and Act* on account of the method it uses. "It is difficult ... to say," he writes, "that the book presents a philosophical theory of the person, that is, a full theory of the structure of the person. It is a study of the cognition of the person through his conscious acts."[lxxxviii] Earlier he notes as follows: "This description, on account of unifying several aspects or starting points of the analysis and not fitting within any traditionally accepted philosophical disciplines, must constitute some separate methodological area, which can preliminarily be called, for instance, a theory of the cognition of the person."[lxxxix]

Assuredly, Prof. Gogacz's view on *Person and Act* is not devoid of originality. Nonetheless, however, the provisional attempts undertaken by the author of that study to explain the etymology of particular terms are not sufficient for qualifying the entire study as a clarification of the linguistic layer instead of a real analysis, that is, as a theory of the cognition of the person based merely on terminological clarifications. It still seems to the author of *Person and Act* that the reflections on the cognition of the person, contained in his study, are proportional to [1a]the need for the cognition of the person himself, which he attempted to include in it[1b]. It also seems that the entire discussion concerning the problem of the philosophical character of *Person and Act* fundamentally confirms his conviction.

2. The Second Circle: The Concept of the Person Contained in *Person and Act* and the Reality of Person and Act in Philosophical Understanding

The second circle of reflections, which winds through the presentations of the discussion participants, in a certain measure remains in the shadow of the first circle, namely, of the methodological or metaphilosophical reflections. Nonetheless, we can distinguish quite clearly the views of the authors of particular presentations on the relation of the concept of the human person presented in *Person and Act* to the reality that the person, in their opinion, constitutes. Thus, the assessment of the concept here is not merely methodological but strictly substantive.

A historical or systematic approach?

Prof. Półtawski approaches this problem *historically*, offering an extensive introduction in the beginning of his presentation entitled *Człowiek a świadomość* [Man and consciousness]. Prof. Półtawski rightly holds that "every philosophical work should ... be understood both in its objective reference and in its place in history: to see whence and whereto its author tends."[xc] In the name of this premise, he first gives a concise and very accurate outline of the issues concerning man in post-Cartesian thought.

Other presentations have above all a systematic *character*. Prof. Krąpiec indicates what hinders the acceptance of *Person and Act* as a full philosophical anthropology. In particular, it is "the lack of the analysis of man's spiritual acts from the side of [their] subjective objectivity" (his point principally concerns the cognitive acts).[xci] At the same time, however, he sees the study as "an *aspectual anthropology* ... allowing us to more deeply understand man *as the subject of morality*."[xcii] I think that we can agree with this opinion. A certain aspectuality—precisely the one indicated by Fr. Krąpiec—is presupposed in *Person and Act*. In fact, it is already noted in the title. Fr. Styczeń attempts to answer the question: "Why the cognition of the person precisely through the act?"—Why the method of analyzing human dynamism? Fr. Tischner poses the question of whether the way through value would not be more proper than the way through the act.

When we agree to the aspectuality of *Person and Act*, we nonetheless at the same time need to state that the point here concerns *the aspect that most fully and most deeply reveals man precisely as a person*. The author of *Person and Act* chose this aspect consciously, and not only on account of the fact that it reveals man as a person. In a certain sense it also reveals man both as the *subject* and as the *object of morality*, that is, of personal, or authentically human, *praxis*. It seems that this is primarily the focus of the presentation by Fr. Forycki, who deals with the metaphysics of the fulfillment of the human person contained in *Person and Act*. Hence, he writes: "We can ... pose a question: in what kind of experience are the particular propositions of metaphysics thus understood verified? And it seems that this experience is the one that the author of *Person and Act* tries to take advantage of in his analyses. One of the fundamental *criteria of truthfulness or untruthfulness, rightness or wrongness of metaphysical propositions* is their *suitability in the realization of the human acts*, and through them, and in them, of *the human person*."[xciii] For, as we continue to read, "man becomes more and more free and realizes himself in the true act not so much when he becomes dependent on factual norms (although this too can be expedient for him at a certain stage) as when he attempts to imitate the personalization of the norm of humanity, as the person-ideal becomes for him a call to perform particular acts."[xciv]

It seems that Fr. Tischner draws attention to the same thing by stating that *Person and Act* is more than merely a synthesis that generates the need for a twofold interpretation of the theses of Thomism and phenomenology. Namely, it concerns "the style of Christian *praxis*," at the root of which is the fundamental conviction that "the person is a good."[xcv]

Thus, through the aspect chosen by himself, the author of *Person and Act* was in a sense forced to investigate the reality of the person not only from the side of the subject of morality, but also from the side of the object, which above all is also the person. This objectivity of approach manifested itself in the analysis of consciousness and freedom and distinguished the concept of transcendence and the integration of the person in the act. Certainly, this entails many years of reflection on Kant's ethics, especially on the so-called second imperative, but perhaps even more on the concept of *praxis* in St. Thomas, in which *theoria* finds not only its reflection but also its completion, so that it can in turn be fully found there. We find ourselves, together with the act, in the very center of the dynamism proper to the person; we also indirectly find ourselves at the gates of the fullest theory of the person. Thus, *the attempt to understand the person through the act* was undertaken due to the objective richness of that source. At the same time, as Fr. Styczeń writes, "the act is a way for the person to reveal himself, and its objective reality does not arouse any reservations but puts up the most decisive resistance and limits to the arbitrariness of interpretation."[xcvi]

In his extensive presentation entitled *Człowiek a świadomość* [Man and consciousness], Prof. Półtawski rendered a very fundamental service to the book *Person and Act*; namely, he showed in what way the book is located *at the meeting point between modern*, post-Cartesian anthropology, which attempts to overcome the subjectivism and idealism inherent in it, *and the realistic tradition of classical philosophy*. Among other things, he writes,

> It seems ... that the more modern examinations of living beings, and of man in particular, lead to a dynamic conception that is closer to the Aristotelian-Thomistic than to the Cartesian tradition. If we interpret this classical definition [which grasps man as *animal rationale*—K.W.] in this spirit, then we should say that in every living being there exists a certain original dynamic of the organism, which in its highest human form assumes a new shape and gains a new quality thanks to the capacity for rational action, that is, the conscious choice of an end and means, a capacity characteristic of man. Thus, on the one hand, man uses his innate dynamic of a living being for this new form of life, also changing the original character of this dynamic. On the other hand, there arises a particular tension that is specific to man between the original actuations related to drives and instinct and the free act.[xcvii]

The concept of consciousness on the basis of the dynamism of the person

In his presentation, Prof. Półtawski perceived above all that the entire *concept of consciousness*, which found its expression in *Person and Act*, cannot be correctly considered if separated from an analysis of human dynamism based on a realistic interpretation of man. The analysis of the concept of consciousness in *Person and Act*, undertaken in that way by Prof. Półtawski, in a certain measure, seems to validate this concept. This has particular significance for the author of the study, especially in view of the difficulties that Prof. Stępień and Dr. Grygiel expressed regarding this concept. It seems that Prof. Półtawski's exegesis, which is based on an earlier critical analysis of the Husserlian concept of "pure consciousness," somehow helps in accepting the concept of consciousness that is identified neither with knowledge nor with self-knowledge (this does not mean that it can be separated from them), and which therefore in itself does not demonstrate *intentionality*. This is precisely the principal difficulty seen by Prof. Stępień, who on this point formulates main questions concerning the concept of consciousness sketched in *Person and*

Act. Dr. Grygiel advances the question a bit further, perceiving in this concept, and especially in the reciprocal relations of self-knowledge and consciousness, a "certain play *in infinitum*."[xcviii] It seems, however, that such a "play" is not a necessary consequence of the reciprocal relation of self-knowledge and consciousness in the way outlined in *Person and Act*. Rather, the author sees here a certain continuity of the hidden boundary that runs between the processes of objectivization and subjectivization, ensuring their reciprocal equilibrium within the whole "rational nature" of man.

While accepting the concept of consciousness sketched in *Person and Act* in principle due to the fact that this concept *corresponds to the realistic and dynamic vision of man*, Prof. Półtawski, as we stated, in turn offers his own view on the matter either by distinguishing consciousness in the nounal and adjectival senses or by distinguishing the mirroring function of consciousness from its reflexive function. As a result of his analysis, he writes,

It seems ... that according to the realistic and dynamic concept of man as laid out by the author, the definition of mirroring and subjectivization as two functions of consciousness *is not completely precise* [my emphasis—K.W.], that consciousness understood in a nounal sense must be treated in this understanding as in a sense irreal; the mirroring and subjectivization would constitute the functions of respective real powers and at the same time correspond to two fundamental dimensions of having lived-experience or, as Ey states, to its "vertical" and "horizontal" structure.[xcix]

(Prof. Półtawski devoted a separate article entitled "Czyn a świadomość" [Act and consciousness] to the analogies that occur between the concept of consciousness by the distinguished French psychiatrist Henri Ey and the one in *Person and Act*.)[c] We need to consider whether *reflexivity* does not constitute a specific analogy, characteristic of consciousness, of the intentional act [*akt*], the act that, by penetrating "inside" the act [*czyn*] of the person, would safeguard in this case the consciousness-related form of the lived-experience of the act [*czyn*].[ci]

Inasmuch as Prof. Półtawski, in my opinion, accurately demonstrates in what way the study *Person and Act* situates itself at the meeting point of post-Cartesian anthropology with the realistic and dynamic Aristotelian-Thomistic tradition, Prof. Gogacz cannot agree on several points regarding the expression of the latter in that study. Although in the beginning of his presentation Prof. Gogacz notes that the author of *Person and Act* "by using so many languages in his book and considering the person from the position of so many philosophical disciplines, presents a lucid, exactly clear, and intelligible exposition," he later arrives at the meaning of particular terms and formulations exclusively from the position of so-called "existential Thomism."[cii] The author of *Person and Act*, feeling himself connected with that position, very eagerly accepts these remarks and is ready to improve his text wherever there is an essential need for it. At the same time, however, he asks to consider the fact that this study contains a "plurality of languages and aspects"[ciii] (in the opinions of both the author of *Person and Act* and many participants of the discussion there is chiefly a duality of them) and allows *a fuller analogy of metaphysical terms*, for instance, the terms *actus* and *actus-potentia*. The author of *Person and Act* knows that he performs a kind of *rendering of one philosophical language into another*. This is precisely why he cares that his rendering be well understood. Thus, for example, when he reads the following passage in Prof. Gogacz's presentation, "Because the person expresses himself in the act, because he transcends himself in it, it is the act that most fully becomes an expression of the person and the very person himself. The person has the form of the act. This unity ... is the primacy of action over the subject. The act not only allows us to know the person, the act is a person transcending himself,"[civ] then he must ask whether his rendering was in fact understood correctly.

For it seems that the concept of the transcendence of the person in the act together with its correlative concept of integration, as included in *Person and Act*, sufficiently explains the specificity of the efficacy of the person in its manifold richness—of course, it does so in another language, one that is closer to experience—and at the same time this approach adequately *safeguards the primacy of the subject of action*, that is, the person, *over his action, that is, the act*. At the same time, in light of this primacy, we see the basis for affirming the personal act of existence at the root of all dynamisms of the person and, above all, for affirming the strictly personal dynamism, which is the act itself.

I would like to propose this criterion—and a request to take into consideration the demands of rendering one philosophical language into another—with respect to *the problem of "nature" in relation to "person,"* broached by several discussion participants, but first and foremost by Prof. Kalinowski. It seems that this problem could not be ignored while making this rendering, nor could it be unilaterally solved. Rather, it was fitting to work toward manifesting all that "rational nature" *de facto* is in the person with all its richness and incommensurability in relation to other "natures" in the world of nature. There is a very interesting remark by Dr. Gałkowski, to whom the "notion of human nature, which fundamentally encompasses the whole man, seems ... overly complex."[cv] Dr. Grygiel approaches this problem in yet another way. Nonetheless, the author of *Person and Act* perceives the importance of the reservations put forth at this point by Prof. Kalinowski and fully agrees with them, although this author wants to face the difficulties that are linked with this problem, especially when transitioning from the classical mentality, which is more philosophically stabilized than the contemporary mentality, which is more searching.

In order to conclude the reflections evoked by presentations in the discussion on the topic of rendering the reality of the person in philosophy from one language to another, it is necessary to focus on Dr. Gałkowski's entire presentation. It seems that he emphasizes an issue that is very important for this philosophical rendering when he writes,

Speaking in a most general manner, the analysis of freedom, in fact, just like the entire anthropological analysis, differs in both philosophical orders by a certain fundamental basis, by a fundamental point of reference—they confronted each other precisely in *Person and Act. In Thomism*, this *basis* (a basic concept) is the concept of the person understood as *substance*, as the concrete rational nature of man, whereas *in phenomenology* (and perhaps also in existentialism) this concept is the person as a certain *center* [all emphasis mine—K.W.] or, depending on the view, the highest or deepest layer of man.[cvi]

Personally I think that by moving between the one and the other basic concept in *Person and Act* (and this results from the function of rendering: the translator always remains in the middle between two languages), I attempted as far as possible to reveal one of these concepts through the other, and not to obscure, that is, not to exclude it. I am thankful to Dr. Gałkowski for drawing attention to the problem of freedom in *Person and Act.*

The postulate of the relational concept of the person

One more presentation remains to be considered, namely, the one by Fr. Kuc, which among all these published here contains perhaps the most advanced critique of *Person and Act*, quite a thorough questioning of this study. Fr. Kuc himself describes his presentation as "a constructive opposition to some statements, methodologies, and presuppositions of *Person and Act*."[cvii] I think that what is constructive in this case is *above all the proposition or suggestion* that results from the remarks of our disputant. What he is after is "the philosophy of man that takes for its starting point the relation of persons, which determines human development, and not the co-relation of the person and the act."[cviii] The author of *Person and Act* simply considers the proposition of developing a relative concept of the human person as a task that he assigns to himself. He thinks, however, that a thorough examination of this concept is impossible without at least a simultaneous study of the person based on the "person-act" co-relation.

I think that Fr. Kuc deviates from *Person and Act* in three points, namely, in the understanding of the concept of participation that the study really contains, in a certain simplification of the problem of inter-personal relations, and in the concept of human dynamism. As far as *participation* is concerned, we can agree with the opinion of Fr. Kuc that it is "at least insufficient" as an "interpretation of the existing of the community of persons"[cix] only to the extent that the task of the author in this chapter was not an exhaustive interpretation. His point was above all to emphasize one aspect that Prof. Zdybicka accurately grasps in her presentation: "The human person's ability to act with other persons, by which man realizes the authentic personalistic value: he performs the act and fulfills himself in it."[cx] Emphasizing this aspect is important for the author of *Person and Act* due to various anti-personalistic tendencies of contemporary life and on account of conceptions of the common good that contradict the true good of the person. This aspect is important if we are to prevent a certain oversimplification of *the problem of inter-personal relations*. It seems that the study, *Person and Act*, sufficiently, though concisely, outlines the complexity that takes place in this area due to the fact that relations to other persons do not only have a direct character but also occur through various circles of social life. The point is to ensure that man realizes the authentic personalistic value in all of them.

Returning once more to the issue of the dynamism proper to the human person, the author of *Person and Act* holds that we must thoroughly understand the *dynamism of the "person-act" co-relation* in order to correctly understand and express the *dynamism of the "person-person" relation*, in the case of "person" written both with the lowercase and with the uppercase "P" (i.e., in the relation of man and God). The author of *Person and Act* thinks, for example, that, without a thorough penetration into all that by which the structure of self-governance and self-possession is revealed in the human person, it is impossible to picture correctly and with entire personalistic realism, man's relation to other human persons or to God, which is what above all concerns Fr. Kuc. We can thus say that the analysis of the person based on the "person-act" co-relation contains at the same time an indispensable implication of the relational concept of the person. And the latter cannot be correctly constructed without a thorough understanding of the person in his interior dynamism.

3. The Third Circle: The Concept of the Person as a Basis for Manifold Practice

The participants of the discussion on *Person and Act*, perhaps a majority, note the *theoretical* meaning of the concept of man that is contained in this study. At the same time, however, the *practical meaning* of this concept is brought to light. And so, Fr. Wojciechowski attempts from the position of the anthropologist to view *Person and Act* in a synthetic way and to define the character of this study on the basis of contemporary philosophical anthropology, of which it is characteristic "to grasp man as a bodily-spiritual unity, and not, as used to be done in the past, as a being composed of the soul and the body." Fr. Wojciechowski adds that "this grasp does not remove the difference between the soul and the body, but only presents their relation to each other in a different way."[cxi] At the end of his presentation, he says that the study that proceeds precisely from these presuppositions "enriches the matters concerning the soul and ... leads us further toward a deeper understanding of the spiritual and bodily elements in man."[cxii] According to Fr. Wojciechowski, the author of *Person and Act* "attempts not so much to 'prove' the existence of the spiritual element in man, for he leaves this to metaphysical analyses, as to make it available or draw closer and in a sense 'touch' it in the lived-experience of the person." Fr. Wojciechowski joins the methodological discussion when he further writes that "these analyses constitute a direct preparation for metaphysics to draw the final conclusion."[cxiii]

Otherwise, Sr. Zdybicka, who in the beginning of her presentation briefly recapitulates the theoretical aspects of *Person and Act*, emphasizes right afterward the "practical role" of the book, and does so "in the full context of today's cultural situation." "The truth about the human person," she writes, "is necessary so that one conducts oneself properly, lives in a human way, and responsibly fulfills the human—the personal and social—task. For many reasons, it is more needed and more important today than at any other time."[cxiv] Thus, at the conclusion of the work emerges that which was presupposed at its beginning. Although the issue of morality was "placed outside the parentheses" in the beginning, the *human, personal* praxis, which constitutes the basis of morality, makes itself heard through all theoretical analyses and inquiries—and orients the entire study in its direction.

Three participants of the discussion on *Person and Act*, namely, Bp. Stroba, Prof. Kukołowicz, and Dr. Półtawska, clearly speak along these lines. Each of these presentations has a slightly different dimension and its own character. What they contain is perhaps the announcement of a discussion, rather than a full discussion, in the sphere of various areas of human *praxis*, areas for which the conception of the man-person will always be fundamental. In connection with reading *Person and Act*, Bp. Stroba poses a question "*concerning the consequences that result from it for pastoral ministry* [my emphasis—K.W.], in which, especially after Vatican II, there is an increasing sensibility to personal values."[cxv] For he thinks that "a pastor who experienced the greatness of the person and its role determining the value of man will not be able to forget about it in pastoral ministry."[cxvi] In the name of these reasons, Bp. Stroba sees a need for a symposium "which would take up pastoral aspects" in connection to *Person and Act*.[cxvii]

Prof. Kukołowicz goes *in the direction of pedagogy*, especially in the direction of education in the family. Relying on the concept of man outlined in the discussed study, he sees the possibility "to formulate a program, though a general one, of the complete education of man." He also claims that this study creates an occasion "*to confront the meaning of the family* [my emphasis—K.W.] in the realization of this program." The formulation of this particular program in pedagogy imposes itself because the understanding of the ends of education that proceeds from "seeing man in the somatic-psychical categories," while ignoring his side "whose name is the person," must lead to an incomplete education that cannot be fully humanistic due to being "turned to a 'part' of man."[cxviii]

The most extensive presentation is that of Dr. Półtawska. Properly speaking, it is a small monograph, within which the author links her *conception of the objectivizing psychotherapy* (this is what she called the method of psychotherapy applied by her for many years and proven in experience) *with the concept of the person*, or, more strictly speaking, with the concept of self-possession developed in the study *Person and Act*. In the first sentences of her work, Dr. Półtawska already states the necessity of the concept of man at the foundation of psychotherapy: "Psychotherapy as a method of healing requires being based on some concept of man. The older trends of psychotherapy, which grew from psychoanalysis, seemed unacceptable because the image of man, which was emerging in the interpretation of, for instance, Freud, Adler, and Jung, did not exhaust the observed reality and seemed to be an impoverishment in relation to human existence."[cxix] Furthermore, Dr. Półtawska tries to demonstrate how the concept of man, which—within the method of objectivizing therapy and with this method—"was created ... so to speak in an 'intuitive,' supra-scientific way and based in a certain sense on 'sound reason,'"[cxx] meets with the concept of *Person and Act*, with its particular components, and how it can constitute a system of reference for this unusual area of practice that is psychotherapy.

We must admit that we are transported here into a somewhat different world, being in a sense removed from the disputes carried on by philosophers and methodologists concerning the verification of the concept contained in *Person and Act*. At the same time, we are led *to this verification* by a different path, as it were, which only ostensibly leads in the opposite direction. For ultimately this path, which is traveled by the author who proceeds from her psychotherapeutic practice, runs precisely within the experience of man; it continues in the field that not only particularly requires a theory of man but also to a certain extent tests this theory. By her one sentence about the image of man that emerges in the interpretation of Freud, Adler, or Jung, Dr. Półtawska broached a sphere of discussion about man that is not lesser than the ones discussed by all previous disputants, who appealed either to Plato, Aristotle, and Thomas Aquinas or to Husserl, Heidegger, and Ricoeur. Obviously, the discussion in this area would require the participation of not only philosophers or the representatives of Christian *praxis* having a pastoral character, as indicated by Bp. Stroba, but also other specialists representing the manifold concerns for man—of course, under the condition that they will see, similar to the discussion participants recently listed here, the indispensable *need for the theory of the person at the basis of their* praxis.

※

Concluding this afterword of mine, I wish to express once more the conviction that all who agreed to take part in the discussion rendered an enormous service not only to the author of *Person and Act*, but perhaps also to the entire issue concerning the cognition of man. Of course, this issue is greater than any of its realizations, and, in particular, greater than the one that found its place in the study we have discussed. Nonetheless, our discussion certainly became an occasion for a multilateral deepening of the cognitive subject matter, which constantly shapes philosophical anthropology anew. The *discussion* perhaps very considerably *contributed* to defining the directions of this *novum*, and to establishing, or even specifying, the distinctions "between the new and the old" (or perhaps we ought rather to say "between the new and that which additionally deserves to be called *perenne*"). Perhaps it also contributed to a better identification of the transitions that lead from one to the other in a correct way and that can, and even must, be followed. Assessing the discussion as a whole, I once more arrive at the conclusion that our philosophical thinking about man in which we find ourselves is neither the situation of an irrevocable rift nor the situation of a severance—we can advance, trying to join a plurality of paths into one.

And advance we must. For at the same time the discussion reveals yet again *the whole importance of the problem of man*, its whole specific weight, together with the multilateral pressure of practice on theory. It is necessary to know man better and better, and to understand ever more comprehensively the reality of the person, which is both immanent and relational, "personal" and "communal"—and the paths toward grasping all this richness continue to call us to follow them.

Thus, concluding this discussion, I wish that all that the esteemed participants willed to say in it, together with the study *Person and Act* itself, continues to work for a more thorough cognition of man; that it serves not only the author of this study but also all who will apply themselves to the work of knowing man. Therefore, I am especially thankful for the possibility of publishing the entire discussion in *Analecta Cracoviensia*.

4 ❦ The Personal Structure of Self-Determination

(A Lecture for the Conference on St. Thomas)

1.

By means of this lecture,[cxxi] I do not merely wish to discuss the problem that seems key to me for the concept of the human person and for a creative continuation of the thought of St. Thomas in this field and in relation to manifold trends of contemporary thought, especially phenomenology, but I also wish to inform you of the state of this problem among contemporary Catholic philosophers in Poland. I take as a starting point the discussion that developed after the publication of my book entitled *Person and Act*.[1] This *discussion* was initiated by the meeting of philosophy professors in December 1970 at the Catholic University of Lublin and was carried on through a number of written presentations (about twenty), which are to be published in *Analecta Cracoviensia*.[2] Representatives of several Catholic academic environments, above all those from Lublin, Warsaw, and Kraków, and representing somewhat diverse philosophical orientations, all took part in this discussion. The discussion laid a strong emphasis on the methodological aspect of the problem, though it also did not lack statements concerning the very theory of the person and even the application of this theory in pastoral ministry, pedagogy,

---

1. Karol Wojtyła, *Osoba i czyn* (Kraków: Polskie Towarzystwo Teologiczne, 1969). [Editorial note: The second Polish edition was published in 1985 by Polskie Towarzystwo Teologiczne (Kraków), and the third Polish edition in 1994 and 2000 by Wydawnictwo Towarzystwa Naukowego Katolickiego Uniwersytetu Lubelskiego (Lublin).]
2. *Analecta Cracoviensia* 5–6 (1973–74): 49–272.

and contemporary psychiatry. Simplifying a little, we could say that the Lublin representatives were interested above all in a *methodological clarification of St. Thomas's thought,* and in this case in a certain attempt to translate his thought into modern language. The Kraków representatives, however, were more interested in the *possibilities of a modern reading of St. Thomas's thought* in light of phenomenology properly understood. The study *Person and Act* also evoked certain interest among Marxist writers, who sporadically voiced their opinions about it, though they did not take part in the aforementioned discussion.

Let the above information also serve as a specific introduction to the problem that I intend to present here. The problem of the personal structure of self-determination resides at the very center of my study *Person and Act*. By presenting it here, I wish at the same time to emphasize its connection with the domestic, that is, Polish, philosophical environment, with its interests and creative pursuits, which, in fact, most clearly refer to pan-European currents. Engaging in these currents, Polish science has its own domestic profile, which at times makes itself known to the wide "market" of philosophical output (for instance, as was the case with the works of the logicians from the Lviv-Warsaw school or with the phenomenology of Roman Ingarden from Kraków), though it—in a sense, on an everyday basis—shapes Polish intellectual culture in its own native country.

2.

After this introductory remark, I turn to the subject matter at hand. In order to investigate the personal structure of self-determination, we must proceed from the broadly understood *experience of man*. The experience of man, of course, may be understood phenomenalistically, but this understanding presupposes a theory of cognition that assumes the interior split of cognition between the functions of the senses and of the mind as well as between sensory and conceptual contents. Without denying the distinctiveness of these functions and their corresponding contents, we must state that human cognition constitutes an organic (and not merely an organizational) unity. The first and fundamental stage of human knowing is always experience, which, in accord with the dual structure of the knowing subject, contains not only the sensory but also the intellectual element. For this reason, we can say that human experience is already always *some understanding*. Thereby, it is also the beginning of the whole process of understanding, which is shaped in its own proper ways, but always in relation to that first stage, that is, experience. Without this there seems to be no possibility for consistent realism in philosophy or in science. Then the image of the world we create in them could be fundamentally inconsistent with reality.

The same relates to man as the object of philosophical anthropology. It is in experience that we must seek the basis for understanding man—and a full and comprehensive experience at that, which is free from any systemic a priori. Concerning the analysis of the personal structure of self-determination, its starting point is *the experience of man*, and in particular the *human act*, the experience that contains the "lived-experience" of moral good and evil as the essential and particularly important moment, which we can describe separately as the *experience of morality*. Properly speaking, we can never completely separate these two experiences—of man and of morality—although in this whole process of reflection we can, in turn, concern ourselves with one more than the other. In the former case, philosophical reflection will lead us in the direction of anthropology, whereas, in the latter case, in the direction of ethics.

The experience of the human act is concentrated on the *lived-experience* of the fact "*I act*." This fact is completely original, unique, and unrepeatable every time. Nonetheless, all facts of the type "I act" contain their proper sameness both in the lived-experience of the same person and in intersubjective dimensions. The lived-experience of the fact "I act" is distinguished from all other facts, which only "happen" in the personal subject. This clear diversification of the "happening" in the subject and the "acting" of the subject—that is, the act—allows us, in turn, to grasp the moment that decisively distinguishes action in the integral experience of man, that is, the act of the person from all that only happens in him. *We call this moment self-determination.*

The first description of self-determination in the experience of the human act contains the *grasp of the efficacy of the personal "I"*: "I act" means "I am the efficient cause" of my action, of the actualization of the subject. This is different in the case of all that only "happens" in me, because then the lived-experience of the efficacy of the personal "I" does not occur. The grasp of the efficacy of the acting subject in relation to his action is closely linked with the *grasp of his responsibility* for action, a fact that especially concerns the axiological and ethical content of the act. All this belongs organically, as it were, to the experience of self-determination, though this is manifested in it to varying degrees. This depends—one could say—on the personal maturity of the act. The greater this maturity, the more clearly the acting subject experiences self-determination. The greater the consciousness of action and the consciousness of value, the more clearly the man-subject experiences self-determination. The more clearly he experiences self-determination, the more clearly does his own efficacy and responsibility appear in lived-experience and in consciousness.

Self-determination as a property of the human act, which is manifested in experience, *draws the attention of the analyst of this act to the moment of the will* as a power of the person. The will is the power of the person's self-determination, as is evident by closer inspection of its acts, both the so-called simple act of the will ("I will") and the developed act, or so-called "process" of the will (to use the terminology of psychologists such as Ach, Michotte, or Fr. Dybowski in Poland).[3] Self-determination is manifested both in the elementary volition ("I will") and in choice and decision, which are the fruit of man's cognition of values, deliberation of motives, and sometimes their struggling and fighting inside man. When comparing the inquiries of the aforementioned psychologists of the will with the concept of the developed and mature act of the will that we find in St. Thomas, we observe quite a significant convergence of positions.

At this point, however, we are not concerned with the comparative analysis of the act of the will. By stating that the will is the power of self-determination, we do not mean the will itself in any methodical isolation, which would aim at penetrating its own dynamic. Here we have the whole person in mind by necessity. The *self-determination* of the person is accomplished *through acts of the will* as a central power of the human soul. However, self-determination is not identified with acts of

---

3. See, for instance, Mieczysław Dybowski, *Zależność wykonania od cech procesu woli* (Warsaw: Drukarnia Instytutu Głuchoniemych i Ociemniałych 1926), and Dybowski, *Działanie woli: Na tle badań eksperymentalnych* (Poznań: Księgarnia Akademicka, 1946).

the will in any form they have, because it is a *property of the person himself*. At this point—even though our reflection is still keeping to the phenomenological plane of experience—what becomes particularly clear in this light is St. Thomas's distinction between substance and accident, between the soul and its power, namely, the will. The analysis here conducted, though brief, allows us to perceive that self-determination is a property of the person, of whom the well-known definition speaks: "*rationalis naturae individua* substantia." However, this property is realized through the will, which is a power-accident. *Self-determination is the essence of the freedom of man.* It is not limited in man to the accidental dimension only, but belongs to the substantial dimension of the person: it is the freedom of man and not only the freedom of the will in man, though undoubtedly the freedom of man through the will.

3.

When we state that self-determination given in the integral experience of man directs our analysis toward the act of the will, then at the same time we must notice that the analysis that grasps this reality in the phenomenological categories of the intentional act is insufficient. Understanding the will merely as a "volition" that is directed to its proper object—a value or an end—does not fully explain the will's specific dynamic. Such an analysis indicates only one aspect of the will and only one aspect of the transcendence proper to it. The act of the will is an *active orientation* of the subject, that is, of the power, toward the object, that is, the value willed as the end and in this way constituting the object strived for. This active orientation (which, *nota bene*, distinguishes the act of the will from various "volitions" or "wants" happening in the subject) also contains the transcendence of this subject toward the value, that is, the end; the subject actively "goes out," as it were, beyond himself toward this value, while still remaining the "I" that specifically decides to go toward the value. We can call this transcendence horizontal. It seems that the analysis of the act of the will in psychology is in some sense exhausted in the aspect of *intentionality* and "*horizontal*" *transcendence*. In the transmission of the teaching of St. Thomas concerning the act of the will, this aspect was often presented in a somewhat unilateral way.

It seems, however, that with the help of the integral experience of man and his act, we can more fully grasp the dynamism of the will, thereby drawing closer to the totality of the conceptions inherited from St. Thomas. Precisely the reality of self-determination tells us about it. For self-determination expresses the fact that what occurs in the act of the will is not only an active orientation of the subject toward a value. Something more is contained in it, namely, *man*, by *orienting* himself by this act *toward* a given *value*, not only determines this orientation, but he also *determines himself* through this orientation. The concept of self-determination contains more than the concept of efficacy: man is not only the agent of his acts, but through these acts he is in some way a "maker of himself" at the same time. Becoming accompanies action—moreover, it is organically joined to action. Therefore, self-determination, and not only the very efficacy of the personal "I," explains the *realness and the personal character of moral values*; it explains the realness of the fact that through his acts, *man becomes "good" or "evil"*—and since he became, he also is "good" or "evil" *precisely as man*, as was grasped in an excellent way by St. Thomas.[4]

If we continued to analyze the will as an intentional act, assuming only its horizontal transcendence, then this realism and personal character of moral values, of good and evil in man, would remain completely inexplicable. Thus, we must accept the personal structure of self-determination: this self-determination, which is expressed in particular volitions, surpasses the pure intentionality of these volitions (it does not matter whether these are simple volitions or complex processes of the will). Intentionality indicates in a sense the external, toward the object, which is a value and thus attracts the will to itself. Self-determination, however, indicates in a sense the internal, the subject, who through the willing of a given value, through the choice of it, at the same time defines himself as a value, for he becomes "good" or "evil." Man determines

---

4. See what St. Thomas says about moral habits: "Ab huiusmodi habitibus *simpliciter* dicitur homo bonum *operari, et esse* bonus." [From having habits of the latter sort, man is said *simply* to *do* good, and to *be* good (Wojtyła's emphasis).] *Summa theologiae* I-II, q. 56, a. 3. (*Simpliciter* here means "fundamentally," thus "as man" and not merely "in some respect.") We read further on in the same place: "Non enim dicitur simpliciter aliquis homo bonus, ex hoc quod est sciens vel artifex, sed dicitur bonus solum secundum quid, puta bonus grammaticus, aut bonus faber." [For through being gifted in science or art, a man is said to be good, not simply, but relatively; for instance, a good grammarian, or a good smith.]

not only his action but also himself in view of the most essential quality. In this way, the *becoming of man as man corresponds to self-determination.* (Thanks to this, he becomes more "somebody" in the personal-ethical sense, since in the ontic sense he is "somebody" from the very beginning. Let us add here that the Polish pronoun *ktoś* [somebody] as the opposite of the pronoun *coś* [something] most succinctly grasps the personal distinctness of man.)

It seems that the experience of self-determination—with its fundamentally phenomenological character—introduces us to a fuller understanding of the reality that St. Thomas called *actus humanus* or *voluntarium*. For the personal structure of self-determination turns out to be a condition of the full understanding of what the phenomenon "I act" contains. If we accept, as does St. Thomas, the full realness of moral values in the object "man," then at the same time we must accept that the person as the subject in the act of self-determination stands as an "object" with respect to himself. Self-determination reveals the personality of the structure inside the person; being ontically one, he is in his dynamism somebody specifically complex; the person-subject is then revealed in the relation to the person-object. *Self-determination* in a sense "*objectivizes*" *the subject* acting in his own action. This objectivization of the person is by no means his "reification"; the person cannot become a thing for himself, although he is for himself so to speak an inseparable "partner." In this sense, he is the first and fundamental object that he himself determines. Precisely in this determination of himself, his subjectivity is revealed in its deepest possibilities, in the essential qualifications that attest to what is human (*humanum*) and personal at the same time.

If self-determination reveals that man is the object of his own subject, it thereby simultaneously manifests a particular *complexity, which is proper to man as a person.* St. Thomas, and with him the whole tradition of Christian thought, emphasizes that "*persona est sui iuris et alteri incommunicabilis.*" Following this experience of man, the key moment of which is self-determination, we must acknowledge the direct evidentness of these traditional formulations. For self-determination reveals the *structure of self-possession and self-governance* as proper to the person. If man determines himself, then he must possess himself and govern himself. These realities explain each other because they contain each other. Each of them reveals the specific complexity that is proper to man as a person. (*Nota bene*, the Thomistic adage also stresses that the point concerns the person: "persona *est sui iuris et alteri incommunicabilis.*") The point concerns not the metaphysical complexity of the soul and body (*materia prima + forma substantialis*), which is proper to man as a being, but the *complexity that is more "phenomenological."* The phenomenological experience reveals man as one who possesses himself and at the same time is possessed by himself. It also reveals him as one who governs himself and at the same time remains under his own governance. The one and the other are revealed through self-determination, are its implication, and enrich its content. Through self-possession and self-governance, the personal structure of self-determination is brought to light in all its proper fullness.

By determining himself—and this is accomplished through the act of the will—man becomes conscious and at the same time witnesses to others that he possesses himself and governs himself. In this way *human acts provide us with a specific insight into the structure of the person*. From the perspective of the method, this structure presents itself to us as a group of necessary conditions for what is visually, and thus experientially, given to us to take place. Thanks to self-determination, man experiences that he is a person in a relatively direct way. Of course, the path from this experience to the understanding that would be a full theory of the person must lead through metaphysical analysis. Among other things, this analysis will allow us to situate the personal structure of self-determination in ontic contingency, in the limitations of the human being. Nevertheless, experience is the indispensable beginning of this entire cognitive path, while the lived-experience of self-determination seems to be the central point of that beginning. At any rate, if full affirmation of the personal value of human acts requires a theory of the person as its basis, then the construction of that theory seems impossible without an analytical penetration into the dynamic reality of the act and, above all, into the structure of self-determination that is essential to that act and that is, in a sense, revealed as a personal structure from the beginning.

4.

In the pastoral constitution of Vatican II we read among other things that "Man, *who is the only creature on earth which God willed for itself, cannot fully find himself except through a sincere gift of self.*"[5] With these words, the document of the most recent council seems in a sense to *summarize* the centuries-old *traditions and pursuits of Christian anthropology*, the anthropology for which divine revelation became the liberating light. The anthropology of St. Thomas Aquinas is deeply seated in the current of this tradition and is, at the same time, open to all achievements of human thought, which from various sides complement the concept of the person developed within Thomistic thought, thus confirming the realistic character of that concept. These quoted words of Vatican II seem to emphasize above all the axiological aspect, for they speak of the person who is a particular value in himself, and for this reason he is particularly enabled for the gift of self. However, *under* this *axiological aspect*, the ontological aspect, which is deeper than the other, can be easily revealed. The ontology of the person suggested by the quoted text seems again to meet closely with the experience to which we referred here. In other words, if we want to fully accept the truth about the human person manifested by *Gaudium et spes*, we must investigate once again the personal structure of self-determination.

As we already stated above, the human person is revealed to us in the experience of self-determination as a specific structure of self-possession and self-governance. The one and the other, however, do not mean a closing in on oneself. Quite the contrary: both *self-possession and self-governance denote a particular disposition for a "gift of self,"* and precisely for a "sincere" gift.[cxxii] For only the one who possesses himself can give himself, and give himself sincerely at that. And only the one who governs himself can make of himself a gift, again, a sincere gift. The problem of sincerity certainly deserves a separate analysis, which we do not undertake here. The understanding of the person in the categories of the gift, which was highlighted anew by the teaching of Vatican II, seems to reach even deeper into the dimensions revealed by the present analysis. It

---

5. Second Vatican Council, Pastoral Constitution on the Church in the Modern World *Gaudium et spes* (December 7, 1965) [Vatican translation].

seems to reveal the personal structure of self-determination even further.

For only *the one who can determine himself*—as we already attempted to outline—*can also become a gift for others*. The conciliar statement that "man ... cannot fully find himself except through a sincere gift of self" allows us to conclude that precisely when man becomes a gift for others does he most fully become himself. The "law of the gift," to put it this way, is inscribed in the depth of the dynamic structure of the person. The text of Vatican II certainly draws from the inspiration of revelation and sketches this particular image of the man-person in its light. We can say that this is the image in which the person becomes defined both as a being willed by God "for its own sake" and as a being oriented "toward" others. However, this relational image of the person necessarily presupposes the immanent (and indirectly "substantial") image, which is revealed to us through analysis of the personal structure of self-determination.

In this last point, by necessity we limited ourselves to indicating the problem. In concluding the present discourse on the personal structure of self-determination, we ought to add that by necessity it was concise and passed over an entire series of elements deserving a broader analysis (which does take place in the study *Person and Act*, mentioned in the beginning). However, even in this concise discourse, we attempted to manifest the *very current need for confrontation* of the metaphysical conception of the person, which we encounter in St. Thomas and in the traditions of Thomistic philosophy, with the integral experience of man. By this confrontation, the cognitive sources, from which the Angelic Doctor drew his metaphysical notions, are becoming more widely open. In this instance, all the richness contained in these sources and the possibilities to draw from them are also revealed. At the same time, both the possibilities of meeting with contemporary thought and the points of inevitable divergence from it in the name of the truth about reality are perhaps better revealed.

5 ❊ The Person

Subject and Community

Introductory Information

The totality of the reflections that I intend to present in this work[cxxiii] refers to my study *Person and Act* and is rooted in it.[1] On the basis of the analyses conducted there, I intend to investigate anew the connection that occurs between the subjectivity of the man-person and the structure of the human community. This problem was already sketched out in *Person and Act*, especially in the last part of that work entitled "Participation." Here I intend to somewhat expand that outline, starting from the conception of the person that was quite widely developed in that previous study of mine. Many analyses conducted in *Person and Act* remain closely connected to the problem of the subjectivity of the human person, and we can even say that all of them help us to understand and manifest it in some way. It is difficult to reproduce these analyses here in their entirety. Some fragments could be assembled as an appendix to our present reflections. In addition, we should mention the discussion that was conducted in connection with *Person and Act* at a certain meeting of philosophy professors. All the statements from that discussion constitute an extensive contribution to Polish philosophical anthropology, and that is the reason for their publication in *Analecta Cracoviensia*.[2]

---

1. [15a] Karol Wojtyła, *Osoba i czyn* (Kraków: Polskie Towarzystwo Teologiczne, 1969) [henceforth cited in notes as *Person and Act*].[15b] [Editorial note: The second Polish edition was published in 1985 by Polskie Towarzystwo Teologiczne (Kraków), and the third Polish edition in 1994 and 2000 by Wydawnictwo Towarzystwa Naukowego Katolickiego Uniwersytetu Lubelskiego (Lublin).]

2. *Analecta Cracoviensia* 5–6 (1973–74): 49–263: Andrzej Szostek, "Dyskusja nad dziełem Kardynała Karola Wojtyły 'Osoba i czyn': Wprowadzenie," 49–51; Karol Wojtyła, "Wypowiedź wstępna

The problem of man's subjectivity is of great philosophical significance today.[1a] On the basis of this problem, manifold cognitive tendencies, presuppositions, and orientations compete with one another, often conferring diametrically different forms and senses of it. The philosophy of consciousness seems to suggest that it only just discovered the human subject. The philosophy of being is ready to demonstrate that, quite the contrary, purely consciousness-related analysis must, as a result, lead to the annihilation of that subject. There exists a need to find a right boundary, according to which the phenomenological analyses generated from presuppositions of the philosophy of consciousness will start to work toward the enrichment of the realistic image of the person. Also, a need exists to authenticate the foundations of such a philosophy of the person.

Additionally, the problem of the subjectivity of the person, and in particular this problem in relation to the human community, imposes itself today as *one of the central worldview problems* that lie *at the very foundations of human praxis*, at the foundations of morality (and thus ethics), and at the foundations of culture, civilization, and politics. What comes to light here is philosophy in its essential function, philosophy as an expression of fundamental understandings and ultimate substantiations. The need for such understandings and substantiations constantly accom-

---

w czasie dyskusji nad 'Osobą i czynem' w Katolickim Uniwersytecie Lubelskim dnia 16 grudnia 1970 r.," 53–55; Mieczysław Albert Krąpiec, "Książka Kardynała Karola Wojtyły monografią osoby jako podmiotu moralności," 57–61; Jerzy Kalinowski, "Metafizyka i fenomenologia osoby ludzkiej: Pytania wywołane przez 'Osobę i czyn,'" 63–71; Stanisław Kamiński, "Jak filozofować o człowieku?" 73–79; Kazimierz Kłósak, "Teoria doświadczenia człowieka w ujęciu Kardynała Karola Wojtyły," 81–84; Józef Tischner, "Metodologiczna strona dzieła 'Osoba i czyn,'" 85–89; Marian Jaworski, "Koncepcja antropologii filozoficznej w ujęciu Kardynała Karola Wojtyły (próba odczytania w oparciu o studium 'Osoba i czyn')," 91–106; Tadeusz Styczeń, "Metoda antropologii filozoficznej w 'Osobie i czynie' Kardynała Karola Wojtyły," 107–15; Roman Forycki, "Antropologia w ujęciu Kardynała Karola Wojtyły (na podstawie książki 'Osoba i czyn,' Kraków 1969)," 117–24; Mieczysław Gogacz, "Hermeneutyka 'Osoby i czynu' (recenzja książki Księdza Kardynała Wojtyły 'Osoba i czyn,' Kraków 1969)," 125–38; Stanisław Grygiel, "Hermeneutyka czynu oraz nowy model świadomości," 139–51; Antoni B. Stępień, "Fenomenologia tomizująca w książce 'Osoba i czyn,'" 153–57; Andrzej Półtawski, "Człowiek a świadomość (w związku z książką Kardynała Karola Wojtyły 'Osoba i czyn')," 159–75; Jerzy W. Gałkowski, "Natura, osoba, wolność," 177–82; Leszek Kuc, "Uczestnictwo w człowieczeństwie 'innych'?" 183–90; Tadeusz Wojciechowski, "Jedność duchowo-cielesna człowieka w książce 'Osoba i czyn,'" 191–99; Zofia Józefa Zdybicka, "Praktyczne aspekty dociekań przedstawionych w dziele 'Osoba i czyn,'" 201–5; Jerzy Stroba, "Refleksje duszpasterskie," 207–9; Teresa Kukołowicz, "'Osoba i czyn' a wychowanie w rodzinie," 211–21; Wanda Półtawska, "Koncepcja samoposiadania—podstawą psychoterapii obiektywizującej (w świetle książki Kardynała Karola Wojtyły 'Osoba i czyn')," 223–41; Karol Wojtyła, "Słowo końcowe," 243–63.

panies man's existence on earth and is particularly intensified in certain moments of history. These are the moments of great breakthroughs and confrontations. To such moments also belongs the contemporary moment. It is a time of a great dispute about man, a dispute about the very sense of his existence and thus about the nature and meaning of his being. It is not for the first time that *Christian philosophy* faces *a materialistic interpretation*, but it is the first time that this interpretation has so many means at its disposal and expresses itself in so many currents. This is precisely the case in Poland with respect to its entire political reality, which grew from Marxism, from dialectic materialism, and which tries to win minds to it.

It is known that such situations in history have already contributed many times to a more thorough rethinking of the totality of Christian truth and its particular elements. It is so in our case. The truth about man gains a clearly privileged place in the entire process of which we speak. Already almost twenty years ago in the context of the discussion in Poland concerning the worldview, it became clear that what remains at the center of it is not cosmology or the philosophy of nature [*przyroda*] alone, but precisely philosophical anthropology and ethics: *the great and fundamental dispute about man.*

From the viewpoint of Christian philosophy as well as theology, this turn of events (which also found its expression in the entire magisterium of the Second Vatican Council, and especially in the constitution *Gaudium et spes*) favors an undertaking of the topic of the human person from different sides. (The author in some sense constantly remains in this vein through his publications.)[3] The present work also grows out of the same substratum.

---

3. See, for example, "Osobowa struktura samostanowienia," a lecture given on March 12, 1974, at the 17th Philosophical Week of the Catholic University of Lublin entitled "The Relevance of Thomism: On the 700th Anniversary of St. Thomas's Death." This lecture was also given on April 23, 1974, in Naples at the conference for the 700th anniversary of St. Thomas's death (appearing in the records of the conference as "The Personal Structure of Self-Determination"), organized by the Order of Preachers and held on April 17–24, 1974, in Rome and Naples [see p. 457 in this volume]. See also the lecture given at this conference entitled "Act and Lived-Experience" in the "Phenomenology and Metaphysics" section. Also see the author's earlier works such as "Problem oderwania przeżycia od aktu w etyce na tle poglądów Kanta i Schelera," *Roczniki filozoficzne* 5, no. 3 (1955–57): 113–40. [16a]

1. Between *Suppositum* and the Human "I" (Reflections on the Subjectivity of the Person)

The experience of man

In the field of experience, man appears as a particular *suppositum* and at the same time as a concrete "I," every time unique and unrepeatable. This is the experience of man in the twofold sense, for he who experiences is man and he whom the subject of experience experiences is man as well—man as both a subject and an object. His subjectivity belongs to the essence of experience, for experience is always an experience of "something" or "somebody" (as is the case in the experience of man). The tendency to retreat toward the "pure subjectivity" of experience is characteristic of the philosophy of consciousness, of which we shall speak a little later. Yet what belongs to the essence of experience is its objectivity, and hence *the man-subject is given in experience also in an objective way*. Experience in a sense displaces the concept of "pure consciousness" in human cognition, or rather it summons to the dimensions of objective reality all that, on the basis of this concept, deepens our knowledge of man.

In experience man is given to us as the one who exists (is) and acts. "I" am also such a man, as is any "other" outside me. The experience of existing (being) and acting is shared by all people, including me ("I"), and at the same time all "others" and the "I" are the object of this experience. This happens in various ways because "I" experience myself as existing (being) and acting differently from all other people, and in turn the same can be said about every "other" as a concrete "I." It is clear, however, that I must include both the others and my own "I" in the whole process of understanding man. In this process I can proceed from the "others" or from the "I." Taking this "I" into particular consideration is important especially for a full understanding of man's subjectivity, because *in no other object of* the *experience* of man *are the elements constitutive to this subjectivity given to me* in so direct and manifest way *as in my own "I."*[4]

---

4. See Mieczysław Albert Krąpiec, *Ja—człowiek: Zarys antropologii filozoficznej* (Lublin: Towarzystwo Naukowe Katolickiego Uniwersytetu Lubelskiego, 1974). In this work, the "I" understood as a subsisting subject is located at the starting point and constitutes the basis of philosophical

In creating the image of the person-subject based on the experience of man, a great deal is drawn from the experience of one's own "I," but never in isolation from the "others" or in opposition to them. All analyses aimed at elucidating human subjectivity have their "categorial" boundaries, which we cannot cross and from which we cannot completely separate ourselves. They are closely linked with the objectivity of experience. We depart from this objectivity of experience, which allows us to understand and explain fully the subjectivity of man, when we begin to accept *"pure consciousness" or the "pure subject"*—but then we do not interpret the real subjectivity of man any longer.

We do not yet interpret this subjectivity when we concern ourselves in a purely "phenomenal" or "symptomatic" way with particular functions or even selected structural wholes in man, as is done by various *particular sciences* that occupy themselves with man under different aspects. We cannot deny that in this way they gather *more and more "material"* for understanding the man-person and the subjectivity proper to him. However, they do not yet constitute this understanding itself. Taking into account the constant increase of the empirical knowledge of man, we ought to note a constant necessity for the philosophical renewing (in a sense "reinterpreting") of the man-person's image in all its essential fabric. This necessity also increases through all the richness of phenomenological analyses, which, in the name of the objectivity of experience, require to be transferred, as it were, from the plane of consciousness and integration into the full reality of the person. We must admit that these analyses are particularly valuable and fertile for the entire process of understanding and explaining the subjectivity of the person.

This state of inquiries about man, and particularly the quite thoroughly clarified and diversified relation to the fundamental source of knowing him that is the entire and comprehensive experience of man, allow us to fully accept and at the same time to understand the old concept of *suppositum* in a new way. If we say that man—both every "other" as well as "I"—is given in experience as a *suppositum*, then we state

---

anthropology. The author gives us an outline of a full philosophy of man. In the study *Person and Act*, the analyses connected with the experience of the human "I" constitute rather the basis of man's revelation as a person. We encounter yet another approach in the work of Fr. Józef Tischner, "Aksjologiczne podstawy doświadczenia 'ja' jako całości cielesno-przestrzennej," in *Logos i ethos: Rozprawy filozoficzne* (Kraków: Polskie Towarzystwo Teologiczne, 1971), 33–82.

that the entire experience of man, which reveals him to us as the one who exists, lives, and acts, allows and bids us to think correctly about him as the subject of his own existence and action. Precisely this is contained in the concept of *suppositum*. This concept *is used to state the subjectivity of man in the metaphysical sense*. When we say "metaphysical," we mean not so much "extra-phenomenal" but "through-phenomenal," that is, "trans-phenomenal." For through all "phenomena," that is, manifestations, which in experience comprise the totality of man as the one who exists (is) and acts, we perceive—in a sense we must perceive—the subject of this existence and action. Or rather we perceive that man is—must be—precisely this "sub-ject," because without this, the entire being and acting that is given to us in experience as "his" being and acting (in the concrete case of my own "I" as "my" being and acting) could not be "his" ("my") being and acting. The metaphysical subjectivity, that is, *suppositum, as the transphenomenal and thereby precisely fundamental expression of the experience of man* is at the same time a guarantee of the identity of this man in being and acting.

By stating that *suppositum* constitutes the fundamental expression of the entire experience of man, we want to state at the same time that this expression is *in a sense inviolable*—experience cannot be separated from it—and that it is also *open* to everything that the experience of man, and in particular the experience of one's own "I," can contribute to the understanding of the subjectivity of the person. For although we accept the specificity and distinctness of metaphysical cognition, we defend ourselves against severing it from all the rest of human cognition. In fact, all cognition is at its root metaphysical—it touches a being—and this cannot obscure the significance of particular aspects of this being for understanding it in all its richness.

Operari sequitur esse

The discovery of the human *suppositum*, that is, of the subjectivity of man in the metaphysical sense, contains at the same time a fundamental grasp of the relation between existence and action. This relation is expressed by the philosophical adage *"operari sequitur esse."*[5] Despite

---

5. [17a][18a] Prof. Mieczysław Gogacz also took part in the discussion on *Person and Act*. Gogacz returns to this same problem in the interdisciplinary session organized by the Academy of Catholic

the fact that its tone seems to indicate a unilateral relation, namely, the causal dependence of action on existence, this adage conceals in itself yet another relation between *operari* and *esse*. For since *operari* results from *esse*, it constitutes at the same time—proceeding in the opposite direction—the most proper way to know this *esse*. Thus, this dependence is gnoseological. In this way we draw from the human *operari* the cognition not only of the fact that *man is its "sub-ject,"* but also *who man is as the subject of his action*. *Operari*, that is, the integrally understood dynamism of man, allows us to better and more properly understand the subjectivity of man. The point here is not only *suppositum* as the subject in the metaphysical sense, but also, on the basis of *suppositum* thus understood, everything through which man is an individual and personal subject.

The dynamism proper to man is complex and diversified. Disregarding other distinctions for the time being, we must state that the totality of human dynamism (*operari* in the broadest sense of the word) consists of all that in different ways only *"happens"* in man in addition to what man *"does"* [*działa*] or more strictly speaking what he "does by acts" [*czyni*]. The act is a separate form of the human *operari*, and above all man reveals himself as a person in and through it. A full analysis of man's dynamism, not only of acts but also of all that "happens" in him—here we mean both the somatic and the psychical (the somatic-reactive and

---

Theology on February 15–16, 1973, on the topic of "The Hermeneutics of Theological Anthropology." Mieczysław Gogacz, "Filozofia człowieka wobec teologii," *Studia theologica Varsaviensia* 12, no. 1 (1974): 177–92. In addition, Gogacz published his various statements in the book *Wokół problemu osoby* (Warsaw: Pax, 1974), which also contains the text printed in *Analecta Cracoviensia* from the discussion on *Person and Act*. Following all these statements and referring to what was already said in the afterword ["Słowo końcowe"] to the discussion in relation to "Hermeneutyka 'Osoby i czynu,'" the author of *Person and Act* sees the need to respond to the position held by Prof. Gogacz. For it seems that the fundamental concept of *Person and Act* was wrongly read by him and is wrongly interpreted, there being many traces of this especially in the book *Wokół problemu osoby*. In the text published in *Studia theologica Varsaviensia* on the topic of *Person and Act*, we read: "According to the book, the person is a *subject* [my emphasis—K.W.] of conscious and creative activities of man, of his acts manifesting the person outwardly" (190). However, according to the author of *Person and Act*, the person is above all *the agent of the act* (see chapter 2, "The Analysis of Efficacy in Relation to the Dynamism of Man").[17b] The entire study *Person and Act* is in its fundamental conception based on the conviction that *operari sequitur esse*; the act of personal existence finds its immediate consequences in the action of the person (that is, in his act). Therefore, the act is on its part the basis for the revelation and understanding of the person. Without expressing an opinion on the schemas within which Mieczysław Gogacz divides the notions of the person into existentialistic and essentialistic, I—as in the afterword [to the discussion on *Person and Act*]—question only the correctness of his reading of *Person and Act*.[18b]

psycho-emotive) dimensions[6]—would lead us to a full image of human subjectivity. For *the subjectivity of man corresponds* beyond a doubt *to the complexity of his nature, and thus it is, so to speak, multi-layered.* A more precise analysis conducted on the basis of the relation *"operari sequitur esse"* and always on the basis of the human *suppositum*, that is, the metaphysical subjectivity, would help to show in what the somatic and the psychical subjectivity of man consist—in what way the man-person is a subject through his body and his psyche. We must at least mention the enormous significance of the entire human emotivity for the shaping of concrete human subjectivity, for what sort of subject a concrete man is, as both an individual and a person.

When, however, we forgo this entire group of analyses, we do this with the conviction that what has the fundamental and *essential significance* for knowing the subjectivity of the man-person *is above all* the form of the human *operari* that is the *"act"*: man's conscious action in which the freedom belonging to the human person is both expressed and concretized. In this way, remaining still on the ground of *suppositum*—of course—*humanum*, which is to say, subjectivity in the metaphysical and fundamental sense, we can arrive at *grasping and explaining subjectivity* in the sense proper to man, that is, *in the personal sense*. For the metaphysical subjectivity *suppositum* belongs to everything that in some way exists and acts; it belongs to various beings existing and acting in accord with the analogy of proportionality. But the subjectivity proper to man, that is, personal subjectivity, is more fittingly described by taking for its basis the totality of human dynamism (*operari*) and above all that which is, strictly speaking, the action of man as a person, that is, the act.

Starting with the act, we will have to state that the personal subjectivity of man is a specific and rich structure, which is revealed through an analysis of the act, conducted in the most comprehensive way possible. Man, as a person, is constituted in the metaphysical sense as a being through his own *suppositum*: he is the one who exists and acts from the beginning, though the fully human action (*actus humanus*), that is, the act, appears only at a certain stage of his development. This is a consequence of the complexity of nature. The spiritual element of

---

6. See Wojtyła, *Person and Act*, part 3, "The Integration of the Person in the Act," chapter 5, "Integration and Somaticity," and chapter 6, "Integration and the Psyche."

cognition-consciousness and freedom-self-determination gradually takes over the somatic and originally psychical layers of humanity. The entire development of the individual clearly progresses toward the revelation of the person and his proper subjectivity in the human *suppositum*. Thus, it is in a sense on the foundation of this *suppositum* that *the concrete human "I" gradually reveals and at the same constitutes itself*—it reveals itself also by constituting itself.

The human "I" constitutes itself precisely through acts—through *operari* proper to man as a person. It also constitutes itself through the totality of the psycho-somatic dynamism, through the entire sphere of *operari* that only "happens" in the subject, but which also somehow shapes the subjectivity of the individual. Of course, the human "I" constitutes itself through all this, thanks to the fact that it was already and is fundamentally and principally constituted as a *suppositum*. The *suppositum humanum*, in a sense, must reveal itself as the human "I"—the metaphysical subjectivity as the personal subjectivity.

This "must" is the strongest argument for the metaphysical conception of nature. Man is a person "by nature." It is "by nature" that the subjectivity proper to the person belongs to him. The fact that the human *suppositum*, the metaphysical subjectivity, *in certain cases does not manifest the features of personal subjectivity* (these are the cases of psycho-somatic or purely psychical underdevelopment, in which the normal human "I" was not formed or was deformed) does not allow us to question the very foundations of this subjectivity, for they inhere in the essentially human *suppositum*.

Nonetheless, we shall continue to concern ourselves with the normally shaped human "I," for it reveals to us the correct features of the subjectivity proper to the person.

Consciousness and lived-experience

When indicating the act as the form of the dynamism proper to man, of the human *operari*, which above all allows us to know man as a personal subject, we must note at once that it (i.e., the act) is conscious action. While attempting to understand the subjectivity of the person precisely through the act, we must realize what particular significance consciousness has for this subjectivity. We must admit that this aspect was not developed in the scholastic tradition, in which the *actus humanus* was submitted to a detailed analysis above all under the aspect of *voluntarium*. Clearly, *voluntarium* could occur only on the basis of understanding—above all, the understanding of the good and the end—because *voluntas* is nothing else but *appetitus intellectivus* expressed in *liberum arbitrium*, although *consciousness is not the ordinary understanding* that directs the will and action. In turn, the aspect of consciousness received a kind of absolutization since the time of Descartes, and which in contemporary times entered phenomenology through Husserl. The gnoseological approach in philosophy displaced the metaphysical approach. A being is constituted in consciousness and in a sense through consciousness, whereas *the reality of the person requires the reinstatement of the concept of a conscious being*, that is, a being not constituted in consciousness and through consciousness, but, on the contrary, in a sense constituting consciousness. A similar case occurs with the reality of the act as conscious action.

For if we can accept that the person and act, or, in other words, one's own existing and acting "I," is constituted in consciousness inasmuch as this consciousness consistently mirrors the being (*esse*) and action (*operari*) of that "I," then at the same time the experience of man (and in particular the experience of one's own "I") clearly reveals that consciousness is always grounded in that "I," that is, that its root is always the *suppositum humanum*. *Consciousness is not an autonomous subject*, though by way of a certain abstraction or exclusion, which in the Husserlian terminology was called *epoché*, it can be treated as if it was a subject. This way of treating consciousness stands at the basis of the entire so-called transcendental philosophy, which considers cognitive acts as consciousness-related intentional acts, thus as turned toward the extra-subjective, and thus objective, contents (phenomena). As long as this type of analysis of consciousness has the character of a cognitive method, it can bear and does bear wonderful fruit. Nonetheless, due to the fact that, at its basis, there stands an exclusion (*epoché*) of consciousness from reality, from the being that really exists, this method cannot be considered a philosophy of reality itself, especially of the reality of man, of the reality of the human person. Undoubtedly, however, we must widely take advantage of it in the philosophy of man.

Consciousness is not an autonomous subject, although *it possesses a key significance for understanding the personal subjectivity of man*. In no way can the relation between the *suppositum humanum* and the human "I" be grasped and objectivized without considering consciousness and its function. The function of consciousness is not exclusively cognitive in the sense in which human acts of knowledge or even self-knowledge are cognitive. We can accept with Husserl that these acts exist in consciousness, though it is another matter whether they are acts proper to consciousness, and whether they genetically correspond to its function. For insofar as consciousness indubitably mirrors what is cognitively objectivized by man, at the same time, it especially *confers on all of this the subjective dimension* proper to man precisely because he is a subject. Consciousness interiorizes all that man cognizes—also that which he cognizes in himself in the acts of self-knowledge—and *makes it all the content of the lived-experience of the subject*.[7]

These are two completely different dimensions: to be a subject (*suppositum*) and to experience oneself as a subject. Only in the second dimension do we touch upon the proper reality of the human "I." Consciousness has the key and constitutive significance for the shaping of the second dimension of man's personal subjectivity. We can also say that the human *suppositum* becomes the human "I" and is revealed as such thanks to consciousness. This, however, does not mean in the least that the human "I" is completely reducible to consciousness or to so-called self-consciousness. It is merely constituted in the *suppositum humanum* by means of consciousness on the basis of the entire being (*esse*) and acting (*operari*) proper to this *suppositum*. This ought not to be understood in the sense of particular acts or rather moments of consciousness, consciousness that, as we know, is manifested as dynamic as well as noncontinuous and fluctuating (as is sufficiently evident by periods of sleep) in addition to being connected in various ways with the so-called subconscious.

Taking all this into account, we cannot, however, fail to admit that *man is a subject—that he is one so to speak fully* in actu—*only when he experiences himself as a subject*. And precisely this presupposes consciousness.

---

7. See Wojtyła, *Person and Act*, chapter 1, "Person and Act in the Aspect of Consciousness," and Andrzej Półtawski, "Czyn a świadomość," in *Logos i ethos*, 83.

Of course, according to this understanding, the very meaning of the subject and subjectivity is enriched and, in a sense, modified. What belongs to the concept of subjectivity is a specific inwardness of action and of existence itself—*inwardness* but also *"in-selfness"* [*w-sobność*]. Man exists "in himself" [*w sobie*] and thereby his actions have also an "in-transitive" dimension. However, the inselfness and inwardness of man's action and existence understood precisely in this way is nothing other than a more proximate, still philosophical description of what is virtually contained in the concept *suppositum humanum*. In order to arrive at the image of the person, who is always a concrete human "I," and thus to explicate the full meaning of the personal subjectivity of man, there is a need to develop this virtuality, that is, to explicate as fully as possible what is contained in the *suppositum humanum*. And this is precisely what the analysis of man from the side of consciousness and lived-experience helps us to do.

A view exists saying that through this analysis we separate ourselves from metaphysical subjectivity and enter onto the plane of purely psychological subjectivity, which differs fundamentally from metaphysical subjectivity. This view ultimately appeals to the experience of man and to the way of methodically exploiting this experience. However, it seems that nothing stands in the way of *the analysis of man* conducted *from the side of consciousness* and lived-experience to help us *gain a fuller understanding of the* suppositum humanum *itself* and above all this *suppositum* as a concrete and unrepeatable "I," that is, the person. For the reality of the person is not "extra-phenomenal" but only "trans-phenomenal." In other words, we must thoroughly and comprehensively enter into the "phenomenon" of man in order to fully understand and objectivize this reality.

Efficacy and self-determination

After these remarks, we can return to the form of the human *operari* that is the act—conscious action. Having discussed the aspect of consciousness, which is essential for that action, we are better prepared to understand the particular connection between the act and the personal subjectivity of man. The act, which in traditional terminology was called *actus humanus*, deserves rather the name *actus personae*. The reason for calling the act by this particular name is the moment of efficacy, the efficacy that stands at the basis of the act; this is the efficacy of the person. A close connection exists between a concrete human act and a particular "I," a connection having a causal and efficacious character. In virtue of this connection, the act cannot be separated from the given "I" and ascribed to somebody else as its agent. This connection is of a completely different kind from the connection that occurs between that human "I" and all that merely "happens" in it. We ascribe the act—thus conscious action—to that "I" as an agent that is also conscious; this *efficacy* contains *the moment of the will, thus the moment of freedom,* and consequently the moment of *responsibility having a moral character.* In this way we enter the essential dimension of the personal subjectivity of the person.[8]

We should analyze this dimension gradually, for what is united to—and in a sense accumulated in—this dimension is such richness of the specifically human reality that it is impossible to have simultaneous insight into all essential elements of that reality. Although the analysis of the responsibility having a moral character brings us even further into matters of the will and the freedom proper to man as a person—thus in a sense sharpening insight into them—it is nonetheless fitting to place in the foreground the analysis of the personal efficacy itself.

Although it is undeniably grounded in the experience of man, the concept of efficacy is imprecise here, insofar as efficacy can point to causal dependence on an external effect that resides outside the efficacious subject. In this case, action itself has a transitive character, and clearly this occurs often in man's actions. Through his activity man is an agent of many effects outside himself; by his action he shapes the surrounding reality. This type of efficacious dependence is also contained in the concept of the act, although in this case it is not the most fundamental type. *Another type of efficacious dependence* is the most fundamental for the act: *the one that links man's conscious action with his own subject.* Of course, this other type of efficacious dependence, having an intransitive character, is open in every particular case only to introspection, to interior experience. For this reason, perhaps even our linguistic wonts link the concept of the act to its fundamental dimension to a lesser degree

---

8. Roman Ingarden, *Über die Verantwortung: Ihre ontischen Fundamente* (Stuttgart: Philipp Reclam Jun., 1970); translated by Adam Węgrzecki as *O odpowiedzialności i jej podstawach ontycznych,* in *Książeczka o człowieku* (Kraków: Wydawnictwo Literackie, 1972), 75–184.

than is the case in reality. Exterior experience must be completed with interior experience in order to recover the full sense of the reality of this dimension. It is fundamentally important for the vision of the personal subjectivity of man.

For only then, that is, with the full sense of the reality of man's interior dimension, does this *efficacy*, which appears to us with undeniable evidentness in the experience of the act, *turn out to be not only efficacy but also self-determination*. By acting consciously, I not only am an agent of the act and of its transitive and intransitive effects, but also determine myself, by myself. Self-determination is a deeper and more fundamental dimension of the efficacy of the human "I," through which man reveals himself as a personal subject in the act. Mere efficacy, the causal dependence of the act on one's own "I," does not yet tell us everything about this subjectivity. We could understand it by analogy to other subjects of existence and action, to other *supposita* in the world, to which we also ascribe efficacy and the effects of this efficacy befitting their nature and the powers that they command. But this efficacy that results from the subject (*suppositum*) does not penetrate it, does not return to it, as it were, and does not relate first and foremost to it itself. It also does not reveal the particular subjective structure revealed through the act and through the efficacy of the person contained in the act. It is this efficacy, which is at the same time self-determination, that fully reveals the person to us as a subjective structure of self-governance and self-possession.[9]

Human action, that is, the act, has various ends, objects, and values toward which it turns. However, by turning toward these various ends, objects, and values, *man cannot but turn toward himself as an end in his conscious action, for he cannot relate to various objects of action and choose various values without thereby determining himself* (and therefore he becomes the first object for himself-the subject) and his own value. The structure of the human act is auto-teleological in a particular way. This is not only a dimension of biological life and the instinct connected with it, nor is this merely the dimension of elementary attractions and repulsions subordinated to diversified spheres of pleasure or pain. The

---

9. See Wojtyła, *Person and Act*, chapter 3, "Self-Determination." [Editorial note: Since the time of writing this article, Wojtyła changed the title of this chapter to "The Personal Structure of Self-Determination," which is how it appears on p. 207 in this volume.]

self-determination, contained in the acts, and contained in the authentically human efficacy, indicates yet another dimension of auto-teleology, one ultimately connected with truth and good in an absolute and sincere sense (*bonum honestum*). Therefore, *transcendence*, which is, in a sense, the second name of the person, is revealed in human acts. It is precisely transcendence that manifests the subjectivity proper to man. If subjectivity reveals itself through self-determination, it does so because what is expressed in self-determination is the transcendent dimension of the essentially human action, which at the same time remains in the person as in a subject and cannot bypass him, for it is above all in him that it finds its reason for being and its meaning. In this way, the efficacy of the person ultimately manifests his proper subjectivity—every time, and in every act, choice, and decision; it, so to speak, brings this subjectivity out of obscurity and makes it a vivid "phenomenon" of human experience.

Already we touch upon the further stages of the analysis, which, as we indicated in the beginning, cannot be conducted all at once, but must be gradual and successive. At the same time, however, it is not easy to divide these stages through analysis and hermetically close them off from one another. Therefore, before we continue, let us consider for a moment *the structure of efficacy-self-determination, through which the personal subjectivity* of man is not only cognitively revealed before us, but also *really constituted* in itself as a specific reality that is essentially different from all the other *supposita* that we encounter in the world that surrounds us. It is precisely this human *suppositum*, thus constituted and constituting itself through acts of self-determination, that we call the "I." Of course, we say this especially and properly about our own *suppositum*, but indirectly about any other as well.

We mentioned previously that the "I" is irreducible to consciousness itself even though it is constituted through consciousness; consciousness, and especially self-consciousness, is an indispensable condition for the constituting of the human "I." But the real constitution of this "I" on the basis of the human *suppositum* is fundamentally owed to acts of self-determination. As aforementioned, it is in them that man's proper structure and profile of self-possession and self-governance are revealed. They are revealed because in every act of self-determination this structure is, in a sense, realized anew. Precisely *in this realizing of the structure of self-possession and self-governance, the concrete human "I," which is a person, really constitutes itself.* Here we can see even better the close connection between the "I" and the *suppositum*. The "I" is nothing else but a concrete *suppositum humanum*, which, when given to itself in lived-experience—and thus through consciousness (self-consciousness)—and precisely in the lived-experience of the act, is identified with the self-possession and self-governance that are revealed thanks to the personal dynamic of efficacy, which is self-determination.

Thus the "I" is not only self-consciousness, but also self-possession and self-governance, which are proper to the concrete human *suppositum* and reveal themselves primarily through the act. If we said above that the "I" cannot be reduced to self-consciousness only, then we must now add that the full dimension of the human "I," to which self-possession and self-governance belong, is in turn conditioned by self-consciousness. On this is also based the full relation of this "I" to personal subjectivity, which is proper to man. We stated previously that this is not only the subjectivity of a being, but also the subjectivity of lived-experience. Consciousness has a fundamental significance for constituting precisely this subjectivity through its proper function of interiorizing, which in *Person and Act* was called the reflexive function. Consequently, that which is revealed in the experience of man (above all as a given "I") is the "inwardness" and "inselfness" proper to the concrete human *esse* and *operari*. As we said, the very concept of *suppositum* does not reveal such meanings of the subject and subjectivity.

This "inwardness" and "inselfness" as the full (*in the sense of pertaining to experience and lived-experience*) *realization of the personal subjectivity of the human "I" are manifested and at once realized in self-possession and self-governance.* Man experiences himself as a personal subject inasmuch as he becomes conscious that he possesses himself and governs himself. Consciousness, or more strictly speaking self-consciousness connected with the act, connected with efficacy as self-determination, conditions this lived-experience. In this sense, we can say that both the concrete human "I" and its corresponding concrete human personal subjectivity are constituted through consciousness (or with its help).

From the point of view of the person as a being that "exists and acts," and thus as a *suppositum*, we perceive in this analysis no fundamental fracture, no hiatus. For the lived-experience of one's own personal subjectivity is nothing else but the full actualization of all that is virtually contained in the *suppositum humanum*, in the metaphysical subjectivity. This is at once the full and profound revelation of this subjectivity and the full and profound realization of the being in lived-experience. This seems to be both the possible and, in a sense, philosophically definitive sense of what the old adage proclaims: "*Operari sequitur esse.*" The *suppositum humanum* and the human "I" are two poles of one and the same experience of man.

Fulfillment and transcendence

The image of the personal subjectivity of man, which is revealed before us in lived-experience and experience, would not be complete if we failed to introduce the moment of fulfillment into it. If the path to know the person is the act ("*operari sequitur esse*"), then it is impossible not to pay attention to the expression "to perform an act," which seems to correspond most thoroughly not only to the reality of the act itself, *actus humanus*, but also to that of man, the subject who performs this act. This expression is not accidental. In its proper content it indicates the striving of what is not complete toward its own proper fullness. The act as *actus humanus* is this actual fullness in the order of *operari*. However, the person always remains in its field of performance. Therefore, precisely because the act as *actus humanus* reveals his inwardness and inselfness while at the same time activating the structures of self-possession and self-governance proper to him, a problem arises: *how much is the performance of the act also the fulfillment of oneself, the fulfillment of the person who performs the act?*[10]

This is a real and, in a sense, the deepest and most fundamental problem among the problems that must be undertaken in the analysis of the personal subjectivity of man. In the dynamic structure of this subjectivity, the striving for self-fulfillment that dwells at the root of the entire human *operari* and especially of the acts, attests at once to contingency and auto-teleology. The striving for fulfilling oneself, for fulfilling one's "I," in a sense manifests the fact that this "I" is incomplete; an incompleteness that does not denote the being's contingency but allows itself to be re-

---

10. See Wojtyła, *Person and Act*, chapter 4, "Self-Determination and Fulfillment."

duced to it. At the same time, the very striving manifests auto-teleology, for the end of the being—of the *suppositum* that experiences its own incompleteness—is the fulfillment of itself, that is, "self-fulfillment." The discovery of this striving supplements our image of the human "I," the "I" that is constituted by means of consciousness and self-consciousness in its own acts. In these acts, through the moment of self-determination, the human "I" not only reveals itself to itself as self-possession and self-governance, but also *as a striving for self-fulfillment*. This undeniably indicates that *the personal subjectivity of man is not a closed structure*. Neither self-consciousness nor self-possession close man, the human "I," in his own subject. Quite the contrary, this whole "turning toward oneself," for which consciousness and self-determination work, ultimately turns out to be the source of the fullest opening of this subject to reality. A close connection occurs in man, in the human "I" as a personal subject, between the fulfillment of oneself and transcendence. We said previously that transcendence is in a sense another name for the person in contemporary mentality.

The philosophical meaning of transcendence is manifold. In metaphysics it denotes being as a reality surpassing all categories while at the same time constituting their foundation. The case is similar with truth or the good as transcendentals parallel to being. In philosophical anthropology, transcendence—in accord with its etymology, *trans-scendere*—also denotes sur-passing (or out-growing), inasmuch as it is verifiable in the integral experience of man, inasmuch as it is manifested in the dynamic totality of his being and acting, his *esse* and *operari*. *Manifold manifestations of* this *transcendence* ultimately meet in one source that constantly pulsates in man as a subject, as a *suppositum*, and which in the ultimate analysis attests to the fact that the *suppositum humanum* is also of a spiritual nature. Transcendence constitutes the revelation of man's spirituality.

Here we neither intend to submit this problem to a metaphysical analysis nor attempt to comprehensively elucidate the transcendence proper to the human person. We shall limit ourselves *to stating only one moment of transcendence*, namely, the one that is manifested *through the specific personal form conferred on the acts of man by conscience*. For this moment of transcendence is clearly linked with the profile of fulfillment, which closely belongs to the personal subjectivity of man. Moral subjectivity is often spoken of by analogy to psychological subjectivity when we take into consideration the aspect of consciousness and lived-experience. However, these distinctions cannot break up the image of the fundamental unity of the personal subject. The personal subjectivity of man is one that we experience as our own "I" in our acts, and which appears to us in its proper depth in the lived-experience of moral value—good or evil—the lived-experience that remains in experiential connection with the moment of conscience in human acts.

Why does the moment of conscience in the act reveal the transcendence of the person? The answer to this question would require a number of analyses, which we attempted to conduct in *Person and Act*.[11] Here, out of necessity, we must briefly reply by stating that *truth as the source of moral* or "categorical" (to use Kantian language) *duty is heard in conscience*. It is heard *as a condition constitutive for the freedom* proper to the act, in which this freedom is revealed as the self-determination of the person. To be free means not only "to will" but also "to choose" and "to decide," and all of this tells us about the transcendent subordination of good to truth in action, in the act. However, only conscience is, so to speak, the proper place of this subordination. In conscience, the authentic transcendence of the person in the act is realized, for, thanks to the conscience, *actus humanus* is shaped as the volition and choice of the "true good." In this way the moment of conscience reveals in the act, and in its efficacious subject, the transcendence of truth and freedom, for freedom is realized precisely through the volition and choice of the true good.

In order to "do good and avoid evil" (as the original principle of conscience-synderesis, and the elementary formula of the entire human *praxis*, declares), man must constantly in a sense surpass himself toward the true good in his conscience: this is the fundamental direction of the transcendence that constitutes a property of the human person, a *proprium personae*. Without this transcendence—without *surpassing* and, in a sense, rising above *oneself* in the direction of truth and *in the direction of the good willed and chosen in the light of truth*—the person, or personal subject, is not in a sense himself. Therefore, we do not yet emphasize the personal property of man when we analyze the acts of his cognition and

---

11. See Wojtyła, *Person and Act*, part 2, "The Transcendence of the Person in the Act."

will, or the world of values connected to them, unless we, at the same time, bring to light the transcendence that inheres in these acts through the relation to truth and to good as "true" (or "honorable"), that is, willed and chosen on the basis of truth. All this becomes obvious to us through the analysis of conscience.

At the same time the analysis of conscience shows us the close connection between transcendence and fulfillment. It is not only a question of the participation of conscience in the dynamic of the performed act, but also of the fulfillment of oneself in this act. By performing the act, *I fulfill myself in it insofar as this act is "good,"* that is, in conformity with conscience (let us add: with a good or right conscience). Through such an act, I myself "become" good and "am" good as man. The moral value reaches into the full depth of the ontic structure of the *suppositum humanum*. The opposite of this is an act incompatible with conscience, a morally evil act. Then I "become" evil and "am" evil as man. In that case, the performance of the act does not bring me fulfillment of myself. It is rather the *non-fulfillment of myself*. To negative moral value (which we could also call anti-value, especially from the viewpoint of the judgment and verdict of conscience) corresponds the lived-experience of the non-fulfillment of oneself. It would be fitting to analyze separately these two meanings of the fulfillment and the non-fulfillment of oneself—one metaphysical: I "become" and "am" good or evil as man; and the other experiential, given in consciousness and the lived-experience of the moral value of "good" and "evil." If we do not do this, we must at any rate observe a particular closeness of both these senses. This is one more proof that the *suppositum humanum* and the human "I" constitute only two poles of the one and the same experience of man.

We can clearly see that *the fulfillment of oneself is not identified with the very performance of the act but depends on the moral value of this act*. I fulfill myself not through performing an act, but through becoming good when this act is morally good. Evidently, the fulfillment of the person remains in connection with transcendence, with the transcendent dimension of the act objectivized in conscience. I fulfill myself through good, whereas evil brings me non-fulfillment. It is also clear that self-fulfillment is a distinct structure of the personal subject, which differs both from self-possession and from self-determination. This structure is actualized in the act through its moral value—through good—but only in the dimension of this act *per modum actus*. The experience of morality shows us further possibilities of grounding and consolidating good—the moral value—in the subject, as it also indicates further possibilities of deepening and consolidating evil in him. The ethics of Aristotle and Thomas Aquinas, as well as the contemporary characterology, speak in this case *de habitibus*—about the wonts and moral habits, about the virtues and vices of man. All this contains the manifold form of self-fulfillment, or on the contrary, the non-fulfillment of oneself. Both speak about man, about the human "I" as a personal subject.

It is essential that fulfillment as a subjective reality, which is given to us among other things in the lived-experience of conscience, but which of course is not limited nor reduced to it, is clearly linked with transcendence. *Man fulfills himself*, he realizes the auto-teleology of his personal "I," *through the transcendent dimension of his* operari. The transcendence of truth and good has a decisive influence on the shaping of the human "I," on its becoming in the whole reality of the personal subject, as is perfectly seen in the analysis of conscience and morality. The same analysis also deepens our vision of man's contingency, both by emphasizing how essential the striving for fulfilling himself is for him, and especially by showing how he is constantly found between good and evil in this striving, between fulfillment and non-fulfillment, how he must steadfastly overcome the forces that act against self-fulfillment from without and from within.

This, at least, partial self-fulfillment, brought by the moral good of the act, also discloses to us the moment of peace and felicity, so essential for the lived-experiences of conscience (whereas the moral evil is manifested in the lived-experience of conscience with despondency and despair). All this points to transcendence as *the common, so to speak, perspective of self-fulfillment and happiness*. However, we do not intend to consider this matter more extensively here, but limit ourselves to only mentioning it.

2. Various Dimensions of the Community

Status quaestionis

Bringing together the subject and the community in the title of this article does not determine in advance how these two topics will be joined in our analysis. The course of our reflections thus far—in accord with the declaration made in the beginning—directs this analysis toward the connection that occurs between the subjectivity of the man-person and the structure of the human community. I intend to investigate this connection anew—and I understand this investigation in relation to the previous one in *Person and Act*.[12] We introduce this qualification while at the same time emphasizing that the elaboration in the aforementioned study is by no means exhaustive; neither do I now intend to perform an exhaustive elaboration of the problem. However, perhaps I will manage to add some new thoughts to what has already been said.

First and foremost, we ought to state that the study *Person and Act* contains no *theory of community*, but only concerns itself with considering the elementary condition in which the man-person's being and acting "together with others" serve self-fulfillment, or at least do not hinder it. For in no way can we contradict the relevant facts. We should keep in mind these (negative) facts, known to us from the history of peoples and human societies, when we consider the problem of the personal subject in the community. This is, in fact, to what the last chapter of *Person and Act* limits itself. A theory of community is not adequately elaborated in that chapter, although certain elements of this theory are contained there *implicite*. Such an element is above all *the concept of "participation,"* which in the last chapter of *Person and Act is understood in a twofold way.* First, participation is understood as the property of the person, which is expressed in the ability to confer a personal (personalistic) dimension on his own being and acting when he exists and acts together with other people. On the other hand, participation is understood in *Person and Act* as a positive relation to the humanity of other people, although we do not understand "humanity" as an abstract idea of man, but—in conformity with the total vision of him in that study—as a personal "I," every time unique and unrepeatable. "Humanity" is not an abstraction or a generality but has in every man a specific weight of personal being (as we see, in this case this "specific weight" is not derived from the concept "specific"). *To participate in the humanity of another man means to remain in a live relation to the fact that he is this man in particular* and not only in

---

12. See Wojtyła, *Person and Act*, chapter 7, "An Outline of the Theory of Participation." [19a]

relation to the fact by which he is (*in abstracto*) man. On this is based the entire specificity of the evangelical concept of "neighbor."

If the first meaning of participation indicates not this positive relation to the humanity of another man, but the property of the person in virtue of which man by being and acting together with others is nonetheless able to fulfill himself in this acting and being, then this way of positing the problem indicates the indispensable primacy of the personal subject with respect to the community. This primacy is *both metaphysical (thus factual) and methodological*. This means not only that people *de facto* exist and act together as a multitude of personal subjects, but also that we can say nothing essential about this coexistence and cooperation in the personalistic sense—that is, as a community—unless we proceed from man precisely as a personal subject.[13]

In my opinion, it is to this that all *problems of alienation* are ultimately reduced. They are significant not on account of man as an individual of the species "man," but on account of man as a personal subject. Man, as an individual of a species, is and does not cease to be man regardless of any configurations of inter-human or social relations. However, man as a personal subject can undergo alienation in these relations, that is, a sort of "de-humanization." Precisely for this reason, *Person and Act* thinks of participation first and foremost as a property in virtue of which man, by being and acting together with others, and thus in various configurations

---

13. Fr. Leszek Kuc participated in the discussion on *Person and Act* ("Uczestnictwo w człowieczeństwie 'innych'?," *Analecta Cracoviensia* 5–6 [1973–74]: 183–90). Also see the afterword ["Słowo końcowe"], in which the author responds to Fr. Kuc's statement. At this point, however, we speak to the very view presented by Fr. Kuc concerning the problem of the person and community, which—besides the cited statements in the discussion on *Person and Act*—he expressed both in the aforementioned interdisciplinary session ("Przyczynek do konstrukcji tematyki antropologii chrześcijańskiej," *Studia theologica Varsaviensia* 12, no. 1 [1974]: 289–302) and in the article "Zagadnienia antropologii chrześcijańskiej," *Studia theologica Varsaviensia* 9, no. 2 (1971): 95–109. In these pronouncements, Fr. Kuc indicates his position rather than presenting a full conception. Among other things, we read the following in *Analecta Cracoviensia*: "Precisely here, in the presence of other people in the concrete person, we perceive reality, the ontic basis of the community. In our opinion, we can and ought to treat every human person both as a separate and autonomous person and as a really existing and acting community of persons" (187). Nonetheless, it must be added that the above by no means exempts us from investigating what this community as an objective unity of the real plurality of persons-subjects is. Just as the personal subjectivity of man is an objective reality, so—in the given case—is the plurality of these subjects and their community, that is, the unity through the common good, above all in relations of the "we" type—something that we shall discuss in a further analysis.

of inter-human and social relations, is able to be himself and fulfill himself. *Participation is, in a sense, the antithesis of alienation.* If in *Person and Act* we speak of participation as a specific property of the man-person, then it means that man strives for participation and defends himself against alienation, and the basis of the one and the other is not his specific essence alone but his personal subjectivity.

Therefore, in considering the community, we cannot attach fundamental significance to the fact that man exists and acts "together" with others as to a "material" fact. As such this fact says nothing about the community, but only about the plurality of beings, of acting subjects that are people. The "material" fact itself of the being and acting of many people together, or—as is the case in the analyses of *Person and Act*—by man together with others, is not yet a community. *By the community, we understand* not the *plurality of subjects* alone but always the *specific unity of this plurality.* This unity is *accidental* in relation to each one and to all. It arises as a relation or a sum of relations existing among them. These relations can be examined as an objective reality, which qualifies all and each in a certain plurality of people. We then speak of a society (or commune, or, using other language, social groups, etc.). Although particular people (personal subjects), who are members of such society, are themselves and each separately substantial subjects (*supposita*), and the society, in itself, constitutes exclusively a group of relations, and thus is an accidental being, this accidental being nonetheless moves (i.e., in the conception of society), in a sense, to the foreground and constitutes the basis for the predication of people, of the persons belonging to it. Thus, we speak of a person from the viewpoint of social affiliation, for example, a "Pole," a "Catholic," a "townsman," a "laborer," and so on.

We can also examine the same relation or the same group of relations, through which a definite plurality of people—of personal subjects—constitutes a social unity, *not merely as an objective reality*, which qualifies all and each one in this plurality, *but rather from the viewpoint of the consciousness and lived-experience of all its members* and, in a sense, of each of them. Only then do *we enter the reality of community* and touch on its proper meaning. It is clear that there exists—from both the factual (thus metaphysical) and the methodological viewpoints—a close connection, correspondence, and adequateness between the community and the personal subjectivity of man, as the latter was elucidated in the first part of our reflections. By analyzing the plurality alone of human *supposita* and the unity of the objective inter-human or social relations corresponding to them, we obtain a somewhat different image from the one that arises *when considering personal subjectivity*,[14] namely, consciousness and the lived-experience of inter-human or social relations in a given human plurality. It seems that only the second image corresponds to the concept of community.

We frequently use the words "community" and "society" interchangeably. This is justified in light of everything said above. At the same time, however, what has been said so far also points to a reason for distinction. A community is not simply a society, nor is a society simply a community. Even if, to a considerable extent, the same elements determine both realities, nonetheless we grasp these elements in different aspects, and this, in fact, creates an important difference. In a sense we can also say that *it is through the community of its members that a society* (a commune, a social group, etc.) *is itself*. As a result, a community seems to be something more essential, at least from the viewpoint of the personal subjectivity of all members of a given society or social group. In this way it also becomes clear that the social relations in the given (thus one and the same) society can become a source of alienation as the community; that is, the social relation, bond, and unity that is made conscious and experienced by particular subjects, vanishes.

Hence, we can conclude, at least from what has been said so far, that the concept of community has both a *real* and an ideal *sense*: both a certain reality and an idea or principle are at stake here. This sense is ontological as well as axiological, thus *normative*. It is impossible to fully elucidate here all these senses of the community; we can only mention them. To a certain extent the previous analysis of personal subjectivity can lead us toward understanding these various senses of the community, and help us explicate them. The community is an essential reality for human coexistence and cooperation, and it is also their fundamental norm. Accordingly, it is clear that there exists a special value of the community, which perhaps cannot be simply identified with the so-called common

---

14. In this sense, we can also speak of the person-community coupling, of which Fr. Leszek Kuc speaks in the statements previously cited.

good. In a sense, we detect this value by investigating the co-existence and cooperation of people from the perspective of the personal subjectivity of each of them. The common good seems to be rather an objectivization of the axiological sense of every society, commune, environment, social group, etc. If we speak of the so-called social nature of man, then the *discovery of the value of the community denotes a direct argument for that thesis.*

It is in this context that the problem of the relation *between the community*—the value of the community—*and the auto-teleology of man* emerges before us. It seems indubitable that man fulfills himself in community with others, and that he fulfills himself through this community. Does this mean, however, that we can, in a sense, reduce the person's self-fulfillment to the community, and auto-teleology to the teleology of the community, or many communities? We shall try to consider this matter later by sketching two profiles or dimensions of the human community, which are also, as it seems, irreducible to each other. One of them is the dimension of inter-human or inter-personal relations, whose symbol can be the "I-thou" relationship. The second dimension of relations, which we can symbolize by the "we" relationship, seems not to have so much of an inter-human as a social character. In both cases, the previously analyzed personal subjectivity of man must constitute an element of not only a further analysis, but also a gradual—we can say, retrospective—verification.

"I-thou": The inter-personal dimension of the community

In this and the next component of our analysis, we could speak about the profile of the community, though it seems better to speak about its dimension. For in each of these relationships that we intend to analyze, the community is not only a distinct fact, but also—together with its factual structure (which we seem to indicate by the word "profile")—has a different axiological and normative sense, and thus a different measure. In our analysis we will attempt to discover and, to a certain extent, also define this measure of the "I-thou" relationships and consequently the "we" relationships. These relationships *develop on the basis of* the facts of the *coexistence and cooperation of people*; they belong both to the experiences of man and to the fundamental (pre-scientific and even in a sense pre-reflective) understanding of these experiences. The coming to be of man, the origins of his being, and his relatively long period of development are realized in the "I-thou" and the "we" relationships, although man reflects on neither its meaning nor its structure while he inheres in these profiles of the community with all his existence. The studies of developmental psychology can shed much light on this matter. There is no doubt that the "I-thou" and the "we" relationships as the experienced facts, thus as the facts given in the experience of man, are in each of us much older than any attempts—especially *methodical attempts—of the reflective objectivization of these relationships.*

While fully appreciating this fact, or rather a rich and very influential group of facts, we wish in the present analysis to take the later situation as a basis, namely, a situation that allows us to speak about the sufficient stage of the development of man's personal subjectivity.

For what is at stake, both in the present and in further analyses, is not only the *suppositum humanum*, but also the human "I." It seems that only from the position of a sufficiently formed personal subjectivity of man can we submit the "I-thou" and then the "we" relationships to full analysis, in view of the communal reality contained in these relationships. It also seems that the profile or dimension of the community, which is contained in each of these relationships when we analyze them *at a stage of sufficiently formed personal subjectivities, should work retrospectively*, that is, should explain these relationships at earlier stages, and not vice versa. Let us first refer to the "I-thou" relationship, in which (to a certain degree in contradistinction to the "we" relationship) we perceive above all the inter-human, that is, inter-personal, dimension of the community.

If it is sometimes maintained that, so to speak, the "I" is constituted through the "thou,"[15] then this capital mental shortcut certainly requires to be developed and expanded. In this explication, we cannot ignore the fundamental fact that, just as with the "I," the "thou" is always a

---

15. In his work, "Człowiek a Bóg: Zagadnienie relacji znaczeniowej pomiędzy osobą ludzką i Bogiem a problem ateizmu" (*Logos i ethos*, 127), Fr. Marian Jaworski writes the following, among other things: "To the essential moments, which determine the human person, we ought to add the relation to the 'thou.'" The article is devoted fully to the relation of man ("I") to God as the unconditional "Thou" of man, as the principle of the personal being of man. Noting this position, the author wishes to add that within the present study he does not undertake an analysis of this significant relation, but keeps to the inter-personal relations.

somebody, that is, another "I." For the same reason, a certain plurality of personal subjects exists at the starting point of the "I-thou" relation. Although this plurality is minimal (one + one), we must nonetheless base the analysis of unity, which is essential for the concept of community, on acknowledging this plurality. *"Thou" is another "I" different from me.* By thinking and saying "thou," I also express a relation that, in a sense, proceeds outside of me but simultaneously returns to me. The "thou" is not only an expression of division, but also an expression of contact. For this word always contains a clear *distinction of one from many others.* This distinction does not necessarily have to be formal—it can be virtual; it does not have to constitute the very "text" of the relation, for it can belong to its "subtext." Nonetheless, by thinking and saying "thou," I am always somehow conscious that this concrete man whom I address this way is one of many whom I can address this way, that in this way I also address (and experience) different people—in other moments and situations—and that I could address everyone this way. Thus, the "I-thou" relation is potentially oriented from me toward all people, but actually it always binds me to one. If it actually binds me to many, then it is not the relation to "thou" but to "we," though it can very easily be distributed into a series of "thou" relations.

At the same time, this manifests a particular revertibility of that relation. The *relation to "thou"* is in its essential structure always the relation to the other and only "I" in this relationship, and therefore it *demonstrates*, in a way proper only to itself, *the ability to return to this "I" from which it proceeded.* We do not treat here of the function of the counter-relation, for the "thou" as an "I" can be related to me (to my "I") in the same way as to "thou"—to him "I" am a "thou." Our point concerns the same relation proceeding from my "I" to a "thou," for this relation has its complementary function consisting of returning to that "I" from which it proceeded. Of course, all that we are presently writing about makes complete sense only in the aspect of consciousness and lived-experience, thus in the aspect in which both the "I" and the "thou" as a second "I" are constituted. However, it does not fully make sense as a relation taken as a metaphysical category. For we continue to speak about experiencing relations, which presupposes the "I" and the "thou" as distinct personal subjectivities, and not merely about relations as accidents grounded in distinct *supposita*, though this does not in the least mean that we question this fundamental reality. In any case, what is indispensable for conducting this analysis is the "I" and the "thou" as fully constituted, distinct personal subjects, together with all that determines personal subjectivity for each of them.

If the relation oriented from "I" to "thou" returns to the "I" from which it proceeded, then *this revertibility of relation* (not yet necessarily reciprocity, that is, the counter-relation "thou"-"I") *contains the moment of the specific constitution of the human "I" through the relation to the "thou."* It seems that this moment does not yet determine the community, but rather bears importance for a fuller lived-experience of oneself, of one's own "I," and, in a sense, for testing this "I" "in the light of the other 'I.'" On the basis of this relation a process of imitating personal models can develop, a process that is very important for education and self-education,[16] and ultimately for the fulfillment of oneself, whose original dynamism is rooted in every personal subjectivity (as previously noted). Without going that far, however, we must accept that the "thou" helps me in a normal state of things to acknowledge my own "I" more fully and even to confirm it, to auto-affirm it. In its fundamental form, the "I-thou" relation does not lead me out of my own subjectivity; indeed, in a sense, it embeds me more firmly in that subjectivity. The structure of relation is, in a sense, the confirmation of the structure of the subject and the subject's primacy in relation to it.[17]

---

16. I concerned myself with this problem especially in connection with the analysis of Max Scheler's ethics. See Karol Wojtyła, *Ocena możliwości zbudowania etyki chrześcijańskiej przy założeniach systemu Maksa Schelera*, Rozprawy wydziału filozoficznego 5 (Lublin: Towarzystwo Naukowe Katolickiego Uniwersytetu Lubelskiego, 1959); Wojtyła, "System etyczny Maksa Schelera jako środek do opracowania etyki chrześcijańskiej," *Polonia sacra* 6, no. 2–4 (1953–54): 143–61; and Wojtyła, "Ewangeliczna zasada naśladowania: Nauka źródeł Objawienia a system filozoficzny Maksa Schelera," *Ateneum kapłańskie* 55, no. 1 (1957): 57–67.

17. My work "Uczestnictwo czy alienacja" ("Participation ou aliénation"), sent to the International Phenomenological Colloquium in Freiburg (January 24–28, 1975) and presented in Freiburg to the philosophical department of the University of Freiburg on February 27, 1975, is devoted in an analytical way to the formation of the relation of "I" to "thou." [20a]The general topic of the colloquium organized by the Société Internationale pour l'étude de Husserl et de la phénoménologie—Internationale Forschungsgesellschaft für Phänomenologie was "Soi et autrui: La crise de l'irréductible dans l'homme." Because the text of the lecture has not yet been published, I am providing the chapter titles: "The Necessity of Establishing the Starting Point—'I'-*Soi*: Self-Determination and Self-Possesion"; "'The Other'-*Autrui*"; "The 'I-the Other' (*Soi-Autrui*) Relationship: Its Potentiality and Actualization"; "Participation as a Task"; "Alienation." The titles of the lectures

The relation of "I" to "thou" considered in this way *already constitutes a real lived-experience of the inter-personal relationship*, although *its full lived-experience* occurs *when* the "I-thou" relation *possesses a reciprocal character*, namely, when the "thou," who has become the other (the other-man) for the "I," makes me his "thou," that is, when two people become for each other reciprocally "I" and "thou" and in this way experience their relation. It also seems that only then can we follow the full specificity of the community that is proper to the "I-thou" inter-personal relationship. Nonetheless, we should repeat once more that, even without this reciprocity, the "I-thou" relation constitutes a real lived-experience of the inter-personal relationship, and on this basis we can also analyze the participation that was defined in *Person and Act* as participation in the very humanity of the other man. It seems that the reciprocity of the "I-thou" relation is not necessary for this participation, but only allows us to ascertain that precisely this participation, and nothing else, becomes the essential *constitutivum* of a community that has an inter-human, inter-personal character in the case of the reciprocity of the "I-thou" relation.

In this reflection *we do not undertake an analysis of particular forms and variations of "I-thou" inter-personal relations* or of particular forms and variations of the community that is shaped in them (or through which these relations are shaped; for the community, as was said, is an essential element of such reciprocal relations). It is known that some forms of "I-thou" inter-personal relations, above all friendship and love, have been the objects of multiple and diverse expositions and studies, and still do not cease to be a privileged topic of human reflection. In this study, passing over the analysis and characteristics of the "I-thou" relations them-

---

given at the colloquium are as follows: Karol Wojtyła (Kraków), "Participation ou aliénation"; Hans Köchler (Innsbruck), "Die personale Selbstbestimmung und die Dialektik"; A. de Muralt (Geneva), "L'acte fondé et l'aperception d'autrui"; E. Maarbach (Louvain—Archives Husserl), "Zum Problem der Doppel-Reduktion"; Jérome Danek (Québec), "L'intersubjectivité et la monadologie chez Husserl"; Ph. Secrétan (Fribourg), "Soi et autrui dans la conception de la personne chez Edith Stein"; S. Strasser (Nijmegen), "Der Einzige und sein Anderer"; Alonso Lingis (State College), "Lévinas's Critic [sic] of Heidegger on Intersubjectivity"; Jan De Greef (Louvain), "L'aliénation irréductible de soi"; M. Nédoncelle (Strasbourg), "Altérité et causalité"; C. Valenziano (Cefalù), "La réciprocité des consciences"; M. D. Philippe (Fribourg), "L'amour de soi, obstacle ou moyen privilégié?"; J. C. Piguet (Lausanne), "Le langage entre soi et autrui"; A.-T. Tymieniecka (Boston): "Autrui et interprétation créatrice"; E. A. Montsopoulos (Athens), "Plaisir et aliénation."[20b]

selves, we wish to *emphasize what is essential for the community* contained in them, *from the viewpoint of the subjects themselves*, or, more strictly speaking, from the viewpoint encompassed by reciprocity, the relation of the concrete "I" and "thou" in their personal subjectivity. Thus, our point is rather to show the moment of a certain regularity analogously common to all the relations in which two persons as "I" and "thou" are linked with each other, regardless of the detailed characteristics of the relations themselves. For we keep an eye on the inter-personal dimension of the community, proper to all the "I-thou" relationships, independently of their particular formation. Therefore, this analysis includes the "I-thou" of the spouses or the betrothed, the "I-thou" of the mother and the child, and the "I-thou" of two persons who do not know each other but, unexpectedly to themselves, discover themselves in this relationship.

Apart from any detailed characteristics of the relations themselves, perhaps we must realize and emphasize one thing. For man, both the "I" and the "thou," is not only the existing but also the acting subject, and in this action the "thou" becomes an object for the "I" at every step, even while this objectivity, together with the entire relation, returns to the "I" on the basis of a specific interaction: the "I" becomes in a particular way an object for itself in the actions objectively directed toward the "thou." This, in fact, belongs organically, so to speak, to the process of the particular constituting of the "I" through the "thou," of which we already spoke. If—as we already stated in the first part—the "I" is constituted through its acts and in the same way the "thou" is constituted as another "I", then the "I-thou" relation and the relational effects of this relationship in both its subjects (the "I" and the "thou") are also constituted in the same way. The subject "I" experiences the relation to the "thou" in the action whose object is the "thou," and, of course, vice versa. *Through* this action *objectively directed toward the "thou," the subject "I" not only experiences himself in relation to the "thou," but also experiences himself in a new way in his own subjectivity.* The objectivity of action (action and interaction) is the source of the confirmation of the subjectivity of the agent, perhaps simply because this object is in itself a subject and represents a personal subjectivity proper to it.

Thus, we can define *the fundamental dimension of the inter-personal community* by limiting ourselves to the "I-thou" relationship in, so to speak, its elementary form, without any detailed specifications of the reciprocal relation of both persons, but while taking into consideration that, in this relationship, the "I" is the subject of actions objectively directed at the "thou," and vice versa. This dimension is simultaneously a fact and a postulate; it has a metaphysical and normative (ethical) sense, according to what we previously said about the concept of community. This dimension *is reduced to treating*, that is, *to actually experiencing the "other as oneself."* We take this formulation straight from the Gospel, and our entire analysis refers us to what was said in the last chapters of *Person and Act* about the meaning of "neighbor."[2a]

In order to more fully specify this dimension of the community, which is proper to the "I-thou" inter-personal relations, we must state that precisely in these relations does the reciprocal revelation of man in his personal subjectivity, in all that constitutes this subjectivity, take place. The "thou" stands with respect to the "I" as a true and full "other 'I,'" which is determined—similarly to my own "I"—not only by self-consciousness but above all by self-possession and self-governance. In this subjective structure, the "thou" as the "other 'I'" represents its own transcendence and its own striving for self-fulfillment. This entire *structure of personal subjectivity*, which is proper to the "I" and the "thou" as the "other 'I,'" *is reciprocally revealed through the community proper to the "I-thou" relation* because, thanks to the reciprocity of the relation, "I" am at the same time a "thou" for this "other 'I,'" which is "my 'thou.'" In this way, the "I-thou" relation as the reciprocal relation of two subjects (*supposita*) not only acquires the meaning of, but really becomes an authentic subjective community.

When we say that the reciprocal revelation of man in his personal subjectivity takes place in this community, we indicate the factual meaning of community proper to the "I-thou" inter-personal relation. We cannot forget that this community also has a normative meaning. From this point of view we ought to say that what should take place through this dimension of the community, which is proper to the "I-thou" inter-personal relation, is the reciprocal revelation of man, the revelation of man to man, in his personal subjectivity and in all that determines it. Through the "I-thou" relation, man should be revealed to man in his profound structure of self-possession and self-governance and especially in the striving for self-fulfillment; a striving that, while culminating in the acts of conscience, attests to the transcendence proper to man as a person. *In this truth of his personal reality, man should be* not only revealed to man in the "I-thou" inter-personal relations but also *accepted and affirmed in this truth*. This acceptance and affirmation is an expression of the moral (ethical) sense of the inter-personal community.

This sense both shapes and—in another aspect—verifies the inter-personal community in its particular realizations, in the particular variations of the reciprocal relations of the human "I" and "thou," such as friendship and love. The deeper, the more integral, the more intensive is the interconnection of the "I" and the "thou" in these reciprocal relations, the more does this interconnection acquire the character of trust, self-giving, a specific (i.e., possible only in the relation of a person to a person) belonging, and the more does there arise the necessity of the reciprocal acceptance and affirmation of the "I" by the "thou" in its personal subjectivity, in the entire structure of self-possession and with the entire regularity of personal transcendence, which is expressed in acts of conscience. In this way, on the basis of the "I-thou" relation, from the very nature of the inter-personal community, *the reciprocal responsibility of a person for a person* also increases.[18] This responsibility is a reflex of conscience and transcendence; it stands both on the part of the "I" and of the "thou" on the path to self-fulfillment, and at the same time it conditions the proper, that is, the authentically personal, dimension of the community.

By "community" we understand that which joins together. In the "I-thou" relation, the authentic inter-personal community is shaped (in any form or variation) if the "I" and the "thou" remain in a reciprocal affirmation of the person's transcendent value (which we can also call dignity), confirming this by their acts. It seems that only this relationship deserves the name of *communio personarum*.[19]

---

18. My ethical study *Love and Responsibility* is built on this basis.
19. See also the Pastoral Constitution on the Church in the Modern World *Gaudium et spes*, no. 12: "But God did not create man as a solitary, for from the beginning 'male and female he created them' (Genesis 1:27). Their companionship produces the primary form of interpersonal communion (*communio personarum*)" [Vatican translation].

"We": The social dimension of the community

It seems indispensable to distinguish the social dimension of the community from the inter-human (inter-personal) one. This distinction is dictated by different profiles of this community, which—in a sense both symbolically and very precisely—are expressed by the pronouns "I-thou" and "we." The "I" and "thou" only indirectly indicate the plurality of persons joined by a relation (one + one) while they directly indicate the persons themselves, whereas the "we" indicates directly the plurality and indirectly the persons belonging to this plurality. "We" indicates above all a collection; of course, this collection consists of people, that is, of persons. Although this collection, which we can call a society, a commune, a group, etc., does not possess by itself a substantial being, nonetheless, as we recalled above, that which results from the accident, from the relation between people-persons, advances in a sense into the foreground, thus providing *the basis for predicating* primarily *of all and only secondarily of each in this collection*. This is precisely what is contained in the pronoun "*we.*"

It is therefore clear that the "we" introduces us into the world of other human relations and indicates another dimension of the community. This is the social dimension, which differs from the previous one, namely, the inter-human dimension of the community in the "I – thou" relation. Undertaking in turn the analysis of the social dimension of the community, we continue to hold that the community has its specific adequateness with respect to the person as a subject, with respect to the personal subjectivity of man, and thus with respect to the fact that every man is an "I" or a "thou," and not only a "he." The "he," similarly to the "they," seems to mean above all a man-object. We intend to conduct an analysis of the social dimension of the community not so much from the position of the "he" and "they," but in parallel to the previous analysis, thus, still in a sense from the position of the "I" and "thou." *Also, we do not intend to speak about society but only about the social dimension of the human community*, which is indicated by the pronoun "we." For we ought to state right at the beginning of this analysis that this pronoun indicates not only many subjects, many human "I's," but *also the specific subjectivity of this plurality*. In this way, the "we" differs from the "they."

When we say that the "we" denotes many human "I's," we grasp this plurality and try to understand it though action, similar to our attempt to understand the "I." The "we" means many people, many subjects, who in some way exist and act together. Our point, however, is not the plurality of actions, which progress next to each other, so to speak. "Together" means that these actions, as well as the existence of these many "I's," remain in relation to some single value, which thereby deserves to be called the common good (by speaking in this way, we do not intend to use interchangeably nor to confuse the concepts of the value and the good). *The relation of the many "I's" to the common good* seems to constitute *the very core of the social community*. Thanks to this relation, while experiencing their personal subjectivity—and thus the factual plurality of the human "I's"—people are conscious that they constitute a specific "we" and experience themselves in this new dimension. This is the social dimension, different from the "I-thou" dimension, though in this dimension the person remains himself. Thus, both the "I" and the "thou" remain, but the direction of the relation fundamentally changes. This direction is set by the common good. In this relation, the "I" and the "thou" also find their reciprocal relation in a new dimension; *they find their "I-thou" through the common good*, which determines a new unity between them.

The best example here can be marriage, in which the vividly delineated "I-thou" relation, the inter-personal relation, acquires a social dimension when the spouses accept in this relation the group of values that can be called the common good of marriage and—at least potentially—of the family. In relation to this good, their community appears as having a new profile and a new dimension in action and existence. This is the "we" profile and, at the same time, the *social dimension of the community of the two* (not only one + one, but two), who in this dimension do not cease to be the "I" and the "thou." They also do not cease to remain in the "I-thou" inter-personal relation; indeed, that relation draws from the "we" relation in its own way and is enriched through it. This, of course, means that this new social relation posits new tasks and demands essential to the "I-thou" inter-personal relation.

Having before our eyes the elementary outline of the "we" relation, we can ask—by analogy to the previous analysis—to what extent and in what sense the process of the specific constitution of every "I" through the "we" takes place, just as it takes place in the inter-personal relation where the "I" is constituted through the "thou," as discussed earlier. Human experience confirms this. Of course, when speaking about the constituting of the human "I," we take into consideration all that was said in the first part concerning the personal subjectivity of man. We do not mean here constituting in the metaphysical sense, because in this sense every "I" is constituted in its own *suppositum*. But *the constituting of the concrete "I" in its personal subjectivity takes place in a particular way through acting and existing "together with others" in a social community, in the dimension of various "we's."* It takes place in a different way than in the "I-thou" dimension; the relation to the common good has the decisive sense here. Through this relation, man, the concrete "I," finds another confirmation of his personal subjectivity besides the inter-personal relation. Nonetheless, this confirmation of the subject "I" in the community of the "we" deeply agrees with the nature of this subject. Perhaps this verification stands at the basis of all that has ever been said about the social nature of man.

By its essence, the *"we" denotes neither a diminishment nor a deformation of the "I."* If this happens *de facto* (this was noted in *Person and Act*), we ought to seek causes in the sphere of the relation to the common good. This relation can be defective in different ways—both on the part of the human "I" (or many human "I's") and on the part of what is accepted as the common good for many "I's."

This is an extensive field of philosophy and, above all, social ethics, which we do not intend to enter substantively and comprehensively here. Just as in the analysis of the inter-personal relations ("I-thou"), we do not intend to introduce into our reflections here the manifold forms and varieties of the social community, that is, the manifold forms and varieties of the social reality in which every man exists and acts (such as societies, communes, social groups, or environments). What we fundamentally also intend to do here in the analysis of the social dimension of the community is to especially grasp and elucidate the meaning of this dimension *in the aspect of man's personal subjectivity*—due to their adequateness. In this aspect, in which the auto-teleology of man is naturally manifested, the entire issue of his "self-fulfillment," thus also the community, must appear not only in its factual (i.e., ontological or meta-physical) sense, but also in its normative, that is, ethical, sense.

Thus, we first ought to state that the "common" relation of many "I's" to the common good, through which this plurality of subjects is revealed to itself (and to others) as a specific "we" (and is this "we"), constitutes a particular expression of the transcendence proper to man as a person. The relation to the common good realizes this transcendence in a particular way. It is fitting to refer here to what we said in the first part of this study on the topic of transcendence and its close connection with the self-fulfillment of the subjective "I." Conscience, as the key point of the personal subject's self-fulfillment, indicates transcendence in a particular way and inheres, so to speak, in its own subjective center. *Transcendence is objectively realized in the relation* to truth and to the good as "true" (that is, "honorable"). The relation *to the common good*, which unites the plurality of subjects into one "we," ought to be likewise grounded in the relation to truth and to the "true," that is, "honorable," good.[20] It is then that the proper measure of the common good will be manifested. The common good is by its essence the good of many, and in its fullest dimension it is the good of all. This plurality can be quantitatively different: a couple in the case of marriage (no longer one + one, but precisely a couple), several in the case of the family, millions when particular nations are concerned, and billions when we consider all mankind. The concept of the common good is thus an analogous concept because the very reality of this good is subjected to differentiation, thus, to the analogy of proportionality. The common good is something different for marriage or the family, for a nation, for mankind, and within them for every distinct society, commune, or social group, in which the human "we" is also realized in an analogous way. Nevertheless, in all these realizations *the common good corresponds to the transcendence of persons being the objective basis for their constitution in the social community as "we."*

The reality of the common good *in its proper richness of analogy* de-

---

20. See also *Gaudium et spes*, no. 24: "Indeed, the Lord Jesus, when He prayed to the Father, 'that all may be one ... as we are one' (John 17:21–22) opened up vistas closed to human reason, for He implied a certain likeness between the union of the divine Persons, and the unity of God's sons in truth and charity" [Vatican translation].

termines the direction of the transcendence that stands at the root of the human "we." This transcendence, however, belongs to the structure of the human "I," and is not opposed to the personal subjectivity of man but instead fundamentally corresponds to it. Of course, this does not mean that social life is a collision-free zone; we know from experience that the case is quite the contrary. In *Person and Act* we attempted to identify some variations of such collisions, only mentioning their manifold form and scope.[21] No less fundamentally does the social dimension of the community adequately enter the striving for self-fulfillment, the striving proper to the human subject. The common good as the objective basis of this dimension constitutes a greater fullness of value than the individual good of each separate "I" in a given community. Therefore, the common good has a superior character, and it corresponds to the subjective transcendence of the person in this character. The superior character of the common good, the greater fullness of the value that determines it, ultimately consists in the fact that the good of each of the subjects in the community, which calls itself "we," is expressed and realized more fully in that good. Thus, *through the common good, the human "I" finds itself more fully and thoroughly in the human "we."*

The common good is at times a difficult good; perhaps it is such even in principle. We Poles know from our history how much at various times this good, which is called "Poland" or "Homeland," cost particular people and entire generations of our compatriots. The measure of the effort put into the realization of the common good, the measure of sacrificing so many individual goods, such as in exile, prison, and death, witnessed, and constantly witnesses, to the greatness of this good, to its superiority. The situations presented here as examples—and these examples are very eloquent—and especially the extreme, boundary situations, also convincingly manifest the truth that *the common good by itself conditions the individual goods* of particular members of the community, of the human "we." In extreme situations, it seems that, without the common good, these goods lose, as it were, their reason for being in the lived-experience of certain members of the community. However, this in no way means

---

21. See especially in chapter 7 sections such as "Individualism and anti-individualism" [Editorial note: In this edition, the section just referred to is entitled "The systems limiting participation"], "The analysis of attitudes: Authentic attitudes," and "The analysis of attitudes: Non-authentic attitudes."

that self-dedication or the sacrifice of one's life for the common good is reduced to a simple "over-appreciation" between that good and the good of the individual in this or that community.

Precisely the fact that the common good is a superior good—and as such corresponds to the transcendence of the person, meets with his conscience, is embraced by him, or causes conflicts—*must the problem of the common good be the central problem of social ethics*. The history of societies and, at the same time, the evolution of social systems indicate that although we constantly struggle for the "true" common good, which corresponds to the very essence of the social community proper to the human "we" and the personal transcendence proper to the human "I," the facts nonetheless speak of the constant appearance of various kinds of utilitarianisms, totalisms, and social egoisms. In the smallest and, at the same, time most fundamental human "we," namely, marriage and the family, we already encounter manifestations of various deviations, which of course correspond to both this community and its own specificity. The more the plurality of the human "I's" increases, the more difficult, in a certain sense, becomes the social community, the unity proper to the human "we," in its various dimensions. After all, as we said, the common good is a difficult good.

The property of this good, the reason for its superiority in relation to individual goods, is, as was stated, that the good of each of the subjects of the community, which on the basis of the common good determines and experiences itself as "we," is more fully expressed and more fully realized in this good. This also explains the fact of the social community, the fact of the constitution of the "we" by many human "I's." This fact itself is fundamentally free from utilitarianism; it remains on the foundation of the objective and authentically experienced truth about good, also as a truth of conscience. In the name of precisely this truth, people as members of a community undertake efforts connected with the realization of the common good, sometimes even in the extreme situations mentioned above. But also, in the name of the same truth about the common good, people pursue all the values constituting the true and inviolable good of the person. This is expressed in our own epoch in a particular way, as attested by numerous statements and actions. For *the community*, the human "we" in various dimensions, *denotes the form of human pluralities in which the person as a subject is maximally realized*. Such then will be the sense of the common good in its various analogies, such will be the reason for its superiority, sometimes experienced dramatically, though in a fundamental way always ethically, by a personal subject.

As we said in the beginning, the "we" does not denote only a simple fact of human multi-subjectivity; it indicates not only many human "I's" but also the specific subjectivity of this plurality—at least, it indicates a decisive striving for attaining this subjectivity. Clearly, this is a manifold striving, which ought to be understood and realized as befitting the various "we's," in accord with the communal specificity proper to each of them. This striving, and in the wake of it the realization of the subjectivity of the many, is shaped differently in the case of the "we" of marriage or the family, differently when the given environment, commune, or social group is concerned, and differently when we consider a nation, country, or even all mankind. The expression "human family" is in this respect very eloquent. In these various dimensions, the human "I's" carry the readiness not only to think about themselves in the categories of "we," but also to realize *what is essential for the "we"*—and thus for the social community. Therefore, based on this community, and hence in conformity with its human essence, they carry *the readiness to realize the subjectivity of the many and, in the universal dimension, the subjectivity of all*. For this denotes the full realization of the human "we." It seems that only on the basis of the social community thus understood, in which the factual multi-subjectivity is developed in the direction of the subjectivity of the many, can we perceive an authentic *communio personarum* in the human "we."

It is known, however, how many obstacles, how many counter-dispositions, oppose this readiness of which we speak here, outgrowing it from different sides. It is also known how far we have yet to go to realize the human "we" in various areas, by way of both progressing and regressing in so many sectors. The issue is what prevails in different stages and how the balances of realizing different "we's," and ultimately the universal "we," are shaped.

In any case, the analysis of the social community demonstrates at this point the *fundamental homogeneity of the personal subject and of the human community*. What is at stake in the shaping of various "we's"—in all the richness of the analogies proper to it—is a clear reflex of the human "I," of the personal subjectivity of man, which is not opposed to that subjectivity. And if it is opposed, man as a subject must introduce corrections. The social community "we" is not only given to him but also constantly entrusted to him as a task. All this confirms the thesis of the specific primacy of the subject-person over the community. Without this, there is no way to defend not only the auto-teleology of the human "I," but also even the teleology of man.

Alienation as the antithesis of participation

It seems that the analyses of the inter-personal and social communities conducted here can result in manifold consequences. Above all, the concept of community cannot be applied univocally, because it indicates different realities. The reality of the social community cannot be fully reduced to the reality of the inter-human, inter-personal reality, and vice versa, the latter cannot be reduced to the former. Between the "I-thou" relationship and the "we" relationship, a distinctness of profiles exists, which reaches down to perhaps the very roots of both relationships. We can only—and even must—state that the "I-thou" relationship exists in different "we" relationships; "we" relationships do not eliminate it and definitely should not eliminate it; quite the contrary, they should facilitate and evoke it. Similarly, we can and ought to state that "we" relationships of different types progress through the "I-thou" relationship. The social and the inter-personal dimensions of the community *in different ways permeate, contain, and even condition each other*. Nonetheless, the profiles of these relationships *remain fundamentally distinct and separate*. From the normative point of view, we should strive to shape, support, and develop the "I-thou" and the "we" relationships in their authentic form. This denotes the possibly full regularity of the communal and the personal life, which is indicated by the known principle of subsidiarity (*principium subsidiarietatis*).

In turn, and based on our previous reflections, the meaning of participation and alienation as its antithesis can be more fully delineated. Indeed, in perceiving the distinctness of the community in the "I-thou" and the "we" relations, that is, the separate dimension of the inter-human and the social communities, we ascertain that in the entire analysis it is man as a person who is and remains the basis for the analogy in relation to them. Moreover, it seems that conducting analyses of the community from the viewpoint of man's personal subjectivity, as has been accomplished (or, rather, only outlined), allows us to establish fundamental theses concerning the community, that is, to discover the essential framework of the communal reality. The reversal of this order seems to be not only dangerous for the truth of the image at stake, but also simply impossible. For *we can sensibly speak of the community only in the world of persons*, thus only on the basis of the person as the proper subject of existing and acting, both personal and communal, and, moreover, *in relation to man's personal subjectivity itself*. For only this aspect allows us to grasp the essential properties of the human "I's" and the relations between them, both the inter-personal and the social alike. And therefore, it seems that the plane of the subject (which nonetheless is objective from the epistemological and methodological point of view) allows us to understand more fully both participation and alienation.

If we see alienation as the opposite—the antithesis—of participation, then we have before our eyes the person and the two dimensions of the community, both the "we" and the "I-thou" dimensions. In each of these dimensions, participation is bound with transcendence, and thereby is grounded in the person as a subject and in the striving for the self-realization proper to that person, for self-fulfillment. Man as a person fulfills himself through the "I-thou" inter-personal relations and through the relation to the common good, which allows him to exist and act together with the others as a "we." These two variations of the relation and the dimensions of the community connected with these variations also carry with themselves two distinct profiles of participation, and that was at least partially pictured in *Person and Act*. As we noted, this picture requires further analyses and clarifications, which to a certain extent is the purpose of this study.

The present analysis rather confirms the author in the conviction that participation ought to be understood as *a property of man corresponding to his personal subjectivity*. This subjectivity does not close man in himself, does not make him an impermeable monad, but, quite the contrary, it opens him to others in a way proper to a person. Thus, we can and should see in participation—both when the "I-thou" inter-personal and the "we" social dimensions of the community are concerned—the authentic expression of personal transcendence and its subjective confirmation in the person. Inasmuch as it could seem that the transcendence toward the common good, in a sense, draws man away from himself, or, speaking more broadly, draws everyone away from man, a thorough analysis of this good must nonetheless lead us to the conviction that *man is firmly inscribed in the true sense of the common good*, and not only man in his specific definition, but precisely man as a person and a subject. Therefore, this true sense of the common good, its full "honorableness," is and must be the central object of social ethics in science and the object of the greatest responsibility in practice.

And although the "I-thou" and the "we" profiles of the community are separate from and irreducible to each other, they nonetheless must permeate and condition each other in the experience and the formation of communal life. Man in his full truthfulness, man as a person, one whose personal identity is revealed through the "I-thou" relations, inasmuch as these relations have the profile of the authentic *communio personarum*, is inscribed and must constantly be inscribed in the true sense of the common good if this good is to correspond to its definition, and thus to its essence. Therefore, it seems that in *Person and Act* we could describe participation (in the social profile) as the property by virtue of which man strives (also) for self-fulfillment and fulfills himself by acting and existing together with others. Although this description originates from the person as a subject and not from the community—from the "I" and not from the "we," and thus it seems aspectual and not integral—it nonetheless allows us equally well to find the social profile of the community. For *participation thus understood conditions the entire authenticity of the human "we,"* the "we" that is objectively shaped on the basis of the relation to the common good. At the same time, however, and on the basis of that relation in particular—as we showed in the present analysis—it aims at shaping the true subjectivity of all who belong to the social community. The transition from multi-subjectivity to the subjectivity of the many is the proper and full sense of the human "we." Participation understood as the property of every "I," by virtue of which the "I" fulfills itself by existing and acting "together," does not oppose this meaning of the social community. Indeed, it seems that participation only thus understood can ensure both that meaning and above all the realization of the social community: the realization of the human "we" in all its authenticity as the true subjectivity of the many.

Participation thus understood, namely as the property of the person, by virtue of which he is and remains himself in the social community, seems to condition the authentic *communio personarum* both in the "we" relations and in the "I-thou" inter-personal relations. Both consist in opening; both are shaped on the basis of the transcendence proper to the person. The "I-thou" relation opens man directly to man. *To participate means in this case to turn to the other "I" on the basis of personal transcendence, and thus to turn to the full truth about this man and, in this sense, to his humanity.* This humanity is given in the "I-thou" relation not as an abstract idea of man (this problem belongs in *Person and Act* rather to epistemological foundations), but as a "thou" for an "I." In this relationship, participation is nothing else but the realization of the inter-personal community in which the personal subjectivity "thou" is revealed through the "I" (and, in a sense, reciprocally), and above all the personal subjectivity of the one and the other is grounded, secured, and grows in this community.

Alienation is the opposite of participation; it is the antithesis of participation. It is known that the concept of alienation was used in Marxist philosophy. Regardless of this, however, it constitutes one of the elements of modern anthropology, of contemporary thought about man. Therefore, we ask ourselves the question: What is this alienation? How should we understand its essence? It seems that, regardless of the interpretations already presented concerning what in fact or allegedly was or is alienation, it is suitable and indeed fundamental to continue to ask the question and to inquire *what alienation is in itself.* Indeed, *only the answer to this question can authenticate our judgments on the factual variations of alienation,* on what it was, is, and can be.[22]

If we say that alienation is the antithesis of participation, then this statement remains connected to what we said previously, formulating the *status quaestionis* of this—second—part of the statement about the

---

22. Concerning this issue, see Fr. Zbigniew Majchrzyk's study "Problem alienacji u polskich marksistów" (a doctoral dissertation written in 1973 and directed by Fr. Tadeusz Styczeń at the philosophical department of the Catholic University of Lublin; a copy is available in the university's library).

person. What was said is that the entire problem of alienation cannot be considered with respect to man as an individual of a species, thus not with respect to his specific definition, but only with respect to man as a personal subject. We hold *that alienation is in its essence a personalistic problem* and in this sense, of course, both a humanistic and an ethical one.

As the antithesis of participation, alienation contributes to or (depending on what the alienating factor is) creates an occasion for *man to be* to some extent *deprived of the possibility of fulfilling himself in the community*—either in the *social* community *"we"* or in the *inter-personal* community *"I"-"thou."* For alienation can and does occur in a manifold way in both these dimensions of the community. As far as the social dimension is concerned, the presence of alienating factors is manifested in the fact that the plurality of human subjects, in whom each is a given "I," cannot correctly develop toward the authentic "we." The social process that should lead to the true subjectivity of all is then hindered or even reverted because man cannot find himself as a subject in this process. In a sense, the social life goes on outside him—not so much against him, but rather "at his expense." He, on the other hand, by existing and acting "together with others," does not fulfill himself in this life, either because he estranged himself or because the society, by its defective structures, does not give him the basis for it or, what is more, denies him appropriate rights.

This, of course, is not a full and exhaustive picture, but *merely an outline leading us* to understand alienation as the antithesis of participation in the social sense. Depending on its dimensions, alienation of this type limits or even destroys the human "we," not only on the part of this or that "I" (as in the case of estrangement), but—as history and contemporariness teach us—in the dimensions of entire social groups, environments, classes, or even nations. In no way do we undertake here the analysis of this social phenomenon. The point is to grasp the outline that will allow us to define more closely the essence of alienation. Analogously—while retaining all the distinctness of the relationship to which we paid attention in previous analyses—we can reveal this outline in the inter-personal dimension of the community, in the "I-thou" relations. This dimension is in general quantitatively incomparable, though sometimes qualitatively even more afflictive. For perhaps human life progresses more in the "I-thou" than in the "we" dimensions. *Alienation as* the antithesis of participation means in this dimension the *limitation or destruction of all through which man is for man another "I."* The lived-experience of the truth of humanity, of the essential value of the person in the human "thou," is then upset. The "I" remains cut off and not contacted, and thereby not fully discovered also for itself. Then in inter-human relations the "neighbor" vanishes, and the "other," the "alien," or even the "hostile" remains.

This is also only an outline leading us to the meaning of alienation in the inter-human dimensions. The community is deformed in this dimension and vanishes just as the lived-experience of humanity, which authentically brings people closer to one another and unifies them, vanishes as well. If we hold that alienation is the antithesis of participation with respect to both these dimensions of the community, we thereby wish to highlight—from the negative viewpoint—all that was the content of this entire analysis, namely, that the reality of the human community in both its dimensions—the "I-thou" and the "we"—is shaped on the basis of man's personal subjectivity, particularly and above all in relation to it. Alienation as the antithesis of participation, and thus the opposition or negation of participation, not so much "dehumanizes" man as an individual of a species as it strikes at the person as a subject. On the other hand, *participation as the antithesis of alienation confirms and enhances the person as a subject*, and in this sense, it can also be accepted as a specific "property" of the person. For it serves his self-fulfillment in both the inter-human and social relations. In every dimension it secures the transcendence proper to the person.

❦

Our reflections are coming to an end. We do not intend to conduct in them an analysis of alienation alone. What we said a moment ago constitutes neither a description of the phenomenon nor an attempt to systematize it. It is known that much has been written on that topic. The concept of alienation became one of the important, if not downright fundamental, categories of contemporary thought about man. At the same time, with the plurality of declarations on what alienation is—at least the declarations known from Marxist philosophy—we see no fully established view on what alienation is, what constitutes its essence.

The author of this sketch does not *ex professo* concern himself with this topic. The proper object of the analyses collected under the title "The Person: Subject and Community" was to examine the connections that occur between the (inter-human and social) community and the personal subjectivity of man. However, at the conclusion of these analyses, the author sees the *possibility of proposing the reduction of various factual descriptions of alienation* (which contain only a statement or suggestion that it occurs in given situations) *onto the plane of the person as a subject and community*. It seems that by way of this reduction—and this analysis can also serve as its instrument—the essence of alienation will be more fully revealed. Only a fuller knowledge of what alienation is can constitute the basis for stating what thing it is (in the given cases or situations) and why.

We stated several times in the second part of the present reflections that we cannot speak of alienation on the basis of the specific concept of "man" alone, but only in relation to the personal subjectivity of this man. This statement is introductory and, in a sense, intuitive. Nevertheless, the author expresses the conviction that the analysis of the personal subjectivity of man conducted here in the context of "the person: subject-community" can also serve, thanks to this intuition, to examine the nature of alienation.

6 ❧ Participation or Alienation

[1a]

[2a]Introduction

In this lecture I wish to take up one of the problems that lie at the center of the contemporary thought about man.[cxxiv] The problem "participation or alienation" lies at the center of thought because it is also located in the center of life: of the existence and coexistence of people, societies, environments, and systems. The very concepts of "participation" and "alienation" carry various connotations. They are linked with the areas of sociology, economics, and politics, and at the same time progress through the sphere of ethics and theology. Both these concepts have a rich philosophical genealogy, which cannot be exhaustively presented here.[2b]

[3a] [4a]"Participation" originates from the philosophy of Plato,[1] thus, it remains linked with his idealism from its beginnings; though later—in Christian philosophy and theology—it finds its new interpretation, namely, a realistic one. By using this concept in this lecture, I accept that interpretation in particular and confer a personalistic sense on the concept of "participation." For I see a possibility and need to introduce "participation" into the philosophy of the person precisely on account of "alienation," which also finds its proper application in the philosophy of the person.

---

1. Plato, *Parmenides* 132d, 151e; *Symposium* 510a, 511a and others. [Editorial note: Wojtyła most likely used *Platonis opera: Graece et latine* (Paris: Firmin-Didot, 1891–1900).] See Louis-Bertrand Geiger, *La participation dans la philosophie de S. Thomas d'Aquin* (Paris: Vrin, 1942), 92; Cornelio Fabro, *Participation et causalité selon S. Thomas d'Aquin* (Louvain: Publications Universitaires de Louvain, 1961), 426. See also Zofia J. Zdybicka, *Partycypacja bytu: Próba wyjaśnienia relacji między światem a Bogiem* (Lublin: Towarzystwo Naukowe Katolickiego Uniwersytetu Lubelskiego, 1972), 20–38.

Participation or Alienation | 515

The very concept of "alienation" originates from nineteenth-century philosophy.[2] This concept gained specific popularity in contemporary thought through Marxist philosophy. For according to Marx, the entire revolutionary practice is to serve to overcome the manifold alienation of man. Marx considered alienation to be the system of private property, the state holding this system, the work in this system, the social-economic relations shaped by this system, and religion. Marx and Marxists understand alienation as all that by which man deprives himself or is deprived of what is essentially human, what belongs to humanity or to man. In this way the concept of alienation stands at the same time at the very center of Marxist anthropology. This concept is a constant topic of interest for contemporary Marxist and non-Marxist thinkers,[3] among others in Poland.[4] They state that various revolutionary changes within

2. Wincenty Granat, "Alienacja," in *Encyklopedia Katolicka* (Lublin: Wydawnictwo Towarzystwa Naukowego Katolickiego Uniwersytetu Lubelskiego, 1973), 1:367–69.

3. The bibliography concerning this problem is very rich. I offer a few works as examples: Marcella D'Abbiero, *Alienazione in Hegel: Usi e significati de Entäusserung, Entfremdung, Veräusserung* (Rome: Edizioni dell'Ateneo, 1971); Nicola Badaloni, "Alienazione e libertà nel pensiero di Marx," *Critica Marxista* 6, nos. 4–5 (1968): 139–64; Daniel Bell, "The Debate on Alienation," in *Revisionism: Essays on the History of Marxist Ideas*, ed. Leopold Labedz (London: Allen and Unwin, 1962); Peter L. Berger, *La religion dans la conscience moderne* (Paris: Centurion, 1971), 137–67; Pierre Bigo, *Marxisme et humanisme* (Paris: Presses Universitaires de France, 1954); Robert Blauner, *Alienation and Freedom: The Factory Worker and His Industry* (Chicago: University of Chicago Press, 1964); David Braybroocke, "Diagnosis and Remedy in Marx's Doctrine of Alienation," *Social Research* 25, no. 3 (1958): 325–45; Jean-Yves Calvez, *La pensée de Karl Marx* (Paris: Éditions du Seuil, 1956); Raya Dunayevskaya, *Marxism and Freedom* (New York: Bookman Associates, 1958); Loyd D. Easton, "Alienation and History in the Early Marx," *Philosophy and Phenomenological Research* 22, no. 2 (1961): 193–205; Auguste Etcheverry, *Le conflit actuel des humanistes* (Paris: Presses Universitaires de France, 1955); Iring Fetscher, "Przemiany marksistowskiej krytyki religii," *Concilium* 1 (1968): 477–91; Erich Fromm, *Marx's Concept of Man* (New York: Frederick Ungar, 1961); Fromm, *Beyond the Chains of Illusion: My Encounter with Marx and Freud* (New York: Simon and Schuster, 1962); Fromm, *The Sane Society* (New York: Holt, Rinehart and Winston, 1960); Roger Garaudy, *La liberté* (Paris: Éditions Sociales, 1955); Garaudy, *Humanisme marxiste: Cinq essais polémiques* (Paris: Éditions Sociales, 1957); Garaudy, *Perspectives de l'homme: Existentialisme, pensée catholique, marxisme* (Paris: Presses Universitaires de France, 1959), translated by by Zdzisław Butkiewicz and Julian Rogoziński as *Perspektywy człowieka: Egzystencjalizm, myśl katolicka, marksizm* (Warsaw: Książka i Wiedza, 1968); Garaudy, *Marxisme du XXe siecle* (Paris: La Palatine, 1966); Patrick Masterson, *Atheism and Alienation: A Study of the Philosophical Sources of Contemporary Atheism* (Dublin: Gill and Macmillan, 1971); Fritz Pappenheim, *The Alienation of Modern Man: An Interpretation Based on Marx and Tönnies* (New York: Monthly Review Press, 1959); Aldo Zanardo, "Forme e problemi del marxismo contemporaneo (a proposito della fortuna del pensiero giovanile di Marx)," *Studi storici* 3, no. 4 (1962): 667–730.

4. See especially Adam Schaff, *Marksizm a jednostka ludzka: Przyczynek do marksistowskiej filozofii człowieka* (Warsaw: Państwowe Wydawnictwo Naukowe, 1965); Andrzej Werblan et al., "Dyskusja nad książką Adama Schaffa pt. 'Marksizm a jednostka ludzka,'" *Nowe drogi* 19, no. 12

the economic-social or the economic-political systems do not necessarily contribute to the elimination of the phenomenon of alienation; sometimes new variations of alienation appear on that basis.[5]

Precisely these reflections incline us, among other things, to consider the problem of alienation on the basis of philosophical anthropology, and in particular on the basis of the philosophy of the person. For it seems that the very concept of alienation can contribute a great deal to the contemporary understanding of the problem of man. The philosophy of the person manifests the proper dimension of this problem and shows more fully the subjectivity of man, inter-subjective relations, and the relation between the man-subject and the human community.

Precisely on the basis of these relations, I wish to attempt to show the oppositions between alienation and participation[6] (in the personalistic sense of this term) in this lecture. Of course, the attempt to address the

---

(1965): 57–186; "Dyskusja nad książką A. Schaffa pt. 'Marksizm a jednostka ludzka,'" *Studia filozoficzne*, no. 1 (1966): 3–50; Schaff, "Marksizm a jednostka ludzka (podsumowanie dyskusji)," *Studia filozoficzne*, no. 2 (1966): 87–106; Schaff, "Alienacja a działanie społeczne," in *Fragmenty filozoficzne, seria III: Księga pamiątkowa ku czci Profesora Tadeusza Kotarbińskiego w osiemdziesiątą rocznicę urodzin*, ed. Tadeusz Czeżowski, 481–98 (Warsaw: Państwowe Wydawnictwo Naukowe, 1967).

See also Bronisław Baczko, "Wokół problemów alienacji," *Studia filozoficzne*, no. 6 (1959): 19–52; Baczko, "Hegel, Marks i problemy alienacji," *Studia filozoficzne*, no. 1 (1957): 36–58; Jan Danecki, *Czas wolny: Mity i potrzeby* (Warsaw: Książka i Wiedza, 1967); Stanisław Grygiel, "Człowiek czy Bóg?" *Znak* 22 (1970), 145–76; Tadeusz M. Jaroszewski, *Alienacja?* (Warsaw: Książka i Wiedza, 1965); Leszek Kołakowski, *Kultura i fetysze: Zbiór rozpraw* (Warsaw: Państwowe Wydawnicto Naukowe, 1967); Janusz Kuczyński, *Porządek nadchodzącego świata: Katolicyzm, laicyzm, humanizm* (Warsaw: Książka i Wiedza, 1964); Zbigniew Kuderowicz, "Marks i Engels wobec alternatywy: Jednostka-społeczeństwo," *Studia filozoficzne*, no. 2 (1969): 113–30; Marek Fritzhand, *Myśl etyczna młodego Marksa* (Warsaw: Książka i Wiedza, 1961); Fritzhand, *O niektórych właściwościach etyki marksistowskiej* (Warsaw: Państwowe Wydawnicto Naukowe, 1974).

5. See especially Schaff, *Marksizm a jednostka ludzka*, 176–95; see also Kołakowski, *Kultura i fetysze*, 79, 115, 269, and 270.

6. The author of this article does not *ex professo* concern himself with the topic of alienation. He sees, however, the possibility to propose performing a reduction of various factual descriptions of alienation (which contain a statement or suggestion that alienation occurs in given situations) onto the plane of the person as a subject and of the community. It seems that the essence of alienation will be more fully revealed by way of this reduction. We cannot speak about alienation on the basis of the specific concept "man" alone, but only in relation to the personal subjectivity of that man. Although this is an introductory and, in a sense, still intuitive statement, the author nonetheless expresses the conviction that the analysis of the personal subjectivity of man in the context of the person as both subject and community can also serve, with the help of this intuition, an examination of the nature of alienation. See the author's study "The Person: Subject and Community," [pp. 467–513 in this edition]. See especially part 2, section 4, "Alienation as the antithesis of participation." See also my study *Person and Act* [Osoba i czyn], (Kraków: Polskie Towarzystwo Teologiczne, 1969), part 4, "Participation," 283–326 [pp. 377–414 in this edition].

problem "participation or alienation" also requires one's own elaboration of both these concepts. I wish to do so by analyzing two types of relations. The first one is the inter-human relation that can be grasped by the "I–the other" formula (I would not identify it immediately with the "I-thou" relation, which undoubtedly is a particular form of the "I–the other" relation). I intend to devote a little more time to the analysis of this relation, also because I have dealt with it more.[7] Besides, I think that the inter-personal relation is perhaps more fundamental—also from the viewpoint of the antinomy that occurs between participation and alienation. From the same viewpoint, I intend to analyze the relation of the "we" type, which indicates the social (and not only the inter-personal) dimension of human existence.

In all these reflections I bear in mind not only an "academic" and abstract problem, but also a problem that truly seems to lie in the very center of the lives of contemporary people—and in different dimensions at that. For it is in different dimensions that man—each and every one—happens to exist and act "together with others." It is thus first and foremost on this basis that we should seek both what confirms man, what serves his autorealization, and what in any way deprives him of "humanity."[4b]

An enormous and diverse body of literature, not only a philosophical one, corresponds to the problems that I will consider here. In this relatively brief statement, I will only be able to refer to a few authors, namely, to those whose works I personally came in contact with. Although, as I indicated, I attempt to present the entire problem on the basis of my own reflections, [5a]I should underscore that there is also a rich body of literature in the Polish language[5b].[8] My statement will certainly have the

---

7. My work entitled "Participation or Alienation (Participation ou aliénation)" is devoted in an analytical way to shaping the relation of "I" to "thou." It was sent to the International Phenomenological Colloquium in Swiss Fribourg, which took place January 24–28, 1975, and was in turn delivered at the invitation of the Department of Philosophy at the University of Fribourg on February 27 of the same year. The general topic of the colloquium organized by the Société Internationale pour l'étude de Husserl et de la phénoménologie—Internationale Forschungsgesellschaft für Phänomenologie was: "Soi et autrui—la crise de l'irréductible dans l'homme."

8. I list only some works: Mieczysław Gogacz, Wokół problemu osoby (Warsaw: Pax, 1974); Wincenty Granat, Osoba ludzka: Próba definicji (Sandomierz: Wydawnictwo Diecezjalne w Sandomierzu, 1961); Roman Ingarden, Książeczka o człowieku (Kraków: Wydawnictwo Literackie, 1972). Ingarden's collection contains among others the following discourses: "Człowiek i przyroda"—a Polish translation of the lecture "L'homme et la nature" delivered during the discussion on the problem of "Man and nature [przyroda]" at the plenary session of the XII International Congress of Phi-

most in common both with their reflections and with the situation of the human person in my homeland.[3b]

[6a]1. The Form of Participation and Alienation Connected with the Relation of the "I–the Other" Type[6b]

[7a]What does it mean to participate in the humanity of man?

Above all, a question arises as to how we understand man, whom in this relation we describe with the pronoun "I."[7b]

[8a]The "I" does not merely denote the content of consciousness but *denotes the real subject* who, through consciousness, experiences himself (i.e., precisely the "I") and experiences "the other" outside himself. *That which most fully and most penetratingly reveals man as the "I"—indeed, as the person—is the act.*[9] And the moment of self-determination is essential for every act performed consciously by a concrete man.[8b]

Self-determination, which in the simplest and full way reveals the

---

losophy in Venice in 1958; "O naturze ludzkiej"—a Polish translation of the theses of the lecture "La nature humaine," delivered at the XI Congress of the Philosophical Associations of the French Language in Montpellier in 1961 (announced in the acts of this congress in Paris in 1961); *O odpowiedzialności i jej podstawach ontycznych* (*Über die Verantwortung: Ihre ontischen Fundamente*), a discourse printed in German as a separate book by Philipp Reclam Jun., Stuttgart, 1970 (translated from German by Adam Węgrzecki). Marek Fritzhand, *Człowiek, humanizm, moralność: Ze studiów nad Marksem* (Warsaw: Książka i Wiedza, 1961); Tadeusz M. Jaroszewski, *Osobowość i wspólnota: Problemy osobowości we współczesnej antropologii filozoficznej—marksizm, strukturalizm, egzystencjalizm, personalizm chrześcijański* (Warsaw: Książka i Wiedza, 1970); Marian Jaworski, "Człowiek i Bóg: Zagadnienie relacji znaczeniowej pomiędzy osobą ludzką i Bogiem a problemem ateizmu," in *Logos i ethos: Rozprawy filozoficzne*, 115–28 (Kraków: Polskie Towarzystwo Teologiczne, 1971); Mieczysław Albert Krąpiec, *Ja—człowiek: Zarys antropologii filozoficznej* (Lublin: Towarzystwo Naukowe Katolickiego Uniwersytetu Lubelskiego, 1974); Krąpiec, *Człowiek i prawo naturalne* (Lublin: Towarzystwo Naukowe Katolickiego Uniwersytetu Lubelskiego, 1975); Bohdan Bejze, ed., *O człowieku dziś*, vol. 2 of *Aby poznać Boga i człowieka* (Warsaw: Wydawnictwo Sióstr Loretanek, 1974); Adam Schaff, *Filozofia człowieka*, 3rd ed. (Warsaw: Książka i Wiedza, 1965); Thomas Aquinas, *Traktat o człowieku* [Treatise on man], *Summa theologiae I, 75–89*, trans. and ed. Stefan Świeżawski (Poznań: Pallotinum, 1956); Marian Jaworski and Adam Kubiś, eds., *Teologia a antropologia: Kongres teologów polskich 21–23 IX 1971* (Kraków: Polskie Towarzystwo Teologiczne, 1971); Józef Tischner, "Aksjologiczne podstawy doświadczenia 'ja' jako całości cielesno-przestrzennej," in *Logos i ethos*, 33–79.

9. My study entitled *Person and Act* (Kraków: Polskie Towarzystwo Teologiczne, 1969) is built precisely on this conviction. [21a]See also the discussion on that study published in *Analecta Cracoviensia* 5–6 (1973–74): 49–272. See also Andrzej Półtawski, "Czyn i świadomość," in *Logos i ethos*, 83–113.[21b]

freedom of the will and the freedom of man, *allows us at the same time to define that by which everyone is his own "I."* It allows us in a sense to touch what the concept *soi* expresses.[10] Here man, the subject of the act, through the moment of self-determination manifested in this act, discovers and confirms himself as one who possesses himself. *Not only self-consciousness but above all self-possession belongs to the essence of* soi-*"I." Self-consciousness* conditions self-possession, and this is manifested above all in the act. [9a](This is in some sense manifested also when the action of man demonstrates essential deficiencies of self-possession, when man "allows himself to be governed" by affections or passions.)[9b] Thus the act introduces us into the very depth of the human "I"-*soi*.[10a] This happens by way of experience.

[11a]Who, in that case, is "the other"?[11b]

"The other"-*autrui* is located outside the field of this experience. Self-consciousness and self-possession, as their very names indicate, are untransferable outside this one concrete "I"-*soi*, which experiences and consequently understands itself in this way. However, the impossibility of experientially transferring outside oneself what constitutes one's own "I" does not mean the impossibility of *understanding* that *"the other" is constituted in a similar way, that he is also an "I."* What will be essential for his constitution is self-possession conditioned by his own self-consciousness. In some measure, understanding this truth defines the relation of the concrete "I" to all people. They are not only "other" in relation to the "I," but each of them is at the same time "an other 'I.'" "The other"-*autrui* is always one of them—an "other 'I'" remaining in a relation to my own "I," a relation experienced in some way.

[12a]*The consciousness that "the other" is "an other 'I'"* determines a capacity to participate in the very humanity of other people and initiates this participation. Thanks to this, everyone can be a "neighbor" to me. For *"the other" does not only denote the sameness of the being* that exists next to me and that even acts together with me in some system of actions. On the basis of this real situation, *"the other"* denotes a no less real, though

---

10. [22a]See Karol Wojtyła, "The Personal Structure of Self-Determination," trans. Andrzej Potocki, in *Tommaso d'Aquino nel suo VII Centenario: Congresso Internationale, Roma-Napoli, 17–24 aprile 1974*, 379–90. [see p. 457 in this edition]. [22b]

above all subjective, participation in humanity, proceeding from the consciousness that the other man is "an other 'I,'" that is, "also an I."[12b]

Thus, the reality of "the other" does not result primarily from the categorial cognition alone, from humanity as a conceptualization of the being "man," but from the even fuller lived-experience, in which *a transfer, as it were, occurs of what is given to us as our own "I"* outside ourselves onto "one of the others" who thereby appears before me as "an other 'I'"—"a second 'I'"—a "neighbor." (This lived-experience could be described perhaps even more accurately as the "reception" of another man as the "other 'I.'" It seems, however, that this "reception" does not take place without the previous "transfer" of which we spoke above.) The neighbor is another man, not only on the basis of the general sameness of humanity but also, and above all, *on the basis of being "an other I."*

[13a]The "I–the other" relationship demands actualization[13b]

Participation in the humanity of other people—of the others, of neighbors—is not foremost shaped by a mere understanding of the being "man," which by its nature is general and does not sufficiently approach man as a concrete "I." Participation is shaped *by way of the consciousness-related approach that proceeds from the lived-experience of one's own "I."* This does not mean that the understanding of the being "man" bears no significance for participation, being alien, or even opposite to it. By no means. The understanding of the being opens a way to participation, but by itself does not yet determine participation. Also, it alone does not shape the "I–the other" (*soi-autrui*) relationship. This relationship is not yet shaped by the fact that we have a [14a]general[14b] concept of man, in which we encompass all people without exception. *The "I–the other" relationship is* not [15a]general[15b] but *always* [16a]concrete[16b], *every time unique and unrepeatable*—both when we, proceeding from "I," consider it as a one-directional relationship, and when we consider its reciprocal character, since "the other" is also a distinct "I" for whom I can be precisely "the other."

[17a] It is known that very many people exist and act in the world; all these are conceptually apprehended by everyone who thinks "man." In this apprehension, however, no one is yet "the other" in relation to "I." *The very concept "man" does not yet create this relationship.* Does it only indicate the possibility of this relationship? It seems that it is something

more—it is the first potentiality of this relationship, *making it fundamentally possible*. This concept makes this relationship possible in relation to all people, without exception, that is, in relation to every man. The concept "man" fundamentally opens the path to the lived-experience of "the other 'I'" in relation to everyone who is included in this *concept just as my own "I" is included in it—and because this "I" is included in it as well*. Thus, that which determines the potentiality of the "I–the other" (*soi-autrui*) relationship is above all the fact of both partners of this relationship being man, a fact that is made conscious by them.

In what way is participation realized? [18a] If "the other" (*autrui*) or the "neighbor" (*prochain*) appears to me as "the other 'I'"—and it is only this that we can call participation in concrete humanity—then *in my consciousness and lived-experience* on the basis of general properties of the other as "man" there *must come into being that which also determines my own "I," for this determines the relation to the other as to an "I."* As we previously stated, that which determines the lived-experience of my own "I" (that is, the lived-experience of man who is me as "myself") is not only self-consciousness but also and even more so the self-possession conditioned by it. [19a] I possess myself not so much through becoming self-conscious as through self-determination. It tells me of full subjectivity and of the objective unity of actions with the being that I am as their subject. Thus it—self-possession—attests to my own "I" as a person. The category of the person objectivizes and expresses in philosophical (and colloquial) language what is given in experience as the "I."

The actualization of the "I–the other" (soi-autrui) relationship proceeds from becoming conscious of the fact of the humanity of a specific man outside me, one of many, *but is accomplished in the lived-experience of the other "I" as a person*. Participation means the fundamental personalization of the relation of man to man. I cannot experience another man as myself, for my own "I" as such is untransferable. When I experience him as a person, I approach in a maximal way what determines his "I" as a unique and unrepeatable realness of man.

Participation as a task

The analysis thus far leads us to the conviction that, although people exist and act together within different societies, communities, or environments, and although these existence and action are accompanied by the fundamental becoming conscious of the humanity of each of them, the participation itself in humanity is nonetheless not yet actualized in this. The actualization of participation in relation to every man emerges before everyone as a task. It also seems that precisely this is what explains *the fundamental need for the commandment contained in the Gospel*, the commandment whose fullest rightness, that is, whose key ethical meaning, is largely accepted by people regardless of professed religion or worldview. We should state that what we call *the commandment to love in its fundamental*, elementary (in a sense still pre-ethical) *layer, constitutes a call to experience the other man as "the other 'I'"*—that is, a call to participate in his humanity concretized in his person, just like my humanity is concretized in my person.

For, as we said, the "I–the other" relationship is not ready-made but only potential; experience demonstrates a need for a certain *impulse to realize it*. If this impulse was expressed in the commandment, that does not mean that it could remain only external. It must be born internally. The commandment to love only indicates that every man must, as a task, constantly posit actual participation in the humanity of other people, that is, the lived-experience of the other as "I," as a person. Thus, the *impulse* expressed from without by the commandment *must* every time *proceed from within*. Is this impulse exclusively emotional, as Max Scheler seems to claim, and does it have a completely spontaneous character?

[20a]It is difficult to deny the significance of human spontaneity in the shaping of the relations of man to man, above all the significance of affections, of emotional spontaneity.[20b] Certainly, this is an enormous capital distributed in people differently and differently influences the shaping of the "I–the other" relationships. *Scheler's analyses*[11] [21a] also provide an

---

11. See especially Max Scheler, *Der Formalismus in der Ethik und die materiale Wertethik: Neuer Versuch der Grundlegung eines ethischen Personalismus*, vol. 2, 5th ed. (Bern: Francke, 1966). Fragments (including "Z fenomenologii życia emocjonalnego człowieka") translated by Adam Węgrzecki in his *Scheler*, Myśli i ludzie (Warsaw: Wiedza Powszechna, 1975), part 2, pp. 131–219. See also Scheler, *Wesen und Formen der Sympathie*, 3rd ed. (Bonn: F. Cohen, 1926).

[23a]See my articles "System etyczny Maksa Schelera jako środek do opracowania etyki chrześcijańskiej," *Polonia sacra* 6, nos. 2–4 (1953–54): 143–61; "Problem oderwania przeżycia od aktu w etyce na tle poglądów Kanta i Schelera," *Roczniki filozoficzne* 5, no. 3 (1955–57): 113–40; "O metafizycznej i fenomenologicznej podstawie normy moralnej (w oparciu o koncepcję św. Tomasza z Akwinu oraz Maksa Schelera)," *Roczniki teologiczno-kanoniczne* nos. 1–2 (1959): 99–124.[23b]

additional argument for the fact that there is a fundamental disposition to participate in humanity as a value that inheres in man, and thus *a disposition to a spontaneous opening toward others; something that seems to be contradicted by Sartre,*[12] whose analysis of consciousness leads to a definitive closing of the subject with respect to "others."[22a]

Thus, without at all diminishing the importance of emotions and spontaneity in the shaping of the authentic "I–the other" (*soi-autrui*) relationship, it is nonetheless difficult not to accept that, since every man faces this relationship as a certain task, then its *actualization always fundamentally depends on the will*. The lived-experience of man, of one of others, as the other "I," always contains a discreet choice. First of all, it is a choice of precisely this man among others, which after all is reduced to the fact that precisely this man among others is *hic et nunc* given or "entrusted as a task" to me. The choice spoken of here consists in the fact that *I accept his "I," that is, I affirm the person,* and in this way, I *in a sense "choose him in myself," that is, in my "I,"* for I do not have another access to the other man as an "I" except through my own "I." Emotional disposition and purely emotional spontaneity can help with this choice, but they can also hinder it. The expression *"emotional spontaneity"* was used here on purpose, for we must accept that there additionally exists a *spontaneity of the will.* [23a] The choice spoken of here lies on the plane of that spontaneity. The constituting of the "other 'I'" in my consciousness and will is not a result of a choice among people, among others. As was said, we are concerned with the man who is *hic et nunc* given and entrusted as a task to me, and therefore this "choice" is not necessarily experienced as a choice. It is *rather a simple identification of "one of the others" as "the other 'I'"* on the basis of the lived-experience of my own "I"—an identification of the person and the value—and this identification does not require a longer process of the will, an acknowledgment or struggle of motives, etc.[23b]

Nonetheless this does not at all change the fact that we deal here with a certain choice, and that participation in the humanity of the other man is a certain task. This task can and should be posited at the foundations of a strictly ethical order and valuation. Although its own meaning seems to

---

12. See especially Jean-Paul Sartre, *L'être et le néant: Essai d'ontologie phénoménologique* (Paris: Gallimard, 1957), 310ff and 502.

be above all personalistic, to an enormous extent a strictly ethical order of values depends precisely on it. The so-called *second categorical imperative*, as formulated by Immanuel Kant, may serve as a confirmation of this thesis.[13] [24a]

[25a]Alienation is the opposite of participation

The statement that the "I–the other" relationship is not something ready-made and completely spontaneous, but a particular task, helps us to interpret the manifold reality of inter-human relations. In short, we can describe them as "I-thou." In the "I-thou" relation, we discover different forms of the path followed by the *soi-autrui* ("I–the other") relationship, if this relationship is to be shaped as the authentic *communio personarum*. Here it seems that the old analyses of such a master as Aristotle,[14] concentrated on both the axiological and ethical essence of friendship, still tell us very much. All these are "positive" verifications of participation.[25b]

However, we should pay more attention to the *negative verifications* than to the other ones. They speak [26a], perhaps even more, of reality being the participation in the humanity of the other man. With a more penetrating analysis of their subjective complexity, affections or attitudes such as hate, reluctance, aggression, and envy demonstrate that nothing else *lies at their bottom but the lived-experience of the other man as the other* "I"—not of the one whom I encompass in an abstract way by the very concept "man," but precisely of the one whom in I "choose in my 'I'" (or "on the basis of my 'I'") a certain way. Only this can explain the spiritual onerousness of affections or attitudes such as reluctance, hate, aggression, or envy. The suffering that accompanies this, indicates in any case that man as the other "I" is not indifferent to me. Perhaps even these *neg-*

---

13. See Immanuel Kant, *Grundlegung zur Metaphysik der Sitten*; translated by Mścisław Wartenberg as *Uzasadnienie metafizyki moralności*, ed. Roman Ingarden, 2nd ed. (Warsaw: Państwowe Wydawnictwo Naukowe, 1953; first published in 1906). [24a]See my article "O kierowniczej lub służebnej roli rozumu w etyce: Na tle poglądów Tomasza z Akwinu, Hume'a i Kanta," *Roczniki filozoficzne* 6, no. 2 (1958): 13–31.[24b]

14. See Aristotle, *Nicomachean Ethics* 8.5.1157b25–30, 8.8.1159a25–35, 1159b; 8.13.1162b35, 1163a1. [Editorial note: For all of Aristotle's works, Wojtyła most likely used *Aristotelis opera omnia: graece et latine* (Paris: Firmin Didot, 1848–83) or *Aristotelis opera*, 5 vols. (Berlin: Academia Regia Borussica, 1831–70).] In the Polish translation by Daniela Gromska (Warsaw: Państwowe Wydawnictwo Naukowe, 1956), 294–95, 302–3, 316–17.

ative affections or attitudes sharpen even more *the elementary reality itself of participating in the humanity of the other* and show how I am bound in myself, bound from within, by this humanity.

[27a]So, precisely in this place and at this point of our reflections, it seems that we discover an experiential basis for understanding the essence of alienation. It is vividly delineated precisely against the background of the "negative" verification of participation. *For alienation denotes nothing else but the denial of participation, an attenuation or outright annihilation of the possibility of experiencing the other man as "the other 'I,'" and thereby a devastation of the "I–the other" relationship.* Inasmuch as various "negative" affections or attitudes, in a sense, verify a capacity for participation in the humanity of "the other," alienation resides outside the field of such verification. Alienation denotes the situation in man, the state, the attitude in which he is not, in a sense, able to experience the other man as "the other 'I.'" The causes of this can be various and very complicated—we do not intend to inquire about them here. But a closer analysis of this situation, state, or attitude at hand would show us the absence, or rather the suppression, of all the *elements through which the "I–the other" relationship is built*, the elements of its actualization. We stated that the very concept of man does not yet actualize this relationship. We must receive the other as an "I," accept him, and choose him in a sense on the basis of our own "I"; we must do this while in a sense crossing the boundary of self-consciousness, so as to experience the reality of self-possession, which determines "the other 'I'" just as it does our own.

Alienation cancels all that. The concept of man remains in consciousness, but it is, in a sense, impermeable to the lived-experience of "the other 'I'" in it, estranged from the essential elements of this lived-experience. There exists no shortage of examples. The history of concentration camps, prisons, and tortures provides these examples in our epoch—and in monstrous dimensions at that. A question arises as to whether our entire civilization, especially the Atlantic one with its primacy of business and technology, is not threatened by the danger of alienation. In addition, daily life provides—certainly in less drastic, though often very acute dimensions—examples of such alienation. *The estrangement of inter-human relations from the fundamental elements of the lived-experience of "the other" as the "I" is a wide terrain of the confrontation* that we must carry on between participation and alienation. It not only pertains to the sphere of inter-human relations but also reaches human interiority. For every one of us experiences his own humanity in proportion to how capable he is of participating in the humanity of others, of experiencing them as "the other 'I.'"[27b]

[28a] [29a] 2. The Form of Participation and Alienation Connected with the Relation of the "We" Type[29b]
Between plurality and community

Proceeding now to the second part of our reflections, it is fitting to indicate another meaning of participation, its other form. The other meaning and other form of alienation will also be manifested on that basis. For, as was stated above, alienation is the antithesis, the opposite of participation. In order to show this opposite more fully, it is fitting to submit to at least a concise (and, I am afraid, too cursory) analysis of what is concealed in the pronoun "we." It seems that it indicates the social dimension of human existence, which ought to be distinguished from the inter-personal dimension, which we had before our eyes when analyzing the "I–the other" (in a sense the "I–thou") relationship. We can say that the relationship of the "I–the other" ("I-thou") type also indirectly indicates the plurality of persons connected by a relation (one + one); this relationship directly indicates the persons themselves, each of them. *The pronoun "we," however, rather seems to indicate the plurality and, indirectly only, the persons belonging to this plurality.* "We" above all indicates a collection—of course, this collection consists of people, that is, persons. This collection, which we can call society, community, a social group, etc., does not in itself possess a substantial but only an accidental being (speaking in the categories of traditional philosophy), for it is based on a system of relations between people. And so, that which results from accident, from the relation between people, moves into the foreground, as it were, providing the basis for predicating primarily of all and only secondarily of each in this collection. The pronoun "we" seems to contain exactly that. [30a] And that posits the entire problem of participation in an entirely new way.[30b]

At the same time, however, "we" hides in itself a great richness of the reality that is authentically human. We should take into consideration the enormous plasticity and analogousness of this expression. Since it speaks of the plurality of human subjects, each plurality, as it were, can be defined by it: the members of a family, of some social group—and not even necessarily a durable group—can think and call themselves "we." People who belong to the same nation, citizens of a country, and ultimately all people who feel that they belong to humanity as the great human family can also think and call themselves so. However, *"we" indicates not only the plurality of human subjects*, but also the fact that they are in some way linked to one another, that they constitute a unity. Therefore, *the expression "we" draws its proper sense from the good* (value), which—by uniting many people—deserves the name of *the common good*. The name *"common good"* is also interpreted as a call to community, which is to be constituted by people who refer to themselves by the pronoun "we." Thus, this pronoun contains *at least a call to community*. [31a]This call must proceed through the consciousness and freedom of every "I"-man who feels that he belongs to a certain "we."[15] [31b]

[32a]Participation is also a right[32b]

It is not my intention, however, to conduct in these reflections a comprehensive analysis of the social or communal reality of human existence. It is sufficient to state—as was already done in the beginning of the analysis of the "I–the other" relation—that every man not only exists and acts among others but also exists and acts "together with others." This statement is in a sense more original than the objectivization of the very relationships in which this existing and acting "together with others" takes place, than the more proximate definition of the nature of various "we's," which are thereby manifested and even, simply speaking, shaped. It is known that not only does the "we" as a distinct social unity of existence cause action "together with others," but also vice versa: such action at times evokes a unity and community of existence, a "we." On this social unity we confer various names depending on the relations on which it is based.

---

15. [25a]See Karol Wojtyła, *Osoba i czyn* [Person and act], 302–25. See also by the same author "Osoba: podmiot i wspólnota" [The Person: Subject and Community; pp. 467–513 in this volume]. Also see Leszek Kuc, "Uczestnictwo w człowieczeństwie 'innych,'" in *Dyskusja nad dziełem Kardynała Karola Wojtyły "Osoba i czyn," Analecta Cracoviensia*, 5–6 (1973–4): 183–90.[25b]

However, man always remains *the fundamental problem: man who exists and acts together with others*. Precisely this action, as well as existence "together with others" within various "we's," turns our thought for the second time to the meaning of participation. If man exists and acts "together with others," this means that he takes part in a whole greater than himself, thus, he participates in it. However, we cannot be content with stating the purely objective or, in a sense, "material," state of affairs. For the one who in this way "takes part," that is, "participates," is a person. Participation cannot be something merely outside him, outside his human subjectivity. It must define or determine his self in a certain—and at that a fundamental—way. In this way, as it seems, we arrive at the personalistic understanding of participation. *Participation is in a sense a property of the person* acting and existing together with others. It consists in the fact that *man fulfills himself* by existing and *acting in this way*.

In this second understanding of participation, we must, in a sense, go beyond the previous meaning, which is proper to the inter-human relations of the "I–the other" ("I-thou") type. The social community of being and action, which we define in various ways by the pronoun "we," is formed in reference to a common good. In this case, participation must take into consideration the fundamental fact that both self-determination (as was mentioned previously) and the striving for fulfilling oneself are proper to every man, to every "I" within the given "we." It is precisely thanks to this that man is a person. No human "we" may suppress or destroy this! Participation is a property of the person, which comes to light precisely when man acts (and exists) together with others. In virtue of this property, man is *able to realize the personalistic value of his act while realizing what results from the community of action and being. He is also entitled to this*. We take the position of personalism against individualism and totalism, for these two concepts destroy in the human person the possibility and, in a sense, the very capacity for participation. They deprive man of the right to participation.

The second meaning of alienation

[33a]Hence a second meaning of alienation arises.[33b] By alienation we mean here all that limits and prevents man from fulfilling himself on the basis of acting and existing "together with others" within various

"we's," within which man in fact exists and acts. When we speak about self-fulfillment, we do not accept the subjectivistic sense of this fulfillment, but rather the objectively legitimized striving of the personal subject. Alienation is everything that deprives man as a person of the potency for self-fulfillment thus understood. As long as participation indicates *the structure* of the human "we's" (of groups, societies, nations, or countries)—that is, *the order* in them, thanks to which each of the persons who exists and acts within these "we's" can be himself and fulfill himself—*alienation is the opposite of this structure and this order*.

Rightly then, alienation, in this sense, is linked with a defective social, economic, political, or international system. However, the criterion of mending the system can be neither merely economic, political, nor sociological; it must be personalistic. The way to overcome alienation in this second dimension, which is determined by the necessity of every man's existing and acting "together with others," is to find the authentic sense of participation and contribute to its realization.

Only in this way will man not be lost in various systems of his social existence.

Conclusion

As I say this, I remember well the four-year work of the Second Vatican Council, in which I participated. The constitution *Gaudium et spes*, adopted on December 7, 1965, devotes much attention to the correct proportion of the processes of socialization and personalization in the modern world. Above all, however, I remember the following statement: "The Church, by reason of her role and competence, is not identified in any way with the political community nor bound to any political system. She is [and wishes to be—K.W.] at once a sign and a safeguard of the transcendent character of the human person."[16]

[34a]This transcendental character of the human person still remains the starting point and at the same time the task and arrival point of the inter-personal and social relationships of human existence. According to Marxist philosophy, man is alienated in a sense by his own products:

---

16. *Gaudium et spes*, no. 76 [Vatican translation].

economic and political systems, property, work, and power. Marxist philosophy also includes religion in these products.

Hence a conclusion emerges that one can transform the human world on the plane of these products, change economic and political systems, take up the fight with religion—and the age of alienation will cease, and the "kingdom of freedom," that is, of the full autorealization of each and all, will come.

The need for the transformation of the human world on the plane of the products of man cannot be denied. However, some Marxists, as was mentioned in the beginning, already noted that this direction of transformations causes new forms of alienation, which in turn require to be overcome.[17] Ultimately, a conviction must arise that the entire human world

---

17. See note 5 [p. 516] and especially Adam Schaff, "Jednostka a jej twory (problem alienacji)" and "Komunizm a jednostka ludzka," chapters 2 and 5, respectively, in *Marksizm a jednostka ludzka*, 147–96 and 255–347. [26a] In chapter 2, Schaff considers the problem of the existence of alienation in socialistic countries (the problem of the alienation of the state, of work, of the family, of the nation, and of national feelings). The author concludes this chapter with the following statement:

> Alienation thus also takes place in the socialistic society—both one that is an ordinary, not-yet-overcome relic of the past and one that is more organically, more durably linked with the conditions of the new system. In any case, this problem exists and must constitute the object of reflection and real concern. It is clear that in inter-human social relations the issue of the development of the human individual, the issue of the full development of his personhood, depends first and foremost on the existence and character of the occurring alienations. Man must always exteriorize his spiritual life if he wants to communicate with others, must objectivize and reify his activity if he wants to—and he must—live socially. The objectivization and reification of man's activity make the substratum for the alienation of this activity and its products in suitable social conditions. The alienation of man's products and activity, which subjects him to the power of things and subordinates him to the blind necessity of the vehement development of reality, alienates man himself because it deprives him of the possibility of fully conscious activity, which is characteristic in nature [*przyroda*] only of the species *Homo sapiens*.
>
> The estranged man, because he lives and acts in the world of alienation, is a man of crippled personhood, of limited possibilities for development. The ideal type of the man of the epoch of Communism is the man liberated from the power of alienation, the universal man. Even if this ideal is unattainable, as is the "limit" of a mathematical sequence, it can and ought to be pursued, of course, by fighting manifold alienations, because generally this ideal cannot be otherwise pursued. However, in order to fight consciously, one ought to have a good recognition of the situation, to know where and which alienation occurs or threatens, and not to close one's eyes to reality and proclaim with dogmatic faith that the new system is the realization of a society without alienation because alienation is *ex definitione* not possible in it.
>
> Even if Marx proclaimed something similar, such a view ought to be rejected as erroneous. Fortunately, we do not have to be so radical—Marx did not proclaim this. The writings from the period of his youth, especially the *Manuscripts*, contain in this respect a sizeable dosage of insurmountable utopism, announcing the automatic terminus of all alienation together with abolishing private property; however, in the mature Marx these sins of youth no longer

can be thoroughly transformed only on the plane of man himself, thus "by safeguarding the transcendent character of the human person." This way, the firm conviction arises that it is impossible to exclude the commandment to love contained in the Gospel from any program of transforming the human world. This commandment appears to us on the final horizon of our reflections and determines all perspectives—the more and most distant—of man's development. Perhaps this analysis devoted to the topics of participation and alienation will help us all to acknowledge this truth, just as it helped the author of these reflections.[34b] [28b]

---

exist. Shortly after the *Manuscripts*—in *German Ideology*—Marx speaks about the process of overcoming alienation in Communism and not about its immediate and one-time liquidation: "Communism is for us a state that ought to be introduced, and not an ideal that the reality should follow. We call Communism the real movement that abolishes the present state."

Precisely here lies the solution to the problem: alienations and their dangers ought to be seen and consciously fought. Evil does not consist in the fact that there are alienations in socialism but begins to exist when they are not consciously fought. In this respect the superiority of the socialistic system over the capitalistic one does not consist in the fact that the former is free from all alienation, but in the fact that better conditions exist in socialism for a conscious overcoming of alienation. What needs to be done is to skillfully take advantage of those conditions, which means, among other things, that the existence of alienation ought not to be denied "in principle" when it is a fact, but to be examined and overcome. (Schaff, "Jednostka a jej twory [problem alienacji]," in *Marksizm a jednostka ludzka*, 193–95.)

The doctoral dissertation of Fr. Adam Zbigniew Majchrzyk entitled *Problem alienacji u polskich marksistów* (Lublin, 1973), directed by Fr. Prof. Tadeusz Styczeń in the Department of Christian Philosophy at the Catholic University of Lublin, contains much valuable material. [26b]

7 ❧ A Letter to Anna-Teresa Tymieniecka

To Professor Teresa Anna Tymieniecka[cxxv]
Fribourg, Suisse
May 11, 1975

Dear Professor,

I wish to cordially thank you for the invitation to Paris for the International Colloquium on June 13 and 14 of this year. I feel very honored by this invitation. I am also convinced that participating in the colloquium, in which such distinguished representatives of contemporary phenomenology, both philosophers and psychologists, are to take part, would be for me an extraordinary opportunity to enrich my own understanding of the topic so close to me. You know my certain works on this particular topic. The study *Person and Act*[1] is probably their fullest expression, though perhaps not the most mature because I constantly undertake certain problems selected from within the totality of the understanding that I attempted to outline in *Person and Act*.

This was the case during the conference in Rome and Naples marking the 700th anniversary of the death of St. Thomas Aquinas, where I spoke on the topic of "the personal structure of self-determination." Additionally, during the sessions of the "metaphysics and phenomenology" group at this same conference, I spoke on the topic of "the act and lived-experience" and provided that speech in writing. In that paper I primarily refer to Max Scheler and conduct a critical analysis of his conception of action, and especially of the act representing a given moral value. Both the lecture on the personal structure of self-determination

---

1. Karol Wojtyła, *Osoba i czyn* (Kraków: Polskie Towarzystwo Teologiczne, 1969).

and the statement on the relation of the act to lived-experience grow out of my long-standing philosophical interests, the synthesis of which is, in a sense, the aforementioned study *Person and Act*.

My interests were shaped on the basis of research and lectures that I conducted at the theological department of the Jagiellonian University in Kraków and in the philosophical department of the Catholic University in Lublin. These lectures were primarily in the fields of theological, and especially philosophical, ethics. However, I gradually began to concentrate my interests more and more on the human person as the fundamental ethical—and not only ethical—reality. The path in that direction led through a study anterior to *Person and Act* entitled *Love and Responsibility*,[2] in which I attempted to manifest the profound personalistic sense of conjugal morality (indirectly of the entire so-called sexual morality). After having written that ethical study, I concluded that yet a much more thorough work aiming at revealing the fundamental structures constituting the personal "I" of man is indispensable, so that the personalistic sense of the entire human morality (and not only—though perhaps in some measure—conjugal and so-called sexual morality) is revealed more and more fully. Thus, although the purely normative subject-matter was already, in a sense, placed outside the parentheses in *Person and Act* in order to make the man-person above all the topic of analyses, nonetheless a distinct relation to the values through which man becomes good or evil as man, that is, to moral values, constantly inheres in my entire work. I have never lost the conviction that the personal world of these values, their immanence in action, in a sense, most deeply reveals man in himself, in his interior drama, manifesting the proper measure of his personal greatness.

In *Person and Act* I conduct an entire analysis of the personal subject, starting from the conviction that precisely the act most thoroughly reveals to us that subject's dynamic structure—and precisely the act through the value of good or evil that is expressed in it. Lately, I again analyzed the same problem in an extensive article entitled "The Person: Subject and Community." I permit myself to attach this text, for it too can help in illuminating new stages of work on the topic that—as we see from the above information—lies at the very center of my interests. In

---

2. Karol Wojtyła, *Miłość i odpowiedzialność: Studium etyczne*, 2nd ed. (Kraków: Znak, 1962).

the latter work, I devote more attention to the analysis of the community than in *Person and Act*, seeing this community in two dimensions: the inter-human "I-thou" and the social "we." A certain new impulse for reflections in this direction came from the last colloquium in Swiss Fribourg, which was on the topic of "*Soi et autrui*," and to which I was also invited in January 1975 to present the lecture entitled "*Participation ou aliénation*" ("Participation or Alienation"). In this lecture I analyzed (with respect to *Person and Act*) the problem of the relation of man (the I) to the "other" man in a new way.

Because I will most likely not be able to come personally to the colloquium in Paris (as was the case with the colloquium in Fribourg), I therefore permit myself to send this present information, which is by no means a résumé, but rather merely a notification on works, publications, and orientations. I am undeniably philosophically connected with the Aristotelian-Thomistic foundation. However, I work on that foundation while taking advantage of the method and achievements of phenomenology to a large extent. I do not know whether I succeed in sufficiently overcoming the fundamental divergence of these two directions—this was a great point of interest for my colleagues in the discussion on the book *Person and Act*, which within days will be published in *Analecta Cracoviensia*. I must admit that the object or problem itself absorbs me perhaps less than "systemic" accuracy—I have never (perhaps for the last time in my habilitation thesis) practiced a purely systemic or commentatorial exegesis. It is very difficult to take full responsibility for someone else's thought.

I am aware that my present communication (and my entire participation in the Parisian colloquium on "*L'homme agissant*") faces one difficulty, namely, that everything or almost everything that I have written on this topic remains in its original Polish. Therefore, out of necessity, I here inform you of the facts almost completely unknown and foreign to the participants of the colloquium. I appreciate the invitation to take an active part in it all the more. Because my philosophical pursuits occupy, out of necessity, only a certain amount of time in my vocation (although in my own episcopal and pastoral vocation I find a thorough justification for the philosophy I practice), therefore I kindly ask that you and all esteemed participants accept (in addition to the information presented here) my concise statement on the topic of "*La Subjectivité et l'irréductible dans l'homme*," which I am attaching. This statement relies on all my previous reflections, and especially on the most recent "The Person: Subject and Community," whose full text (in Polish) I have also attached to this letter.

With expressions of respect and spiritual connection,

Karol Cardinal Wojtyła

8 ✻ [1a]Subjectivity and "the Irreducible" in Man[1b]

1. *Status quaestionis*

It seems that the problem of the subjectivity of man resides today at the center of various interests.[cxxvi] It would be difficult to explain concisely why and in what way this situation developed and is constantly developing. Perhaps there are numerous reasons, though not all of them ought to be sought in the fields of philosophy or science. Nonetheless philosophy—and above all philosophical anthropology and ethics—is a particular locus concerning the manifestation of this problem, its objectivization. For the essence of the problem lies precisely in this point: we feel *a need stronger than ever*—and we also see *a greater possibility—for the objectivization of the problem of man's subjectivity.*[1]

In this respect, contemporary thought seems in a sense to be leaving aside old antinomies, which grew, above all, on the grounds of the theory of cognition (epistemology), and which constituted the inviolable, as it were, demarcation line between fundamental orientations in philosophy. The antinomy of subjectivism-objectivism and the antinomy of idealism-realism (which is concealed in the former) created unfavorable conditions for studying the subjectivity of man, on account of the fear that it would inevitably lead to subjectivism. Among thinkers who maintained realism and epistemological objectivism, these apprehensions were somewhat justified by the subjectivistic and idealistic char-

---

1. [27a]Here the author also wishes to refer to Anna-Teresa Tymieniecka's study "Beyond Ingarden's Idealism/Realism Controversy with Husserl: The New Contextual Phase of Phenomenology," in *Ingardeniana*, ed. Anna-Teresa Tymieniecka, 241–418, Analecta Husserliana 4 (Dordrecht: D. Reidel, 1976).[27b]

acter, or at least "overtone," of analyses conducted on the basis of "pure consciousness." As a result, the line of demarcation and opposition was strengthened between the "objective" understanding of man, which at the same time was an ontological understanding (man as a being), and the "subjective" understanding, which seemed to inevitably sever itself from the other reality.

However, we are witnessing, in a sense, the breaking down of this demarcation line due to the same reasons that contributed to its creation. "Due to the same reasons" means: also under the influence of phenomenological analyses conducted on the grounds of "pure consciousness" by means of the Husserlian *epoché*, thus, by placing existence, that is, the reality of the conscious subject, in parentheses. In the opinion of the person writing these words, this *demarcation line between subjectivistic (idealistic) and objectivistic (realistic) understandings* in anthropology and ethics must break down and in fact *does break down on the basis of man's experience*. As a matter of fact, this experience liberates us from pure consciousness as a subject thought of and presupposed a priori and introduces us into the whole concreteness of man's existence, that is, into the reality of the conscious subject. However, having completed all the phenomenological analyses conducted on the basis of that presupposed subject, that is, pure consciousness, we can no longer study man merely as an objective being, but, in a sense, we must study him as a subject under the dimension determined by consciousness that concerns this specifically human subjectivity of man.

It seems that this subjectivity is, in fact, personal.

2. The Historical Background of the Problem

This matter requires a more extensive elucidation, within which we must touch on the problem of *"l'irréductible dans l'homme"* (the irreducible in man), that is, what is originally, or fundamentally, human; what determines the total originality of man in the world.

As is well known, traditional Aristotelian anthropology was based on the definition ὁ ἄνθρωπος ζῷον νοητικόν, *homo est animal rationale*.[2] This definition does not only correspond to the Aristotelian demands of

---

2. [28a] See Aristotle, *Nicomachean Ethics* 1098a.[28b]

denoting the species (man) through the most proximate genus (a living being) and the factor differentiating the given species in this genus (endowed with reason). *This definition* is also built in a way that excludes—at least when we take it directly and immediately—the possibility of manifesting what is "*l'irréductible dans l'homme.*" It contains—at least in the foreground—*a conviction of the reducibility of man to the world.* The reason for this reducibility was and is the need to understand man. We can call this *type of understanding cosmological.*

It is impossible to question the usefulness of the Aristotelian definition, which established its rule on the basis of metaphysical anthropology and sponsored the creation of many particular sciences concerning man understood precisely as *animal* with the distinguishing feature of rationality. The entire tradition of the science about the complexity of human nature, about the spiritual-bodily *compositum humanum*, which passed from the Greeks through the scholastics to Descartes, moves within this definition, thus on the basis of the conviction of the reducibility of what is essentially human to the "world."[3] It cannot be denied that the vast regions of experience and the particular knowledge based on it follow this conviction and work to strengthen it.

On the other hand, however, it seems that the *conviction of the primordial originality of the human being,* of his *fundamental irreducibility to the "world,"* to nature [*przyroda*], is as old as the need expressed by Aristotle's definition for that reduction. This conviction stands at the foundation of understanding man as a "person," which in the course of philosophy also has a long history. Today it stands at the foundation of a growing manifestation of the person as a subject and of many efforts aiming at personal interpretation of the subjectivity of man.[4] [2a]

In the philosophical and scientific tradition originating from the definition *homo—animal rationale, man was* first and foremost an object, *one of the objects of the world,* visibly and physically belonging to it. Ob-

---

3. [29a] The conviction of the fundamental reducibility of man to the "world" inheres above all in the entire philosophical tradition of materialism, and in dialectic materialism. The expression of this is both the Marxist conception of anthropogenesis (work "generates" man) and the view that the human being is explained by the sum or resultant of the existing relations of production.[29b]

4. One such effort is the author's study entitled *Osoba i czyn* [Person and act] (Kraków: Polskie Towarzystwo Teologiczne, 1969), and the work pertaining more to this topic, entitled "Osoba: Podmiot i wspólnota" [The Person: Subject and Community; pp. 467–513 in this volume], *Roczniki filozoficzne* 24, no. 2 (1976): 5–39.

jectivity, thus understood, *was linked* with the general presupposition of *man's reducibility*. Subjectivity, on the other hand, is, so to speak, a term bringing forth the fact that in his proper essence man cannot be reduced and completely explained by the most proximate genus and the specific difference. Thus, in a sense, *subjectivity* is *a synonym of the entire* l'irréductible dans l'homme. If we make an opposition in this context, this opposition is not between objectivism and subjectivism but only between two ways of a philosophical (but also common and practical) treatment of man: as an object and a subject. For we cannot forget that the subjectivity of the man-person is also something objective.[5] [3a]

We should also state that the way of treating man as an object does not result directly from the Aristotelian definition itself and especially does not belong to the metaphysical concept of man in this philosophical current. It is known that the very objectivity of the concept of man as a being required, *first*, the acknowledgment that man constitutes a separate *suppositum* (a subject of being and acting) and, *second*, the *affirmation* that he is a person (*persona*). However, the traditional teaching of man as a person, which has been signified by the definition of Boethius—*rationalis naturae individua substantia*—expressed the individuality of man as a substantial being who possesses a rational, that is, spiritual, nature rather than the whole specificity of subjectivity, essential for man as a person. In this way the Boethian definition above all defines, so to speak, the "metaphysical terrain," that is, the dimension of the being in which the personal subjectivity of man is realized, creating in a sense a condition for "developing" this terrain on the basis of experience.[6]

---

5. See *Person and Act*, chapter 1, "Person and Act in the Aspect of Consciousness," section 6, "Subjectivity and subjectivism."

6. [30a]We ought to note the fundamental difference that occurs between the Aristotelian definition of man as *animal rationale* and the Boethian definition of the person. In the latter case, the fact of reducing man "to the world" by indicating the most proximate genus (*animal*) does not occur. The Boethian definition of the person only manifests the category of being—*substantia*, indicating the fact of existing in oneself (*in se*) as fundamental for man as a person. If we say that this definition defines in a sense a "metaphysical terrain," which is prepared "for development" on the basis of experience, we thereby wish to state that the structure of being, expressed in this definition, also corresponds to the experience of man as a person. Furthermore, we also wish to state that this structure is most fundamental, corresponding to what in our experience of man as a person is also most fundamental—thus to what structurally conditions and determines the totality of these experiences thanks to which the man-person is revealed before us in all his subjectivity. This is important for our discourse, in which we concern ourselves with lived-experience as an indispensable element of interpretation.[30b]

3. Lived-Experience as an Element of Interpretation

It seems that the category that we must reach in order to accomplish that "development" is the category of lived-experience. It is not known in the metaphysics of Aristotle. The categories that could seem relatively closest to lived-experience, namely, the Greek categories of *agere* and *pati*, cannot be identified with it. These categories serve to define the dynamic of being; they also perfectly differentiate what merely "happens" in man from what man "does," that is, his "acts."[7] [4a] However, as a result of explaining the dynamic reality of man this way, the corresponding lived-experience remains every time (both in the case of *agere* and *pati*) as an aspect that is not directly grasped by this metaphysical interpretation or "reduction," as *l'irréductible*: the ir-reducible element. From the viewpoint of the meta-physical structure of being and acting, thus from the viewpoint of man's dynamism understood meta-physically, grasping this element can seem unnecessary.[8] For even without it we obtain a sufficient understanding of man, of the fact that man "acts" and that something "happens" in him. The entire edifice of anthropology and ethics has been based on this understanding throughout many centuries.

However, *as* the need to understand man as a unique and unrepeatable person *increases*, especially *the need to understand the personal subjectivity of man* in the entire dynamism of action (the act) and happening that is proper to man, *the category of lived-experience gains its significance*, and a key significance at that. For it is a question not only of a metaphysical objectivization of man as the acting subject, that is, the agent of his acts, but also of a presentation of the person as the subject experiencing his acts, his experiences, and, in all this, his subjectivity. Once such a demand is put forward in the interpretation of the acting man (*l'homme agissant*), the category of lived-experience must find its place in anthropology and ethics; moreover, to a certain degree it must stand in the center of respective interpretations.[9] [5a]

---

7. The study *Person and Act* is to a large extent built on this basis.

8. [31a] This does not at all change the fact that the experiential access to "action" (the act) and to "happening" as two different forms of the dynamization of the human subject creates nothing else but precisely lived-experience. The anthropology constructed by means of metaphysical objectivization abstracts in this objectivization from lived-experience as a moment shaping the image of the man-person. The anthropology concerned about the full manifestation of his subjectivity must consider how to introduce the moment of lived-experience into that image. [31b]

9. It seems that a certain illustration of this problem can be provided by comparing the study

A question may immediately arise whether we do not inevitably doom ourselves to subjectivism by conferring this key function onto lived-experience in the interpretation of man as a personal subject. Passing over excessively detailed reflections on this problem, we can briefly state that by binding ourselves firmly enough in that interpretation with the integral experience of man, we do not doom ourselves to subjectivism of understanding, but instead *we protect the authentic subjectivity of man*, that is, his personal subjectivity, *in the realistic interpretation of his being.*

4. The Necessity of Dwelling on the Irreducible

The interpretation of man on the basis of lived-experience requires the aspect of consciousness to be introduced into the analysis of the human being.[10] In this way man is given to us not only as a being defined specifically, but also as a concrete "I," as a subject experiencing himself. The subjective being together with the existence proper to him (*suppositum*) appears to us in experience precisely as the subject experiencing himself. If we consider him, he will reveal to us the structures that determine him as a concrete "I." Revealing these structures that constitute the human "I" does not in the least have to denote a break with reduction and the specific definition of man, but denotes in itself a methodological procedure that can be described *as dwelling on* l'irréductible. We must remain in the process of reduction, which leads us in the direction of understanding man in the world (the cosmological type of understanding), *in order to understand man* in himself. That second type of understanding can be called personalistic. The *personalistic type of understanding man* is not an antinomy to the cosmological type, but its complement. We

---

Person and Act with the recently published work by Fr. Albert Krąpiec entitled *Ja—człowiek: Zarys antropologii filozoficznej* (Lublin: Towarzystwo Naukowe Katolickiego Uniwersytetu Lubelskiego, 1974).

10. [32a]Introducing the aspect of consciousness into the analysis of the human being is an indispensable condition for restoring the moment of lived-experience to the entire interpretation of man. This does not mean, however, that we understand lived-experience only as some content of consciousness. What this means is that only consciousness reveals the reality of a concrete man as a subject experiencing himself. Thus, every lived-experience is not constituted "in consciousness" but "through consciousness." What constitutes its proper essence is another matter. According to E. Lévinas it lies in a specific *jouissance*. See Emmanuel Lévinas, *Totalité et infini: Essai sur l'extériorité*, 3rd ed. (The Hague: Martinus Nijhoff, 1968), 83.[32a]

already said that the definition of the person formulated by Boethius designated only, so to speak, the "metaphysical terrain" for the personal interpretation of the subjectivity of man.

The experience of man cannot be exhausted by means of the "cosmological" reduction. We must consider *l'irréductible*, what in every man is unique and unrepeatable, through which he is not only "in particular" this man—an individual of a species—but through which he is a person: a subject. Only then is the image of man correct and complete. It is impossible to complete it by way of reduction alone, and we cannot remain within *l'irréductible* alone (for this would mean the inability of stepping outside the pure "I")—we must cognitively complement one with the other. However, taking into account various circumstances of the real existence of people, we must constantly make more room for *l'irréductible* in this cognitive effort; *we must give it a certain predominance, as it were*, in the thinking about man, in theory and in practice. For *l'irréductible* also signifies all that is invisible in man, all that is completely interior, and *by which every man is* in a sense *an eyewitness of himself*, his humanity, and his person.

Not only are the acts and experiences in their deepest dependencies on their own "I" revealed in lived-experience, but also the entire personal structure of self-determination, in which man finds his "I" as one who possesses himself and governs himself, or at any rate can and should possess himself and govern himself. The dynamic structure of self-determination tells man every time that he is both given and entrusted as a task to himself. Precisely in this way man appears to himself in his acts, in interior decisions of conscience, as one who is constantly entrusted as a task to himself, who must constantly confirm, verify, and thereby, in a sense, constantly "achieve" the dynamic structure of his "I," given to him as "self-possession" and self-governance.[11] For at the same time, this structure is completely interior, immanent; it constitutes the real endowment of the personal subject; it is in a sense that subject himself. *In the lived-experience of self-possession and self-governance, man experiences that he is a person and that he is a subject.*

---

11. [33a] What opens before us in this direction is the perspective of a number of analyses, which would show what the transcendence of the person in action, in the act, is, and in what it consists. [33b]

The structure of self-possession and self-governance as essential for the personal "I," as shaping the personal subjectivity of man, is experienced by each of us in the lived-experience of the moral value of good or evil. This reality appears to him perhaps even more intensely when it is threatened by evil than when nothing endangers it—at least for the time being. Anyway, experience teaches us that *morale* is thoroughly rooted in *humanum*, and more strictly speaking in what ought to be called *personale*. Morality defines the personalistic dimension of man in a fundamental way, is grounded in this dimension, and can only be properly understood in this dimension. At the same time, *morale is a fundamental expression of the transcendence proper to the personal "I."* The decisions of conscience show at every step that man as a person fulfills himself by rising above himself toward the values accepted in truth and therefore realized with a deep sense of responsibility.

5. Perspective

All this deserved many insightful analyses, some of which were already accomplished while others are still being continued. Without undertaking these analyses, however, we only wish to state that this whole rich and manifold reality of lived-experience constitutes not so much an element or aspect as a specific dimension in our cognition of man. We should especially dwell on this particular dimension if the subjective and, in this sense, also personal structure of man is to appear in all its fullness.

What does this cognitive *dwelling on lived-experience* mean?[12] We must understand it *in relation to* l'irréductible. For traditions of philosophical anthropology do teach us that one can, in a sense, pass through

---

12. [34a] The cognitive dwelling on lived-experience, upon *l'irréductible*, denotes—as already follows from the previous remarks—an opening of a new field of objectivization, namely, one that is organically linked with consciousness. In this field man appears as a subject experiencing himself. This subject experiencing himself not only is a concrete "I," but also—being such beyond all doubt—experiences himself as a person and confirms himself as a person. All this enters into the sphere of implication on the basis of the "cosmological" reduction. The attribute *rationale* in the Aristotelian definition *homo animal rationale* speaks of this in an indirect way. However, it takes a very long time to explicate from this "rationality" of a living being (*animal*) the aspect of consciousness proper to the experience of man, the aspect in which man appears to himself as a subject experiencing himself. In this way the cognitive dwelling on *l'irréductible*, on the ir-reducible, becomes in fact the beginning of a new reduction: of a new explanation of the essence of man. Man is then objectivized as a person, as a subject conscious of himself and determining himself. [34b]

this dimension, one can cognitively bypass it by way of abstraction aiming at the specific definition of the man-being, that is, at the reduction of a cosmological type (*homo—animal rationale*). However, a question arises whether, when defining the essence of man, we do not then also, in a sense, lose what is most human, since *humanum* is expressed and realized as *personale*. In that case *l'irréductible* would indicate that one cannot know man only in that way, cannot understand him only in that way. This is what the contemporary philosophy of the subject seems to say to the traditional philosophy of the object.

However, this is not all. *L'irréductible* denotes what by its essence cannot be subjected to reduction, what cannot be "reduced" but can only be manifested, revealed. *By its essence, lived-experience opposes reduction;* this, however, does not mean that it breaks away from our cognition. It only demands *to be known in another way*, namely, by such a method, *by way of such an analysis that only reveals and manifests its essence*. The method of phenomenological analysis allows us to dwell on lived-experience as *l'irréductible*. This method is not in the least only a description that individually registers phenomena (phenomena in the Kantian sense: as contents falling under the senses). By dwelling on the lived-experience of *l'irréductible* we attempt to cognitively penetrate its entire essence. In this way, we grasp not only the structure of lived-experience, subjective in its essence, but also its structural bond with the subjectivity of man. Thus, phenomenological analysis contributes to transphenomenal understanding and, at the same time, to the revelation of the richness that is proper to the human being in all the complexity of the *compositum humanum*.[13]

So, this manifestation—one that is as profound as possible—seems to be an indispensable way to know man on account of his personal subjectivity. This subjectivity is also a distinct reality, a reality we attempt to understand in the objective totality whose name is "man." At the same time, this determines the character of the entire way of understanding. After all, *lived-experience too—and above all—is reality*. The correct method of manifesting it can only contribute to *enriching and deepening the*

---

13. [35a] Therefore, what at once appears together with the perspective of the analyses, which would show what the transcendence of the person in the act is and in what it consists, is a similar perspective of analyses, which would show in what the integration of the person in the act consists. We understand the integration here not so much as the realization but as the revelation of the unity of the *compositum humanum*. [35b]

entire realism of the concept of man. Then the personal profile of man enters the sphere of cognitive vision; the complexity of his nature is not blurred but is more accurately delineated. The thinker seeking the ultimate truth—in the philosophical sense—about man already moves not in a "purely metaphysical terrain," but finds an abundance of elements attesting to both the bodiliness and the spirituality of man, and better manifesting the one and the other. These are the elements of further philosophical development.

However, the question always remains: Do the "cosmological" type of understanding man and the "personalistic" type ultimately exclude each other? In which place, if at all, do reduction and the manifestation of *l'irréductible* in man meet? In what sense is the philosophy of the subject to manifest the objectivity of man in his personal subjectivity itself? It seems that these are the *questions that determine today the perspective* of thinking about man, the perspective of contemporary anthropology and ethics. These are essential and burning questions. Anthropology and ethics must be practiced today from this difficult but promising perspective.

9 ❈ [1a]The Degrees of Being in Phenomenology and in Classical Metaphysics[1b]

Introduction (to the Discussion, from the Point of View of the Phenomenology of Action)

[2a]
1. *Actus humanus*

We should ask ourselves to what extent the main topic of this colloquium,[cxxvii] and of the degree of being, justifies this introduction (and the discussion that is expected to follow), to what extent human action—for the discussion is to carry on in this aspect after my introduction—has to do with the issue of degrees of being. By posing this question in the beginning, we wish to ask about the relation between anthropology and metaphysics. At least, this is how this problem is portrayed from the point of view of traditional philosophy, especially Thomism. It is known that Thomistic anthropology has a metaphysical character. This means that it concerns itself with man as a being, as somebody really existing. What remains in connection with this is in turn the entire conceptual "apparatus," through which man and his action are philosophically defined.

It is difficult to examine here all the details of this construction. It is necessary, however, to emphasize that the grasp of human action by the category *actus* is in a sense irreplaceable if we want to express the dynamism essential for this action. There is no other category in the philosophical language that, in its essence, expresses and adequately renders this dynamism—both the dynamic character of being in general and the dynamism contained in every concrete action of man in particular, as this action is given to us in experience. The essential strength of the concept *actus humanus*—the concept used in the language of Thomistic philosophy to denote an act, that is, a conscious human action—is precisely that it manifests a dynamism, that is, that which is essential to all action and to human action in particular.

2. *Operari sequitur esse*

In this consists the significance of Thomism, and especially of its "existential" version (à la Gilson, Świeżawski, or Krąpiec), for the philosophy of action, for the analysis of the human *praxis*. This philosophy and all the analyses undertaken on its foundation proceed from the statement *operari sequitur esse*. This sentence, this adage contains a fundamental proposition on the topic of the experience of action and, in particular, a fundamental understanding that is born in the experience of human action. On the basis of this experience, we ascertain the fact that "man acts," of which a particular and, in a sense, initial form is the fact "I act." In what manner the fact "I act" and the fact "man acts" are given to us in experience is another matter. We do not intend to undertake this matter here. (I did that in the introduction to my book *Person and Act*. The further thoughts that I intend to present in these opening remarks will refer to that book to some degree.)

The very fact that we appeal to experience when fundamentally verifying the concept *actus humanus* as grasping that which is most essential in human action already attests that we do not intend to posit our problem only on a systemic plane. The strength of the system (in this case, of Thomism and its conceptions of *actus* in particular and *praxis* in general) is the fundamental conformity with experience which, in turn, allows us on the basis of that experience of man (which here constitutes the proper source of cognition) to see and grasp anew, as it were, the entire specificity of human action. The point here, of course, is not some exchange of terminological elements, a change of language, but essentially new perceptions (intuitions) of the same object, which is not so much the "action of man" (understood so to speak in a certain isolation) as the "acting man" in the specificity of the human *operari sequitur esse*, proper to this dynamic whole.

3. The Essential Moments of the Act

I express the conviction—which I also communicated in the aforementioned work—that phenomenology can and should enter precisely here into the whole basically realistic analysis of human action. The experience of man—just as every other experience—is closely linked to manifesting the moments through which the fact "I act—man acts" is essentially constituted. "Essentially" means that outside this moment, that without this moment, the action of man as an act of a person is not given to us in reality. There is a need to closely differentiate between the action of man and what merely "happens" in man in various ways. Precisely in light of this differentiation, these moments, through which the human act is essentially constituted in our consciousness (and simultaneously in our experience), possess fundamental significance.

4. Intentionality and Transcendence

The human act (that is, the action of man in the proper sense) is constituted through the moment of a particular transcendence of the person. Our point here is not the transcendence proper to the acts of cognition (consciousness); our point is not the transcendence that is identified with the intentional character (intentionality) of these acts. This cognitive intentionality undoubtedly resides at the basis of the act and the transcendence of the person, which is connected with the act, but it alone does not yet constitute this transcendence. The cognition of values through intentional acts, tinted in various ways by emotion, conditions human action, conditions the act, in which man also intentionally turns toward cognitive values, wants these values, chooses or rejects them, and sometimes makes decisions about them with difficulty. However, the very intentionality of volition, which is most fully manifested in the act of choice, does not create the essential dimension of the transcendence that appears in the human act while being its constitutive moment. Therefore, the sole analysis of intentional acts fails here. The transcendence of the person in action (the act) is irreducible to the intentionality of cognitive acts and even to the intentionality of volitions themselves.

5. Self-Determination and Transcendence

The moment of the transcendence of the person in the act proceeds from self-determination, that is, from the will, through which man is the subject and agent of his action. Self-determination as a fact that constitutes the experiential core itself of the fact "I act—man acts" reveals the will as the proper source of the freedom of the person. The essential function of the acts of the will—whether it be a simple volition or a more complex choice as a result of clashing between motives—is not the striving itself for the object (for the value as an object), but the determination of the subject. The term "self-determination" means that man, as a subject of action, not only determines this action as its agent (that is, as the efficient cause), but also that, through this, he determines himself. The moment of the transcendence of the person in the act is based precisely on self-determination. Through self-determination, man performs an act, that is, he confers a properly human quality and content onto his action. In this way human action not only "transits" beyond its subject, but at the same time remains in it, retains its "intransitiveness" in the subject "man." Thanks to the structure of self-determination, man—who in his acts is their agent—also stands as if above them. While he determines his acts, he also has the consciousness that they determine him through their personal quality, through their positive or negative moral value. And they will continue to determine him even when they pass away, when they belong to the past.

As is evident even from this concise analysis, the transcendence of the person in the act is constituted through moral consciousness, through conscience, through the lived-experience of value and especially of duty, through responsibility. All this appears before us as our analysis progresses inside human action, inside every fact "man acts"—in particular when we penetrate it through our own experience, through the fact "I act."

6. The Integration of the Person in the Act

Hand in hand with this discovery, with the experiential revelation of the transcendence of the person in the act, goes the no less experiential revelation of the complementary aspect, which we shall call the integration of the person in the act. It is something obvious that the act—*actus humanus*—is in every case a specific synthesis of man's dynamism. If it is essentially constituted through the moment of transcendence, which fundamentally reveals the dynamism of the human spirit, then it is known that the manifold action of man is not limited to nor exhausted in this moment. Even when the entire sphere of actions, which are traditionally called *actus interni*, is concerned, they also occur with a commitment of the whole man. The structures of his bodiliness, sensuality, and affectivity unified in one subjective "whole" take part in different ways in performing these actions, which are traditionally called *actus interni*.

In addition, however, an enormous quantity of human acts possesses the character of *actus externi*: they are performed in a visible way, externally perceptible, in the dimension of the human bodiliness, sensuality, and affectivity. To man's bodiliness, sensuality, and affectivity correspond their own interiorly diverse forms of dynamism. We speak here of the spontaneous dynamism proceeding from nature itself, that is, from the innate organization of both the human somaticity and psyche. We can say that the human somaticity is above all reactive, whereas the psyche is above all emotive. (I do not substantiate here this characterization, although I do attempt to do so in the aforementioned publication *Person and Act*.) At any rate, our experience of action reveals to us that the moment of the integration of the person in the act must occur in it together with the moment of transcendence, since the dynamisms of the human psyche and somaticity in the essentially human action enter, in a sense, into the one dynamic "whole," which appears in experience as the act of the person.

Nota bene, we can understand the integration of the person in the act either as a function of joining, that is, creating one whole, that is, the act, out of different dynamisms, or we can also understand it as the revelation of this unity on the basis of plurality and diversification of dynamisms (this is closer to the thinking of a phenomenologist). Phenomenology is not directed to explain causes. Nonetheless, the essential diversification of the dynamisms that enter into the structure of human action certainly lies in the sphere of the inquiries of phenomenology. What will be perhaps not even completely alien to these inquiries is the defining and diversifying of potentiality as the permanent source of various dynamisms in the subject man.

7. Gradi dell'essere

Do any conclusions proceed from this analysis, cursory by necessity, concerning the gradualization of the being itself, the diversification of the degrees of being? It seems so. Furthermore, our conducted analysis leads us to formulate these opinions: first, that man is a particular subject in whom the gradation of being occurs in such close connectedness and unity; and, second, that this gradation already distinctly appears in the phenomenological analysis itself or, if we proceed from a metaphysical analysis, acquires through it a particular vividness.

So, with all evidentness, there emerges in the experience of man the superiority of what determines the transcendence of the person in the act in relation to what enters into the structures of integration. Precisely in the act and through the act is this superiority manifested so vividly. This superiority is within the one and the same man. Transcendence reveals this, by which this man determines himself and thus also governs and possesses himself, whereas the integration of the person in the act reveals this, which must be in some way "integrated," that is, also subjected and mastered in man when he performs the act. (Here I am not yet speaking of the virtue of self-mastery, that is, an ethical habit, but of the purely praxeological dimension.) Thus, a distinct subordination is made manifest. The phenomenological analysis of human action allows us to speak about the "higher" and the "lower" man, the way in which traditional anthropology and the theology of interior life speak about him.

It is another matter whether, as a result of the analysis thus conducted, even with all vividness in the revelation of what is spiritual in man in relation to what is "non-spiritual," we can make on the basis of this analysis the distinction between spirit and body (matter). It is clear that this distinction belongs to metaphysics. Phenomenology, in a sense, "does not reach" the complexity of man expressed in the categories of the body as the first matter and the soul as the substantial form. Nevertheless, it seems that phenomenological analysis in its own manner further illumines the mystery of that complexity. We can ask ourselves whether phenomenological analysis, without crossing the boundaries of its "competency," speaks in a way "for" the hylomorphic solution of the concept of man. It is difficult to say. At any rate, it seems that this analysis clearly does not oppose this solution. It seems, however, that it clearly reveals both the complexity of man and the gradation within this complexity.

We ascertained that this gradation consists in the superiority of that which determines the transcendence of the person in the act with respect to that which must be personally "integrated" in action, so that this action is a true act of the person. It seems that within integration itself we can also ascertain the superiority of the psyche over somaticity, and, in particular, the superiority of emotivity proper to the human psyche in relation to the reactivity proper to somaticity. It is sufficient to state that the totality of the somatic reactions comprising the totality of the functions of the human organism occurs ("happens") in man without the contribution of consciousness: they are not made conscious and are unable to be made conscious. But all that occurs in man in an emotive way—regardless of the extent to which it proceeds from the reactive-somatic substratum—always "happens" at the same time in consciousness. Emotions are by their nature able to be made conscious. In this way, they grow, so to speak, above the threshold of human somaticity. Phenomenologically they belong to the manifestations of the "soul" and not the "body," although they are not "spiritual"; they do not constitute by themselves the transcendence of the person in the act.

A look at the problem of the gradation of human being through the—to a considerable extent phenomenological—analysis of human action shows a diversification of the "degrees of being" within the metaphysical unity of man. A look based on this analysis requires us to exclude the materialistic interpretation of man, according to which his spiritual structure would be merely an epiphenomenon of the structures of matter. In that case, we would clearly have to relinquish the gradation of being that was manifested here. However, the experience to which we appeal, namely, the experience of human action, does not permit us to do so. This experience clearly manifests the moment of the transcendence of the person as a moment that is essential and constitutive for the act; and even though the act is undoubtedly conditioned by integration at the same time, nonetheless, the integration of both the human somaticity and the psyche is dependent on self-determination. In this way, the moment of the transcendence of the person is not only constitutive for the act but also really superior in it—and superior with all conditionings at that. It is not possible to demonstrate on the basis of the (phenomenological) analysis of the human act that the spiritual structure—that is, precisely the moment of transcendence—is merely a reflex in the act, an epiphenomenon of material structures. Also, in this way, the thesis about the gradation (about the degrees) of human being, which we have stated here, obtains its confirmation.

10 ❦ The Transcendence of the Person in the Act and the Auto-teleology of Man

1. The Historical Connection

Against the background of the rich program of the conference in Siena and Arezzo,[cxxviii] devoted to the problem of teleology in manifold aspects and meanings, I wish to posit the problem of the auto-teleology of man. By positing this problem, I refer to my several previous statements,[1] but above all I am undertaking yet another attempt to more deeply develop the concepts contained in my study entitled *Person and Act*.[2] Hence the full title of this lecture is "The Transcendence of the Per-

---

1. I hold that we discover the auto-teleology of man through the analysis of self-determination. My works were built on that conviction, for instance: *Miłość i odpowiedzialność: Studium etyczne* (Lublin: Towarzystwo Naukowe Katolickiego Uniwersytetu Lubelskiego, 1960; 2nd edition, Krakow: Znak, 1962); "Osoba i czyn w aspekcie świadomości," in Pastori et magistro: *Praca zbiorowa wydana dla uczczenia jubileuszu 50-lecia kapłaństwa Jego Ekscelencji Księdza Biskupa Doktora Piotra Kałwy, Profesora i Wielkiego Kanclerza KUL*, ed. Andrzej Ludwik Krupa (Lublin: Towarzystwo Naukowe Katolickiego Uniwersytetu Lubelskiego, 1966), 293–304; "Problem teorii moralności," in *W nurcie zagadnień posoborowych: Praca zbiorowa*, ed. Bohdan Bejze, 3:217–50 (Warsaw: Wydawnictwo Sióstr Loretanek-Benedyktynek, 1969).

2. This study was published in 1969 by Polskie Towarzystwo Teologiczne in Kraków. An effort was undertaken to translate this study into English. See also "Dyskusja nad dziełem Kardynała Karola Wojtyły 'Osoba i czyn,'" in *Analecta Cracoviensia* 5–6 (1973–74): 49–272. This discussion includes contributions from Mieczysław Albert Krąpiec, "Książka Kardynała Karola Wojtyły monografią osoby jako podmiotu moralności"; Jerzy Kalinowski, "Metafizyka i fenomenologia osoby ludzkiej: Pytania wywołane przez 'Osobę i czyn'"; Stanisław Kamiński, "Jak filozofować o człowieku?"; Kazimierz Kłósak, "Teoria doświadczenia człowieka w ujęciu Kardynała Karola Wojtyły"; Józef Tischner, "Metodologiczna strona dzieła 'Osoba i czyn'"; Marian Jaworski, "Koncepcja antropologii filozoficznej w ujęciu Kardynała Karola Wojtyły (próba odczytania w oparciu o studium 'Osoba i czyn')"; Tadeusz Styczeń, "Metoda antropologii filozoficznej w 'Osobie i czynie' Kardynała Karola Wojtyły"; Roman Forycki, "Antropologia w ujęciu Kardynała Karola Wojtyły (na podstawie książki 'Osoba i czyn,' Kraków 1969)"; Mieczysław Gogacz, "Hermeneutyka 'Osoby i czynu' (recenzja książki Księdza Kardynała Karola Wojtyły 'Osoba i czyn,' Kraków 1969)"; Stanisław Grygiel, "Hermeneutyka czynu

son in the Act and the Auto-teleology of Man." Within the problem thus posited, I see the possibility for a new interpretation of the perennial topic of the philosophy of man and morality. I mean anthropology and ethics still built on the foundation of the Aristotelian philosophy of being, within which τέλος constituted one of four causes, that is, sources for understanding reality, and one of the principles for the metaphysical explanation of reality.[3] It is on this basis that *teleology*, that is, the principle of finality (*nota bene*, τέλος means not only "end" [*cel*] but also "terminus" [*kres*]!), *entered into the interpretation of human action, of human* πρᾶξις, and into the interpretation of morality, *of human ethos*: ἦθος.

It seems that it is impossible to question the rightness of the principle *omnis agens* (and not only *omne agens*), *agit propter finem*. Therefore, the teleological interpretation of human action constantly persists in philosophy and science. A contemporary confirmation of that can be so-called praxeology, that is, the science about purposeful action ("about good labor," as a title of a treatise by Tadeusz Kotarbiński says).[4] From

---

oraz nowy model świadomości"; Antoni B. Stępień, "Fenomenologia tomizująca w książce 'Osoba i czyn'"; Andrzej Półtawski, "Człowiek a świadomość (w związku z książką Kardynała Karola Wojtyły 'Osoba i czyn')"; Jerzy W. Gałkowski, "Natura, osoba, wolność"; Leszek Kuc, "Uczestnictwo w człowieczeństwie 'innych'?"; Tadeusz Wojciechowski, "Jedność duchowo-cielesna człowieka w książce 'Osoba i czyn'"; Zofia J. Zdybicka, "Praktyczne aspekty dociekań przedstawionych w dziele 'Osoba i czyn'"; Jerzy Stroba, "Refleksje duszpasterskie"; Teresa Kukołowicz, "'Osoba i czyn' a wychowanie w rodzinie"; Wanda Półtawska, "Koncepcja samoposiadania—podstawą psychoterapii obiektywizującej (w świetle książki Kardynała Karola Wojtyły 'Osoba i czyn')."

3. Aristotle, *Metaphysics* 1.3.983a24–33; *Physics* 2.3.195a—see in parallel *Metaphysics* 5.2.1013a–1014a. *Aristotelis opera*, 5 vols. (Berlin: Academia Regia Borussica, 1831–70); Polish translation in *Filozofia starożytna Grecji i Rzymu*, texts selected and prefaced by Jan Legowicz, 2nd ed., Wybrane teksty z historii filozofii (Warsaw: Państwowe Wydawnictwo Naukowe, 1970), 190–91.

4. Tadeusz Kotarbiński, *Traktat o dobrej robocie*, 6th ed. (Wrocław: Zakład Narodowy im. Ossolińskich, 1975; first published in Łódź in 1955). The sixth edition contains an extensive bibliography of Polish and foreign publications concerning praxeology, pp. 515–29. We mention only some of the many publications of T. Kotarbiński: "La notion de l'action," in *Psychologie philosophique*, vol. 7 of *Actes du XIème Congrès International de Philosophie, Bruxelles, 20–26 août*, 169–74 (Amsterdam: North-Holland, 1953); *Hasło dobrej roboty* (Warsaw: Wiedza Powszechna, 1968); "Praxiology and Economics," in *On Political Economy and Econometrics: Essays in Honour of Oskar Lange*, 303–12 (Warsaw: Państwowe Wydawnicto Naukowe, 1964); *Les origines de la praxéologie* (Warsaw: Państwowe Wydawnicto Naukowe, 1965); "L'évolution de la praxéologie en Pologne," in *Philosophie des sciences*, vol. 2 of *La philosophie contemporaine: Chroniques*, ed. Raymond Klibansky, 438–50 (Florence: La Nuova Italia Editrice, 1968); *Sprawność i błąd: Z myślą o dobrej robocie nauczyciela*, 5th ed. (Warsaw: Państwowe Zakłady Wydawnictw Szkolnych, 1970); *Studia z zakresu filozofii, etyki i nauk społecznych* (Wrocław: Zakład Narodowy im. Ossolińskich, 1970); "Teleologia a prakseologia," *Prakseologia*, nos. 3–4 (1973): 7–13. See also Henry Duméry, "Philosophie de l'action et praxéologie," in *Fragmenty filozoficzne, seria III: Księga pamiątkowa ku czci Profesora Tadeusza Kotarbińskiego w*

the viewpoint of the analysis of human praxis, it seems that there are no reasons to question teleology as an interpretative principle; however, *for already two centuries it has been questioned in ethics* as a sufficient principle for interpreting the morality of human ethos. *This criticism was carried out by Kant,*[5] and the direct basis for it was provided by the Anglo-Saxon (and not only the Anglo-Saxon) utilitarianism of the seventeenth and eighteenth centuries.[6] [1a]

It seems that Kant's criticism in this case was correct and fertile.[7] [2a] Kant came to the defense of the very essence of human morality, which utilitarianism attempted to reduce to the level of pure utility. At the same time, Kant also came to the defense of the transcendence of the human person, which, on the basis of morality, not only is realized but also—in a most direct way, as it seems—is revealed and manifested.[cxxix] However, *it is not to Kant that we owe* the key to *the cognitive manifestation itself of the transcendence of man* in the ethical dimension of his action and existence. The obstacle here was the radical break of human cognition into two mutually independent spheres: the sensual phenomena and the intellectual noumena. If Kant's criticism in relation to teleology of a utilitarian type in ethics was—as I said—fertile for perceiving anew and for expressing in philosophical categories the transcendence of the human person, then we owe this very perception and expression to Kant only in an indirect way. For directly *we owe it much more to phenomenology.*[8] [3a] The point

---

osiemdziesiątą rocznicę urodzin, ed. Tadeusz Czeżowski, 301–16 (Warsaw: Państwowe Wydawnictwo Naukowe, 1967).

5. Immanuel Kant, *Grundlegung zur Metaphysik der Sitten*, translated by Mścisław Wartenberg as *Uzasadnienie metafizyki moralności*, ed. Roman Ingarden, 2nd ed. (Kraków: Państwowe Wydawnictwo Naukowe, 1953). Kant, *Kritik der praktischen Vernuft*, translated by Benedykt Bornstein as *Krytyka praktycznego rozumu* (Warsaw: E. Wende, 1911); Second edition translated by Jerzy Gałecki (Warsaw: Państwowe Wydawnicto Naukowe, 1972). See Tadeusz Kroński, *Kant* (Warsaw: Wiedza Powszechna, 1966).

6. Especially the theories of Thomas Hobbes and Jeremy Bentham. See Maria Ossowska, *Myśl moralna Oświecenia angielskiego* (Warsaw: Państwowe Wydawnictwo Naukowe, 1966). See also Tadeusz Styczeń, *Metaetyka*, part 1 of *Zarys etyki* (Lublin: Katolicki Uniwersytet Lubelski, 1974), 66–67.

7. Max Scheler, *Der Formalismus in der Ethik und die materiale Wertethik: Neuer Versuch der Grundlegung eines ethischen Personalismus*, 4th ed. (Bern: Francke,1954); Karol Wojtyła, "O kierowniczej lub służebnej roli rozumu w etyce: Na tle poglądów Tomasza z Akwinu, Hume'a i Kanta," *Roczniki filozoficzne* 6, no. 2 (1958): 13–31; Wojtyła, ch. 1 in *Miłość i odpowiedzialność*; Tadeusz Styczeń, ch. 3 in *Problem możliwości etyki jako empirycznie uprawomocnionej i ogólnie ważnej teorii moralności: Studium metaetyczne* (Lublin: Towarzystwo Naukowe Katolickiego Uniwersytetu Lubelskiego, 1972); Styczeń, *Metaetyka*, 67–71.

8. Here we especially ought to include M. Scheler. Taking advantage of certain ideas of E.

in this case concerns phenomenology not only as a philosophy of "pure consciousness," but also as a method that allows many contemporaries a new and deepened entry into perennial and never outdated philosophical topics, especially in the areas of anthropology and ethics.

2. We Discover the Auto-teleology of Man through the Analysis of Self-Determination

This entry and the attempt connected with it, the attempt of a renewed interpretation of this fundamental fact of our experience, which is the fact "I act–man acts," help us to grasp and understand, as well as to make particularly manifest, the transcendence of man (the person) in the act. It seems that the traditional interpretation of the act, of human action (*actus humanus*), did not reveal this transcendence in its proper meaning. *The traditional interpretation of* actus humanus *was closely connected with the analysis of* voluntarium, that is, the act of the will understood—surely rightly—as an active basis and source (*potentia*) of man's striving for the end. This certainly corresponds to the characteristic of human volitions, which always appear in the field of our consciousness as a striving "for something." This striving arises in an unprompted way (spontaneously) in the subject. In order to explain its spontaneous appearing, we must, on the one hand, consider the potentiality of the subject, which we call the will (in the broad sense), and we must, on the other hand, accept the ax-

---

Husserl and F. Nietzsche, he created the so-called material ethics of value, which is the most developed form of ethics proposed by phenomenologists. N. Hartmann then developed Scheler's views, which were assimilated into Christian ethics and used in the spirit of realism by D. von Hildebrand and others. See Karol Wojtyła, *Ocena możliwości zbudowania etyki chrześcijańskiej przy założeniach systemu Maksa Schelera*, Rozprawy wydziału filozoficznego 5 (Lublin: Towarzystwo Naukowe Katolickiego Uniwersytetu Lubelskiego, 1959); Wojtyła, "O metafizycznej i fenomenologicznej podstawie normy moralnej (w oparciu o koncepcję św. Tomasza z Akwinu oraz Maksa Schelera)" *Roczniki teologiczno-kanoniczne* 6, nos. 1–2 (1959): 99–124; Tadeusz Styczeń, "O pewnej koncepcji etyki: Na marginesie 'Badań etycznych' Husserla," in *Zeszyty Naukowe KUL* 11, no. 1 (1968): 59–65; Styczeń, "Czy empiryczność i apodyktyczność," chapter 10.3 in *Problem możliwości etyki*, 91–126; Styczeń, *Metaetyka*, 78–80; Józef Tischner, "Wartości etyczne i ich poznanie," *Znak* 24, no. 5 (1972): 629–46; Jerzy Trębicki, *Etyka Maxa Schelera* (Warsaw: Państwowe Wydawnictwo Naukowe, 1973). In Poland, R. Ingarden practiced ethics in the phenomenological spirit. Roman Ingarden, *Książeczka o człowieku* (Kraków: Wydawnictwo Literackie, 1972); Ingarden, *Przeżycie, dzieło, wartość* (Kraków: Wydawnictwo Literackie, 1966). See also Maria Gołaszewska, "Romana Ingardena filozofia moralności," *Etyka* 9 (1971): 113–44.

iological nature of the end, that is, of that to which this volition-striving spontaneously turns. According to this understanding, volition is nothing else but a spontaneous turning toward value.

It is insufficient, however, merely to state the very spontaneity of volition in relation to value in order to explain the nature of the will, or in order to offer an adequate interpretation of the fact "I act–man acts." This very fact is undoubtedly explained by the dynamism of the will; indeed, *human action (agere humanum) grows from a spontaneous relation to value, as from a rich substratum*. However, within this action (*agere humanum*), the human act, we do not only ascertain the sole spontaneity of volitions. The spontaneous turning to value is subjected in the process of the will—if not always, then at any rate very often—to a specific "necessity" of choice, which ultimately confers a character of decision on human *voluntarium*. In this form, this *voluntarium* is contained in the experience of the act, in facts of the "I act–man acts" type.

When we speak about the "necessity" of choice, this necessity does not oppose freedom but, on the contrary, determines it. *The freedom of the will is revealed in man as the "necessity" of choosing among values and deciding*. The necessity of choosing and deciding does not destroy the original (or fundamental) spontaneity of human volitions and the turning toward values that is connected with these volitions. Quite the contrary, it draws from that turning and, so to speak, is accomplished "in it." Spontaneous volitions and the values that intentionally correspond to them constitute a specific material of choice and decision characteristic of the will while shaping the specific dynamism of the acts, which we find in the facts of the "I act–man acts" type.

We ought to add that these *volitions* spontaneously turned toward various values (very often still in the rather passive form of desires: "I feel like"), and appearing in consciousness, *have the character of specific intentional acts*: emerging from the subject, from various layers and centers of his potentiality, they are directed toward the object whose name is "value." This object is diversified as to content and, above all, quality; however, in every individual case of this diversification, it can and even must be identified as a value. As is thus evident, value is the objective reason for the being of every volition. Volition by its nature relates to values, and outside this relation it neither is constituted in the subject nor does it subsequently appear in consciousness. *Thus, nothing stands in the way of considering value as the object and the rationale of human volitions* (with their entire diversification and indispensable hierarchization) *to be an end*. In this way, the axiological image of the diversified and hierarchized dynamism (and potentiality) of man becomes a teleological image. Of course, we do not touch here on the whole rich specificity of the cognition of values, but only accept the intentionality of volitions, which consists in referencing values somehow already cognized.

However, we do not identify—and cannot identify—this intentionality of volitions, broadly understood here, with the will, with *voluntarium* as the dynamic *constitutivum* of the act. What is essential for the will is not the very intentionality of volitions, but the personal structure of self-determination. Only this structure explains the proper dynamism of the acts, what is contained in the experience of facts of the "I act–man acts" type. The dynamic *essence of the act is not constituted by volition alone as an intentional turning toward values, but by the determination of oneself, that is, self-determination, connected with that turning* and engaging the personal subject in its own way.[9] Thus, the proper *voluntarium* is not contained in the very lived-experience of willing something but in the lived-experience of determining oneself (the lived-experience of self-determination) that permeates this willing.

We ought to note that the term "self-determination" indicates at once that the determining (and acting) one is only the subject himself, that is, the personal "I," and that this personal "I" determines himself as the subject. Thus, in this dynamic relation, the "I" becomes an object for itself: an object of the will as a power of a determining subject. It is precisely in this relation that *the nucleus, as it were, of the auto-teleology of man* is contained. We said already that τέλος denotes not only "end" but also "terminus." The analysis of self-determination indicates that *voluntarium* as the interior dynamic structure of the person, constituting the act, finds its proper *"terminus"* not in the values to which human volitions are intentionally turned, but *in the subjective "I" itself, which* both determines

---

9. My study *Person and Act* is built precisely on this conviction. See also the discussion on this study published in *Analecta Cracoviensia* 5–6 [see note 2 on p. 554 in this article] and Karol Wojtyła, "The Personal Structure of Self-Determination," trans. Andrzej Potocki, in *Tommaso d'Aquino nel suo VII centenario: Congresso Internazionale Roma-Napoli, 17–24 aprile 1974*, 379–90 (Rome, 1974) [see p. 457 in this edition].

himself and *in a certain way wills and chooses himself through the volition of any values*, through the definite choice of them.

In this first approach, the auto-teleology of man appears to us to be a cycle that is closed and constantly being closed within the man-subject, who in action becomes for himself not only an object but also a terminus and end. At first glance, this picture can strike us as containing a climate of some solipsism, bringing to mind a monad closed in on itself. However, a more thorough reflection, including on what has been said thus far, must lead to conclusions that radically change this first, self-imposing picture. *Auto-teleology presupposes teleology: man does not become the terminus of self-determination, the terminus for his choices and volitions, independently from all values to which these choices and volitions turn*. The auto-teleology of man does not mean, above all, a closing in on oneself but, as is proper to the structure of self-determination, a vital contact with all of reality and a dynamic exchange with the world of values diversified and hierarchized in itself. The auto-teleology of man merely indicates that this contact and life-giving exchange are accomplished on the level of, and in accord with, the personal "I." In it they find their points of departure and arrival, they, in a sense, originate from it and are ultimately grounded in it, they draw their form from it and confer a form on it.

3. The Transcendence of the Person in the Act Confers Sense on Human Auto-teleology

In order to confer, on the basis of experience itself, full vividness on the above statement—and on the discovery of what constitutes the very core (*nucleus*) of the auto-teleology of man—we must make more fully manifest what the transcendence of the person in the act consists in. This transcendence is contained in facts of the "I act–man acts" type; its revelation is accomplished by a thorough penetration into the interior structure of these facts, and thus on the basis of experience. It is evident that *man, as the subject of action, "surpasses" himself* in that action *by turning toward the objects, that is, willing various values and choosing them*. However, as we demonstrated previously, the intentional dynamism itself of the will, the dynamism of volitions and choices turned toward a value as the object and end, is not essential for the act. What is essential for the will and the act is the personal structure of self-determination. Therefore, it is that structure that we fundamentally have in mind when speaking of the transcendence of the person in the act. The object of action is transcendent in relation to the acting subject; the value as the end of volition or choice is transcendent. However, the transcendence proper to the human act and linked with the personal structure of self-determination is not exhausted in this, let us say, horizontal direction.

A thorough analysis of the will as the personal structure of self-determination indicates that its every *fully mature decision, choice, or mature volition* of a given value *presupposes a subjective relation to truth*. We find the simplest and the most transparent confirmation of this fact in the analysis of conscience on the basis of the experience of human morality. This confirmation is the simplest but not the only one. Conscience judges on the moral—that is, subjective and personal—value of our acts, thus also of our volitions and choices directed to various objective values; it defines them as morally good or morally evil. The relation to truth, which in the case of conscience is, above all, the truth of the good (or the truth about the good), indicates a different dimension of transcendence proper to the person than the one that is expressed in the very crossing of the horizontal boundary of the subject when he turns toward the objective value regardless of the judgment of conscience. We can call this dimension "vertical" transcendence, for precisely in virtue of the relation to truth, in virtue of conscience, in which this relation is expressed and concretized, the man-person stands in a sense "above" his acting, choosing, and willing. He acquires a specific mastery over them.[10]

This dimension of the transcendence proper to the human person is constituted through the relation to truth, good, and beauty in the transcendent and somewhat absolute sense. *This relation does not remain a separated dimension of the human spirit but enters the real structures of the person's acting and existing.* In particular, it enters the personal structure of self-determination and constitutes this structure in its own way, especially through the judgments of conscience, which express the truth about the moral value of action, yet also (though in a different way) through the judgments that express the truth about the logical value of thinking or the aesthetic value of production, creativity, etc.

---

10. See Wojtyła, *Person and Act*, part 2, "The Transcendence of the Person in the Act."

In these reflections we shall continue (*brevitatis causa*) to dwell on action itself, emphasizing the transcendence of the person in the act, the transcendence proceeding from the moment of conscience, the moment that is central and decisive for the constitution of the act of the person in relation to truth. This moment as the real expression of the transcendence of the person in the act suffices for gaining a more thorough look at the issue of the auto-teleology of man. The expression τέλος itself means both "end" and "terminus." Thus, the auto-teleology of man also indicates that man is an end for himself. This conviction finds justification and basis in the analysis of human acts and, above all, of the core dynamism of these acts, which is *voluntarium* as the personal structure of self-determination. An accurate analysis of this structure allows us to confer on the auto-teleology of man a sense that results from the transcendence of the person in the act, namely, from its experience and interpretation. *Man is an end for himself inasmuch as, and in such a way, that his acts*—and the volitions, choices, and decisions contained in them—*find in man himself their terminus.* They find this terminus *on the basis of the transcendent relation to truth* (and with it also to good or to beauty, which, however, we do not submit to separate analyses here).

The relation to truth contains in some way the "terminus" of the personal structure of self-determination. When man as the subject of action attains this "terminus," then in some measure he fulfills himself. [4a]Therefore, he also attains the "end" that he is for himself.[4b] The personal structure of this fulfillment corresponds on the basis of experience to the auto-teleology of man. This fulfillment is not absolute, although it has in itself something of the absolute, for it is accomplished on the basis of the "absoluteness of good."[11] [5a] It can be accomplished on this basis precisely because it grows in the act of the person on the foundation of the transcendent relation to truth, in the profile of the "vertical" transcendence of the subject. The essential greatness of conscience consists in its being upright and speaking the truth. If such a conscience is also called the voice of God, it is because it reveals that *in which man not only "surpasses" the horizontal boundaries of his subject but also "rises above*

---

11. See Władysław Tatarkiewicz, *O bezwzględności dobra* (Warsaw: Gebether i Wolff, 1919); Tatarkiewicz, "On the Four Types of Ethical Judgements," in *Proceedings of the Seventh International Congress of Philosophy, Held at Oxford, England, September 1–6, 1930*, ed. Gilbert Ryle, 398–401 (London: H. Milford, 1931).

himself," thus attaining at the same time a thorough conformity with himself. Precisely *this conformity* with himself, which is realized on the basis of the transcendence of the person, of the transcendent relation to truth, *enters, so to speak, into the definition of self-fulfillment,* that is, the auto-teleology of man.[6a]

The fulfillment of oneself, which, in a sense, is demanded by the entire personal structure of self-determination, contains the "moment of the absolute" (certainly this also bade Kant speak of the absolute imperative): the fulfillment of oneself in the act is accomplished on the basis of the absoluteness of good. At the same time, however, the subject of this fulfillment retains full consciousness of his own non-absoluteness, that is, the contingency, limitation, and relativity of being. For in virtue of the transcendence proper to himself, he does not stand "beyond good and evil" but only—as experience very vividly confirms—"rises above himself," so as through the relation to truth—thus spiritually—to possess himself in the area of his volitions and to fulfill himself in this way. He is constantly a task for himself: he is entrusted to himself as a task, and every time—in every action, volition, choice, and decision—he is being entrusted anew. [7a]In this way, the whole existence of man in the dimension of the "world" is constantly accompanied, in a sense, by the *"auto-teleology of the terminus," which conditions the entire "auto-teleology of the end."* [8a] Through this auto-teleology the man-person, in a sense, constantly inscribes himself in the structure of the "world," permeates it, so as to surpass it at the same time.[7b]

4. Auto-teleology in the Dimension of the "Terminus" and "End"

It was already said in the previous stage of this analysis (in the context of reflection on the personal structure of self-determination) that the auto-teleology of man presupposes the entire teleology of volitions and choices, through which man is constantly being included in the axiological (and, in turn, teleological) structure of reality, within which he exists and acts. It was also said that the auto-teleology of man does not mean a solipsistic closing in the likeness of an impassable monad, but, on the contrary, means an opening toward values, and potentially toward all of them. Auto-teleology means only *a personal "modus" of this opening*. This "modus" must be manifold, thus, for instance, *different in relation to things and different in relation to persons*. [9a]This "modus" must yet be different in relation to God.[9b]

In relation to things it concerns, for instance, the whole enormous sphere of human work, production, technology, economy, and civilization—we must in a sense presuppose and postulate the auto-teleology of man in each of them. We must presuppose it all the more if these spheres, growing objectively, can serve not only man's fulfillment in himself but also his alienation.

The relation to persons is in some measure tangled up with the relation to things, although it has, above all, its own dimension in the existence and action of every man. The auto-teleology of the human person constitutes, so to speak, the threshold of relation, which fundamentally conditions the correct creation of any community, whether inter-personal or social. At the same time, however, if man spontaneously "surpasses" himself toward the other, toward the others, toward the community (and in this "surpassing" there is also a "rising above oneself"), then it is proof that self-fulfillment, that is, auto-teleology, carries in itself an opening of the subject.[10a] Man fulfills himself *"through the others,"* realizes himself by living "for the others"—precisely in which what most comes to light is *not only the surpassing of oneself toward the others but also the rising above oneself*.[12] These matters were analyzed multiple times and are constantly the object of analyses, most expedient in an epoch such as ours, in which the processes of socialization must be balanced by the effort of personalization.[11a]

[12a]Finally, what should the "modus" of opening oneself in relation to God be like, a "modus" proper to the personal auto-teleology of man? Here is the question that both the old and the contemporary philosophy of the person must ask itself. The analysis of revealed sources, which is

---

12. My work entitled "Participation or Alienation" (Participation ou aliénation) [pp. 514–31 in this edition] is devoted in an analytical way to shaping the relation of "I" to "thou." It was sent to the International Phenomenological Colloquium, which took place January 24–28, 1975, in Swiss Fribourg, and it was in turn delivered at the invitation of the Department of Philosophy at the University of Fribourg on February 27 of the same year. The general topic of the colloquium organized by Société Internationale pour l'étude de Husserl et de la phénoménologie—Internationale Forschungsgesellschaft für Phänomenologie was "*Soi* et *autrui*: La crise de l'irréductible dans l'homme."

expressed by the old and the contemporary teaching (Magisterium) of the Church, facilitates the theological answer to that same question. Particularly, much seems to be said in this respect by the following formulation of the most recent council, one that is concise but at the same time pregnant with content: "Man, *who is the only creature on earth which God willed for itself, cannot fully find himself except through a sincere gift of self.*"[13] It is known from the same sources that man makes this "gift of self" not merely to the "world" or to the people in the world, but ultimately to God himself. To this man was called and invited by God; this is the deepest content of revelation and the covenant. In this respect, both the theology emerging in an organic reflection on the Word of God and the philosophy of religion manifest the auto-teleology of man. This auto- teleology constitutes, so to speak, a mature fruit of the transcendence of the person, who most fully "surpasses" and "rises above" himself in a personal relation to God. It is known that this view is under fire by the modern criticism of religion. It seems, however, that we cannot seek the grounds for explaining it primarily in this criticism, but in religious experience, which is simply one of man's fundamental and essential experiences.

By analyzing, in the present reflections, the auto-teleology of man on the basis of the transcendence of the person in the act, we arrive at the conclusion (already previously expressed) that *the "auto-teleology of the terminus" is existentially proper to man existing and acting in the world.* This terminus is the truth of human acts. Conscience constitutes the fundamental condition of self-fulfillment. By fulfilling himself, man attains the end that he is for himself; he becomes the good that he "is" and at the same time that he constantly "should be." Under the necessity of judgment that proceeds from the very depth of personal being or, we can say, under the entire wonderful dimension of the "auto-teleology of the terminus" that is linked with the existential situation of man existing and acting "in the world," *another dimension, as it were, is constantly revealed— the "auto-teleology of the end."* The more the relation of man to things, persons, and God is mature, that is, the more it is based on truth about them, the more man fulfills himself. The more good and beauty he draws out—of course, always in the light of truth—from his relation to things, persons, and God, the more he fulfills himself, the more he becomes the

---

13. *Gaudium et spes*, no. 24 [Vatican translation].

good he constantly "is" and constantly "should be." Auto-teleology is thus at the same time a fuller way of speaking about man as value.

And perhaps in this way of personalistic analysis, the perennial concept of happiness (εὐδαιμονία),[14] which in his time Kant rightly questioned in ethics while opposing utilitarianism, can return to our reflections on the auto-teleology of man. For it is impossible not to perceive that man, in fulfilling himself, always finds a verification of that which he calls happiness. Kant perceived this as well. However, we do not intend to analyze here the problem of the connection in which this "authentic" happiness remains with the auto-teleology of man, in particular with respect to his relation to things, persons, and God. For we, above all, intended to show the very fact of the auto-teleology of man and to indicate the roots of this fact, which are revealed together with the analysis of the transcendence of the person in an indispensable way.[12b]

---

14. Aristotle, *Nicomachean Ethics* 1.6.1097a15–1097b5; translated by Daniela Gromska (Warsaw: Państwowe Wydawnictwo Naukowe, 1956), 220–21.

We can approach the problem of happiness from different points of view. See Władysław Tatarkiewicz, *O szczęściu*, 2nd ed. (Kraków: Wiedza, Zawód, Kultura, 1949), 3rd ed. (Warsaw: Państwowe Wydawnictwo Naukowe, 1962); Tatarkiewicz, *O doskonałości* (Warsaw: Państwowe Wydawnictwo Naukowe, 1976).

11 ❧ *Theoria* and *Praxis* in the Philosophy of the Human Person

1a

1. Introduction—positing the problem

I wish to begin these reflections[cxxx] by quoting certain statements found in the introduction to my study *Person and Act*:

In its full, experiential content, the fact "man acts" can be understood ... as an act of the person.... For we hold that the act is a particular moment of the vision—that is, the experience—*of the person.* Of course, this experience is at the same time a closely specified understanding.... The act is undoubtedly action. Action corresponds to various agents. However, *we definitely cannot ascribe the action that is the act to any other agent except the person.* According to this understanding, *the act presupposes the person.* This understanding was adopted in various areas of knowledge that had human action as their object; in particular, however, this understanding was adopted in ethics. Ethics was and is a science about the act that presupposes the person: man as a person.

In this study, however, we intend to turn this understanding around. Although it bears the title *Person and Act*, the study nevertheless will not be of the act that presupposes the person. We adopt a different direction of experience and understanding. Namely, *this study will concern the act that reveals the person; it will be a study of the person through the act.* For such is the nature of the correlation inhering in experience, in the fact "man acts": the act constitutes a particular moment of revealing the person. The act allows us to have the most proper insight into his essence and to understand it most fully. We experience that man is a person, and we are convinced of this because he performs acts.[1]

---

1. Karol Wojtyła, introduction to *Person and Act* [pp. 102–4 of this edition].

567

I took the liberty of quoting this more extensive passage from the introduction to my study *Person and Act* because—to a certain degree—this passage shows in what direction I would like to conduct these reflections on the topic of *theoria* and *praxis*. Although the quoted statements do not directly speak on the topic of *praxis*, but only on the act as a particular source of knowing man-person, it is difficult to deny that precisely the act as an essentially human action constitutes the very core of the philosophical reflection on the topic of *praxis*. Permit me to quote one more fragment, which speaks precisely on that issue:

> We can say that the person-act relation is for everyone first and foremost a lived-experience, a subjective fact. Thanks to induction [2a](*sensu Aristotelico*)[2b], it becomes [3a]in a sense[3b] a topic and a problem. Then it enters the area of theoretical inquiry. For as a lived-experience, that is, as an experiential fact, the person-act relation at the same time constitutes that which the philosophical tradition called "praxis." It is accompanied by "practical" understanding, namely, the understanding that is sufficient and required for man to live and act consciously.[2]

It seems that this fragment contains the ground, as it were, for distinguishing and contrasting the practical in relation to the theoretical in the traditional understanding of these terms. Specifically, this will require commentary over the course of our reflections. At this time, however, I merely mention this in order to finish the text that again defines the new and proper direction of my inquiries: "Our chosen *direction of understanding and interpretation leads through the theorization of this praxis*. The point [4a](in the study *Person and Act*)[4b] is not how to act consciously, but to ascertain what conscious action, or the act, is and how this act reveals the person to us and helps us fully and comprehensively understand him."[3]

2. Commentary

The further reflections that I intend to conduct here on the topic of *theoria* and *praxis* will be, to a certain degree, a commentary on the posi-

---

2. Wojtyła, introduction to *Person and Act* [p. 109 of this edition].
3. Wojtyła, introduction to *Person and Act* [pp. 109–10 of this edition].

tion that I took in my study. In that study, we find an attempt to reverse—or rather to complete—the course of philosophical thinking that was characteristic of traditional philosophy. According to my conviction, this course was expressed in the view that practice presupposes theory, that theoretical philosophy is in a sense the foundation of so-called practical philosophy, which principally encompasses ethics and its various branches (thus, for example, the ethics of social life, economic life, professional life, conjugal life, etc.). It is proper to stress here that I myself lectured on ethics at the Theological Faculty of the Jagiellonian University in Kraków and the Catholic University of Lublin, and that it was specifically this discipline that led me to gradually concentrate my interests on man as a person. The path to this focus was led by the need to substantiate the norms of Catholic conjugal ethics, and this fact found its expression, among others, in the book *Love and Responsibility*. These inquiries and analyses presented me with an interior need—a command, as it were—to concern myself with the theory of the person, which, in turn, found its expression in the study cited above. Thus, the path to theory—in this case, to the theory of the person—was led from "practice," or in any event from ethics, which, at the beginning of my academic activities, I considered a discipline that belonged to practical philosophy, and to be, in fact, a central division of that philosophy.

However, I must admit that quite quickly I began to question the rightness of this inclusion. Already during my active engagement with the philosophical faculty in Lublin, where a division was introduced into the theoretical and practical sections, I favored assigning ethics to the theoretical section or at least linking it with both sections. Of course, this position did not have a purely organizational significance but proceeded from essential premises—that is, precisely from my new view on the relation between the theoretical and the practical in ethics, a view that developed as I practiced my discipline.

The traditional approach inherited from Aristotle and consolidated in the teaching of St. Thomas and the Thomistic tradition seems to provide grounds for making the practical dependent on the theoretical. Based on this philosophical tradition, we must speak of the primacy of *theoria* before *praxis*, for, at first glance, it would be difficult to speak of the primacy of *praxis*. In some sense, this position finds its rationale in the adage *op-*

erari sequitur esse. Since "*sequitur*," then we must first state *that the agent is*, and *what* or *who* he is, in order to speak correctly on the topic of his *operari*, especially if we are to speak on this topic in a normative sense, as ethics does concerning human *operari*. In this way, the adage *operari sequitur esse* should be read in the sense of *praxis sequitur theoriam*. I am still convinced that this consequence is correct, particularly in the area of ethics. For it is impossible to formulate right, that is, practically true (and, at the same time, theoretically justified), norms of human conduct without a thorough answer to the question of what man is. Therefore, the path of *praxis sequitur theoriam* is unavoidable in ethics; it necessarily obligates. However, a question arises as to whether this path has only one direction, from theory to *praxis*, and whether it does not to some degree lead also in the opposite direction, namely, from *operari* to *esse*—and thus, at the same time, from *praxis* to *theoria*. Is our cognition of the acting subject—the one who acts—not shaped in a fundamental measure through the experience and understanding of "that" and "how" this acting subject acts?

Thus, the adage *operari sequitur esse* indicates the ontic dependence of action on the existence of the acting subject, while it also seems to indicate the cognitive order in which action allows us to understand the existence and the nature of the one who acts. In this way, *praxis* is located in a sense at the origin of *theoria*. This position does not at all change the rightness of the statement that "a good theory is the best practice." For the point here is not the fundamental dependence of practice on theory, of action on cognition, but the path on which this cognition or understanding is obtained. This path leads from *praxis*, from action.

This position seems particularly close to contemporary philosophy, in which the epistemological current—inductive and, above all, reductive—prevails. This, however, does not mean that we cannot seek a basis for this position in the philosophy of St. Thomas, which, as is known, has a decisive metaphysical profile. It concerns itself above all with the order of being and not human cognition alone. If, for St. Thomas, the very core of human *praxis* is the act [*czyn*]—*actus humanus*—then we should remember that *actus* denotes perfection, the fulfillment of a potency. Thus, this perfection resides precisely in *praxis*. In it, any being—and, above all, man—realizes itself by fulfilling its potencies. In turn, then, we must accept that we can draw the fullest experience and understanding of this being—and particularly man—precisely from its *praxis*. What man is and which potencies, powers, and habits he has at his disposal are best manifested in this *praxis*. *Praxis* as the human act gives us in a sense the fullest insight into all this.

This position also speaks of the close coherence between *operari* and *esse*—and indirectly also of the coherence between *praxis* and *theoria*. Man can act only in accord with what he is and what he is like. Likewise, a theory of man is true inasmuch as it is a comprehensive reflection of his *praxis*. To a certain extent, we can also say that *praxis* is a dimension that verifies theory. This entire principle, however, must not be understood in a simplistic way. For it is known that not only "factuality" (the fact that man acts, that he does this or that) but also "duty" (the fact that man should act in a certain way) belongs to human *praxis*. We are unable to build a correct theory of man if we ground it only on what composes the "factuality" of his *praxis* and disregard "duty," which also belongs to this *praxis*. What is essential for a correct theory of man is the dynamism of the tension between factuality and duty. This is the proper and adequate sense of the adage *operari sequitur esse* in relation to man.

3. Conclusions

In this way, our reflection on the topic of *theoria* and *praxis* clearly approaches the area of morality as a group of facts that are thoroughly rooted in human *operari* and bear in themselves the deep mark of the tension between "factuality" and "duty." Thus, in order to provide proper elements for a theory of man as well as for any humanistic (personalistic) theory of reality, we must more penetratingly look at the internal structure of human action (the act [*czyn*]) and the connection of this action with the personal subject. St. Thomas already noted that the human act possesses at once transitive and intransitive profiles. It possesses the transitive (*transiens*) profile inasmuch as it turns to objects, and especially inasmuch as it contributes to a certain objectivization in a product. We then say that while acting, man "makes," creates, or produces something. At the same time, however, both the action of this type and every other human act possess their intransitive profile inasmuch as they remain in the subject (*immanens*), inasmuch as it is in him that they evoke a specific effect. We can observe these immanent effects of action in various dimensions of man's subjective being, thus both in the somatic and psychical dimensions. However, the fundamental, immanent effect of human action is in the essentially human and, thereby, strictly personal dimension. This effect is moral good or evil as a value or anti-value of the human person, one that makes man himself—man as such—good or evil.

This is an ingenious observation of St. Thomas. He states that through his action in the transitive dimension (*actio transiens*) toward this or that objectivization, man becomes, for example, a good engineer, physician, writer, artist, etc. However, each of these qualifications considered in the intransitive dimension (*immanens*) does not make man fundamentally (*simpliciter*) good or evil, good or evil as man, but makes him as such in a certain respect (*secundum quid*). Only ethical qualification—that is, moral value or anti-value—constitutes the objective good or evil of man, makes man good or evil as man.

We ought to state that this distinction—which, in my opinion, corresponds to the profound and full eloquence of man's experience—constitutes an essential key to shaping the whole *theoria-praxis* problem. Let us organize the conclusions that suggest themselves here.

The first conclusion pertains to a narrower problem, namely, the problem of practicing anthropology, ethics, and other sciences linked to man. Based on the above, albeit concise, reflections, there is no doubt that this problem lies on the plane of the encounter between *praxis* and *theoria*. Also, there is no doubt that this human *praxis* is manifold, which is expressed, after all, overabundantly in history, culture, civilization, technology, etc. However, among these manifold (historical and contemporary) manifestations of human *praxis*, we must resolutely seek that which is essentially human. In this respect, the analysis of human action conducted by St. Thomas—which distinguished two elements in this action, *transiens* and *immanens*, and stated that the moral value is that which makes man as man good (or evil)—possesses the significance of a fundamental and permanent directive. Regardless of which method we use to form a philosophical anthropology, these elements must find expression in it. In a sense, they condition both the strict inviolability of *humanum* in the analysis of the whole of reality and the real transcendence of the person in relation to the world. Without considering and emphasizing these elements, which belong to the permanent heritage of St. Thomas's philosophy, we ought to doubt the accuracy of reading human *praxis* in a given *theoria*. We also should doubt the rightness of the influence of a given *theoria* on a given *praxis*.

The second conclusion pertains to the relation that occurs *de facto*—and should occur—between *theoria* and *praxis*. Thus, this conclusion is broader, more general. Based on the above, albeit concise, reflections, we see that the relation between *theoria* and *praxis* has a two-sided character. Taking into consideration not only the dynamic character of man but also that of the whole of reality, we must accept as obvious that there cannot exist a theory that would, in some way, fail to presuppose and explain *praxis*, that is, simply speaking, action and the dynamism of reality. In this aspect, we can state that *praxis* precedes *theoria*, or that *praxis* is anterior to *theoria*. This primacy is epistemological, which also includes *implicite* that our relation to reality starts with experience. At the same time, however, it is clear that what we experience and what we cognize, namely, this reality, is anterior to our cognition—we do not produce it while cognizing but find it already present. It is not reality that presupposes cognition, but cognition that presupposes reality. Hence, our cognition tends from *praxis* to *theoria*, that is, to grasping the reality that we cognize in a sense "in itself." The cognitive striving from *praxis* to *theoria* is explained not merely by the need to grasp reality "in itself"—as it is. This striving is also explained by considering *praxis*. For we try to possess the fullest possible vision of reality in itself (namely, *theoria*) in order to confer a greater maturity, perfection, and fullness onto *our* praxis.

These reflections seem to emphasize greatly the moment of reduction in our cognition and the necessity of constantly making deduction dependent on reduction. The "purely deductive" systems seem to be threatened by the loss of creative contact between *praxis* and *theoria*; therefore, the possibility of their service to truth is quite limited and doubtful.

In order to close these reflections, I should add that the fundamental system of causes, or the ultimate reasons that explain every reality—the system that was fundamental for the philosophy of Aristotle and that of St. Thomas after him—moves the final cause to the foreground. It seems that this systematic presupposition in a sense opens the gate to any—and primarily to human—*praxis* and, moreover, to its definite primacy. Since, in explaining reality, we are to proceed from the end as the fundamental reason, this means that in the process of understanding this reality, we must in a sense constantly posit questions linked with action and the entire dynamism of being. Thus, questions about *praxis* constitute the fundamental elements for constructing a picture of reality—and we call this picture *theoria*.

12 ❦ [1a]*Theoria* and *Praxis*

A Universally Human and Christian Topic[1b]

1. Introduction

Speaking at the beginning of the conference devoted to the topic of *theoria* and *praxis*, I wish first of all to thank the organizers for the initiative and for the invitation, by which I feel much honored.[cxxxi] The very program of the conference reveals how rich and multifaceted, how perennial and still relevant this topic is today. Certainly, what awaits us at this conference is not only a *historical look* at the problem of *theoria* and *praxis* but also its *live actualization*. Actualization proceeds from the need to look at the old and, in a sense, *perennial problem in ever-new contexts*. In this case, the contemporary epoch determines the context—first, as both a defined and being-defined totality of the facts of human existence, and second, as a group of cognitive solutions and conditionings in the sphere of human thought.

The topic of *theoria* and *praxis* inheres in the very center of philosophical reflection, whose contemporary paths are manifold but are not necessarily separated from the old ones. Nonetheless, the plurality of these paths, their diverseness, requires in a sense a manifold reinterpretation of the topic, its undertaking in the context of various conceptions of philosophizing, and a search for new formulations of problems based on new presuppositions. The form conferred on the topic of *theoria* and *praxis* by traditional philosophy is certainly distinct—at least in the two great currents that reach down to *Plato and Aristotle*. But we must expect another form of the *theoria–praxis* problem in post-Cartesian philosophy. We know what *Kant*, on the one hand, and the philosophy that in a certain sense aimed to overcome Kant's position, on the other hand, contributed to this great topic. As to the latter, I have in mind, above all, *phenomenology*, such as the one championed by Max Scheler (with which I concerned myself in a particular way and which perhaps will also find some resonance in this lecture).[1]

Marxism as a philosophical current introduced a particular affirmation of *praxis*, placing it at the foundation of the entire diamatic system and its own materialistic concept of man. Man became man through *praxis*—through work: *Marxism* presupposes *praxis* (human action) not only at the foundation of cognition, of theory, but also at the foundation of anthropogenesis itself. In turn, it sees in this *praxis* the fundamental factor of transforming the world by way of revolutionary practice.[2]

All of this indicates the great richness of the *theoria–praxis* problem, its particular relevance, and, finally, a plurality of meanings stratified in and around it. It is not my task in this inaugural lecture to anticipate all that will in turn be said and analyzed from many sides by so many excellent thinkers—philosophers and scholars. However, speaking at the

---

1. Karol Wojtyła, "System etyczny Maksa Schelera jako środek do opracowania etyki chrześcijańskiej," *Polonia sacra* 6, nos. 2–4 (1953–54): 143–61; Wojtyła, "Zagadnienie woli w analizie aktu etycznego," *Roczniki filozoficzne* 5, no. 1 (1955–57): 111–35; Wojtyła, "Ewangeliczna zasada naśladowania: Nauka źródeł Objawienia a system filozoficzny Maksa Schelera," *Ateneum kapłańskie* 55, no. 1 (1957): 57–67; Wojtyła, "O metafizycznej i fenomenologicznej podstawie normy moralnej (w oparciu o koncepcję św. Tomasza z Akwinu oraz Maksa Schelera)," *Roczniki teologiczno-kanoniczne* 6, nos. 1–2 (1959): 99–124; Wojtyła, *Ocena możliwości zbudowania etyki chrześcijańskiej przy założeniach systemu Maksa Schelera*, Rozprawy wydziału filozoficznego 5 (Lublin: Towarzystwo Naukowe Katolickiego Uniwersytetu Lubelskiego, 1959).

2. See Tadeusz M. Jaroszewski, "Marksowska kategoria 'praktyki' a antropologia filozoficzna," *Człowiek i Światopogląd*, no. 2 (37), (1968), 11–16; Jaroszewski, "Marksowska kategoria 'praktyki' oraz jej rola w filozofii dialektycznego materializmu," *Studia filozoficzne*, no. 2, (1969), 3–20; Jaroszewski, *Osobowość i wspólnota: Problemy osobowości we współczesnej antropologii filozoficznej—marksizm, strukturalizm, egzystencjalizm, personalizm chrześcijański* (Warsaw: Książka i Wiedza, 1970), especially pp. 63–66: "Dialektyczna filozofia *praxis* a problem osobowości dynamicznej"; Jaroszewski, *Rozważania o praktyce. Wokół interpretacji filozofii Karola Marksa* (Warsaw: Państwowe Wydawnictwo Naukowe, 1974); Roger Garaudy, *Perspectives de l'homme: Existentialisme, pensée catholique, marxisme* (Paris: Presses universitaires de France, 1959), published in Polish as *Perspektywy człowieka: Egzystencjalizm, myśl katolicka, marksizm*, trans. Z. Butkiewicz and J. Rogoziński (Warsaw: Książka i Wiedza, 1968); Lucien Sève, *Marxisme et theorie de la personnalité* (Paris: Editions sociales, 1972), published in Polish as *Marksizm a teoria osobowości*, trans. Kazimierz Piechocki (Warsaw: Książka i Wiedza, 1975). See also: Tadeusz Ślipko, "Pojęcie człowieka w świetle współczesnej filozoficznej antropologii marksistowskiej w Polsce," *Zeszyty Naukowe KUL* 10, no. 2, (1967), 3–16; Ślipko, "Marksizm a osoba ludzka (Zarys pewnej interpretacji)," in *Aby poznać Boga i człowieka*, Part 2: "O człowieku dziś," ed. Bohdan Bejze, 177–204 (Warsaw: Wydawnictwo Sióstr Loretanek, 1974).

beginning of this long and rich series of analyses and comprehensive approaches, I would like to take a look in a rather synthetic way at *the problem of* theoria *and* praxis *as a topic that is both human and Christian.*

What do I mean by such a formulation? The subject matter of *theoria* and *praxis* remains in fundamental relation to man. It is human in both its objective and subjective senses. First, I will try to explain somewhat more broadly how I understand its human specificity and its human dimension—which is precisely the dimension that philosophy examines. I think that the issue of *theoria* and *praxis*, also as a gnoseological problem, is principally a topic of *anthropology as well as ethics*, to which, in my opinion, we ought to grant a central position here.

To what extent is the topic of *theoria* and *praxis* a Christian topic? I think that it is such primarily through the entire human dimension that philosophy continually examines anew under different aspects. But it is so also according to the dimension of man and the world that faith and consequently theology discover *in light of the Word of God*. There is no doubt that this Word, particularly concentrated on man, constitutes at the same time a *profound sense* of the reciprocal relation in which *theoria* and *praxis* abide.

The program of this conference also includes a theological approach to the topic of *theoria* and *praxis*. Therefore, while delivering the inaugural address, I wish to address it as a topic that is both human and Christian.

2. *Theoria–praxis*: A Two-Directional System

The classical approach inherited from Aristotle and consolidated in the teaching of St. Thomas[3] and the Thomistic school seems to provide grounds for making the practical dependent on the theoretical. It also seems to provide grounds for acknowledging the primacy of theory over practice. In some sense, this position finds its rationale in the adage *operari sequitur esse*. Since "*sequitur*," then we must first state *that the agent*

---

3. See *Summa theologiae* I-II, q. 9, a. 1: *Utrum voluntas moveatur ab intellectu* [Whether the will is moved by the intellect?]; q. 3, a. 5: *Utrum beatitudo sit operatio intellectus speculativi an practice* [If it be an operation of the intellect, whether happiness is an operation of the speculative or of the practical intellect?]; q. 58, a. 4: *Utrum moralis virtus possit esse sine intellectuali* [Whether there can be moral without intellectual virtue?].

is, and *what or who he is*, in order to speak correctly on the topic of his *operari*, especially if we are to speak on this topic in a normative sense, as we do in ethics. In this way, the adage *operari sequitur esse* is read in the sense of *praxis sequitur theoriam*. I am convinced that this consequence is correct, especially in the area of ethics. For it is impossible to formulate right, that is, practically true (and, at the same time, theoretically justifiable), norms, that is, principles of human conduct (*operari*), without a thorough answer to the question of what man is.

Therefore, the path of *praxis sequitur theoriam*, the *path from theory to practice*, is unavoidable not only in ethics but also in all other sciences concerning action (in medicine, technology, art, etc.). However, a question arises as to whether this path has only one direction, from theory to *praxis*, and whether it does not lead simultaneously *in the opposite direction*, namely, *from* praxis *to* theoria, or at least from *operari* to *esse* (if we already agree to a certain identifiability between these two pairs of concepts). The question is whether our cognition of the one who acts is not shaped in a fundamental measure through the experience and understanding of "that" and "how" this acting subject acts.

The adage *operari sequitur esse* indicates the essential (in a dynamic sense) dependence of action on the existence of the acting subject—and this is its objective sense. At the same time, however, the same adage seems to indicate the cognitive order in which action allows us to understand not only the existence but also the nature of the "agent": the one who acts. In this way, *praxis* is also located in a sense at the origin of theory, at its foundation, as it were.

This position seems *particularly close to contemporary philosophy*, in which the epistemological approach prevails over the metaphysical. This, however, does not mean that we cannot seek a basis for this position in the philosophy of St. Thomas, which, as is known, has a decisively metaphysical profile. It concerns itself above all with being and with cognition on the basis of being. If, for St. Thomas, the very core of human *praxis* is *actus humanus* (the act [*czyn*]), then we should remember that this *actus* denotes at once the perfection and fulfillment[4] dependent on a certain

---

4. See *Summa theologiae* I-II, q. 1, a. 3: *Utrum actus humani recipiant speciem ex fine* [Whether a man's actions are specified by their end?]; q. 8, a. 2: *Utrum voluntas sit tantum finis, an etiam eorum quae sunt ad finem* [Whether the will is of the end only, or also of the means?]; q. 9, a. 1: *Utrum voluntas moveatur ab intellectu* [Whether the will is moved by the intellect?]. See also Karol Wojtyła,

power, thus, potency (*potentia*)—namely, on the will. Hence, by way of *praxis*, man performs acts (*actus humanus*) and, at the same time, fulfills himself, actualizing his potencies. Once we move from the metaphysical to the epistemological approach, it can and should be stated that we can attain the fullest experience and, consequently, *the fullest understanding of who man*—the acting subject—*is* through *a thorough analysis of the act, and thus, by way of* praxis. We must therefore undertake the trouble of a penetrating, in-depth, and comprehensive analysis.

3. *Praxis* as a Starting Point for a Theory of Man

As is evident, the position taken here, linked to the epistemological approach of contemporary philosophy (particularly phenomenology), refers at the same time to key tenets in St. Thomas's anthropology. The coherence between human *operari* and human *esse* becomes in a particular way a basis for the coherence between *praxis* and *theoria*. Man can act only in accord with what he is and what he is like. A theory of man is true inasmuch as it is a profound reflection of his *praxis*. To a certain extent, we can also say that *praxis* is a dimension that verifies theory.

This entire conception, however, must not be understood in a simplistic way. It is known that *not only the "factuality" of* praxis (the fact that man acts, that he does this or that) *but also its "duty"* (the fact that man should act in a certain way) *belongs to human* praxis. A unilateral emphasis on the sole "factuality" of human *praxis*—an emphasis that we encounter in positivistic approaches (for instance, even in the so-called sociology of morality or psychology of morality)—falls short of building an adequate theory of man. We are unable to build such a theory if we rely only on what composes the "factuality" of man's action, of his *praxis*, and disregard "duty," which more deeply explains the reality of man as an acting subject.[5] Thus, the basis for a correct theory of man must

---

chapter 4: "Self-Determination and Fulfillment" in *Person and Act* [page 251 of this volume]. See also Wojtyła, "The Personal Structure of Self-Determination," trans. Andrzej Potocki, in *Tommaso d'Aquino nel suo VII centenario: Congresso Internazionale, Roma-Napoli, 17–24 aprile 1974*, 379–90 (Rome, 1974) [see p. 457 in this edition].

5. Duty is not treated as such. See Immanuel Kant, *Grundlegung zur Metaphysik der Sitten* (Leipzig: Philipp Reclam Jun., 1904). Translated by Mścisław Wartenberg as *Uzasadnienie metafizyki moralności*, ed. Roman Ingarden, 2nd ed. (Warsaw: Państwowe Wydawnictwo Naukowe,

grasp the entire dynamism of the tension between factuality itself and the authentically personal duty in man's action. For *duty is the properly human, personal dimension of the factuality of the whole of human* praxis. We must always keep this dimension before our eyes when forming a theory of man.

In order to provide proper elements for an adequate theory of man as well as for any truly humanistic (personalistic) theory of reality, we must constantly keep before our eyes that which St. Thomas noted in a capital way in his teaching on the act [*czyn*]. The act (*actus humanus*) possesses at once a transitive and intransitive profile.[6] It possesses *the transitive* (*transiens*) *profile* inasmuch as it turns to objects outside of man, and especially inasmuch as it contributes to a certain objectivization in a product. We then can say that while acting, man "makes," creates, or produces something. However, both the action of this type and every other *actus humanus* also possess their *intransitive* (*immanens*) *profile inasmuch as they remain in the subject*—inasmuch as it is in him that they evoke a specific effect.

4. *Praxis* and Ethos

Taking into account the complex structure of man as an acting subject, we can observe these immanent effects of action in various layers of this structure, thus in both the somatic and the psychical layers. However, the fundamental, immanent effect of the act is one that occurs in the essentially human and thereby strictly personal dimension. This effect is *moral good or evil* as a value or anti-value of the human person, one that makes man himself—man as such—good or evil.

This is an ingenious observation of St. Thomas. He states that through his action in the transitive (*transiens*) dimension, toward this or

---

1953). Translated and edited by Mary Gregor as *Groundwork of the Metaphysics of Morals*, Cambridge Texts in the History of Philosophy (Cambridge: Cambridge University Press, 1997).

Instead, duty is treated as a personal element of the act and morality. See Wojtyła, *Person and Act*, especially part 2, "The Transcendence of the Person in the Act," chapter 4, "Self-Determination and Fulfillment," section 4, "Duty as the expression of the call to fulfill oneself" [pp. 265–70 in this edition].

6. See Gerbert Meyer, "Actio immanens, actio transiens," in *Historisches Wörterbuch der Philosophie*, vol. 1, ed. Joachim Ritter, col. 76–78 (Basel: Schwabe, 1971).

that objectivization of things, toward this or that product, man becomes good (or evil) only in a certain respect (*secundum quid*). Thus, he becomes, for instance, a good worker, physician, engineer, speaker, writer, artist, etc. However, none of these qualifications considered in the intransitive (*immanens*) dimension of the act makes man fundamentally (*simpliciter*) good or evil, good or evil as man. Only *ethical qualification*—that is, *moral value or anti-value*—constitutes the objective good or evil of the acting subject, *makes man good or evil as man.*[7]

I think that this distinction has a fundamental significance for the correct understanding of *praxis* in its constitutive connection with man, with the human subject. It is also a specific key to shaping the whole *theoria–praxis* problem as a human topic. The strength of the distinction made by St. Thomas is also, in my opinion, due to the fact that it *corresponds* to the profound and *full eloquence of man's experience*, which always is (and must be) also the experience of morality. In this experience, we do not find man as acting only in relation to objects, as producing certain transitive (*transiens*) effects by his action, but always as most deeply determining himself in this action in the dimension of good or evil.

This has fundamental *consequences for a theory of man* as a person but also for every authentically human, that is, *also personalistic, theory of reality*. There is no doubt that the entire human *praxis*—both in the historical, diachronic approach and in the "contemporary," that is, simultaneously synchronic one—is expressed, so to speak, overabundantly by the plurality and diversification of objectivization, products, and works. It is expressed in this way in culture, civilization, technology, economy, politics, and art. However, among these manifold objectivizations of human *praxis*, in which above all what is transitive (*transiens*) in man's actions is expressed, we must resolutely seek what is in-transitive—precisely what makes man good (or evil) as man.

To discover this in the entire complex richness of human *praxis* is an essential and necessary *condition for identifying the very humanum in the analysis of the complex reality of the "world."* This is also a condition for the

---

7. See Thomas Aquinas, *Summa theologiae* I, q. 5: *De bono in communi* [Of goodness in general]. See Wojtyła, *Ocena możliwości zbudowania etyki chrześcijańskiej przy założeniach systemu Maksa Schelera*, Rozprawy wydziału filozoficznego 5 (Lublin: Towarzystwo Naukowe Katolickiego Uniwersytetu Lubelskiego, 1959); Wojtyła, *Person and Act*, part 2: "The Transcendence of the Person in the Act."

real transcendence of man as a person. Thus, a correct, that is, in-depth, analysis (and, at the same time, concept) of human praxis has a decisive significance both for the very theory of man (what man is) and for the authentically human (that is, personalistic) theory of entire reality. The concept of *praxis* that unilaterally concentrates on the mere material objectivizations of human action without considering the "intransitive" dimension in this action, and without acknowledging the essential primacy of this dimension, conceals in itself premises to cancel the personal transcendence of man, to efface the identity of *humanum*. On the basis of such a concept, there can be no possibility of *transforming the world with regard to man*, of making the world "more human." The only consequence of the theory originating from this concept of human *praxis* can be the practice of reducing humanity. It seems that historical experiences provide quite a few proofs for that.

5. The Identification of *Humanum*

Already in the beginning we said—and now we can repeat it with much greater justification—that the relation between *theoria* and *praxis* has a two-sided character. Taking into consideration both the dynamism of man himself, who essentially expresses himself in his acts, and the dynamic character of the entirety of reality, we must accept that there cannot exist a theory that would fail in some way to explain—and thereby to presuppose—both these dynamisms. According to this understanding, we can and ought to state that *praxis* precedes *theoria*, that *praxis is* in a sense *anterior to theoria*. This is an epistemological primacy based on the fact that our entire cognitive relation to reality starts with experience. At the same time, however, it is clear that what we experience and what we cognize, namely, this dynamic reality, is objectively and really anterior to our cognition—we do not produce it while cognizing but find it already present. It is not reality that presupposes cognition, but cognition that presupposes reality.

Hence, our cognition tends from *praxis* to *theoria*, that is, to grasping the reality that we wish to cognize and cognize in a sense "in itself." *The cognitive striving from* praxis *to* theoria is explained by the need to grasp reality *"in itself"—as it is*. This striving is also explained by considering *praxis*. For we try to possess *the fullest possible "vision"* of reality in itself (vision, in fact, means theoria) *in order to confer a greater maturity*, perfection, and fullness onto *our* praxis. For we try to possess the fullest possible vision of man "in himself" in order to confer the greatest possible fullness of the auto-realization that his acts bring about.

Thus, without revealing and manifesting the elements through which *the very* "humanum" of human actions—that is, also the transcendence of the person—*is identified*, we ought to fundamentally doubt the accuracy of the reading of authentic human *praxis* by a particular theory of man or of entire reality. We should also doubt the legitimacy of placing such a theory at the basis of human *praxis* in order to influence it. Such a theory can even be temporarily advantageous, can serve to enrich the world of man's products, especially material ones; however, it does not deepen *humanum* itself, does not serve it, but rather endangers it. By way of such *praxis*, man can even have more, can possess more things, but he definitely cannot be more and be more fully—be as man.[8]

6. *Humanum* and *Christianum*

The above contradistinction undoubtedly occupies contemporary thought, which concentrates on man and perceives the significance of the connections between *theoria* and *praxis* in a new way. It is known that the very contradistinction "to have more—to be more" appeared in existentialism (Gabriel Marcel), but also entered the Magisterium of the Church and was fixed on the pages of the Second Vatican Council. This is not the first stage of the encounter between *humanum* and *christianum*, but only the next, contemporary stage.

It seems that our reflections on the topic of *theoria* and *praxis* as simply a human topic find full justification in the Word of God. Faith and theology attend to man not only as the one whom the Creator commanded *"to subdue the earth,"*[9] but also as one whose entire being and acting is posited from the beginning *in the dimension of the mysterious tree*

---

8. See Gabriel Marcel, Être et avoir (Paris: Editions Aubier-Montaigne, 1935), published in Polish as *Być i mieć*, trans. Donata Eska (Warszawa: Pax, 1962). See also the Second Vatican Council, The Pastoral Constitution on the Church in the Modern World *Gaudium et spes* (December 7, 1965), especially articles 12, 14, 15, 33, and 39.

9. Gen 1:28.

of the knowledge of good and evil.[10] A close correspondence occurs here between the eloquence of the Word of God and the experience of man together with the reflection to which this experience obligates us. In light of this, we cannot build either a theory of man or an authentically human theory of reality and, in turn, of practice, in which only the aspect expressed by the words "subdue the earth" is considered.

These words do not contain the whole dimension of human *praxis*—therefore, they cannot constitute an exclusive foundation for a theory of man and reality. This foundation must be praxis *also understood as ethos*. After all, the very expression of subduing the earth is by no means and cannot be indifferent to ethos. We cannot build a theory that would correctly proceed from human *praxis*—and, in turn, correctly influence it—without taking into consideration the "supra-material" element that inheres in the very essence of ethos and which essentially conditions the mastery of man "over the earth." Thus, from the viewpoint of both *humanum* and *christianum*, we ought to accept the superiority of ethos. We also ought to accept its primacy as the element that explains man in himself and confers an essentially human character on his entire *praxis*, which, in turn, also conditions the more human character of this world, to which man ontically and dynamically belongs.

However, *christianum* does not end here. It decisively introduces *yet another dimension* into the two-sided (or two-directional) relation of praxis–theory and *theoria–praxis*, with which we concern ourselves here. When St. Paul writes to the Corinthians: "*But we proclaim Christ crucified, a stumbling block to Jews and foolishness to Gentiles, but to those who are called, Jews and Greeks alike, Christ the power of God and the wisdom of God,*"[11] he indicates this other dimension of [2a]*Praxis*[2b]. This is the dimension that, on the basis of *christianum*, constitutes an indispensable foundation for building a theory of man and the world.

Christianum differs from *humanum* itself by the fact *that ethos*—which, we said, constitutes the constitutive element of human *praxis*—opens itself to "the power of God and the wisdom of God"[12] according to the quoted words of St. Paul *ad Corinthios*. Precisely for this reason

---

10. See Gen 2:17.
11. 1 Cor 1:23–24.
12. 1 Cor 1:24.

and following the full eloquence of these words, *christianum* must in the whole two-sided system of *theoria–praxis* include the proclamation of "*Christ crucified, a stumbling block to Jews and foolishness to Gentiles*"; it must include the whole *Mysterium Paschale*. Is not this *mysterium*, the Cross, the fundamental fact in the area of *Praxis* that requires an adequate theory of man and a theory of the world in which man lives and acts?

Of course, this entire dimension of the problem belongs *to the sphere of faith and, consequently, to theology*, which is a methodical reflection on the fact and content of the Church's faith. The fundamental task for theology is and will remain the building of a theory of man and an authentically human reality, for which one of the fundamental starting points is precisely *the* Praxis *of the Cross and* the Mysterium Paschale. This is the mystery of God Incarnate that nonetheless remains in the human dimensions of history. Theology accepts as its starting point the faith of the Church, the faith in which man responds to the Word of the living and incarnate God—to the Word of God revealing himself to man when man entrusts himself to this God and his Word.[13]

In turn, this is human *praxis*—the praxis of faith in which ethos opens itself, as was said, to "the power of God and the wisdom of God."

It is our deepest conviction—a conviction that we draw from both the experience of man and morality—that this opening of human *praxis* to God does not deprive *humanum* of its authentic content and value; it does not alienate it. Quite the contrary, it *allows* this humanum *to find itself in the full dimension of Transcendence*, which inheres deeply in the personal structure of man.[14] Thus, the task of theology is also to show *christianum* as a particular shape of the identification of *humanum*.

The extensive reflections and analyses on the topic of *theoria* and *praxis* will certainly provide many possibilities for that.

---

13. See the Second Vatican Council, The Dogmatic Constitution on Revelation *Dei Verbum*, no. 5 (November 18, 1965).

14. See *Gaudium et spes*, nos. 12, 14, 15, 16, 17, and 22.

13 ❦ The Author's Preface to the First English Edition of *Person and Act*

Now that the present work will emerge from the limited readership to which the original language of composition confined it, I would like to preface it with several introductory remarks.[cxxxii]

First of all, as audacious as it may seem in the present day, in which philosophical thinking is not merely nourished and based upon history but even, it may be ventured, reduced to reflecting upon theories about theories, the present work cannot be seen otherwise than as a personal effort to disentangle the intricacies of a crucial state of affairs and to clarify the basic elements of their problem. I have, indeed, tried to face the major issues themselves concerning nature, life, and the existence of man, with its limitations as well as with its privileges as they directly present themselves to man in his struggles to survive with the dignity of a human being, to set himself goals, and in his striving to accomplish them; of man, who is torn apart between his all too limited condition and highest aspirations to set himself free.

These struggles of man are reflected by the struggles of the author himself who attempts here to unravel the subjacent apparatus of man's operations as it may lead either to his victories or to his defeats, and only as such should the present work be seen. May it contribute to this disentangling of the conflicting issues facing man that are crucial for man's own clarification of his existence and for directing his conduct.

Our approach also runs against another trend of modern philosophy. Since Descartes, the knowledge of man and his world has been identified with the cognitive function. As if only in cognition, and especially through the knowledge of himself, would man manifest his nature and his prerogative.

Preface to the First English Edition | 587

And yet, in reality, does man reveal himself in thinking or in the actual enacting of his existence?—in observing, interpreting, speculating or reasoning are changeable, flexible already in their acts, and mostly futile when confronted with the facts of reality, or in this confrontation itself when he has to take an active stand upon issues of vital decisions and with vital consequences and repercussions?

In fact, it is in reversing the classic attitude toward man that we undertake our study: by approaching him through action. Considering the enormous spread of issues confronting the philosopher who seeks a new approach to man and attempts to apply it, it is only natural that our work must at this point be only too sketchy. We are perfectly aware of both the past and present literature sharing this approach, but it [1a]appeared[1b] to us imperative to undertake it [2a]ourselves[2b].

The author's acquaintance with traditional Aristotelian thought granted, it is however the work of Max Scheler that has been a major influence upon his reflection. In my overall conception of the person envisaged through the mechanisms of his operative systems and their [3a]variations[3b], as presented here, may indeed be seen the Schelerian foundation studied in my previous work.

First of all, it is Scheler's value-theory that comes into question. However, when the differentiation of issues concerning man reached its peak in our times, introducing most artificial cleavages into the heart of the matter of the issues themselves, it is the unity of the human being that seems imperative to be investigated. And in spite of the fundamental Schelerian, and for that matter phenomenological, efforts conducive to the cognition of the complete man, the quest often [4a]for[4b] this unity, its basis as well as its primordial manifestation, remains extant.

In traditional Aristotelian thought, it was the very conception of the "human act," as such seen as the manifestation of man's unity as well as its source.

It seems then that by introducing here the above-mentioned approach to man through action, this may yield necessary insights into the unity of man.

And it is certainly not necessary to emphasize the importance of an inquiry into the unifying factors of man for the present-day outlook on life, sanity, culture, and their prospects.

(One more point must be mentioned.) An important question has still to be raised. In the lapse of time between its first appearance in the Polish language and the present version of this book, not only the author's participation in the philosophical life but also a numerous series of philosophical discussions have contributed to greater precision on many points. There were first discussions with several Polish philosophers (published in *Analecta Cracoviensia* 1973/74). However, those with Professor Anna-Teresa Tymieniecka of Boston were most important for the present publication. They have added to the clarification of numerous concepts and, consequently, to an improved presentation. Professor A.-T. Tymieniecka, having consented to become the philosophical editor of this work, has proposed some changes that have been incorporated into the definitive version with full [5a]approval[5b] of the author. The author is also pleased that this definitive version of his book appears in the distinguished Analecta Series.

And last, but not least, I would like to thank the translator, Mr. Andrew Potocki who has attempted most expertly and with great devotion and care to render this rather difficult Polish text into the English language.

Cardinal Karol Wojtyła

TEXTS MARKED BY THE CRITICAL APPARATUS

I: Pre-1969 Synopsis and Fragments

1. *Person and Act*: A Synopsis

[1a] [1b] [the manuscript notes above this phrase] (*homo artisticus, homo ludens*)

[2a] [here begins the marginal note] (a) The experience of morality *ex se* (in a sense, a priori) shows us man with moral value in him—both *quoad fieri* and *quoad esse* of this value. It is precisely this that allows us to most thoroughly penetrate what man (the person-act) is.

(b) The need to (1) complement and (2) verify the anthropology brought forth from the experience of morality with the anthropology developed "outside" this experience.

(c) The clear boundary of the experience of morality: only man, only a being endowed with intellectual consciousness.

[3a] [here is placed the marginal note] (?)

[4a] [here begins the marginal note] However, this is "another experience" in the sense that it is another cognitive entry into the same object.

[5a] [5b] [noted above this phrase] (*iuxtapositio*: the moral value—man)

[6a] [6b] [here is placed the marginal note] ?

[7a] [here begins the marginal note] Consciousness and sensation (feeling, self-feeling)

[8a] [here begins the marginal note] Consciousness does not reveal "itself" as the subject of consciousness-related acts—but it *reveals a concrete "I"* as the subject of these acts (among other things).

Problems: (a) do not hypostasize consciousness, because this contradicts experience, (b) determine what the "I"-*suppositum* relation depends on.

[9a] [here begins the marginal note] Only *attributive*

[10a] [here begins the marginal note] The relation of:

(1) self-experience and self-observation
(2) both of these to self-knowledge
(3) self-knowledge to the knowledge of man in general

[11a] [here begins the marginal note] *Nota bene*, consciousness grasps some efficacy insofar as it grasps (a) and (b) as proceeding from the "I" and constituting its property. Thus, consciousness does not grasp so much the efficacy of the "I" in relation to (a) and (b) as it excludes the possibility of another efficacy at their origin.

[12a] [here begins the marginal note] Thus: the "act" *sensu analogico*

[13a] [here begins the marginal note] To what extent the "act" and the relation "*potentia*-act" are given intuitively, that is, constitute the object read in experience itself, and to what extent they already constitute interpretation.

[14a] [here begins the marginal note] Introspection (consciousness) is correlated here with observation.

[15a] [here begins the marginal note] See *praecedentia* de hac re!

[16a] [here begins the marginal note] *Nota bene*, we can posit the problem of the extent to which observation does not contradict this.

[17a] [here is placed the marginal note] ?

[18a] [here begins the marginal note] *The power of striving*

[19a] [here begins the marginal note] *Nota bene*, that which conditions efficacy simultaneously conditions freedom.

[20a] [here begins the marginal note] Hence the consciousness-related-subjective image of the person is also irregular.

[21a] [here begins the marginal note] It is fitting to emphasize that the body is the first factor of the concretization of man: the concrete man is the one that possesses this particular body.

[22a] [here begins the marginal note] Although the reactions of the body are in some way reducible to physico-chemical reactions, they are nonetheless not identifiable with them. They possess their own specificity, as does the entire reactivity of the human body.

[23a] [here begins the marginal note] These are two somewhat different problems: *actus externus*, in which we observe the subordination of the body (*soma*) to the will; we infer this subordination from the direct observation of such an act. A somewhat different problem is the relation between conscious efficacy and the reactivity proper to the body (the *soma*-organism).

[24a] [here begins the marginal note] Experience teaches that this content has a cause outside itself and is not its own source.

[25a] [here begins the marginal note] At any rate, we ought not to understand this

connection between affections and cognition—or, better, between emotivity and cognition—too simplistically (what does this look like in the case of bodily affections?).

26a [here begins the marginal note] Or in the previous paragraph (4).

27a [here begins the marginal note] Emotivity is something original.

28a [here begins the marginal note] Emotivity is fundamentally irreducible to appetition, though indirectly it has a great significance for appetition.

29a [here begins the marginal note] (If need be: "drive and self-determination" as no. 1 in the next section B.)

2–5. *Person and Act*: Fragments

1a 1b [the 1966 typescript] unverifiability

2a [the 1966 typescript] The introductory and fundamental reflections contained in the previous chapter have prepared us for such work.

3a [the 1966 typescript] We warned against this in the previous chapter's reflections.

4a 4b [the 1969 *Person and Act* edition] constitution

5a 5b [the 1969 *Person and Act* edition] directly

6a 6b [the 1966 typescript] This is a proper collapse

7a 7b [the 1968 published text] prior

8a 8b [the 1966 typescript] affections

9a 9b [the 1969 *Person and Act* edition] internal

10a 10b [the 1966 typescript] acts

II: *Person and Act*

Introduction

1a [1979/1985] on the plane of consciousness,

2a 2b [1979/1985: removed]

3a 3b [1979/1985] data

4a 4b [1979/1985] momentary sensory phenomenon, but also man himself, who emerges from all experiences

5a 5b [1979/1985] when it receives impressions

6a 6b [1979/1985] an actual group of sensory data or a series of such groups

7a [1994/2000] and in a sense the richer

[8a] [1994/2000] proceeding from experience

[9a] [1969] The sources of

[10a] [1994/2000] and we concentrate above all on this fact

[11a 11b] [2000] specifically placing ethics

[12a 12b] [1979/1985] *must correspond to*

[13a 13b] [1979/1985: removed]

[14a 14b] [1969: added]

[15a 15b] [1969] At the beginning of this book, we adopted the following words as our motto: "*The Church, by reason of her role and competence, is not identified in any way with the political community nor bound to any political system. She is at once a sign and a safeguard of the transcendent character of the human person.*" The author sees a need to explain not so much the content of these words for their own sake as the motive that influenced their placement at the beginning of this book. The cited passage was taken from a document of the Second Vatican Council, namely, the Pastoral Constitution on the Church in the Modern World starting with the words "*Gaudium et spes*." Citing this passage, the author wishes to refer to the period in which the study of person and act was being formed in its initial phase. He also wishes to refer to the particular climate that accompanied the reflections contained in this study. It was the climate of the Second Vatican Council, and in particular of the group that at the council undertook work on the Constitution on the Church in the Modern World. The author was fortunate to participate in this work. For a time, his own study of person and act and the aforementioned conciliar document were being created simultaneously.

We do not intend to emphasize this circumstance in this book, because in accord with the author's intention—at least as attested by the introductory reflections conducted thus far—the study of person and act should have a philosophical character. However, it is difficult to disregard this circumstance of its origin. By undertaking work on the problem of the person, the author is aware of the fact that this philosophical problem also possesses a capital significance for theology. We are content simply to state this, for at this point nothing more would be proper or possible. The significance of personalism in theology is an enormous problem. In the present study, we do not consciously intend at any point to cross the threshold of this problem. Perhaps we will be able to do so one day after a thorough preparation. At any rate, the present study can also serve as a preparation of thought for undertaking personalism in the field of theology. The passage from the conciliar document cited in the beginning does not indicate in the least that personalistic subject matter has already been undertaken in this field.

However, it indicates the universal significance of this subject matter, its primary importance for every man and for the entire, ever-growing human family.

[16a] [1969]—namely, the world of culture and civilization, that is, the "contemporary world" over which we stooped with such concern and attention as the authors of the constitution *Gaudium et spes*.

The present study to some extent also refers to the book *Love and Responsibility*, published seven years ago. This book was described as "an ethical study," but for the reasons presented above we do not intend to repeat this. Nonetheless, person and act are rooted also in that study. It generated the need to take a closer look at the person, a look in a sense for his own sake, and to verify the reality that he is on the basis of even more elementary and universal experiences. Perhaps this vision of the person that we wish to attain in the present study will confirm in its own way the rightness of the statements and principles formulated in the ethical study entitled *Love and Responsibility*. If this will be an effect of this work, it will be only a secondary and additional effect. For here we strive above all toward an understanding of the human person for his own sake.

17a [the 1979/1985 edition places footnote 8 here]

18a 18b [1979/1985: removed]

Chapter 1: Person and Act in the Aspect of Consciousness

1a 1b [1969] The Act: "Conscious Action" and "*Actus humanus*"

2a 2b [1979/1985] It also seems that all attempts—which in taking on this subject matter endeavor to investigate the whole fullness of the act's essential components and constitutive interconnections—must in some way accept the philosophical content hidden in the expressions *actus humanus* and *actus voluntarius*. This content is also presupposed by the attempt undertaken in this study (in further inquiries, we intend to develop and elucidate it in a number of aspects)*. We must only state that this historical conception. [*Editorial note: The text in parentheses was added in the 1994/2000 edition.]

3a 3b [1979/1985] By approaching the person through the act, we intend to retain this fundamental philosophical intuition, which seems to be irreplaceable with respect to the grasp and philosophical interpretation of every dynamism, including the dynamism of the act, that is, of conscious action. We must undertake as full and comprehensive an interpretation of this dynamism as possible, because only in this way can we bring to light the whole reality of the person.

4a 4b [1979/1985] as it seems, philosophical reflection up until now has not developed a more fundamental concept that would express dynamism apart from the concept of *actus*

5a 5b [1969] Conscious Action and the Consciousness of Action

6a 6b [1969] It concerned itself with consciousness as something incorporated into human being and human action. According to this conception, man exists and acts consciously, but he does not exist and act through consciousness. We have already said—in positing the matter this way—that we do not intend an absolutization of consciousness. *Our goal is only to open an aspect that was too confined* and that remained only an implication *in the traditional conception*. This was an implication contained in man's rationality (referring to the definition *homo—animal rationale*);

concerning the act, this was an implication of *voluntarium*. Thus, our task in this study is a certain "explication" of consciousness (the Latin term clearly indicates the opposite of implication).

⁷ᵃ [1969 marginal note] (Possibly a note by A.T.) The problem of the identity of consciousness, like that of its continuity, runs through the entirety of Western philosophical reflection from Plato through Descartes and Kant till Ingarden. We would not claim to bring to the network of its problems a new solution but merely to elaborate a novel basis for the reformulation of some of its issues. [*Editorial note: This note was originally composed in English (except the text in parentheses). It is reproduced here with slight stylistic changes.]

⁸ᵃ ⁸ᵇ [1969] In reply to this important question, we must say that all of this is in consciousness in a way proper only to it—we can call it *a consciousness-related way*. The thinkers who absolutized consciousness by making it in their conceptions the single subject of all content—here lies the common foundation of idealistic thinking—perhaps did not adequately consider the way in which everything that inheres in consciousness does so. For this way—"consciousness-related," as we said—indicates that consciousness neither fulfills the cognitive function in the proper sense of the word nor possesses its own subjectivity; it is not a *suppositum* or a power from which this function could develop organically.

⁹ᵃ ⁹ᵇ [1969] Therefore, cognitive acts have an intentional character; they are clearly turned toward the cognized object. Properly speaking, the intentionality characteristic of, for example, acts of understanding is foreign to consciousness. For the cognitive role of consciousness (that the role is cognitive is difficult to question) is completely different. It does not consist in penetrating the object, in objectivization for the sake of understanding. Consciousness is understanding—for its intellectual character is beyond doubt—but it is always an understanding of something already understood, of course, in accord with the degree and manner of understanding. Acts of consciousness do not possess an intentional character, although objects of cognition also exist in consciousness through an intellectual image—but the intellectual formation of this image is neither a task nor a work of consciousness. For mirroring alone belongs to consciousness. In this consists the consciousness-related character of cognition, both when particular acts of consciousness and when the totality of such acts—hence either a sum or a resultant—are concerned.

¹⁰ᵃ [1979/1985] Unlike classic phenomenology, we think that

¹¹ᵃ [1979/1985] or the constitution

¹²ᵃ ¹²ᵇ [1979/1985] ontic substratum of lived-experiences

¹³ᵃ ¹³ᵇ [1979/1985] The full substantiation of this thesis does not belong to the scope of our study but to psychology or the appropriate area of anthropology.

¹⁴ᵃ ¹⁴ᵇ [1979/1985: removed]

¹⁵ᵃ ¹⁵ᵇ [1979/1985] referring to man's own "I" as the object of direct cognition

¹⁶ᵃ [1979/1985] nor to anything else

[17a] [1969] The root of consciousness is the cognitive ability and efficiency to which man owes all processes of understanding. Consciousness appears, so to speak, on the margin of these processes, but also more "inside" the personal subject. Therefore, its work is all "interiorization" and "subjectivization," which we shall discuss later.

[18a] [1979/1985] (or of knowledge, in our particular understanding of these terms)

[19a 19b] [1979/1985] the knowledge thus understood

[20a 20b] [1979/1985: removed]

[21a 21b] [1979/1985] being and function

[22a 22b] [1979/1985] a potentiality that rests on the substratum of the objectivizing permeation of one's own "I" in its entire concreteness

[23a 23b] [1969] The Reflexive Feature of Consciousness and Lived-Experience

[24a 24b] [1969] The analysis of self-knowledge allows us to better understand consciousness in its mirroring function, consciousness as reflection. It may indeed seem that this function is actually "lost" in self-knowledge—so much did the previous analysis subordinate the consciousness-related mirroring to self-knowledge.

A question thus arises: according to this understanding, does consciousness have a separate reason for being? This question is linked to another of a methodological nature: how do we arrive at precisely this conception of consciousness and at this conviction concerning the dependence of consciousness on self-knowledge? Precisely because of these questions, the analysis now undertaken seems extremely important. Of course, the entire conception of consciousness with its relation to self-knowledge is not explained separately, is not explained for its own sake. It is explained by the integral conception of man as a person, the conception that we intend to develop in this study. What seems decisive for solving the problem of consciousness and its immanent relation to self-knowledge is the issue of both the objectivity and subjectivity of man. We have touched upon this issue in the previous analysis. The moment of self-knowledge as immanent to consciousness seems to possess key significance for grasping the objectivity of the subject that is one's own "I." In turn, however, we must penetrate this objective subject precisely in the perspective of his subjectivity. Here, consciousness must play a decisive role.

[25a 25b] [1969] However, as we have already mentioned several times, the mirroring function is neither the sole nor the complete function of consciousness. In addition to reflection, lived-experience is also linked to consciousness—both are proper to man, both are extremely important for understanding the person in his relation to the act and the act in its relation to the person. The aspect of consciousness is not exhausted in the role of a mirror placed next to acts in order to reflect them to one's own "I"—a mirror placed from without, as it were. The mirror of consciousness introduces us certainly into the interiority of acts and into the interiority of their dynamic relation to one's own "I," while the role of consciousness itself does not

change so much as finds a complement. *It allows us not only to interiorly see our acts and their connection with our own "I," but also to experience them as acts and as our own acts at that. We owe to consciousness the full subjectivization of what is objective.* In it, person and act in their reciprocal relation (which is a close correlation), as well as all that constitutes the intentional "world of the person," are subjectivized. We are fully justified in analyzing this world in its objective content—at this point, however, we undertake a study of subjectivization.

26a 26b [1969] A feature that we can call reflexive is proper to consciousness. This feature is characteristic of both the particular acts of consciousness and the sum of these acts (or possibly their resultant in man), which compose the actual state of consciousness. The reflexivity of consciousness denotes its natural turning toward an object as such. Reflexivity is something other than the reflectivity proper to the human mind and its acts. For reflectivity presupposes the intentionality of acts of thinking, that is, their turning toward an object. Thinking becomes reflective when we turn to the act previously performed in order to more fully grasp its objective content or possibly also its character or structure. Reflective thinking is an important element in the coming to be of all understanding, all knowledge—including knowledge about oneself, that is, self-knowledge. This thinking directly serves consciousness and its development in man, a fact that is completely clear in light of reflections from the previous point—however, this thinking does not constitute consciousness itself. *What is constitutive of consciousness is its turning toward the subject as such—consciousness is reflexive, not reflective.*

27a 27b [1969] This turning is different from reflection itself. In reflection, the subject still appears as an object. The reflexive turning of consciousness causes this object, which ontologically is a subject, to experience himself as a subject—that is, to experience his own "I." This is something new and different from all previous categories: being a subject differs from being known (objectivized) as a subject, even as this occurs in consciousness-related mirroring, which is still different from the subjective lived-experience of the subject. Man is the subject of his being and acting; he is this subject as a being of a given nature, and this fact has its consequence in action. This subject of being and acting, which is man, is denoted in ontology by the word *suppositum*. The word *suppositum* is used to denote the subject in an utterly objective manner while abstracting from the aspect of lived-experience, in which this subject is given to himself as his own "I." The word *suppositum* in a sense abstracts from the aspect of consciousness, the consciousness thanks to which the object, which is a subject, experiences himself as a subject—and objectivizes this lived-experience with the help of the word "I." In fact, the word "I" contains more than *suppositum*, for it contains the subjective lived-experience of subjectivity and implicates the object that is a subject (that is, subjectivity in the objective and ontological sense—precisely that which *suppositum* denotes). However, if we severed the word "I" from its implication, which is the *suppositum*, then this "I" would merely denote the consciousness-related aspect or, in other words, the psychological aspect of subjectivity.

In the present reflections—in accord with the cognitive presuppositions made in the introductory chapter—*we do not intend to sever the "I" from its ontological impli-*

cations. Every man is given in integral, that is, simple, experience as a *suppositum*—as a being that is the subject of existence and action. At the same time, however, he is given to himself as an "I"—and not only in a consciousness-related way but also in self-knowing objectivization. Self-knowledge reveals this: the suppositum that is me is my own "I," since in it I experience myself as a subject. I not only possess consciousness of my own "I" but also, thanks to consciousness, experience this "I," that is, experience myself as a subject. Consciousness is thus an aspect but not only an aspect—it is also a real factor that constitutes subjectivity in a psychological way, or, rather, in a way related to lived-experience. Thus, in a sense, consciousness constitutes one's own "I." Without consciousness, this "I" would remain merely a *suppositum*.

28a [1969 marginal footnote (marked with a question mark)] (In contemporary ontology of the Ingardenian type, faced with the greatly advanced differentiation of an individual real being's fundamental structure, we perhaps ought to speak of the "constitutive nature" of this individual being rather than of a "*suppositum*.")

29a 29b [1969] It is worthwhile to consider the path that leads from reflection to lived-experience. This is precisely the path of consciousness. Consciousness is linked with a being, that is, with a concrete man "who is myself," who objectively is some "I." Consciousness neither obscures this being nor absorbs it into itself, as would follow from the basic premise of idealistic thinking, according to which *esse* is *percipi* ("to be" is the same as "to be the content of consciousness," while no being outside consciousness is accepted). Quite the contrary; consciousness *inwardly, as it were, reveals* this being, the human being—the person, to speak concretely. Its reflexive function consists in this, provided we understand this function integrally. Thanks to this function, man exists in full conformity with his mental essence and exists "inwardly." This existence is identified with lived-experience. Lived-experience is not a reflex that appears on the surface of man's being and acting. Quite the contrary—it is *the mode of the actualization of being and acting that man owes to consciousness*. It is, in a sense, a final and definitive mode in which the real and objective energies contained in man as a being are actualized not only objectively but also in the profile of his subjectivity, *finding their subjective completion in lived-experience.*

30a [1969 marginal note] (We could venture to say that as did cognition for Bergson, so for us experience appears as this definitive and ultimate form.) [*Editorial note: This note was originally composed in English (except the text in parentheses). It is reproduced here with slight stylistic changes.]

31a 31b [1969] This fact also indirectly confirms and verifies *the spirituality of man.*

32a 32b [1969] In what way does man experience his acts? We know already what his being conscious of them means—that is, we know how we ought to understand the consciousness-related reflection of the act.

33a 33b [1969] Man experiences his act as "action" that is causally linked with his own "I."

34a 34b [1969] Only in connection with action (that is, the act) does man experience his morality, moral values, good and evil ("morality" or "immorality," as is commonly though erroneously said). Again, man not only is conscious of the morality of his acts but also experiences it authentically. *The act and morality, moral values, function not only objectively in the meaning mirrored by consciousness, but also in an utterly subjective manner in the lived-experience that consciousness directly conditions.* Because it constantly turns to the subject as a subject, consciousness evokes the lived-experience of the subjectivity of every act and its moral value. At the same time—thanks to its mirroring function, closely linked with self-knowledge—it allows us to both become objectively conscious of and to experience the act (i.e., the action causally connected with our own "I") and its moral value (which is also the moral value of this "I," that is, of a person, by virtue of the causal connection). As we already stated, lived-experience is not an additional and "superficial" reflex of the act but constitutes a reflexive reduction inward, thanks to which the act becomes a fully subjective reality in man. In a sense, it gains its completion in his subjectivity.

Together with this completion, it acquires an experiential expression through which it becomes an object of understanding—a more and more thorough understanding, as was outlined in the introductory chapter. However, the present chapter treats experience as something broader than self-experience, and understanding as something broader than self-understanding, which remains exclusively within self-knowledge and consciousness in both its functions. Drawing from self-experience and self-understanding, we attempt to cross their boundaries toward an understanding of man, an understanding of act in its relation to the person. Already at the starting point we position ourselves—as is evident—differently; we position ourselves, in a sense, outside of our own "I" since this understanding's object is not one's own "I" but man. However, this "man" is also myself, is my own "I."

35a 35b [1969] Consciousness mirrors man's own "I" and his acts while at the same time allowing him to experience himself and his acts.

36a 36b [1969] We do not take "first" and "later" in a chronological sense, but only in the sense of a natural adequation of the object and subjective acts.

37a 37b [1969] Hand in hand with the emotionalization of reflection goes the emotionalization of lived-experience. As we said, consciousness does not cease to mirror—even in the greatest intensity of emotions and sensations, we still discover a consciousness-related reflection, although this reflection no longer possesses the proper significance for the emotional sphere of interior life. The reflexive function of consciousness, the one that shapes lived-experience, also loses its decisive influence. It is worth noting that with a significant intensification of affections or passions, man, properly speaking, ceases to experience them and instead only lives by them. For emotive facts, though very subjective in themselves—that is, closely connected with the subjective concrete "I"—do not possess the reflexivity, the ability to subjectivize, that is at the disposal of consciousness. In a certain sense, affective lived-experience is posterior to the actualization of emotions and the invasion of sensations in consciousness. Faced with this invasion, the reflexive function of consciousness is also in a sense hindered, and man *lives by his affections objectively rather than experiencing them subjectively.* The truly human lived-experience of affections, indeed, emotional lived-experience itself, again demands the threshold of consciousness that we mentioned earlier. At a certain degree of intensity of sensations, consciousness functions normally with respect to both mirroring and reflexivity. What can then be formed are authentic, affective lived-experiences in all their subjective completion and not merely the objective, emotive facts onto which consciousness cannot confer a subjective completion, even though they undoubtedly reside in the subject. For the emotionalization of consciousness impedes or even prevents the actualization proper to it.

38a 38b [1969] reducing acts exclusively to lived-experience

39a 39b [1969] We ought to emphasize the adverb "exclusively" used in the previous sentence, for it indicates what was described previously as the absolutization of an aspect.

40a 40b [1969] an exclusive subject

41a [1969] their objective equivalents, that is,

42a 42b [1979/1985: removed]

43a 43b [1969] In this sense and with this status, it is only the key to the subjectivity of man—that is, the basis for a full understanding of the subjectivity of man in his relation to his own acts—and not the basis for subjectivism.

Chapter 2: The Analysis of Efficacy in Relation to the Dynamism of Man

1a 1b [1969] The Fundamental Directions of the Dynamism of Man: *Agere–pati.* The Concept of *Actus.*

2a [1979/1985] alone

3a 3b [1979/1985] in another way

4a 4b [1979/1985] It seems that the experience of human action and of what happens in man could greatly help

5a 5b [1979/1985] and even a certain equivalence

6a 6b [1979/1985: removed]

7a 7b [1979/1985] Both have their source in man; however, if we speak of *agere* and *pati* as two different directions of this dynamism, we must also state that the direction "from within" is common to them both, for, after all, this direction belongs to the essence of every dynamism. *Agere* and *pati* diversify this dynamism without depriving it of the unity of proceeding from the same dynamic subject; this, however, in no way changes the fact that the *agere*-act differs from the rest of the dynamic manifestations of the subject "man" that are described by the category *pati*.

8a [1979/1985], in fulfillment

9a 9b [1979/1985] two modes of existence

10a [1979/1985] What is made apparent here, of course, is the need for a factor thanks to which this transition or fulfillment is accomplished. For the time being, however, we set this problem aside.

11a 11b [1969] The Dynamism of Man and Efficacy

12a 12b [1979/1985] We wish to attempt such an explanation, and in this explanation we shall try to follow the starting points that were established precisely in the previous analysis.

13a 13b [1979/1985] a cause

14a 14b [1979/1985] finds himself at the origin of his action

15a 15b [1979/1985] Without investigating this thesis in its entirety, we must nonetheless emphasize the part of it that consists in ascertaining a particular evidentness of man's efficacious causation in action, of the person in the act.

16a 16b [1979/1985: removed]

17a 17b [1979/1985] For we cannot simply and definitively identify the "man-maker" with human action and the "man-material" with what happens in the human subject. Nonetheless, the act is always some mastery of human passivity.

18a 18b [1979/1985: removed]

19a 19b [1979/1985] *an operation leading to*

20a [1979/1985] even if we continue to fundamentally distinguish nature from the person

21a [1979/1985] What is more, they do not allow him to be and to act in any other way.

22a 22b [1979/1985] draws from this humanity its real constitution

23a [1979/1985]—it indicates the forces that constitute the being and action of man at the level of the person

24a 24b [1979/1985: removed]

25a 25b [1979/1985: removed]

26a 26b [1979/1985] interior

27a [1979/1985] and guarding the threshold of consciousness

28a 28b [1979/1985] However, inasmuch as the dynamism of the vegetative layer resides almost completely outside the scope of consciousness, the emotive dynamism—which we shall attempt to examine more closely further on—seems to greatly facilitate the psychical representation and manifestation of contents, including the contents from which consciousness and the will have severed themselves.

29a 29b [1969] rootedness

30a [1979/1985] and ultimately on conscience,

Texts Marked by Critical Apparatus | 601

Chapter 3: The Personal Structure of Self-Determination

1a 1b [1969] Self-Determination: The Will as a Property of the Person

2a 2b [1979/1985] This is precisely the *fieri* of the person that has its own phenomenological specificity and indicates its own ontic distinctness

3a [1979/1985] or obscures

4a [1979/1985] truly human

5a 5b [1979/1985] structure of the person

6a [1979/1985] reveals,

7a 7b [1979/1985] through

8a 8b [1979/1985: removed]

9a 9b [1969] "Objectivization" and Intentionality

10a 10b [1979/1985] in each of these structural intrapersonal relations,

11a [1979/1985] At the same time, objectivity thus understood constitutes an essential correlate of the specific complexity that is revealed in man, in the human person, together with the structures of self-possession and self-governance.

12a [1979/1985] as a specific dimension of human, personal existence, the dimension that is both subjective and objective

13a [1979/1985] "purely"

14a [1979/1985] but concerns in an essential way the problem of the interpretation of the act

15a 15b [1979/1985: removed]

16a 16b [1979/1985] Nonetheless, experience, vision, and the phenomenological analysis connected with it allow us to look in a new way at the entire relation of the person to the act,

17a 17b [1979/1985] In a sense, a new dimension of this synthesis emerges as we deepen our understanding of efficacy: the objectivity proper to efficacy is revealed because self-determination identifiable with the lived-experience "I want" constitutes the dynamic core of this objectivity [or: "of this efficacy"].

18a 18b [1979/1985] In the integral dynamic of the will, as well as in the specific structure of the person, what corresponds to this objectivization originating from self-determination is the subjectivization that—as was shown in the analysis of chapter 2—emerges through consciousness in this structure of the person.

19a 19b [1979/1985] which thus becomes an utterly subjective fact. Hence there proceeds, in a sense, a constant discovery of the subject in his profound objectivity—a discovery, so to speak, of the objective construction of one's own subject. When consciousness introduces all of this into the orbit of lived-experience, the interior objectivity of the act, the objectivization proper to self-determination, is clearly delineated in the profile of the full subjectivity of the person, who experiences himself as the acting "I." The person, this acting "I," then experiences the fact

20a 20b [1969] Self-Determination: The Fundamental Meaning of Freedom

21a 21b [1979/1985] while being a subject, is at the same time the first object that we determine by an act of the will

22a 22b [1979/1985] because we then efficaciously determine ourselves, the subject himself is an object for himself. In this way, the "objectivization" enters into the fundamental meaning of freedom. And

23a 23b [1969] The Second Aspect: The Will as a Power

24a 24b [1994/2000: removed]

25a 25b [1969] The Developed Meaning of Freedom: The Analysis of Decision

26a 26b [1979/1985] emphasize

27a 27b [1979/1985] namely, the transcendence of the person in the act, the transcendence in which the very reality of the person, his structure, is manifested in an experiential way

28a [1979/1985] or Michotte

29a 29b [1979/1985] *absorption or commitment of the will*

30a [1979/1985] Now we ought to examine the structure of human decisions.

31a [1979/1985] What is more, it itself determines and forms this transcendence.

32a [1979/1985] Thus if man chooses the "lesser" good in the given case, this happens because it was presented to him *hic et nunc* as "greater."

33a 33b [1979/1985] the essential activity of the will

34a 34b [1969] The Subordination to Objects—or Truth as the Basis of Transcendence

35a [1979/1985] (the person is inexpressible, i.e., cannot be fully grasped conceptually)

36a 36b [1979/1985] expands this relation to the dimensions of the principle of decision, choice, and act

37a 37b [1969] Cognition as a Condition of the Transcendence of the Person in the Act: The Lived-Experience of Value

38a 38b [1979/1985], first, we should state the fundamental significance of this truth about the good, the truth that the will "demands" from cognition, and, second, we should assume that this demand particularly conditions cognition and exerts a specific influence on it

39a 39b [1969] Cognition as a Condition of the Transcendence of the Person in the Act: The Judgment and the Intuition of Value

40a 40b [1979/1985] Of course, by saying "I cognize" and "I think" we do not intend to simply identify thinking with cognition. We only wish to state for the time being that,

41a 41b [1979/1985: removed]

42a 42b [1979/1985] perception

43a 43b [1979/1985] perception

44a 44b [1979/1985] This property, that is, the relation to truth—the relation that is not only transcendent but also experienced—also manifests the spiritual nature of the personal subject.

45a 45b [1979/1985] namely, the truth about the good, the moment that confers on the act the form of the authentic *actus personae*

46a 46b [1979/1985] the moment of cognitive action

47a 47b [1979/1985] intentionally

48a [1979/1985] in the act

Chapter 4: Self-Determination and Fulfillment

1a [1979/1985] We intend to do so presently, taking the analysis conducted thus far of the personal structure of self-determination as our starting point. Our further reflections will continue the analysis of the same structure under the aspect of fulfillment, for fulfillment in the act corresponds precisely to self-determination, which is deeply rooted—as we attempted to demonstrate—in the dynamic structure of the person.

2a 2b [1979/1985] Right at the beginning of these reflections, we should state that we concern ourselves first and foremost (if not exclusively) with the act as the internal and intransitive effect of the person's efficacy. In this respect, we intend to analyze the entire dynamism of performing the act, starting from the personal structure of self-determination. The previously outlined dynamic of the will explains the fact that acts

3a 3b [1979/1985: removed]

4a [1979/1985] and therefore at the same time thoroughly subjective

5a [1979/1985] this existential

6a 6b [1969] An Introduction to the Interpretation of Conscience

7a 7b [1979/1985] through moral good or the non-fulfillment of oneself through moral evil

8a [1979/1985] The precise point here is the truth about good, the truth experienced in conscience.

9a 9b [1979/1985] in relation to transcendentals such as being, truth, good, and beauty. Man has access to them through cognition, and in the wake of cognition, in the wake of the mind, through the will and the act.

[10a 10b] [1979/1985: removed]

[11a] [1979/1985] when we appeal to experience, especially to the experience of morality

[12a 12b] [1979/1985: removed]

[13a 13b] [1979/1985] forming the duty corresponding to that good

[14a] [1979/1985] cognition and

[15a 15b] [1979/1985] This fulfillment or non-fulfillment depends directly on conscience, on its judgment. As we can see, the function of conscience is determined by the ontology of the person and act, and in particular by the dependence of freedom on truth, proper only to the person—the very center of the person's transcendence in the act and man's spirituality.

[16a 16b] [1969] Truthfulness and Conscience

[17a] [1979/1985], his will,

[18a 18b] [1979/1985] how deeply the relation to truth is rooted in the very potentiality of man's personal being. We speak of this relation in particular when we ascribe "rational nature" to man or when we appeal to his mind as the power to cognize truth and to distinguish truth from falsehood. The mind is commonly understood as an organ of thinking, although the very function of thinking, and at the same time of understanding, is linked rather to reason.

[19a 19b] [1979/1985] is expressed in the ability to think and to understand

[20a 20b] [1979/1985] The mind as a property of man and his power allows him to remain in potentially comprehensive contact with reality—*Intellectus est quodammodo omnia*, as Thomas Aquinas used to say. Every being can become the content of the mind. It is truthfulness that is essential to this cognitive relation of the mind to being.

[21a 21b] [1979/1985] This superiority belongs to the totality of the experience of the transcendence of the person and, in particular, of the transcendence we consider here, namely, that of the person in the act. *This is the superiority—the transcendence through truthfulness and not through consciousness alone.* We appeal here to the previously conducted analyses (in chapter 2) that indicate this fact. Although human consciousness undoubtedly has a mental character, its proper function does not consist in the very inquiry after truth and in the active differentiation of truth from non-truth, the fact accomplished in judgments. Consciousness in its mirroring function draws its semantic content from the active processes of the mind directed toward truth. Thanks to this, truthfulness also belongs to it, and through its reflexive function consciousness conditions the lived-experience of truthfulness. However, as we stated in the analyses of chapter 2, the proper function of consciousness is not knowledge, the active understanding and investigation of truth. This fact must bear

on grasping the transcendence of the person in the act, especially when the function of conscience is concerned, for it is on conscience that we base this transcendence.

²²ᵃ ²²ᵇ [1979/1985] seems to be

²³ᵃ ²³ᵇ [1979/1985] By truthfulness we understand here precisely this effort and the mental activity of man at its essential point. Grasping truth is linked with a specific striving. Truth is the end of this striving.

²⁴ᵃ ²⁴ᵇ [1979/1985] a specific superiority through truth; it is the "superiority of truth" connected with a certain distance from objects, as it were, and inscribed in the spiritual nature of the person

²⁵ᵃ ²⁵ᵇ [1979/1985] Both the lived-experience of truthfulness and the lived-experience of duty belong to conscience. It is duty that we shall now analyze.

²⁶ᵃ ²⁶ᵇ [1979/1985], although in light of our previous and present analyses it seems clear that consciousness ensures the subjective lived-experience of truthfulness in judgments of conscience. It likewise ensures in such judgments the lived-experience of certainty. In a different case, the work of consciousness will be the lived-experience of the uncertainty of conscience or—as the worst possibility—the lived-experience of bad faith, that is, of the "falsehood of conscience."

²⁷ᵃ [1979/1985] will and

²⁸ᵃ [1979/1985] of thinking and

²⁹ᵃ ²⁹ᵇ [1969] Duty: Vocation

³⁰ᵃ [1979/1985] (in a sense all ready and present)

³¹ᵃ [1979/1985] which obligates the person

³²ᵃ [1979/1985] the very evoking of

³³ᵃ [1979/1985], thus, of duty

³⁴ᵃ ³⁴ᵇ [1979/1985] in a sense with the absolute freedom

³⁵ᵃ [1979/1985], which is also expressed in rejecting the ethical "law of nature"

³⁶ᵃ ³⁶ᵇ [1979/1985] the basis of this transcendence, especially of transcendence in action. As we have noted, however, it seems that the metaphysical reduction proper to this definition emphasizes the intellectual nature (the rational nature) *more than it does the person* in cognitive transcendence through the relation to truth. In this study, we attempt to reveal this particular transcendence as constituting the person.

³⁷ᵃ ³⁷ᵇ [1979/1985] However, this content and the power of attraction stop, in a sense, at the threshold of the person, which is the threshold of conscience, that is, the threshold of the truthfulness of the good—the truthfulness from which duty begins.

³⁸ᵃ ³⁸ᵇ [1979/1985] with the system of norms understood above all as prohibitions; and the positive way, which is identified with the attraction and acceptance of values

39a [1979/1985], namely, the boundaries of the reality within which man is to fulfill himself

40a 40b [1969] Efficacy and Responsibility

41a 41b [1979/1985] in which duty as the normative power of truth is rooted

42a 42b [1979/1985] One has a duty to relate to the object according to its true value. A responsibility for the object with respect to its value, that is, to put it briefly, *a responsibility for value*, is born together with this duty. This responsibility is, in a sense, already contained in the coming to be of duty itself and at the same time results from this coming to be. Duty conditions responsibility, and at the same time, responsibility is already somehow present in the constitution of duty.

43a 43b [1979/1985: removed]

44a 44b [1979/1985] transfer onto

45a 45b [1979/1985: removed]

46a 46b [1979/1985] (in the sense of being a person). The structure of responsibility is most closely connected with the action of man, with the act of the person. However, it is not linked with what only happens in man, unless what happens is itself dependent on non-action as its effect. The structure of responsibility is first of all proper to the person from within, whereas on the basis of participation—of coexistence and cooperation with others—it becomes responsibility "to somebody." The proper personal meaning of responsibility to God would require a separate and thorough theological analysis, which we have not undertaken in this text.

47a 47b [1969] Fulfillment and Felicity: Remarks on the Relation of Felicity to Pleasure

48a 48b [1979/1985] sensual

49a 49b [1979/1985], with the transcendence of the person in the act. The case is similar when the opposite of felicity is concerned

50a 50b [1979/1985: removed]

51a 51b [1979/1985] Pleasure, as well as pain, "happens" in man. This perhaps belongs to its essence, and this too seems to differentiate pleasure from felicity, which corresponds to the content of personal fulfillment. Insofar as felicity indicates the personal structure, we can link pleasure with the natural structure, appealing to certain elements of the comparison between person and nature, which we conducted earlier.

52a 52b [1979/1985] manifests spirituality

Chapter 5: Integration and Somaticity

1a [1979/1985] conscious

2a [1979/1985] conscious

Texts Marked by Critical Apparatus | 607

³ᵃ [1979/1985] conscious

⁴ᵃ ⁴ᵇ [1979/1985] above all in a dynamic understanding

⁵ᵃ [1979/1985]—we touch the defects inhering in it itself

⁶ᵃ ⁶ᵇ [1979/1985] the indispensability of the anterior grasp of transcendence and integration for understanding the psycho-physical unity of man

⁷ᵃ ⁷ᵇ [1979/1985] manifested

⁸ᵃ ⁸ᵇ [1979/1985: removed]

⁹ᵃ [1979/1985], and for freedom in the dynamic relation to truth

¹⁰ᵃ [1979/1985] And although in our study we do not intend to undertake the problem of the soul and its relation to the body as our own philosophical topic, we nevertheless wish to express this problem as correctly as possible within the analysis of person and act.

¹¹ᵃ [1979/1985] (for example, an entire series of movements inheres in the act of going to school; these movements are connected with walking or marching)

Chapter 6: Integration and the Psyche

¹ᵃ ¹ᵇ [1979/1985] manifest

²ᵃ ²ᵇ [1979/1985] coherence

³ᵃ [1979/1985] internally

⁴ᵃ [1979/1985] not only spirituality, which we have already considered (see sections 7 and 8 of chapter 4), but also

⁵ᵃ [1979/1985] and the behaviors and relations connected with them

⁶ᵃ ⁶ᵇ [1994/2000] (*emotio: e/ex* = from, *movere* = to move) which originates from "within," and this is attested by the prefix *e/ex*

⁷ᵃ [1979/1985] and its somatic dynamism. Thus, without anticipating all that will subsequently be said on the topic of human emotivity, it is fitting to note already the essential irreducibility of emotion to reaction, of emotivity to reactivity. Emotion is not a somatic reaction but a psychical fact essentially distinct and qualitatively different from the reaction of the body

⁸ᵃ ⁸ᵇ [1979/1985] is contained in the human act through the ever-specific integration of the personal subject's somaticity

⁹ᵃ ⁹ᵇ [1979/1985] *is contained in a particular way in the human act through the integration of the entire psycho-emotivity of man*

¹⁰ᵃ [1979/1985] There exists a need for a multilateral analysis of human emotivity in order to manifest the separate profile of psychical integration.

¹¹ᵃ ¹¹ᵇ [1979/1985] of the human soul is revealed

12a [1979/1985] As we can see from this, we do not intend here to identify emotivity with sensuality.

13a [1979/1985] Man draws the vividness of his actions from emotion as well.

14a 14b [1979/1985] The Sensorial and Motor Reactions

15a 15b [1979/1985] The sensorial reaction fundamentally differs from the motor reaction

16a 16b [1979/1985: removed]

17a 17b [1979/1985] sensations

18a 18b [1979/1985] connected with the body

19a [1979/1985], and this is conditioned by sensation and consciousness

20a 20b [1979/1985] by the human mind in its proper way

21a 21b [1979/1985: removed]

22a 22b [1979/1985] true value

23a 23b [1979/1985] contact objects directly and at the same time provide the mind with material, as it were

24a 24b [1979/1985] the objects of this world by means of mental generalization

25a 25b [1979/1985] originally and fundamentally

26a [1979/1985] but are most often linked with it

27a [1979/1985], two different subjective facts

28a 28b [1979/1985] seems to be different from the one that accompanies excitement

29a 29b [1969] Integration: Emotivity and Efficacy

30a 30b [1979/1985] a particular task to be fulfilled opens before man due to the fact that self-possession and self-governance are proper to him as a person.

31a [1994/2000] of integration

32a [1979/1985] Thus we wish to state that this tension between the emotivity of the human subject and his personal efficacy in acts is specifically creative.

33a 33b [1969] Integration on the Basis of the Relation to Value

34a 34b [1979/1985] Then man lives only by his emotion, excitement, or passion—he undoubtedly lives subjectively, though this "subjectivity" brings negative effects concerning efficacy, self-determination, and the transcendence of the person in the act.

35a 35b [1979/1985] the particular "value" of his lived-experiences that is their subjective vividness. This does not remain without significance, even when the cognitive aspect of these lived-experiences is concerned.

36a 36b [1979/1985] relation to truth, a dynamic relation to truth in the will itself

37a [1979/1985] spontaneously experienced

38a 38b [1979/1985] the intellectual relation to truth

39a 39b [1979/1985] the mind

40a [1979/1985]—the truth about good and evil in this case

41a [1979/1985] on the basis of the psychical subjectivity shaped in a self-projected way by rich and diversified emotive facts with their proper spontaneous attraction or repulsion

42a [1979/1985] transcendent

43a [1979/1985] For instance, the man-child learns necessary movements and appropriate skills sooner than appropriate virtues.

44a 44b [1979/1985] grasp (and not merely its description)

45a 45b [1979/1985] What is eloquent is their complementarity. Much is revealed by the fact that man as a person is at once the one who possesses and governs himself as well as the one who is possessed by and subordinated to himself.

46a [1979/1985] without, however, achieving that grasp

47a 47b [1979/1985: removed]

48a 48b [1979/1985] *seems*

49a 49b [1979/1985] who know nothing of metaphysics and of the metaphysical meaning of form, matter, and their reciprocal relation

50a [1979/1985] Thus the categories of phenomenological vision, which allow us to show the complexity of man on the basis of experience and vision, and the ability to grasp the limits of this vision are both important here.

51a [1979/1985] where we emphasized the connection between the transcendence and the spirituality of man

52a 52b [1979/1985] and even—indirectly—the emotive dynamism proper to the human psyche have their proper source in the body, then the integration of these dynamisms in the act of the person requires us to seek a source they would share in common with transcendence, in relation to which, as was said in the beginning, integration plays a supplementary role. Is this ultimate source—or, speaking in other words, the principle of both the transcendence and the integration of the person in the act—in fact the soul? It seems that in our approach we have drawn much closer to it.

Chapter 7: (*Supplementum*): An Outline of the Theory of Participation

1a 1b [1979/1985] the will as a power seems, in a sense, to limit the meaning of the act when both its ontology and axiology (including "ethical axiology") are concerned

2a 2b [1979/1985] authenticity of the personalistic value. This value itself is not yet an ethical value, but it proceeds from the dynamic depth of the person, reveals and confirms this depth;* this, in turn, allows us to better understand ethical values in their close correspondence to the person and to the entire "world of persons." [*Editorial note: This clause can also be read as saying that the personalistic value reveals and confirms the person.]

3a 3b [1979/1985: removed]

4a 4b [1969] Individualism and Anti-Individualism

[1979/1985] Individualism and Totalism as a Contradiction of Participation

5a 5b [1979/1985] the common good understood in a particular way

6a 6b [1969] Participation and Community Membership

7a 7b [1979/1985] to take up participation

8a [1979/1985] personal and

9a 9b [1994/2000] subordinating

Afterword

1a 1b [1969: added]

III: Post-1969 Related Essays

3. The Afterword to the Discussion on *Person and Act*

1a 1b [the published text] expressing what the person himself is

5. The Person: Subject and Community

1a [The English edition sent by Wojtyła to the Catholic University of America in 1977 places footnote 1 here, written in English as follows:] This work continues the investigations initiated in my study *Person and Act* (Kraków: Polskie Towarzystwo Teologiczne, 1969). It examines anew the connection between the subjectivity of man as a person and the structure of human community. This problem was sketched in the last chapter of *Person and Act*, entitled "Participation" [sic]. Here, I intend to develop this, beginning with the conception of the person that was extensively treated in the aforementioned work. The many analyses carried out there are closely connected with the problem of human subjectivity; even all of them may be said to lead in some way to its understanding and articulation. Discussions of *Person and Act* have been printed in *Analecta Cracoviensia*, 5–6 (1973–74): 49–272.

2a [The English edition sent by Wojtyła to the Catholic University of America places footnote 17 here, containing the second part of the sentence, originally located in the main text.] The whole analysis refers to what has been said in the final chapters of *Person and Act* about the meaning of "neighbor."

6. Participation or Alienation

[1a] [original typescript of the 1976 Harvard version] (Second edition of the lecture at Harvard University on July 27[, 1976])

[2a 2b] [1978 *Summarium* edition (1975 Fribourg version)]

1. An Introductory Remark

I wish to add my reflections to those of everyone speaking at this colloquium on the topic of *Soi et autrui* (I and the other). I wish to do so by referring to my own considerations devoted to the philosophy of man. Their main expression is the study *Person and Act*,* as of yet not translated from the Polish language. Because I cannot refer my lecture to a text that would be known to you in its entirety, distinguished participants of the colloquium, I permitted myself to have the last two sections of the book, which I enclose in the appendix, translated.† They pertain—in a broad sense—to the meaning of the commandment to love one's neighbor, which we know from the Gospel, in light of the personalistic interpretation of human action, that is, the act. The first of the enclosed sections analyzes what we denote by the concept "neighbor" in contradistinction to the concept "member of the community" (here we mean any community, any social group or society). The second section grasps the commandment to love in relation to the concept of alienation as it entered the context of contemporary anthropology, especially as a consequence of Marxism. It seems to me that the second section is only supplementary (from the viewpoint of this colloquium and even from the viewpoint of my study); the reflections concerning the "neighbor" seem to be fundamental. What I intend to say now is, in a sense, a commentary on the translated fragment of the study *Person and Act* that is enclosed in the appendix.

* Karol Wojtyła, *Osoba i czyn* (Kraków: Polskie Towarzystwo Teologiczne, 1969).

† Wojtyła, *Osoba i czyn*, 319–26. "'Człowiek wspólnoty' a 'bliźni'" [The "member of the community" and the "neighbor"] and "Znaczenie przykazania miłości" [The meaning of the commandment to love].

[2000 KUL edition]

Introduction

In this lecture, I wish to elucidate a problem that seems to lie at the center of contemporary thought about man. It lies at the center of this thought because it is also located at the center of the life and interaction of people. The very concepts of "participation" and "alienation" carry various connotations. They have a long philosophical genealogy. They are linked with the fields of sociology, economics, and politics, and they progress through the sphere of ethics and theology. It is difficult to disregard all these fields, for each of them also corresponds to distinct dimensions of human existence. If each of these dimensions can be considered in terms of participation or alienation, it is precisely on account of man—moreover, on account of the fact that man is a person. Hence, I intend to speak here about participation and alienation from the viewpoint of personalism, the philosophy of the person. From this viewpoint, an antinomy appears between participation and alienation—it appears most essentially and simultaneously, in a sense, from its very foundations.

³ª ³ᵇ [1978 Summarium edition (1975 Fribourg version): absent]

⁴ª ⁴ᵇ [2000 KUL edition] For this purpose, I wish to analyze two types of relation, in which the two meanings of participation and alienation will simultaneously come to light. The first is the "I-the other" relation, in which the inter-human bond is expressed, and the second is the relation of the "we" type, in which the social community is expressed in various ways.

⁵ª ⁵ᵇ [2000 KUL edition] I should underscore, however, that it also has a rich literature in my homeland, in the Polish language, for our thinkers are keenly concerned with it

⁶ª ⁶ᵇ [1978 Summarium edition (1975 Fribourg version): absent]

[2000 KUL edition] 1. The Analysis of the "I–the other" Relation

⁷ª ⁷ᵇ [1978 Summarium edition (1975 Fribourg version)]]
2. The Necessity of Establishing a Starting Point

It seems that in the very posing of the problem "I-the other, *soi-autrui*, we proceed simultaneously from two cognitive situations. One of them is the ascertainment of the fact of the existence and action of the concrete man, denoted by the pronoun "I," together with other people: "the other" is one of these, a man who exists next to me, who at the same time is "the other" and "one of the others" who exist and act together with me. Let us immediately add for the sake of precision that the circle of "others" is as wide as the totality of people; anyone from that totality can be "the other," and in reality he is always somebody remaining in the factual, that is, somehow experienced, relation to me. Here we already approach the second cognitive situation that we must in turn define more closely. Its basis is not so much consciousness as self-consciousness conditioning the entire structure of the lived-experience of "oneself," that is, of a concrete "I."* For its part, this consciousness constitutes the entire world that is at the same time given to us as a fact—in this world, consciousness constitutes all and each of the people, both the closer and the more distant ones. It constitutes them as "other" than me. It constitutes among them "the other" (*autrui*), who is at the same time "other" and "one of the others," thereby defining his relation to me, that is, to my "I."

* As is evident, I intend to continue to understand *soi* as "I," which expresses an attempt to find the unity of both cognitive situations discussed here.

[Editorial note: There is no text emphasis in the entire 1978 version of this article.]

[2000 KUL edition] The necessity of establishing a starting point

It seems that in the very posing of the problem "I–the other" (*soi-autrui*), we proceed simultaneously from two cognitive situations. *One is the ascertainment of the fact of the existence and action* of the concrete man denoted by the pronoun "I," who exists and acts among others and *together with other people*: "the other" is one of these, a man who exists next to me, who at the same time is "the other" and "one of the others." Let us immediately add for the sake of precision that the circle of "others" is as wide as the totality of people; anyone from that totality can be "the other," and in reality he is always somebody remaining in the factual, that is, somehow experienced, relation to me. Here we already approach the *second cognitive situation* that we must in turn define more closely. Its basis is not so much consciousness as *self-consciousness conditioning the entire structure of the lived-experience of "oneself,"* that is, of *a concrete "I."* For its part, this consciousness constitutes the entire world that is at the same time given to us as a fact—in this world, consciousness constitutes all and each of the people, both the closer and the more distant ones. It constitutes them as "other" than me. It constitutes among them "the other" (*autrui*), who at the same time is "other" and "one of the others," thereby defining his relation to me, that is, to my "I."

8a 8b [1978 Summarium edition (1975 Fribourg version)] We must necessarily consider both of these cognitive situations at the starting point of our reflections, because the problem of *soi-autrui* is not limited to ascertaining being itself, that is, existence, but requires us to analyze lived-experience—the lived-experience in relation to two subjects who really exist and really act. I wish to highlight the problem of "I-the other, *soi-autrui*" from the perspective of actions, that is, acts.

3. "I-*soi*": Self-Determination and Self-Possession

The act most fully and most penetratingly reveals man as an "I," indeed, as a person. For what in the categories of being is expressed by the concept "person" is in experience and lived-experience given precisely as "*soi*-I." Consciousness alone does not yet constitute this "I," though it conditions its full appearance through the act. One's own "I" fully appears through the act to the consciousness of this "I." Accounting for this would require a separate analysis of consciousness itself in connection with the act, an analysis I attempted to conduct in the aforementioned study, *Person and Act*. Here, however, I wish to pass over these reflections in order to emphasize above all the moment of the act, that is, conscious action, for the constitution of the human "I-*soi*." This constitution is also in consciousness, though not through consciousness alone. Consciousness, however, although conditioning the act (as conscious action), does not itself create or shape it. The act is created and shaped from other foundations, from other sources of man's potentiality. The essential potentiality that constitutes the act in itself, that confers on the act its whole proper realness, is the will. Although we ascertain this, we do not intend to concern ourselves with the act as an act of the will, because this has been done many times already.

It is fitting to essentially grasp that by which the act reveals, in a sense, the totality, originality, and unrepeatability of every man and thereby reveals the "I-*soi*" of the agent in a way different from self-consciousness—we can say, in a more profound and definitive way. What is essential for every act performed consciously by the concrete man is the moment of self-determination. It seems that in this moment the will is most essentially manifested as a property of the person and as his potentiality—not the will considered as a power in itself, but as a property of the person and his essential potentiality. For through the will, man himself can determine himself and does determine himself every time he accomplishes an act. Man is the agent of the act, and his efficacy in this act, that is, the will ("I will"), turns out to be self-determination.

[2000 KUL edition] By understanding *soi* as "I," we accept the unity of both cognitive situations being discussed. *Soi* not only denotes the content of consciousness but also *the real subject* who, through consciousness, experiences himself (i.e., precisely his "I") and experiences "the other" (*autrui*) outside himself. At the same time, we notice at the starting point that the problem of *soi-autrui* is not limited to ascertaining two subjects who really exist and act. It also requires us *to analyze the lived-experience that confers* on this existence and action *the sense of existing and acting precisely as* soi *and* autrui. The key to understanding this sense is action, that is, the act.

"I"-*soi*

The act most fully and most penetratingly reveals man as an "I," indeed, as a person.* For what in the categories of being is expressed by the concept "person" is in experience and lived-experience given precisely as "*soi*-I." *Consciousness* alone does not yet constitute this "I," though it *conditions its full appearance through the act.* One's own "I" fully appears through the act to the consciousness of this "I." Consciousness, however, although conditioning the act (as conscious action), does not itself create or shape it. The act is created and shaped from other foundations, from other sources of man's potentiality. The essential *potentiality that constitutes the act in itself, that confers on the act its whole proper realness, is the will.*

It is fitting to essentially grasp that by which the act reveals, in a sense, the totality, originality, and unrepeatability of every man and thereby reveals the "I"-*soi* of the agent in a way different from self-consciousness—we can say, in a more profound and definitive way. What is essential for every act performed consciously by the concrete man is the moment of self-determination. It seems that in this moment the will is most essentially manifested as a property of the person and as his potentiality—the will considered not only as a faculty of the subject "man," but as a property of the person, which determines in an essential way the potentiality of that person. For through the will, man himself can determine himself and does determine himself every time he accomplishes an act. Man is the agent of the act, and his efficacy in this act, that is, the will ("I will"), turns out to be self-determination.

* My study entitled *Person and Act* [Osoba i czyn] (Kraków: Polskie Towarzystwo Teologiczne, 1969) is built precisely on this conviction.

9a 9b [the 1978 *Summarium* edition (1975 Fribourg version): absent]

10a [the 1978 *Summarium* edition (1975 Fribourg version) places the following footnote here] See Karol Wojtyła, "The Personal Structure of Self-Determination" [Osobowa struktura samostanowienia], in *Tommaso d'Aquino nel suo VII centenario: Congresso internazionale, Roma-Napoli, 17–24 aprile 1974* (Rome: 1974), 379–90.

11a 11b [1978 Summarium edition (1975 Fribourg version)] 4. "The Other-*Autrui*" [2000 KUL edition] "The other"-*autrui*

12a 12b [1978 Summarium edition (1975 Fribourg version)] The consciousness that "the other" is "an other I" stands at the basis of what I called "participation" in *Person and Act* and of what I wish to clarify here. For the concept of participation in my study helps above all to emphasize the property of man as a person that allows him to remain himself and to continue to fulfill himself in action, in his acts, while also being and acting together with others. This conception of participation does not have much to do with the Platonic or the Scholastic one, but, as we see, it serves to define and emphasize that which in existence and action together with others in various systems of social life in a sense safeguards the person and the personalistic property and value of his action. This is what I called "participation" in *Person and Act*. Namely, it is an ability to be and to act with others so as to remain oneself and to realize oneself (*soi*-I).

At the end of this analysis, precisely in the sections that I referred to in the beginning, a still deeper property of participation, its more fundamental meaning, is revealed. Behold, man has the ability to participate in the very humanity of other people, and thanks to this, everyone can be a "neighbor" to him. Precisely here we encounter this reflection on the topic of "the other-*autrui*." For "the other" not only denotes the sameness of the being that exists next to me and even acts together with me in some system of actions. On the basis of this real situation, "the other" also denotes a no less real, though above all subjective, participation in humanity, proceeding from the consciousness that the other man is "an other 'I,'" that is, "also an I."

13a 13b [1978 Summarium edition (1975 Fribourg version)]
5. The "I–the Other, *Soi-Autrui*" Relationship: Its Potentiality and Actualization

Thus the "I–the other, *soi-autrui*" relationship is outlined in its proper structure. As we see, this structure is not only ontic but also concerns consciousness and lived-experience. This structure is what we understand here as participation.

[2000 KUL edition]
The first meaning of participation: What does it mean to participate in humanity?

Thus the "I"-"the other" (*soi-autrui*) relationship is outlined in its proper structure. As we see, this structure is not only ontic, but also concerns consciousness and lived-experience. This structure is what we understand here as participation.

14a 14b [1978 Summarium edition (1975 Fribourg version)] universal

15a 15b [1978 Summarium edition (1975 Fribourg version)] universal

16a 16b [1978 Summarium edition (1975 Fribourg version)] interpersonal

17a [1978 Summarium edition (1975 Fribourg version)] The problem of the potentiality of the relationship "I–the other, *soi-autrui*" and the need for actualizing participation, through which this relationship is properly formed, are clearly delineated along with the universality of the concept "man."

[18a] [1978 Summarium edition (1975 Fribourg version)] Certainly, it is not yet ready-made in conceptualization itself or in awareness of the fact of humanity.

[19a] [1978 Summarium edition (1975 Fribourg version)] It is linked more with the will than with cognition.

[20a] [20b] [1978 Summarium edition (1975 Fribourg version)] It is difficult to deny the significance of human spontaneity and affections in the shaping of the relations of man to man.

[21a] [The 1978 Summarium edition (1975 Fribourg version) places the following footnote here:] See especially *Der Formalismus in der Ethik und die materiale Wertethik*, Halle, 1921, *Wesen und Formen der Sympathie*, 4th edition, Bonn, 1929, and others.

[The 2000 KUL edition places the following footnote here:] See especially Max Scheler, *Der Formalismus in der Ethik und die materiale Wertethik: Neuer Versuch der Grundlegung eines ethischen Personalismus*, um ein Vorwort vermehrt (Halle: Niemeyer, 1916); in addition, and among others, Max Scheler, *Wesen und Formen der Sympathie: Der "Phänomenologie der Sympathiegefühle,"* vol. 1 of *Die Sinngesetze des emotionalen Lebens*, 2nd ed. (Bonn: F. Cohen, 1923).

[22a] [the 1978 Summarium edition (1975 Fribourg version) places the following footnote here] See especially Jean-Paul Sartre, *L'être et le néant* (Paris: Gallimard, 1973).

[the 2000 KUL edition places the following footnote here] See principally Jean-Paul Sartre, *L'être et le néant* (Paris: Gallimard, 1957), especially p. 310.

[23a] [23b] [1978 Summarium edition (1975 Fribourg version)] It seems that the choice spoken of here lies on the plane of that spontaneity. This constitution, in a sense, of the "other 'I'" in my consciousness and will is not a result of a choice among people, among others; as was said, we are concerned with the man who is *hic et nunc* given and entrusted as a task to me—and therefore this "choice" is not experienced as a choice. It is rather a simple identification of one of the others as "the other 'I,'" an identification that does not require a longer process of the will, an acknowledgment or struggle of motives, etc.

[24a] [the 1978 Summarium edition (1975 Fribourg version) places the following footnote here] See Immanuel Kant, *Krytyka praktycznego rozumu* [*Kritik der praktischen Vernunft*], trans. and ed. Jerzy Gałecki (Warsaw: Państwowe Wydawnictwo Naukowe, 1972), pt. 1, bk. 1, ch. 3; Immanuel Kant, *Uzasadnienie metafizyki moralności* [*Grundlegung zur Metaphysik der Sitten*], trans. Mścisław Wartenberg, ed. Roman Ingarden, 2nd ed. (Warsaw: Państwowe Wydawnictwo Naukowe, 1953).

[the 2000 KUL edition places the following footnote here] See Immanuel Kant, *Uzasadnienie metafizyki moralności* [*Grundlegung zur Metaphysik der Sitten*], trans. Mścisław Wartenberg, ed. Roman Ingarden, 2nd ed. (Warsaw: Państwowe Wydawnictwo Naukowe, 1953).

25a 25b [1978 Summarium edition (1975 Fribourg version)]

7. The Verification of Participation

The statement that the "I-the other" relationship is not something ready-made and completely spontaneous but a particular task undoubtedly helps us to interpret manifold realities such as "friendship" and *communio personarum*. We ought to clearly distinguish *communio*—which is above all the "I-the other, *moi-autrui*" relationship, one that matures interiorly into the "I-thou" interpersonal relationship—from "community"-*communitas*, which encompasses a greater number of persons. Friendship has already been analyzed many times. We can state with full certainty that the relationship "I—the other man as another I" stands at the basis of friendship. Friendship is simply an evolution of this relationship and a revelation of its richness in proportion to the love that both people are able to bring into it. To a considerable extent, Aristotle has already explained this matter.*

* See *Nicomachean Ethics*, translated into Polish by Daniela Gromska (Warsaw: Państwowe Wydawnictwo Naukowe, 1956), especially bk. 7.

26a [1978 Summarium edition (1975 Fribourg version)] indirectly

27a 27b [1978 Summarium edition (1975 Fribourg version)] The Gospel also indicates this by using the expression "neighbor" (*prochain*) instead of the expression "the other" (*autrui*).

8. Alienation

It seems that the concept of alienation, introduced into the philosophy of the nineteenth century and discussed by Marx, enjoys great popularity today. This concept is not too precise and is not even unequivocal—therefore, it seems to cause serious problems for contemporary Marxists. Here we do not intend to recount these problems or to disambiguate this concept. Regardless of its weak points, the concept of alienation seems to be needed precisely in the philosophy of man. It is justified by the state of human existence, the contingency and limitedness of every realization of a concrete "I," that is, a person. The concept of alienation, correctly used, can help us in analyzing human reality—and, above all, not on the plane of external conditionings from the extra-human world but within strictly human and inter-human relations—and thus in analyzing the *soi-autrui*, the "I–the other" relationship. According to Marxist philosophy, man is alienated by his products: economic and political systems, property, and work. Marx also included religion in this category. The problem thus posited leads, of course, to a conclusion that it is sufficient to transform the world of these products, to change economic and political systems, to take up a fight with religion. Thus, the age of alienation will cease, and the "kingdom of freedom," that is, of the full auto-realization of each and all, will come. Independently from what the experience of our epoch will demonstrate—or, rather, what it already demonstrates—we should state that such a conception of alienation, properly speaking, shifts the problem outside of man toward, so to speak, the structures of his social existence, and thus it overlooks the essential issue. For the relation to man himself is essential—even, in a sense, regardless of these structures. We know that in concentration camps there were people who were able to attain a relation to another man as to "another I," as to a neighbor—and at times did so to a heroic degree.

This does not mean that the transformation of the structures of people's social existence in the conditions of contemporary civilization is unnecessary. What it means is that the issue of every man's participation in the humanity of another man, of other people, will always remain a fundamental issue. It is here that we should seek the roots and the first seeds of alienation. For alienation denotes above all the denial of participation, its inhibition or prevention, the destruction of the "I-the other" relationship, an attenuation of the ability to experience the other man as "the other I," and an attenuation of the possibility of friendship and spontaneous forces of the community understood as a *communio personarum*. The transfer of the problem of alienation into the sphere of human products and structures can itself contribute to producing alienation, as some contemporary Marxists have already pointed out.*
The structures of man's social existence in the conditions of contemporary civilization, and even this civilization itself and its so-called progress, should be definitively assessed in light of the following fundamental criterion: does this civilization create the conditions—because this is its only proper function—for the development of participation; does it facilitate the lived-experience of man, of other people, as "the other I"? Or, quite the contrary, does it hinder this, does it impede and destroy this fundamental issue of human existence and action that, after all, must always be realized together with others? Thus, the central problem of the life of humanity in our epoch—and perhaps in every epoch—is this problem: participation or alienation? Currently, it seems to appear in sharper contour and is also made more conscious.

* See Adam Schaff, *Marksizm a jednostka ludzka: Przyczynek do marksistowskiej filozofii człowieka* (Warsaw: Państwowe Wydawnictwo Naukowe, 1965).

28a 28b [1978 Summarium edition (1975 Fribourg version): absent]

29a 29b [2000 KUL edition] 2. The Analysis of the "We" Relation

30a 30b [2000 KUL edition: absent]

31a 31b [2000 KUL edition: absent]

32a 32b [2000 KUL edition] Second meaning of participation

33a 33b [2000 KUL edition] Both individualism and totalism are sources of alienation.

34a 34b [2000 KUL edition] It seems that the concept of alienation, introduced into the philosophy of the nineteenth century and discussed by Marx, enjoys great popularity today. The content of this concept, however, is not clear or comprehensively verified. According to Marxist philosophy, man is alienated by his products: economic and political systems, property, and work. Marx also included religion here. Hence, a conclusion is drawn that it is sufficient to transform the world on the plane of these products, to change economic and political systems, to take up a fight with religion. Thus, the age of alienation will cease, and the "kingdom of freedom," that is, of the full autorealization of each and all, will come. However, some contemporary Marxists rightly note that in this way various forms of alienation are not overcome; indeed, new ones come into being, ones that in turn must be overcome.* For this reason, the following question arises: *on what basis was that which Marxism considered to be alienation acknowledged as such*? In order to answer the question of what truly alienates man, we must first answer the question of who man himself truly is. Moreover, we must decisively want to "safeguard the transcendent character of the human person."†

This is, at the same time, the key to overcoming alienation and to building various domains of human existence in the dimension of participation. I am convinced that this key remains the commandment to love contained in the Gospel.

* See, for instance, Adam Schaff, *Marksizm a jednostka ludzka: Przyczynek do marksistowskiej filozofii człowieka* (Warsaw: Państwowe Wydawnictwo Naukowe, 1965), 176–95.

† Second Vatican Council, Pastoral Constitution on the Church in the Modern World, *Gaudium et spes*, no. 76.

8. Subjectivity and "the Irreducible" in Man

[1a] [1b] [the original manuscript and typescript] *La Subjectivité et l'irréductible dans l'homme*

[2a] [the published Polish and English editions place the first footnote here (footnote 4 of this article)]

[3a] [the published Polish and English editions place the second footnote here (footnote 5 of this article)]

[4a] [the published Polish and English editions place the third footnote here (footnote 7 of this article)]

[5a] [the published Polish and English editions place the fourth and last footnote here (footnote 9 of this article)]

9. The Degrees of Being in Phenomenology and in Classical Metaphysics

[1a] [1b] [the original manuscript and typescript] *I gradi dell'essere nella fenomenologia e nella metafisica classica: Introduzione* (*dal punto di vista di una fenomenologia dell'azione*).

620 | Texts Marked by Critical Apparatus

²ᵃ [the English version stored in the Kraków archive has the following text at this point] The present paper is a brief outline of the key concepts and ideas contained in my more extensive study, *Person and Act.* Its English translation is now being prepared.

10. The Transcendence of the Person in the Act and the Auto-teleology of Man

¹ᵃ [the 1994/2000 Polish edition places footnote 5 here]

²ᵃ [the 1994/2000 Polish edition places footnote 6 here]

³ᵃ [the 1994/2000 Polish edition places footnote 7 here]

⁴ᵃ ⁴ᵇ [1994/2000 Polish edition: removed]

⁵ᵃ [the 1994/2000 Polish edition places footnote 8 here]

⁶ᵃ [the 1994/2000 Polish edition places footnote 9 here]

⁷ᵃ ⁷ᵇ [1994/2000 Polish edition] On the basis of the entire human experience, especially that of the fundamental contents of the fact of acting ("I act–man acts"), we arrive at the conviction that what is proper to man is above all the "auto-teleology of the terminus," which conditions the entire "auto-teleology of the end."

⁸ᵃ [the 1994/2000 Polish edition places footnote 10 here]

⁹ᵃ ⁹ᵇ [1994/2000 Polish edition: removed]

¹⁰ᵃ [the 1994/2000 Polish edition places footnote 12 here]

¹¹ᵃ [the 1994/2000 Polish edition places footnote 11 here]

¹²ᵃ ¹²ᵇ [the 1994/2000 Polish edition offers the following ending] In concluding these reflections on the auto-teleology of man, it is difficult to resist one more reflection, which remains quite closely connected to the dual meaning of the Greek τέλος, indicating the "end" and "terminus." It is known that in the long philosophical tradition of antiquity and the Middle Ages, anthropology and ethics, constructed in accord with the teleological conception, were closely connected with the *category of happiness* (εὐδαιμονία) as the end for which man ultimately strives through all he does and undertakes.* Christianity built its theological synthesis on the same premise.† As was mentioned in the beginning, Kant questioned the legitimacy of introducing eudaimonism into ethics (the problem directly concerned the version of eudaimonism represented by utilitarianism). Thereby, it seems, the auto-teleology of man was, in a sense, further bound with the transcendence of the person in the act.

By analyzing in the present reflections man's auto-teleology precisely on the basis of the transcendence of the person in the act, we can arrive at the conclusion (previously expressed) that *above all the "auto-teleology of the terminus" is existentially proper to man existing and acting in the world.* This terminus is the truth of human acts. Conscience constitutes the fundamental condition of self-fulfillment. The "world" means for every man the necessity of judgment, which proceeds from the very depth of his personal being. However, under this necessity, so to speak, under the entire wonderful dimension of the "auto-teleology of the terminus," connected with the existential situation of man existing and acting in the world, *another dimension, as it were, is constantly disclosed—the "auto-teleology of the end,"* which ancient and medieval thinkers linked with the concept of happiness‡—and theologians conferred a concrete form on it by drawing from revelation, from the Word of God. Regardless of how, in various aspects, we assess Kant's criticism aimed at teleological presuppositions in ethics, we cannot rule out the fact that through this criticism we were indirectly better prepared to understand the human "auto-teleology of the end" precisely as the ultimate culmination of the transcendence of the person in the act.

* Aristotle, *Nicomachean Ethics* 1.6.1097a15–1097b5; Polish translation by Daniela Gromska (Warsaw: Państwowe Wydawnictwo Naukowe, 1956), 220–21.

† See Thomas Aquinas, *Summa theologiae* I-II.

‡ We can approach the problem of happiness from different points of view. See Władysław Tatarkiewicz, *O szczęściu*, 2nd ed. (Kraków: Wiedza, Zawód, Kultura, 1949, 3rd ed. (Warsaw: Państwowe Wydawnictwo Naukowe, 1962); Tatarkiewicz, *O doskonałości* (Warsaw: Państwowe Wydawnictwo Naukowe, 1976).

11. *Theoria* and *Praxis* in the Philosophy of the Human Person

1a [the original manuscript has here the Polish title repeated in Italian] Riflessioni sulla teoria e prassi nella filosofia della persona umana

2a 2b [added by the author—not in the cited work]

3a 3b [added by the author—not in the cited work]

4a 4b [added by the author—not in the cited work]

12. *Theoria* and *Praxis*: A Universally Human and Christian Topic

1a 1b [the original manuscript and typescript] Teoria–prassi—un tema umano e cristiano

2a 2b [the original typescript and the 2000 KUL edition (but not the original manuscript)] PRAXIS

13. The Author's Preface to the First English Edition of *Person and Act*

1a 1b [the original typescript] appeased

2a 2b [the original typescript] our own

3a 3b [the original typescript] various

4a 4b [absent in the original typescript]

5a 5b [the original typescript] approach

FOOTNOTES MARKED BY THE CRITICAL APPARATUS

II: *Person and Act*

1a 1b [1979/1985 and 1994/2000] In the phenomenological approach, experience is the source and basis of all knowledge about objects. However, this does not mean that only one kind of experience exists and that this experience is "sensory" perception, either "external or internal," as modern empiricists used to claim. For phenomenologists "direct experience" is every cognitive act in which the object itself is given, in the original, that is—as Husserl states—as "bodily self-present" (*leibhafte selbstgegebenheit*). However, many varieties of experience exist in which individual objects are given, for example, the experience of somebody else's individual psychical facts, the aesthetic experience in which works of art, etc., are given to us.

2a 2b [1979/1985 and 1994/2000] This direction of investigation concurs with that expressed by Maurice Blondel in his classical work *L'action*, new ed. (Paris: Presses Universitaires de France, 1963).

3a 3b [1979/1985 and 1994/2000] They call this cognition "intuition of essence" or "ideation," and define it as being a priori. However, ideation proceeds from what is individual as an example and—as some emphasized (see, e.g., Maurice Merleau-Ponty, *Le problème des sciences de l'homme selon Husserl*, introduction and part 1 of *Les sciences de l'homme et la phénoménologie* [Paris: Tournier et Constans, 1953])—is precisely an attempt to deepen the traditional understanding of induction as opposed to its positivistic understanding as a generalization from a series of cases, in which elements co-occur as alien to one another, to other similar cases.

4a 4b [1979/1985 and 1994/2000] This tendency can also be seen in the writings of Roman Ingarden (the first edition of the present work appeared before Ingarden published his treatise *O odpowiedzialności i jej podstawach ontycznych*, i.e., *Über die Verantwortung: Ihre ontischen Fundamente* [Stuttgart: Philipp Reclam Jun., 1970]).

5a 5b [1979/1985] not "in consciousness" and not only "in consciousness" [1994/2000] not "in consciousness"

6a 6b [1979/1985 and 1994/2000: removed]

7a 7b [1979/1985 and 1994/2000] However, we must stress that in this study our point is to present the reality of the person in the aspect of consciousness, not to analyze consciousness for its own sake.

Therefore, this chapter constitutes only a sketch of the epistemological foundations of our reflections. This sketch, however, has a fundamental significance for the whole conception of man presented in this book.

"Knowledge" or "self-knowledge" in the sense employed here does not denote an abstract result or product of the cognitive process but the actualized potentiality that enables the cognition of the object and actually realizes this cognition.

8a 8b [1979/1985 and 1994/2000: removed]

9a 9b [1979/1985 and 1994/2000: removed]

10a 10b [1979/1985 and 1994/2000] Thus a problem arises: does consciousness (in its reflexive function) constitute lived-experience, or does it only condition the constitution of lived-experience as *jouissance*?

11a 11b [1979/1985 and 1994/2000: removed]

12a 12b [1979/1985 and 1994/2000] Because the problem of the subconscious is marginal to our reflections, we do not take into consideration or discuss the Freudian distinction between the preconscious (*das Vorbewußte*) and the properly unconscious (*das Unbewußte*), i.e., pushed out of consciousness; thus, we use the general term "the subconscious."

13a 13b [1979/1985 and 1994/2000: removed]

14a 14b [1979/1985 and 1994/2000: removed]

III: Post-1969 Related Essays

5. The Person: Subject and Community

15a 15b [English version under AKKW CII 21/158] This work continues the investigations initiated in my study *Person and Act* (Kraków: Polskie Towarzystwo Teologiczne, 1969). It examines anew the connection between the subjectivity of man as a person and the structure of the human community. This problem was sketched in the final chapter of *Person and Act*, entitled "Participation." Here I intend to develop this, beginning with the conception of the person that was extensively treated in the aforementioned work. The many analyses carried out there are closely connected to the problem of human subjectivity; they may even all be said to lead in some way to its understanding and articulation. Discussions of *Person and Act* have been printed in *Analecta Cracoviensia* 5–6 (1973–74): 49–272.

16a [English version under AKKW CII 21/158] *Miłość i odpowiedzialność: Studium etyczne* [*Love and Responsibility: An Ethical Study*] (Lublin: Towarzystwo Naukowe Katolickiego Uniwersytetu Lubelskiego, 1960; 2nd ed. Kraków: Znak, 1962); translations: *Amour et responsabilité. Etude de morale sexuelle* (Paris: Société d'Editions Internationales, 1965); *Amore e responsabilità* (Turin: Marietti, 1969); *Amor y responsibilidad* (Madrid: Editorial Razon y Fe S.A., 1969). [Editorial note: Since 1969, two English editions of *Love and Responsibility* have appeared, the first published in London in 1981 by William Collins Sons (reprinted in London by Fount in 1982 and in San Francisco by Ignatius Press in 1993) and the second in 2013 by Pauline Books and Media (Boston).]

17a 17b [2000 Polish edition moves this section to the end of the previous footnote]

18a 18b [English version under AKKW CII 21/158] The entire study *Person and Act* (hereafter referred to as PA) in its fundamental conception is based on the conviction that *operari sequitur esse*. The act of personal existence finds its strict consequences in the activity of the person, or in other words, in the act. This is why the act is the basis of the manifestation and understanding of the person.

19a [English version under AKKW CII 21/158] *Person and Act* did not contain a theory of community but considered only the elementary conditions required in order that the existence and action of man as a person "together with others" serve, or at least not hinder, self-fulfillment. These negative facts, known to us from the history of man and of human societies, ought to be kept in mind while considering the problem of the personal subject in the community. The final chapter of *Person and Act* is limited to this; it does not sufficiently elaborate it but does contain implicitly some elements of this theory. [*Editorial note: To improve style and readability, slight modifications have been made to the original English text of this note.]

20a 20b [English version under AKKW CII 21/158: removed]

6. Participation or Alienation

21a 21b [2000 KUL edition: removed]

22a 22b [2000 KUL edition: removed]

23a 23b [2000 KUL edition: removed]

24a 24b [2000 KUL edition: removed]

25a 25b [2000 KUL edition: removed]

26a 26b [2000 KUL edition: removed]

8. Subjectivity and "the Irreducible" in Man

27a 27b [2000 KUL edition: removed]

28a 28b [2000 KUL edition: removed]

29a 29b [2000 KUL edition: removed]

30a 30b [2000 KUL edition: removed]

31a 31b [2000 KUL edition: removed]

32a 32b [2000 KUL edition: removed]

33a 33b [2000 KUL edition: removed]

34a 34b [2000 KUL edition: removed]

35a 35b [2000 KUL edition: removed]

EDITORIAL NOTES

I. Pre-1969 Synopsis and Fragments

1. *Person and Act*: A Synopsis

i. This piece entitled "Osoba i czyn (konspekt)" and completed on November 16, 1965, had not been published in any language prior to appearing in the present volume. The manuscript is catalogued in the Archive of the Metropolitan Curia in Kraków under AKKW CII 12/122a. All the marginal notes accompanying this text indicate its working character.

ii. The Polish adjective świadomościowy is translated here as "consciousness-related," because there is no word in English expressing the Polish meaning. It functions in relation to "consciousness" as do the English adjectives "accidental" and "factual" in relation to the nouns "accident" and "fact." In contrast to świadomościowy, the adjective świadomy (conscious) refers more to cognitive objectivization than to the proper function of consciousness. Hence, Wojtyła distinguishes between conscious action and the consciousness of action. The word "consciousness-related" refers to consciousness with its two main functions: the mirroring (reflective) function and the reflexive function. Consciousness does not cognitively objectivize but (a) mirrors what one in a sense already knows and (b) interiorizes or subjectivizes what it mirrors, thus forming a lived-experience of oneself as a subject.

iii. These three groups concern:

(a) somatic/vegetative processes, of which the person is never conscious (such as the production of blood cells or adrenaline by the organism) unless indirectly through knowledge;

(b) sensations and emotions, of which the person is aware as they happen in him;

(c) human acts, of which the person is conscious as being their agent.

iv. While the original manuscript has "(a)" in this sentence, it is conceivable given the context that Wojtyła intended to write "(c)."

v. In order to distinguish between the Polish words *czyn* and *akt* (which are both translated by the English "act"), the Polish is presented in brackets if these terms appear close to each other in the text. See the note on *czyn* and *akt* within *Person and Act* below.

vi. The phrase "this striving" can also be read as "this knowing."

2. *Person and Act*: The Introductory and Fundamental Reflections

vii. This is the initial chapter of the text that Wojtyła sent in 1965 to be published by the Catholic University of Lublin in a collection entitled Pastori et magistro commemorating the fiftieth anniversary of the priesthood of Bishop Piotr Kałwa. Unfortunately, this introductory chapter was not published in the Lublin collection and appeared in a heavily truncated form as the introduction to the first Polish edition of *Person and Act*.

viii. In order to distinguish between the Polish words *czyn* and *akt* (which are both translated by the English "act"), the Polish is presented in brackets if these terms appear close to each other in the text. See the note on *czyn* and *akt* within *Person and Act* below.

3. Person and Act in the Aspect of Consciousness: A Fragment of the Study *Person and Act*

ix. This is the first part of the second chapter of the text sent by Wojtyła in 1965 to the Catholic University of Lublin. This part was published in 1966 as "Osoba i czyn w aspekcie świadomości (fragment studium 'Osoba i czyn')," in Pastori et magistro: *Praca zbiorowa wydana dla uczczenia jubileuszu 50-lecia kapłaństwa Jego Ekscelencji Księdza Biskupa Doktora Piotra Kałwy, Profesora i Wielkiego Kanclerza KUL*, ed. Andrzej Ludwik Krupa (Lublin: Towarzystwo Naukowe Katolickiego Uniwersytetu Lubelskiego), 293–305, and consists of the first part of chapter 1 of *Person and Act*.

x. This résumé was translated from the French by Michael Camacho.

4. *Person and Act*: The Reflexive Functioning of Consciousness and Its Emotionalization

xi. This is the second part of the second chapter of the text sent by Wojtyła in 1965 to the Catholic University of Lublin. This part was published as "Osoba i czyn: Refleksywne funkcjonowanie świadomości i jej emocjonalizacja," *Studia theologica Varsaviensia* 6, no. 1 (1968): 101–19, and is the middle part of chapter 1 of *Person and Act*

xii. Here the published fragment contained a summary in French. This summary was a French translation of the beginning of the published article itself (specifically, the introduction and section 1, "The Person and the Act in the Aspect of Consciousness"). The summary concluded with the following paragraph: "In the sections to follow, which are currently under preparation, the author analyzes in turn: person and act against the background of the dynamism of man; the transcendence of the person in act; the problem of self-determination; the problem of the relation between self-determination and fulfillment, in particular self-fulfillment; and the integration of the person in act (integration and the somatic, integration and the psyche)."

Editorial notes to pages 87–121 | 629

5. *Person and Act*: Subjectivity and Subjectivism

xiii. This is the third (and last) part of the second chapter of the text sent by Wojtyła in 1965 to the Catholic University of Lublin. This unpublished fragment is the last part of chapter 1 in the first Polish edition of *Person and Act*. Although it does not significantly differ from the published text, we include it for the sake of completeness.

6. Person and Act in Light of Man's Dynamism

xiv. This fragment was published in 1968 as "Osoba i czyn na tle dynamizmu człowieka," in *Problemy filozoficzne*, vol. 1 of the collection *O Bogu i o człowieku*, ed. Bohdan Bejze, 201–26 (Warsaw: Wydawnictwo SS. Loretanek-Benedyktynek, 1968). We publish only its first part, which provides a summary of the previous chapter, a summary that has not been published in the book editions. The rest of this fragment contains the first five sections of chapter 2 of the 1969 edition of *Person and Act*. Because these five sections differ from the book edition only slightly, we do not reproduce them here, in the interest of avoiding duplication.

II: *Person and Act*

Introduction

xv. Second Vatican Council, Pastoral Constitution on the Church in the Modern World *Gaudium et spes* (December 7, 1965). The English translation is taken from the Vatican website, www.vatican.va.

xvi. The Polish text is ambiguous. The meaning can be either that "the *fieri* of moral values reveals the person more than the act does" or that "this *fieri* reveals the person more than it reveals the act."

xvii. This subtitle is a bit misleading because the text—both here and in "Person and Act: A Synopsis"—speaks of placing person and act outside the parentheses, leaving the problem of morality within them. However, it does not matter whether the person and his action are placed within or outside the parentheses. The point is that this very procedure allows us to focus on person and act without losing sight of the ethical order.

xviii. Another possible reading is "characteristic of man and only of him."

Chapter 1: Person and Act in the Aspect of Consciousness

xix. Wojtyła points out a link between the Polish word *czyn* and the Latin word *actus*, whose polonized form is *akt*. In order to distinguish between them, the Polish words *czyn* and *akt* (which are both translated by the English "act") are presented in brackets if they appear close to each other in the text.

For example, Wojtyła uses *akt* in the following phrases: act morally good or evil; act of choice; act of cognition; act of conjugal intercourse; act of consciousness; act of desire; act of experience; act of faith; act of human nature; act of interior life; act of love; act of man; act of mercy; act of reproduction; act of self-knowledge; act of the conscience; act of cult; act of the emotive sphere; act of the vegetative sphere; act of the Magisterium; act of the will ; act of virtue; act of volition; affective act; cognitive act; conjugal act; creative act; emotional-cognitive act; ethical act; experiential act; external act; human act; intentional act; internal act; legislative act; moral act; psychical act; religious act; sensual act; sexual act.

He uses *czyn* in the following phrases: act of spouses; human act; morally good or evil act; person and act; person-act.

xx. "A.T." probably refers to Anna-Teresa Tymieniecka.

xxi. The Polish adjective świadomościowy is translated here as "consciousness-related," because there is no word in English expressing the Polish meaning. It functions in relation to "consciousness" as do the English adjectives "accidental" and "factual" in relation to the nouns "accident" and "fact." In contrast to świadomościowy, the adjective świadomy (conscious) refers more to cognitive objectivization than to the proper function of consciousness. Hence, Wojtyła distinguishes between conscious action and the consciousness of action. The word "consciousness-related" refers to consciousness with its two main functions: the mirroring (reflective) function and the reflexive function. Consciousness does not cognitively objectivize but (a) mirrors what one in a sense already knows and (b) interiorizes or subjectivizes what it mirrors, thus forming a lived-experience of oneself as a subject.

xxii. Another possible translation is "the relation's last 'reflection.'"

xxiii. The word *czucie* is translated consistently as "sensation," although it could also be translated as "feeling" because the verb *czuć* means "to sense" or "to feel." Therefore, in a few instances, the noun *czucie* and the verb *czuć* were rendered as "feeling" and "to feel," respectively.

Chapter 2: The Analysis of Efficacy in Relation to the Dynamism of Man

xxiv. Another possible reading of the phrase "the subject's properties" is "its properties," namely, "the properties of the dynamism."

xxv. The phrase "the man reveals himself" can also be read as "intuition reveals itself."

Chapter 3: The Personal Structure of Self-Determination

xxvi. As he makes clear in his *"Person and Act*: A Synopsis," Wojtyła distinguishes the acts of which we are made conscious (*uświadomione*; that is, those that we become aware of as they happen in us) from properly conscious acts (*świadome*). The made-conscious acts are not properly conscious, though properly conscious acts are also made-conscious. We could link made-conscious acts to sensual cognition (also present in animals). However, only properly conscious acts possess the consciousness-related character resulting from the fact that "consciousness not only mirrors but also in a particular way 'interiorizes' what it mirrors, giving to it all a place in the person's own 'I'" (*Person and Act*, ch. 1, p. 131).

xxvii. This sentence can be read in two ways. First, it emphasizes this "directing" as a directing of the person and not merely of one of his powers. Second, it stresses that it is the person himself who does the "directing" without being determined by the object.

Chapter 4: Self-Determination and Fulfillment

xxviii. The Polish verb *spełniać* can be translated as "to fulfill" or "to perform," depending on the meaning. Hence, the English phrases "to perform an act" and "to fulfill oneself" use the same Polish verb: *spełniać*.

xxix. The word *sprawczość* is consistently translated as "efficacy" and the word *sprawca* as "agent." The word "agency" is another valid translation of the word *sprawczość*.

xxx. Due to the Polish pronoun used, "it" in this sentence and the next may refer to truth, dependence on truth, or freedom.

xxxi. According to the present translation, the last part of this sentence says that conscience confers on norms its own normative force. However, the Polish text may also be understood as saying that conscience confers on norms their own normative power. The next sentence contains a similar problem. In translation, it refers to conscience's own ground, whereas the Polish text could also be read as referring to the norms' own ground.

xxxii. The phrase "his immaturity," referring to the immaturity of the person, may also be read as "its immaturity," that is, the immaturity of transcendence.

xxxiii. Because Wojtyła notes this distinction, we will apply it consistently throughout all volumes. Therefore, we translate, on the one hand, *szczęście* as "happiness" and, on the other hand, *szczęśliwość* and *uszczęśliwienie* as "felicity," even though the latter terms could be translated as "happiness," "beatitude," or even "bliss." The word "felicity" was chosen to render these latter terms not only because it accords with the work of different thinkers (such as Aristotle, St. Thomas, Kant, and Scheler), but also because it seems to include the subjective aspect of lived-experience. It may be helpful to note that the Thomistic tradition distinguishes between *beatitudo objectiva* as the desired good taken objectively and *felicitas*, *beatitudo subjectiva*, or *beatitudo formalis* as the state or operation of the subject enjoying possession of the objective good.

xxxiv. The first English and German editions mistakenly place a heavily truncated footnote 10 here (pp. 289–90 in this edition), altogether absent from the Polish editions. The original form of the footnote has been restored and inserted in the correct place.

xxxv. The meaning of this sentence is that the author's analyses in this study take advantage of the light of traditional reflections more than they shed light on them.

Chapter 5: Integration and Somaticity

xxxvi. Another possibility is to read the final clause as "*when* my own 'I' becomes for myself the first object in action," which would indicate this objectivization of the "I" as a condition for the "unity of objectivization."

xxxvii. According to this sentence, reactivity and emotivity are ascribed to the psycho-somatic dynamism of man, not to man himself—though the latter meaning is also possible.

xxxviii. This sentence can be read in two ways. In the first, more immediate sense, Aristotle's attitude underpinned his metaphysics and anthropology differently than Plato's did—implying that Plato's attitude also underpinned Aristotle's metaphysics and anthropology, just in a different way. In the second sense, Plato's attitude informed his own metaphysics and anthropology so that these latter were different from Aristotle's.

xxxix. Another possible reading of the second part of this sentence is "contact with consciousness maintains the drive for self-preservation with the help of so-called bodily sensations."

xl. This sentence can also be read as saying that the natural striving to maintain one's existence and to be with another person of the other sex is *a* basis of marriage and *a* basis of the family rather than *the* basis. Both readings make sense, because marriage and the family ultimately originate from God, who bestows on man a nature that is indispensable for marriage and the family. Hence, while marriage and the family are not simply the result of biological determination, neither is it the case that nature has nothing to do with them.

Chapter 6: Integration and the Psyche

xli. The comparison of Aristotle to the Stoics and of Scheler to Kant concern their logical (pertaining to the school of thought) rather than chronological relationship.

Chapter 7: (*Supplementum*): An Outline of the Theory of Participation

xlii. The Polish word *współdziałanie*, which is translated here as "co-operation," can also be translated as "co-action."

xliii. The Polish word *pełnowartościowy*, which literally means "having full value," is translated here as "fully-mature."

xliv. According to Wojtyła, "norming" refers to the rational governance of the human being (of his acts) in order to realize the good, which is the proper end of his rational nature. Hence, norming is based on valuation, that is, on rationally grasping and acknowledging the good (*ratio boni*), and is formed by way of judgments. To summarize, "to norm" means "to introduce into every human act the conformity with reason." See vol. 2 of this collection, especially *The Lublin Lectures*.

xlv. This sentence speaks of the discovery of participation in the community. However, another possible reading is the discovery of participation in the person.

xlvi. Wojtyła compares the word *wspólnota* (community) with *społeczeństwo* (society), as they have the same semantic stem in Polish, for *wspólnota* is related to *wspólnie* (together) and *społeczeństwo* is related to *społem* (together). In English, the link is not so evident.

xlvii. The words "being" and "existence" are used here interchangeably. Hence, the phrase "existing together with others" means also "being together with others."

xlviii. The Polish adjective *gruntowny* means "encompassing the whole and entering into the details." In other words, the noun *gruntowność* denotes not only breadth but also depth, since the root of the word is *grunt*, that is, "ground."

xlix. The Polish word *bliźni* denotes the evangelical neighbor (see Matthew 5:43 or Luke 10:29), not merely the person living next door (for which the word *sąsiad* is used).

Afterword

l. The afterword did not appear in the first Polish edition of *Person and Act* but was added by Wojtyła before the second Polish edition.

III: Post-1969 Related Essays

1. Introductory Statement during the Discussion on *Person and Act* at the Catholic University of Lublin on December 16, 1970

li. This text was originally published as "Wypowiedź wstępna w czasie dyskusji nad 'Osobą i czynem' w Katolickim Uniwersytecie Lubelskim dnia 16 grudnia 1970 r.," *Analecta Cracoviensia* 5–6 (1973–74): 53–55.

lii. The Learned Society of the Catholic University of Lublin (Towarzystwo Naukowe KUL) is an academic institution and publisher, operating as an entity separate from but complementary to the university. It consists of members from various faculties within the university, such as the Faculty of Theology, the Faculty of Philosophy, the Faculty of History and Philology, the Faculty of Social Sciences, and others.

liii. This, of course, was true only for the first Polish edition of *Person and Act*, published in 1969.

2. Symposium on *Person and Act* (Lublin—Catholic University of Lublin, 1971)

liv. This text, entitled in Polish "Sympozjum nt. książki 'Osoba i czyn': Lublin—KUL—1971 r." has never been published. It is catalogued in the Archive of the Metropolitan Curia in Kraków under AKKW CII 14/131. Because this text closely resembles "The Introductory Statement during the Discussion on *Person and Act* at the Catholic University of Lublin on December 16, 1970" and has a very informal character, it seems to be a direct transcription of the actual introduction by Card.

Wojtyła during the December 1970 discussion. Hence, the date on the original typescript should be 1970, not 1971, for there is evidence of only one symposium on *Person and Act* in Lublin.

lv. The Polish phrase *krakowskim targiem* (translated as "a Kraków compromise") means more or less "to split the difference," that is, to compromise by meeting halfway.

lvi. The paragraph to which Wojtyła refers here is located at the end of the introduction, rather than chapter 1, of *Person and Act*.

lvii. Again, this was true only for the first Polish edition of *Person and Act* from 1969.

lviii. Wojtyła probably refers to Fr. Kamiński here.

3. The Afterword to the Discussion on *Person and Act*

lix. This text was originally published as "Słowo końcowe" in *Analecta Cracoviensia* 5–6 (1973–74): 243–63. It was also published as "Słowo końcowe po dyskusji nad *Osobą i czynem*" in the collection *Osoba i czyn oraz inne studia antropologiczne*, ed. Tadeusz Styczeń, Wojciech Chudy, Jerzy W. Gałkowski, Adam Rodziński, and Andrzej Szostek, 349–69 (Lublin: Towarzystwo Naukowe Katolickiego Uniwersytetu Lubelskiego, 2000).

lx. All statements of the participants of this discussion were published in *Analecta Cracoviensia* 5–6 (1973–74): 49–263. Footnote 2 (pp. 467–68) to the article "The Person: Subject and Community" in this volume contains a detailed list of all authors.

lxi. Roman Ingarden, *Książeczka o człowieku* (Kraków: Wydawnictwo Literackie, 1972).

lxii. Marian Jaworski, "Koncepcja antropologii filozoficznej w ujęciu Kardynała Karola Wojtyły (Próba odczytania w oparciu o studium 'Osoba i czyn')," in *Analecta Cracoviensia* 5–6 (1973–74): 94 (emphasis original).

lxiii. Jaworski, "Koncepcja antropologii filozoficznej," 97.

lxiv. Jaworski, "Koncepcja antropologii filozoficznej," 96.

lxv. Jerzy Kalinowski, "Metafizyka i fenomenologia osoby ludzkiej: Pytania wywołane przez 'Osobę i czyn,'" in *Analecta Cracoviensia* 5–6 (1973–74): 68 (emphasis original).

lxvi. Mieczysław Gogacz, "Hermeneutyka 'Osoby i czynu' (Recenzja książki Księdza Kardynała Wojtyły 'Osoba i czyn,' Kraków 1969)," in *Analecta Cracoviensia* 5–6 (1973–74): 131 (emphasis original).

lxvii. Kalinowski, "Metafizyka i fenomenologia osoby ludzkiej," 69.

lxviii. Stanisław Kamiński, "Jak filozofować o człowieku?" in *Analecta Cracoviensia* 5–6 (1973–74): 75.

lxix. Kamiński, "Jak filozofować o człowieku?" 75.

lxx. Jaworski, "Koncepcja antropologii filozoficznej," 94.

lxxi. Jaworski, "Koncepcja antropologii filozoficznej," 93.

lxxii. Tadeusz Styczeń, "Metoda antropologii filozoficznej w 'Osobie i czynie' Kardynała Karola Wojtyły," in *Analecta Cracoviensia* 5–6 (1973–74): 108 (emphasis added).

lxxiii. Styczeń, "Metoda antropologii filozoficznej," 112.
lxxiv. Styczeń, "Metoda antropologii filozoficznej," 112 (emphasis added).
lxxv. Styczeń, "Metoda antropologii filozoficznej," 113.
lxxvi. Kamiński, "Jak filozofować o człowieku?" 78.
lxxvii. Jaworski, "Koncepcja antropologii filozoficznej," 100.
lxxviii. Kamiński, "Jak filozofować o człowieku?" 76.
lxxix. Kamiński, "Jak filozofować o człowieku?" 76.
lxxx. Stanisław Grygiel, "Hermeneutyka czynu oraz nowy model świadomości," in *Analecta Cracoviensia* 5–6 (1973–74): 144.
lxxxi. Kamiński, "Jak filozofować o człowieku?" 78.
lxxxii. Mieczysław Albert Krąpiec, "Książka Kardynała Karola Wojtyły monografią osoby jako podmiotu moralności," in *Analecta Cracoviensia* 5–6 (1973–74): 61.
lxxxiii. Jaworski, "Koncepcja antropologii filozoficznej," 99.
lxxxiv. Jaworski, "Koncepcja antropologii filozoficznej," 105–6.
lxxxv. Grygiel, "Hermeneutyka czynu oraz nowy model świadomości," 142.
lxxxvi. Gogacz, "Hermeneutyka 'Osoby i czynu,'" 126.
lxxxvii. Gogacz, "Hermeneutyka 'Osoby i czynu,'" 126–27.
lxxxviii. Gogacz, "Hermeneutyka 'Osoby i czynu,'" 130.
lxxxix. Gogacz, "Hermeneutyka 'Osoby i czynu,'" 129–30.
xc. Andrzej Półtawski, "Człowiek a świadomość (W związku z książką Kardynała Karola Wojtyły 'Osoba i czyn')," in *Analecta Cracoviensia* 5–6 (1973–74): 159.
xci. Krąpiec, "Książka Kardynała Karola Wojtyły," 60.
xcii. Krąpiec, "Książka Kardynała Karola Wojtyły," 57–58.
xciii. Roman Forycki, "Antropologia w ujęciu Kardynała Karola Wojtyły (Na podstawie książki 'Osoba i czyn,' Kraków 1969)," in *Analecta Cracoviensia* 5–6 (1973–74): 122 (emphasis added).
xciv. Forycki, "Antropologia w ujęciu Kardynała Karola Wojtyły," 123.
xcv. Józef Tischner, "Metodologiczna strona dzieła 'Osoba i czyn,'" in *Analecta Cracoviensia* 5–6 (1973–74): 86.
xcvi. Styczeń, "Metoda antropologii filozoficznej," 110.
xcvii. Półtawski, "Człowiek a świadomość," 164–65.
xcviii. Grygiel, "Hermeneutyka czynu oraz nowy model świadomości," 149.
xcix. Półtawski, "Człowiek a świadomość," 175 (emphasis added).
c. This article by Prof. Andrzej Półtawski was published as "Czyn a świadomość" in *Logos i ethos: Rozprawy filozoficzne* (Kraków: Polskie Towarzystwo Teologiczne, 1971), 83–113.
ci. The Polish adjective *świadomościowy* is translated here as "consciousness-related," because there is no word in English expressing the Polish meaning. It functions in relation to "consciousness" as do the English adjectives "accidental" and "factual" in relation to the nouns "accident" and "fact." In contrast to *świadomościowy*, the adjective *świadomy* (conscious) refers more to cognitive objectivization than to the proper function of consciousness. Hence, Wojtyła distinguishes between conscious action and the consciousness of action. The word "consciousness-related" refers to consciousness with its two main functions: the mirroring (reflective) function and the reflexive function. Consciousness does not cognitively objectivize but

(a) mirrors what one in a sense already knows and (b) interiorizes or subjectivizes what it mirrors, thus forming a lived-experience of oneself as a subject.

cii. Gogacz, "Hermeneutyka 'Osoby i czynu,'" 127 and 132.
ciii. Gogacz, "Hermeneutyka 'Osoby i czynu,'" 128.
civ. Gogacz, "Hermeneutyka 'Osoby i czynu,'" 137.
cv. Jerzy W. Gałkowski, "Natura, osoba, wolność," in *Analecta Cracoviensia* 5–6 (1973–74): 179.
cvi. Gałkowski, "Natura, osoba, wolność," 179 (emphasis added).
cvii. Leszek Kuc, "Uczestnictwo w człowieczeństwie 'innych'?" in *Analecta Cracoviensia* 5–6 (1973–74): 190.
cviii. Kuc, "Uczestnictwo w człowieczeństwie 'innych'?" 189.
cix. Kuc, "Uczestnictwo w człowieczeństwie 'innych'?" 186.
cx. Zofia Józefa Zdybicka, "Praktyczne aspekty dociekań przedstawionych w dziele 'Osoba i czyn,'" in *Analecta Cracoviensia* 5–6 (1973–74): 204.
cxi. Tadeusz Wojciechowski, "Jedność duchowo-cielesna człowieka w książce 'Osoba i czyn,'" in *Analecta Cracoviensia* 5–6 (1973–74): 191.
cxii. Wojciechowski, "Jedność duchowo-cielesna człowieka w książce 'Osoba i czyn,'" 197.
cxiii. Wojciechowski, "Jedność duchowo-cielesna człowieka w książce 'Osoba i czyn,'" 198.
cxiv. Zdybicka, "Praktyczne aspekty," 202.
cxv. Jerzy Stroba, "Refleksje duszpasterskie," in *Analecta Cracoviensia* 5–6 (1973–74): 207 (emphasis added).
cxvi. Stroba, "Refleksje duszpasterskie," 208.
cxvii. Stroba, "Refleksje duszpasterskie," 209.
cxviii. Teresa Kukołowicz, "'Osoba i czyn' a wychowanie w rodzinie," in *Analecta Cracoviensia* 5–6 (1973–74): 212 (emphasis added).
cxix. Wanda Półtawska, "Koncepcja samoposiadania—podstawą psychoterapii obiektywizującej (w świetle książki Kardynała Karola Wojtyły 'Osoba i czyn')," in *Analecta Cracoviensia* 5–6 (1973–74): 223.
cxx. Półtawska, "Koncepcja samoposiadania," 224.

4. The Personal Structure of Self-Determination (A Lecture for the Conference on St. Thomas)

cxxi. This lecture "Osobowa struktura samostanowienia" was given by Wojtyła on March 12, 1974, at the 17th Philosophical Week of the Catholic University of Lublin, entitled "The Relevance of Thomism: On the 700th Anniversary of St. Thomas's Death." It was also published in the collection *Osoba i czyn oraz inne studia antropologiczne*, ed. Tadeusz Styczeń, Wojciech Chudy, Jerzy W. Gałkowski, Adam Rodziński, and Andrzej Szostek, 423–32 (Lublin: Towarzystwo Naukowe Katolickiego Uniwersytetu Lubelskiego, 2000). In addition, it was delivered on April 23, 1974, in Naples at the conference marking the 700th anniversary of the death of St. Thomas. Subsequently, it was published in English as "The Personal Structure of Self-Determination," trans. Andrzej Potocki, in *Tommaso d'Aquino nel suo VII centenario: Congresso Internazionale, Roma-Napoli, 17–24 aprile 1974*, 379–90 (Rome-Naples, 1974), and in *Person and Community: Selected Essays*, trans. Theresa Sandok, 187–95 (New York: Peter Lang, 1993). An Italian edition of this article entitled "La struttura generale dell'autodecisione" appeared in *Asprenas* 21, no. 4 (1974): 337–46. A Spanish edition entitled "La estructura general de la autodecision" was published in Karol Wojtyła, *El hombre y su destino: Ensayos de antropología*, trans. Pilar Ferrer, 171–85 (Madrid: Palabra, 1998).

cxxii. The Latin term *sincerum donum* was translated into English as "a sincere gift" and into Polish as *bezinteresowny dar*. The adjective *bezinteresowny* literally means "disinterested," not in the sense of being indifferent or impartial but in the sense of having no selfish motivation for gain, of being sincere. Hence, I prefer to translate *bezinteresowny* as "sincere."

5. The Person: Subject and Community

cxxiii. Although written between 1974 and 1975 (and completed before May 1975), this article was originally published as "Osoba: Podmiot i wspólnota," *Roczniki filozoficzne* 24, no. 2 (1976): 5–39. It was also published in the collection *Osoba i czyn oraz inne studia antropologiczne*, ed. Tadeusz Styczeń, Wojciech Chudy, Jerzy W. Gałkowski, Adam Rodziński, and Andrzej Szostek, 373–414 (Lublin: Towarzystwo Naukowe Katolickiego Uniwersytetu Lubelskiego, 2000). An English translation entitled "The Person: Subject and Community" was sent for publication to the Catholic University of America on January 3, 1977. English translations of this article were published in *The Review of Metaphysics* 33 (1979–80): 273–308, and in *Person and Community: Selected Essays*, trans. Theresa Sandok, 219–61 (New York: Peter Lang, 1993). A German translation was published as "Person: Ich und Gemeinschaft," *Klerusblatt* 57, no. 9 (1977): 189–92. Wojtyła also presented this article on June 23, 1977, upon receiving an honorary doctorate from Johannes Gutenberg University in Mainz, Germany. A Spanish edition entitled "La persona: Sujeto y comunidad" appeared in Karol Wojtyła, *El hombre y su destino: Ensayos de antropología*, trans. Pilar Ferrer, 41–109 (Madrid: Palabra, 1998).

6. Participation or Alienation

cxxiv. In Polish, this article was published as "Uczestnictwo czy alienacja" in *Summarium: Sprawozdania towarzystwa naukowego KUL* 7 (1978): 7–16, and in *Osoba i czyn oraz inne studia antropologiczne*, ed. Tadeusz Styczeń, Wojciech Chudy, Jerzy W. Gałkowski, Adam Rodziński, and Andrzej Szostek, 447–61 (Lublin: Towarzystwo Naukowe Katolickiego Uniwersytetu Lubelskiego, 2000). Originally, this article (entitled "Participation ou aliénation") was sent to the International Phenomenological Colloquium in Swiss Fribourg, which took place on January 24–28, 1975. There, it was delivered on February 27, 1975. On July 27, 1976, Wojtyła delivered the article as a lecture at Harvard University, Boston. This article appeared in English as

"Participation or Alienation?" in *The Self and the Other*, ed. Anna-Teresa Tymieniecka, 61–73, Analecta Husserliana 6 (Dordrecht: D. Reidel, 1977), and in *Person and Community: Selected Essays*, trans. Theresa Sandok, 197–207 (New York: Peter Lang, 1993). A Spanish version of this article entitled "Participatión o alienación" appeared in Karol Wojtyła, *El hombre y su destino: Ensayos de antropología*, trans. Pilar Ferrer, 111–31 (Madrid: Palabra, 1998).

Overall, there are three different Polish editions of the article "Participation or Alienation." The edition published by *Summarium* in 1978 is based on the 1975 version of the article sent to the International Phenomenological Colloquium in Swiss Fribourg. Another edition was presented at Harvard University in 1976 but never published in print. The third edition was published by the Catholic University of Lublin (KUL) in 2000. This edition is an amalgamation of the 1975 and 1976 versions, although it is impossible to ascertain the time of its creation. Because neither original manuscripts nor original typescripts of the 2000 KUL edition exist in the Kraków archive, the ECE uses the original Polish text of the 1976 Harvard version as the main edition and those published in 1978 and 2000 as supplementary texts (to which the reader has access through the critical apparatus).

7. A Letter to Anna-Teresa Tymieniecka

cxxv. This letter, published for the first time in the present volume, is catalogued in the Archive of the Metropolitan Curia in Kraków under AKKW BI 4208.

8. Subjectivity and "the Irreducible" in Man

cxxvi. An English version of this article (entitled "Subjectivity and the Irreducible in Man") was sent to an international colloquium taking place in Paris on June 13–14, 1975. It was subsequently published as "Podmiotowość i 'to, co nieredukowalne' w człowieku," *Ethos* 1, nos. 2–3 (1988): 21–28. It was also published under the same title in *Osoba i czyn oraz inne studia antropologiczne*, ed. Tadeusz Styczeń, Wojciech Chudy, Jerzy W. Gałkowski, Adam Rodziński, and Andrzej Szostek, 435–43 (Lublin: Towarzystwo Naukowe Katolickiego Uniwersytetu Lubelskiego, 2000). It appeared in English as "Subjectivity and the Irreducible in Man" in *The Human Being in Action*, ed. Anna-Teresa Tymieniecka, 107–14, Analecta Husserliana 7 (Dordrecht: D. Reidel, 1978), and in *Person and Community: Selected Essays*, trans. Theresa Sandok, 209–17 (New York: Peter Lang, 1993). An Italian edition of this article entitled "La soggettività e l'irriducibilità nell'uomo" appeared in *Il Nuovo Areopago* 6, no. 1 (1987): 7–16. A Spanish edition was published under the title "La subjetividad y lo irreductible en el hombre" in Karol Wojtyła, *El hombre y su destino: Ensayos de antropología*, trans. Pilar Ferrer, 25–39 (Madrid: Palabra, 1998).

Editorial notes to pages 546–567 | 639

9. The Degrees of Being in Phenomenology and in Classical Metaphysics: Introduction (to the Discussion from the Point of View of the Phenomenology of Action)

cxxvii. This article is an introduction to the discussion on the phenomenology of action ("Introduzione del punto di vista di una fenomenologia dell'azione") given by Cardinal Wojtyła on March 28, 1976, during the conference "I gradi dell'essere nella fenomenologia e nella metafisica classica" at the Gregorian University in Rome. It was published in English as "The Degrees of Being from the Point of View of the Phenomenology of Action," in *The Great Chain of Being and Italian Phenomenology*, ed. Angela Ales Bello, 125–30, Analecta Husserliana 11 (Dordrecht: Kluwer, 1981).

10. The Transcendence of the Person in the Act and the Auto-teleology of Man

cxxviii. This article was published as "Transcendencja osoby w czynie a autoteleologia człowieka," in *Osoba i czyn oraz inne studia antropologiczne*, ed. Tadeusz Styczeń, Wojciech Chudy, Jerzy W. Gałkowski, Adam Rodziński, and Andrzej Szostek, 479–90 (Lublin: Towarzystwo Naukowe Katolickiego Uniwersytetu Lubelskiego, 2000). It was also submitted for the 6th International Philosophical Congress, organized by Facoltà di Lettere in Siena and Facoltà di Maggistri in Arezzo, June 1–5, 1976, under the title "L'autoteleologia dell'uomo e la trascendenza della persona nell'atto." On July 29, 1976, Wojtyła delivered it in English as "The Transcendence of the Person in Act and Man's Auto-teleology" at The Catholic University of America in Washington, D.C. A slightly different English version of this article was published as "The Transcendence of the Person in Action and Man's Self-Teleology," in *The Teleologies in Husserlian Phenomenology*, ed. Anna-Teresa Tymieniecka, 203–12, Analecta Husserliana 9 (Dordrecht: D. Reidel, 1979.) An Italian edition of this article entitled "Trascendenza della persona nell'agire e autoteleologia dell'uomo" appeared in *Il nuovo areopago* 7, no. 1 (1988): 6–18. It was also published in Spanish as "Trascendencia de la persona en el obrar y autoteleología del hombre" in Karol Wojtyła, *El hombre y su destino: Ensayos de antropología*, trans. Pilar Ferrer, 133–51 (Madrid: Palabra, 1998).

cxxix. This sentence may also be read as saying that it is the human person (not transcendence) who manifests and realizes himself—though the next sentence speaks of transcendence as the subject of manifestation.

11. *Theoria* and *Praxis* in the Philosophy of the Human Person

cxxx. The manuscript of this text, entitled in Polish "*Teoria i praxis* w filozofii osoby ludzkiej," is catalogued in the Archive of the Metropolitan Curia in Kraków under AKKW CII 21/163a. It has never been published in Polish, though it appeared in Italian as "Teoria e prassi nella filosofia della persona umana" in *Sapienza* 29, no. 4 (1976): 377–84. On April 1, 1976, Wojtyła delivered this Italian version as "Riflessioni sul tema: 'Teoria e prassi' nella filosofia della persona umana" at the Angelicum in

Rome. This article closely resembles "*Theoria* and *Praxis*: A Universally Human and Christian Topic."

12. *Theoria* and *Praxis*: A Universally Human and Christian Topic

cxxxi. This article was published as "*Teoria–praxis*: Temat ogólnoludzki i chrześcijański," in *Osoba i czyn oraz inne studia antropologiczne*, ed. Tadeusz Styczeń, Wojciech Chudy, Jerzy W. Gałkowski, Adam Rodziński, and Andrzej Szostek, 465–75 (Lublin: Towarzystwo Naukowe Katolickiego Uniwersytetu Lubelskiego, 2000). The Polish text has been translated into Italian and delivered by Wojtyła at the international philosophical conference "Teoria e prassi" in Genoa, Italy, on September 8, 1976. It was published in Italian as "Teoria–prassi—un tema umano e cristiano" in *Atti del congresso internazionale*, vol. 1, 31–41 (Napoli: Edizioni Domenicane Italiane, 1979). Due to their close resemblance, this article seems to be a more developed version of Wojtyła's lecture "*Theoria* and *Praxis* in the Philosophy of the Human Person."

13. The Author's Preface to the First English Edition of *Person and Act*

cxxxii. This text of Wojtyła's preface to the 1979 English edition of *Person and Act* is reproduced from original typescripts found in the Archive of the Metropolitan Curia in Kraków, catalogued under AKKW CII 16/134 and CII 17/136d. This version differs only slightly from the published one. It is uncertain whether Wojtyła wrote it in English or in Polish, or whether he wrote it himself. Any obvious errors in the text from the archive were corrected in light of the published version and marked by the critical apparatus. The text has also been copyedited to improve its style and legibility.

BIBLIOGRAPHY

Note: The works listed are the sources Wojtyła used. Some bibliographic information regarding translations and new editions of these works has also been provided by the editors.

Ach, Narziss. *Über den willensakt und das temperament*. Leipzig: Quelle and Meyer, 1910.
Aquinas, Thomas. *S. Thomae Aquinatis Summa theologica*. Paris: Firmin-Didot, 1891–1900. Translated by Fathers of the English Dominican Province as *Summa theologiae*, 5 vols. (Notre Dame, Ind.: Christian Classics, 1981; first edition, 1911).
———. *Traktat o człowieku* [Treatise on man], *Summa theologiae 1, 75–89*. Translated and edited by Stefan Świeżawski. Poznań: Pallotinum, 1956.
Aristotle. *De Anima*. In *Aristotelis opera omnia: Graece et latine*. Paris: Firmin-Didot, 1848–83. Or in *Aristotelis opera*. 5 vols. Berlin: Academia Regia Borussica, 1831–70.
———. *The Basic Works of Aristotle*. Edited by Richard McKeon. New York: Modern Library, 2001.
———. *Etyka Nikomachejska* [Nicomachean ethics]. Translated by Daniela Gromska. Warsaw: Państwowe Wydawnictwo Naukowe, 1956.
———. *Filozofia starożytna grecji i rzymu*. Texts selected by Jan Legowicz. 2nd ed. Wybrane teksty z historii filozofii. Warsaw: Państwowe Wydawnictwo Naukowe, 1970.
———. *Metaphysics*. In *Aristotelis opera*. 5 vols. Berlin: Academia Regia Borussica, 1831–70.
———. *Physics*. In *Aristotelis opera*. 5 vols. Berlin: Academia Regia Borussica, 1831–70.
———. *Politics*. In *Aristotelis opera omnia: Graece et latine*. Paris: Firmin Didot, 1848–83. Or in *Aristotelis opera*. 5 vols. Berlin: Academia Regia Borussica, 1831–70.
Ayer, Alfred Jules. *Language, Truth and Logic*. London: Victor Gollancz, 1936.
Baczko, Bronisław. "Hegel, Marks i problemy alienacji." *Studia filozoficzne*, no. 1 (1957): 36–58.
———. "Wokół problemów alienacji." *Studia filozoficzne*, no. 6 (1959): 19–52.
Badaloni, Nicola. "Alienazione e libertà nel pensiero di Marx." *Critica marxista* 6, nos. 4–5 (1968): 139–64.
Bejze, Bohdan, ed. *O człowieku dziś*. Vol. 2 of *Aby poznać Boga i człowieka*. Warsaw: Wydawnictwo Sióstr Loretanek, 1974.

Bell, Daniel. "The Debate on Alienation." In *Revisionism: Essays on the History of Marxist Ideas*, edited by Leopold Labedz, 195–211. London: Allen and Unwin, 1962.
Bentham, Jeremy. *Introduction to the Principles of Morals and Legislation*. London: T. Payne, 1789.
Berger, Peter L. *La religion dans la conscience moderne*. Paris: Centurion, 1971.
Bergson, Henri. "L'âme et le corps." In *Oeuvres*. 2nd ed. Paris: Presses Universitaires de France, 1963.
Bigo, Pierre. *Marxisme et humanisme*. Paris: Presses Universitaires de France, 1954.
Blauner, Robert. *Alienation and Freedom: The Factory Worker and His Industry*. Chicago: University of Chicago Press, 1964.
Blondel, Maurice. *L'action humaine et les conditions de son aboutissement*. Vol. 2 of *L'action*. New ed. Paris: Presses Universitaires de France, 1963.
Boethius. *Liber de persona et duabus naturis*. Patrologiae cursus completus, series Latina, vol. 64, edited by J.-P. Migne. Paris: Migne, 1860.
Brandt, Richard Booker. *Ethical Theory: The Problems of Normative and Critical Ethics*. Englewood Cliffs, N.J.: Prentice Hall, 1959.
Braybroocke, David. "Diagnosis and Remedy in Marx's Doctrine of Alienation." *Social Research* 25, no. 3 (1958): 325–45.
Calvez, Jean-Yves. *La pensée de Karl Marx*. Paris: Éditions du Seuil, 1956.
D'Abbiero, Marcella. *Alienazione in Hegel: Usi e significati di Entäusserung, Entfremdung, Veräusserung*. Rome: Edizioni dell'Ateneo, 1970.
Dąbrowski, Kazimierz. *La désintégration positive: Problèmes choisis*. Warsaw: Państwowe Wydawnictwo Naukowe, 1964.
———. *Personnalité, psychonévroses et santé mentale d'après la théorie de la désintégration positive*. Warsaw: Państwowe Wydawnictwo Naukowe, 1965.
———. *Psychothérapie des névroses et des psychonévroses: L'instinct de la mort d'après la théorie de la désintégration positive*. Warsaw: Państwowe Wydawnictwo Naukowe, 1965.
Danecki, Jan. *Czas wolny: Mity i potrzeby*. Warsaw: Książka i Wiedza, 1967.
de Finance, Joseph. *Être et agir dans la philosophie de Saint Thomas*. Rome: Presses de l'Université Grégorienne, 1965.
Duméry, Henry. "Philosophie de l'action et praxéologie." In *Fragmenty filozoficzne, seria III: Księga pamiątkowa ku czci profesora Tadeusza Kotarbińskiego w osiemdziesiątą rocznicę urodzin*, edited by Tadeusz Czeżowski, 301–16. Warsaw: Państwowe Wydawnictwo Naukowe, 1967.
Dunayevskaya, Raya. *Marxism and Freedom*. New York: Bookman Associates, 1958.
Dybowski, Mieczysław. *Zależność wykonania od cech procesu woli*. Warsaw: Drukarnia Instytutu Głuchoniemych i Ociemniałych, 1926.
———. *O typach woli: Badania eksperymentalne*. Lwów-Warsaw: Książnica-Atlas, 1928.
———. *Działanie woli: Na tle badań eksperymentalnych*. Poznań: Księgarnia Akademicka, 1946.
"Dyskusja nad książką A. Schaffa pt. 'Marksizm a jednostka ludzka.'" *Studia filozoficzne*, no. 1 (1966): 3–50.

Easton, Loyd D. "Alienation and History in the Early Marx." *Philosophy and Phenomenological Research* 22, no. 2 (1961): 193–205.
Etcheverry, Auguste. *Le conflit actuel des humanistes*. Paris: Presses Universitaires de France, 1955.
Fabro, Cornelio. *Participation et causalité selon S. Thomas d'Aquin*. Louvain: Publications Universitaires de Louvain, 1961.
Fetscher, Iring. "Przemiany marksistowskiej krytyki religii." *Concilium* 1 (1968): 477–91.
Florkowski, Eugeniusz, ed. *Analecta Cracoviensia* 5–6 (1973–74).
Forycki, Roman. "Antropologia w ujęciu Kardynała Karola Wojtyły (na podstawie książki 'Osoba i czyn,' Kraków 1969)." *Analecta Cracoviensia* 5–6 (1973–74): 117–24.
Freud, Sigmund. *Das Ich und das Es und andere metapsychologische Schriften*. Frankfurt: Fischer Taschenbuch Verlag, 1960. Translated by Joan Riviere as *The Ego and the Id*, ed. James Strachey (New York: W. W. Norton, 1960).
Fritzhand, Marek. *Człowiek, humanizm, moralność: Ze studiów nad Marksem*. Warsaw: Książka i Wiedza, 1961. (Second edition, 1962.)
———. *Myśl etyczna młodego Marksa*. Warsaw: Książka i Wiedza, 1961.
———. *O niektórych właściwościach etyki marksistowskiej*. Warsaw: Państwowe Wydawnictwo Naukowe, 1974.
Fromm, Erich. *The Sane Society*. New York: Holt, Rinehart and Winston, 1960.
———. *Marx's Concept of Man*. New York: Frederick Ungar, 1961.
———. *Beyond the Chains of Illusion: My Encounter with Marx and Freud*. New York: Simon and Schuster, 1962.
Gałkowski, Jerzy W. "Natura, osoba, wolność." *Analecta Cracoviensia* 5–6 (1973–74): 177–82.
Garaudy, Roger. *La liberté*. Paris: Éditions Sociales, 1955.
———. *Humanisme marxiste: Cinq essais polémiques*. Paris: Éditions Sociales, 1957.
———. *Perspectives de l'homme: Existentialisme, pensée catholique, marxisme*. Paris: Presses Universitaires de France, 1959. Translated by Zdzisław Butkiewicz and Julian Rogoziński as *Perspektywy człowieka: Egzystencjalizm, myśl katolicka, marksizm* (Warsaw: Książka i Wiedza, 1968).
———. *Marxisme du XXe siècle*. Paris: La Palatine, 1966.
Geiger, Louis-Bertrand. *La participation dans la philosophie de S. Thomas d'Aquin*. Paris: Vrin, 1942.
Gogacz, Mieczysław. "Hermeneutyka 'Osoby i czynu' (recenzja książki Księdza Kardynała Wojtyły 'Osoba i czyn,' Kraków 1969)." *Analecta Cracoviensia* 5–6 (1973–74): 125–38.
———. "Filozofia człowieka wobec teologii." *Studia theologica Varsaviensia* 12, no. 1 (1974): 177–92.
———. *Wokół problemu osoby*. Warsaw: Pax, 1974.
Gołaszewska, Maria. "Romana Ingardena filozofia moralności." *Etyka* 9 (1971): 113–44.
Granat, Wincenty. *Osoba ludzka: Próba definicji*. Sandomierz: Wydawnictwo Diecezjalne w Sandomierzu, 1961.

Bibliography

———. "Alienacja." In *Encyklopedia Katolicka*. Vol. 1, 367–69. Lublin: Wydawnictwo Towarzystwa Naukowego Katolickiego Uniwersytetu Lubelskiego, 1973.
Grygiel, Stanisław. "Człowiek czy Bóg?" *Znak* 22 (1970): 145–76.
———. "Hermeneutyka czynu oraz nowy model świadomości." *Analecta Cracoviensia* 5–6 (1973–74): 139–51.
Hare, Richard Mervyn. *The Language of Morals*. Oxford: Clarendon Press, 1952.
Hartmann, Nicolai. *Ethik*. 4th ed. Berlin: Walter de Gruyter, 1962. (First edition, 1926.)
Hume, David. *A Treatise of Human Nature*. London: Printed for John Noon, 1739.
Husserl, Edmund. *Allgemeine Einführung in die reine Phänomenologie*. Vol. 1 of *Ideen zu einer reinen Phänomenologie und phänomenologischen Philosophie*. Halle: Max Niemeyer, 1913. Translated by W. R. Boyce Gibson as *Ideas: General Introduction to Pure Phenomenology* (London: Allen and Unwin, 1931). Translated by Danuta Gierulanka as *Idee czystej fenomenologii i fenomenologicznej filozofii* (Warsaw: Państwowe Wydawnictwo Naukowe, 1967).
———. "Vergemeinschaftung der Monaden und die erste Form der Objektivität: die intersubjektive Natur." In *Cartesianische Meditationen und Pariser Vorträge*. The Hague: Nijhoff, 1963.
Ingarden, Roman. *Z badań nad filozofią współczesną*. Warsaw: Państwowe Wydawnictwo Naukowe, 1963.
———. *Formalontologie*. Vol. 2 of *Der Streit um die Existenz der Welt*. Tübingen: Max Niemeyer, 1965. Translated by Arthur Szylewicz as *Controversy over the Existence of the World*, vol. 2 (Frankfurt am Main: Peter Lang, 2016).
———. *Przeżycie, dzieło, wartość*. Kraków: Wydawnictwo Literackie, 1966.
———. *Über die Verantwortung: Ihre ontischen Fundamente*. Stuttgart: Philipp Reclam Jun., 1970. Translated by Adam Węgrzecki as *O odpowiedzialności i jej podstawach ontycznych*, in *Książeczka o człowieku*, 75–184 (Kraków: Wydawnictwo Literackie, 1972). Translated by Arthur Szylewicz as *On Responsibility: Its Ontic Foundations*, in *Man and Value*, 53–117 (Washington, D.C.: The Catholic University of America Press, 1983).
———. *U podstaw teorii poznania*. Warsaw: Państwowe Wydawnicto Naukowe, 1971.
———. "Człowiek i czas." In *Książeczka o człowieku*, 41–74. Kraków: Wydawnictwo Literackie, 1972.
———. *Książeczka o człowieku*. 3rd ed. Kraków: Wydawnictwo Literackie, 1975. (First edition 1972; second edition, 1973.)
Jaroszewski, Tadeusz M. *Alienacja?* Warsaw: Książka i Wiedza, 1965.
———. "Marksowska kategoria 'praktyki' a antropologia filozoficzna." *Człowiek i światopogląd*, no. 2 (37) (1968), 11–16.
———. "Marksowska kategoria 'praktyki' oraz jej rola w filozofii dialektycznego materializmu." *Studia filozoficzne*, no. 2, (1969), 3–20.
———. *Osobowość i wspólnota: Problemy osobowości we współczesnej antropologii filozoficznej—marksizm, strukturalizm, egzystencjalizm, personalizm chrześcijański*. Warsaw: Książka i Wiedza, 1970.
———. *Rozważania o praktyce wokół interpretacji filozofii Karola Marksa*. Warsaw: Państwowe Wydawnictwo Naukowe, 1974.
Jaworski, Marian. "Człowiek a Bóg: Zagadnienie relacji znaczeniowej pomiędzy

osobą ludzką i Bogiem a problem ateizmu." In *Logos i ethos: Rozprawy filozoficzne*, 115–28. Kraków: Polskie Towarzystwo Teologiczne, 1971.

———. "Koncepcja antropologii filozoficznej w ujęciu Kardynała Karola Wojtyły (próba odczytania w oparciu o studium 'Osoba i czyn')." *Analecta Cracoviensia* 5–6 (1973–74): 91–106.

Jaworski, Marian and Adam Kubiś, eds. *Teologia a antropologia: Kongres teologów polskich 21–23 IX 1971*. Kraków: Polskie Towarzystwo Teologiczne, 1971.

Kalinowski, Jerzy. *Teoria poznania praktycznego*. Lublin: Towarzystwo Naukowe Katolickiego Uniwersytetu Lubelskiego, 1960.

———. "Metafizyka i fenomenologia osoby ludzkiej: Pytania wywołane przez 'Osobę i czyn.'" *Analecta Cracoviensia* 5–6 (1973–74): 63–71.

Kamiński, Stanisław. "Jak filozofować o człowieku?" *Analecta Cracoviensia* 5–6 (1973–74): 73–79.

Kant, Immanuel. *Grundlegung zur Metaphysik der Sitten*. Leipzig: Philipp Reclam Jun., 1904. The original edition (Riga, 1785) later appeared in a collective publication of the Berlin Academy of Sciences: *Kants gesammelte Schriften, herausgegeben von der Königlich Preussischen Akademie der Wissenschaft*, vol. 4 (Berlin: G. Reimer, 1903). Translated by Mścisław Wartenberg as *Uzasadnienie metafizyki moralności*, ed. Roman Ingarden, 2nd ed. (Warsaw: Państwowe Wydawnictwo Naukowe, 1953; first edition, 1906). Translated and edited by Mary Gregor as *Groundwork of the Metaphysics of Morals*, Cambridge Texts in the History of Philosophy (Cambridge: Cambridge University Press, 1997).

———. *Krytyka praktycznego rozumu* [Critique of practical reason]. Translated by Benedykt Bornstein. Warsaw: E. Wende, 1911. Second edition translated by Jerzy Gałecki (Warsaw: Państwowe Wydawnicto Naukowe, 1972).

Kłósak, Kazimierz. "Teoria doświadczenia człowieka w ujęciu Kardynała Karola Wojtyły." *Analecta Cracoviensia* 5–6 (1973–74): 81–84.

Kołakowski, Leszek. *Kultura i fetysze: Zbiór rozpraw*. Warsaw: Państwowe Wydawnicto Naukowe, 1967.

Kotarbiński, Tadeusz. "La notion de l'action." In *Psychologie philosophique*, 169–74. Vol. 7 of *Actes du XI^{éme} Congrès international de philosophie, Bruxelles, 20–26 août*. Amsterdam: North-Holland, 1953.

———. "Praxiology and Economics." In *On Political Economy and Econometrics: Essays in Honour of Oskar Lange*, 303–12. Warsaw: Państwowe Wydawnicto Naukowe, 1964.

———. *Les origines de la praxéologie*. Warsaw: Państwowe Wydawnicto Naukowe, 1965.

———. *Hasło dobrej roboty*. Warsaw: Wiedza Powszechna, 1968.

———. "L'évolution de la praxéologie en Pologne." In *Philosophie des sciences*. Vol. 2 of *La philosophie contemporaine: Chroniques*, edited by Raymond Klibansky, 438–50. Florence: La Nuova Italia Editrice, 1968.

———. *Sprawność i błąd: Z myślą o dobrej robocie nauczyciela*. 5th ed. Warsaw: Państwowe Zakłady Wydawnictw Szkolnych, 1970.

———. *Studia z zakresu filozofii, etyki i nauk społecznych*. Wrocław: Zakład Narodowy im. Ossolińskich, 1970.

———. "Teleologia a prakseologia." *Prakseologia*, nos. 3–4 (1973): 7–13.

———. *Traktat o dobrej robocie*. 6th ed. Wrocław: Zakład Narodowy im. Ossolińskich, 1975. (First edition, 1955.)

Krąpiec, Mieczysław Albert. "Książka Kardynała Karola Wojtyły monografią osoby jako podmiotu moralności." *Analecta Cracoviensia* 5–6 (1973–74): 57–61.

———. *Ja—człowiek: Zarys antropologii filozoficznej*. Lublin: Towarzystwo Naukowe Katolickiego Uniwersytetu Lubelskiego, 1974.

———. *Człowiek i prawo naturalne*. Lublin: Towarzystwo Naukowe Katolickiego Uniwersytetu Lubelskiego, 1975.

Kretschmer, Ernst. *Körperbau und Charakter: Untersuchungen zum Konstitutionsproblem und zur Lehre von den Temperamenten*. 24th ed. Berlin: Springer, 1961.

Kroński, Tadeusz. *Kant*. Warsaw: Wiedza Powszechna, 1966.

Kuc, Leszek. "Zagadnienia antropologii chrześcijańskiej." *Studia theologica Varsaviensia* 9, no. 2 (1971): 95–109.

———. "Uczestnictwo w człowieczeństwie 'innych'?" *Analecta Cracoviensia* 5–6 (1973–74): 183–90.

———. "Przyczynek do konstrukcji tematyki antropologii chrześcijańskiej." *Studia theologica Varsaviensia* 12, no. 1 (1974): 289–302.

Kuczyński, Janusz. *Porządek nadchodzącego świata: Katolicyzm, laicyzm, humanizm*. Warsaw: Książka i Wiedza, 1964.

Kuderowicz, Zbigniew. "Marks i Engels wobec alternatywy: Jednostka-społeczeństwo." *Studia filozoficzne*, no. 2 (1969): 113–30.

Kukołowicz, Teresa. "'Osoba i czyn' a wychowanie w rodzinie." *Analecta Cracoviensia* 5–6 (1973–74): 211–21.

Lévinas, Emmanuel. *Totalité et infini: Essai sur l'extériorité*. 4th ed. The Hague: Martinus Nijhoff, 1971. (Third edition, 1968.) Translated by Alphonso Lingis as *Totality and Infinity: An Essay on Exteriority* (Dordrecht: Kluwer Academic Publishers, 1991).

Luijpen, Wilhelmus Antonius. *Existential Phenomenology*. 3rd ed. Pittsburgh, Pa.: Duquesne University Press, 1963.

Majchrzyk, Zbigniew. "Problem alienacji u polskich marksistów." Doctoral diss., directed by Fr. Tadeusz Styczeń. Catholic University of Lublin, 1973.

Marcel, Gabriel. *Être et avoir*. Paris: Editions Aubier-Montaigne, 1935. Translated by Donata Eska as *Być i mieć* (Warsaw: Pax, 1962).

Masterson, Patrick. *Atheism and Alienation: A Study of the Philosophical Sources of Contemporary Atheism*. Dublin: Gill and Macmillian, 1971.

Merleau-Ponty, Maurice. *Le problème des sciences de l'homme selon Husserl*. Introduction and part 1 of *Les sciences de l'homme et la phénoménologie*. Paris: Tournier et Constans, 1953.

Meyer, Gerbert. "Actio immanens, actio transiens." In *Historisches Wörterbuch der Philosophie*, vol. 1, edited by Joachim Ritter, col. 76–78. Basel: Schwabe, 1971.

Michotte, Albert and Emile Prüm. "Étude expérimentale sur le choix volontaire et ses antécédents immédiats." *Archives de psychologie* 10 (1911): 113–320.

Nuttin, Joseph. *La structure de la personnalité*. Paris: Presses Universitaires de France, 1971.

Ossowska, Maria. *Myśl moralna oświecenia angielskiego*. Warsaw: Państwowe Wydawnictwo Naukowe, 1966.

Pappenheim, Fritz. *The Alienation of Modern Man: An Interpretation Based on Marx and Tönnies*. New York: Monthly Review Press, 1959.

Plato. "Parmenides." In *Platonis opera: Graece et latine*. Paris: Firmin-Didot, 1891–1900.

———. "Symposium." In *Platonis opera: Graece et latine*. Paris: Firmin-Didot, 1891–1900.

Półtawska, Wanda. "Koncepcja samoposiadania—podstawą psychoterapii obiektywizującej (w świetle książki Kardynała Karola Wojtyły 'Osoba i czyn')." *Analecta Cracoviensia* 5–6 (1973–74): 223–41.

Półtawski, Andrzej. "Czyn a świadomość." In *Logos i ethos: Rozprawy filozoficzne*, 83–113. Kraków: Polskie Towarzystwo Teologiczne, 1971. Translated as "Ethical Action and Consciousness," in *The Human Being in Action*, ed. Anna-Teresa Tymieniecka, 115–50, Analecta Husserliana 7 (Dordrecht: D. Reidel, 1978).

———. "Człowiek a świadomość (w związku z książką Kardynała Karola Wojtyły 'Osoba i czyn')." *Analecta Cracoviensia* 5–6 (1973–74): 159–75.

Ricoeur, Paul. *Le volontaire et l'involontaire*. Vol. 1 of *Philosophie de la volonté*. Paris: Aubier, 1967. Translated by Erazim V. Kohák as *Freedom and Nature: The Voluntary and the Involuntary* (Evanston, Ill.: Northwestern University Press, 1966).

Sartre, Jean-Paul. *L'être et le néant: Essai d'ontologie phénoménologique*. Paris: Gallimard, 1943. (Subsequent editions, 1957 and 1973.)

Schaff, Adam. *Filozofia człowieka*. 3rd ed. Warsaw: Książka i Wiedza, 1965.

———. *Marksizm a jednostka ludzka: Przyczynek do marksistowskiej filozofii człowieka*. Warsaw: Państwowe Wydawnictwo Naukowe, 1965.

———. "Marksizm a jednostka ludzka (podsumowanie dyskusji)." *Studia filozoficzne*, no. 2 (1966): 87–106.

———. "Alienacja a działanie społeczne." In *Fragmenty filozoficzne, seria III: Księga pamiątkowa ku czci Profesora Tadeusza Kotarbińskiego w osiemdziesiątą rocznicę urodzin*, edited by Tadeusz Czeżowski, 481–98. Warsaw: Państwowe Wydawnictwo Naukowe, 1967.

Scheler, Max. *Wesen und Formen der Sympathie: Der "Phänomenologie der Sympathiegefühle*. Vol. 1 of *Die Sinngesetze des emotionalen Lebens*, 2nd ed. Bonn: F. Cohen, 1923. (Third edition, 1926; fourth edition, 1929.)

———. *Der Formalismus in der Ethik und die materiale Wertethik: Neuer Versuch der Grundlegung eines ethischen Personalismus*. 5th ed. Bern: Francke, 1966. (First edition, 1913–16; fourth edition, 1954.) Translated by Manfred S. Frings and Roger L. Funk as *Formalism in Ethics and Non-Formal Ethics of Values: A New Attempt toward the Foundation of an Ethical Personalism* (Evanston, Ill.: Northwestern University Press, 1973). Fragments translated by Adam Węgrzecki in *Scheler, Myśli i ludzie* (Warsaw: Wiedza Powszechna, 1975).

Second Vatican Council. *Dei Verbum*. Dogmatic Constitution. November 18, 1965.

———. *Gaudium et spes*. Pastoral Constitution on the Church in the Modern World. December 7, 1965.

Sève, Luien. *Marxisme et theorie de la personnalité*. Paris: Editions sociales, 1972. Translated by Kazimierz Piechocki as *Marksizm a teoria osobowości* (Warsaw: Książka i Wiedza, 1975).

648 | Bibliography

Shoemaker, Sydney. *Self-Knowledge and Self-Identity*. Ithaca: Cornell University Press, 1963.
Ślipko, Tadeusz. "Pojęcie człowieka w świetle współczesnej filozoficznej antropologii marksistowskiej w Polsce," *Zeszyty naukowe KUL* 10, no. 2, (1967), 3–16.
———. "Marksizm a osoba ludzka (zarys pewnej interpretacji)." In "O człowieku dziś." Part 2 of *Aby poznać Boga i człowieka*, edited by Bohdan Bejze, 177–204. Warsaw: Wydawnictwo Sióstr Loretanek, 1974.
Stępień, Antoni B. "Fenomenologia tomizująca w książce 'Osoba i czyn.'" *Analecta Cracoviensia* 5–6 (1973–74): 153–57.
Stevenson, Charles Leslie. *Ethics and Language*. New Haven: Yale University Press, 1944.
Stroba, Jerzy. "Refleksje duszpasterskie." *Analecta Cracoviensia* 5–6 (1973–74): 207–9.
Styczeń, Tadeusz. "O pewnej koncepcji etyki: Na marginesie 'Badań etycznych' Husserla." *Zeszyty naukowe KUL* 11, no. 1 (1968): 59–65.
———. *Problem możliwości etyki jako empirycznie uprawomocnionej i ogólnie ważnej teorii moralności: Studium metaetyczne*. Lublin: Towarzystwo Naukowe Katolickiego Uniwersytetu Lubelskiego, 1972.
———. "Metoda antropologii filozoficznej w 'Osobie i czynie' Kardynała Karola Wojtyły." *Analecta Cracoviensia* 5–6 (1973–74): 107–15.
———. *Metaetyka*. Part 1 of *Zarys etyki*. Lublin: Katolicki Uniwersytet Lubelski, 1974.
Szostek, Andrzej. "Dyskusja nad dziełem Kardynała Karola Wojtyły 'Osoba i czyn': Wprowadzenie." *Analecta Cracoviensia* 5–6 (1973–74): 49–51.
Tatarkiewicz, Władysław. *O bezwzględności dobra*. Warsaw: Gebether i Wolff, 1919.
———. "On the Four Types of Ethical Judgements." In *Proceedings of the Seventh International Congress of Philosophy, held at Oxford, England, September 1–6, 1930*, edited by Gilbert Ryle, 398–401. London: H. Milford, 1931.
———. *O szczęściu*. 2nd ed. Kraków: Wiedza, Zawód, Kultura, 1949. (Subsequent editions, Państwowe Wydawnictwo Naukowe, 1962 and 1973.) Translated by Edward Rothert and Danuta Zielińska as *Analysis of Happiness*, Melbourne International Philosophy Series 3 (Warsaw: Państwowe Wydawnictwo Naukowe, 1976).
———. *O doskonałości*. Warsaw: Państwowe Wydawnictwo Naukowe, 1976.
Tischner, Józef. "Aksjologiczne podstawy doświadczenia 'ja' jako całości cielesno-przestrzennej." In *Logos i ethos: Rozprawy filozoficzne*, 33–82. Kraków: Polskie Towarzystwo Teologiczne, 1971.
———. "Wartości etyczne i ich poznanie." *Znak* 24, no. 5 (1972): 629–46.
———. "Metodologiczna strona dzieła 'Osoba i czyn.'" *Analecta Cracoviensia* 5–6 (1973–74): 85–89.
Trębicki, Jerzy. *Etyka Maxa Schelera*. Warsaw: Państwowe Wydawnictwo Naukowe, 1973.
Tresmontant, Claude. *Le problème de l'âme*. Paris: Seuil, 1971.
Tymieniecka, Anna-Teresa. "Beyond Ingarden's Idealism/Realism Controversy with Husserl: The New Contextual Phase of Phenomenology." In *Ingardeniana*, edited by Anna-Teresa Tymieniecka, 241–418. Analecta Husserliana 4. Dordrecht: D. Reidel, 1976.
———, ed. *Ingardeniana*. Analecta Husserliana 4. Dordrecht: D. Reidel, 1976.

———. "Initial Spontaneity and the Modalities of Human Life." In *The Crisis of Culture*, edited by Anna-Teresa Tymieniecka, 15–37. Analecta Husserliana 5. Dordrecht: D. Reidel, 1976.
von Hildebrand, Dietrich. *Wahre Sittlichkeit und Situationsethik*. Düsseldorf: Patmos-Verlag, 1957.
———. *Ethik*. Vol. 2 of *Gesammelte Werke*. Regensburg: J. Habbel, 1973. Translated as *Christian Ethics* (New York: David McKay Company, 1953).
Werblan, Andrzej, Wincenty Kraśko, Jerzy Wiatr, Tadeusz M. Jaroszewski, Stefan Żółkiewski, Bronisław Baczko, Jarosław Ładosz, et al. "Dyskusja nad książką Adama Schaffa pt. 'Marksizm a jednostka ludzka.'" *Nowe drogi* 19, no. 12 (1965): 57–186.
Wojciechowski, Tadeusz. "Jedność duchowo-cielesna człowieka w książce 'Osoba i czyn.'" *Analecta Cracoviensia* 5–6 (1973–74): 191–99.
Wojtyła, Karol. "System etyczny Maksa Schelera jako środek do opracowania etyki chrześcijańskiej." *Polonia sacra* 6, nos. 2–4 (1953–54): 143–61.
———. "Problem oderwania przeżycia od aktu w etyce na tle poglądów Kanta i Schelera." *Roczniki filozoficzne* 5, no. 3 (1955–57): 113–40. Published under the same title in *Zagadnienie podmiotu moralności*, ed. Tadeusz Styczeń, Jerzy W. Gałkowski, Adam Rodziński, and Andrzej Szostek, 161–80 (Lublin: Towarzystwo Naukowe Katolickiego Uniwersytetu Lubelskiego, 2001).
———. "Zagadnienie woli w analizie aktu etycznego." *Roczniki filozoficzne* 5, no. 1 (1955–57): 111–35.
———. "Ewangeliczna zasada naśladowania: Nauka źródeł objawienia a system filozoficzny Maxa Schelera." *Ateneum kapłańskie* 55, no. 1 (1957): 57–67.
———. "O kierowniczej lub służebnej roli rozumu w etyce: Na tle poglądów Tomasza z Akwinu, Hume'a i Kanta." *Roczniki filozoficzne* 6, no. 2 (1958): 13–31.
———. *Ocena możliwości zbudowania etyki chrześcijańskiej przy założeniach systemu Maksa Schelera*. Rozprawy wydziału filozoficznego 5. Lublin: Towarzystwo Naukowe Katolickiego Uniwersytetu Lubelskiego, 1959.
———. "O metafizycznej i fenomenologicznej podstawie normy moralnej (w oparciu o koncepcję św. Tomasza z Akwinu oraz Maksa Schelera)." *Roczniki teologiczno-kanoniczne* 6, nos. 1–2 (1959): 99–124.
———. *Miłość i odpowiedzialność: Studium etyczne* [Love and responsibility: An ethical study]. Lublin: Towarzystwo Naukowe Katolickiego Uniwersytetu Lubelskiego, 1960. (Second edition, Kraków, 1962. Fourth edition, Lublin, 1986.) Translated by Thérèse Sas as *Amour et responsabilité: Étude de morale sexuelle*, with an introduction by Henri de Lubac (Paris: Société d'Éditions Internationales, 1965). Translated by Ambretta Berti Milanoli as *Amore e responsabilità: Studio di morale sessuale*, with an introduction by Giovanni Colombo (Turin: Marietti, 1969). Translated by Juan Antonio Segarra as *Amor y responsabilidad: Estudio de moral sexual*, with an introduction by Henri de Lubac (Madrid: Razón y Fe, 1969). Translated by August Berz as *Liebe und Verantwortung: Eine ethische Studie*, (Munich: Kösel, 1979). Translated by Josef Spindelböck as *Liebe und Verantwortung: Eine ethische Studie* (Kleinhain: Verlag St. Josef, 2007). Translated by João Jarski and Lino Carrera as *Amor e responsabilidade: Estudo ético* (São Paulo: Loyola, 1982). Translated by H. T. Willets as *Love and Responsi-*

bility (London: Fount, 1981). Translated by Grzegorz Ignatik as *Love and Responsibility* (Boston: Pauline Books and Media, 2013).

———. "Osoba i czyn (konspekt)." November 16, 1965. Archive of the Metropolitan Curia in Kraków. AKKW CII 12/122a.

———. "Osoba i czyn w aspekcie świadomości (fragment studium 'Osoba i czyn')." In *Pastori et magistro: Praca zbiorowa wydana dla uczczenia jubileuszu 50-lecia kapłaństwa Jego Ekscelencji Księdza Biskupa Doktora Piotra Kałwy, Profesora i Wielkiego Kanclerza KUL*, edited by Andrzej Ludwik Krupa, 293–305. Lublin: Towarzystwo Naukowe Katolickiego Uniwersytetu Lubelskiego, 1966. The complete text Wojtyła's submitted: "Osoba i czyn: artykuł do księgi pamiątkowej na 50-lecie kapłaństwa Bpa Piotra Kałwy," Archive of the Metropolitan Curia in Kraków, AKKW CII 13/128.

———. "Osoba i czyn na tle dynamizmu człowieka." In *Problemy filozoficzne*. Vol. 1 of *O Bogu i o człowieku*, edited by Bohdan Bejze, 201–26. Warsaw: Wydawnictwo SS. Loretanek-Benedyktynek, 1968.

———. "Osoba i czyn: Refleksywne funkcjonowanie świadomości i jej emocjonalizacja." *Studia theologica Varsaviensia* 6, no. 1 (1968): 101–19.

———. *Osoba i czyn* [Person and act]. Edited by Marian Jaworski. Kraków: Polskie Towarzystwo Teologiczne, 1969. (Second edition, ed. Andrzej Półtawski, 1985.) Third edition: *Osoba i czyn oraz inne studia antropologiczne*, ed. Tadeusz Styczeń, Wojciech Chudy, Jerzy W. Gałkowski, Adam Rodziński, and Andrzej Szostek (Lublin: Towarzystwo Naukowe Katolickiego Uniwersytetu Lubelskiego, 1994; repr. 2000). Wojtyła's revisions of *Person and Act*, 1969–79, Archive of the Metropolitan Curia in Kraków, AKKW CII 13/127. Translated by Andrzej Potocki as *The Acting Person* (Dordrecht: D. Reidel, 1979). Translated by Herbert Springer as *Person und Tat* (Freiburg im Breisgau: Herder, 1981). Translated by Stanisław Morawski, Renzo Panzone, and Rosa Liotta as *Persona e atto* (Vatican City: Libreria editrice Vaticana, 1982). Translated by Jesús Fernández Zulaica as *Persona y acción* Biblioteca de autores crisitanos (Madrid: La Edit. Católica, 1982). Translated by Gwendoline Jarczyk as *Personne et acte* (Paris: Le Centurion, 1983).

———. "Problem teorii moralności." In *W nurcie zagadnień posoborowych: Praca zbiorowa*, edited by Bohdan Bejze, vol. 3, 217–50. Warsaw: Wydawnictwo Sióstr Loretanek-Benedyktynek, 1969.

———. "Sympozjum nt. książki 'Osoba i czyn': Lublin—KUL—1971 r." Archive of the Metropolitan Curia in Kraków. AKKW CII 14/131.

———. "Praktyczne aspekty dociekań przedstawionych w dziele 'Osoba i czyn.'" *Analecta Cracoviensia* 5–6 (1973–74): 201–5.

———. "Słowo końcowe." *Analecta Cracoviensia* 5–6 (1973–74): 243–63.

———. "Wypowiedź wstępna w czasie dyskusji nad 'Osobą i czynem' w Katolickim Uniwersytecie Lubelskim dnia 16 grudnia 1970 r." *Analecta Cracoviensia* 5–6 (1973–74): 53–55.

———. "The Personal Structure of Self-Determination." Translated by Andrzej Potocki. In *Tommaso d'Aquino nel suo VII centenario: Congresso internazionale, Roma-Napoli, 17–24 aprile 1974*, 379–90. Rome, 1974.

———. Wojtyła to Anna-Teresa Tymieniecka, May 11, 1975. Archive of the Metropolitan Curia in Kraków. AKKW BI 4208.

———. "Osoba: Podmiot i wspólnota." *Roczniki filozoficzne* 24, no. 2 (1976): 5–39. Also published in *Osoba i czyn oraz inne studia antropologiczne*, ed. Tadeusz Styczeń, Wojciech Chudy, Jerzy W. Gałkowski, Adam Rodziński, and Andrzej Szostek, 373–414 (Lublin: Towarzystwo Naukowe Katolickiego Uniwersytetu Lubelskiego, 2000). Translated as "The Person: Subject and Community," in *The Review of Metaphysics* 33 (1979–80): 273–308, and in *Person and Community: Selected Essays*, trans. Theresa Sandok, 219–61 (New York: Peter Lang, 1993). Translated as "Person: Ich und Gemeinschaft," *Klerusblatt* 57, no. 9 (1977): 189–92. Translated as "La persona: Sujeto y comunidad" in Karol Wojtyła, *El hombre y su destino: Ensayos de antropología*, trans. Pilar Ferrer, 41–109 (Madrid: Palabra, 1998).

———. "*Teoria i praxis* w filozofii osoby ludzkiej." Archive of the Metropolitan Curia in Kraków. AKKW CII 21/163a. Published as "Teoria e prassi nella filosofia della persona umana." *Sapienza* 29, no. 4 (1976): 377–84.

———. "The Intentional Act and the Human Act, That Is, Act and Experience." In *The Crisis of Culture*, edited by Anna-Teresa Tymieniecka, 269–80. Analecta Husserliana 5. Dordrecht: D. Reidel, 1976.

———. Wojtyła to unknown recipient, "Sprawy związane z tłumaczeniem *Osoby i czynu*" [Matters concerning the translation of *Person and Act*], March 1977. Archive of the Metropolitan Curia in Kraków. AKKW CII 17/136a.

———. Preface to the 1979 English edition of *Person and Act*. Archive of the Metropolitan Curia in Kraków. AKKW CII 16/134 and CII 17/136d.

———. "The Degrees of Being from the Point of View of the Phenomenology of Action." In *The Great Chain of Being and Italian Phenomenology*, edited by Angela Ales Bello, 125–30. Analecta Husserliana 11. Dordrecht: Kluwer, 1981.

———. Wojtyła to unknown recipient, "Notatki JP2 Styczeń 1981" [Notes concerning the translation of *Person and Act*], January 1981. Archive of the Center for Documentation and Research of the Pontificate of John Paul II in Rome. AODiSP - EE/X.

———. "Podmiotowość i 'to, co nieredukowalne' w człowieku." *Ethos* 1, nos. 2–3 (1988): 21–28. Published under the same title in *Osoba i czyn oraz inne studia antropologiczne*, ed. Tadeusz Styczeń, Wojciech Chudy, Jerzy W. Gałkowski, Adam Rodziński, and Andrzej Szostek, 435–43 (Lublin: Towarzystwo Naukowe Katolickiego Uniwersytetu Lubelskiego, 2000). Translated as "Subjectivity and the Irreducible in Man" in *The Human Being in Action*, ed. Anna-Teresa Tymieniecka, 107–14, Analecta Husserliana 7 (Dordrecht: D. Reidel, 1978). Translated as "Subjectivity and the Irreducible in the Human Being," in *Person and Community: Selected Essays*, trans. Theresa Sandok, 209–17 (New York: Peter Lang, 1993). Translated as "La soggettività e l'irriducibilità nell'uomo," in *Il Nuovo Areopago* 6, no. 1 (1987): 7–16. Translated as "La subjetividad y lo irreductible en el hombre," in Karol Wojtyła, *El hombre y su destino: Ensayos de antropología*, trans. Pilar Ferrer, 25–39 (Madrid: Palabra, 1998).

———. "Osobowa struktura samostanowienia." In *Osoba i czyn oraz inne studia antropologiczne*, edited by Tadeusz Styczeń, Wojciech Chudy, Jerzy W. Gałkowski, Adam Rodziński, and Andrzej Szostek, 423–32. Lublin: Towarzystwo

Naukowe Katolickiego Uniwersytetu Lubelskiego, 2000. Translated by Andrzej Potocki as "The Personal Structure of Self-Determination," in *Tommaso d'Aquino nel suo VII centenario: Congresso internazionale, Roma-Napoli, 17–24 aprile 1974*, 379–90 (Rome-Naples, 1974). Translated as "The Personal Structure of Self-Determination," in *Person and Community: Selected Essays*, trans. Theresa Sandok, 187–95 (New York: Peter Lang, 1993). Translated as "La struttura generale dell'autodecisione" in *Asprenas* 21, no. 4 (1974): 337–46. Translated as "La estructura general de la autodecision" in Karol Wojtyła, *El hombre y su destino: Ensayos de antropología*, trans. Pilar Ferrer, 171–85 (Madrid: Palabra, 1998).

———. "*Teoria-praxis*: Temat ogólnoludzki i chrześcijański." In *Osoba i czyn oraz inne studia antropologiczne*, edited by Tadeusz Styczeń, Wojciech Chudy, Jerzy W. Gałkowski, Adam Rodziński, and Andrzej Szostek, 465–75. Lublin: Towarzystwo Naukowe Katolickiego Uniwersytetu Lubelskiego, 2000. Published as "Teoria-prassi—un tema umano e Cristiano," in *Atti del congresso internazionale*, vol. 1, 31–41 (Napoli: Edizioni Domenicane Italiane, 1979).

———. "Transcendencja osoby w czynie a autoteleologia człowieka." In *Osoba i czyn oraz inne studia antropologiczne*, edited by Tadeusz Styczeń, Wojciech Chudy, Jerzy W. Gałkowski, Adam Rodziński, and Andrzej Szostek, 479–90. Lublin: Towarzystwo Naukowe Katolickiego Uniwersytetu Lubelskiego, 2000. Translated as "Transcendenza della persona nell'agire e autoteleologia dell'uomo," in *Il nuovo areopago* 7, no. 1 (1988): 6–18. Translated as "Trascendencia de la persona en el obrar y autoteleología del hombre," in Karol Wojtyła, *El hombre y su destino: Ensayos de antropología*, trans. Pilar Ferrer, 133–51 (Madrid: Palabra, 1998).

———. "Uczestnictwo czy alienacja?" [Participation or alienation?]. In *Osoba i czyn oraz inne studia antropologiczne*, edited by Tadeusz Styczeń, Wojciech Chudy, Jerzy W. Gałkowski, Adam Rodziński, and Andrzej Szostek, 447–61. Lublin: Towarzystwo Naukowe Katolickiego Uniwersytetu Lubelskiego, 2000. Also published in *Summarium: Sprawozdania towarzystwa naukowego KUL* 7 (1978): 7–16. Translated as "Participation or Alienation?" in *The Self and the Other*, ed. Anna-Teresa Tymieniecka, 61–73, Analecta Husserliana 6 (Dordrecht: D. Reidel, 1977). Translated by Theresa Sandok as "Participation or Alienation?" in Karol Wojtyła, *Person and Community: Selected Essays*, 197–207 (New York: Peter Lang, 1993). Translated as "Participatión o alienación," in Karol Wojtyła, *El hombre y su destino: Ensayos de antropología*, trans. Pilar Ferrer, 111–31 (Madrid: Palabra, 1998).

Zanardo, Aldo. "Forme e problemi del marxismo contemporaneo (a proposito della fortuna del pensiero giovanile di Marx)." *Studi storici* 3, no. 4 (1962): 667–730.

Zdybicka, Zofia Józefa. *Partycypacja bytu: Próba wyjaśnienia relacji między światem a Bogiem*. Lublin: Towarzystwo Naukowe Katolickiego Uniwersytetu Lubelskiego, 1972.

INDEX

Absoluteness of good, 562–63
Absolutization, 5, 88, 158; of consciousness, 63, 64, 124, 127n4, 131, 476, 593n6, 594n8; of experience of man, 57, 112–13; of relation of person and body, 310–11
Accident (*accidens*), 184, 461, 627, 630, 635
Accidental being, 16, 200, 490, 500, 526
Ach, Narziss, 13–14, 18, 229, 460
Acognitivism, 264n5
Act: actuation differentiated from, 171; call to fulfillment in, 269–70; capacities for actualization and, 23–24; causal connection with person, 169–70; conception of, 112–17; conduct and, 366; conscious, 14–17; creativity of, 171–73, 462, 571–72; distinguished from action, 37, 61; efficacy and freedom in, 13–15; essentialization of, 23; essential moments of, 548; existence as first and fundamental, 175; experience and, 38–41; experience of morality and, 3–6; fact of performing, 36; hermeneutics and, 443–44; immanence of person in, 23–32, 572; integration of person in, 114–15, 549–51; internal and intransitive effect of, 252–53, 255; made-conscious, 14–17; meaning of, 15–17; morality as property of, 104; moral qualification of, moment of truth about good and, 241–42; moral reality and, 253–54; moral value of, person revealed through, 105; and moral world, 36–37; non-made-conscious, 14–17; as particular moment of vision of person, 102–4; performance of ("I perform an act"), 251–54; performance of, as value, 380–81; personalistic value of, 380–83; personal maturity of, 460; person as efficient cause of, 22–24; Polish *czyn* vs.

akt, 627, 628, 629–30; problem of drives in, 31–32; psycho-emotive sphere and, 25, 27–31; in reflection of consciousness, 10–11; relation to lived-experience, 24; semantic wealth of word, 124; significance of topic, 36–37; somatic-reactive sphere and, 25–26; structure of, 22–35; "together with others," 377–80; transcendence of person in, 24, 32–35, 114–15, 560–63. *See also specific topics*
"The Act and Ethical Lived-Experience," 420–21
"The Act and Lived-Experience," 429
Actio, 81, 148
Action: act distinguished from, 37, 61; *agere-pati* and, 163–64, 167; ambiguity in concept of *actus* and, 167; appearance of, behavior and, 366–67; body and, 313–15; cognition and, 247; and complexity of man-person, 286; conduct and, 366; consciousness of, 62–65, 72, 125–26, 630–31; drives as source of, 32; and existence, 175, 183–84; felicity-pleasure boundary and, 279–81; foundations in potentiality, 189–90; happening differentiated from, 11, 16–17, 81, 128, 148, 162–64, 167–73, 540, 548; happening synthesized with, 177–78; instinctive, 225–26; lived-experience of efficacy and, 168–73; nature and defining subject of, 178–79; nature and defining way of, 179–80; Scheler's conception of, 532–33; and *suppositum*, 176–77; teleological interpretation of, 555–56; Wojtyła's elucidation on, xx. *See also* Conscious action
Activity, 163–73. *See also* Agere
Act of will: analysis of, 17–21; developed, 18; dialectic, 18; differences with other acts, 15–16; dynamic, 18; freedom and, 21–22;

653

Act of will: (*cont.*)
intentionality and, 16; motivation and, 231–33; originality of, 231–38; originality of, determinism vs., 235–37; as response to values, 237–38; simple (phenomenological moment), 14, 18, 460; somatic reactivity in, 26

Actualization, 16–17; act of will and, 19–21; *actus humanus* and, 60, 123; capacities for, 23–24; configuration of existence in, 166–67; consciousness and, 79–80, 135, 597; emotivity and, 27–28; in "I–other" relationship, 520–24, 615–17; of lived-experience, 146; morality and, 4; participation and, 388, 520–24; personalistic value of act and, 382; *potentia–actus*, 166–67; of potentiality, 23–24, 146–47; of *praxis*, 575, 579; psycho-emotive sphere and, 25, 27–31; self-determination and, 459; self-knowledge and, 68–69, 135; somatic-reactive sphere and, 25–26; will and, 523

Actuations, 171. *See also* Happenings (actuations)

Actus, 4, 23, 61, 123–24, 165–66, 170–71, 546–47; ambiguity of concept, 167; coupling with potentia, 59–60, 121–22, 165–67

Actus externus, 217, 550, 590

Actus hominis, 32, 168

Actus humanus, 59–62, 72, 463, 546–47, 550, 557, 593; *actus hominis* vs., 168; *actus personae* vs., 478–79; conscience and, 485; consciousness implicated in, 126–28, 475–76; philosophical richness of, 121–25; *praxis* as, 570–71, 578–79; self-determination and, 213–14

Actus individui, 221–22

Actus internus, 26, 216–17, 550

Actus personae, 23, 31, 33, 114, 122–24, 478–79; self-determination and, 213–14, 220; transfer by analogy to individual, 221–22

Actus voluntarius, 59–61, 122, 124–25, 593

Adler, Alfred, 195, 454–55

Aesthetic emotional stirring, 351

Affections, 27–31, 334, 351–58; bodily, 27–28; central vs. peripheral, 353; and conscious action, 83–84; consciousness and, 9–10; differentiating, by emotive content, 354–55; differentiating, criteria for, 353–54; emotionalization by, 82–86, 150–57; excitability and excitement in, 349; and lived-experience of value, 358–62; lower vs. higher, 353–54; and participation, 522–25; participation in act, 27–31; permeation into will, 357–58; qualificative element of, 28; richness and diversity of, 352–53; subjectivity of, 352–53, 354, 356–57

Affectivity, 82, 151, 350–54, 550; and disintegration, 355–56; emotional stirring as core of, 351–52; sublimation and, 353. *See also* Affections

Agency, 631

Agent, 168–73, 182, 570, 577–78, 631

Agent of thinking, 247–48

Agere, 25, 59, 121, 163–73, 237–38, 540; cognition and, 247; dynamism with *pati*, 163–64, 167, 173, 246–47, 540, 599; foundations in potentiality, 189–90; moment of truth and, 246. *See also* Act; Action

Agere humanum, 558

Aggression, 524–25

Agit propter finem, 555

Alienation, 412–13, 489–90, 507–13, 617–19; at center of contemporary lives, 517, 611; at center of contemporary thought, 514, 611; concept of, 514–16; as deprivation of fulfillment, 528–29; "I–other" relation and, 517–26, 612–17; Marxism and, 511, 512, 515–16, 529–31, 617–19; negative verifications of participation and, 524–25; "Participation or Alienation," 514–35, 611–19, 625, 637–38; as personalistic problem, 511, 611–12; reduction of descriptions, 513; "we" relation and, 517

Analecta Cracoviensia, xxvii, 101n1, 433–35, 456–57, 467, 534, 588. *See also* Person and Act; specific authors

Analecta Husserliana, xxvii, 172n4, 413n4

Analogy: *actus personae* and individual, 221–22; common good, 503–4; formation of "man acts" in, 161; limit to, 278; moral subjectivity and psychological subjectivity, 485; principle of, 278–79; "we," 506–7

Analogy of being, 176–77

Analogy of proportion, 178

Anger, 352, 354, 363

Animal rationale, 63, 130, 311, 317, 447, 537–39, 544, 593–94

Anima vegetativa, 192

Anthropology: Aristotelian, 537–39;

aspectual, 445; Christian, 465; connection with ethics, 41–43, 58, 75, 104, 106–7; "ethical," 3; methodology using, 75; of morality, 4–5; *Person and Act* as study of, 430; *praxis* and *theoria* in, 577; relation with metaphysics, 546; transition "toward the position of the person" in, 383–84. *See also* Philosophical anthropology
Anti-individualism, 389, 391–93, 397
Antimonies, 536–37
Anti-personalistic thinking, 392, 451–52
Anti-value, 257, 363–65, 486, 572, 580–82
A-personalistic thinking, 392
Appetition, 28–29, 31, 227–29, 346–47
Appetitus, 227–28, 346–47
Appetitus concupiscibilis, 30, 346–47, 348
Appetitus intellectivus, 476
Appetitus irascibilis, 30, 346–47, 348
Appetitus rationalis, 127, 227–28, 238, 346, 356
Appetitus sensitivus, 346–47, 356
Apriorism: cognitive, 47, 98–99; emotivity and disintegration in, 355–56; rationalistic, 238n10
Aristotelian anthropology, 537–39
Aristotelian philosophy: problem of act vs. product in, 171; and teleology, 555; Wojtyła's connection to, 534, 587
Aristotle, xxxiii, 116–17, 632; on *actus*, 60, 121–23; on affectivity and disintegration, 355; on *agere-pati*, 163–64; comparison to Stoics, 632; on dynamic vision of man, 301; on dynamism of being, 165; on efficient cause, 22–23; on good and end, 232; on habit, 362, 487; on happiness, 22; on human action, 33; on induction, 53–54, 107; on intentionality of volition, 19; on meaning of act, 15; on metaphysics, 257; *Nicomachean Ethics*, 41, 104; on *praxis* and *theoria*, 569–70, 573–74, 575–76, 577; on soul-body relation, 371; on *suppositum*, 174–75; on teleology of act of will, 22; on temperament, 30; on unity of man-person, 289; Wojtyła's references to, xxix, xxxii, 420–21
Aspectuality of *Person and Act*, 445–46
Atheism, xviii
Attitudes, 400–407; authentic, 400–403; non-authentic, 404–7; pre-ethical meaning of, 400–401
Attraction, 269, 362–64, 480, 605

Augustine, vii, xvii, 421–22, 426
Authentic attitudes, 400–403; non-authentic attitudes vs., 404–5
Authenticity, 344–45, 404–5, 610
Authority, personal, responsibility linked with, 273–75
Auto-creationism, 172n4
Auto-determination, 21–22, 31, 243, 256
Auto-determinism, 222–24, 235
Autonomy, 217–18n3, 257, 267
Auto-realization, 583, 617–18
Auto-teleology, 480–84, 487, 554–66, 620–21, 639; community and, 492, 502–3, 507; core (nucleus) of, 559–60; in dimension of terminus and end, 563–66; fulfillment and, 483–84, 487, 492, 562–66; and happiness, 566; as personal *modus*, 564–65; positing problem of, 554–55; self-determination and, 554n1, 557–63; teleology presupposed by, 560; as threshold of relation, 564; transcendence and sense conferred on, 560–63; will, volition, and value in, 557–60
Avoidance, 35, 404–7
Awareness: act–motion synthesis and, 323; self-awareness, 103–4n2, 290n10
Axiological order, common good in, 398
Axiological reality, morality as, 254–56
Axiological truth, 246
Axiological typology, 347
Axiology of person, 381, 465
Ayer, Alfred Jules, 264n5

Baczko, Bronisław, 516n4
Badaloni, Nicola, 515n3
Balthasar, Hans Urs von, xviii
Beatifying, 277
Beatitude, 351, 631
Beauty: and emotional stirring, 351; as transcendental, 33, 257–58, 603–4
Becoming (*fieri*), 16, 166, 199–202; causal connection and, 169–70; lived experience of efficacy and, 169; meaning of, 199, 629; morality (good and evil acts), 202; moral value, 4, 6–7, 9, 11–13, 24, 105, 629; *potentia-actus* and, 166; reciprocal relations with *esse* and *operari*, 199–200; self-determination and, 32, 207–8, 462–63; and spheres of potentiality, 200–201
Behavior, 313, 366–67; and integration, 367; meaning of, 366–67

Behaviorism, 313
Being, degrees of, 546–53, 619–20
Bejze, Bohdan, xxvin4, 518n8, 554n1, 576n2, 629
Bell, Daniel, 515n3
Belonging, social, 394–95
Bentham, Jeremy, 280n8, 556n6
Berger, Peter L., 515n3
Bergson, Henri, 139n9, 314n4, 597
Berkeley, George, 159n15
Bigo, Pierre, 515n3
Birth, nature as, 178–80
Blauner, Robert, 515n3
Blondel, Maurice, 103n2, 123n2, 623
Bodiliness, 82, 151, 311, 337, 545, 550
Bodily affections, 27–28
Bodily self-present, 101n1, 623
Body, 151–52; act and motion of, 319–24; coherence of experience of man with, 331–32; consciousness and, 9–10, 82, 151–52, 192–93, 339; drives and, 324–29; dynamism of, 162, 315–19; efficacy of, 320; excitement and, 348; habit and, 322–23; hylomorphism and, 310–11; independence from self-determination, 319–21; lived-experience of one's own, 337–41; man-person's possession and use of, 313–15; as matter, 286, 308, 371; meaning of, 25; obedience of, 315; outwardness and inwardness of, 308–9; participation in act, 25–26; as part of nature, 317–19; personal unity of man as, 288; potentiality of, 317–19; potentiality of, and instinctive action, 225–26; psyche vs., 332–33; reactivity of, 25–26, 315–19, 326, 338, 550, 590; relation of soul to, 367–73, 452–53, 551–52, 607; relation to person, 310–24; self-feeling and, 339–40; sensing one's own, 339; somatic–vegetative potentiality and, 192–93, 200–201; as sphere and means of express of person, 312–13; subjectivity of, 319–21; unity with spirit, in man-person, 286–91; vitality of, 318–19. *See also* Somaticity
Boethius (Boethian), 147, 175–76, 185, 261, 539, 542
Bonum arduum, 347
Bonum honestum, 481
Bonum operari, 462n4
Bonum per se, 22
Boyce Gibson, W. R., 129n6
Brandt, Richard Booker, 105n3

Brayboocke, David, 515n3
Brentano, Franz, 129n6

Calvez, Jean-Yves, 515n3
Camacho, Michael, 628
Cartesian philosophy, 128n5, 161n1, 377n1, 447, 476, 538, 586, 594
Catechesis on Human Love, xviii, xx
Catechism of the Catholic Church, xix
Categorical imperative, 217n3, 258n2, 355, 446, 524, 563
Causality: connection between person and act, 169–70; of nature, 182–83
Certainty, 262, 267–68, 605
Choice, 460; ability to decide manifested in, 233–34; action by, 32; and act of will, 19–22; autonomous determination of object, 234–35; cognition and, 243–46; conscience and, 34; motivation of, 232–33; necessity of, 558; originality of, 240; simple volition vs., 232–34. *See also* Decision
Christ: and concept of "we," 503n20; and "gift of self," xix; growing into mystery of, xv; origin of Church in, xii–xvii; *praxis-christianum* and, 584–85; triune and mystery of person, xviii–xix
Christian anthropology, 465
Christianity: contemporary, worldview of, 428; heritage of, Wojtyła on, ix; *praxis* and *theoria* in, 577, 583–85
Christian philosophy: fundamental dispute about man, 469; materialistic interpretation of, 469
Christianum, 583–85
Church: concept of person in, 428; contemporary, worldview of, 428; origin and time, and significance of saint, xii–xvii; transcendence of, 93, 117n9, 529, 592
Citizen/citizenship, 394, 403, 527
Co-action, 632
Coexistence (co-existence), 410, 489, 491–93, 514, 606
Cognition: act of will and, 18–21; *agere* (action) and, 247; conscious action and, 125–26; consciousness and, 7–10, 64–65, 128–30, 594–95; creative role of intuition and, 249–50; efficacy and, 246–47; emotion and, 27–29, 590–91; experience and, 38–41, 51–52; experience of man and, 44–50, 95–96, 100–107; happenings vs.

actions, 17; intentionality of, 64, 129, 548, 594; mental, 8, 17, 28–29, 40, 346, 361; morality and, 4; and motivation, 231–32; objectivization in, 64–65, 66, 125–26, 129–30; organic unity of, 458; practical, 109–10, 246; *praxis*-to-*theoria*, 573, 582–83; a priori, 107n5, 623; reality presupposed by, 582; and self-determination, 215–16, 458–59; sensual, 8, 28, 31, 40; and sensuality–rationality demarcation, 346; subjectivizing function of, 216; theory of (epistemology), 536–37; and transcendence, 243–46, 281, 548; transition to spontaneity to reflectivity in, 52; understanding and conception in, 49–58; of value, 232, 242–46, 249–50; will directed by, 215–16
Cognitive apriorism, 47, 98–99
Cognitive contact: experience of man and, 44–45, 50, 95–96, 102; sensations or feelings and, 344
Cognitive dynamism, 129–30
Cognitive emotional stirring, 351
Coherence: dynamic, of person, nature and, 182–87; dynamic, of person, personal existence and, 185–86; experience of man with body, 331–32; nature and, 184; *operari* with *esse*, 185–86, 571, 579; person with act, 184, 282–83, 384; *praxis* with *theoria*, 571, 579; reality of person, 251, 254; self-governance with transcendence, 296; self-knowledge with consciousness, 66–67, 133, 134; somatic "I" with personal "I," 340; subconscious and, 197; truth with cognition, 240
Collective life, 35
Commandment to love, 411–14; demands concerning existing and acting "together with others," 413–14; roots of alienation revealed in, 412–13, 611, 619
Common good, 396–99, 491–92; analogy of, 503–4; avoidance and, 404–7; challenge of, 504–5; conformism and, 404–6; as foundation of authentic community, 399; "I-thou" and, 501; meaning of, 397, 398; opposition and, 402–3; primacy of, 399; solidarity and, 401–2; teleological and personalistic conceptions of, 397–98; thoroughness of, 399; totalism and, 391; transcendence and, 509; "we" and, 501, 503–6, 526

Common language analysis, 104–5n3
Communio, 432, 617
Communion, xviii–xix
Communio personarum, 499, 506, 509–10, 524, 617–18
Communism, 530n17
Community, 379–80; afterword on, 415–16; attitudes and, 400–407; auto-teleology and, 492, 502–3, 507; avoidance and, 404–7; axiologies of, 393; commandment to love and, 411–14; common good and, 396–99, 491–92; concept of, 393; conformism and, 404–6; consciousness and, 490; dialogue and, 403; dimensions of, 487–513; dimensions of, irreducibility of, 492, 509; editorial notes on, 632–33; etymology of, 394; and fulfillment, 488, 498–99, 502–3, 504, 511; homogeneity of, 506; "I-thou" and (inter-personal dimension), 492–99, 534; lived-experience and, 490; member of, 407–8; membership in, participation *vs.*, 395–96; membership in, social belonging and, 394–95; neighbor concept and, 407–11; opposition and, 402–3; participation and, 392–96; person as subject of action *vs.*, 393–94; "The Person: Subject and Community," xxvii–xxviii, 467–513, 533–35, 610, 624–25, 637; real and ideal sense of, 491–92; society *vs.*, 491; solidarity and, 401–2; subjectivity and, 468–69; theory, not present in *Person and Act*, 488; totalism and, 391; unity of plurality in, 490–91; "we" (social dimension), 492–93, 500–507, 526–27, 534
Complexity: in experience of man, 44–49, 100, 107–8; man-person, 286–91; person-act, 124–25; psycho-somatic, 303–10, 331; self-determination and, 207–8, 463–64; self-governance and, 208; transcendence and integration in, 367–69
Compositum humanum, 289, 538, 544
Conception, 49–58; as expression of understanding, 50, 111–12; of person and act, 112–17
Conceptual apparatus, 546
Conceptual contents of cognition, 458
Conceptualization, 248, 520, 616
Conceptual totality, 39
Concreteness of person, 24–25, 175–77, 186, 537, 590

Concretization of person, somatic constitution and, 311–12
Concupiscence, 30, 346–47, 348, 363–64
Conduct, 366–67; and integration, 367; meaning of, 366
Conference on St. Thomas lecture, 457–66, 636–37
Conformism, 35, 404–7
Conformistic avoidance, 407
Conformity with self, 562–63
Conjugal morality, 533, 569
Conscience, 484–87; and attitudes, 404; and common good, 503; as condition of efficacy, 33–34; creative character of, 267–68; dependence on truth, 256–64, 485–86, 561–63, 604–5; duty and, 262–70, 485; emotional stirring and, 351; fulfillment conditioned by, 259; as intrapersonal source of duty, 265–66; normative character of, 12, 34, 631; as normative reality inside person, 258–59; objective character of, 34; and responsibility, 272; responsibility to self in, 275–76; self-fulfillment and, 255–59; threshold of, 605; and transcendence, 33–34, 256–59, 484–87, 561–63, 604–5; truthfulness of, 261–63
Conscious action: and *actus humanus*, 59–61, 72, 121–25; and consciousness of action, 62–65, 72, 125–26, 630–31; dynamism and, 90–92; emotion and, 83–84; experience and, 38–41; meaning of, 61; structure of, 125–32; understanding and conception of, 49–58
Conscious decision, 226
Conscious efficacy, 7, 13–15, 30–31
Consciousness, 6–13, 593–99; absolutization of, 63, 64, 476; access to spirituality through, 147; *actus humanus* and implication of, 126–28, 475–76; as aspect, 88–89, 113–14, 593–94, 624; in attributive sense, 68, 83; as basis of dynamism of person, 447–50; body and, 9–10, 82, 151–52, 192–93, 339; cognition and, 7–10, 64–65, 128–30, 594–95; and community, 490; continuity of, 127–28; of duty, 12; dynamism relationship to, 161–63; and efficacy, 11–15, 114, 590; emotionalization of, 10, 82–86, 150–57, 357–58; enrichment of person and act in context of, xxxii; experience of morality and, 4–5; explication of, 63, 594; and freedom, 11–15; functions of, 75–77, 128–30, 139–50; human act in reflection of, 10–11; introductory analysis of, 7–8; and lived-experience, 11, 139–50, 475–78, 624; in lived-experience of one's own body, 337–41; meaning of, 128–30; mind and, 260–61; mirroring (reflecting) by, 7–11, 64–65, 72–73, 76–81, 128–34, 139–41, 595–99; moral, 33–34; morality as content of, 6–7; moral value in reflection of, 7, 11–13, 598; in nounal sense, 68, 83, 126–27; objectivization of, 67–71, 72–73; permeation of sensation into, 342–43; philosophy of and character of study, 440–42; potentiality and, 135, 187–99; psychological, person and act in, 71–73; pure, 447, 470–71, 536–37, 556–57; reflexive feature of, 76–81, 142–44, 482, 596; self-determination shaped by, 214–16; self-determination unity with, 216; and self-knowledge, 9–10, 595; self-knowledge and, 9–10, 66–71, 72–73, 76, 132–39; stream of, 139n9, 198; and subject, 8–9; subjective, 6–7, 69, 139–50, 475–78; subjectivism and, 158–60; subjectivization of, 76–81; substantialization of, 9; superiority over sensations, 340–41; threshold of, 197; in totality of human dynamisms, 130–32; transillumination by, 130–34, 139–41; as understanding, 64–65; vitality characteristics of, 139; and voluntarium, 124–25
Consciousness of action, 62–65, 72, 125–26, 630–31
Consciousness-related way, 64–66, 130–31, 594, 627, 630, 635
Consent, consciousness and, 11
Constitution: concept of, 311–12; somatic, 311–12, 323–24, 332–33
Constitution on Divine Revelation. *See Dei Verbum*
Contingency, 416; possibility of fulfillment manifested as, 256, 483–84
Continuity of consciousness, 127–28
Conversion, 351
Cooperation (co-operation), 265, 377–80, 385–89, 396, 410, 489, 491–93, 606, 632. *See also* Participation
Cosmological understanding, 420, 429, 469, 538, 541–45

Courage, 363
Creativity: of conscience, 267–68; in emotivity–efficacy tension, 356; of intuition, 249–50; man's creation through act, 171–73, 462, 571–72; union of truth and freedom in, 277
Crowd psychology, 387

D'Abbiero, Marcella, 515n3
Dąbrowski, Kazimierz, 301n1
Danecki, Jan, 516n4
Danek, Jérome, 496n17
Decision, 460; as center of free will, 226–31; cognition and, 243–46; judgment and, 248–49; moment of, 229–30; motivation and, 231–33; originality in act of will and, 231–38; originality of, 240; presentation of object and, 236–37; relation to truth as interior principle of, 239–40, 603; as response to values, 237–38; simple volition vs. choice, 232–34; "truth about good" and, 238–42; will's readiness to go toward good and, 230–31
Deduction, 6, 573
Deed, 366
De Finance, Joseph, 121n1, 175n5
"Degrees of Being in Phenomenology and in Classical Metaphysics," 546–53, 619–20, 639
Dehumanization, 412–13, 489–90
Dei verbum, 420, 428–30, 585n13
Dependence: efficacious, 479–80; on "I," and freedom, 219–22; on truth, 240–41, 256–64, 485–86, 561–63, 604–5. *See also* Self-dependence
Descartes, René. *See* Cartesian philosophy
Desire, sensual, 347
Despair, 278–79, 351, 487
Despondency, 351, 487
Determination: auto-determination, 21–22, 31, 243, 256; of object, autonomous, 234–35; will as power of, 222–26, 460–64. *See also* Self-determination
Determinism, 21–22, 228–29; auto-determinism, 222–24, 235; materialistic, 235–36; motivation and, 236; originality of act of will vs., 235–37
Development, as growing into mystery of Christ, xv
Dialectic act of will, 18
Dialectic materialism, 469

Dialogue, 403
Dignity, ix, xviii, 499, 586
Direct experience, 101n1, 289, 623
Discourse, intuition and, 250
Disintegration, 298–302; affectivity and, 355–56; as deficiency of self-possession and self-governance, 300–301; degrees of intensity, 301–2; somatic, 324; understanding fundamental of integration through, 301–2; varied usage of term, 298–99
Disposition, 30, 31
Doubt, 384
Dramatis persona, 270
Drives: attraction and repulsion in, 363; communication to psyche, 325; complex character of, 324–25; conditioning on basis of body's reactivity, 326; consciousness and, 9–10; etymology of, 324–25; excitability as component of, 349–50; and instinctive action, 225–26; instinct *vs.*, 31–32, 324–25; and integration, 324–29; meaning of, 31–32; problem of, 31–32; proper interpretation of, 328–29; reproductive (sexual), 32, 325, 327–28, 632; for self-preservation, 32, 325, 326–27, 632; as source of action, 32; subconscious and, 195
Dualism (duality): ethical, 242n12; experience of man, 113, 440–42, 458–59; freedom–nature paradox, 186n7; function of consciousness, 80, 147; interpretation of man, 285; language and aspects, 449; meaning of nature, 178; self-determination, 33, 209n1; self-governance and self-possession, 296; self-possession and self-governance, 296; subject, 477–78; subject–object, 76
Duméry, Henry, 555n4
Dunayevskaya, Raya, 515n3
Duty, 262–70, 605–6; conscience as intrapersonal source of, 265–66, 485; consciousness of, 12; drama of, and transcendence, 270; as expression of call to fulfillment, 265–71; linking of truthfulness with, 263–64; lived-experience of, 266; personalistic synonym of, 268; and *praxis*, 571, 579–80; response to values through, 272–73; responsibility linked to efficacy through, 271; transition of value into, 268–70

Duty ethics, 12
Duty-responsibility, 272-73
Duty stage of norm, 12
Dybowski, Mieczysław, 18, 229n8, 460
Dynamic act of will, 18
Dynamic coherence of person: nature as basis of, 182-87; personal existence and, 185-86
Dynamic readiness, 180
Dynamism, 90-92, 140, 549-51, 593, 599-600; *actus* (*actus humanus*), 546-47; *agere-pati*, 163-64, 167, 173, 246-47, 540, 599; analysis of efficacy in relation to, 160, 161-204; body, 162, 315-19; cognitive, 129-30; consciousness-efficacy, 114; consciousness in totality of, 130-32; editorial notes on, 630; emotive, 337-38; etymology and meaning of, 188; freedom and, 202-4; fundamental visualizations and concepts concerning, 161-64; humanity as basis of, 183-84; of nature, and instinctive action, 225-26; nature's orientation toward, 179; of person, consciousness as basis of, 447-50; of person, transcendence as, 221; *potentia-actus*, 59-60, 121-22, 165-67; potentiality and source of, 188-89; psycho-somatic, 303-10, 330-33, 550, 607, 609, 632; relation to consciousness, 161-63; self-determination and, 209-10, 218-22, 223-24; subconscious and, 193-99; variants and layers of, 190-91; vegetative, 162; *volitum-praecognitum*, 238-39, 242-43, 248-49; will, 210-17, 601

Easton, Lloyd D., 515n3
Efficacious dependence, 479-80
Efficacy: act of will and, 17-21; analysis of, 160, 161-204; of body, 320; and causality of nature, 182-83; conduct and, 366; conscience as condition of, 33-34; conscious, 7, 13-15, 30-31; conscious action and, 126; consciousness and, 11-15, 114, 590; emotivity and, 354-59, 608; experience of man and, 479; freedom and, 203-4, 219; and integration, 297, 330; morality and, 21-22; responsibility linked to, through duty, 271; self-determination and, 33, 214, 219, 222, 459-60, 478-83; specificity of, 160, 168-73; subjectivity and, 157, 173-78, 478-83; and thinking, 246-47; translation from Polish, 631

Efficiency, of self-knowledge, 84-85, 154
Efficient cause: of act, person as, 22-24; meaning of, 22-23
Ego, 128n5, 137, 198n10, 275n7, 290n10, 314n4, 368n8
Egotism, self-knowledge vs., 137-38
Ehrlich, Emilia, xxvi
Eidetic method, 106n4, 275n7
Eidos, 106n4
Elation, 348-49
Emotion, 27-31, 627; act and, 362-65; appetitive character of, 28-29; cognition and, 27-29, 590-91; cognitive contact in, 344; and conscious action, 83-84; consciousness and, 9-10; consciousness-related governance over, 153; etymology of, 333-35; and participation, 522-25; participation in act, 27-31; spiritual struggle with, 29-30; and vividness of lived-experience, 359
Emotionalists, 344
Emotionalization: of consciousness, 10, 82-86, 150-57, 357-58; essence of, 152-54; of lived-experience, 86, 155-57, 598-99; threshold for, 155
Emotional stirring, 232, 350-54; as core of affectivity, 351-52; excitement vs., 350-51, 353; and lived-experience of value, 360
Emotive dynamism, 337-38
Emotive excitability, 346-50
Emotivism, 264n5
Emotivity, 27-28, 333-65; affections differentiated by, 354-55; analysis of influence, 152-54; as concentrator of lived-experiences, 337-38; consciousness-related element and, 150-52; drives and, 325; and efficacy, 354-59, 608; etymology of, 333-35; and lived-experience of value, 358-62; and psyche, 152, 333-37, 550; and reactivity, 335-36, 607; as sensibility to values, 336-37; as source of limitation to conscious efficacy, 358-59; spontaneity and, 354-55, 360-62
Empiricism, experience of man in, 100-101
End, 555, 559-66, 620-21. See also Teleology
Enjoyment, of lived-experience, 144n10
Envy, 524-25
Epiphenomenon, 552-53
Epistemology, 536-37, 570, 578
Epoché, 106n4, 476, 537, 574

Error, 49, 100, 242, 260, 271
Esse, 25, 175; causal connection and, 169–70; coherence with *operari*, 185–86, 571, 579; consciousness and, 476; nature and, 178–80; *operari sequitur esse*, 175, 183–84, 253, 381, 472–75, 547, 569–71, 625; reciprocal relations with *operari* and *fieri*, 199–200; subjectivity and, 482; and *suppositum*, 176–77; transcendence and, 484. See also Existence
Esse contingens, 416
Essence: intuition of, 107n5, 623; nature and, 179, 183–84
Etcheverry, Auguste, 515n3
"Ethical" anthropology, 3
Ethical norms, truthfulness of, 265–68
Ethical order, 383, 388–89, 392, 523–24, 629
Ethical value: actualization and, 382; personalistic value preceding and conditioning, 381–82. See also Value(s)
Ethics: connection with anthropology, 41–43, 58, 75, 104, 106–7; duty, 12; fulfillment and, 255; material, of value, 556–57n8; moral reality in, 254; norms of, 259; person and act in philosophy of, 3–6; placement outside parentheses, 42, 106–7, 364; *praxis* and *theoria* in, 567–74, 577; social, 393; value, 12
Ethos: creation through act, 171–73; *praxis* and, 555–56, 580–82, 584–85; primacy of, 584; teleology and, 555
Eucharist, xiii
Eudaimonism, 280n8, 620
Evaluational nihilism, 264n5
Evidentness, 102–3, 170, 266, 463, 480, 551, 600
Evil: anthropology–ethics relationship and, 41–42; consciousness of act and, 147–49; degradation of person, xviii; dynamism and, 91–92; and emotional stirring, 351; *fieri* and, 202; freedom and, 202–3; lived-experience and, 147–49; *praxis* and, 580–82; as property of human acts, 104; repulsion from, 362–64; responsibility for, 273; revelation by moral value of act, 105; self-determination and, 273, 462–63
Evolution, 317, 505
Excitability, 346–50; as capacity for excitement, 349; as component of drives, 349–50; etymology of, 349
Excitement: elation vs., 348–49; emotional stirring vs., 350–51, 353; excitability as capacity for, 349; intentionality of, 348; as separate emotive core, 347–48
Existence: action (*operari*) and, 175, 183–84; auto-teleology and, 565–66; Berkeley on ways of, 159n15; causal connection between person and act in, 169–70; contemporary dispute about, 468–69; creation through act, 171–73; drive for self-preservation, 32, 325, 326–27; as first and fundamental act, 175; nature and, 178–80; personal, and dynamic coherence of person, 185–86; person as *suppositum* in, 175–77; *potentia–actus* and, 166–67; subjectivity and, 470–71; "together with others," 377–80
Existentialism: act ("I perform an act") in, 251–54; concept of *actus*, 166–67; morality as existential reality in, 253–54; *operari sequitur esse*, 175, 183–84, 253, 381, 472–75; status of man, 416; "to have more–to be more," 583
Existential Thomism, 133, 449, 547
Experience: *actio* vs. *passio* in, 81, 148; act of will and, 17–19; as basis of knowledge, 38–41, 96–97; conscious relation to, 51–52; datum of, person–act relation and, 74–75; dynamism and, 90–92; efficacy and freedom in, 13–14; empirical view of, 100–101; experience of man vs., 97; exterior, 13, 24–25, 48, 57, 99–100, 479–80; Grygiel on types of, 441; "I" and "man" in field of, 97–98; in-depth reading of, 5–6; interior, 13, 24–25, 47–48, 57, 99–100, 479–80; phenomenalistic view of, 39, 45, 95–96, 100–102, 623; philosophical anthropology and, 436–40; problem of, 38–41, 101n1; subject–object relation of, 44; understanding and conception of, 49–58. See also Lived-experience
Experience of man, 95–107, 470–72, 548; act as particular moment of vision of person in, 102–4; cognition of person on basis of, 100–107; cognitive contact in, 44–45, 50, 95–96, 102; coherence with body, 331–32; disproportional understanding of, 57–58; duality of, 113, 440–42, 458–59; and efficacy, 479; experience vs., 97; fact of "man acts" and, 101–2; fundamental sameness of, 46–47, 54–55, 97, 107–8;

Experience of man, (*cont.*)
incommensurability of, 46–48, 57, 97–98, 112–13, 162, 441; integral, integral dynamism given in, 161–62; meaning of, 95–96; reduction as exploration of, 108–9; and self-determination, 458–59; simplicity and complexity of, 44–49, 100, 107–8; stabilization of, 47, 98–99, 107; totality of (interior and exterior aspects), 99–100; understanding of, 95–96, 98–99, 107–12, 459; union with experience of morality, 106–7

Experience of morality, 459, 589; boundary of, 589; reflections on person and act from, 3–6; union with experience of man, 106–7

Experiential expression of spirituality, 146–47

Exterior experience, 13, 24–25, 48, 57, 99–100, 479–80

Exteriorization, 216–17, 313, 322

Ey, Henri, 139–40n9, 448

Fabro, Cornelio, 514n1
Fact, 627, 630
Factuality, 571, 579–80
Faculty, 188. *See also* Potentiality
Faith: Augustine's account of, xvii; concept of person (image of man) in, xviii; doctrine of, disputes concerning, 428; heritage of, Wojtyła on, ix; Paul, St., on, xiv–xv; *praxis-christianum* and, 584–85; *praxis-theoria* and, 577, 583–84
Falsehood, 604, 605
Familial community, 394–95
Family: common good of, 501, 503; membership in, 399, 408; pedagogy and, 453–54; reproductive drive as basis of, 327, 632; "we" and, 505–6, 527
Father, xii–xv; Jesus praying to, xix, 503n20; triune and mystery of person, xviii–xix
Fault, 242, 351, 382
Fear, 363
Feeling, 334; direction to values, 344–45
Felicific calculus, 280n8
Felicity, 276–81, 606; boundary line between pleasure and, 279–80; correspondence of personal structure to, 278–79; eternal, relationship with God and, 277–78; happiness vs., 276, 631; intra-personal profile of, 278; self-fulfillment as, 276;

translation from Polish, 631; truthfulness and freedom as source of, 276–77
Fetscher, Iring, 515n3
Fides et ratio, xviii
Fieri, 16, 166, 199–202; causal connection and, 169–70; lived experience of efficacy and, 169; meaning of, 199, 629; morality (good and evil acts), 202; moral value, 4, 6–7, 9, 11–13, 24, 105, 629; *potentia–actus* and, 166; reciprocal relations with *esse* and *operari*, 199–200; self-determination and, 32, 207–8, 462–63; and spheres of potentiality, 200–201
Finality, 218–19, 319, 326–28, 555. *See also* Teleology
Formalism, 20, 116n8, 148n13, 244n13, 344n3, 360n6
Forycki, Roman, 445–46, 468n2, 554n2, 635
Freedom: as auto-determination, 256; as basis of transcendence, 217–22, 256–57; body and, 315; conscience and, 267–68, 485; consciousness and, 11–15; and decision, 226–31; dependence on truth, 258; determinism vs., 235–37; developed meaning of, 222–23, 226, 241, 252; discovery and interpretation of, 21–22; and efficacy, 203–4, 219; independence from objects in, 234–35; instinct of, 225; Kant on a priori of, 217n3; lack, as necessity, 219; and morality, 13, 202–3; and nature, paradox of, 186n7; and objectivization of "I," 222; person subjected to, xvii; and potentiality, 202–4; as real attribute of person, 217–18; religious, Wojtyła's elucidation on, xx; self-dependence and, 219–22; self-determination and, 33, 461, 518–19; as source of felicity, 276–77; spontaneity of, 226–27; union with truth, 277; will as power of, 224

Free will: as basis of transcendence, 217–22; decision as center of, 226–31; expression in autonomous determination of object, 234–35; necessity of choice and, 558

Freud, Sigmund, 195, 197–98n10, 454–55, 624
Friendship, 496, 499, 524, 617, 618
Fritzhand, Marek, 516n4, 518n8
Fromm, Erich, 515n3
Fulfillment: act ("to perform an act") and, 252–54, 483, 631; acting together with others and, 383–84; in acts, 269–70;

alienation and deprivation of, 528–29; and auto-teleology, 483–84, 487, 492, 562–66; community and, 488, 492, 498–99, 502–3, 504, 511; conscience and, 259, 484–87; duty as expression of call to, 265–71; editorial notes on, 631; ethical dimension of, 255; felicity and, 276–81; Forycki on, 445–46; ontology of, 256, 259, 262; participation and, 528; relinquishing, conformism and, 405; self-determination and, 251–91, 603–6; spirituality and, 284–86; and transcendence, 483–87; truthfulness of conscience as basis of, 261–63

Gałkowski, Jerzy W., xxviin6, 450, 468n2, 555n2, 634, 636–40
Garaudy, Roger, 515n3
Gaudium et spes, 619, 629; citation by John Paul II, xixn3; on *communio personarum*, 499n19; on concept of "we," 503n20; on "gift of self," 565; participation of Wojtyła in, xxv; on *praxis*, 583, 585; on reality and concept of person, 420, 427–28, 465, 469; on transcendence of Church, 93, 117n9, 529
Geiger, Louis-Bertrand, 514n1
Generalizations: formation of "man acts" in, 161; in self-knowledge, 70–71, 138–39
"Gift of self," xix, 465–66, 565
Gnoseological approach, 476, 577
Gogacz, Mieczysław, 437–38, 443–44, 448–49, 517n8, 554n2, 634, 635, 636
Gołaszewska, Maria, 557n8
Good: absoluteness of, 562; act of will and, 20–21, 237–38; anthropology-ethics relationship and, 41–42; attraction to, 362–64; auto-determination and, 22; cognition of, 244–45; consciousness of act and, 147–49; dynamism and, 91–92; and emotional stirring, 351; *fieri* and, 202; freedom and, 22, 202–3; lived-experience and, 147–49; norm and, 12; *praxis* and, 580–82; as property of human acts, 104; responsibility for, 273; revelation by moral value of act, 105; self-determination and, 273, 462–63; as transcendental, 33, 257–58, 603–4; truth about, and lived-experience of value, 244–45; truth about, as basis for moral qualification of acts, 241–42; truth about, as basis of decision and transcendence, 238–42, 561; truth about,

manifestation in conscience, 256–59, 485–86, 561–63, 604–5; will's readiness to go toward, 230–31
Good, common. *See* Common good
Gospel: Christ as origin of Church in, xii–xv; commandment to love in, 411–14, 522, 531, 611, 619; on experiencing other as oneself, 498; "neighbor" in, 617, 633
Gradi dell'essere (degrees of being), 546–53, 619–20
Granat, Wincenty, 515n2, 517n8
Greef, Jan De, 496n17
Grygiel, Stanisław, 431, 441, 447–48, 516n4, 635
Grzybek, Stanisław, 425

Habit, 322–23, 487; in act and emotion, 362–65; in act and motion, 322–23; moral, 364–65, 462n4
Habitus, 322
Habitus innati, 31
Happenings (actuations), 459–60, 473–74, 540, 548; action differentiated from, 11, 16–17, 81, 128, 148, 162–64, 167–73, 540, 548; action synthesized with, 177–78; actuation as, 171; affections as, 353, 356–57; *agere-pati* and, 163–64, 167; ambiguity in concept of *actus* and, 167; and complexity of man-person, 286; drive and, 32; emotional stirring as, 350–51; emotion (sensation) and, 82–86, 151–56; excitement as, 347–48; felicity–pleasure boundary and, 279–81, 606; foundations in potentiality, 189–90; instinct and, 218–19; intuition and, 250; lived-experience of efficacy and, 168–73; man as subject in, 173–74; psychosomaticity and, 305–6; thinking and, 247–48; volition and, 212–13
Happiness: act of will and, 22; auto-teleology and, 566; felicity vs., 276, 631; fulfillment and, 487; lived-experience of, 22; proceeding from relations to other persons, 277–78; translation from Polish, 631
Hare, Richard Mervyn, 264n5
Hartmann, Nicolai, 244n13, 339n2, 557n8
Hate, 352, 354, 524–25
Hedonism, 280–81
Heidegger, Martin, xxix, 172n4, 455, 496n17
Hermeneutics, 442–44

Hierarchy: of potentiality, 198; of sensation, 82–83, 152; of soul, 290n10; of values, 269, 381, 384, 411, 559–60; world of, will and, 231
Hildebrand, Dietrich von, 198n11, 244n13, 557n8
Historical approach, 445–47
Hobbes, Thomas, 556n6
Holy Spirit, xiv, xviii–xix
Homo, 63, 538–39, 544, 593–94
Homo aeconomicus, 3
Homogeneity: of community, 506; of personal subject, 506; of will, 234
Horizontal transcendence, 221, 227, 281, 461–62
Human family, 506
Humanity: as basis of dynamism, 183–84; defending, Wojtyła on, ix; estrangement from, 412–13; meaning of, 488; nature and, 183; participation in, as core of participation, 410–11, 488–89; participation in, meaning of, 518–19, 615–17; subordination to, neighbor concept and, 409–10
Human nature. *See* Nature
Humanum, 463, 543–44, 572–73, 581–85; *agere humanum*, 558; and *christianum*, 583–85; *compositum humanum*, 289, 538, 544; identifying, *praxis* and, 581–83; inviolability of, 572; *studium humanum*, 430; *suppositum humanum*, 199–200, 474–78, 482–86, 493
Hume, David, 13, 334n1
Husserl, Edmund: on act and self, 275n7; on consciousness, 447, 476–77, 537; *epoché* terminology of, 106n4, 476, 537, 574; on experience, 101n1, 623; Ingarden and, 117n8, 536n1; on intentionality, 129n6; on intersubjectivity, 377–78n1; phenomenological method of, 106n4; Scheler and, 556–57n8
Hylomorphism, 310–11, 371, 552

"I," 470–87; act of will and, 14, 17–21; affections and, 356–57; as agent, 168–73, 182; as concrete object, 134–35; consciousness and, 8, 11, 80; constitution as subject through lived-experience, 145–46; dependence on, and freedom, 219–22; dynamism and, 90–92; efficacy and, 13–15, 478–83; emotionalization and, 85–86; experience of man and, 44–49, 57–58, 95–107, 470–72; freedom and, 21–22; integral vision of, 71; integration of nature in, 181–87; irreducibility of, 481, 541–43; man as subject, 173–74; ontology of, 145, 596–97; *operari sequitur esse* and, 472–75; reflexivity and, 76–81, 142–44; relationship with "thou," 492–99, 534; self-determination and relation to, 210–12, 214–17; self-knowledge and, 66–71, 132–39; specific governance of, 21; subjectivity and, 89; *suppositum* and, 76–79; synthesis as object and subject, 216; understanding "man" from, 149–50
Idealism, 536–37; antinomy with realism, 536; consciousness-absolute and, 131; deviation from *fieri* of morality, 13; experience and, 9, 57–58, 220; freedom and, 217; objectivity of consciousness vs., 216; overcoming, 447; and participation, 514; pessimism and, 356; Plato and, 514; reflexivity and, 77; subjectivism and, 88–89, 158–59
Ideality, 12–13
Idealness, 13
Ideation, 107n5, 623
Identity, problem of, 128n5
Identity of consciousness, 127–28
"I feel like," 212–13
Immanence: experience and understanding, 50–51; of person in act, 23–32, 572; *praxis* and, 580–82; of spirit, 284–85
Imperative, 217n3, 258n2, 355, 446, 524, 563
Impression, 13, 28, 31, 45, 247, 343
Incommensurability, in experience of man, 46–48, 57, 97–98, 112–13, 162, 441
Incommunicabilis, 33, 209, 463–64
Independence, 220; in sphere of intentional objects of volition, 222–23; of will, dependence in truth and, 240–41
Indetermination, 242–43
Indeterminism, 222–23, 235
Indifference, 231
Individua, 98
Individual, 220–22
Individualism, 389–92; a-personalistic (anti-personalistic) thinking at root of, 392; denial of participation in, 390–91, 528; principle of, 390
"Individualism *à rebours*," 391
Individuality, 539

Individualization, 176
Individua substantia, 127, 132, 147, 175–76, 185, 261, 437, 461, 539
Individuum in actu, 221–22
Induction, 53–56, 107–8, 442; inter-subjectivization in, 109–10; phenomenologist view of, 107n5
Ingarden, Roman, xxxii, 116–17, 434, 458, 479n8, 517n8, 557n8, 623; on act and self, 275n7; on consciousness, 128n5, 139n9, 159n15; on creativity (formation of act), 172n4; on existence, 159n15; on experience, 101n1, 103–4n2; Husserl and, 101n1, 117n8, 536n11; on intentional vs. intentive, 228n7; on linking man to time, 198n11; on a priori cognition, 107n5; on responsibility, 282–83n9; on self-knowledge, 133n7, 137–38n8; on soul, 139n9, 289–90n10, 314n4, 368n8
In-selfness, 478, 482
Insight, 567; into person, 102–4; phenomenology and, 283; into spirituality, 147, 284
Instinct: consciousness and, 9–10; drives vs., 31–32, 324–25; dynamism of, vs. self-determination, 218–22; meaning of, 218; reactions/dynamism of body, 318–26; as source of action, 32; subconscious and, 195, 198n10
Instinctive action, 225–26
Instinct of freedom, 225
Integrality, 124, 309–10, 313, 316, 320–21, 331–33
Integration, 114–15, 549–51; as aspect complementary to transcendence, 295–96, 330, 550; concept of, 296–98; conduct and behavior in, 367; consciousness-related governance over emotion and, 153; discovery of man's complexity through, 367–69; drives and, 324–29; editorial notes on, 632; emotivity and, 333–65; etymology of, 297–98; fundamental meaning of, 300, 301–2, 330; fundamentals concerning, 295–98; habit and, 322–23, 362–65; manifestation through disintegration, 298–302; of nature in person, 181–87; and psyche, 330–73, 607–9; psycho-somatic unity and, 303–10; as realization and manifestation of wholeness (unity), 297–98; self-possession/self-governance and, 296, 298, 330; and somaticity, 295–329, 606–7; soul as principle of, 372–73; soul-body relation and, 369–70; of truthfulness, 344
Intellect: and conceptualization, 248; and consciousness, 64–65, 80; and emotionalization, 82–86, 154; and experience of man, 47–49, 98–100; intuitive function of, 5–6, 9; and language, 37; and mind, 260; reasoning function of, 6; and self-knowledge, 66–67, 82, 132–34; and spirituality, 288; and understanding, 50–56, 66, 132–33
Intellectualistic approach, 20–21, 34, 262
Intellectualistic determinism, 21
Intellectual reduction, 88, 158
Intentionality, 16; act ("to perform an act") and, 252–54, 483; of cognition, 64, 129, 548, 594; of excitement, 348; of psycho-emotive sphere, 31; of reflectivity, 78; of self-knowledge, 71, 135, 137; and transcendence, 548; of volition, 16, 19, 20, 211–12, 222–23, 228–29, 245, 462, 548, 558–59; and will, 228–29, 461–63
Inter-human relations, 385, 410, 415–16, 489–92, 612, 617. *See also* Community; Participation; Relationships
Interior experience, 13, 24–25, 47–48, 57, 99–100, 479–80
Interiority, 99–100, 113
Interiorization, 131, 135, 162, 216–17, 260, 291, 341, 358, 595
Inter-personal relationships: "I–other," 517–26, 534, 612–17; "I–thou," 492–99, 534
Interpretation, 6; *actus humanus* and, 59; conception and, 111–12; direction of, 107–12; lived-experience as element of, 540–41; *praxis* and, 109–10; reduction and, 6, 53, 56, 58, 109–12; subjectivistic deviation and, 12; teleology and, 555–56
Intersubjectivity, 91, 161, 264, 377–78n1, 386n2, 413n4, 459, 516
Inter-subjectivization, 109–10, 442
Intransitiveness, 252–55, 274–77, 478–80, 571–72, 580–81
Introspection, 141, 212, 590
Intuition, 5–6, 547; creative meaning of, 249–50; and discourse, 250
Intuition of essence, 107n5, 623
Intuitiveness, 343
Involuntary, 186n7, 242n12
Inwardness, 308–9, 478, 482

"I-other," 517–26, 534, 612–17; actualization in, 520–24, 615–17; emotions (affections) and, 522–24; meaning of "other," 519–20, 612–13
"I perform an act," 251–54
Irascibility, 30, 346–47, 348, 363–64
Irrationality, affections and, 353
Irreducibility in man: consciousness and, 10–11, 481; efficacy and, 174; emotivity and, 29; experience of man and, 46, 49, 97, 100; historical background of problem, 537–39; of "I," 481, 541–45; lived-experience and, 540–41; necessity of dwelling on, 541; reducibility vs., 537–39; self-preservation and, 327; subjectivity and, 174, 481, 536–45, 619
Irreducibility of felicity, 281
Irreducibility of spirituality, 284–86, 289
Isolation, individualism and, 390–91
"I–thou," 492–99, 534; common good and, 501; constitution of "I" from "thou," 493–97; as fundamental dimension of community, 497–98; in marriage, 501; participation and, 507–10; plurality of, 494; reciprocal character of relationship, 496–99; revertibility of relationship, 494–95; "thou" as "I" different from me, 494; "we" vs., 500–501
"I will," 460; "I feel like" vs., 212–13; moment of decision and, 229–30; self-determination and, 208–15; self-possession and, 208; subjective shaping by consciousness, 214–15; volition vs., 212

James, Henry, 139n9
Jaroszewski, Tadeusz M., 516n4, 518n8, 576n2
Jaworski, Marian, xxvi, 101n1, 421; on philosophical character of study, 436, 438, 440, 442–43; on relation to "thou," 493n15
Jesus: and concept of "we," 503n20; and "gift of self," xix; growing into mystery of, xv; origin of Church in, xii–xvii; *praxis–christianum* and, 584–85; triune and mystery of person, xviii–xix
John Paul II, St. *See* Wojtyła, Karol; *specific topics and works*
Joy, 279, 352, 354, 363
Judgment, 8, 20, 21, 28, 246–50, 262; and decision, 248–49; ethical, 264n5; mental activity of, 248; moment of, 248; and norm, 33–34; true or false, 266. *See also* Conscience
Jung, Carl, 195, 454–55
Justification, 351, 356
Juxtaposition, 33, 238n10, 269, 411

Kalinowski, Jerzy, 101n1, 421, 428, 468n2, 554n2; on philosophical character of study, 436–38; on practical cognition, 110n6; on problem of nature in relation to, 450; on relation of person to nature, 186n7, 449–50; on theory of person, 442
Kalwa, Piotr, 75
Kamiński, Stanisław, 101n1, 419, 421, 423, 468n2; on philosophical character of study, 437–42
Kant, Immanuel, xxxiii, 116; on affectivity and disintegration, 355–56; on categorical imperative, 217n3, 258n2, 355, 446, 524, 563; on conscience, 267; criticism of teleology, 556; on freedom, 217n3; on freedom of will, 13; on intellectualistic determinism, 21; on lived-experience of value, 361–62; on personalism, 116n8; on *praxis* and *theoria*, 575–76; reaction to Bentham's utilitarianism, 280n8; Scheler and, 258n2, 632; on transcendence, 221n4; on *volitum* and *praecognitum*, 238
Kłósak, Kazimierz, 101n1, 419, 423–24, 431, 433; on philosophical character of study, 436–37
Knowledge: cognitive characters of, 66; consciousness and, 8, 9–10; experience and, 38–41, 96–97; experience of man and, 45–46; Paul, St., on, xiv–xv. *See also* Self-knowledge
Köchler, Hans, 496n17
Kołakowski, Leszek, 516n4
Kotarbiński, Tadeusz, 555
Krąpiec, Albert, 419, 421, 431, 468n2, 518n8, 540–41n9, 547, 554n2; on "I," 470–71n4; on *Person and Act* as philosophical anthropology, 445; on self-knowledge, 133n7; on theory of person, 442
Kretschmer, Ernst, 30, 312n3
Kroński, Tadeusz, 556n5
Kubiś, Adam, 518n8
Kuc, Leszek, 431, 451–52, 468n2, 489n13, 491n14, 527n15, 555n2, 636
Kuczyński, Januscz, 516n4

Kuderowicz, Zbigniew, 516n4
Kukołowicz, Teresa, 453–54, 468n2, 555n2, 636

Lange, Oskar, 555n4
Law of nature, 605
Leibniz, Gottfried Wilhelm, 161n1
Letter to Families, xviii
Lévinas, Emmanuel, 144n9, 198n11, 496n17, 541n10
Libertas contradictionis, 22
Libertas contrarictatis, 22
Libertas specificationis, 22
Liberum arbitrium, 212n2, 223n5, 476
Lingis, Alphonso, 144n10, 496n17
Lived-experience, 55–56, 459, 532–33; "The Act and Ethical Lived-Experience," 420–21; "The Act and Lived-Experience," 429; actualization of, 146; body and, 151–52; of body (one's own), 337–41; and community, 490; conscience and, 34; consciousness and, 11, 139–50, 475–78, 624; constitution of "I" as subject through, 145–46; of duty, 266; dwelling on, 543–45; dynamism and, 90–92; as element of interpretation, 540–41; emotionalization of, 86, 155–57, 598–99; emotive dynamism as concentrator of, 337–38; enjoyment of, 144n10; experience of man and, 97–98; expression of spirituality through, 146–47; fact of "man acts" in, 161–62; of happiness, 22; and irreducibility in man, 540–45; meaning of, 14; mirroring (reflection) and, 139–41, 597; and moral values, 147–49; *praxis* and, 109–10; reflexive feature of consciousness and, 77–81, 142–44; relation of act to, 24; of soul, 289–91, 370; subjectivism and, 88, 158–60; subjectivity of, 87–89, 139–50, 157–58, 161; of truthfulness, 266; of value, cognitive, 242–46; of value, moment of truth about good and, 244–45; vividness of, emotion and, 359. *See also specific lived-experiences*
Lived-experience of efficacy, 168–73; causal connection between person and act revealed in, 169–70; transcendence manifested in, 170–71
Love, 352, 354, 363; *Catechesis on Human Love*, xviii, xx; commandment to love, 411–14, 522, 531, 611, 619; human, Wojtyła's elucidation on, xx; as "I-thou" relationship, 496, 499; mystery of triune and, xviii–xix
Love and Responsibility (*Miłość i odpowiedzialność*), 328, 419, 427, 533, 569, 593
Lubac, Henri de, xviii, 328n5
The Lublin Lectures, xx, xxii, 423–33; afterword to discussion, 433–56, 610; concluding synthesis of, 435; decision to publish, 433–34; editorial notes on, 633–36; first circle presentations (philosophical character of study), 435–44; introductory statement during, 419–22; second circle presentations (concept and reality of person), 435, 444–52; service and contributions of, 455–56; third circle presentations (concept of person as basis for manifold practice), 435, 452–55
Luijpen, Wilhemus Antonius, 314n4

Maarbach, E., 496n17
Majchrzyk, Zbigniew, 510n22, 531n17
"Man-maker," 173, 600
"Man-material," 173, 600
Marcel, Gabriel, 583
Marriage: common good in, 503; "I-thou" and "we" in, 501, 505–6; reproductive (sexual) drive as basis of, 327–28, 632
Marx, Karl, 515, 530n17, 617–19
Marxism, 458, 469, 510, 512, 515, 529–31, 538n3, 576, 611, 617–19; alienation in, 510, 512, 515–16, 529–31, 617–19; interest in *Person and Act*, 458; political reality in Poland, 469; *praxis* in, 576
Masterson, Patrick, 515n3
Material ethics of value, 556–57n8
Materialism, 469, 538n3, 576
Materialistic determinism, 21, 235–36
Materiality, denial of, 284
Materia prima, 371, 464
Mental cognition, 8, 17, 28–29, 40, 346, 361
Merleau-Ponty, Maurice, 623
Metaphysical terrain, 539
Metaphysics: *actus humanus* in, 60, 63, 127; contingency in, 256; degrees of being in, 546–53; integration of nature in, 181–87; linkage with phenomenological method, 6; *potentia–actus* in, 165–67; relation with anthropology, 546; transcendence in, 484; transcendentals in, 257–58; trans-phenomenal in, 472;

Metaphysics: (*cont.*)
Wojtyła's references to, xxxii, xxxiii. *See also* Suppositum; *specific topics*
Method, 38, 75, 436–42. *See also specific methods*
Meyer, Gerbert, 580n6
Michotte, Albert, 18, 229n8, 460
Mill, John Stuart, 53, 107
Mind, 260–64, 604; conscience linked with, 262–63; and definition of person, 268; effort of conscience as task of, 261–63; engagement in experience, 39; as man's property, 260; wonder as function of, 116
Mirroring: by consciousness, 7–11, 64–65, 72–73, 76–81, 128–34, 139–41, 595–99; consciousness of act as, 65; dynamism in, 162; emotionalization and, 153–57
Mobility. *See* Motion
Montsopoulos, E. A., 496n17
Moral consciousness, 33–34
Moral habits, 364–65, 462n4
Morality: anthropology of, 4–5; conjugal (sexual), 533, 569; consciousness and, 4–7, 11–13, 598; dynamism and, 91–92; efficacy and, 13, 21–22; emotivity-efficacy tension and, 356; essence of, Kant on, 556; experience of, 459, 589; experience of, boundary of, 589; experience of, reflections on person and act from, 3–6; experience of, union with experience of man, 106–7; experience of man and, 44; *fieri* of, 202; freedom and, 13, 202–3; human, personal *praxis* as basis of, 453; lived-experience of, 91–92; moment of truth about good and, 241–42; objectivization in, 253; personalistic sense of, 533, 543; practice and theory in, 567–74; as property of human acts, 104; psychology of, 4; as reality, axiological, 254–56; as reality, existential and personal, 253–54; as reality grounded in person and act, 4; sociology of, 4; subjectivity and, 468–69; world of, 36–37
Moral order, 36–37
Moral personhood, 12, 34, 300
Moral self-knowledge, 70, 137
Moral subjectivity, 485
Moral value: of act, person revealed through, 105; conscience and, 485–87; consciousness and, 4–7, 11–13, 598; consciousness of act and, 147–49; *fieri* of, 4, 6–7, 9, 11–13, 24, 105, 629; lived-experience and, 147–49; personalistic value preceding and conditioning, 381–82; person and act in, 4; *praxis* and, 580–82; self-determination and, 33, 273, 462–63; subjectivism and, 158–60. *See also* Value(s)
Motion (mobility), 305, 312, 316, 319–24; emotivity and, 334–35; habit and, 322–23; and somatic constitution, 323–24; synthesis with act, 321–23
Motivation, 231–33; and act of will, 19–21; and determinism, 236; emotional stirring vs., 232; meaning and composition of, 231–32; simple volition vs. choice, 232–33; will led out of initial indetermination by, 242–43
Motor stimulus, 338
Movement: in action, 123n2, 305; of sensation or emotion, 27, 156, 305, 334–35; of will, 212n2, 232, 237. *See also* Motion (mobility)
Mulieres dignitatem, xviii
Muralt, A. de, 496n17

Natura rationalis, 268, 285
Nature, 178–87; as basis for dynamic coherence of person, 182–87; body as part of, 317–19; drives and, 325; duality of, 178; dynamism of, and instinctive action, 225–26; dynamism of, vs. self-determination, 218–22; efficacy of person and causality of, 182–83; etymology of, 178–79; existence as person, 186–87; integration in person, 181–87; law of, 605; opposition to, 180–81; orientation toward dynamism, 179; person differentiated from, 187–88; position of, 384; in relation to person, problem of, 449–50; subject of action defined by, 178–79; theology of, 420, 429; way of action defined by, 179–80; world of, 181
Necessity, 219, 558
Nédoncelle, M., 496n17
Negative verifications of participation, 524–25
Neighbor, 407–11, 489, 498, 610–11, 615; alienation and, 512; commandment to love and, 411–14; community membership and, 407–8; Gospel usage of term, 617, 633; "I–other" relationship and, 519–21, 617–18; subordination of people to humanity manifested in, 409–10
Neighbor system of reference, 35

Nicomachean Ethics, 41, 104
Nietzche, Friedrich, 556–57n8
Nihilism, 264n5
Non-authentic attitudes, 404–7
Noncontradiction, 285
Non-fulfillment, 486–87
Norm(s): act of will and, 21; conscience and, 12, 34, 258–59, 631; consciousness and, 12–13; duty and, 262–71; of ethics, 259; moral habits and, 364; objectivization in, 266; realization of conscious efficacy in relation to, 7; right or wrong, 266; stages of, 12; truth and, 260–64; truthfulness and rightness of, 265–68
Normative power of truth, 260–64
Normative profile of ethics, 254
Normative reality, conscience as, 258–59
Normative sense of community, 491
Norming, 632
Nuttin, Joseph, 138n8, 152n14

Obedience of body, 315
Obiectum formale, 32, 248
Obiectum materiale, 32, 248
Object: autonomous determination of, 234–35; experientially given person–act relation as, 74–75; "I" as, 134–35, 210–12, 214–17; man as, 538–39; presentation of, and determinism, 236–37; synthesis with subject, 216
Objective totalism, 389–90. *See also* Totalism
Objectivism, 57–58, 536–37; *actus humanus* and, 121; subjectivity and, 87, 89, 157–58
Objectivity, 538–39; boundary of, self-knowledge and, 159; content of consciousness, 6–7; simultaneous with subjectivity, 140; synthesis of, self-determination and, 214–15
Objectivization: body and, 313–15; boundary with subjectivization, 448; cognition and, 64–65, 66, 125–26, 129–30; dialectic with subjectivization, 216; emotionalization vs., 84–86; experience of man and, 95, 96–98, 102; freedom and, 222; induction and, 55; of "man acts," dynamism and, 161–62; mind and, 261; in morality, 253; norms and, 266; *potentia–actus* and, 166; of problem of subjectivity, 536–37; in psycho-somatic complexity, 306; of relationships, 493; self-determination and, 210–12, 214–17,

463, 601–2; self-knowledge and, 67–73, 76, 133–36
Objectivizing psychotherapy, 454–55
Obligation, 34, 265–68, 279, 400–401, 570, 584
Obsequium, 268
Observation (exterior experience), 13, 24–25, 48, 57, 99–100
Omnis agens, 555
Ontic continency of man, 416
Ontological structure of person, 34
Ontology, 465; of fulfillment, 256, 262; of "I," 145, 596–97; self-knowledge, 136, 138; of self-knowledge, 71
Operari, 25; coherence with *esse*, 185–86, 571, 579; consciousness and, 476; reciprocal relations with *esse* and *fieri*, 199–200; subjectivity and, 482; transcendence and, 484. *See also* Activity
Operari sequitur esse, 175, 183–84, 253, 381, 472–75, 547, 625; *praxis–theoria* and, 569–71, 577–79
Opposition, 400–403; as authentic attitude, 404; change into avoidance, 404–7
Ordinary, threat of, 115–16
Organism, 25–26, 151, 192–93, 308–9, 590
Originality, in act of will, 231–38
Originality, of choice and decision, 240
Ossowska, Maria, 556n6
"Others," 470–71; experiencing the other as oneself, 498; "I–other" relation, 517–24, 534, 612–17; meaning of, 519–20, 612–13; "thou," 492–99, 534; "we," 492–93, 500–507, 534. *See also* "Together with others"
Outwardness, 99–100, 113

Pain, 27, 29, 192, 196, 225, 278–81, 339, 480, 606
Pappenheim, Fritz, 515n3
Participation, 377–413, 609–10; and actualization, 388, 520–24; afterword on, 415–16; alienation as antithesis to, 412–13, 489–90, 507–13, 516–17, 524–26; attitudes and, 400–407; avoidance and, 404–7; at center of contemporary lives, 517, 611; at center of contemporary thought, 514, 611; colloquial sense of, 385; commandment to love and, 411–14, 522, 531, 611, 619; and common good, 396–99; community and, 392–96, 487–513; community membership vs., 395–96; conformism and, 404–6; dialogue and, 403; editorial notes on,

632–33; emotion (affections) and, 522–25; and fulfillment, 528; in humanity, as core of participation, 410–11, 488–89; in humanity, meaning of, 518–19, 615–17; individualism and denial of, 390–91, 528; introducing concept of, 377–80; "I-other" relation and, 517–26, 612–17; Kuc on, 451; as manifold ability for person to relate to "others," 387–88; more precise definition of, 383–88; negative verifications of, 524–25; neighbor concept and, 407–11; opposition and, 402–3; philosophical sense of, 385; Plato on, 514; positive verifications of, 524; as property of acting "together with others," 384–85; as property of person, 386–88, 488–89, 508–10; as right, 527–28; semantic specificity of, 386n2; solidarity and, 401–2; spontaneity and, 522–23; systems limiting, 388–92, 528; as task, 521–24; totalism and denial of, 389–92, 528; and transcendence, 385, 508–10, 529–31; "we" relation and, 507–10, 517

"Participation or Alienation," 514–35, 611–19, 625, 637–38

Pasja, 349

Passio, 28–29, 81, 148, 350, 387

Passion, 29, 156, 347–50. *See also* Affections

Passiones animales, 349–50

Passivity, 163–73, 201. *See also* Pati

Pastoral ministry, 453, 457–58

Pastori et magistro, xxvi

Pati, 163–73, 237–38, 540; and conformism, 405; dynamism with *agere*, 163–64, 167, 173, 246–47, 540, 599; foundations in potentiality, 189–90

Paul, St., xiv–xv, 268, 370n9, 584–85

Pedagogy, 453–54, 457–58

Perception, 101n1, 138n8, 547, 623

Perfection, 25, 230, 570, 573, 578–79, 583

Performance: of act, as value, 380–81; of act, fact of, 36; "I perform an act," 251–54

Person: axiology of, 381, 465; causal connection with act, 169–70; cognition of, experience of man and, 100–107; concept and reality in *The Lublin Lectures*, 435, 444–52; concept as basis for manifold practice, 435, 452–55; conception of, 112–17; concreteness of, 175–77, 186, 537, 590; as concrete objective whole, 24–25; dynamic coherence of, nature and, 182–87; dynamic coherence of, personal existence and, 185–86; as efficient cause of act, 22–24; experience of morality and, 3–6; as focus of Wojtyła's writings, viii–ix, xviii; fundamental dispute about man, 469; human being as created gift, xix; immanence, in act, 23–32, 572; integration, in act, 114–15, 549–51; integration of nature in, 181–87; moral value of act and revelation of, 105; nature differentiated from, 187–88; nature in relation to, problem of, 449–50; ontological structure of, 34, 465; opposition to nature in, 180–81; participation as property of, 386–88, 488–89, 508–10; psycho-emotive sphere of, 25, 27–31; reduction to object, xvii–xviii; relational concept of, postulate of, 451–52; relation of body to, 310–24; significance of topic, 36–37; somatic-reactive sphere of, 25–26; as subject, 87–89; subjectivity of, 8–9; as *suppositum*, 173–77; theology of, 420, 429; theory of, 442–44, 569; transcendence, in act, 24, 32–35, 114–15, 560–63; triune of God and, xviii–xix; uniqueness of, 176; unity and complexity of man-person, 286–91; unrepeatability of, 176; vision of, act as particular moment of, 102–4; world of, 66, 78, 141, 181, 508, 596. *See also* specific topics

"The Person: Subject and Community" ("Osoba: Podmiot i wspólnota"), xxvii–xxviii, 467–513, 533–35, 610, 624–25; editorial notes on, 637; introductory information, 467–69; reflections on subjectivity of person, 470–87; status quaestionis, 487–92

Persona, 539

Person–act unity, 303–5

Persona in actu, 23, 31, 33, 221–22

Personal authority, responsibility linked with, 273–75

Personalism (personalistic view): and alienation, 511, 611–12; anti-personalistic thinking vs., 451–52; and attitudes, 400–401, 404; and commandment to love, 412; and common good, 397–98; and irreducibility in man, 541–43; Kant on, 116n8; and morality, 533, 543; and reality, 581–82; and revelation, 428; and self-determination, 207–51, 457–66, 532–33,

542–43, 601–3, 636–37; significance of, 115–17, 419–20; and theology, 428–29
Personalistic value of act, 380–83; acting "together with others" and, 382–83; actualization in, 382; preceding and conditioning ethical value, 381–82
Personal maturity of act, 460
Person and Act (*Osoba i czyn*): afterword, 415–16; aspectuality of, 445–46; book editions of, xxvi–xxvii; chronological genesis of, xxv–xxviii; critical apparatus and, xxi–xxiii, xxxiv–xxxvii, 589–621; current translation of, textual basis for, xxxi–xxxiii; editorial interventions in, xxviii–xxx; editorial notes, 627–40; first English translation of, xxvi–xxvii; first English translation of, author's preface to, 586–87, 640; first English translation of, controversies surrounding, xxviii–xxx; hermeneutics and, 443–44; Kuc's critique of, 451–52; last chapter as complement, 377n1; Lublin symposium on, introductory statement during, 419–22; Marxist interest in, 458; philosophical character of, 429–30, 435–44; post-*1969* writings related to, xxvii–xxviii; pre-*1969* fragments of, xxv–xxvi; present critical edition of, xxviii–xxxiii; as reflections, not scholarship, 421, 430; reverence for work, xxxiii–xxxiv; significance of topic, 36–37; Wojtyła's reasons and motives for writing, 419–20, 426–29. *See also specific topics*
Personhood, 187–88; moral, 12, 34, 300; psychological, 300; structure of responsibility and, 275–76
Pessimism, 356
Pharisaism, 263n4
Phenomenalism, experience of man in, 45, 95–96, 100–102
Phenomenological moment of will, 14, 18
Phenomenologists, editorial interventions by, xxviii–xxx
Phenomenology, 443–44; anthropology and ethics in, 41; cognition and induction in, 107n5; degrees of being in, 546–53, 619–20; entry into philosophical topics via, 556–57; experience in, 39, 102, 623; linkage with philosophy, 5–6, 436–37; nature in, 180–87; *praxis* and *theoria* in, 576; soul-body relation in, 367–73; spirituality in, 284;

and teleology, 556–57; Thomism and, 440, 446, 450; transcendence in, 283; unity and complexity of man-person in, 286–87; vision of man, 115, 609; volition in, 212–13; Wojtyła's references to, 420–21
Phenomenon, 34, 61, 124, 163, 478
Philippe, M. D., 496n17
Philosophical anthropology, 4–5, 75, 190, 436–43, 459, 536; alienation in, 516; dwelling on lived-experience in, 543–44; reality of person and act in, 311; transcendence in, 484; will as power in, 224; Wojtyła's work as, 445, 452, 455, 467, 469
Philosophy: antimonies in, 536–37; currents in Poland, 116–17; in essential function, 468–69; fundamental dispute about man, 469; linkage with phenomenology, 5–6, 436–37; materialistic interpretation of, 469; phenomenology as method of entry, 556–57; philosophical character of *Person and Act*, 429–30, 435–44; practical, 569; rendering languages of one into another, 449–50; renewing of man-person's image in, 471; self-knowledge in, 70; theoretical, 569
Philosophy of being, xxxii, 5, 440–42, 555; and *actus humanus*, 122, 126n4; and character of study, 440–42; and dualistic interpretation of man, 285; and experience of man, 112–13, 370; and linking man to time, 198n11; and lived-experience, 429; and philosophical anthropology, 5, 438; and sensuality vs. rationality, 346; and subjectivity, 468; subjectivity in, 468; and transcendence, 281; and transitive vs. intransitive, 252n1
Philosophy of consciousness, xxxii, 112, 281, 440; and *actus humanus*, 126n4; and character of study, 440–42; and contingency of person, 256; and experience of man, 112–13; and lived-experience, 429; and subjectivity, 468, 470; subjectivity in, 468; and transcendence, 281
Philosophy of man. *See* Anthropology
Piguet, J. C., 496n17
"Placement outside parentheses," 42, 106–7, 364, 423, 453, 629
Plato, xxxiii, 33, 257, 514, 575, 594, 632
Pleasure, 279–81, 347n4, 480, 606; boundary line between felicity and, 279–80; lived-experience of, 280; natural structure of, 279–80; person-act in sphere of, 280–81

Plurality: of common good, 503; of experiential facts, 108; of "I–thou" relationship, 494, 500; of languages and aspects, 449–50; of subjects, 490; unity, in community, 490–91; of "we," 500–501, 505–6, 526–27

Poland: absence from consciousness of Church, 431–32; common good and, 504–5; literature on participation or alienation in, 517–18; Marxist philosophy in, 515–16; philosophical currents in, 116–17, 457–58; political reality of, 469

Półtawska, Wanda, 305n2, 453–55, 468n2, 555n2, 636

Półtawski, Andrzej, xxvi–xxvii, xxix, 431; on consciousness, 447–48; on historical approach, 445; on meeting point between post-Cartesian and classical philosophy, 447

"Position of nature," 384

"Position of the person," transition toward, 383–84

Positive disintegration, 301n1

Positive verifications of participation, 524

Positivistic approaches (positivists), 41, 53, 104, 107, 579, 623

Possibility, actus and, 61

Post-Cartesian philosophy, 445–48, 575–76

Potency: consciousness and, 11–13; coupling with actus (*potentia–actus*), 59–60, 121–22, 165–67; meaning of, 165–66; praxis and, 578–79

Potentia, 557

Potentia–actus, 59–60, 121–22, 165–67, 590

Potentiality, 557–58; actualization of, 23–24, 146–47; *actus humanus* and, 121–23; becoming (*fieri*) and, 200–201; of body, 317–19; of body, and instinctive action, 225–26; consciousness and, 135, 187–99; emotive, 335; etymology and meaning of, 188; excitement and, 349; foundations of *agere* and *pati* in, 189–90; freedom and, 202–4; fulfillment and, 256; hierarchy of, 198; priority of, 193–96; psychical, 334; psycho-emotive, 190–91, 201; somatic-vegetative, 190–93, 200–201; source of dynamization indicated in, 188–89; spiritual, 287–88; subconscious and, 193–99; sublimation and, 353; variants and layers of, 190–91

Potocki, Andrzej, xxvi, xxviii–xxix

Power, 165–67, 188–89; normative, of truth, 260–64; will as power of person's determination, 222–26, 460–64. *See also* Potency; Potentiality

Practical cognition, 109–10, 246

Practical philosophy, 569

Practical truth, 246

Practice: manifold, concept of person as basis of, 435, 452–55. *See also* Praxis

Praecognitum, 238–39, 242–43, 248–49

Praxeology, 555

Praxis, 547, 555–56, 567–85, 621; actualization of, 575; 579; Aristotle on, 569–70, 573–74, 575–76, 577; Christian, pastoral character of, 455; Christian, style of, 446; as Christian topic, 577; and *christianum*, 583–85; coherence with *theoria*, 571, 579; commentary on, 568–71; conclusions on, 571–74; duty and, 571, 579–80; and ethos, 555–56, 580–82, 584–85; factuality of, 571, 579–80; human, personal, as basis of morality, 453; as human act, 570–71; as human topic, 577, 581; and identification of *humanum*, 581–83; Marxism and, 576; *operari sequitur esse* and, 569–71, 577–79; Paul, St., on, 584–85; preceding or anterior to *theoria*, 573, 582; primacy of, 569–70, 573–74, 582–84; reduction and interpretation proceeding from, 109–10; reflections on, 567–68; relevance and richness of topic, 575–77; as starting point for theory of man, 579–80; subjectivity and, 468–69; Thomas Aquinas (Thomism) on, 446, 547, 569–74, 577–79; two-dimensional system with *theoria*, 577–79

Praxis sequitur theoriam, 570, 578

Preconscious, 624

Presentiment, 334

Primacy: of common good, 399; of conception of person and act, 415–16, 449; of ethos, 584; of personal subject, 489, 495, 507; of *praxis*, 569–70, 573–74, 582–84; of *theoria*, 569–70, 577

Principium subsidiarietatis, 507

Principle(s): of act, free will and, 223–24n5; conscience and, 267; consciousness and, 124–25, 129n6; duty and, 265; responsibility and, 271. *See also specific principles and topics*

Principle of analogy, 278–79
Principle of decision, interior, 239–40
Principle of dialogue, 403
Principle of participation, 388–90, 398, 401
Principle of philosophizing, 5
Principle of soul, 289, 313, 372–73
Prüm, Emile, 229n8
Psyche, 27; boundary with somaticity, 194–95; characterization of, 333–37; conditioning by somaticity, and integrality of man, 309–10; drives and, 325; dynamisms of, 307–10, 609; editorial notes on, 632; emotivity and, 152, 333–37, 550; higher sensations and, 83; integration and, 330–73, 607–9; meaning of, 309, 331–32; sensibility and, 342–46; as sensorial stimulus, 338; unity with somaticity (psycho-somatic unity), 303–10, 330–33, 550
Psychical, meaning of, 331–32
Psychical integrality, 332–33
Psychical potentiality, 334
Psychical reactions, 335–36
Psychical reflex, 340–41
Psychical subjectivity, 338–39, 609
Psycho-emotive potentiality, 190–91, 201
Psycho-emotive sphere, 25, 27–31; concept of emotivity, 27–28; intentionality of, 31; relation to conscious efficacy, 30–31; relation to values, 28–30; rootedness of, 31; spiritual struggle with, 29–30; subjectivity of, 31; temperature and disposition in, 30, 31
Psychological consciousness, person and act in, 71–73
Psychological personhood, 300
Psychological subjectivity, 485
Psychology: crowd, 387; disintegration in, 298–301; of morality, 4; self-knowledge in, 70; of will, 18
Psycho-physical unity, 304
Psycho-somatic integrality, 309–10
Psycho-somatic unity of man, 303–10, 330–33, 550; actuations and, 305–6; superiority of person–act unity to, 303–5
Psychotherapy, objectivizing, 454–55
Pure consciousness, 447, 470–71, 536–37, 556–57
Pure subject, 471
Purification, 351

Quasi-*subiectum*, 9
Quasi-subjectivity, 321, 393–94
Quodammodo omnia, 76, 260, 604

Rationabile obsequium, 268
Rationalism, 238n10, 436–38
Rationalis naturae individua substantia, 127, 132, 147, 176, 185, 437, 461, 539
Rationality, 63, 72, 127, 593–94; demarcation between sensuality and, 346
Reaction–emotion, 335
Reactivity: emotivity and, 335–36, 607; somatic, 25–26, 315–19, 326, 338, 550, 590, 607
Realism, 57–58, 536–37; *actus humanus* and, 121; antimony with idealism, 536; boundary of, self-knowledge and, 159; of concept of man, 544–45; subjectivity and, 87, 89, 157–58; Thomas Aquinas on, 238n10
Reality: axiological, 254–56; deepest, mind as, 260; efficacy and freedom in, 13; freedom and, 217–18; morality as, 4, 253–56; most proper point of, 116; normative, conscience as, 258–59; of person, in *The Lublin Lectures*, 435, 444–52; person–act and fragment of, 36–37, 50; personalistic theory of, 581–82; *praxis–theoria* and, 571–74, 580–82; presupposed by cognition, 582; reduction and penetration in, 110–11
Reason, 285, 361–62
Reasoning, 6, 52–58
Redemptor hominis, xviii, xx
Reducibility, 537–39
Reduction, 52–53, 55–58, 108–12, 442, 537–45, 573; of alienation descriptions, 513; equivalent Polish word for, 53; as exploration of experience of man, 108–9; integration of nature in person, 181–87; interpretation in, 6, 53, 56, 58, 109–12; meaning of, 110; *praxis* and, 109–10; reality and object explained in, 110–11; subjectivism in, 88
Reflection, emotionalization and, 153–57
Reflectivity: of consciousness (mirroring), 7–11, 64–65, 72–73, 76–81, 128–34, 139–41, 595–99; intentionality of, 78; and lived-experience, 139–41, 597; reflexivity vs., 142; transition from spontaneity to, 52; understanding and, 51–52

674 | Index

Reflex(es), 322–25; consciousness-related, 34; feeling as, 29, 360; instinct of freedom as, 225; lived-experience vs., 79, 81, 146, 149, 597–98; moment of transcendence as, 553; responsibility as, 499; sensation and, 338–41, 348, 360; "we" as, 506–7

Reflexivity, 76–81, 142–44, 482, 596; emotionalization and, 153–57; reflectivity vs., 142

Reification, 77, 463, 530

Relational concept of person, postulate of, 451–52

Relationships: happiness proceeding from, 277–78; "I–other," 517–26, 534, 612–17; "I–thou," 492–99, 534; marriage, 327–28, 501, 503, 506; reflective objectivization of, 493; "we," 492–93, 500–507, 534. *See also* "Together with others"

Religion: auto-teleology and, 565; commandment to love and, 522; lived-experience of transcendentals and, 35; Marxism on, 515, 530, 617–19; world of persons in, 274. *See also specific topics*

Religious responsibility, 274

Religious self-knowledge, 70, 137

Reluctance, 524–25

Reproductive drive, 32, 325, 327–28, 632

Repulsion, 29, 362–64, 480

Responding-responsibility, 272

Responsibility, 271–76, 460; as intrapersonal fact, 272; linked with personal authority, 273–75; link to efficacy, through duty, 271; to self, in conscience, 275–76; self-determination and, 273; for values, 272–73, 606

"Responsibility to," 273–75

Retractatio, 426, 431, 434–35, 441–42

Revelation: divine, 420, 438–30, 585n13; personalistic conception of, 428

Ricoeur, Paul, 186n7, 230n9, 275n7, 347n4, 455

Right, participation as, 527–28

Rightness: etymology of, 266; of norms, 265–68

Rilke, Rainer Maria, 172n4

Rootedness: in body, 314n4; of emotions, 357; of emotivity, 27–28, 357; of person, in soul, 290n10; of psycho-emotive sphere, 31; of truth, 241; of will, 212

Saints, mission of: perceiving depth and meaning of, xi–xvii; persecution and rejection of, xvi; prophetic dimension of, xvi; synthesis of human questioning and God's response in, xiv–xvi

Sameness: experience of man, 46–47, 54–55, 97, 107–8; induction and semantic unity of, 54–55

Sartre, Jean-Paul, 13, 41, 104, 523

Schaff, Adam, 515–16nn4–5, 518n8, 530–31n17, 618, 619

Scheler, Max, xxii, xxxiii, 116–17, 420–21, 587; on action, 172n4, 532–33; on emotion/emotionality, 29, 34, 280n8, 344, 351, 353n5, 360n6; on felicity, 280, 631; on "I–thou," 495n16; and Kant, 258n2, 632; on lived-experience of value, 244n13; on material ethics of value, 556–57n8; on moral values, 148–49n13, 263n4; on participation, 522–23; on *praxis* and *theoria*, 576; on transcendence, 221n4

Scholastics, 32–33, 59–60, 122, 220, 475–76, 538

Second categorical imperative, 218n3, 258n2, 446, 524

Second Vatican Council: fundamental dispute about man, 469; on "gift of self," 465–66; on personalization and transcendence, 529–31; on "to have more–to be more," 583; Wojtyła's participation in, xxv, 117n9, 529. *See also Gaudium et spes*

Secrétan, Ph., 496n17

Self-affirmation, 275n7

Self-awareness, 103–4n2, 290n10

Self-consciousness, 8, 70, 85, 135–36, 481–83, 498, 519

Self-dependence: act ("to perform an act") and, 252–54, 483; and freedom, 219–22; independence conditioned by, 222–23; independence of body from, 319–21; moral habits and, 364–65

Self-determination, 32–35, 518–19; autonomous determination of object and, 235; and auto-teleology 554n1, 557–63; as basis of transcendence, 32–33, 213–14, 217–22, 226–27, 241, 461–62, 549, 557–60; cognition and, 243–46; cognitive direction in, 215–16; Conference on St. Thomas lecture, 457–66, 636–37; consciousness and shaping of, 214–15; consciousness unity with, 216; duality in analysis of,

33, 209n1; dynamism of, using will and, 223–24; dynamism of, vs. nature (instinct), 218–22; editorial notes on, 630–31, 636–37; and efficacy, 33, 214, 219, 222, 459–60, 478–83; emotivity (affections) and, 354–58; experience of man and, 458–59; exteriorization of, 216–17; *fieri* and, 32, 207–8, 462–63; and freedom, 33, 461, 518–19; and fulfillment, 251–91, 603–6; "gift of self" and, 465–66; integral dynamic of will and, 210–17, 601; "I will" vs. "I feel like," 212–13; lived-experience of value and, 361–62; objectivization in, 210–12, 214–17, 463, 601–2; personal structure of, 207–51, 457–66, 532–33, 542–43, 601–3, 636–37; reactivity of body and, 315–19; and responsibility for moral value, 273, 462–63; society system vs. neighbor system, 35; spontaneity and, 354–55, 361–62; will as power of, 222–26, 460–64; will manifested as property of person in, 207–10, 460–61
Self-direction, 229
Self-experience, 149–50
Self-feeling, 334, 339–40
Self-fulfillment: and conscience, 255–59; as felicity, 276. *See also* Fulfillment
Self-governance, 32–33, 208–10, 463–64, 481–82, 542–43; body and, 315; coherence with transcendence, 296; disintegration as deficiency of, 300–301; duality of, 296; "gift of self" and, 465–66; and integration, 296, 298, 330; "I-thou" and, 498–99; personalistic value of act and, 382; self-possession presupposed in, 209–10; subjectivity of, 210
Self-knowledge, 70–71; acknowledgement, boundary of objectivity and realism in, 159; *actio* vs. *passio* in, 81, 148; actualization of, 68–69; collapse, in emotionalization, 82–86, 153–54; consciousness and, 9–10, 66–71, 76, 132–39, 595; efficiency of, 84–85, 154; generalizations in, 70–71, 138–39; intentionality of, 71, 135, 137; knowledge about man vs., 71; moral, 70, 137; objectivization in, 67–73, 76, 133–36; ontology of, 136, 138; religious, 70, 137; and self-consciousness, 70; self-consciousness from, 70, 85, 135–36; sensation and, 82–83; social, 70, 137; specificity of, 137–39; subjectivity and, 89; *suppositum*

and, 79; transillumination and, 130–34; and understanding of "man," 149–50; understanding through, 133
Self-observation, 590
Self-possession, 208–10, 463–64, 481–82, 519, 542–43; body and, 315; disintegration as deficiency of, 300–301; duality of, 296; "gift of self" and, 465–66; and integration, 296, 298, 330; "I-thou" and, 498–99; objectivizing psychotherapy and, 454–55; personalistic value of act and, 382; presupposed in self-governance, 209–10; subjectivity of, 210
Self-preservation, drive for, 32, 325, 326–27, 632
Self-responsibility, 275–76
Self-understanding, 149–50
Semantic unity, 54–55, 107–8
Sensation, 27–29, 627; bodily, 151–52; cognitive contact in, 344; direction to values, 344–45; and emotionalization, 82–86, 150–57; emotivity and, 334; excitement and, 348; governance over, 85; hierarchy of, 83, 152; in lived-experience of one's own body, 337–41; permeation into consciousness, 342–43; richness of, 152; superiority of consciousness over, 340–41; translation from Polish, 630. *See also* Sensibility
Senses, 27–29, 39, 47, 98, 101–2, 288. *See also* Sensation
Sensibility, 342–46; individual, formation of, 342–43; meaning and etymology of, 342–45; as particular richness of psyche, 345–46; permeation by truthfulness, 343–45
Sensing, 334
Sensing of one's own body, 339
Sensorial stimulus, 338
Sensual cognition, 8, 28, 31, 40
Sensual desire, 347
Sensuality, 82, 151, 337, 550, 556; demarcation between rationality and, 346; excitement and, 348
Sexual (reproductive) drive, 32, 325, 327–28, 632
Sexual (conjugal) morality, 533, 569
Shoemaker, Sydney, 201n12
Simplicity, in experience of man, 44–49, 100, 107–8

Sin, 242
Social belonging, 394–95
Social dimension of community ("we"), 492–93, 500–507, 534
Social ethics, 393
Social nature, 384, 410, 413–14
Social unity, 490–91
Society, 379–80, 394–95, 490–91, 500, 526–27
Society system of reference, 35
Sociology, 379–80; of morality, 4
Solidarity, 400–403; as authentic attitude, 404; change into conformism, 404–6
Solipsism, 216, 560, 563–64
Soma, 25–26, 309–10, 340, 590
Somatic constitution, 311–12, 323–24, 332–33
Somaticity, 627; act and motion of, 319–24; boundary with psyche, 194–95; conditioning of psyche, and integrality of man, 309–10; drives and, 324–29; dynamisms of, 307–10, 315–19, 607; editorial notes on, 632; habit and, 322–23; integration and, 295–329, 606–7; as motor stimulus, 338; outwardness and inwardness of body and, 308–9; possession and use of body, 313–15; relation of person and body, 310–24; self-feeling and, 339–40; unity with psyche (psycho-somatic unity), 303–10, 330–33, 550
Somatic reactivity, 25–26, 315–19, 326, 338, 550, 590, 607
Somatic-vegetative potentiality, 190–93, 200–201
Somebody, person as, 176–77
Sorrow, 352, 354, 363
Soul: colloquial understanding of, 371; concept of psyche and, 309, 331–32; as form, 371; lived-experience of, 289–91, 370; as principle of transcendence and integration, 372–73; relation to body, 367–73, 452–53, 551–52, 607; unity with body, in man-person, 286–91
Specialization, 42–43
Spirit: immanence of, 284–85; unity with body, in man-person, 286–91. *See also* Soul
Spirituality: elation in, 348–49; emotional stirring and, 351; emotional struggle with, 29–30; emotivity and, 337; experiential expression of, 146–47; higher sensations and, 83, 152; manifestations of, immanence of spirit and, 284–85; negation of materiality in, 284; transcendence as basis of, 284–86, 484; understandings of, proper succession in, 285–86; unity and complexity of man-person in, 286–91
Spiritual potentiality, 287–88
Spontaneity: and attraction to or repulsion from value, 362–64; of freedom, 226–27; of habits, 365; and instinctive action, 225–26; of lived-experience of value, 360–62; and participation, 522–23; and self-determination, 354–55, 361–62; transition to reflectivity from, 52; of volitions, 557–58
Stagirite, 310
Stein, Edith, 496n17
Stępień, Antoni, 431, 433, 437, 447–48, 468n2, 555n2
Stevenson, Charles Louis, 105n3
Stoics, 355–56, 361–62, 632
Stream of consciousness, 139n9, 198
Striving, *appetitus* as, 227–28
Stroba, Jerzy, 453, 455, 468n2, 555n2, 636
Studium humanum, 430
Styczeń, Tadeusz, 101n1, 421, 431, 438–39, 445–46
Subconscious, 624; as expression of potentiality–consciousness relationship, 193–99; indication of consciousness as sphere of realization in, 197–98
"Subdue the earth," 583–84
Subject: of action, definition by nature, 178–79; consciousness and, 8–9, 475–78; constitution of "I" as, through lived-experience, 145–46; duality of, 477–78; man ("I") as, 173–74, 539; personal, homogeneity of, 506; person as, 87–89; person as, vs. community, 393–94; potentiality of, 187–99; pure, 471; synthesis with object, 216. *See also* "The Person: Subject and Community"
Subjectivism, 7, 57–58, 87–89, 157–60, 536–37, 541; affections and, 357; deviation from *fieri* of morality, 13; difference of subjectivity from, 158–60; overcoming, 447; *status quaestionis*, 536–37
Subjectivity, 8–9, 87–89, 157–60; affections and, 352–53, 354, 356–57; authentic, of man, 541; of body, 319–21; categorical boundaries of, 471; community and, 393–94, 487–513; content of consciousness, 6–7, 69; difference from subjectivism,

158–60; efficacy and, 157, 173–78, 478–83; emotion, 27–28; experience of man and, 470–72; fulfillment and, 483–87; historical background of problem, 537–39; and integration, 297; and irreducibility, 174, 481, 536–45, 619; "I-thou" and, 492–99; layers of, 190–91; lived-experience and, 139–50; of man, attempt to render, 112–13; moral, 485; objectivization of problem, 536–37; participation and, 507–13; philosophy of being and, 468; philosophy of consciousness and, 468, 470; problem of, 468–69; psychical, 338–39, 609; of psycho-emotive sphere, 31; psychological, 485; in reality of person and act, 87, 89, 157–58; reflexivity and, 142–44; of self-governance, 210; of self-possession, 210; simultaneous with objectivity, 140; transcendence and, 481; "we" and, 500–507

"Subjectivity and 'the Irreducible' in Man," 536–45, 619, 625–26, 638

Subjectivization, 595, 596; body and, 341; boundary with objectivization, 448; cognition and, 215–16; dialectic with objectivization, 216; emotivity and, 358; induction and, 109–10; lived-experience and, 91, 141, 162, 214–15; mirroring by consciousness and, 68, 134; reflexive feature of consciousness and, 76–81; self-determination and, 215–17, 601; self-knowledge and, 134–35

Sublimation, 353

Submission, and conformism, 405

Subordination to truth, 240

Subsidiarity, 507

Substance (substantial being), 16, 200, 285–88, 313, 450, 461, 539. *See also* Suppositum

Substantialization, 9

Suffering, 524–25

Sufficient reason, 285

Summa theologiae, 41, 104

Suppositum, 76–79, 87–88, 143, 470–87, xxxn9; act and, 16; act of will and, 20; consciousness and, 8–9, 11, 64–65, 76–79, 87–88, 131, 143–45, 157, 476; difference between nature and person in, 187–88; efficacy and, 478–83; etymology of, 175; experience of man and, 470–72; fulfillment and, 483–87; integration of nature in, 183; irreducibility and, 539, 541; man as, 173–78;

ontology of, 78–79, 143; *operari sequitur esse* and, 472–75; principles of, 174–75; reciprocal relations of *esse-operari-fieri* in, 199–200; subjectivism and, 76–79, 87–88, 143–45, 157; subjectivity and, 157; transcendence and, 484; understanding in new way, 471–72

Świeżawski, Stefan, 421, 518n8, 547

Systematic approach, 445–47

Teleology, 554–66; act of will, 19–21, 22; common good in, 397–98; human action, 33; as interpretative principle, 555–56; Kant's criticism of, 556; presupposed by auto-teleology, 560. *See also* Auto-teleology

Temperament, 28, 30, 31, 324, 333

Terminus, 555, 559–66, 620–21. *See also* Teleology

Theology: of nature, 420, 429; of person, 420, 429; personalistic conception of, 428–29; *Person and Act* and, 420, 428–29; *praxis* and *theoria* in, 577, 583–85. *See also* specific topics

Theoretical philosophy, 569

Theoria, 443, 446, 567–85; Aristotle on, 569–70, 573–74, 575–76; commentary on, 568–71; conclusions on, 571–74; *operari sequitur esse* and, 569–71, 577–79; *praxis* preceding or anterior to, 573, 582; primacy of, 569–70, 577; reflections on, 567–68; relevance and richness of topic, 575–77; Thomas Aquinas and Thomism on, 446, 547, 569–74; two-dimensional system with *praxis*, 577–79

"*Theoria* and *Praxis*: A Universally Human and Christian Topic," 575–85, 621, 640

"*Theoria* and *Praxis* in the Philosophy of the Human Person," 567–74, 621, 639

Theory of person, 442–44, 569

"They," 500

Thinking, 246–49; agent of, 247–48; perspective of efficacy on, 246–47. *See also* Cognition

Thomas Aquinas, xxxiii, 116–17; on *actus*, 121–23, 571–73, 578–79; on affection/emotion, 28–29; anthropology of, 465; on *appetitus*, 346–47; classification of affections, 363; on existence, 175, 176; on habit, 362, 462n4, 487; on intentionality of will, 228–29; methodological clarification of, 458;

Thomas Aquinas, (*cont.*)
on mind, 260, 604; modern reading of, 458; *passio* of, 28–29; and philosophical character of study, 436, 442–43; on *praxis* and *theoria*, 446, 569–74, 577–79; on realism, 238n10; on self-determination and will, 457–58, 460–66; on soul–body relation, 371; *Summa theologiae*, 41, 104; on *suppositum*, 174–75; on teleology of act of will, 22; on unity of man-person, 289; on volition and act of will, 19–21; on volitum and praecognitum, 238–39; Wojtyła's references to, xxix, xxx, xxxii, 420–21

Thomism: act (*actus*) in, 15, 60, 121–23, 546–47, 571–73, 578–79; anthropology and metaphysics in, 546; dynamic vision of man in, 301; existential, 133, 449, 547; obedience of body in, 315; *passio* in, 350; phenomenology and, 440, 446, 450; *praxis* and *theoria* in, 446, 547, 569–74, 577–79; Wojtyła's connection to, 449, 534

Thomistic typology, 30, 347

"Thou," 492–99, 534; constitution of "I" through, 493–97; as "I" different from me, 494

Tischner, Józef, 445

"Together with others," 377–80, 488, 527–28, 633; afterword on, 415–16; attitudes and, 400–407; avoidance and, 404–7; commandment to love and, 411–14; community and, 392–96; conformism and, 404–6; individualism and, 390–91; opposition and, 402–3; participation as property of, 384–85; participation as property of person, 386–88; and personalistic value of act, 382–83; solidarity and, 401–2; totalism and, 391. *See also* "We"

Totalism, 389–92, 528; a-personalistic (anti-personalistic) thinking at root of, 392; principle of, 390

Transcendence, 114–15, 281–86, 548–49; and auto-teleology, 554–66, 620–21, 639; Church, 93, 117n9, 529, 592; cognition and, 243–46, 281, 548; and common good, 509; common good and, 503, 505; conscience and, 33–34, 256–59, 484–87, 561–63, 604–5; discovery of man's complexity through, 367–69; drama of value and duty attesting to, 270; emotivity and, 336–37; etymology of, 221, 484; experience and understanding, 50–51; expression and explanation of "man acts" in, 282–84; felicity and, 276–81; freedom of will as basis of, 217–22, 256–57; fulfillment and, 483–87; horizontal, 221, 227, 281, 461–62; integration as aspect complementary to, 295–96, 330, 550; intentionality and, 548; manifested in lived-experience of efficacy, 170–71; meanings of, 281, 484; mind and, 260–61; participation and, 385, 508–10, 529–31; of person in act, 24, 32–35, 114–15, 560–63; *praxis* and, 572–73, 581–83, 585; as property of dynamism of person, 221; psycho-somatic unity and, 303; self-determination as basis of, 32–33, 213–14, 217–22, 226–27, 241, 461–62, 549, 557–60; self-governance and, 296; society system vs. neighbor system, 35; soul as principle of, 372–73; soul–body relation and, 369–70; spirituality based on, 284–86; subjectivity manifested in, 481; transcendentals, 33, 35, 257–58, 281, 484, 603–4; "truth about good" and, 238–42, 268, 561; truthfulness and, 260–64; unity and complexity of man-person in, 286–91; vertical, 221, 226–27, 281–84, 561

"Transcendence of the Person in the Act and the Auto-teleology of Man," xxxiii, 554–66, 620–21, 639

Transcendentals, 33, 35, 257–58, 281, 484, 603–4

Transilluminating, 130–34, 139–41

Transitiveness, 252–55, 480, 571–72, 580–81

Trans-phenomenal, 370, 472, 478

Tresmontant, Claude, 193n9

Triune of God, and mystery of person, xviii–xix

Truth: act of will and, 20–21; and attitudes, 404; auto-determination and, 22; axiological, 246; dependence on, and conscience, 256–64, 485–86, 561–63, 604–5; dependence on, and freedom, 258; dependence on, and independence of will, 240–41; duty and, 262–64; and emotional stirring, 351; grasping, 248, 260–61; norm and, 12; normative power of, 260–64; practical, 246; relation to, 239–46, 604; relation to, as interior principle of decision, 239–40, 603; subordination to, 239; superiority of, 261, 604–5; and

transcendence, 33, 238–42, 260–64, 268, 561; as transcendental, 257–58, 603–4; union with freedom, 277
Truth about good, moment of: as basis of decision and transcendence, 238–42, 561; as basis of moral qualification of acts, 241–42; and lived-experience of value, 244–45; manifestation in conscience, 256–59, 485–86, 561–63, 604–5
Truthfulness: of conscience, 261–63; integration of, 344; lived-experience of, 266; of norms, 265–68; and response to values, 272; sensibility and, 342–46; as source of felicity, 276–77
Tymieniecka, Anna-Teresa, xxvii, xxviii–xxx, 226n6; editorial interventions by, xxviii–xxx; as editor of English edition, xxvi–xxvii, 588; on Ingarden, 117n8, 172n4, 536n1; on spontaneity, 226n6; Wojtyła's letter to, xxviii, 532–35, 638
Typology, 30, 333; axiological, 347; Thomistic, 30, 347

Uncertainty, 605
Unconsciousness, 193n9, 196, 624
Understanding, 49–58; conception as expression of, 50, 111–12; conscious action and, 90; conscious cognitive process in, 51–52; consciousness as, 64–65; experience of man, 95–96, 98–99, 107–12, 459; first and elementary, 51; induction and, 53–56; knowledge and, 66; of "man," from "I," 149–50; philosophical, concept and reality of person in, 444–52; reasoning and, 52–58; reduction and, 52–53, 55–58; stages of, 107–12. *See also* Self-knowledge
Uniformity, 406
Uniqueness of person, 176
Unity: integration as realization and manifestation of, 297–98; organic, in cognition, 458; person–act, superiority of, 303–5; of plurality, in community, 490–91; psycho-physical, 304; psycho-somatic, 303–10, 330–33, 550
Unity of man-person, 286–91; awakening of need to understand complexity of human being in experience of, 289; determination by spirituality, 288
"Unknown being," 115
Unrepeatability of person, 176

Usus, 322
Usus passivus, 315
Utilitarianism, 280–81, 505, 556, 566, 620
Utility, 20, 556

Valuation, 523–24, 632
Value(s): ability to respond to and responsibility for, 272–73, 606; of act, person revealed through, 105; *appetitus* and, 347; attraction to or repulsion from, 269, 362–64, 480, 605; and auto-teleology, 557–60; cognition of, 232, 246–47, 249–50; conscience and, 485–87, 561; consciousness and, 7, 11–13; drama of, and transcendence, 270; dynamism and, 91–92; emotivity as sensibility to, 336–37; freedom and, 22; hierarchy of, 269, 381, 384, 411, 559–60; judgment concerning, 246–50; lived-experience of, emotivity and, 358–62; lived-experience of, moment of truth about good and, 244–45; lived-experience of, sensibility and, 343–45; material ethics of, 556–57n8; performance of act as, 380–81; personalistic, of act, 380–83; person and act in, 4; *praxis* and, 580–82; problem of, 245; psycho-emotion sphere and, 28–30; self-determination and, 33, 273, 361–62, 462–63; spontaneous relation to, 360–64; subjectivity and, 480–81; transition into duty, 268–70; volition as spontaneous turning toward, 557–58; will and response to, 237–38
Value ethics, 12
Vegetation, 318–19, 627
Vegetative dynamism, 162
Vegetative life, 26, 151
Vegetative potentiality, 190–93
Veritatis splendor, xviii
Vertical transcendence, 221, 226–27, 281–84, 561
Virtue, 364–65, 562–63
Vision into person, 102–4
Vitality, 318–19
Vocation, 117n9, 269–70
Volition, 460–63; act of will and, 18–21; autonomous determination of object, 234–35; and auto-teleology, 557–60; cognitive lived-experience of value and, 245; consciousness and, 11; defined in respect to object, 223; freedom (independence) and, 22, 222–23; intentionality of, 16, 19, 20,

Volition, intentionality of, (*cont.*)
211–12, 222–23, 228–29, 245, 462, 548, 558–59;
"I will" vs., 212; moment of decision and,
229–30; self-determination and, 211–13;
simple, motivation of, 232–33; simple, vs.
choice, 232–34; spontaneity of, 557–58;
thinking vs., 247

Volitum, 238–39, 242–43, 248–49

Voluntarium, 127, 463, 476, 557–58, 593–94;
actus voluntarius and, 59–61; conscious
action and, 62–63; consciousness and,
124–25; dynamism and, 90; emotion and,
83–84, 152; modifications of, 150–51

Voluntarium perfectum, 25, 382

Voluntary, 122, 186n7, 242n12; action, 62, 72

"We," 492–93, 500–507, 534; alienation
and, 517; analogies of, 506–7; analysis of
pronoun, 526–27; and common good, 501,
503–6, 526; common good and, 501, 503–6;
constitution of "I" through, 501–2; family
as, 506; "I–thou" vs., 500–501; marriage
as, 501; participation and, 507–10, 517;
plurality of, 500–501, 505–6, 526–27

Wholeness: integration as realization and
manifestation of, 297–98. *See also* Unity

Will: and actualization, 523; *actus humanus*
and, 126–28; *actus voluntarius* and, 124–25;
analysis of, 18; appetition and, 227–28,
346–47; autonomous determination
of object by, 234–35; and auto-teleology,
557–60; cognitive action and, 125–26;
cognitive direction of, 215–16; conception
of, 18; consciousness and, 11–13; and
decision, 226–31; emotivity and conscious
response of, 336–37; freedom of, as basis
of transcendence, 217–22; homogeneity
of, 234; independence of, dependence in
truth, 240–41; initial indetermination of,
motivation and, 242–43; integral dynamic
of, 210–17, 601; intentionality and, 228–29,
461–63; manifested as property of person,
207–10, 460–61; necessity of choice and,
558; objectivization of subject of, 210–12;
permeation of affections into, 357–58;
as power of person's self-determination,
222–26, 460–64; process of, 18, 460;
toward good, 230–31; using, and dynamism
of self-determination, 223–24. *See also* Act
of will; *Voluntarium*

Witness: of act and motion, 321–24; of
Church time, xii; of consciousness, 13–17,
162–63; of cosmological to personalistic
transition, 420, 428–29; of integral
experience, 171; of irreducibility in man,
542; of person and act, 91–92, 114, 253, 264,
464; by saint, xv–xvii; by Wojtyła, xviii,
xxxiii

Wojciechowski, Tadeusz, 452–53, 468n2,
555n2, 636

Wojtyła, Karol: critical apparatus and works
of, xxi–xxiii, xxxiv–xxxvii, 589–621;
letter to Tymieniecka, xxviii, 532–35,
638; participation in Second Vatican
Council, xxv, 117n9; perceiving depth and
meaning of mission, xi–xvii; person as
focus of writings, viii–ix, xviii; quantity
of and access to work, vii; reasons and
motives for writing *Person and Act*, 419–20,
426–29; relationship of pre-papal works
to pontificate, xx–xxi; reverence for work
of, xxxiii–xxxiv. *See also specific topics and
works*

Wonder, 116

Work, Wojtyła's elucidation on, xx

World: irreducibility of human to, 538;
man as object of, 538–39; of morality,
36–37; of nature, 181; new, person–act and
introduction to, 36; of the person, 66, 78,
141, 181, 508, 596; of persons, 274

Zdybicka, Zofia Józefa, 451, 453, 468n2, 514n1,
555n2, 636